The Best in Children's Books

The Best in Children's Books

The University of Chicago
Guide to Children's Literature
1985-1990

Written and edited by
Zena Sutherland, Betsy Hearne,
and Roger Sutton

The University of Chicago Press
Chicago and London

Zena Sutherland is professor emeritus in the Graduate Library School at the University of Chicago and former editor of the *Bulletin*. Betsy Hearne is editor of the *Bulletin*; Roger Sutton is executive editor of the *Bulletin*.

The University of Chicago Press, Chicago 60637
The University of Chicago Press, Ltd., London
© 1991 by The University of Chicago
All rights reserved. Published 1991
Printed in the United States of America
00 99 98 97 96 95 94 93 92 91   5 4 3 2 1

ISBN (cloth): 0-226-78064-3

Library of Congress Cataloging-in-Publication Data

Sutherland, Zena
    The best in children's books : the University of Chicago guide to children's
literature, 1985–1990 / written and edited by Zena Sutherland, Betsy Hearne, and
Roger Sutton.
        p.   cm.
    1. Bibliography—Best books—Children's literature.   2. Children's literature
Bibliography.   3. Children's literature—Book Reviews.
I. Hearne, Betsy Gould.   II. Sutton, Roger.   III. Title.
Z1037.S96 1991
[PN1009.A1]   91-23100
                                                                                CIP

⊛ The paper used in this publication meets the minimum requirements of the American National Standard for Information Sciences--Permanence of Paper for Printed Library Materials, ANSI Z39.48-1984.

Contents

Acknowledgments

The critical evaluations used in this books are based on the judgments of past and present members of *The Bulletin of the Center for Children's Books* advisory committee who served during the years 1985-1990. They include Alba Endicott, Isabel McCaul, Hazel Rochman, Robert Strang, and Elizabeth Taylor; those who have contributed reviews include Kathryn Pierson Jennings, Ruth Ann Smith, and Deborah Stevenson in addition to editors Betsy Hearne, Zena Sutherland, and Roger Sutton. Special thanks to Deborah Stevenson for her assistance in production.

Introduction

When the Center for Children's Books was established at the University of Chicago in 1945, one of its goals in setting up a collection of trade books written for children was the evaluation and analysis of books in terms of uses, appeals, and literary quality. *The Bulletin of the Center for Children's Books*, which grew out of a memorandum that circulated within the Graduate School of Education, now has international circulation.

Review copies of all children's trade books are sent to the center by publishers. Once each week, members of the advisory committee meet to examine the books and discuss the reviews prepared by the staff. The committee comprises teachers and librarians in public and private schools and libraries.

Books for children and young people of all ages are reviewed, and occasionally an adult book that may be of particular interest to adolescent readers is included. It is clear from the reading level index that some spans are heavily represented. There are many more citations listed for grades 4-6, for example, than for grades 4-7; however, material may also be found for the 7th grade reader in such groups as 5-7, 6-9, or 7-10. The book has not been planned as a balanced list in respect to an individual grade or age, or to subject or genre. The editors' selections have been made primarily on the basis of literary quality, with representation of subjects as a secondary consideration. The goal is a list of the best books published in the years 1985-1990.

Why is it important to select children's books with discrimination? For one thing, the years in which such books are appropriate are fleeting, although some books can gratify readers of any age. There are so many activities and competing interests that fill children's time today that only the most inveterate readers read more than half a dozen books yearly beyond those required by their schools.

Second, studies of the adult reading population show how easy it is to fall into the pattern of reading only superficial material. Children exposed to flimsy mass market books, comics, and pedestrian series books will not necessarily proceed to good literature. It is possible for a child to acquire discrimination, but it isn't likely to happen unless some adult—a parent, a teacher, a librarian—suggests better books, encourages the ownership of books, and discusses good books with enthusiasm and understanding. It is incumbent on adults who are concerned with children's reading to select and counsel wisely, to appreciate the importance of both the content of books and the reading habit itself, and to comprehend what the elements of good children's books are.

In many ways, the literary criteria that apply to adult books and children's books are the same. The best books have that most elusive component, a distinctive literary style. A well-constructed plot; sound characterization with no stereotypes; dialogue that flows naturally and is appropriate to the speaker's age, education, and milieu; and a subtly developed theme are equally important in children's and adults' fiction. Authoritative knowledge, logical organization of material, and accuracy are major considerations in informational books for any age.

In books for children, there are additional considerations based on limitations of comprehension and experience. Comparatively few children enjoy a story without action or conflict, however delicate the nuances of style, and most young readers abjure the tedious presentation of information in the guise of conversation. For very young children, it is important that a book not contain so much information as to confuse them. The vocabulary need not be rigidly controlled, but it should not include so many terms that the reader is discouraged. The concepts must be clear but not simplistic. Format (type size, distribution of print, placement on page) and illustrations should be consistent with the level of the text, and maps or diagrams should be very carefully placed and labeled.

Because children are forming ideas of themselves and their society and are testing and acquiring ethical values, it is imperative that the books they read foster and nurture opinions and attitudes that are intelligent and flexible. Will the books they read serve to do this? The best ones will. Adults should be wary, however, of their own bias and should evaluate very carefully the author's values and assumptions lest agreement with their own ideas be confused with objectivity.

Each book must be judged on its own merits, and each book should be chosen—whether for an individual child, a library, or a classroom collection— with consideration for its strength even though it may have some weaknesses. This has been a precept in critical evaluation of books for *The Bulletin*. It is often illuminating to compare a book with other books by the same author or with similar books on a subject, but the judgment of each book is made on that book alone. With the spate of publication of children's books, selection is difficult. It is our hope that through this bibliography and its indexes, readers may more easily find the best in children's books.

Zena Sutherland

Suggestions for Using This Book

The reviews included here have been selected by the editors from those already published in the Bulletin of the Center for Children's Books. Except for a few titles originally coded as "Additional" or "Special Reader," all of the books listed here had received a rating of "Recommended." An asterisk is used to denote books of special distinction. The reviews are listed alphabetically by the author's name and are numbered in sequence to facilitate the use of the six indexes at the back of this book.

Of the indexes, only the title index does not refer the reader to the number assigned each book but gives instead the last name of the author.

The developmental values index is based on the analysis of each book for those elements that illuminate some aspect of achieving maturity, solving problems, or establishing relationships at any developmental stage in the life of a child or young reader. The developmental values covered range from the young child's acquisition of environmental concepts or adjustment to a new baby in the family, to the adolescent's attitudes toward his or her role in marriage.

The curricular use index suggests books for incorporation into the school curriculum, for supplemental reading in relation to curricular units. Susan Kuklin's Fighting Back (no. 576), for example, is included under "Sex Education" in the curricular use index, whereas it is cited under "AIDS" in the subject index.

The reading level index is arranged progressively by grades following the books for preschool children, which are listed by age. Books for independent reading begin with first grade, usually age six. The reading levels are given in a span that is intended to suggest probably use rather than to impose limits. A volume of poetry, for example, may be graded 4-6, indicating widest use in grades 4, 5, and 6; it may, however, be read aloud to young children, used independently by proficient readers in grade 3 or even grade 2, or be read by older children or adults. The levels of reading difficulty have been determined by the Bulletin advisory committee after consideration of the vocabulary the length and complexity of the writing, subject interest, latent content, organization of material, and the appropriateness of content, difficulty, and format to the maturity of the intended reader.

The subject index entries include both fiction and nonfiction. Nonfiction books about Africa, for example, are grouped according to subject matter into various subheadings under the general heading "Africa." Fictional stories set in that region will be found under the "Africa, stories" subheading.

The type of literature index makes it possible for the reader to find citations for all of the books of poetry, all of the mystery stories, and so on, that have been selected to be grouped together. The temptation to break this index down into fine categories has been sternly resisted, lest the book become inordinately massive. It is hoped that the separate indexes give ample access to the material in the volume.

Reviews of Books

1   **Abells**, Chana Byers. *The Children We Remember*. Greenwillow, 1986. Library ed. ISBN 0-688-06372-1; Trade ed. ISBN 0-688-06371-3. 45p. illus. with photographs. Library ed. $10.88; Trade ed. $9.95.

3-7   A heartrending photodocumentary of Jewish children's typical existence before and after the Nazis came to power shows school, synagogue, and playtime pictures in contrast to scenes of poverty, starvation, and persecution. This is a book of few words, assuming some background knowledge of World War II and the Holocaust. And in this case, less is more, for the carefully selected photos dominate the unobtrusive statements describing scenes of children helping each other, children dying, children surviving. In acknowledging, along with the book jacket, that this is "a story that must be told to all of today's children," one also hopes there is an adult nearby to help share the shock of scenes like the one in which a soldier is shooting a mother and her baby.

2   **Abercrombie**, Barbara. *Charlie Anderson*; illus. by Mark Graham. McElderry, 1990. ISBN 0-689-50486-1. 32p. $12.95.

4-6 yrs.   Charlie is a gray striped cat that appears out of the woods to sleep on Elizabeth's bed every night. It's not till a storm keeps him away that Elizabeth and her sister, Sarah, go looking for him and discover that he spends the day with another family. The question Elizabeth asks Charlie, "Who do you love best?" is a loaded one, for she and her sister spend weekends with their father and stepmother in the city. So it's wise of Charlie to purr his affection in the dark. "Just like Elizabeth and Sarah, Charlie has two houses, two beds, two families who love him. He's a lucky cat." The message is overt but carried by an appealing story and by pictures softened with pensive blue-grays and fuzzy textures. This gentle fable will reassure many children who feel lost between allegiances to divorced parents.

3   **Ackerman**, Karen. *Song and Dance Man*; illus. by Stephen Gammell. Knopf, 1988. Library ed. ISBN 0-394-99330-6; Trade ed. ISBN 0-394-89330-1. 32p. Library ed. $11.99; Trade ed. $11.95.

K-2   Grandpa is a bit tubby, bald and bespectacled in Gammell's bright, clean pictures (nice shading, nice composition) for a picture book told

1

in the second person. Grandpa takes three grandchildren up to the attic, where he arranges lights and gives a performance that enchants his audience. They tell him they wish they could have seen him dance in "the good old days" but he says he wouldn't trade a million good old days for the time he spends with the narrators. Still—he glances back up the attic stairs, and "we wonder how much he really misses that time on the vaudeville stage . . . ." There's an engaging warmth to the story, a little humor, a poignant note, and a refreshingly different role for a grandparent. Nice, too, to have an elderly person who is still active and capable.

4   **Ackerman,** Karen. *The Tin Heart*; illus. by Michael Hays. Atheneum, 1990. ISBN 0-689-31461-2. 32p. $13.95.

5-8 yrs.   Soft in line and color, nicely composed paintings are carefully integrated with the text of a simply written Civil War story. Mahaley's father operates a ferry from the northern side of the Ohio River; Flora's father has a store on the Kentucky side. The two girls, best friends, play together while passengers are buying and loading goods. Flora's father has made a tin heart, cut in half, for the girls to wear as a symbol of their friendship. When war comes the fathers are on opposite sides of the conflict, and the ferry dock is changed. There is one dramatic episode, when Mahaley's father is helping slaves escape (via the old dock) and Mahaley falls overboard. She is rescued, and her father returns for her; both fathers begin to understand what the children already know. "Not the river, not the war, was strong enough to keep the two halves of a tin heart, of a friendship, apart forever." Oversimplified, perhaps, but for the read-aloud audience the story is at a comprehensible level. It's told with subdued momentum and in a restrained style that adds to the effectiveness of the story by providing contrast with the drama of war's tension and the flight to freedom.

5   **Adler,** C. S. *Eddie's Blue-Winged Dragon*. Putnam, 1988. ISBN 0-399-21535-2. 144p. $13.95.

4-6   Eddie hoped his little sister would like the dragon, elegantly crafted of brass and with transparent blue glass wings. Mina didn't like it at all; she said it was alive and it was watching her—but then Mina was only six. It soon becomes clear to the reader as it does to Eddie, that the dragon does come to life, and that it acts as an instrument of vengeance against those who are unpleasant to Eddie. The fantasy element is nicely incorporated into a story that has perceptive treatment of familial and peer relationships, of Eddie's growing self-confidence in dealing with a bully and overcoming shyness, and of the delicate balance of classroom life, especially for a child with cerebral palsy. Well done.

6   Adoff, Arnold. *Chocolate Dreams;* illus. by Turi MacCombie. Lothrop, 1989. Library ed. ISBN 0-688-06823-5; Trade ed. ISBN 0-688-06822-7. 64p. Library ed. $13.88; Trade ed. $13.95.

3-6   A rich confection of wordplay, rhythms, and unexpected twists of rhyme and meaning from a poet in his element—chocolate. Adoff has managed to turn chocolate into a metaphor for love, disappointment, delight, sadness, and experience with forty-five poems that take a reader by surprise and at the same time resonate with the familiar. Some are straight-out funny, as in the case of "Chocolate Dreams. Five." Other samples are tongue-in-cheek; the greedy narrator in "I Believe In The Theory That Says We Were Visited Long Ago" says pompously, "and, of course, I chew my chocolate in the/ cause of interplanetary peace." Extraterrestrials turn out to have a keen taste for chocolate, which also inspires a "Horror Fantasy Chiller." There are "Mathematical Metric Conversion" schemes, dreams, riddles, stories, fairy tales, embarrassments ("In Public, I Pick A Piece Or Two From The Plate"), myths, rescue missions, philosophies, geographies, profundities, slices of life ("In The Moments Of Our Cookies"), cheers, and warnings ("Let The Biter Beware . . . In the center of each dark deep/ chocolate hunk/ there is a caramel/ chunk just waiting to glue/ your teeth together/ forever./ Take care"). In all the poems Adoff shows a combination of invention and control, depth and delight, that marks his best work. The assortment of brown and full-color pop-art pictures is luscious. (N.B. The reviewer is not a chocoholic and thus brings unbiased perspective.)

7   Adoff, Arnold. *Sports Pages;* illus. by Steve Kuzma. Lippincott, 1986. Library ed. ISBN 0-397-32103-1; Trade ed. ISBN 0-397-32102-3. 74p. Library ed. $10.89; Trade ed.. $11.50.

3-6   Soft, grayed pictures that are remarkable for the economy of line with which the artist shows action reflect the range of sports in Adoff's poems and the diversity of emotions and experiences they portray. The poems are in the voices of young athletes of both sexes, and they capture hope or despair, excitement or exhaustion, the bonding in a team sport, the isolation of the single participant. Adoff writes with a control of structure that never impedes the movement of the poem. This is one of his best collections.

8   Adoff, Arnold. *The Cabbages Are Chasing the Rabbits;* illus. by Janet Stevens. Harcourt, 1985. ISBN 0-15-213875-7. 32p. $13.95.

K-2   There's just a touch of cumulating comic frenzy in the illustrations, colorful scenes of flora and fauna in mixed media (ink, watercolor, and colored pencil) that echo the fanciful role reversal of vegetables chasing rabbits who are chasing dogs who are chasing leaves while, in contrapuntal fashion, the birds sit stubbornly on the ground waiting to be fed and a scandalized owl makes pointed comments about such laziness. The poem has a blithe, romping quality that should appeal to children whether or not they are aware of the controlled structure or such devices as refrain and accumulation.

9   **Aesop**. *The Town Mouse and the Country Mouse*; ad. and illus. by Janet Stevens. Holiday House, 1987. ISBN 0-8234-0633-4. 28p. $13.95.

4-6 yrs.   Stevens extends the Aesop fable with dialogue and detail to serve her funny, full-page spreads, resounding with brisk watercolors, lively line work, and expressive animal characters. The city mouse, in particular, resembles a child playing dress-up, draped with an earring for a hat and other oversize jewelry. The close-ups of the larger animals—a cow, a cat, a pig's tail, human feet, and two ferocious dogs—make effective contrasts in perspective. Whether the backdrop for dramatic action is a field of cabbages or a table full of sweets, blatant moral has rarely had such playful context.

10   **Ahlberg**, Allan. *Ten in a Bed*; illus. by André Amstutz. Viking, 1989. ISBN 0-670-82042-3. 95p. $11.95.

4-6
*

The ten in this witty and literary bed include three bears; a wicked, er, wonderful witch; a puss-in-boots; an oh-so-sleeping beauty; a big bad wolf ("*Tra la la la la*—that's a weak line"); Simple Simon ("though it would have been *Brainy Simon* or *Captain Dynamite Simon*, if I had written it"); a frog in search of a kiss; and a hungry giant. "*Fish gotta swim, birds gotta fly*—and I have to eat people." It's easy to be clever with this sort of material, but Ahlberg's satiric twigs brush gently, always remaining true to the fairytale source and spirit. The bed belongs to Dinah, a commonsensical Scheherazade who encounters each of the creatures sleeping in it on successive nights, and gets them to leave by telling stories—*their* stories, as they would like to hear them. Most of the visitors turn out to know each other, and the stories turn into stories within stories within stories ("'I have heard it already *already*!' said the baby bear") as Dinah and her guests ponder the mysteries of tales and tradition: "'Yes, well there's other versions,' said the wolf over his shoulder. 'Lots of 'em.'" The fresh tone and humor will recommend this to young sophisticates who believe themselves too old for fairy tales.

11   **Aiken**, Joan. *Mortimer Says Nothing*; illus. by Quentin Blake. Harper/Charlotte Zolotow, 1987. Library ed. ISBN 0-06-020039-1; Trade ed. ISBN 0-06-020038-3. 185p. Library ed. $12.89; Trade ed. $12.70.

5-7   Funny short stories continue the adventures of Arabel Jones and her raven, Mortimer, who can (and does) swallow anything from garden tools to gold bricks. In the first tale, Mortimer stymies an ornithologist who is trying to record the bird's call of "Nevermore!" Mortimer also complicates a frenetic series of events in which Mrs. Jones runs amok in her preparations for a visit from a snooty ladies' club. In a second story, Mortimer foils a spoiled visiting cousin and catches a criminal gang singlehanded; in the third, he accompanies the family on a chaotic "rest cure" for Mr. Jones; and in the fourth, he disappears during a crisis over a mysterious telephone caller. Occasionally the humor here becomes predictable in its exaggeration, but children will enjoy the slapstick effects and pileup of incidents. This is illustrated with Quentin Blake's cartoon drawings in much the same format as earlier books in the series.

12   **Aiken**, Joan. *The Teeth of the Gale*. Harper, 1988. Library ed. ISBN 0-06-020045-6; Trade ed. ISBN 0-06-020044-8. 307p. Library ed. $14.89; Trade ed. $14.95.

7-10   Continuing the successful combination of adventure, romance, and history that distinguished the first two books of this trilogy, *Go Saddle the Sea* and *Bridle the Wind* , this is set in a turbulent period of Spanish history, the 1820's. Felix, now a college student, is called home by his Spanish grandfather to respond to a written request that Felix help the beautiful Dona Conchita find and retrieve the three children who have been spirited away by her husband, declared evil and probably mad. Felix responds with alacrity, since his name had been forwarded by his beloved Juana (now preparing to take her vows as a nun). Aiken has managed again to knit enough colorful characters and cliffhanger situations for two books into a coherent whole, and if now and then Felix, the narrator, or wily Conchita or evil Don Ignacio seems to be more theatrical than real, few Aiken fans will care.

13   **Alcock**, Vivien. *The Cuckoo Sister*. Delacorte, 1986. ISBN 0-385-29467-0. $14.95.

6-9   First published in Great Britain, this is a remarkably effective story, effective in its perceptiveness, its credibility as the voice of a child, and its dramatic suspense. Kate, eleven, is shocked when she accidentally discovers an older sister had been stolen from her pram as a baby. She's even more shocked when tough, vulgar thirteen-year-old Rosie shows up with a sealed letter that says the sender (Rosie's "Mum") confesses to having kidnapped her and announces that she's going to disappear and Rosie is all theirs, that she is their long-lost Emma, Kate's older sister. But is it true? Is Rosie-Emma going to oust Kate from her position as does the fledgling cuckoo hatching in another bird's nest? Rosie, by the way, is angry, vituperative, and not at all interested in being part of an upper middle class family. Alcock does a fine job of showing the ambivalence of both girls as their relationship changes, and she builds suspense without making a big fuss about doing so.

14   **Alcock**, Vivien. *The Monster Garden*. Delacorte, 1988. ISBN 0-440-50053-2. 134p. $13.95.

5-9   Whether she writes realistic fiction like *The Cuckoo Sister*, or more often—as here—fantasy, Alcock is a superb craftsman. Her books have well-sustained pace and narrative flow, innovative plots, and strong characters. Here the protagonist is the rather lonely daughter of a widowed father, who pays as little attention to Frankie as do her older brothers. "My father is a high-up scientist and a low-down male chauvinist pig." When she discovers that one brother has stolen some "goo" from Dad's genetic engineering lab, Frankie demands a share as the price of silence. And from that grayish lump grows a living thing, a monster ("Monnie") who becomes more and more responsive and whose existence must be kept a secret shared with few other people. Eventually, for its own safety, Monnie has to leave, although it and a mourning Frankie meet one last time after the monster has become a beautiful, gleaming sea creature. *The Monster Garden* is a deft fantasy; it is also a story of compassionate love and growing self-reliance.

15   **Alcock**, Vivien. *The Mysterious Mr. Ross*. Delacorte, 1987. ISBN 0-385-29581-2. 161p. $14.95.

5-8
*
"'Don't talk to strange men,' she said, 'And remember, you're not to go anywhere near the Gray Gulls.'" Feeling truly at home only along the rough seashore rockline of the Gray Gulls, Felicity habitually defies the second of her mother's instructions; the first is ignored when she spots a young stranger trapped by a dangerous tide. For a few triumphant days, Felicity is a heroine ("I particularly liked the way you waved aside their compliments with your bandaged hand. Such a big bandage too! Most effective" says one amused observer) and the fished-out Mr. "Albert Ross" a celebrity, but the town and Felicity's family begin to tire of them both, leaving Felicity alone but for the albatross around her neck as both comfort and curse. As in her previous novels, Alcock here invests a gripping, elemental suspense story with mythic resonances and psychological complexity. Felicity is a bright but awkward girl who fills her head with impossible romantic stories; Ross, the quintessential stranger "who might be anyone. Anything." satisfies her dreams in a way unexpected both to readers and Felicity herself. There's a hint of the supernatural in the denouement, not enough to classify this as a ghost story, but enough to make us question the possibility, an ambiguity in the best gothic tradition.

16   **Alcock**, Vivien. *Travelers by Night*. Delacorte, 1985. ISBN 0-385-29406-9. 182p. $14.95.

4-6   Belle and Charlie are circus children, he an orphan who'd been taken in by her parents (his aunt and uncle) and she a once-flamboyant tightrope walker who had lost her courage and garnered a facial scar in an accident. Now the circus has failed financially, Belle's parents have gone to America, and the two children are having a farm vacation before the school term and a new life with a hospitable aunt begin. The crisis that changes their plans is the discovery that Tessie, an old elephant they both love, is destined for the slaughter-house because her owner is old and ill. That's when Belle conceives the idea of stealing Tessie and, traveling by night and hiding by day, taking her to a safari park and sneaking her in. The situation and successful conclusion are improbable, but Alcock makes them believable and enjoyable, as Belle and Charlie have a series of adventures and encounters en route. They spend the money they have been hoarding to pay for plastic surgery for Belle, but she considers it spent in a good cause and indeed she finds, after inevitable publicity, that she has adjusted to having a scarred face. The pace is brisk, the children appealing, the mission one with which most readers will sympathize, and the book substantial in structure and style.

17   **Alderson**, Brian, ed. *The Helen Oxenbury Nursery Rhyme Book*; illus. by Helen Oxenbury. Morrow, 1987. ISBN 0-688-06899-5. 67p. $15.00.

3-5 yrs.   About half the length of the 156-page *Cakes and Custards* , from which
  *   these verses are drawn, this book is even more exciting visually than the original. The page size is larger; the images are given more space and their reproduction sharpened. In some cases the drawings themselves have been revised, and in general the format is cleaner. Those who missed the first book will be delighted at the full range of color, textural contrast, expression, and variation of page design here. There's refreshing wit in depictions of the humorous verse. The hungry cow considering the piper's song about corn rigs is memorable, as is the "Don't Care" child being squashed into a pot by a ring of outraged adults, or the married man whose troubles begin with two glaring mothers-in-law ("Needles and Pins"), or Good King Arthur's bleary-eyed wife tottering out in her robe to fry last night's pudding. On the other hand, "I Am a Little Beggar Girl" is accompanied by a haunting, full-page portrait of a ragged child gazing through the window with her whole heart in her face. Illustrations appear variously framed and in shapes contrasting from circular to rectangular but always coordinated for a smooth transition from page to page. The drawing is structurally sound and the coloration subtle but vivid. Alderson's selection and editing bring out the best in Mother Goose, street rhymes, and childhood chants, with a blend of popular and lesser-known choices. A prime pick.

18   **Alexander**, Ellen. *Llama and the Great Flood: A Folktale from Peru*; written and illus. by Ellen Alexander. Crowell, 1989. Library ed. ISBN 0-

690-04729-0; Trade ed. ISBN 0-690-04727-4. 39p. Library ed. $13.89; Trade ed. $13.95.

5-8 yrs.   A welcome addition to the picture-book folklore collection, this will be a logical companion to present with the many available versions of Noah and the Ark. After an introduction to the Andean people of Peru, the narration picks up the Quechuan story of a great flood, about which a llama dreams and warns his owner. The two of them, with the owner's wife and child, take food to the top of the highest mountain, Willka Qutu, where they find animals of every kind already gathered. "Almost at once the sea began to overflow and they all remained stranded there. . . . Only the top of Willka Qutu remained above water. It is said that the water even reached the fox's tail and turned it black. It is still that color today." When the people and animals descend, they find an empty world that they must repopulate. A note explains the background of the story and some of the artist's graphic motifs, which she attributes to "several pre-Inca cultures such as the Wari and the Moche." The full-color wash drawings are vivid even if the human figures are somewhat stiffly drafted, and the rocky landscapes are expressive—literally, when parts of the terrain take on the aspect of faces.

19   Alexander, Lloyd. *The El Dorado Adventure.* Dutton, 1987. ISBN 0-525-44313-4. 164p. $12.95.

5-8   In a sequel to the humorous/picaresque *The Illyrian Adventure,* the intrepid young Philadelphia heiress, Vesper Holly, goes off to the small country of El Dorado, in Central America. The time is the 1870's, the narrator is Vesper's guardian, the bemused and scholarly Professor Brinton Garret, Brinnie. It is Alexander's humor and his zest for the outrageous that make this tale enjoyable, for the plot romps from one frenetic villainy to another, as Vesper rebuffs evil foes, charms the Chirica Indians whose home lands she is saving, and effects enough escapes from captors to rival Pearl White. The wit, the humor, and the doughty protagonist will appeal to readers; the style, the firm characterization, and pointed digs at the foibles of humankind will give them substance.

20   Alexander, Lloyd. *The Illyrian Adventure.* Dutton, 1986. ISBN 0-525-44250-2. 132p. $12.95.

5-8   A gentleman scholar goes to collect his sixteen-year-old ward, Vesper, and straighten out her estate, but instead finds himself embroiled in an adventure halfway around the world. The time is 1872, and the place a small, autocratic kingdom in the Mediterranean, where Illyrian guerillas are carrying on skirmishes against their traditional enemies, the king (not a bad fellow) and his advisor (a very bad fellow). Vesper has stumbled over a secret in her deceased father's research, which eventually leads to the reconciliation of the warring factions, but not before a harrowing series of escapades—all revealed by the stuffy narrator, whose slowness to catch on adds calculably to the reader's suspense and high estimation of Vesper's cleverness. Alexander's archaeological mystery has intricate plotting and witty wording—a romp of a read-aloud for Raiders of the Lost Ark fans. And doesn't the ending hint at more enterprises to come?

21   **Alexander**, Lloyd. *The Philadelphia Adventure.* Dutton, 1990. ISBN 0-525-44564-1. 150p. $12.95.

6-9   Philadelphia is the setting for the fifth book about the intrepid nineteenth-century heroine Vesper Holly. Scheming to control Brazil's natural resources, arch-villain Helvitius is also intent on destroying Vesper, her guardian, Brinnie, and anyone else nearby. An amazingly resourceful young man, Toby ("The Weed") Passavant, has been added to the cast of characters as an innocent love interest for Vesper; bumbling Brinnie is characteristically jealous. Alexander has thoroughly researched the events and personalities surrounding the 1876 World's Fair. The combination of historical fact, non-stop danger and intrigue, and masterful writing style adds up to another energetic predicament for Vesper Holly.

22   **Alexander**, Martha. *Even That Moose Won't Listen to Me;* written and illus. by Martha Alexander. Dial, 1988. Library ed. ISBN 0-8037-0188-8; Trade ed. ISBN 0-8037-0187-X. 26p. Library ed. $9.89; Trade ed. $9.95.

K-2   Softly colored, neatly executed line and wash pictures in Alexander's distinctively low-keyed style illustrate a story in the *Nobody Listens to Andrew* tradition. As a moose calmly munches his way through the family vegetable garden, Rebecca's urgent pleas for intervention are dismissed by each member of her family; even the moose, when she tries to frighten him off, ignores Rebecca. When, too late, the others see the destruction in the garden and ask Rebecca what in the world happened, she answers "I'm busy now," and promises to tell them when she finishes building her toy rocket ship. Not a new idea, but an attractive development of the concept, amusing, but—because of Rebecca's calm—not quite convincing.

23   **Aliki**. *Dinosaur Bones;* written and illus by Aliki. Crowell, 1988. Library ed. ISBN 0-690-04550-6; Trade ed. ISBN 0-690-04549-2. 32p. Library ed. $12.89; Trade ed. $12.95.

K-3   In a companion volume to three earlier books about dinosaurs, Aliki explains how, based on discoveries of fossil remains and the rock strata in which they were found, scientists have been able to classify species and assign them chronological niches. The text is written simply and clearly, and the cartoon-style drawings give additional information through captions and comments-in-balloons. An index-chart gives habitats and geological periods, and the text gives, in addition to facts about scientific history, a sense of the way knowledge is gathered, sifted, organized, and perennially questioned.

24   **Aliki.** *The King's Day: Louis XIV of France*; written and illus. by Aliki. Crowell, 1989. Library ed. ISBN 0-690-04590-5; Trade ed. 0-690-04588-3. 32p. Library ed. $13.89; Trade ed. $13.95.

2-5
*
Louis XIV was the archetypal king: powerful, brilliant, wealthy, and totally committed to personal luxury. He was also a man of routine, so the one day depicted here resembled many others in the seventy-two years of his reign. Aliki has done a masterful job of balancing selective details of daily ritual—the king's Lever, Mass, Council, Petit Couvert, hunt, Appartement, Grand Couvert, and Coucher—with historical complexities of setting. One double spread shows Louis, Queen Marie Thérèse, and the Dauphin on the verso, with two of Louis' mistresses, their eight children, and the governess Louis later married on the recto. We learn that an autopsy showed Louis' stomach to be twice the size of an ordinary one, that five hundred servants were kept busy preparing his meals, that he did not eat between meals and did not talk during them. His courtiers fought to attend him from the moment he arose at 8 A.M. to his bedtime at 1:30 A.M. What we don't learn, even in the concluding précis, is the cost of his rule to the peasantry or anything about the common people whom "he controlled . . . with absolute power." Although it's true that "he knew just what he wanted for his kingdom, and brought spectacular glory to it and to the seventeenth century in which he lived," it would have been more accurate to hint that there was another side to the story. This is a quibble, however, and one that's partly attributable to Aliki's sharply defined scope. The book design combines the appeal of a comic format with carefully researched illustration, including elaborate indoor and outdoor scenes of Versailles. A chronology and list of definitions (without pronunciation) for French words are appended. On balance, this is lively and informative biography.

25   **Aliki.** *Overnight at Mary Bloom's.* Greenwillow, 1987. Library ed. ISBN 0-688-06765-4; Trade ed. ISBN 0-688-06764-6. 31p. illus. Library ed. $11.88; Trade ed. $11.75.

K-2
Breezy, flyaway line drawings with watercolor and crayon echo the ebullience of another story about the joys of visiting an adult friend who loves children. Mary Bloom's invitation to spend the night is accepted with alacrity (no parental permission is mentioned) and the experience, as described by the young visitor, is sheer delight. They cook together, feed the pets and Mary Bloom's baby, clean up, play

games, do bedtime chores and rituals: walk the dogs, brush teeth, read a story, and snuggle happily to sleep. For children, Mary Bloom is, indeed, the hostess with the mostest.

26   **Allard**, Harry. *Miss Nelson Has A Field Day*; illus. by James Marshall. Houghton, 1985. ISBN 0-395-36690-9. 30p. $12.95.

K-2   Staff and pupils at the Horace B. Smedley School are equally dejected; not only is their football team inept, but also the coach has cracked up—and the big Thanksgiving Day game is looming. Pretty Miss Nelson comes to the rescue in the guise of the dreaded, dour Viola Swamp. But there's one thing different here; unlike the other Miss Nelson books, in which it's clear that the teacher is in disguise, the two appear at the same time! Allard's explanation is pat, but children will probably enjoy the contrivance just as they have enjoyed the ebullience and exaggeration of text and pictures in the earlier stories. Anyway, it's hard to take seriously a story in which a struggling team is so quickly made to shape up that they defeat a strong team seventy-seven to three.

27   **Allen**, Jeffrey. *Nosey Mrs. Rat*; illus. by James Marshall. Viking, 1985. ISBN 0-670-80880-6. 30p. $11.95.

4-6   A hilarious read-aloud and look-along introduces someone everyone knows: the peripatetic snoop. Nosey Mrs. Rat does not mind over-hearing and overseeing everyone's business, but she gets her comeuppance when she tattles on Brewster Blackstone's truant activities. He and his gang make a film exposing her favorite tricks: Shirley Rat upside down in the garbage can looking for clues, and again, ballooning her way up to peer into high windows. Properly mortified, Shirley flees the scene and vows to mend her ways, sort of, in an anti-climatic ending. Marshall maintains his flair for naively humorous expressions and silly situations. Mrs. Rat using her special sticky shoes to scale Brewster's wall is memorable.

28   **Ames**, Mildred. *Cassandra-Jamie*. Scribner, 1985. ISBN 0-684-18472-9. 135p. $12.95.

5-7   Jamie liked the new seventh grade English teacher, Ms. Schuyler, right away, but it took a longer time before she realized why the woman looked familiar: she looked like Jamie's mother. What could be nicer than bringing this wonderful teacher to the attention of her widowed father? That becomes Jamie's mission, and the story of her efforts to be a matchmaker, her resentment against the woman her father's dating, and her annoyance with Gavin, the next door neighbor who keeps popping in to chat with Agnes, the housekeeper, is brisk in pace and perceptive in its quasi-humorous, sympathetic development.

Characters have depth and individuality, and the dialogue has an easy, natural flow.

29   **Ancona**, George. *Handtalk Zoo*; by George Ancona and Mary Beth; illus. with photographs by George Ancona. Four Winds, 1989. ISBN 0-02-700801-0. 30p. $14.95.

2-5   Color photographs show the bright faces and deft hands of an interracial group of children who are visiting a zoo with two adults, one of whom is co-author Mary Beth. Like the previous *Handtalk* and *Handtalk Birthday*, this is permeated with the message that physical limitations are a superficial difference; the five boys and girls shown here are lively, responsive, and intelligent guides to the zoo and to the signs used to describe its inhabitants. Signs for sentences ("Let's go see the bear") are demonstrated in sequential photographs; fingerspellings are also given for the animals' names.

30   **Ancona**, George. *Turtle Watch*; written and illus. with photographs by George Ancona. Macmillan, 1987. ISBN 0-02-700910-6. 47p. $13.95.

2-5   A photodocumentary records the work of oceanographers as they try to rebuild the sea turtle population on the northeast coast of Brazil through a project called TAMAR. Every night during the nesting season, they track down the turtles, transfer the eggs to a safer location, and protect the released hatchlings on their way to the sea. An important part of the project is educating fishermen and their children to the importance of preserving what they used to eat or sell—six out of seven species of sea turtles in this hemisphere are endangered. The details of the turtles' egg-laying, of the project's operation, and of two local children's participation are vividly projected in both pictures and text. The ending seems abrupt—one wishes for more information on the habits and characteristics of the sea turtle, but the book is successful within its defined focus; it will serve as a springboard to further exploration on the part of students intrigued by this absorbing, carefully designed presentation.

31   **Anderson**, Joan. *From Map to Museum: Uncovering Mysteries of the Past;* illus. with photographs by George Ancona. Morrow, 1988. Library ed. ISBN 0-688-06915-0; Trade ed. ISBN 0-688-06914-2. 63p. Trade ed. $11.95; Library ed. $11.88.

5-7   This author-illustrator team have collaborated on a "living history" series that includes *Joshua's Westward Journal*. Here they document the work of David Thomas, Curator of Anthropology at the American Museum of Natural History, in his exploration of a Spanish mission site on St. Catherine's island off the coast of Georgia. Following an introduction by Dr. Thomas himself and a description of his exhibit, Anderson backs up to the beginning of his archaeological expedition, from his hunt for the site through the details of mapping, digging, classifying, preserving, and studying. The knowledge that a nail is as important a treasure as a gold medal is crucial to the account: "It's not what you find but what you find out that counts." Thus the stress on any clue that "ecofacts" (fish scales, animal bones, shells) can give about the lifestyle of a people ("It was determined that the Indians who lived under Spanish influence and adopted European agricultural methods developed more tooth decay and bone disease"). Business-like black-and-white photographs and maps on every page expand a balanced report that benefits considerably from an expert's cooperation.

32   **Anderson**, Margaret. *The Druid's Gift*. Knopf, 1989. Library ed. ISBN 0-394-91936-X; Trade ed. ISBN 0-394-81936-5. 211p. Library ed. $13.99; Trade ed. $12.95.

6-9   Carefully crafted and colorfully written, this multi-layered time shift fantasy is particularly appealing in the picture it gives of succeeding generations of the inhabitants of an isolated island off the Scottish coast. There are interlocking events and memories that hold the story together, from the era of Viking invasions to a millennium later; one of the links is the protagonist of each segment (called, variously, Caitlin, Cathan, Catie, or Catriona) who is instrumental in fusing historic themes and in bringing together the traditionally hostile Druids and the islanders. A nicely meshed combination of realism and fantasy, this has a colorful setting, a brisk pace, and characters who come alive.

33   **Andrews**, Jan. *Very Last First Time*; illus. by Ian Wallace. McElderry, 1986. ISBN 0-689-50388-1. 29p. $9.95.

5-7 yrs.   In her Inuit village in northern Canada, Eva Padlyat prepares to "walk on the bottom of the sea" alone for the first time. For years, after the tide goes out, she and her mother have gone under the ice to collect mussels, but doing it by herself is a rite of passage that becomes a mini-adventure when she goes exploring, forgets the time, drops her candle, and barely beats the sea water back to her ice hole. The paint-ings, dominated by deep purple glinting here and there with gold or green, are impressionistic in texture and give an eerie sense of the shadowy shapes, crevasses, and sense of isolation surrounding the child. A unique experience for young listeners and an intriguing introduction to another culture.

34   **Anno**, Mitsumasa. *Anno's Math Games*; written and illus. by Mitsumasa Anno. Philomel, 1987. ISBN 0-399-21151-9. 100p. $18.95.

2-4   Anno's sprightly illustrations and direct, simple text present a series of mathematical concepts for younger children, with questions posed but not answered, so that the book has a game element. It is designed to inculcate concepts of sets, location, capacity, sequence, proportion, etc. in a way that is effective. Most of the questions posed are fairly easy to answer, although a few minor obstacles (a deck of cards that has 11, 12 and 13 rather than the jack, queen, and king familiar to children in this country, for example) may require adult interpretation. Notes for older readers are appended, explaining Anno's purpose and suggesting ways to use the book.

35   **Apfel**, Necia H. *Nebulae: The Birth and Death of Stars*. Lothrop, 1988. Library ed. ISBN 0-688-07229-1; Trade ed. ISBN 0-688-07228-3. 48p. illus. with photographs. Library ed. $13.88; Trade ed. $13.95.

3-5   The coauthor of two college textbooks on astronomy, Apfel writes simply and clearly in an oversize book with large print and a continuous text. Although there are a few instances in which the arrangement of material seems illogical ("One famous stellar nursery is the Rosette Nebula . . ." on the page after a first reference to that nebula, for example) the text is on the whole sequential and authoritative. Apfel describes the way in which nebulae are formed and their consistency and appearance at different times during their dramatic life cycle. An index is provided, as is a brief list of books (ranging broadly in reading level) for further reading.

36   **Arnold**, Caroline. *Kangaroo*; Library ed. ISBN 0-688-06479-5; Trade ed. ISBN 0-688-06478-7. *Koala*; Library ed. ISBN 0-688-06481-7; Trade ed. ISBN 0-688-06480-9. Each book: illus. with photographs by Richard Hewett. Morrow, 1987. 46p. Library ed. $11.88; Trade ed. $11.75.

4-6   Both of these books are smoothly written, with an involving balance between focus on an animal and generalizations about the species. The first book starts out with a couple's adoption of a young orphaned gray kangaroo named Sport, which is raised with the family dog and then released into a nature preserve. Between descriptions of Sport's antics, readers learn about the history, habits, and reproduction cycle of various kinds of kangaroos. Excellent color photography features the animals in both a tame and wild environment. The second book opens with the mating of Frangipani, a three-year-old koala that subsequently has a baby named Karen; both text and photography follow its development from pouch to independence. Here, too, are the facts of marsupial life, with characteristics and diet explained, along with notes of warning about the effects of civilization on wild habitats. Two examples of solid, inviting information.

37   **Arnold**, Caroline. *Trapped in Tar: Fossils from the Ice Age*; illus. with photographs by Richard Hewett. Houghton/Clarion, 1987. ISBN 0-89919-415-X. 54p. $12.95.

4-6   Along with black-and-white photographs of models and reconstructed skeletons from the George C. Page Museum of La Brea Discoveries, an enthusiastic text describes the kinds of fossils found in southern California tar pits. The processes of recovery and paleontologic research are the real emphasis here, but these reveal more than a glimpse of animal and plant life in the Ice Age. In addition to the inherent child appeal of the subject and the clear explanations, the book has a lively format, with pictures dramatically featuring young museum visitors in involved inspection or even hands-on experience of the displays. Closeups of scientists working with bones in excavation pits and laboratories lend a sense of excitement that will inspire students working on prehistoric units and time lines.

38   **Asch**, Frank. *Pearl's Pirates*; written and illus. by Frank Asch. Delacorte, 1987. ISBN 0-385-29546-4. 167p. $13.95.

2-4   In a sequel to *Pearl's Promise* , the intrepid mouse (Pearl is one of a pair of pet mice, and she and Wilbur dote on their boy Jay) is separated from her owner after he is in an accident. Trapped with Wilbur and some other mice on a cargo ship, Pearl escapes by taking over a model of the *Golden Hind* and sailing it away to further adventures, not one of which is convincing but all of which are entertaining. One dire crisis follows another as Pearl and her pals search for pirate treasure. At the close, she and Wilbur are reunited with a happy boy. How? Just don't ask, it's irrelevant. Lots of action here (if little relevance) and a light style that includes plenty of word-play in the sprightly dialogue, and even some characterization.

39   **Ashabranner**, Brent. *Always to Remember: The Story of the Vietnam Veterans Memorial;* illus. with photographs by Jennifer Ashabranner. Dodd/Putnam, 1988. ISBN 0-396-09089-3. 101p. $13.95.

5-8   No current events writer for young people does a better job than Ashabranner in providing an enlightening balance of solid infor-mation, pertinent anecdote, and thoughtful opinion. Beginning with a concise (and fair) chapter on the Vietnam War, the author then recounts the hard work of Jan Scruggs, the vet who began the Vietnam Veterans Memorial Fund, and Maya Lin, the 21-year-old architecture student who won the contest to design the monument. While there is plenty in this book to bring tears, Ashabranner is unobtrusive, allowing the veterans, families, and the memorial to speak for themselves, and his own message that war "is about sacrifice and sorrow, not about glory and reward" is quietly woven in. Although the book lacks pic-tures that convey a sense of the sculpture as a whole (an aerial view would have been helpful), Jennifer Ashabranner's photographs capture the details of flowers and fatigues left along the base of the monument wall but, as the architect intended, viewers will find their attentions primarily caught by the endless rows of names.

40   **Ashabranner**, Brent. *Children of the Maya: A Guatemalan Indian Odyssey*; illus. with photographs by Paul Conklin. Dodd, 1986. ISBN 0-396-08786-8. 97p. $12.95.

5-9   The most intensely focused and moving of all the reportage in this
*   writer-photographer team's series on U.S. minorities provides brief background on the political dynamics behind the genocide of Mayan Indians at the hands of the Guatemalan army. Most of the book is devoted to the stories told by survivors of village massacres, their escapes, experiences as refugees through Mexico and across the border, and their resettlement in Indiantown, Florida, a population center for black, Hispanic, and native American migrant workers. Both the narrative and the photography are informal but clear; as a history and current events resource, this gives not only information but also a sense of immediate involvement in a situation too close and too tragic to be ignored.

41   **Ashabranner**, Brent. *Dark Harvest: Migrant Workers in America*; illus. with photographs by Paul Conklin. Dodd, 1985. ISBN 0-396-08624-1. 150p. $14.95.

7-12   An outstanding combination of coherent narrative and sensitive
*   photography will take readers into the fields with migrant workers who, in many cases, tell their own stories of what life is like following the crops. Using information based on research and interviews, Asha-branner presents facts with a personal sense of involvement that lends urgency to descriptions of children housed and fed below poverty standards, shatters some myths about lazy migrant workers, and yet gives a clear outline of the labor, routes, ethnic groups, agribusiness corporations, and educational/legal problems involved. The black and white photos are expressive and well-composed, a few parent-child portraits classic in the Dorothea Lange tradition. This team, which collaborated on *The New Americans: Changing Patterns in U.S. Immigration*, has an ability to project the people behind the data. Readers will learn to care about these subjects and recognize the strong family traditions they nurture in the face of a devastating system.

42   **Ashabranner**, Brent. *Into a Strange Land*; written by Brent Ashabranner and Melissa Ashabranner. Dodd, 1987. ISBN 0-396-08841-4. 117p. illus. with photographs. $12.95.

5-   Like previous Ashabranner books that document a minority experience in America through the lives and voices of its adolescent members, this conveys both information and humanity. Primarily focusing on Indo-Chinese refugees, the Ashabranners begin (through their interviews) with the reasons these young people leave country and family, their sometimes dangerous escapes and experiences in refugee camps, and their settlement and adjustment in the United States. What comes through most clearly is courage: of the parents, sending their children to a hoped-for better life; of the foster parents, bridging an enormous cultural gap; and of the young people themselves. Most poignant are the stories of Amerasian children fathered by American soldiers: "'I'm always watching on the streets. Maybe that way someday I'll see him. His face will be my face.'" Index and bibliography.

43   **Ashabranner**, Brent. *The Vanishing Border: A Photographic Journey Along Our Frontier With Mexico;* illus. with photographs by Paul Conklin. Dodd, 1987. ISBN   0-396-08900-3. 175p. $14.95.

6-10   In 1986, the U.S. Border patrol apprehended over 1.5 million illegal border crossers from Mexico, according to jacket copy, which continues, "But during the same year, Mexicans crossed the border legally almost 200 million times to work, shop, visit. . ." Ashabranner's investigative journey is recorded in a text that is sympathetic and lucid, based on many interviews on both sides of the border. He points out how interdependent the neighboring areas are, especially in the establishment of U.S.-owned assembly plants in Mexican border cities, in the sharing of conservation or irrigation schemes, in the back-and-forth flow of tourist, family, or business crossovers. The book is marred occasionally by florid passages, but is informative and detailed, is given variety by cited interviews, and is enhanced by the many well-placed photographs. A bibliography and an index are appended.

44   **Asimov**, Isaac. *How Did We Find Out About Robots?;* illus. by David Wool. Walker, 1985. ISBN 0-8027-6563-7. 62p. $9.85.

5-7   The title is misleading here; this isn't about how we found out about robots, but is a history of the development of increasingly sophisticated machines and devices from such early machines as those of Babbage and Hollerith and the early animated figures (automatons) that were designed to amuse rather than perform a useful function. Much of the material here has been included in other books about robots and robotics; Asimov adds information about robots in fiction, he concludes with some interesting conjectures about robots in the future, and he writes with his usual clarity and animation. An index is appended.

45   Avi. *The Man Who Was Poe*. Orchard, 1989. Library ed. ISBN 0-531-08433-7; Trade ed. ISBN 0-531-05833-6. 208p. Library ed. $13.99; Trade ed. $13.95.

6-9   Eleven-year-old Edmund has lost his sister, and Edgar Allan Poe has lost his inspiration. Can they help each other? Informing an intricate detective story with the lurking menace of the real Poe's short stories, Avi has crafted a complex, atmospheric thriller. First mother, then aunt, then Sis having disappeared, a despairing Edmund turns for help to a stranger in the street. "Auguste Dupin" senses a story, as well as some disturbing parallels to his own life, and agrees to investigate. Callous, alcoholic, pursued by private demons, Dupin (Poe) is only intermittently helpful, and just as often hindering, forcing Edmund to do his own searching among shadows he only half comprehends. Avi recreates the gloom of 1840's Baltimore with a storyteller's ease, blending drama, history, and mystery without a hint of pastiche or calculation. And, as in the best mystery stories, readers will be left in the end with both the comfort of puzzles solved and the unease of mysteries remaining.

46   Avi. *Wolf Rider: A Tale of Terror*. Bradbury, 1986. ISBN 0-02-707760-8. 202p. $12.95.

7-10   Fifteen-year-old Andrew Zadinsky receives a call from a mysterious man named Zeke, who says he has just killed a woman named Nina. Everyone Andy talks to, including his father, the school counselor, the police, his friends, and even the girl herself (once he finds her alive) believes the call is a crank, but Andy is convinced the caller is a dangerous psychotic and becomes obsessed with identifying and exposing him. The story is harrowing on two counts: one, the deepening trouble Andy gets into with authorities who believe he is disturbed as a result of his mother's recent death; and two, the approach of the inevitable encounter with the potential killer, who turns out to be a model professor in the mathematics department where Andy's father teaches. The ending is not a standard mystery wrap-up, but a disturbing, ambiguous parting of father and son. Perhaps just a touch too cold and calculating, this is nevertheless a gripping and above-average YA thriller.

47   Babbitt, Natalie. *The Devil's Other Storybook*; written and illus. by Natalie Babbitt. Farrar, 1987. ISBN 0-374-31767-4. 79p. $10.95.

4-7   Ten more stories about the disarming creature featured in *The Devil's Storybook* further characterize him as playing off the foibles of ridiculous human beings and sometimes demonstrating a few human-like failures himself. Plotwise, these are not quite as strong as the first batch, but they're craftily written and mischievous. One pokes fun at a soldier who can hardly wait to go to the next campaign, another recounts the fate of a hunter followed down to Hell by a rhinoceros who pursues him eternally, a third derides the incomprehensible speech of both a pickpocket and his educated victim, and a fourth leaves three snooty sisters boating on the Styx forever because they won't associate with the rabble entering Hell. Babbitt's style is as clean and elegant as ever, the unexpected homey expression contrasting with the classical flow for calculated effect. Her pen-and-ink hatch drawings are equally meticulous. A choice morsel to be savored with tongue in cheek.

48   **Baer**, Edith. *This Is the Way We Go to School: A Book about Children Around the World*; illus. by Steven Björkman. Scholastic, 1990. ISBN 0-590-43161-7. 38p. $13.95.

4-6 yrs.   A first-grade's perfect first-day book. In rhyming couplets and morning watercolors, kids (some in a hurry, some lost in thought, some waving at the reader) go off to school—by foot, car, bus, El train, trolley, bicycle, boat, radio . . . "and the famous Metro line suits Igor and Ilyana fine." The various vehicles ("Bianca, Beppo, Benedetto, ride aboard the *vaporetto*") are informative and interesting, and the multicultural lesson is deftly understated. Pen-and-watercolor illustrations are fresh and optimistic: these kids can't wait to get to school. A closing world map provides geographic context for cultural comparisons. Baer's book makes a boon companion to *Is Anybody Up?*, Ellen Kandoian's introduction to waking up around the world.

49   **Baker**, Jeannie. *Where the Forest Meets the Sea*; written and illus. by Jeannie Baker. Greenwillow, 1988. Library ed. ISBN 0-688-06364-0; Trade ed. ISBN 0-688-06363-2. 28p. Library ed. $11.88; Trade ed. $11.95.

5-8 yrs.   A picture book set in the Daintree Rainforest of northeastern Australia, this features innovative art work—"relief collages . . . constructed from a multitude of materials, including modeling clay, papers, textured materials, preserved natural materials, and paints"— without becoming gimmicky. Colors, textures, and shapes are meticulously and tastefully superimposed for striking effects. The simple text of several lines per page is a first-person narrative about a young boy who boats through a reef with his father to the rainforest. There, he imagines what he would have seen a hundred million years ago, and children will relish finding the shadowy dinosaurs and other creatures that lurk in the tangled trees. After the beauty of these scenes, the last page is provocative. The boy, imagining a real estate development imposed on the area, asks, "But will the forest still be here when we come back?" A silhouette map and brief explanatory note on the Queensland wilderness will prove helpful in establishing the context.

50   **Baker**, Pamela J. *My First Book of Sign*; illus. by Patricia Bellan Gillen.
        Gallaudet University, 1986. ISBN 0-930323-20-3. 76p. $12.95.

K-2   To the hearing-impaired and to those who wish or need to commu-
        nicate with them, signing—communicating by the position and
        movement of hands and fingers—is a boon. This book, meant to be
        used by adults working with young children, is an effective tool for
        teaching signing, provided that adequate explanation is given of the
        illustrative devices used to show motion and direction: the drawing of
        an extra, shadowy hand to show change of position, or the diagrams
        that indicate movements by heavy lines and arrows. A double-page
        spread is used for each letter of the alphabet, and each is shown in
        upper and lower case. A few drawings on each page show words,
        illustrate them, and show the sign. Explanatory material, including
        sign descriptions, a diagram of the manual alphabet, and a letter
        about the author's experiences with a hearing-impaired child are
        appended.

51   **Ball**, Angela. *Vixie.* Oxford, 1988. ISBN 0-19-271555-0. 138p. $13.95

5-7   The time is 1908, the setting the English countryside (Wiltshire), and
        the protagonist, Vixie, is eleven when this record of a year of change
        begins. Economic conditions are already putting pressure on Vixie's
        family when her father, a shepherd, dies on a cold and lonely night.
        Vixie has to leave school and home and go into service as a house-
        maid. No melodramatic events here, but the story of a rural family
        and their community is told with a strong sense of narrative, has well-
        defined characters, and is leavened by humor.

52   **Bang**, Molly. *The Paper Crane;* written and illus. by Molly Bang.
        Greenwillow, 1985. Library ed. ISBN 0-688-04109-4; Trade ed. ISBN 0-
        688-04108-6. 31p. Library ed. $12.88; Trade ed. $13.00.

4-6 yrs. Cranes play an important part in the magical lore of Japan, and
        although the setting appears modern here and the cast multi-cultural,
        there is a distinctly oriental dimension to the simplicity of shapes and
        flat perspectives in Bang's art work. There is also a thoughtful blend of
        story and illustration, with a focal image of paper: paper cut-out
        pictures accompany a tale about a paper crane that comes to life and
        dances as a reward for a poor restaurant owner's generosity to a weary
        old traveler. Earth tones appropriately dominate a warm story that
        ends happily with the restaurant a success once more and the
        stranger flying away on his crane. A mysteriously moving variant
        of the wandering saint/hospitality rewarded legends.

53   **Banks**, Merry. *Animals of the Night*; illus. by Ronald Himler.
        Scribner's, 1990. ISBN 0-684-19093-1. 32p. $13.95.

3-6 yrs.   Because the text is simple without becoming either boring or cloying, and because the watercolor paintings are deeply involving, this is one of those rare bedtime mood pieces that does indeed cast a spell. The opening spread of falling twilight contrasted with a golden bathroom ("Sleepy children go to bed") is reversed in the concluding quiet dawn faced by a page of children bustling to "start a new day." In between come blue-textured scenes of the natural night world, with bullfrogs, skunks, raccoons, rabbits, possums, and of course their predators, the silent owl, the stalking coyote, and a fox. Even armadillos put in an appearance: "To cross a small stream, they hold their breath and walk across the bottom. To cross a wide stream, they swallow air and paddle across." The skillfully varied pictorial frames, the convincing perspectives, and the fine animal drafting invite a long look, while the words will soothe many a fear of the shadowed world beyond reach of electric lights.

54   **Barber**, Antonia. *The Enchanter's Daughter*; illus. by Errol Le Cain. Farrar, 1988. ISBN 0-374-3217-1. 32p. $13.95.

5-8 yrs.
    *   Some of Le Cain's finest painting distinguishes this literary fairy tale about an enchanter who imprisons his daughter in an isolated land of magic. She longs to know her identity and begs for company until finally, preoccupied by his search for the secret of eternal youth, he distracts her with storybooks. These lead her to knowledge and flight, which ends happily in reconciliation with her true family. The story is traditionally structured and sparely told without pretentious embellishment. There are hints of Japanese setting but no notes on origin. Le Cain's art, which can be stylized to the point of coldness, is here softened by a nuance of color and shape sometimes reminiscent of Dulac. The quality of reproduction does unusual justice to these subtleties. The full-page Orientally flavored compositions are elaborate but never out of control, absorbing and reflecting back the impact of the narrative conflict between life and death. A picture book that will extend its hold well beyond the usual preschool audience.

55   **Barrie**, Barbara. *Lone Star*. Delacorte, 1990. ISBN 0-385-30156-1. 182p. $13.95.

5-8   It's 1944, and Jane Miller is trying to adjust to life in Corpus Christi, Texas, where her family has moved to recover from her father's role in defrauding insurance customers. Bereft of her fancy Chicago apartment and extended Jewish family, she begs for a Christmas tree in order to be more like her new best friend. The tiny, secret tree provokes a crisis when Jane's visiting orthodox grandfather discovers it—at the same time as they hear the first news reports of Nazi concentration camps. This is a close and honest look at a child's struggle with being different. A stranger to two worlds, Jane is also

threatened by her brother's leaving to become a soldier, by her
parents' constant fighting, and by her grandfather's exclusive
definitions of Jewish tradition. Indeed, his suspicion of Gentiles is
equaled only by prejudice on the part of a teacher who persecutes
Jane for what he perceives as Yankee impudence. This is a tightly
focused book, its pace heightened by dramatic scenes (especially
Jane's trips downtown with her grandfather to sell his tacky line of dry
goods), closely observed character dynamics, an ending that leaves
important questions open for readers to think about, and enough
emotional momentum to insure that they will.

56   **Barton**, Byron. *I Want to Be an Astronaut*; written and illus. by Byron
       Barton. Crowell, 1988. Library ed. ISBN 0-690-04744-4; Paper ed. ISBN
       0-694-00261-5. 32p. Library ed. $12.89; Paper ed. $7.95.

3-5 yrs. While there is some dissonance between the very young format of this
       picture book and its subject matter, Barton has provided an especially
       evocative early career book. The simple text (no more than a sentence
       per double-spread) expresses the desire of a little girl to "fly on the
       shuttle into outer space." Along with experiencing the joys of ready-to-
       eat meals and zero gravity (a concept that will take some explaining)
       she wants to "help fix a satellite and build a factory in orbit"—a
       welcome nod to the idea, often missing in similar books, that work
       means *work*. The simple paintings place the gleaming white shuttle
       and astronaut suits against deep-purple space, creating a remarkable
       sense of actually seeing the earth from a distance, with perspectives
       close to vertiginous. Adventurous and reassuring at once, this closes
       with the shuttle landing with jaunty agility back on earth.

57   **Bauer**, Marion Dane. *On My Honor*. Houghton/Clarion, 1986. ISBN
       0-89919-462-1. 90p. $11.95.

5-8   In this brief story, Bauer sensitively explores the guilt, both real
  *   and self-made, of a boy whose best friend drowns while the two are
       swimming in a treacherous river. Both twelve, Tony and Joel are
       bicycling to Starved Rock Park, a trip Joel, knowing daredevil Tony
       plans to climb the dangerous bluffs, hoped his father would forbid.
       When Tony changes his mind on the way, deciding instead to swim,
       Joel figures that dangerous as the river is, it is safer than the bluffs,
       and he challenges Tony to a race that results in his friend's drowning.
       Whose fault is it? Joel's, for daring Tony to swim in a river he knew was
       unsafe? Tony's, for not admitting he didn't know how to swim? Or his
       father's, as Joel tries to convince himself, "You should never have let
       me go!" "We all made choices today, Joel. You, me, Tony. Tony's the
       only one who doesn't have to live with his choice." Bauer handles both
       the swift plot and moral dilemmas with a spare, dramatic style, and
       refuses Joel and readers easy answers. The reconciliation between

father and son is poignant, as Joel realizes his father can only offer him love, and the most tentative kind of comfort. "If there is a heaven, I'm sure Tony's gone there. I can't imagine a heaven that could be closed to charming, reckless boys."

58   **Baum**, Louis. *One More Time*; illus. by Paddy Bouma. Morrow, 1986. Library ed. ISBN 0-688-06587-2; Trade ed. ISBN 0-688-06586-4. 27p. Library ed. $10.88; Trade ed. $10.25.

K-2   Watercolor paintings with soft colors and soft line illustrate a story that is told simply and directly, with a good balance of exposition and dialogue. A happy day at the park draws to a close, and small Simon uses the stalling tactics known to all parents, as he asks for just one more this or that before they leave. At the end of a short train journey they reach a small town, and Dad wheels Simon through the twilight to the house where Mom is waiting. Only then is it made explicit that Dad and Mom are divorced, as Simon says goodbye to his father. Few American children will be likely to understand the significance of Dad's request for a "return ticket." Subtly, this says volumes about paternal love, and the poignancy of the relationship is heightened by the cool restraint of Baum's treatment.

59   **Bawden**, Nina. *The Finding*. Lothrop, 1985. ISBN 0-688-04979-6. 153p. $10.25.

4-6
*   In the hands of a lesser writer, the situation and developments used here could easily have become maudlin or melodramatic. Bawden, however, has firm control over her material and discrimination about its treatment, in a fine story about an adopted child who is quiet and gentle and greatly loved. What disrupts Alex's life is the fear that he is upsetting his family because he has inherited a fortune, so he runs away to make things easier for them. This crisis is deftly handled, with a building of suspense as the story moves back and forth from the plight of the runaway to the fearful apprehension of his family. Characterization and dialogue are excellent.

60   **Bawden**, Nina. *Henry*; illus. by Joyce Powzyk. Lothrop, 1988. ISBN 0-688-07894-X. 119p. $13.00.

4-6   Henry is a baby squirrel adopted by a family waiting out the London Blitz on a country farm during World War II. With her characteristic subtlety of craft, Bawden develops scenes and dialogue that bring the reader to realize what Henry means to the narrator, her two brothers, and her mother as they all await her father's return from naval duty. The youngest, Charlie, is particularly touching in his desperate attachments to any strong male figure—a farm hand, an Italian prisoner of war—and in his vague fears about the father he can't quite remember. His question of whether his dad will like the squirrel clearly translates into one of whether his dad will like Charlie. There are many realities here, death in a neighbor's terminal illness, her son's decision to stay with his father on the farm afterwards. This is a story that speaks of family unity in the face of dislocation and separation.

61   **Bawden**, Nina. *The Outside Child.* Lothrop, 1989. ISBN 0-688-08965-8. 232p. $12.95.

5-9
*
Suddenly and accidentally, thirteen-year-old Jane Tucker learns that her widowed father—a ship's engineer whom she rarely sees—is remarried and has two younger children. Inevitably, she defies her adoptive aunts to locate her half-sister and brother. What she doesn't expect to find is a dark secret that seems to spark violent hostility from her stepmother. The realistically piecemeal revelation of Jane's suppressed memory, together with a careful delineation of her friendship with a boy whose family is separated, makes a taut story with faultless characterization as well as sustained pace. Bawden's style in this first-person narrative is deceptively simple. Because of that, young readers will find themselves absorbed in complex relation-ships where the strengths and shortcomings of each individual charge the plot without making it melodramatic. The circumstances of Jane's discovery are unusual, but her situation, and the consequent emotions, are not.

62   **Baynes**, Pauline, comp. *Thanks Be to God: Prayers from around the World*; comp. and illus. by Pauline Baynes. Macmillan, 1990. ISBN 0-02-708541-4. 32p. $9.95.

3-7 yrs.
While most of the thirty-five prayers contained herein are of Christian origin, none get any more specific than "Father," "Lord," "God," or "Chief": "Oh thou great Chief,/ light a candle in my heart,/ that I may see what is therein,/ and sweep the rubbish from thy dwelling place." That is a "prayer of an African schoolgirl"; the others will be similarly new to most children. This is a thoughtful collection of prayers, most brief and many rhyming, that appeal without dogmatic distractions to a child's sense of the Infinite. Delicate ornamentations are scattered throughout the spaciously set text, with the bottom third of each page given over to precise, small-scaled illustrations that unify the prayers/poems on each spread. An Edenic spread nestles an amicable collection of beasts to illustrate two prayers for animals. Children and pets take a crisp sunrise walk to school: "Thank you, God, for this new day/ In my school to work and play." "From ghoulies and ghosties and long-leggety beasties . . ." shares a double-page spread with other bedtime pleas, all gaining credence from the ghostly-green collection of nighttime frights giving way to a sunrise so bright that flowers fly off the bedspread. A reflective resource.

63   **Beatty**, Patricia. *Charley Skedaddle*. Morrow, 1987. ISBN 0-688-06687-
9. 186p. $11.75.

5-7   In one of Beatty's best historical novels, set during the Civil War, a
*   tough boy from a Bowery gang enlists as a drummer boy with the
140th New York Veteran Volunteers. Charley is twelve, anxious to see
battle and gain revenge for the older brother who had been killed at
Gettysburg. Alas, when battle comes, Charley is terrified and runs
away, eventually taking refuge with an elderly, taciturn woman who
lives alone in a rural community. Gradually, Charley learns to care for
Granny Bent and for the beauty of the Blue Ridge Mountains;
gradually, she accepts and becomes fond of him. In time, he expiates
the guilt and shame he feels as a deserter and proves (without melodrama) to himself and others that he does have courage. This is a rite-
of-passage story as well as a wartime adventure story; it speaks out
against war and slavery without obscuring of the medium by the
message. Despite the cute title, this is less flippant than most of
Beatty's books, not as funny but much more substantial. The setting is
vivid, the characterization strong, and the structure solid. The author's
appended notes give background information, distinguish between
what in the book is fact and what is fiction, and explain her modified
use of mountain dialect.

64   **Beck**, Jennifer. *The Choosing Day*; illus. by Robyn Belton.
Hutchinson/David & Charles, 1989. 24p. $13.95.

5-7 yrs.   "In Briar's family, when it is someone's birthday that person can
choose what they want to do all day long." Wow, what a premise! Briar
chooses bananas and ice cream for breakfast—in her mother and
father's great big bed. It's all uphill from there. The bubble bath, the
silver high-heeled shoes, the request that her mother wear a wedding
dress to do the shopping (by bus), an impromptu picnic in the park
with rainbow sponge birthday cake and Briar's soon-to-be-classmates,
a ride home in the back of her father's truck. How could you miss? You
can't. From the endpapers filled with sparkling candles to the free-
floating watercolor illustrations, rose-tinted of course, this is a sure bet
with preschool birthday girls. Any parent who reads it aloud will have
some big wishes on their hands from dawn to dark during the next
celebration.

65   **Beirne**, Barbara. *Under the Lights: A Child Model at Work*; written
and illus. with photographs by Barbara Beirne. Carolrhoda, 1988. ISBN
0-87614-316-8. 56p. $12.95.

4-6   Eleven-year-old Michelle is a professional model who narrates the
story of how she got interested in the job and went about doing it.
Starting out by proving to her parents that she could be responsible
for keeping her grades up, she signed with an agency and began with

go-sees, eventually getting calls for a variety of work from clothing catalogues to fashion shows. The text is careful to include details of the hard work that underpin this fashionable pursuit; there's no time for after-school activities or hanging out with classmates, and Michelle gets fewer calls as she matures and outgrows junior sizes. At the end of the book she announces her decision to retire. However, there aren't many young readers who wouldn't want to trade places for a chance to see what modeling is like, and this book, with its clean design and generous array of color and black-and-white photos, is the next best thing to pounding the pavements of New York.

66   **Bellville**, Cheryl Walsh. *Theater Magic: Behind the Scenes at a Children's Theater*; written and illus. with photographs by Cheryl Walsh Bellville. Carolrhoda Books, 1986. ISBN 0-87614-278-1. 44p. $12.95.

3-6   In an attractive photo-essay that is outstanding for the clarity with which it is written and for the accuracy and breadth of its coverage, author-photographer Belleville makes comprehensible the myriad activities of mounting a play. The pictures (some in color, some in black and white) are of excellent quality, and the two-column text is spaciously set at the bottoms of pages. What the author does is to show how the elements of a production are worked on, separately and together, and what the roles of cast and staff are. The play is an adaptation of Andersen's "The Nightingale."

67   **Bendick**, Jeanne. *Egyptian Tombs*. Watts, 1989. ISBN 0-531-10462-1. 64p. illus. and with photographs. (First Books). $10.90.

3-5   Photographs, drawings, and diagrams show pyramid and rock-tombs, their locations, their design, and some of their contents. The continuous text is divided into brief topics and is written in a clear and simple style; it includes discussion of those theories about death and an afterlife that led, in ancient Egypt, to elaborate embalming, provision of rich supplies, and devious structure of passages leading to burial chambers that have made the tombs of Egypt a fascinating story—and a source of plunder for grave robbers—for millennia. A glossary and an index are provided for a book that serves well as a comprehensible introduction to the subject.

68   **Bennett**, Jill, comp. *Noisy Poems*; illus. by Nick Sharratt. Oxford/Merrimack, 1987. ISBN 0-19-276063-7. 24p. $8.95.

5-8 yrs.   It's hard to resist a picture book of 12 solidly noisy poems by the likes of James Reeves ("The Ceremonial Band"), David McCord ("Song of the Train"), Elizabeth Coatsworth ("Rhyme"), and Jack Prelutsky ("The Yak"). The sound effects alone are tempting enough, from *swush* ("Fishes' Evening Song" by Dahlov Ipcar) to *bash* ("Jazz-Man" by Eleanor Farjeon). Most of the verses have a lively beat and brash imagery. Even the illustrations seem raucous, with loud colors, bold shapes, and wildly varied book design. It's all internally consistent, however, with the ludicrous logic of nonsense. Family or classroom sharing will surely provoke response. Cover your ears.

69   **Berenzy**, Alix. *A Frog Prince*; written and illus. by Alix Berenzy. Holt, 1989. ISBN 0-8050-1123-4. 32p. $13.95.

5-8 yrs.   It's audacious to change motifs of a traditional tale, but Berenzy has replaced the ending of Grimm #1, The Frog Prince, with proven elements of other tales, including Sleeping Beauty, and she has kept the style simple, reserving elaborations for her romantic art. After the capricious princess rebuffs him, this frog travels to the end of the world, tricking a troll and a witch to free their victims, a bird and turtle that help him on his way. Eventually he finds another princess, this one a sleeping frog who responds to his kiss. Berenzy's superlative drafting actually does make these frogs quite heroic without giving up their true native charm. Biologically, they're perfect, whether riding a pony, sleeping under a royal cloak, dancing, or undertaking amphibian activities in the water. The nuances of line, the rich color, and the intensely concentrated compositions add up to some special effects. There are some good lines here, too. It doesn't hurt to find a hero unafraid to acknowledge common nature: "I am only a frog wearing fancy clothes." (Alas, both princesses remain blissfully unaware of inner possibilities.) The Frog Prince is a tale type with many variants. Children familiar with the standard European version will have an interesting time talking about this revision.

70   **Bergman**, Tamar. *The Boy From Over There*; tr. from the Hebrew by Hillel Halkin. Houghton, 1988. ISBN 0-395-43077-1. 181p. $12.95.

5-8   Beginning with the arrival of an orphaned Jewish refugee at the end of World War II, this details his absorption into a Galilee kibbutz until the children's evacuation in the war of 1948. The dynamics among the characters are realistically developed, including one boy's resentment of the allowances made for the newcomer, another's sensitive alliance, and the role played by a dog in bringing the children together. By the end of the book, the protagonist has accepted the loss of his mother, whom he had hoped was still alive, as his best friend has accepted the loss of her father on the European front. There are some touching scenes, as when another refugee relives her bitter past with the evacuation truck's "taking away" her daughter. The focus of the novel, however, is on new lives. While we've had many novels about children's experiences in the Holocaust, this is one of the few and the best on a survivor's adjustment in Israel. There are occasional cases of stylistic awkwardness, but in general the translation is smooth and the dialogue natural.

71   **Bergman**, Thomas. *Finding a Common Language: Children Living with Deafness*; ISBN 1-55532-916-0. *On Our Own Terms: Children Living with Physical Disabilities*; ISBN 1-55532-942-X. *One Day at a Time: Children Living with Leukemia*; ISBN 1-55532-913-6. *Seeing in Special Ways: Children Living with Blindness*; ISBN 1-55532-915-2. *We Laugh, We Love, We Cry: Children Living with Mental Retardation*; ISBN 1-55532-914-4. Each book: written and illus. with photographs by Thomas Bergman. Gareth Stevens, 1989. 48p. (Don't Turn Away). $9.95.

2-6   An exemplary series on deafness, physical disabilities, leukemia,
*   blindness, and mental retardation features straightforward but sensitive texts along with frank, spontaneous, black-and-white photographs. Bergman has tailored each volume to its particular subject: the blind children are interviewed rather than described to reflect how they take in the world through hearing; other books convey information through narrative, always underpinning medical fact with emotional reality. The children here suffer pain, frustration, and fear with courage and patience, though anger and sadness are also clear from some of their reactions. One boy, born without arms or legs but ingenious in the ways he invented to cope, died before the books were finished, a fact the author is honest about acknowledging ("sometimes the weaknesses of a child's body go beyond what you can see in a picture. . . . Ronny died from an infection that his body could not fight"). On the other hand, the benefits of therapy—revealed by detailed shots of special procedures—are apparent, and prognoses often hopeful. The tone of all the books is humane but dignified, with no cuteness, evasion, or sentimentality. Appended sections give valuable information to help readers generalize from the specific children depicted, answering common questions and suggesting things to do and think about, places to write for further information, and relevant children's fiction and nonfiction for further reading. Each book also has a glossary and index. This valuable Swedish import, smoothly translated and adapted for American audiences, is something to which all children should have access: for staring at, considering, and discussing.

72   **Berry**, James. *Spiderman Anancy*. Holt, 1989. ISBN 0-8050-1207-9. 119p. $13.95.

5-   With the same lyrical nuance of dialogue that characterized *A Thief*
*   *in the Village*, Berry has retold twenty Caribbean folktales of West African origin. Like all tricksters, Anancy ranges from hero to villain to fool in his relationships with the other animal characters, but whatever

his role, he becomes so integral to readers by the end of the book that we feel as he does about saying good-bye to his arch enemy: "Bro Anancy is surprised how much he misses Bro Tiger. Anancy decides, to keep the memory of Tiger, he'll tell stories about himself and Bro Tiger. Spider Anancy hides in bedrooms and whispers stories like dreams." The word choices here are irresistibly poetic ("They listen how the Anancy goes on wrapping up his words in tricky traps"), and the prose so rhythmic that sometimes it becomes pure chant. Even the titles have a tongue-rolling sound, as in "Ratbat and Tacooma's Tree." The narrative, which is cast in the present tense, addresses the reader directly, with immediate impact ("Listen to the Anancy calling loud-loud"). The stories themselves are often gripping, either in plot— the kidnapping in "Mrs Dog First-Child and Monkey-Mother," for instance, and the final fight scene between Lion and Tiger—or simply in imagery. The dialect becomes accessible through its musical appeal and is easy to incorporate for either independent readers or storytellers. Like Berry's oral style, the pen-and-ink drawings have an energy that contrasts sharply with many current adaptations that seem tidied to death. There's no question that this is a living tradition.

73 **Berry**, James. *A Thief in the Village and Other Stories.* Orchard/Watts, 1988. Library ed. ISBN 0-531-08345-4; Trade ed. ISBN 0-531-05745-3. 148p. Library ed. $12.99; Trade ed. $12.95

6-10 Nine short stories set in Jamaica portray young characters in the light of some sharply defined incident. A girl gets her longed-for bicycle, two children watch their coconut grove to catch a thief, a child relishes the rituals of Sunday, a boy fights off a bully, another boy is barely saved from being swept out to sea on a horse, yet another yearns to find his father. In some cases, the tone is sad: one crippled lad seems doomed to lose his pet mongoose to heartless peers; a second watches a hurricane destroy the bananas he had hoped would pay for his shoes. In almost all the tales, the voices are true to an experience and to the rhythmic language that expresses it. These scenes will take readers beyond suburban America to a subsistence society that is nonetheless complex in family relationships and community dynamics.

74 **Bess**, Clayton. *Tracks.* Houghton, 1986. ISBN 0-395-40571-8. 180p. $12.95.

7-10 Jess' stepgrandfather in *Big Man and the Burnout* recounts his journey into maturity riding the rails with his brother as a hobo during the Depression. From its opening scene, in which Blue almost gets killed hopping a freight, the book is gripping, with characters making brief but well-defined appearances and action mounting through vivid episodes. There is a cumulatively forceful theme of the dynamics of prejudice, evinced at first in offhand remarks and attitudes and climaxing in the brothers' last harrowing escape from some masked klansmen whose torture of a Mexican they have witnessed. This is a complex book, perceptive of characters such as the Italian woman who harbors the boys, of the hoboes they ride with, and of the brothers themselves. It's also sharply realistic, a rhythmic first-person narrative told in rural dialect and resonant with the experience of hardship.

75   **Bible**, adaptations of. *Adam and Eve: The Bible Story*; retold and illus. by Warwick Hutton. McElderry, 1987. ISBN 0-689-50433-0. 30p. $13.95.

5-7 yrs.   Another of the artist's scenic depictions of Bible literature, this begins with Creation—a small pool of light amidst darkness—and unfolds with charged blue and green washes of increasing complexity as vegetation, beasts, and birds multiply across the landscapes. Adam and Eve appear in their bare anatomical glory, later covered by fig leaves as they experience the shame of guilt after consuming the apple of knowledge. The serpent is persuasively sinuous; indeed, the emphasis here is on height, the perspective vertical, with palm trees, giraffes, waterfalls, and God's sword itself reaching skyward as if to bridge the separation between heaven and earth. This compares handsomely with other versions illustrated by Helen Siegl (Gwendolyn Reed's adaptation) and Jim Russell (Catherine Storr's adaptation).

76   **Bible**, adaptations of. *He Is Risen: The Easter Story*; ad. by Elizabeth Winthrop; illus. by Charles Mikolaycak. Holiday House, 1985. ISBN 0-8234-0547-8. 27p. $14.95.

4-7   Adapted from portions of the King James Version of the Bible, this preserves with sensitivity the mood and the sonorous flow of the original. The artist has matched the adapter's discrimination with strong, dramatic paintings that have deep emotion but no sentimentality, that are effectively composed, and that use color with restraint, so that the predominating reds and browns are rich but subdued.

77   **Bible**, adaptations of. *Moses in the Bulrushes*; ad. and illus. by Warwick Hutton. Atheneum/McElderry, 1986. ISBN 0-689-50393-8. 32p. $12.95.

4-6 yrs.
   *   One of the most dramatic and child-appealing stories from the Old Testament is recounted in a simple, one or two line per page text faced with spacious, light-filled paintings. Hutton's watercolors combine narrative strength with an intensely graceful setting. He has lessened his usual sun-shadow contrasts for a sense of the blazing white air of the Middle East, which lightens all colors except those of the watery depths where Moses is found. The figures are stylized without becoming stiff; even the ducks and geese have a slightly

hieroglyphic stance. Hutton's usually sly slants of humor are here replaced with tenderness for the human aspects of a story with mythical dimensions, the child of destiny born, endangered, and saved.

78   **Bible.** *The Nativity;* illus. by Julie Vivas. Gulliver/Harcourt, 1988. ISBN 0-15-200535-8. 36p. $14.95.

4-6 yrs.   Accompanying a minimal text excerpted from the St. James version of
*   Luke are blissfully exuberant watercolor paintings of the annunciation and birth of Christ. These are tattered angels and poor folk who keep chickens along with their naive sense of humor. Each spread is a spacious new scenario for visual exploration: Mary's expression as she watches her belly grow enormous, her attempts to mount the donkey, the donkey's angle of reluctance in proceeding along a rocky trail, Joseph's cuddling of the baby, the townsfolk crowded onto perches of roof and tree, the shepherd ordering his sheep back to the flock. The compositions are fresh enough to make many another nativity book look like greeting card art. "And she brought forth her firstborn son" shows the baby's head and hands peeking into a dark square of night on one page and tumbling naked into the world the next. In the end, the mottled Angel, his workboots still untied, holds the baby while Joseph helps Mary heave herself back up onto the donkey. This is a book that summons the familial joy of any birth—rainbow colors replace the traditional red and green—with no less reverence for the one celebrated at Christmas.

79   **Bible.** *Noah and the Ark;* illus. by Pauline Baynes. Holt, 1988. ISBN 0-8050-0886-1. 30p. $14.95.

4-8 yrs.   In contrast to Arthur Geisert's *The Ark* (*BCCB* 9/88) with its minimal text and cleverly crabbed etchings, Baynes uses the full flowing text of the Revised Standard Version, and accompanies it with appropriately opulent illustrations. The story begins on the title page, which features a small and delicate frieze of humankind doing terrible things to one another, a realistic detail seen again later in a beautifully peaceful painting of the ark rolling on the water while tiny bodies drown in the waves. Showing imaginatively blended influences of Japanese woodcuts and Persian miniatures, almost every illustration is composed in a sweeping curve—of the animals racing to the Ark, of the waves—filled with echoing details of flicking tails, arching palms, and the suave jump of a swordfish toward the flying dove. The paintings are variously and cleverly framed: waves leap out of trompe l'oeil edges, animals crawl onto the facing page, a volcano erupts into the margin. There is plenty here to hold the eye, and the ear will be caught as well. " . . . and every beast according to its kind, and all the cattle according to their kinds, and every creeping thing that creeps on earth according to its kind, and every bird according to its kind, every bird of every sort."

80   **Bible**, adaptations of. *Noah's Ark*; ad. and illus by Nonny Hogrogian. Knopf, 1986. ISBN 0-394-88191-5. 32p. $12.95.

3-5 yrs.   Actually beginning with the stories of creation and the garden of Eden, this joins the ranks of beautifully illustrated Noahs that include Peter Spier's, Warwick Hutton's, and others. Hogrogian's is ideal for young children because the adaptation is simple, brief, but dignified with Biblical tone and rhythms. The softly colored, textured illustrations are spacious and literal, with a fine balance between gentle humor and gravity. A satisfying addition.

81   **Bible**. *Noah's Ark*; illus. by Jane Ray. Dutton, 1990. ISBN 0-525-44653-2. 32p. $14.95

4-8 yrs.
*   Many of the recent *Noah's Ark* books rely on gimmicks for their distinction; here's one whose simple faith in the story is amply rewarded. The brief text is well-excerpted from the King James Genesis; the illustrations combine the glowing detail of medieval tapestry with the freshness of contemporary quilts. The "wickedness of man" is illustrated with panels showing environmental destruction, argument, and cruelty to animals; God is a great sun-face; Noah is black. There are many eye-filling pictures of the two-by-twos and the stores of food and plants, but the book never gets the schematic look that afflicts so many illustrated version of the tale. Ray's lines and colors are soft, with a use of gold paint in the borders that adds warmth rather than glitz. The animals are stylized but friendly, and Noah's family is emblemized with no loss to their humanity. A final double-page spread shows life renewing itself again, but the tone of the voyage has all along been one of anticipated celebration.

82   **Bierhorst**, John. *Doctor Coyote: A Native American Aesop's Fable*; retold by John Bierhorst; illus. by Wendy Watson. Macmillan, 1987. ISBN 0-02-709780-3. 48p. $14.95.

2-4   A quirky but enticing production combines Wendy Watson's amusing full-color, contemporary-setting cartoon art with 20 fables reworked by Aztec Indians from a Spanish edition of Aesop and reworded again by Bierhorst from a 1628 manuscript. Coyote is the star of the show, whether he's tricking or tricked. The story lines are varied, the morals delicious: "If you don't need it, don't do it"; or, "It doesn't hurt to be clever, if you're too small to be anything else." Watson's animals, decked out as they are in turquoise jewelry and various expressions of greed, remorse, triumph, and defeat, satirize the human in all of us. Some themes will be familiar to children or can be compared to other accessible variants with ease, as in the story of dying old Coyote's directing his sons to dig for their inheritance in his corn fields — thus insuring future crops. Other tales are more unusual and uniquely native American in motif and expression. Largely unavailable before its picture-book debut, this material will be a boon for the study and enjoyment of fables.

83   Bierhorst, John. *The Mythology of Mexico and Central America.* Morrow, 1990. ISBN 0-688-06721-2. 239p. illus. with photographs. $14.95.

9-   The third and last in Bierhorst's scholarly series about myths of North, South, and now Central America, this is organized into three sections: the storytellers, the basic myths, and building the mythologies. These stories and images have not been popularized in the same way as European, Scandinavian, African, or even Asian mythologies; in pioneering their literary dissemination, Bierhorst is careful about regional distinctions, narrative contexts, and preservation of unfamiliar patterns. The resulting array of lore is complex, but advanced students will find striking evidence of common tale types such as the Orpheus-like underworld journey in pursuit of a dead wife. Intriguingly, the Mesoamerican land of the dead varies according to the cause of death. "Among the modern Nahua these are (1) the paradise of the rain dwarfs, where drowning victims go; (2) the sky world, for soldiers killed in battle and women who have died in child-birth; and (3) the regular underworld, for everyone else"—except babies, who "go to a special paradise where they sit beneath a tree of human breasts, catching the milk in their mouths." The races of Adjusters and Defenders, who peopled the earth in its earlier stages, built stone temples, and were destroyed by floods, will appeal to the imagination of science fiction fans. A few of Bierhorst's opinions will provoke argument, as in his assertion that only myth embedded in or giving the illusion of history "can be used today for public as well as private purposes" but his chapter on myths and nationalism makes a valuable conclusion to the study. A glossary of Spanish terms and an extensive section of footnotes and bibliographical references doc-ument the book. Illustrated with maps and photographs of striking traditional art work.

84   Bierhorst, John. *The Mythology of South America.* Morrow, 1988. ISBN 0-688- 06722-0. 269p. illus. with photographs. $14.95.

8-   Like its companion, *The Mythology of North America,* this is a sprawling compendium of myths from many diverse groups. After an introduction characterizing certain traits of the lore, Bierhorst organizes the material geographically: Greater Brazil, Guiana, the Brazilian Highlands, Gran Chaco, the Northwest, and the Central Andes. Within these sections, he proceeds thematically according to elements of the material, grouping tales that treat hostility between men and women, for instance, or variants of ubiquitous tale types such as The Tree and Flood or The Twin Myth. While the imagery is powerful, this is more description than storytelling, and thus more dry than dramatic. Although readers may get bogged down in some of the fragmentary explanations of origin, anyone using the work for research will find it invaluable, especially where the author provides interpretation, as in the lucid conclusion on Inca lore and commentary on cultural contrasts. With exemplary documentation in the form of source notes and an extensive bibliography of references, this is illustrated with black-and-white photos of art objects and drawings by the people represented, along with maps for each region.

85   **Bierhorst**, John. *The Naked Bear: Folktales of the Iroquois.* Morrow, 1987. 123p. ISBN 0-688-06422-1. $13.00.

5-7   Following a brief introduction on the storytelling and culture of the Six Nations of the Iroquois are sixteen folktales with some haunting themes and images. Consistently woven through them all is the close relationship of human and animal, as well as ubiquitous magic powers upon which mortals often call to combat extraordinary forces. In one story, twin brothers retrieve their uncle's eyes from a quilt that two witches have made in cloudland, a "quilt of eyes, all alive and winking." In another, a child whose stepfather has abandoned him in the forest survives with the aid of a porcupine and is adopted by a mother bear, who pays for his life with her own and her cubs'. These tales are easy to read and taut enough to tell, each sustained with the suspense of life and death situations. An appendix lists sources and other works containing information on Native American folklore.

86   **Billings**, Charlene W. *The Loon: Voice of the Wilderness.* Dodd/Putnam, 1988. ISBN 0-396-09244-6. 48p. illus. with photographs. $11.95.

3-6   Organized by phases of the loon's life cycle, Billings' text describes the spring arrival of the birds at their breeding grounds, their nesting, raising chicks, winter migration to the ocean, and loss to environmental threats such as power boats and oil slicks. Color photographs are of uneven quality, some striking and others unclear or even lost in the gutter. On balance, however, the book provides the kind of straightforward information that could supplement more inspiring presentations—films such as *The Loon's Necklace*, for instance—which vividly project the eerie call and characteristics that have given the bird mythological significance among Native Americans.

87   **Björk**, Christina. *Linnea's Windowsill Garden;* tr by Joan Sandin; illus. by Lena Anderson. R&S/Farrar, 1988. ISBN 91-29-59064-7. 59p. $11.95.

4-6   The young plant lover of *Linnea in Monet's Garden* gives information
 *   about every aspect of indoor gardening: choosing, planting, pruning,
        fertilizing, spraying, adjusting light and water. The writing is light and
        crisp; somehow Björk manages to be amusing without ever becoming
        cute. This is informative, accurate, comprehensive, clear and well-
        organized; the illustrations are helpful and are carefully placed in
        relation to textual references. What more could the beginning
        gardener or old green-thumbed hand expect from any horticultural
        how-to-do-it book?

88   **Blegvad**, Lenore. *Anna Banana and Me;* illus. by Erik Blegvad.
        Atheneum, 1985. ISBN 0-689-50274-5. 26p. $9.95.

K-2   Small, deft, softly-tinted sketches add measurably to the appeal of a
        short book that captures the insecurity of a small boy and his
        admiration for the intrepid playmate he calls Anna Banana. The boy,
        who is the narrator, describes a series of encounters in which Anna
        Banana takes the lead and he follows. In the final episode, she
        frightens him with a story about a goblin and runs off; the boy is
        almost paralyzed with apprehension until he finds a feather, when he
        remembers that Anna Banana had said a feather was magic, takes
        heart, and happily trots off toward home. A nicely told story that
        reverses stereotypical sex roles.

89   **Block**, Francesca Lia. *Weetzie Bat.* Harper, 1989. Library ed. ISBN 0-
        06-020536-9; Trade ed. ISBN 0-06-020534-2. 88p. Library ed. $12.89;
        Trade ed. $12.95.

9-   Only in Los Angeles. Like much of the new-wave culture it celebrates,
        there's no doubt that this is the kind of book that's mostly style: "'You
        are my Marilyn. You are my lake full of fishes. . . . my pink Cadillac, my
        highway, my martini, the stage for my heart to rock and roll on, the
        screen where my movies light up,' he said." That's My Secret Agent
        Lover Man comforting Weetzie Bat after the death of her father.
        Weetzie met My Secret Agent Lover Man when a genie gave her
        three wishes. My Secret Agent Lover Man was one, a beautiful house
        was another, and "a Duck for Dirk" the third. Dirk is Weetzie's best
        friend, a Duck is a cute guy, and with the genie's help, Dirk meets the
        perfect Duck named Duck and everybody moves into a beautiful
        house (left to Dirk by his just-dead Grandma Fifi), where they all have
        a baby, Cherokee Love. Oh, and don't forget Cherokee's evil twin,
        Witch Baby: "As soon as she could talk, she would go around
        chanting, 'beasts, beasts, beasts,' over and over again." Stranger than
        any of this is the fact that the author makes it all work. Her theme is
        friendship, her tone affectionate, her imagery sentimental but true to
        type. The prose alternates rhapsodies-in-neon with I-can-read
        conversations: "'I feel weird,' Weetzie said. 'Me too,' Dirk said. Duck

scratched his head." You will too, but despite its startling subject
matter, this is one innocent—*sweet*—book.

90   **Blumberg**, Rhoda. *Commodore Perry in the Land of the Shogun.*
Lothrop, 1985. ISBN 0-688-03723-2. 138p. illus. $13.00.

6-   With matter-of-fact tone and a lively pace and flow in the writing style,
*   Blumberg describes in great detail the visits of Commodore Perry to
Japan in 1853 and 1854. Japan had been a nation in almost complete
isolation for many years, allowing only a few Dutch and Chinese into
the country. Perry, in fact, was dependent on Dutch translators when
he presented President Fillmore's request for a treaty: he encountered
suspicion (the Americans were "evil men") and hostility from con-
firmed isolationists. Guile and patience triumphed, however, and the
treaty opened some ports for trade, guaranteed safety to shipwrecked
Americans, provided for official U.S. representation on a permanent
basis, and included the "most favored nation" clause. The text gives
excellent background information and provides colorful details of the
pageantry, the gifts and entertainment, and the parades and banquets
that proliferated as the treaty preparations progressed. Illustrations
are all from the period, either by Japanese artists and cartoonists or by
the official artists of Perry's party. The text of the treaty, chapter notes,
and a substantial index and bibliography are provided. This is a book
with reference use that reads almost like an adventure story.

91   **Blumberg**, Rhoda. *The Great American Gold Rush.* Bradbury, 1989.
ISBN 0-02-711681-6. 136p. illus. and with photographs. $16.95.

6-   Profusely illustrated with cartoons and sketches from publications of
the gold rush years, 1848-1852, this oversize book is an impressive
combination of good bookmaking, thorough (and documented)
research, a lively writing style, and logical arrangement of material.
Source material, cited in an appended section by chapters, is used
within the text; an extensive relative index is provided, as is a bibliography that is divided into primary and secondary sources. It is rare to
find so illuminating a new book on an old subject.

92   **Blumberg**, Rhoda. *The Incredible Journey of Lewis and Clark.*
Lothrop, 1987. ISBN 0-688-06512-0. 143p. illus. and with photographs.
$15.00.

6-   Profusely illustrated by photographs of artifacts and prints from
*   museums and institutional archives, this is a most impressive addition
to the body of books about the three-year journey of exploration (1803-
1806) led by Meriwether Lewis and William Clark. Their mission was
instigated by President Jefferson, their goals were to chart a route to
the Pacific, to be friendly to the Native American tribes they met, and
to note (for Jefferson's encyclopedic interests) flora, fauna, and other

natural features of the western lands. Blumberg's writing is dignified but never dry, and her sense of narrative makes familiar history an exciting story. Maps are included, as are a bibliography, an index, chapter notes, and an "Aftermath" that describes participants' lives after 1806.

93   Blume, Judy. *Fudge-a-mania.* Dutton, 1990. ISBN 0-525-44672-9. 147p. $12.95.

4-6   Peter, the long-suffering brother of five-year-old Fudge, narrates the ebullient story of a very long three-week vacation. Long, that is, to Peter, because his parents are sharing a summer house with the Tubmans, and Sheila Tubman (*Otherwise Known as Sheila the Great*) is his arch-enemy. Blume manages to avoid slapstick, although she skirts it, probably to the delight of new and old Fudge and Sheila fans. Disasters (minor) accrue, Fudge and his new friend Mitzi are amusingly precocious, and there's wedding-bells romance between Peter's grandmother and Sheila's grandfather. Something for everyone.

94   Blume, Judy. *Just as Long as We're Together.* Orchard/Watts, 1987. Library ed. ISBN 0-531-08329-2; Trade ed. ISBN 0-531-05729-1. 296p. Library ed. $12.99; Trade ed. $12.95.

5-7   The narrator is Stephanie, who's in her first year of junior high, who's distressed by her parents' trial separation (and, when she visits Dad, by his friend Iris), and who finds that best friends are not infallibly understanding or tolerant. Rachel has always been her friend, but both of them like a newcomer (Alison, a Vietnamese adoptee) enough to make it a triumvirate. Blume is, as usual, fine-tuned to the concerns of pre-adolescents and to their speech patterns, so that the minor shifts and crises, joys and woes, of the characters are revealed by Stephanie with a believable immediacy and with all-too-real emotional ups and downs. The vicissitudes of life with friends, families, teachers and classmates, first dates, and physical changes are told with candor for appeal and humor for spice.

95   Bode, Janet. *New Kids on the Block: Oral Histories of Immigrant Teens.* Watts, 1989. ISBN 0-531-10794-9. 126p. $12.90.

7-12   Eleven young people, ranging in age from thirteen to twenty, tell their own stories about coming to the United States. As in Brent Ashabranner's *The New Americans*, Bode focuses on teens from Third World and developing countries: Afghanistan, El Salvador, India, Cuba, the Philippines, China, Mexico, South Korea, the Dominican Republic, Vietnam, and, in a reminder of past immigrant waves, Greece. Most of the subjects have escaped from war, repression, or poverty; all share a carefully qualified admiration for their adopted country. The narratives are distinct in both voice and personal detail, with varying attitudes towards the invariable cultural clashes between old ways and new. Abdul, an Afghani, says, "other immigrants from different cultures who come here get used to the American habits. They date girls. They do what Americans do. But not so much us." But Martha, from the Dominican Republic, rebels: "So what I did was told my mother I was going to the library, but instead I met him." Bode begins the book with a brief chapter on immigration, and introduces each narrative with a paragraph about the country of origin, but the kids speak for themselves. A good collection of personal stories that complements the headlines.

96   **Bode**, Janet. *The Voices of Rape.* Watts, 1990. Library ed. ISBN 0-531-10959-3; Trade ed. ISBN 0-531-15184-0. 144p. Library ed. $12.90; Trade ed. $11.95.

7-12   This is one of those rare nonfiction books that manages to bring both
  *   intensity and evenhandedness to an emotional subject. Through judiciously selected information and well-edited interviews, Bode informs the factual with the personal, addressing the text directly to teenage readers who have been or might be victims or perpetrators of rape—i.e., everyone. After an introductory discussion among ninth-grade classmates revealing many common attitudes, both male and female, Bode alternates victims' and perpetrators' stories before detailing post-rape reactions, treatment, reporting, and court procedures. She talks with police, prosecutors, and defense attorneys, as well as emergency room nurses, crisis intervention center counselors, and psychologists. Yet the resulting text never seems fragmented; it is cohesive, concise, to the point, and up-to-date in terms of research and social realities. The tone is frank but not sensational. Her section on rape prevention is one of the few "you can help do something about this" conclusions that seems both immediately relevant and possible for young people. Source notes document specifics, and there's an extensive, current bibliography of adult and young adult books for further information, along with an index.

97   **Bogart**, Jo Ellen. *Daniel's Dog.* Scholastic, 1990. ISBN 0-590-43402-0. 32p. $11.95.

K-2   Daniel is small, black, engaging, and suffering just a bit from dethronement. To fill the gap, he's invented an imaginary dog, and when his friend Norman (Asian-American) feels unhappy, Daniel solicitously provides him with his own imaginary dog's shaggy friend— also canine, also imaginary. The illustrations are deft paintings, with realistic scenes given just a bit of contrast by the judicious use of abstract design or a ghostly dog. Low-keyed, the story provides a perceptive mother who helps her child adjust to his sibling and who accepts his imaginary companion with equanimity.

98   **Bograd**, Larry. *Poor Gertie*; illus. by Dirk Zimmer. Delacorte, 1986. ISBN 0-385-29487-5. 103p. $12.95.

3-5   An unusually well-developed novel given the confines of brevity and a very simple style, this introduces us to a truly individualistic ten-year-old whose father deserted the family and whose mother can hardly make the rent payments with her low-paying job. Gertie compensates for her lacks with a vivid imagination, but she's honest about the hardships of poverty, about the effects it has on her status at school (" . . . the other kids look right through me") and her environment ("A lot of people in the neighborhood try to act tough because there's not much else to do"). Nevertheless, Gertie, her mother, and her grandfather have a loving relationship that sustains them through the stress of never having enough. Despite its dominant theme, this is a very funny book; Gertie has a humorous eye for describing the antics of classmates and the quirks of living (the buxom school nurse, dressed in white, "looked like a ski area"). Both the first-person narrative and the dialogue are natural and the plot, despite some occasionally exaggerated scenes, carries the episodic chapters to a convincingly happy conclusion.

99   **Bolognese**, Don. *Pen & Ink*. ISBN 0-531-10133-9. *Pencil*. ISBN 0-531-10134-7. Each book: written and illus. by Don Bolognese and Elaine Raphael; Watts, 1986; 60p.; (The Illustrator's Library); $9.90.

5-
*   An unusually articulate discussion of the materials, techniques, practice, and vision required to make pen-and-ink and pencil illustrations. Although some prior knowledge is assumed (templates are mentioned but not defined, for instance, in *Pen and Ink*), most of the explanations are simple without becoming boring: look for the stories of a face; observe the range of textures possible with varied pen tips in five versions of the same drawing; explore the effects of linear, line-and-tone, and tonal drawings in pencil. Although the series introductions are the same for each volume, the texts are carefully tailored to the different media. All of the points made are well illustrated in the accompanying drawings; the description of form and structure in the pencil book, for instance, is rendered all the more lucid by the accompanying sketches. Both books are carefully designed to show what they tell. These are basic lessons in art appreciation as well as creation.

100   **Bond**, Nancy. *Another Shore*. McElderry, 1988. ISBN 0-689-50463-2. 316p. $16.95.

7-   There have recently been several novels that attempt to give
contemporary immediacy to historical event through the device of
time travel, and Bond's is one of the best, both for its immersion in
historical detail and its thoughtful manipulation of the time-travel
theme. 17-year-old Lyn has come to the reconstructed colonial town of
Louisbourg on Nova Scotia with her mother, who has gotten a
commission to photograph the settlement. Lyn gets a job as an
"animator," a costumed guide who pretends to be one of the 18th
century residents, in Lyn's case, 17-year-old Elisabeth Bernard. One
day Lyn falls in the street, and awakens in the old Louisbourg—as
Elisabeth Bernard. Readers will here have to take some time to sort
out new characters and an alien setting; like Lyn, they must grope
along to comprehension. The language is not quite the French that
Lyn understands, the smells are horrendous, Elisabeth's family has no
patience with her fumbling and hysteria. Used to not paying her much
attention, they do not even recognize that Elisabeth is gone and a
stranger in her place. This is a harder world than most depicted in
colonial historical fiction, with little cozy family warmth to keep off the
raging winter storms. There is humor here, especially in the character
of the inept Donald Stewart, another animator who finds himself in
the past, but even he becomes less funny and more pathetic, finally
tragic, trying to find his way home. Bond must be credited for the
integrity of her ending—Lyn cannot come back to the 1980's, and
finally resolves to make a new life with the mercurial (and sexy)
Frenchman she has come to love. It is a passionate relationship, but
its happiness is shadowed by Lyn's loss of her own future, and by the
reader's strong suspicion that in the 1980's there now lives a very
frightened and alone Elisabeth Bernard.

101   **Bowe-Gutman**, Sonia. *Teen Pregnancy*. Lerner, 1987. ISBN 0-8225-
0039-6. 71p. illus. $9.95.

6-10   One of the simplest, most clear-cut guides yet published for young
people on the subject of teen pregnancy, this addresses the reader
directly and explicitly on the responsibilities of sex. The discussion
begins with a few hard-core statistics but launches quickly into a
discussion of developing individual values. There's a healthy
emphasis on the money involved in raising a baby, the restrictions,
and the physical/emotional health problems early pregnancy can
cause teenagers. Explanations of conception and contraception are
accompanied by diagrams and a complete rundown of birth control
methods, including rate of effectiveness and side effects. There's
textual support for the teenager to refuse intercourse, although AIDS
is not cited as an important reason. The disease is mentioned once in
the description of condoms but does not appear in the index. A
chapter of case stories replays scenarios of pregnant teenagers who
have chosen various "solutions," from marriage to abortion. A section

on "where to go for help" lists addresses and phone numbers of
national organizations, along with some books for further reading. The
writing style is easy enough for elementary school children studying
sex and reproduction but will not insult poor or reluctant high school
students.

102   **Boyd**, Candy Dawson. *Breadsticks and Blessing Places*. Macmillan,
1985. ISBN 0-02-709290-9. 210p. $11.95.

5-7   Toni is twelve, black, plump, member of a loving family, a student at
an all-black school in Chicago who hopes to improve her mathematics
performance enough to pass a test that will enable her to be admitted
to a special school, the King Academy. She's doing make-up work in
math but loses her concentration and her interest when one of her two
best friends is killed by a drunken driver. The title refers to two of the
things that are associated with Toni's bereavement; several friends
help her work out her grief and anger. The book ends with Toni
admitted to the King Academy. Boyd deals fully and candidly with a
child's reaction to the death of a close friend as well as to other aspects
of the maturation process that are universal. The tempo lags occasionally but the writing on the whole has good pace and Toni's story is
written with insight and compassion.

103   **Boyd**, Lizi. *The Not-So-Wicked Stepmother*; written and illus. by Lizi
Boyd. Viking Kestrel, 1987. ISBN 0-670-81589-6. 30p. $10.95.

3-6 yrs.   Daddy's new wife, Molly, is easy to hate at a distance, where Hessie
can imagine her to be "wicked, mean, and VERY ugly," with "wrinkled
black dresses." But when Hessie arrives for a summer in Daddy and
Molly's house on the lake, it's hard to resist the warm, friendly woman
who invites her to feed the ducks, pick blueberries, and learn how to
swim. In spite of her fears and a brief attack of homesickness for her
own mother, Hessie finds herself part of a new and happy family. The
story is openly bibliotherapeutic, and the child's emotions and
anxieties are acutely real. The idyllic set-up for resolution will be
reassuring to youngsters in similar situations, even if their own paths
do not run quite so smoothly. Stylized, highly patterned watercolors
show a childlike perspective that echoes the all-important point of
view. The angular, off-beat shapes in flat dimension lend interest to a
text that more traditional art might render stale.

104   **Brandenberg**, Franz. *Otto is Different*; illus. by James Stevenson.
Greenwillow, 1985. Library ed. ISBN 0-688-04254-6; Trade ed. ISBN 0-
688-04253-8. 21p. Library ed. $11.88; Trade ed. $11.75.

K-2   Comical line drawings washed with light, bright colors do all that
picture book illustrations should do for a text, reflecting and
enhancing it while extending in visual details the humor of the

situation. The story is simple; Otto complains about being different
from other creatures but as he progresses through a day, he sees the
patent advantages of having eight arms, or limbs that can function as
arms or legs. Think of the efficiency: "After the meal, Otto did his
homework, swept the floor, and practiced the piano." All at once, of
course. Think of the potential of having an octopus as goalie on one's
hockey team; that's how to be popular. And think of bedtime hugs.
Souffle, but delicious.

105   **Branley**, Franklyn Mansfield. *Journey into a Black Hole.* Crowell,
1986. Library ed. ISBN 0-690-04544-1; Trade ed. ISBN 0-690-04543-3.
28p. Library ed. $11.89; Trade ed. $11.50.

2-3   Simont's paintings effectively convey the mystery and magnitude of
the unimaginable, the space and distance and density of a black hole.
They are deft in interpreting Branley's lucid text, which skilfully
streamlines the explanation of a complicated astronomical phenomenon so that it will be comprehensible to primary grades readers. It
isn't just that Branley is an expert on the subject (he is) but that he's
an expert on what to omit and what to include when writing for
younger children, as he describes what a black hole is, how it is
formed, and what it would be like to travel to one, if one could (or
wanted to) take a journey from which there would be no return.

106   **Branley**, Franklyn Mansfield. *Mysteries of Outer Space;* illus. with
diagrams by Sally J. Bensusen and with photographs. Lodestar, 1985.
ISBN 0-525-67149-8. 69p. $10.95.

5-9   Branley uses a question-and-answer format to provide information
about outer space and man's accommodation to exploring it.
Accurate and authoritative, the author has grouped his questions
logically; the material is under such headings as Kinds of Space,
Weightlessness and Zero Gravity, Uses of Space, and The End of
Space-The End of Time (relax, worriers, there is no foreseeable end to
either). A knowledgeable and interesting survey, illustrated by
diagrams that are carefully placed and captioned. A few books are
suggested for further reading; an index is appended.

107   **Branley**, Franklyn M. *Tornado Alert;* illus. by Giulio Maestro. Crowell,
1988. Library ed. ISBN 0-689-04688-X; Trade ed. ISBN 0-690-04686-3.
32p. (Let's-Read-and-Find-Out-Science Books). Library ed. $12.89;
Trade ed. $12.95.

1-3   Since Dorothy Gale's tornado is a primal scene for many television-
age children, this early science book will probably find a wider than
usual audience. While both text and pictures clearly show the hows
and wheres of tornadoes, they don't skimp on the drama, with almost
every double-page spread dominated by a ferocious twister in an eerie

blue/green/purple sky. The text is brief and simple: "Tornadoes can pick up branches and boards, stones and bricks, cars, and sometimes even people." A concluding section of safety instructions offers a reassuring close.

108   **Brett**, Catherine. *S.P. Likes A.D.* Women's Press, 1990. ISBN 0-88961-142-4. 119p. $6.95

7-10   Lacking the excesses of melodrama that often plague the teenage coming-out novel, this is a simply told, straightforward story about a girl's first realization that she may be a lesbian. Ninth-grader Stephanie finds herself attracted to classmate Anne Delaney, even if she isn't sure exactly why. "In her thoughts Anne Delaney was just— well—there. She wasn't doing anything or saying anything. She was just standing around." A group sculpture project not only allows Stephanie to spend more time with Anne, it brings her friendship with an older lesbian couple enlisted to help with the project. Kate and Mary are a refreshingly relaxed pair of role models whose conversations with Stephanie are enlightening but never didactic. "If you are gay, then sooner or later you'll know for sure. You'll be attracted to someone who's attracted to you. You'll know." And, while her passion for Anne remains unrequited, Stephanie becomes comfortable enough to confide in her best friend, whose response is matter-of-fact: "Why Anne Delaney? She's sort of a jerk." Unassuming and non-threatening, this is a friendly fictional introduction for gay and straight kids alike.

109   **Brooke**, William J. *A Telling of the Tales: Five Stories*; illus. by Richard Egielski. Harper, 1990. Library ed. ISBN 0-06-020689-6; Trade ed. ISBN 0-06-020688-8. 132p. Library ed. $12.89; Trade ed. $12.95.

4-6   Five cleverly styled stories update folklore with a modernized attitude about sex roles. "The Waking of the Prince" features a princess suspicious of the traditional kiss ("Do you have any form of identification with you? . . . You didn't happen to notice any guards on your way up, did you?") and a prince who loses several rounds ("I have failed at hero") to a dragon that invents golden labor-saving devices. "The Growin' of Paul Bunyan" pits Paul's timbercutting ways against Johnny Appleseed's green thumb, the latter winning by a mile when Paul's ax sprouts into a redwood ("there's nobody bigger than a man who learns to grow"). "The Fitting of the Slipper" couples a prince with a peasant girl; "The Working of John Henry" exposes the legendary giant's death as a newsman's fabrication, while the real steel driver takes over the steam hammer. "The Telling of a Tale" is a somewhat confusing tale-within-a-tale that uses "Jack and the Beanstalk" to frame a message about the importance of passing on stories. There's a touch of self-consciousness about these, and a few embarrassing slips (how can an old peasant woman be a wet nurse?) but they're highly entertaining for all that. What's more, female liberation has been a commoner focus among fairy tale revisionists than male sensitivity has been, so this more unusual remodeling will find its way into classroom discussion after some light-hearted readaloud sessions. Each story is illustrated with a black-and-white decoration by Richard Egielski.

110   **Brooks**, Bruce. *Midnight Hour Encores*. Harper, 1986. Library ed. ISBN 0-06-020710-8; Trade ed. ISBN 0-06-020709-4. 263p. Library ed. $13.89; Trade ed. $13.95.

6-12   Sixteeen-year-old Sibilance, self-named at age eight, is a musical prodigy whose flower-child mother left her at birth to the devoted care of her father, whom Sib calls Taxi. After scooping every European prize for her cello playing, Sib tracks down a Russian ex-prodigy, with whom she yearns to study, to San Francisco, where her mother, Connie, also lives. Sib and Taxi's journey from their home on the east Coast across country in a minibus is a journey back in time. Taxi is trying to prepare Sib for meeting her mother by providing a background on the sixties' counterculture. Connie, however, has become a wealthy real-estate broker with a male secretary, exquisite taste, and a sharp business sense. Yet after assuring herself a place in both her mother's life and in the conservatory where her audition wins her a place, Sib realizes her attachment to her father and returns with him. This is an ambitious novel, as was Brooks' previous *The Moves Make the Man*. Although it is somewhat too cleverly written at times, with Sib's dialogue sounding like the technically brilliant "showoff" pieces she detests, the undercurrents of characterization are sharp and strong. Taxi, too, is sometimes as cliched as the phrases with which he describes the sixties (including all the relevant obscenities), yet there's enough individuality to make its mark, as there is with Connie, a setup that is half expected, yet surprising. An intriguing piece, structurally and descriptively, this is vivid if not always convincing.

111   **Brooks**, Jerome. *Naked in Winter*. Jackson/Orchard, 1990. Library ed. ISBN 0-531-08466-3; Trade ed. ISBN 0-531-05866-2. 224p. Library ed. $14.99; Trade ed. $14.95.

7-10
*

Set in late 1940s Chicago, this is an evocative story of adolescence and its rites of passage. A good student at a boys' public high school, Jake Ackerman takes comfort in his group of close friends, hopes to go to college, worries because he isn't aggressive enough with girls. Jake's parents quarrel, and that's upsetting; it's even more upsetting when his father announces that he's bought a house near Midway Airport (in a neighborhood that was almost rural at the time), a move that makes Jake's mother furious and Jake desolate. He commutes to his

old school, but the friendships wane; he falls in love, but there are
tensions and a breach; he realizes how much he loves his father when
Pa becomes ill, and he learns that Ma's bitterness masks an equally
strong love for Pa. While the book is redolent of the period and of
Chicago and of a Jewish family's strength and tenacity, it is in the
characterization of Jake that Brooks excels: Jake is the narrator, and
his honesty, his joy in being loved, his apprehension about himself,
and his need for independence that sometimes vies with his need for
security are vivid, convincing, and moving.

112   Brooks, Martha. *Paradise Café and Other Stories*. Joy Street/Little,
       1990. ISBN 0-316-10978-9. 124p. $14.95.

7-12   First published in Canada in 1988, these fourteen impressively fresh
  *   short stories portray adolescents in aching throes of emotion. The first
       four suggest the range of subjects: "Running with Marty" is about a
       girl who hurts her boyfriend almost beyond recall before she learns to
       value him; "A Boy and his Dog" details the death of an aged pet;
       "King of the Roller Rink" describes a girl jilted because she's from the
       wrong social class; and "The Way Things Are" depicts a retarded boy
       who becomes part of a farm family. Once or twice, the tone seems self-
       conscious, as in "Dying for Love" ("My mother's going through early
       menopause and I'm going through late puberty"), but the writing is
       consistently adroit. Two friends with a crush on the same boy keep
       identical five-year diaries, which one of them describes: "And each
       night under hissing street lamps we sighed, rolling our eyes, before we
       separated to be alone with Karl on the crisply lined pink paper." The
       cast is diverse, including French, Indian, and black characters. All
       share the pain and triumph of maturation with which young adult
       readers can identify.

113   Brooks, Polly Schoyer. *Beyond the Myth: The Story of Joan of Arc*.
       Lippincott, 1990. Library ed. ISBN 0-397-32423-5; Trade ed. ISBN 0-397-
       32422-7. 176p. illus. with photographs. $13.95.

7-10   Brooks, author of *Queen Eleanor* , here focuses on a later medieval
  *   heroine, one who "has been called upon by such diverse extremes as
       communists and monarchists, each claiming her as their champion."
       Carefully distinguishing between fact, speculation, and legend, the
       author traces Joan's destiny from her first visitation, at age thirteen, by
       the spirit of St. Michael. While theologians may argue with the
       assertion that "whether Joan really heard voices or only thought she
       did doesn't matter," few will fail to be impressed with Brooks'
       rendering of Joan's fierce dedication and persistence. The battle
       scenes are vivid, as are the portraits of Joan's followers, bedevilers,
       and beneficiaries—the author's impatience with the wishy-washy King
       Charles has a witty and authoritative tartness. A detailed index,

concisely annotated bibliography, and historical illustrations (including various depictions of Joan) are included. An afterword offers some considerations of how perceptions of Joan have changed over time, and some suggestions for "rational" explanations of her miracles. "Joan herself is not so easy to explain. She is more of a miracle than the many miracles attributed to her."

114   **Brown**, Laurene Krasny. *Visiting the Art Museum*; written and illus. by Laurene Krasny Brown and Marc Brown Dutton, 1986. ISBN 0-525-44233-2. 32p. $11.95

K-3   So there IS something new under the sun, and this book takes a new
*   approach to art appreciation that is both informative and hilarious. It is nicely gauged for the younger child, and it uses a convincing narrative framework (a family visit to a museum) and a believable conversion (the oldest child, reluctant to leave a television set, finds some exciting art objects) to carry nicely integrated information about what one will find in an art museum. Small-scale reproductions of famous pieces of work are accompanied by facts about the artist and the museum in which the work is housed in reality. Balloon-enclosed conversation is funny; appended notes give additional information and tips on how to enjoy an art museum.

115   **Brown**, Marc. *Arthur's Baby*; written and illus. by Marc Tolon Brown. Joy Street/ Little, 1987. ISBN 0-316-11123-6. 32p. $13.95.

4-7 yrs.   Having been through a good many traumas with Arthur already, young listeners won't be too surprised to find he's suffering some pangs of sibling rivalry with the arrival of a new baby sister. And they won't be disappointed in the humor that's injected into Arthur's dose of adaptation. The spacious cartoon strips document a classic sequence: peer reactions ("You'll have to change all those dirty diapers!" says Muffy, holding her nose), Arthur's understated anxiety ("I think babies are taking over the world!"), Mother showing Arthur a snapshot of himself, aged one and crowned with a bowl of mashed peas—and of course the classic conclusion, in which Arthur solves the baby's problem when no one else can. Young listeners know what to expect of Arthur; now they know what to expect of a new baby ("Burp!").

116   **Brown**, Marc, comp. *Hand Rhymes*; comp. and illus. by Marc Brown. Dutton, 1985. ISBN 0-525-44201-4. 30p. $11.95.

1-3 yrs.   Fourteen rhymes culled or adapted from traditional sources and accompanied by miniature pen-and-ink diagrams of hand motions are set into soft watercolor spreads that make this dually useful for reading aloud or remembering in situations where distracting entertainment is desperately called for. The illustrations are consistently engaging while the verses vary. One or two seem artificial, but "Two Little Monkeys" is a nursery school standby, and "The Church" a perpetual favorite. "Five Little Babies" and "Five Little Goblins" will prove popular, the first for every day and the second especially in preparation for sometimes frightening visits of trick-or-treaters. A fit companion volume for Brown's earlier *Finger Rhymes*.

117   Brown, Ruth. *The Big Sneeze*; written and illus. by Ruth Brown. Lothrop, 1985. Library ed. ISBN 0-688-04666-5; Trade ed. ISBN 0-688-04665-7. 24p. Library ed. $11.88; Trade ed. $11.75.

3-5 yrs.   In the grand old tradition of humorous chain reactions, this illustrates the hubbub resulting from a fly's landing on a dozing farmer's nose. The farmer sneezes the fly into a spider's web, an activity that draws a cat that wakes the dog that scatters the hens that panic the donkey that brings the shrieking wife. "I only sneezed!" says the befuddled farmer, with splattered eggs dripping down his head. This is a formula that almost always works with young children, but here it is enhanced with spacious, light-filled artwork that commands attention. The textural variations created by fine lines and brush strokes make every corner of the dusty barn a place to explore, and the perspectives--a closeup of fly-on-nose, an action shot of hurtling cat--put the viewer right in the midst of the commotion. In fact, these seem like motion-picture paintings, with fine focus and a golden-brown glow to each composition.

118   Brown, Tricia. *Hello, Amigos!*; illus. with photographs by Fran Ortiz. Henry Holt, 1986. ISBN 0-8050-0090-9. 38p. $12.95.

K-2   A brief, first-person text captions full-page, lively, black-and-white photographs that follow Frankie Valdez through a school day, made special by his birthday celebration in class and at home. Frankie and his large, traditional Mexican family live in the Mission District of San Francisco. His combined first and second grade is bilingual, and a few Spanish words are sprinkled naturally through the narrative. This will be a good choice not only for Hispanic groups, but also for extending other children's cultural awareness.

119   Browne, Anthony. *Gorilla*; written and illus. by Anthony Browne. Knopf, 1985. Library ed. ISBN 0-394-97525-1; Trade ed. ISBN 0-394-87525-7. 29p. Library ed.$8.99; Trade ed. $7.95.

K-2
*   With an established predilection for gorillas (although she'd never seen one) it isn't surprising that Hannah, whose father always seemed to be too busy to spend time with her, imagines a trip to the zoo with a loving, protective gorilla who serves as a father-substitute. On the morning of her birthday, Father comes through. He gives her a toy gorilla, says "Happy birthday, love," and proposes a trip to the zoo.

Nice fantasy, with a nugget of psychologically sound base, and nicely
told. The best part of the book, for many children, will be the
illustrations, which combine a strong sense of design, effective
handling of color, excellent composition and draughtsmanship, and
fine use of light.

120   Browne, Anthony. *Piggybook*. Knopf, 1986. Library ed. ISBN 0-394-
98416-1; Trade ed. ISBN 0-394-88416-7. 28p. Library ed. $10.99; Trade
ed. $9.95

K-7   Mr. Piggott and his two sons are a male chauvinist lot who, outside of
yelling for their breakfast and dinner, don't exercise themselves much
around the house. When Mrs. Piggott finally tires of the endless
chores that sandwich her workday, she leaves the menfolk on their
own, with a note saying, "You are pigs." Indeed, with the cooking and
housework untended, they soon turn genuinely porcine, a transformation that Browne literally foreshadows with piggy shadows on the
walls, pig faces on the wallpaper, doorknobs, vases, lampshades,
faucets, fireplace, phone. (Observant viewers will note the colonial pig
squire in one familiar painting, with the female figure evacuated from
the bench beside him; also, the shadow of a wolf outside the window as
the household deteriorates without Mrs. Piggott). All ends well with
Mrs. Piggott's return, the male Piggotts grovelling properly for
forgiveness and then leaping into reform with a hand at the chores . . .
while Mrs. Piggott, her shadowy face for the first time clearly defined,
fixes the car. As in most of Browne's art, there is more than a touch of
irony and visual humor here, bringing off the didactic with a light
touch and turning the lesson into satire. There's also a pop-art quality
to many of the shapes and compositions, with smooth coloration and
shiny highlights that emphasize the rounded contours and cari-
catures. Fun to read aloud, this may elicit some discussion on familiar
home situations.

121   Browne, Anthony. *The Tunnel*; written and illus. by Anthony Browne.
Knopf, 1990. Library ed. ISBN 0-394-94582-4; Trade ed. ISBN 0-394-
84582-X. 26p. Library ed. $12.99; Trade ed. $11.95.

5-8 yrs.   "Once upon a time there lived a sister and brother who were not at all
alike. . . . The sister stayed inside on her own reading and dreaming. . . .
The brother played outside with his friends. . . roughing and tumbling." When their mother sends them out together after one
argument too many, Jack decides to explore a tunnel and does not
come back. It is Rose who must brave the underground dark and a
scary forest to rescue Jack, who has been turned to stone. Rose's hug
warms him back to life. Both story and graphics suggest many fairy
tales, including a picture of Little Red Riding Hood on Rose's wall, the
book she reads, her hooded red coat, and creatures that are shaped

Rackham-like from the wood of trees. Motifs from Beauty and the Beast are clear when Jack dons an animal mask to frighten Rose, and of course her name and her courageous love in restoring Jack to human appearance reflect Beauty's role. The exemplary blending of realism and fantasy in picture book format shows how resonantly fairy tales can influence literature beyond the constant replays of illustrated new editions that are currently besieging the market. Close watchers will recognize artistic shades of Browne's *Hansel and Gretel*, *Piggybook*, and *Gorilla*, but this is an imaginative invention unto itself.

122   **Browne**, Anthony. *Willy the Wimp;* written and illus. by Anthony Browne. Knopf, 1985. Library ed. ISBN 0-394-97061-6; Trade ed. ISBN 0-394-87061-1. 28p. Library ed. $8.99; Trade ed. $7.95.

K-3   Chimpanzee characters are shown in pictures that have fine use of color and textural details and that should appeal to the lap audience because of their humor. Willy is small and scrawny and super-polite, even to saying "I'm sorry" when somebody bullies him. He tires of being called a wimp and embarks on a massive body-building program. In time (and possibly due to the passage of time) he gets tall and muscular. Not only is he no longer the prey of the bullies, but also he rescues an extremely appreciative girl chimpanzee. Basking in glory, Willy walks into a lamppost and—just as he did before—says, "Oh, I'm sorry!" An appealing concept, nicely developed and nicely illustrated.

123   **Bröger**, Achim. *The Day Chubby Became Charles;* tr. from the German by Renée Vera Cafiero; illus. by Emily Arnold McCully. Lippincott, 1990. Library ed. ISBN 0-397-32145-7; Trade ed. ISBN 0-397-32144-9. 90p. Library ed. $12.89; Trade ed. $12.95.

2-4   Smoothly translated from the German original, this is a story about alliances and friendship values among younger children that is, for all of its directness and simplicity, subtle and perceptive. Always the odd man out, Chubby trails meekly after Julia and Jacob; one day Julia encounters Chubby after school and hopes that Jacob won't see them walking together. She's rather embarrassed, but as the afternoon goes on, she finds that Chubby (real name Charles) is sympathetic about Julia's concern for her grandmother, apparently ill. The two children exchange confidences, share hiding places, and Julia realizes that Charles is a friend. This is a gentle story, tender but not saccharine.

124   **Bryan**, Ashley. *The Cat's Purr;* written and illus. by Ashley Bryan. Atheneum, 1985. ISBN 0-689-31086-2. 42p. $9.95.

K-2   Based on a story in a collection of folklore of the West Indies, this has been adapted by Bryan, nicely told and illustrated with drawings in which the line is softened and the composition spare. In this version,

Cat and Rat are friends and neighbors, working well together until Rat becomes covetous, wanting to play the tiny drum that Cat had told him was a gift given with the injunction that nobody else play it. Cat discovers Rat's duplicity and chases him; Rat shoves the tiny drum into Cat's mouth so that he inadvertently swallows it. And that's why, with a downplaying of the new enmity and a reminder to readers that the purr of Cat's drum is best heard if one strokes gently, all cats purr. Nice to tell as well as to read aloud.

125   **Bryan**, Ashley, ad. *Lion and the Ostrich Chicks: And Other African Folk Tales*; ad. and illus. by Ashley Bryan. Atheneum, 1986. ISBN 0-689-31311-X. 86p. $13.95.

4-6   Four stories from Masai, Bushman, Angola, and Hausa traditions (exact sources are given in a concluding bibliography) are retold with an unerring sense of rhythm and rhyme that will lure those who feel insecure in storytelling to read these aloud at least. "Lion and the Ostrich Chicks" reveals how the king of beasts gets foiled at chicknapping by a clever mongoose. "Son of the Wind" relates the experience of young Nakati, who plays ball with the wind's son, named Whooree-kuan-kuan Gwow-gwowbootish. "Jackal's Favorite Game" is a funny tale of hide and seek, in which Hare finally gets Jackal to promise not to "tackle and tickle" him any more. "The Foolish Boy" lauds the parents of a simpleton, who turns out better than anyone expected because when he makes mistakes, his parents "didn't get excited./ They didn't get upset./ They didn't howl or holler/ And they didn't throw a fit." Rich in narrative and emotional content, these stories will appeal to independent readers or younger listeners, for whom adults can relish rolling the words around their tongues while reading aloud. Bryan's black-and-white illustrations are scattered throughout the text, with occasional full-page art in red, gold, and black. His style of heavy, swirling lines is full of movement and sometimes touched with folk design motifs. A rich selection.

126   **Buchan**, Elizabeth. *Beatrix Potter*; illus. by Beatrix Potter and Mike Dodd. Hamish Hamilton, 1987. ISBN 0-241-12051-9. 54p. (Profiles). $9.95.

3-5   Capably written in 12 brief chapters and illustrated with a mixture of crosshatch portraits and drawings from Potter's books, this is a sensible, non-adulatory biography of the first modern picture-book artist. Potter's domination by her demanding parents, the untimely death of her fiancé, her brother's alcoholism, and her eventual happiness on a country farm with her husband William Heelis are interwoven with her development of Peter Rabbit, Squirrel Nutkin, The Tailor of Gloucester, and other classic animal characters. U.S. children researching Potter will note with interest her relationship with

Anne Carroll Moore of the New York Public Library and subsequent cordiality to visiting Americans.

127   **Bulla**, Clyde Robert. *The Chalk Box Kid;* illus. by Thomas B. Allen. Random House, 1987. Library ed. ISBN 0-394-99102-8; Paper ed. ISBN 0-394-89102-3. 59p. (Stepping Stone). Library ed. $5.99; Paper ed. $1.95.

2-4   Gregory's ninth birthday is shadowed by a move to a run-down house after his father loses his factory job. Troubled by an insensitive uncle with whom he has to share a room and by his new classmates' rejection, Gregory finds solace in "drawing" the garden he wishes he had on the walls of a burnt-out chalk factory nearby. Then a shy, withdrawn girl who has just won a prize for her art work recognizes Gregory's talent, directs the teacher's attention to his accomplishment, and best of all, offers him her friendship. As usual, Bulla manages a poignant depth within the confines of simple style and narrative. Understated and easy to read, this nevertheless tackles problems that are not easy to solve without exercising the imagination.

128   **Bunting**, Eve. *Ghost's Hour, Spook's Hour;* illus. by Donald Carrick. Clarion, 1987. ISBN 0-89919-484-2. 32. $12.95.

4-7 yrs.   A prize for Halloween but cathartic for any night of the year, this is a powerful evocation of childhood fears. When the narrator is awakened in the middle of the night by scary noises, he and his dog Biff make their way to his parents' room only to find them gone. The trip down the stairs takes a lot of courage, with a bonging clock and a sudden encounter with the mirror scaring boy and dog almost right off the page. All ends well, with both bedded down on the couch beside Mom and Dad, who had moved because of the wind banging a branch against their window. Bunting is proficient at the spare narrative and sound effects that accumulate for such a realistic depiction here. It is Carrick's watercolor paintings, however, that galvanize the text into action. The vivid contrasts of light and dark, along with sudden shifts of shape, color, perspective, build tension, catch the breath, and keep the eye moving. Satisfying as story, art, and empathy.

129   **Bunting**, Eve. *The Wall;* illus. by Ronald Himler. Clarion, 1990. ISBN 0-395-51588-2. 32p. $13.95.

5-8 yrs.   A narrator who appears to be about four years old gives a present-tense account of the visit he makes with his young father to find Grandpa's name on the Vietnam Veterans Memorial. The father's emotions and the boy's perspective are well-realized, and the action is low-key: "He slides out a picture of me, one of the yucky ones they took in school. . . . Dad puts the picture on the grass below Grandpa's name." The watercolor paintings also carry a quiet weight of expression. This is a book that will need some preamble and discussion to be meaningful to a picture book audience, but it does offer possibilities for children to talk about similar experiences of visiting the wall or to acquire an introduction to the Vietnamese conflict that has affected so many of their families.

130   **Bunting**, Eve. *The Wednesday Surprise*; illus. by Donald Carrick. Clarion, 1989. ISBN 0-89919-721-3. 30p. $13.95.

K-3   Every Wednesday night her Mom works late, and big brother Sam waits with Anna until Grandma arrives before he goes to the Y to play basketball. Every Wednesday night Anna and Grandma work on the surprise they are planning for Dad's birthday. It is probable that most readers will be surprised, too: what Grandma has been doing is learning to read, with seven-year-old Anna as her teacher. Bunting's writing is simple and warm and direct, showing rather than telling the book's audience that reading is both a skill and a joy. Carrick's pictures echo the warmth, especially in the faces of the family, painted in realistically detailed watercolors with a careful attention to familial resemblance. A gentle charmer.

131   **Burkert**, Nancy Ekholm. *Valentine & Orson*; ad. and illus. by Nancy Ekholm Burkert. Yearout/Farrar, 1989. ISBN 0-374-38078-3. 48p. $16.95.Sp

7-   In an ambitious recasting of a fourteenth-century French lay known only through subsequent literary reworkings, Burkert reverses most current adapters' practice of casting historical verse into modern prose. Her afterword states that "it was Chaucer's tales that prompted" her to choose a poetic mode, and, although her text has neither Chaucer's narrative irony nor the spare grace of troubadors at ease with the form, it is ingeniously rhymed and metered in iambic pentameter couplets. The chivalric complexity of the tale, about twin boys born to an empress cast out of her realm on the specious charge of adultery, is propounded by its presentation here as a medieval play produced by a family of ragtag actors. The scenes are flawlessly illustrated in Burkert's detailed paintings, for which she freely acknowledges Breugel as inspiration. It is, of course, the art that reveals Burkert's subtlety of technique, style, and content and that is the raison d'être of the book. The graphic tone is in many ways the most varied of Burkert's illustration to date, with robust action, distinctive portraiture, and surrealistic effects coexisting in a rich blend of sharply defined hues and line work. Burkert's irony is visual, surfacing in the depictions of a narrator who plays the wise fool and in a troupe who relish the slapstick of their storytelling trade. Although this appears to be a picture book, it will be of special interest to the junior high and high school students who enjoyed *Proud Knight, Fair*

Lady: The Twelve Laís of Marie de France, or the illustrated
adaptations of Chaucer that appeared in 1988.

132   Burleigh, Robert. *A Man Named Thoreau;* illus. by Lloyd Bloom.
Atheneum, 1985. ISBN 0-689-31122-2. 29p. $11.95.

2-5   An intriguing blend of biographical fact and philosophical summary,
this has more substance than its picture-book format might imply.
The author has smoothly interwoven quotes from *Walden,*
particularly, into a pithy development of Thoreau's thinking there,
which clarifies his independence from traditional society and
therefore his ongoing relevance to today's problems: "Read not the
times. . . read the Eternities." To have simplified concepts so much
without distortion is a gift to the younger reader or listener, and
Bloom's subtly valued pencil drawings facing every page of text lend
further dimension. The list of important dates and bibliography are
unusual features in a book for this audience.

133   Burningham, John. *Hey! Get Off Our Train;* written and illus. by John
Burningham. Crown, 1990. Library ed. ISBN 0-517-57643-0; Trade ed.
ISBN 0-517-57638-4. 48p. Library ed. $14.99; Trade ed. $14.95.

4-7 yrs. Only Burningham could make an ecological fable so much fun. The
child is hero here from the start, as the mother's unsympathetic words
establish immediately: "You aren't still playing with that train are you?
Get into bed immediately. You know you have to be up early for school
tomorrow." The boy does, and dreams that he and his stuffed dog, now
an efficient railroad engineer, are speeding through the countryside
playing games and, by the by, picking up endangered animals ("They
are cutting down the forests where I live, and soon there will be none
of us left," says the tiger). Each time they stop to play (ghosts,
swimming, kite flying, umbrella, snowball throwing), another animal
comes on board until it's time to go home. When the boy's mother
wakes him up for school, there seem to be animals all over the house
("Does this have anything to do with you?"). Spacious drawings
contrasted with deeply textured landscape paintings create a striking
effect as the artist juggles antic humor with a serious message—and
never misses a beat.

134   Bushey, Jerry. *Farming the Land: Modern Farmers and Their
Machines.* Carolrhoda, 1987. ISBN 0-87614-314-1. 36p. illus. with
photographs. $12.95.

3-5   An inviting photodocumentary draws young readers into the country-
*   side for a look at typical sights—"a peaceful small town . . . a newborn
calf being cleaned by its mother . . . or thousands of turkeys just
looking sociable"—before tackling the various machines that farmers
use seasonally for farm work. What's unusual here is the coherent way

in which the text links the organic work of growing things with the technical production aspect. There's also a Ripley's believe-it-or-not appeal: on one $80,000 John Deere tractor, "the tires can cost up to $500 each"; or again, "with an all-wheel drive tractor, today's farmer can plow in ten minutes what would have taken a farmer with one horse all day to do!" The color photographs are well composed and reproduced, with some inspiring rural vistas as well as informative closeups. Words in boldface print are explained in context and defined in a glossary.

135   **Byars**, Betsy. *Bingo Brown and the Language of Love*. Viking, 1989. ISBN 0-670-82791-6. 132p. $11.95.

5-7   Fans of *The Burning Questions of Bingo Brown* need not worry about
*   Byars letting them down with this sequel. It's just as authentically characterized, while the writing builds on the humorous use of free association without losing control. Bingo's true love Melissa has moved to Bixby, Oklahoma; her best friend Cici likes Bingo, but Bingo's macho neighbor Billy has a crush on Cici; and to top it off, Bingo's parents are acting immature about their own relationship because, it turns out, Bingo's mother has become unexpectedly pregnant just when she's secured a job she loves. If the plot sounds popularized, the style is singular. Bingo's first (unnecessary) shave is a classically funny rite-of-passage scene, and the issues of sexual maturity are treated in witty but age-appropriate ways. When buxom Cici finds Bingo cooking dinner as part of his restitution for a $54 phone bill to Melissa, he tries to ease her out of the kitchen: "You will have to excuse me now, I am preparing, er, chicken chests." Enjoy.

136   **Byars**, Betsy. *The Blossoms and the Green Phantom*; illus. by Jacqueline Rogers. Delacorte, 1987. ISBN 0-385-29533-2. 146p. $13.95.

4-6   A third story about the engaging characters of *The Not-Just-Anybody Family* and *The Blossoms Meet the Vulture Lady* is just as funny without being slapstick, just as sweet without being sentimental. Here the members of the Blossom family, as well as several friends, rally to support the ambitious project of the youngest, Jason. His inventive mind has come up with a home-made UFO, concocted of string, air mattresses, garbage bags, day-glo paint and the helium a friend manages to procure. This has vivacity and color, fits nicely with but does not depend on the two books to which it is a sequel, and manages to make the improbable both convincing and entertaining.

137   **Byars**, Betsy. *The Burning Questions of Bingo Brown*. Viking, 1988. ISBN 0-670-81932-8. 166p. $11.95.

5-8
*

With her particular talent for rendering sad situations from a good-humored protagonist's perspective, Byars has written a very funny book about the first love between two classmates whose teacher is desperately lovelorn over an aerobics instructor. While Bingo's girlfriend, Melissa, returns his affection, Mr. Markham is driven to a suicide attempt by rejection. There are many points to admire here. One is the high-spirited reflection of classroom conversations and dynamics, which Bingo observes during his perpetual journeys to the pencil sharpener. A second is the smooth blend of plot and subplot, as the reader realizes that it is the child who is normal and the adult who has lost control. However, neither is stereotyped. Bingo grows wiser with the usual spurts and setbacks of pre-adolescent realization. Mr. Markham is a sensitive, witty, intelligent teacher who is unstable and makes a terrible mistake, but who has the affection of his class and who recovers his balance. The honest, capable handling of Bingo's guilt by his mother, who at first appears to be something of an airhead, is another coup. There is a range of humor, from hilarious ("He, who had been in love three times in one day and had already had four mixed-sex conversations!") to ironic ("Bingo knew his name would not be picked. He had never been chosen for anything in his life"). Maintained in both style and incident, these passages are too numerous to mention, although some, like the description of Bingo's perfect grandmother, are memorable. This is a story that children are going to get a lot out of and love, while adults appreciate both craft and content.

138   **Byars**, Betsy. *Cracker Jackson*. Viking, 1985. ISBN 0-607-80546-7. 146p. $11.95.

5-7

It was Alma who'd given Jackson his nickname when she had been his babysitter; now Alma was married and had her own baby. Jackson, now eleven, still loves Alma and is fearful on her behalf, because—although she won't admit it—her bruises indicate that she's being abused by her hot-tempered, domineering husband, Bill Ray. The latter has threatened Jackson, who is afraid both on his own behalf and Alma's, doesn't feel he can confide in either of his divorced parents, but finally blurts it out during one of his weekly telephone conversations with his father. After Alma, brutally assaulted, admits the situation, Jackson tries to help her; eventually his mother steps in and, in the end, Alma and her baby are taken to another town where they are safe. Any story of wife-battering holds potential for drama and pathos; Byars shows, with depth and conviction, how traumatic this is for the victim, how it can affect others, and how it may be necessary for others to take the initiative in rescuing the victim. The style is excellent, with a smooth narrative flow, a subordination of theme to story, and strong characterization and relationships.

139   **Byars**, Betsy. *The Golly Sisters Go West*; illus. by Sue Truesdell. Harper, 1986. Library ed. ISBN 0-06-020884-8; Trade ed. ISBN 0-06-020883-X. 58p. Library ed. $9.89; Trade ed. $8.95.

1-3   Byars applies her distinctive brand of quirky humor to two adventuresome women determined to dare the frontier with minimum experience. In the first story, they learn the hard way how to make a horse move forward; in the second, they give their first road show to an audience of two dogs; in the third, they get lost; in the fourth, try to incorporate the horse into their act; in the fifth, make up after one of their constant arguments; in the sixth, talk themselves out of a nighttime scare. The dialogue and antics are convincingly like those of rivalrous young siblings anywhere on the block. The story lines are cleverer than much easy to read fare, and the old West setting adds flair. The accompanying water colors, too, add a generous dollop of humor, especially in the horse's expressions and the riotous postures of the two main characters.

140   **Byars**, Betsy. *The Not-Just-Anybody Family*; illus. by Jacqueline Rogers. Delacorte, 1986. ISBN 0-385-29443-3. 149p. $13.95.

5-7
*   Byars is well-known for her ability to shed humorous light on serious situations, and this is no exception. Junior has fallen off the roof in his attempt to fly and been hauled off to the hospital with two broken legs. His sister and brother, after running into the woods to avoid an encounter with the police, are faced with the prospect of rescuing their grandfather, who they correctly assume is in jail (for disturbing the peace after reckless teenagers run their car over some cans he has collected for refund). Their mother is away on her rodeo circuit. Their dog is on the run, looking for Pap. The ins and outs of this plot are so well woven, and often spliced with cliff-hangers, that readers will (a) read fast to see what happens, (b) laugh at the slapstick action, (c) fall in love with this quirky family, and (d) savor the happy ending. A good run for the money, by any account.

141   **Byers**, Rinda M. *Mycca's Baby*; illus. by David Tamura. Orchard, 1990. Library ed. ISBN 0-531-08428-0; Trade ed. ISBN 0-531-05828-X. 32p. Library ed. $13.99; Trade ed. $13.95.

4-7 yrs.   In a close-knit extended family, young Mycca anticipates her Aunt Rose's first baby with longing. She visits her grandparents' house, where Grandma has prepared a crib and diapers ("The baby can sleep in our spare room while you're working, Rose") and begs her own parents to have another baby. This is a hard-working cast of characters: Aunt Rose and her husband Robert live in a trailer, and Rose keeps house for senile, elderly Maudie next door while Robert works in a feed store. Mycca's father admits that he cannot earn enough to support more children than Mycca and her brother, but when the baby arrives, Rose makes sure that Mycca and newborn Serenity share a loving cousinly cuddle. Strokes of cheerful realism raise this common story above the ordinary: "I wish the baby was born. My feet hurt. And I look like a *pig*," complains Rose; later, Mycca bluntly describes Maudie as forgetting everything, including Rose, who takes care of her every day. Rounded shapes and comfortable figures give the warm-hued illustrations a reassuring tone just right for the text as well as for young listeners who are experiencing the anxiety of a new baby coming along.

142 **Calmenson**, Stephanie. *What Am I?: Very First Riddles*; illus. by Karen Gundersheimer. Harper, 1989. Library ed. ISBN 0-06-020998-4; Trade ed. ISBN 0-06-020997-6. 32p. Library ed. $11.89; Trade ed. $11.95.

3-6 yrs. Just one short step up from point-and-name, these rhyming riddles couldn't be simpler: "To guess what I am/ Is easy as can be./ Your sock goes on your foot/ And your foot goes into me." Turn the page for one unmistakable *shoe*. Never tricky and always toddler-tested (keys, flowers, a swing), the riddles provide the appeal of rhyming as well as pride in the accomplishment of figuring out the answer. And, of course, the fun of shouting it out. Tidy drawings on the riddle page provide visual nudges; illustrations of the mystery objects are generic enough to be readily identified while maintaining interest through color (a yellow telephone) and detail (a terrific toy train).

143 **Cameron**, Ann. *Julian's Glorious Summer*; illus. by Dora Leder. Random House, 1987. Library ed. ISBN 0-394-99117-6; Paper ed. ISBN 0-394-89117-1. 62p. (Stepping Stones). Library ed. $5.99; Paper ed. $1.95.

3-5 With spontaneous humor and a natural, easy-to-read style, Cameron shows how a small lie comes to determine young Julian's whole summer. On seeing his best friend, Gloria, tooling along on her new bike, Julian hides his fear of trying it out with a fib about having to work all summer for his dad. Then, of course, he's stuck working—and all for naught; his father rewards him with a new bike. Much to his surprise, however, Julian learns to ride it. The story does several things: it addresses a common fear that rarely surfaces, it portrays a happy, healthy family that just happens to be Black, and it entertains. At one point Julian's mother observes to her exhausted son: "if you nod one more time, your chin is going to make a crash-landing in your creamed corn." Later, Julian confesses to his mother. "Once I began to tell the truth, it seemed like I almost had a taste, like some really delicious food to chew on, that I wanted to have more and more of in my mouth." And he proceeds to detail, with zest, what he hates about bicycles, from tubes and tires to falling off. Modest and honest.

144   **Cameron**, Ann. *More Stories Julian Tells*; illus. by Ann Strugnell. Knopf, 1986. Library ed. ISBN 0-394-96969-3; Trade ed. ISBN 0-394-86969-9. 82p. Library ed. $10.99; Trade ed. $10.95.

2-3   Like the first book of stories narrated by Julian (lively, black, articulate) this has short but carefully constructed anecdotes that are told in a simple but lively style. They have to do with events and relationships that will be familiar to most readers: a squabble with a brother, a harmless trick played by a friend, inventive play. Julian's father plays a major role (and is an exemplary parent, wise and patient) and while Julian and his friend Gloria learn some new things, the book has no trace of didacticism. Black-and-white illustrations show both real and imaginary details, and the page layout—large print, lots of space—facilitates reading.

145   **Cameron**, Ann. *The Most Beautiful Place in the World*; illus. by Thomas B. Allen. Knopf, 1988. Library ed. ISBN 0-394-99463-9; Trade ed. ISBN 0-394-89463-4. 57p. Library ed. $11.99; Trade ed. $10.95

3-5   The narrator starts out with what sounds like a travelogue introduction to his country, Guatemala, but after a bit of description winds into a story of great integrity. Abandoned by his father, he moves into his grandmother's house with his mother, who soon marries another man and leaves him behind. Juan's absorption of his grandmother's values and his learning to trust her love for him help overcome his loss. Her support of his schooling in face of financial need is told with simple power. Cameron's style is succinctly graceful ("Stories are important here, and cars aren't") but realistically natural ("I need my rest. I have had enough sleeping with children. Children kick"). The easy-to-read text, the handsome pencil drawings, and a setting that will take U.S. children into lives led elsewhere make this a winning choice for reading aloud or alone.

146   **Cameron**, Eleanor. *The Private Worlds of Julia Redfern*. Dutton, 1988. ISBN 0-525-44394-0. 218p. $12.95.

6-9   Although several books about a younger Julia have been published in the interim years, this is the direct sequel to the 1971 title *A Room Made of Windows* , the first book about the girl who was a budding writer and passionately loyal friend to her neighbor. This sequel is one of the best books Cameron has produced, both tightly knit and expanding with Julia's growing maturity and her involvement in the lives of others. There are depth and empathy as Julia, now fifteen, finds love and accepts temporary separation from her love, and adjusts to the fact that imperfection of a loved one (her uncle Hugh, primarily) does not mean the end of loving. A far cry from the formula romance, this is a book for thoughtful readers.

147   **Cannon**, A. E. *The Shadow Brothers*. Delacorte, 1990. ISBN 0-385-29982-6. 179p. $14.95.

7-10   Marcus is the narrator, the older child in a Mormon family who had taken in Henry, a Native American, as a foster son when he and Marcus were seven. The boys' fathers had been friends, and Mr. Yazzie had sent his boy to the Jenkins family when Mrs. Yazzie died. Now the boys are adolescents, and Marcus is trying not to be jealous because Henry is spending so much time with a girl. She happens to be the girl Marcus yearns for. She also happens to be the daughter of a well-to-do couple who are not pleased that their lovely Celia is dating a Navajo. Eventually Marcus falls in love with the girl next door, Sutton Rogers. Henry's continuing bouts of cultural conflict culminate in his decision to return to his home and spend more time with his father and grandfather. What happens to Marcus and Henry is not unimportant, but the candor and perception with which Cannon interprets their feelings—about themselves and about each other—looms even larger.

148   **Carkeet**, David. *The Silent Treatment*. Harper, 1988. Library ed. ISBN 0-06-020979-8; Trade ed. ISBN 0-06-020978-X. 280p. Library ed. $13.89; Trade ed. $13.95.

7-10   Ricky, the narrator, has just started high school in his small town in the foothills of the Sierra Nevada mountains, and although he's known as "that nice Appleton boy," he feels he can never live up to the performance of older brother Rodney, a world class egomaniac. There are several plot threads: rivalry with a girl classmate, friendship with an oddball boy of whom Ricky's parents don't approve, a contest, a minor mystery about a ne'er-do-well old prospector, a running feud with Rodney, and a persistent dismay at how Rodney has duped their parents into giving him undeserved kudos. Ah, but it all comes right in the end in a very impressive story that has polished style, a structure deftly meshing all the threads, a cast that is distinctly differentiated, and a core of perceptive exploration of the silent treatment that can be a way of communicating ease or hostility, contempt or shyness, resentment or resolve.

149   **Carle**, Eric, ad. *Eric Carle's Treasury of Classic Stories for Children by Aesop, Hans Christian Andersen and the Brothers Grimm*; ad., comp. and illus. by Eric Carle. Orchard/Watts, 1988. ISBN 0-531-05742-9. 160p. $18.95.

5-8 yrs.   Partially taken from previous collections illustrated by Carle, these twenty-two tales range from commonly anthologized selections such as the Grimms' "Tom Thumb" to less well-known stories such as Andersen's "The Traveling Companion." The retellings are smooth, though they lack the rhythmic power of other versions; the invocation of "Flounder, flounder, in the sea . . ." is missing, for instance, from "The Fisherman and his Wife." The drama of Carle's paintings, however, is undeniable, and they are generously distributed, sometimes full-page and sometimes partial, on every spacious double spread. The picture of tiny Tom Thumb curled up in a snail shell that covers two pages thickly textured with greens, blues, and tans is unforgettable.

150   **Carle**, Eric. *The Very Busy Spider;* written and illus. by Eric Carle. Philomel, 1985. ISBN 0-399-21166-7. 22p. $14.95.

2-5 yrs.   Although the story this tells is slight and has a repetitive pattern, the book should enchant children because the fine lines of the spider's web, as it grows, are raised just enough from the page so that they can be felt and because the collage illustrations are so bright in colors and perky in forms. A spider spins a web between fence posts, and a series of animals comes close, each addressing her, "Neigh! Neigh! Want to go for a ride?" "Moo! Moo! Want to eat some grass?" Each time there is no response to the vapid question which seems to be inserted just so that something will be happening. Each time, the text reads, "The spider didn't answer. She was very busy spinning her web." Web done, the spider catches a fly. There's no mention of what happens to the fly but the book ends with the weary spider falling asleep.

151   **Carlstrom**, Nancy White. *Jesse Bear, What Will You Wear?* illus. by Bruce Degen. Macmillan, 1986. ISBN 0-02-717350-X. 32p. $11.95.

3-5 yrs.   This is one of those lilting chants that parent and child will find themselves saying with or without the book, although the illustrations certainly offer plenty to pore over in lap-sitting sessions. Little Jesse starts out sensibly enough with a "shirt of red/Pulled over my head" but proceeds to "pants that dance," "a rose in my toes," "sun on the run," and "sand on my hand in the morning." Each time of day offers him more opportunities for silly apparel ("juice from a pear/and rice in my hair") until finally he wears bear hugs and kisses to bed, along with some dreams in his head. The big, cheerful watercolor paintings show the baby bear in loving relation to his family and world. Without crossing the line into sentimentality, this offers a happy, humorous soundfest that will associate reading aloud with a sense of play.

152   **Carrick**, Carol. *Left Behind;* illus. by Donald Carrick. Clarion, 1988. ISBN 0-89919-535-0. 30p. $13.95.

5-7 yrs.   Christopher has been the subject of other common crises, including one incident in which he confronts his fear of the water (*Dark and Full of Secrets*) and several others about his dog. Here, he is separated from his class on a field trip downtown when the doors of a crowded train slam shut before he can reboard. Christopher's fear and confusion are realistic without overdramatization, and he's helped by a uniformed official and a policeman before trouble develops. The literal, page-and-a-half watercolor spreads lend just the right amount of low-key tension; a good pick for preschool and primary-grade discussion.

153   **Carrick,** Donald. *Harald and the Great Stag;* written and illus. by Donald Carrick. Clarion, 1988. ISBN 0-89919-514-8. 30p. $14.95.

5-8 yrs.   The young hero of *Harald and the Giant Knight*, who was earlier disillusioned about tournaments and jousting, here challenges the hallowed hunting customs of the Middle Ages. Harald has glimpsed the Great Stag targeted by the baron for sport, and he throws the dogs off track by scattering the Stag's droppings in "a crazy pattern over the forest floor." Saved from discovery by an old hunter who also admires the Stag, Harald escapes the severe punishment that would have accompanied his deed but retains an indelible impression of how it feels to be hunted. The watercolor paintings are rich in woods hues, with occasional spreads featuring festive trappings of medieval attire. The dappled lighting and soft textures graphically emphasize the shadows into which the Stag escapes. A thoughtful blend of historical and contemporary themes.

154   **Carroll,** Lewis. *Alice's Adventures in Wonderland and Through the Looking-Glass;* illus. by Markéta Prachatická. Wellington, 1989. ISBN 0-922984-01-8. 165p. $29.95.

4-   Prague artist Prachatická, who won the 1984 Premio Grafico prize at the Bologna Children's Book Fair for these illustrations, projects a surrealistic tone with meticulous traditional drafting. Imaginatively reflecting the sharp-edged fantasy world of Alice's journeys, her large-scale, pen-and-ink drawings comprise a collector's item worthy of a place near Tenniel's original art. With their eerie figures and illusionary frames and planes, the pictures will fascinate children as well as connoiseurs. Many of the effects derive from minute hatch and crosshatch, a technique drawing the eye deep into textural contrasts and tantalizing perspectives.

155   **Carson,** Jo. *Stories I Ain't Told Nobody Yet: Selections from the People Pieces.* Orchard, 1989. Library ed. ISBN 0-531-08408-6; Trade ed. ISBN 0-531-05808-5. 84p. Library ed. $12.99; Trade ed. $12.95.

7-   Arranged on the page to appear almost as free verse, these are 49 brief excerpts from anecdotes Carson has heard among Appalachians and has adapted for public performance. They are loosely organized into five sections called Neighbors and Kin, Observations, Relationships, Work, and We Say of Ourselves. These are voices roughened by labor and tried by tribulation. They range from a battered woman warning others about her ex-husband ("he does love you, he loves you hurt and he will hit you again") to a black man recalling, after a waitress refuses to serve him and his daughter, the beating he received in jail after a sit-in more than 20 years before ("this is the same story as the one that cracked my head open. The only thing that changed is the law"). There are jokes along with the pain, women's viewpoints as well as men's, fragments of experience shaped into monologues and dialogues, a balance of dialect with straightforward informality of style that's easy to read aloud. Students taking speech or drama classes will find some inspiring pieces here, as will those interested in collecting oral history or researching their roots. "I could fill you up with stories, stories I ain't told nobody yet, stories with your name, your blood in them. Ain't nobody gonna hear them if you don't and you ain't gonna hear them unless you get back home. When I am dead, it will not matter how hard you press your ear to the ground." Listen and learn.

156   **Carter,** Alden R. *RoboDad*. Putnam, 1990. ISBN 0-399-22191-3. 144p. $14.95.

8-12   It's been almost six months since her dad suffered a massive stroke that left him emotionally catatonic, but fourteen-year-old Shar still can't believe that he will never recover. His lethargic behavior, sitting all day in front of the television, eating snacks, earns him the nickname "RoboDad" from Shar's younger brothers, who are both confused and angered by his altered personality. Terrified by his irrational and violent outbursts, the whole family suffers, but Shar most of all. While Mom buries herself in her work, Shar curtails her social life to care for her father. Her formerly gentle "buddy" is cruelly insensitive and sexually threatening: "He looked down at me with that strange stare. Slowly, his big hands came up to cover my breasts. I was so shocked that I went completely rigid. 'These are new,' he said." Most of the characters are carefully drawn and their relationships convincing. Shar's new boyfriend is scared off by her father; their budding friendship cannot stand the stress of his unpredictable behavior. Family dynamics are especially well portrayed, both the love-hate relationship between Shar and her brothers, and Shar's alternating resentment of and dependence on her mother. There is no happy ending, but a gradual reconciliation to the situation: "I remember the dad I lost and miss him. And, I'll give this stranger what love I can in memory of that dad I once had." Powerful and disturbing, the story is told with compassion and honesty.

157   **Carter,** David. *What's In My Pocket?*; written and illus. by David Carter. Putnam, 1989. ISBN 0-399-21685-5. 10p. $8.85.

2-4 yrs.   There aren't many pages in this board-bound paper-engineered book, but they are sturdy, they have a theme, they give information, they have nice composition and bright color in pictures with no clutter, and there's a mild, accessible humor for small children who, after a read-aloud or two, should be able to "read" the text for themselves. Carter uses two devices: one is that the heads of a series of animals pop up and unfold as the pages are turned; two, the flap that forms a "pocket" shows each animal's favorite food for the possibly hungry viewer, save for the very last pocket, which belongs to a kangaroo . . . .

158   **Carter**, Dorothy S. *His Majesty, Queen Hatshepsut;* illus. by Michele Chessare. Lippincott, 1987. Library ed. ISBN 0-397-32179-1; Trade ed. ISBN 0-397-32178-3. 248p. Library ed. $13.89; Trade ed. $13.95.

6-9   Appended material, including historical notes and a bibliography, attest to the research that informs and permeates this excellent historical novel. Like Rosemary Sutcliff, Carter incorporates details of dress and architecture, evidence of contemporary attitudes, and congruous speech patterns to give authenticity. Here the story begins with Hatshepsut's thirteenth year, as she records the pleasures and problems of being royal, female, and Egyptian; it continues with her account of the years of intrigue, power, glory, and—not often, but agonizing—despair. The period and the people come alive.

159   **Caseley**, Judith. *Kisses.* Knopf, 1990. Library ed. ISBN 0-679-90166-3; Trade ed. ISBN 0-679-80166-9. 186p. Library ed. $13.99; Trade ed. $12.95.

9-12   A gifted fifteen-year-old violinist who has just successfully auditioned for a local youth orchestra, Hannah Gold is preoccupied with relationships that seem problematic: her own with boys in her class; her grandmother's with her grandfather, who dies during the course of the book; her parents', when her mother's grief strains her father's patience; her best friend Deirdre's with a boyfriend who abuses her; and Deirdre's parents, who fight viciously and constantly. Sexuality is a subtle but pervasive issue. Hannah observes this among adults as well as experiencing it herself when she breaks off with a sweet but dull boy, is spurned by another who is attractive but arrogant, and finally finds the right match in gentle Bobby, who comforts her when her violin teacher forces a kiss on her. The adolescent girl's alternate fascination with bodies and revulsion from anything "gross" is well portrayed. The point of view is third person, but the story has the immediacy of a first-person narrative without the frequently attendant self-consciousness of one. Caseley's natural voice and realistic detail allow readers an intimate look at both the protagonist and her family, a coup for a first novel.

160   **Cassedy**, Sylvia. *Lucie Babbidge's House*. Crowell, 1989. Library ed.
ISBN 0-690-04798-3; Trade ed. ISBN 0-690-04796-7. 244p. Library ed.
$12.89; Trade ed. $12.95.

4-7   Lucie Babbidge, class scapegoat, has little more to say at school than
"I don't know, Miss Pimm," but at home she is the center of a loving,
eccentric family. Readers will be well into this book before they
discover that Lucie is an orphan, living in "a place for girls who are
neither this nor that," and her "family" exists in a forgotten dollhouse
in the cellar of the orphanage. As in the late author's previous books,
Behind the Attic Wall and *M. E. and Morton*, the setting here is
realistic, but its most intensely detailed landscape is drawn within the
mind of a silent outsider. Lucie's games with her dolls are refuge and
triumph (she can tell Mumma and Dada all about how she won the
game that in reality the other girls wouldn't even let her play) and, she
eventually realizes, powerful, as the events in the dollhouse begin to
happen in the life of Lucie's English pen pal Delia. While the first part
of the novel is somewhat static, readers will be caught by the gothic
mood, and Lucie's brave rescue of Delia's family (one of the other
girls steals the dolls) has an eccentric suspense. Without ever
resorting to superficial psychologizing, Cassedy always showed a deep
understanding of the imaginative obsessions behind children's most
ordinary games, where a paintbox could become a boarding school (in
M. E. and Morton), or here, where a dollhouse can become a home
that brings the world to a girl left too long alone.

161   **Cassedy**, Sylvia. *M. E. and Morton*. Crowell, 1987. Library ed. ISBN 0-
690-04562-X; Trade ed. ISBN 0-690-04560-3. 310p. Library ed. $12.89;
Trade ed. $12.95.

5-8   "If you play something bad, it will come true." Will it? Eleven-year-old
 *   Mary Ella (who nicknames herself M. E., although no one else will call
her that) plays all kinds of games in her head, like Poor Children ("We
make dolls out of cigarette butts,") or Wheelchair or Twins or, best of
all, Easter Egg, where she pretends she lives in one of those translucent eggs, watched over with admiration by a giant girl. In her
games, M. E. can be the center of her own attention, shutting out the
pain caused by her snobbish, private-school classmates, her parents'
weary indifference, her 14-year-old brother Morton—mentally slow,
gullible, and embarrassing. But when M. E. and Morton meet Polly,
who has just moved into the neighborhood, the games change. Their
mother asks "What kind of girl is that who plays with you and with
Morton, too?" Well, Polly is the kind of girl who draws a chalk line
around the block, tying it up with a bow; who makes up races between
the bugs on the ceiling of her squalid apartment; who dares M.E. to
come a bit out of herself, and who sees something special in hapless
Morton. Most of the drama in this book is, like M. E.'s obsessively

detailed fantasies, small but intense, as when M. E. goes to scream at Morton for playing in their mother's jewelry box, but discovers he is instead reverently showing to a friend a prize M. E. received for an essay. M. E.'s ambivalence toward Morton is masterfully portrayed, both in the cruelty with which she can lead the kids in chanting *Morton* without the *t*!" and in her empathy in knowing their parents believe him to be stupid. Though perhaps a trifle too long and studied, this novel, like Cassedy's first *Behind the Attic Wall*, lets us into the private games of a lonely girl and the fantasies children nourish but sometimes must escape—when M. E. believes she has caused a tragic accident by wishing it so, Polly tells her "That's dumb. nothing comes true. Things just happen, no matter what."

162   **Causley**, Charles. *Early in the Morning: A Collection of New Poems;* illus. by Michael Foreman; with music by Anthony Castro. Viking Kestrel, 1987. ISBN 0-670-80810-5. 60p. $14.95.

4-7 yrs.   Contemporary nursery rhymes are tricky; lacking the resonances of
    *   history and familiarity, the poet needs to supply meaning as well as nonsense. A few of the poems here aren't more than funny, tuneful jingling, but the best have a depth made richer by the simple rhymes: "John, John the Baptist/ Worked without any pay/ But he'd hold your hand/ And bring you to land/ And wash your fears away." Causley often moves from the simple to the startling, as in the title poem which begins "Early in the morning/ The water hits the rocks," and ends "And over the back of the chimney stack/ Explodes the silent sun." Even some of the funniest verses here have a melancholy edge, like "Said the Clown," about a clown who can't make anyone laugh, or the several Bobby Shaftoe descendants about a gone-away love, or the one about Nicholas Naylor, tailor: "He sewed up a serpent./ He sewed up a shark,/ He sewed up a sailor/ In a bag of dark." Foreman's drawings and paintings, employing more line than is usual for him, nicely convey the various moods of the poems. Half the poems are set to mostly lovely music; delicately sophisticated (occasionally pretentious), but easy to sing and play, the songs call to mind some of Alec Wilder's compositions for *Lullabies and Night Songs..*

163   **Chaikin**, Miriam. *A Nightmare in History: The Holocaust 1933-1945.* Clarion, 1987. ISBN 0-89919-461-3. 150p. illus. and with photographs. $14.95.

6-9   Clear, well organized, and blunt, this recounts the systematic process with which Hitler organized and perpetrated the destruction of European Jews during World War II. The initial stages of persecution, life in the ghettos, procedures in the concentration and work camps, and resistance movements and rebellion are described with reference to the political and military shifts that affected them. With a careful balance of human detail and general background, Chaikin has done a creditable job of gearing the material to readers younger than the audience for Meltzer's *Never To Forget: The Jews of the Holocaust*. In a few instances, such as the description of a prisoner electrocuted on barbed wire at Auschwitz, the style dramatizes where it doesn't need to—the circumstances project their own horror—but the total effect is a controlled narration of events beyond control. The black-and-white photographs are tragically revealing. The bibliography, some of it annotated, is divided into "Diaries," "Anthologies," "Song Books," etc. for students doing further research. Several eyewitness accounts were collected by the author. Indexed.

164   **Chambers**, Aidan, comp. *Out of Time*. Harper, 1985. Library ed. ISBN 0-06-021202-0; Trade ed. ISBN 0-06-021201-2. 186p. Library ed. $10.89; Trade ed. $11.95.

7-10   In a fresh and varied anthology of fantasy fiction, the work of some major writers for young adults and children is included. There are tales by Joan Aiken, Robert Westall, Jill Paton Walsh, and Jan Mark. Almost all of these stories of the future are distinctive in style and effective in plot, and readers may find special enjoyment in the humor of Marks' "Captain Courage and the Rose Street Gang," in which a hologram designed as a macho hero has been given the voice of a sugary grandmother, or in the taut adventure of "In a Ship Called Darkness 3" by Christopher Leach.

165   **Chang**, Margaret. *In the Eye of War*; by Margaret and Raymond Chang. McElderry, 1990. ISBN 0-689-50503-5. 198p. $14.95.

5-7   The family had moved to Hong Kong, then to Shanghai, to escape the Japanese. In the last year of World War II, Shanghai was (to explain the title reference) a quiet center of the storm, since those Chinese who didn't attract attention were reasonably safe in spite of the presence of the Japanese. This account of what it was like to live there and to welcome the end of the war is based on the experiences of co-author Raymond Chang, who contributes authentic details, the intimacy of memory, and a perspective that may be new to many readers. Added attractions include a smooth writing style, and the candor and depth of characterization of the protagonist, ten-year-old Shao-Shao, Little Brother in a large family.

166   **Charles**, Oz. *How Is a Crayon Made?*; written and illus. with photographs by Oz Charles. Simon, 1988. ISBN 0-671-63756-8. 30p. $9.95.

3-6 yrs.   From the cover photograph of an orderly field of Crayolas through the
    *   clean design of the pages, this book seems to know exactly what it is that kids love about a box of crayons. Order. Rows. Precise and

unpeeled points. And within all this exactness, sensuous spots of pure color. You want to eat them. Even the factory itself (Binney & Smith— in many ways the book resembles a glossy, pint-sized, annual report) is Crayon Heaven, where the machines are brightly covered with crayon dust, performing Willie Wonka-like feats of melting and molding, sorting and sharpening; the device that sorts the different colored crayons together looks like a high-tech gumball machine. The text is clear and minimal, wisely subordinating itself to the close-up, monumentalizing photographs, which, as far as the preschool audience will be concerned, tell the whole titillating story.

167   Chaucer, Geoffrey. *The Canterbury Tales*; ad. by Selina Hastings; illus. by Reg Cartwright. Holt, 1988. ISBN 0-8050-0904-3. 77p. $17.95.

Chaucer, Geoffrey. *Canterbury Tales*; tr. and ad. by Barbara Cohen; illus. by Trina Schart Hyman. Lothrop, 1988. ISBN 0-688-06201-6. 88p. $17.95.

7-12   Two luxuriously illustrated editions of *The Canterbury Tales* published in the same season seems, on the one hand, to be an embarrassment of riches and, on the other, to preempt the question of whether Chaucer's complex, often bawdy poetry should be cast in prose form for children. The books are significantly different in selection, scope, style, and illustration. Cohen's includes four tales—the Nun's Priest's tale, the Pardoner's, the Wife of Bath's, and the Franklin's, with all of their prologues. Hastings' includes these four plus the Knight's tale, the Miller's, and the Reeve's, with no prologues. Both versions give a brief introductory background of Chaucer's work and times, setting the scene for the pilgrimage that frames the stories. Both retain the basic plots, with the difference that Hastings' goal seems to be a graceful recapping of the action, while Cohen has made an effort to retain the original imagery wherever possible. Hastings uses more sophisticated language and sentence structure but shorter versions, having cut so much embellishment; Cohen keeps some of the banter for a longer tale, but her sentences are shorter and easier. Cohen keeps as close to Chaucer's phrases as she can short of melodic end rhymes, while Hastings plays it safe and dispenses with the whole lot. Although the formats are similar, the illustrative effects are diametrically opposite. Trina Schart Hyman's lusty characters and luscious compositions sport details reminiscent of Chaucer's irreverent gleam. Characteristically, her pictures are as elaborately framed as the writer's stories and her scenes full of realistic portraiture and motion. Reg Cartwright's elegantly restrained art is spare, stylized and planar. Its humor is confined to self-mockery save for one lewd scene in the miller's tale, where Absalon brands the bottom of rival Alison, who is mooning him through a window. Indeed, if any summary contrast can be made, it is the slightly more sophisticated look of Hastings' book, rendering it most suitable for young adult consumption, while Cohen's version could easily reach into junior high. Similarly priced, these are extravagantly designed and can jusifiably serve as an introduction where students are not likely to attempt a lilting modern-verse adaptation of the original.

168   Chetwin, Grace. *Box and Cox*; illus. by David Small. Bradbury, 1990. ISBN 0-02-718314-9. 32p. $13.95.

2-4   The story of Mr. Box and Mr. Cox is based on a mid-19th century farce by John Morton. David Small's lively paintings have humor and contribute, through their action and their placement, to the development of the plot, which is incorrigibly slapstick without being heavy-handed. One of the men works at night, the other during the day; both are unaware that they share the same room, a ploy that entails a great deal of frantic moving of the possessions of each by their landlady. Chetwin carries out the pattern by replication within exposition ("Box rents a room, second floor rear, in Mrs. Bouncer's house on Third Street. Cox rents a room, second floor rear, in Mrs. Bouncer's house on Third Street") so that it's a logical extension when each man proposes to the landlady and is accepted (in the same words, of course). And then . . . Cox gets the day off, finds Box in his bed, and learns of the double rent and double engagement. They leave; Mrs. Bouncer is upset at first, but then hangs out a sign: SINGLE ROOM TO RENT. This is the kind of sitcom humor and simple variety that should appeal to primary-grades readers.

169   Chiasson, John. *African Journey*; written and illus. with photographs by John Chiasson. Bradbury, 1987. ISBN 0-02-718530-3. 55p. $16.95.

4-6   With more than half the page space of this oversize book being used for photographs, the text that describes the life-styles in six communities of Africa is fairly brief although it covers salient features of climate, topography, urban-rural contrasts, and the ways in which such factors influence how people live and work. Chiasson, whose color photography is of superior quality, has chosen six cultural groups of diverse kinds (a fishing village, a nomad community, a modern city, farmers, river people, and the drought-stricken provinces of northern Ethiopia) to describe. While the writing style is not comparable to the photography, being rather flat and sedate, it is direct and the material gives a good idea of the vastness of the continent and its enormous diversity. There is no index.

170   Christian, Mary Blount. *Penrod's Pants*; illus. by Jane Dyer. Macmillan, 1986. ISBN 0-02-718520-6. 54p. $9.95.

1-3   The easy-to-read genre abounds with animal friends, but this pair manages to offer a funny twist to each of the situations developed here into five short, short stories. In the first, Penrod Porcupine wants a second pair of pants but can't find exactly the same kind his grandmother sent him (which he loved), even though he and Griswald Bear shop till they drop. Finally, they locate the right kind of pants, but the pockets are empty—unlike the pair Grandmother sent with a five-dollar bill in the pocket! The best two tales are "The Tea Party," in which Griswald vainly tries to teach Penrod the etiquet of denying himself the last cookie, and "The Scary Night," in which the two friends follow each other home till morning because neither is willing to walk alone in the dark. Precise, expressive watercolors of nicely varied size and design will lure young readers on.

171   **Christiansen**, C.B. *A Small Pleasure*. Atheneum, 1988. ISBN 0-689-31369-1. 134p. $12.95

7-12   Less a novel than a series of evocative sketches, this present-tense chronicle of Wray Jean's junior year in a small town in eastern Washington is written with forthright simplicity. Wray Jean wants to *be* somebody. "Last year, I worked on my grades. A girl with goals has to get good grades." This year she plans to work on her social development, memorizing everybody's name from the yearbook, leading the baton twirlers with her fire routine ("The band plays 'Hey, Look Me Over,' while I trace complicated patterns in the night") and joining one of the exclusive girls' clubs. But her gentle father, Daddy Dean, is dying of cancer, and Wray Jean begins to wonder just where all these "leadership points" she's racking up are going to take her. This portrait is as much remarkable for what it doesn't do as for what it does: Wray Jean's search for success is exhausting but never empty, and her small town life is unsophisticated but not sentimentalized. While the success-isn't-everything theme is overstated, and Wray Jean herself overly casual in resisting the message, her narration has a good balance of reflection and conversation and is precisely voiced, with a naive and direct rhythm. Each of the characters is distinctly drawn: best friend Poe is warm, smart, and direct; Mama, a complicated mix of tenderness and withdrawal; Daddy Dean, a gently joking presence who dies quietly offstage.

172   **Christopher**, John. *Dragon Dance*. Dutton, 1986. ISBN 0-525-44227-8. 139p. $12.95.

7-10   In a sequel to *Fireball* and *New Found Land*, in which British Simon and his American cousin Brad had a series of fantasy adventures after they found themselves in a parallel world, the action moves from the New World to China when the boys and their Indian captors are in turn captured by the crew of a Chinese ship. At the court of the Emperor, they claim to be ambassadors from the Roman people (in this parallel world, Rome rules Britain) and are caught in a power struggle for domination of the boy ruler. Sent to a sort of Shangri-la, they are impressed by the beauty and serenity of the mountain colony—until they discover how much is based on illusion. There's a surprise at the close of the book, when an august priest proves to be a famous figure from their own world, and in a conclusion that invites a sequel (despite the fact that this is the third volume in an announced trilogy) Simon decides not to use the fireball to return to his own time but to go adventuring in yet another parallel world with Brad. This lacks the humor that appears occasionally in the first two books, but it has just as much action and suspense; it is written with smooth, fast-paced narrative flow, and it is an adroit fusion of the real and the fanciful.

173   **Christopher**, John. *When the Tripods Came*. Dutton, 1988. ISBN 0-525-44397-5. 151p. $12.95.

6-9   Fans of the Tripods Trilogy (*The White Mountains, The City of Gold and Lead, The Pool of Fire*) will welcome this prequel, and it should win the author new fans as a science fantasy that has nicely controlled action, suspense, and danger. Told convincingly by an adolescent boy, Laurie, this describes the first encounter with the huge hemisphere from space that appeared to be hostile and predatory; with typical Christopher subtlety, the second and more serious drive by the Tripods to control humankind is preceded by a lull. The resolution that follows conflict is believable and, although this sets the stage for the trilogy, it stands sturdily alone. A good read.

174   **Ciardi**, John. *Doodle Soup*; illus. by Merle Nacht. Houghton, 1985. ISBN 0-395-38395-1. 57p. $11.95.

3-5   Ciardi offers a mix of narrative poems, poetic jokes, arrant nonsense, and a bit of word play. Almost every selection is funny, and many are barbed or caustic. Most children find Ciardi's tartness invigorating; most adults find his writing deceptively casual, intrinsically sophisticated.

175   **Clapp**, Patricia. *The Tamarack Tree: A Novel of the Siege of Vicksburg*. Lothrop, 1986. 0-688-02852-7. 214p. $10.25

7-9   A dependably good writer of historical fiction, Clapp has, in this story of the Civil War, used a device that gives both immediacy and a measure of objectivity. Her protagonist is an English girl, Rosemary, who joins her brother in Vicksburg in 1859, when she is fourteen. There is a romantic element, but this is primarily a record of the long siege of the city and it gives, through its British narrator, a good perspective of the tragic division and of the conflicting viewpoints of North and South. The pace of the novel occasionally slows, but the overall tempo is maintained, and the writing style has good structure.

176   **Cleary**, Beverly. *A Girl from Yamhill: A Memoir.* Morrow, 1988. ISBN 0-688-07800-1. 272p. illus. with photographs. $14.95.

6-   While young people who are Cleary fans will certainly enjoy her autobiographical account of childhood and high school years, it is probable that die-hard adult fans will appreciate the book even more as they share memories of the past. The author sees her child self with the same clarity and objectivity as she has seen her fictional characters, and her reminiscences have a resultant integrity and candor. She is honest but not bitter about a mother who was both possessive and domineering, she gives a vivid picture of life during the years of the depression, and she is persuasive rather than dramatic in describing the experiences that are universal to childhood.

177   **Cleaver**, Elizabeth. *ABC;* written and illus. by Elizabeth Cleaver. Atheneum, 1985. ISBN 0-689-31072-2. 52p. $5.95.

2-5 yrs.   In a small, square book one of Canada's most distinguished book illustrators uses a combination of collage and paint in vivid colors on each recto page. The brightness and variety are in sharp and effective contrast to the white verso page, which has an upper and lower case letter and the words for those objects that appear on the facing page, which has a huge letter in color. Most of the words will be familiar to small children: alligator, apple, and ant; banana, beak, blue, button, and so on. There is no attempt to have objects in scale (a stalk of celery is longer than the legs of a cow; a paper-clip is the width of the pineapple next to it) but otherwise this is a functional alphabet book, and it's certainly an attractive one.

178   **Clements**, Bruce. *Tom Loves Anna Loves Tom.* Farrar, 1990. ISBN 0-374-37673-5. 167p. $13.95.

8-12   The title says it all, but the characters are so involving that you want to read their whole story anyway. The question is not whether Tom and Anna will fall in love; they do that as soon as Anna comes to Tom's town for a few weeks' visit with her Aunt Barbara. The question is how they will sustain each other through self-disclosures and mutual experiences. Anna's brother has recently drowned during a storm on Lake Michigan, her brother's best friend tried to rape her afterward, and her beloved aunt dies at the end of the book. Since the first two events happen off stage and in the past, the book can focus on Anna's vulnerability and relationship with Tom instead of on melodramatic action. Even Aunt Barbara's illness, which does add tension to the plot, is low-keyed to suit the subtle nuances of dialogue and dynamics between the two main characters. Tom's quirky best friend, Hank, is something of a distraction, even an anomaly, but he does serve a function as foil for Tom's steadfast good nature. Both families are well realized, too. All in all, it's a reliably handled cast, even down to the villain, who gets most reliably handled of all by trusty Tom.

179   **Clements**, Bruce. *The Treasure of Plunderell Manor.* Farrar, 1987. ISBN 0-374-37746-4. 178p. $12.95.

6-9   Since his first novel in 1974, *I Tell a Lie Every So Often*, Clements has always given us a good read, but this is plot plus. Fourteen-year-old Laurel Bybank, named after the riverside shrub where she was abandoned in mid-nineteenth-century England, has found a "place" as servant to orphaned Mistress Alice, whose aunt and uncle would love to dispose of her before she turns eighteen and comes into her fortune. The suspense is taut, the cast irresistible; but it is wit that sets the book apart. Much of the dialogue goes beyond the function of action and characterization to play with parody. Alice constantly refers to her Intended, for instance, when it is Laurel who consistently rescues her. The girls' friendship is the central relationship of the book, and ultimately, despite their society's sexism, religious prejudice, and class snobbery, they both value each other above all. Laurel's being almost smothered during her "rebirth" into a lady's dress presages her ultimate choice to abandon the wealth and position she has so rightfully earned for further adventure to America—any reader will yearn to follow her after this revel of crafty humor.

180   **Clifford**, Eth. *The Remembering Box*; illus. by Donna Diamond. Houghton, 1985. ISBN 0-395-38476-1. 70p. $12.95.

3-6   A moving remembrance within a remembrance focuses on nine-year-old Joshua's ritual Sabbath with his grandmother, who each week tells him stories inspired by objects in an old battered chest. Sometimes Joshua asks to keep an especially precious treasure, such as the photo of Grandma as a girl, or the old sock stuffed with Grandma and Grandpa's first theater tickets. But always Grandma replies, "Not now, Joshua, not yet." Then the day comes when Grandma has prepared him a memory box of his own. Just before dinner that night, after the story of her silver Sabbath bell, Grandma gives it to him, leans back, and goes to sleep, never to wake again. Joshua, imbued with the quiet strength and love that has grown over his years of visits with the old woman, lights her Sabbath candles one last time and phones his father. Although the movement of the story is unhurried, there is humor in the quiet dialogues. The boy recalls his grandmother's response to his first drawing of her: "Well, at least you gave me four hairs and not three." From such a brief story, the characters emerge full-blown, a warm portrayal of a traditional Jewish family. Also a good companion read-aloud to Mathis' *The Hundred Penny Box*.

181   **Cobb**, Vicki. *Chemically Alive!: Experiments You Can Do at Home;* illus. by Theo Cobb. Lippincott, 1985. Library ed. ISBN 0-397-32080-9; Trade ed. ISBN 0-397-32079-5. 154p. Library ed. $10.89; Trade ed. $11.50.

5-9   Cobb uses home experiments and demonstrations to illustrate chemical principles and processes, her text moving in logical sequence so that it goes from the simple to the more complex, with each section building on what has preceded it. The instructions are clear, the safety warnings frequent, and the "Observations and Suggestions" section that follows each experiment helpful in confirming and extending knowledge obtained from the experiment. A science teacher as well as a practiced writer, Cobb makes the book fun without being too hearty or cute, and her text is both authoritative and readable. An index is provided.

182   **Cobb**, Vicki. *The Trip of a Drip*; illus. by Elliot Kreloff. Little, 1986. ISBN 0-316-14900-4. 50p. (How the World Works). $11.95.

3-5   There are earlier books that clearly explain the water cycle; this book does that, but its emphasis is on the ways that water is provided to people in the city or the country, and how it is made drinkable or processed when it is contaminated waste. The writing is direct, clear, and informal, and the material is logically organized. Cobb provides illustrative examples and home experiments. This should answer most of the questions children may have about "what happens when" or "how does it work?" Diagrams are clear and are adequately labelled.

183   **Cohen**, Miriam. *Liar, Liar, Pants on Fire!;* illus. by Lillian Hoban. Greenwillow, 1985. Library ed. ISBN 0-688-04245-7; Trade ed. ISBN 0-688-04244-9. 28p. Library ed. $11.88; Trade ed. $11.75.

K-2   This is another story that deals capably, albeit briefly, with a common childhood problem: trying to gain recognition or acceptance by exaggerating or telling lies. It doesn't take long for the first graders to see that the new boy, Alex, is doing just that when he tries to top every remark by going a step farther. General disapproval is forcefully expressed in the usual frank way of first graders. However, one intercession by an understanding teacher, one friendly gesture from another child, and one word of praise for an accomplishment combine to make Alex less bumptious. As usual, in this series of stories about a multiethnic classroom, group dynamics works for the good of the individual.

184   **Cohen**, Miriam. *See You in Second Grade!;* illus. by Lillian Hoban. Greenwillow, 1989. Library ed. ISBN 0-688-07139-2; Trade ed. ISBN 0-688-07138-4. 32p. Library ed. $11.88; Trade ed. $11.95.

K-2   The first-grade class made popular by Cohen's insight and humor and by Hoban's everyday-model interracial group here goes on an end-of-year beach picnic. There are none of the problems that are so deftly dealt with in earlier books in this series, just a few skirmishes—Anna Maria's discovery that she's brought her brother's school bag and has neither lunch nor swimsuit, for example—but the low-keyed text gives a clear picture of a day of fun and food and fellowship. There's a dash of poignant nostalgia, but no sentimentality, as they remember events of the year and say goodbye to their beloved teacher and to each other.

185   **Cohen**, Miriam. *Starring First Grade;* illus. by Lillian Hoban. Greenwillow, 1985. Library ed. ISBN 0-688-04030-6; Trade ed. ISBN 0-688-04029-2. 28p. Library ed. $11.88; Trade ed. $11.75.

K-2   As all stage-struck readers know, the limelight can bring out some volatile emotions. Here an understanding teacher copes with the varied reactions of members of her class as they plan and mount a stirring performance of "The Three Billy Goats Gruff." Teacher placidly agrees when one child who's taking dancing lessons wants to be a snowflake, but she has a little more trouble soothing Jim, who wants to be the troll, he doesn't want to be a tree, and he is so angry with Paul (chosen troll) that they argue and stop speaking. All ends well, with the play a success, Jim satisfied with his contribution, and the friendship resumed. The illustrations (with casual line and bright colors) show a multiethnic group, and they echo the light, humorous tone of a story that says a great deal without being didactic.

186   **Cohen**, Susan. *When Someone You Know Is Gay;* by Susan and Daniel Cohen. Evans, 1989. ISBN 0-87131-567-X. 170p. $13.95.

7-12   While it's billed as a "book written for straight teenagers on the subject of homosexuality," gay teens will find much here to inform and reassure themselves as well. Writing in a casual, sympathetic voice, the Cohens discuss the nature of homosexuality and its existence throughout history; theories as to its causes; the relationships of gay people with their families, friends, and churches; and the special concerns of gay youth. Controversial topics such as gay parenting, promiscuity, and AIDS are addressed fairly and responsibly, and throughout there are welcome touches of pithy humor: in responding to the question as to whether homosexuality can be cured, the Cohens write "You can make someone miserable but you can't make them straight." Occasionally, the tone gets a little too laid back (calling Lord Alfred Douglas an "upper-class twerp," for example). A reliance on those handy "experts" who "say" is no substitute for attribution and footnoting; in one case where the experts are named, one would still like to know how Drs. Ellis and Ames arrived at their definitive conclusion that "sexual orientation is determined between the second and fifth months of pregnancy." Far more enlightening (and engaging) are the anecdotal quotes from gay teens as well as kids whose friends or parents are gay. There is neither an index nor a bibliography, although a directory of gay organizations and a list of books and movies of gay interest are appended. Despite its technical flaws, this commonsensical treatment of a controversial topic is the best YA book on homosexuality currently available.

187   Cole, Babette. *Cupid*; written and illus. by Babette Cole. Putnam, 1990. ISBN 0-399-22215-4. 32p. $13.95.

5-8 yrs.   After comically capitalizing on fairy tales with *Prince Cinders*, *Princess Smartypants*, etc., Cole turns to mythology with an updated revision of the god-boy of love, whose mom, the goddess of beauty, decides to move the family down from Olympus to Earth for the Miss World Competition. Cupid's father, the god of thunder ("Bang!"), warns him to behave, but Cupid flies defiantly to the top of the grocery-store canned-goods display, eludes the babysitter, and snatches a neighbor's toy bow, pinging people into lovesickness with suction arrows. After a slapstick kidnapping, Cupid escapes and returns with his parents to the Land of the Gods, where he receives a golden replacement for his broken bow, "and he's been causing trouble ever since." Kids unfamiliar with Cupid may need a background explanation to fully appreciate the spoof, but they'll certainly never forget the manic pink-winged toddler who, with his snaggle-toothed dog, flies through these chaotic scenes keeping cultural literacists from getting too pompous. Pair with Mordicai Gerstein's *Tales of Pan* for a fuller pantheon.

188   Cole, Brock. *Celine*. Farrar, 1989. ISBN 0-374-31234-6. [224p]. $13.95.

7-12   Celine is not even supposed to be in Chicago, but her mother is off
  *   discovering herself, her grandmother can't cope with Celine's creative energy anymore, her father has gone on a lecture tour of Europe, and Celine's stepmother, only six years older than Celine herself, is stuck caring for her. Seven-year-old neighbor Jake latches onto Celine when his mother asks her to babysit; Jake's father's girlfriend turns out to be Celine's art teacher. Celine's crush on Jake's father and her step-mother's temporary attraction to a fossilized art professor slip in as unobtrusive foils to the basic dynamic of the plot. The real love story in the book is between the adolescent protagonist, a veteran of post-divorce arrangements, and second-grade Jake, hurting at every step of his parents' widening separation. What's excluded from this précis, of course, is the wit and stylistic aplomb with which the various episodes develop. Celine is Harriet the Spy turned sixteen. Her observations of adult antics, of peer idiosyncrasies, and of her own irregularities are,

subtly or raucously, irreverent. Celine and Jake are developmentally tuned to a perfect pitch, including mood changes that sometimes make the adolescent act like a child and the child seem old beyond his years. Each member of the large cast is sharply defined, from Celine's would-be boy friend ("He gives his head a shake to restore internal activity") to the high school art teacher ("Her knees crack, as if she has just that moment grown old") and a mismatched couple of Celine's acquaintance ("She arrives at our table, dragging Philip by the hand. A butterfly airlifting a frog"). Child, adolescent, and adult are equally well realized. The adults here will probably be charged with failing to provide adequate role models, but this book is really too good to hold for didactic ransom. Often the characters show unexpected strength as well as weakness; each person is realistically vulnerable, uncertain, flawed—human.

189   **Cole**, Brock. *The Goats;* written and illus. by Brock Cole. Farrar, 1987. ISBN 0-374-32678-9. 184p. $11.95.

5-8
*   Brock Cole's picture books have hinted at his writing talents, but here is proof of an unusual capacity for sustaining fiction. Two outcasts, a boy and a girl, are left by their fellow campers on an island with no food or clothes. In a much larger sense, these two are social misfits, already marooned from their families and peers. They know it and, in an urgent but steadily credible story, they create a relationship that is unique, yet puts them back in touch with the rest of the world. There are many levels here. The action of survival and evasion of authorities when the children run away will hold readers on a plot basis. The main characters' vulnerability, desperate connection, and eventual expansion into trust of some black, inner-city, fresh-air camp kids create a different kind of suspense which is climaxed by a triumphant commitment after their success almost tears them apart. Their progress is marked by the emergence of each from an almost nameless anonymity to comfortable familiarity with each other and themselves. The style does not miss a beat, either in narrative or dialogue, asserting itself without ostentation. Brock hints at sacrificial myth in the boy's story of a haunting experience in a Greek cave, supposedly inhabited by a god to whom worshippers sacrificed goats. Yet the symbolic allusions here and elsewhere reflect rather than obtrude, even when reinforced by references such as a deputy Sheriff's trapping them in his goat-farm jeepster. Several complicated thematic questions of social cruelty and moral obligation arise subtly, through concrete development. This is an unflinching book, and there is a quality of raw emotion that may score some discomfort among adults. Such a first novel restores faith in the cultivation of children's literature. The bookmaking, including Cole's watercolor cover and pen-and-ink chapter heading sketches, is meticulous.

190   **Cole**, Joanna. *Asking About Sex and Growing Up*; illus. by Alan
Tiegreen. Morrow, 1988. Trade ed. ISBN 0-688-06927-4; Paper ed. ISBN
0-688-06928-2. 90p. Trade ed. $11.95; Paper ed. $4.95.

4-6   Considering that a question-and-answer format is inherently rougher
in terms of organization and transition than scientifically structured
approaches to information on sex and reproduction, this is more
effective than one might expect. After an introduction and list of
helpful books for parents and kids, Cole has grouped the questions by
subject: growing up, finding out about sex, the different development
of girls and boys, masturbation, crushes, intercourse, childbirth,
preventing pregnancy, pregnancy, homosexuality, and protection
from sexual abuse and disease. The tone of the text is straightforward
but reassuring, with an emphasis on the emotional as well as the
physical. Cole seems well aware that extensive information may seem
too much for kids of this age, and she keeps her answers brief and to
the point, a few sentences to a few paragraphs each. Whether the
questions actually came from middle-grade readers, the text does not
say; if not, their tenor nevertheless rings true.

191   Cole, Joanna. *Cuts, Breaks, Bruises, and Burns: How Your Body Heals*;
illus. by True Kelley. Crowell, 1985. Library ed. ISBN 0-690-04438-0;
Trade ed. ISBN 0-690-04437-2. 44p. Library ed. $9.89; Trade ed. $10.50.

2-4   Diagrammatic drawings complement the text, showing how different
*   kinds of cells act to form new tissue, prevent or combat infection, stop
bleeding, and dispose of waste materials left from the healing process.
Cole is succinct and explicit in describing (in addition to some
procedures that require the work of medical personnel) how the
human body tends to heal itself. The injuries are those that most
children experience and about which they are usually curious, so this
should be a popular and useful compilation of information.

192   **Cole**, Joanna. *Doctor Change*. Morrow, 1986. Library ed. ISBN 0-688-
06136-2; Trade ed. ISBN 0-688-06135-4. 29p. Library ed. $11.88; Trade
ed. $11.75.

K-2   A shape-changing tale follows the fortunes of clever young Tom, who
hires himself out to a "doctor," discovers the old man's secret book of
wizardry, and finds himself imprisoned till he learns how to turn into
water and trickle under the locked front door. There follows a battle of
wits in which Tom enlists a girl, Kate, whom he's helped, and the two
fool Dr. Change out of a fortune. The story draws on some reliable old
motifs but has a distinctive character of its own, defined partly by
clean writing and partly by Carrick's expressive watercolors, in which
Dr. Change is developed as an eccentrically evil figure, Tom the soul
of jaunty youth, and Kate a good-hearted companion. The turn-of-the-

century, small town and rural scenes have a full crafted quality of composition and coloration that is satisfyingly traditional. This would be fun to use with Brinton Turkle's *Do Not Open*, another suspenseful picturebook in which the villain changes shape once too often.

193   Cole, Joanna. *A Dog's Body;* illus. with photographs by Jim and Ann Monteith. Morrow, 1986. Library ed. ISBN 0-688-04154-X; Trade ed. ISBN 0-688-04153-1. 42p. Library ed. $11.88; Trade ed. $11.75.

K-3   Like others in the author's series (*A Frog's Body*, etc.), this is a first-rate introduction for younger children. Cole emphasizes physical function over anatomical description, answering children's most frequent questions about dogs: how can they run so fast, why do they pant, what do different barks mean? In the simple but thorough text, Cole discusses dogs' lupine ancestry, how different breeds were developed, why certain senses are more important than others. The many black-and-white photographs and diagrams are clear, well-paced, and always informative.

194   Cole, Joanna. *The Human Body: How We Evolved;* illus. by Walter Gaffney-Kessell and Juan Carlos Barberis. Morrow, 1987. Library ed. ISBN 0-688-06720-4; Trade ed. ISBN 0-688-06719-0. 60p. Library ed. $11.88; Trade ed. $11.75.

2-4   Oversize pages afford the space for fine pencil drawings, most of which are anatomical and many of which show comparisons between humans and other primates, without crowding. Cole describes the evolution of human beings, showing how adaptations of form made possible such distinctive human attributes as upright posture, the opposable thumb, and the ability to communicate through words rather than sounds. The continuous text is lucid, sequential in development, and complemented by appended material that includes an index and a time chart.

195   Cole, Joanna. *The Magic School Bus inside the Human Body;* illus. by Bruce Degen. Scholastic, 1989. ISBN 0-590-41426-7. 38p. $13.95.

2-4   Like Ms. Frizzle's class trips to the waterworks and inside the earth, this jaunt uses humorous action to uncover a world of scientific information, including a rough ride through the digestive system, a narrow escape from some white blood cells determined to engulf the germy intruders, to the brain, down the spinal cord, through the nervous system, along some muscles, and out . . . the nose. The kids' comments are part of the fun ("I'll trade you these terrific fish sticks for that horrible peanut butter and banana sandwich"), though the subplot of one boy getting left behind is almost too much—it turns out to be his body which the class tours. There's no question of the value of this addition to the series, however, and the "True-or-False Test" at the end of the book continues a practice of humorous perspective on the information: "If the children really were as small as cells, we couldn't see them without a microscope . . . True! The pictures in this book show the cells and the children greatly enlarged." Cole does a good job of culling facts to be included for primary-grade consumption, and Degen excels at controlling the busyness of the variety-pack cartoon graphics. The bus labelled Burp will go anywhere there's a health unit in the curriculum.

196   Cole, Joanna. *The New Baby at Your House*; illus. with photographs by Hella Hammid. Morrow, 1985. Library ed. ISBN 0-688-05807-8; Trade ed. ISBN 0-688-05806-X. 44p. Library ed. $10.88; Trade ed. $10.25.

2-5 yrs.   A long prefatory note is addressed to parents (most of the remarks are addressed to mothers, in fact), and it gives sensible advice on preparing children for the arrival of a new baby and equally practical suggestions for dealing with older siblings after the baby's birth. Photographs of good quality accompany a text that is direct, sympathetic, and specific as it discusses how one feels, responds, and acts when parental time must be shared and parental love may seem to be withdrawn. The book reassures the child about parental love, about his right to feel resentment but not to demonstrate it with the baby as victim, and about what the future holds for a small big brother or sister. Well done.

197   Collier, James Lincoln. *Louis Armstrong: An American Success Story*. Macmillan, 1985. ISBN 0-02-722830-4. 165p. illus. with photographs. $11.95.

6-10   An annotated bibliography and an index give access to one of the better biographies of the great jazz musician. Collier's writing is based on thorough research, and the research never obtrudes on the life story he is developing. The tone is admiring but never adulatory, and the candor with which Collier describes some of the seamier aspects of Armstrong's childhood is combined with such sympathy that it makes his achievements the more impressive. As the self-taught Armstrong moved from amateur to professional, from honky-tonks to riverboats to Chicago jazz and on to national fame and visibility, his life encompasses much of the history of a uniquely American form of music and a history of black entertainers in the music world.

198   Coltman, Paul. *Tog the Ribber or Granny's Tale*; illus. by Gillian McClure. Farrar, 1985. ISBN 374-37630-1. 29p. $11.95.

3-5   "Your granny had a dreadful flight/And that is why her hair is white/And that is why she doesn't speak right," this eerie narrative poem begins, and Granny takes up the story, describing her terrified run through "the glavering gloom" as a small girl pursued by Tog, the predatory skeleton-spirit. This is reminiscent of Lewis Carroll, but may prove less comprehensible to some readers, since there are both invented words and words that are garbled. However, the story line is clear, the poem has good pace and suspense, and there's humor in the word-play. The illustrations are stunning: McClure paints in a misty ambience that reflects the ghostly quality of the poetry, but there is no vagueness in the splendid intricacy of details, often stressed in the ornamental borders of her paintings. What she achieves is a remarkable combination of richness and restraint.

199   **Conford**, Ellen. *A Royal Pain.* Scholastic, 1986. ISBN 0-590-33269-4. 171p. $11.95.

6-9   Conford has obviously had a good time inventing a tiny European country (Saxony Coburn) and its annual bash (the Gloxinia Festival) and the not-quite-sixteen-year-old Abby who is the narrator. Plucked from her Kansas home (yes there is a dog named Toto) with a story of switched infants and the information that she is the true Princess Florinda XIV of Saxony Coburn, Abby has to cope with homesickness, a jealous ex-Florinda, royal protocol and duties, and the awful fact that she has been betrothed since she was seven to Prince Casimir. Perhaps because she has just fallen in love with a handsome commoner, Geoffrey, she takes an instant dislike to sleek Casimir when they meet. The whole thing is a romp, with a funny mix of stately dialogues and American slang (films are ubiquitous) and lots of action, and no possibility whatsoever that there won't be a happy ending.

200   **Conly**, Jane Leslie. *Racso and the Rats of NIMH*; illus. by Leonard B. Lubin. Harper, 1986. Library ed. ISBN 0-06-021362-0; Trade ed. ISBN 0-06-021361-2. 278p. Library ed. $11.89; Trade ed. $12.50.

5-8   In this sequel to *Mrs. Frisby and the Rats of NIMH* by Robert O'Brien (Conly's father), the super-intelligent rats have established their new home at Thorn Valley, and fieldmouse Timothy, featured in the first book, is a student at their school. On his way to the valley after summer vacation, Timothy meets Racso, a hip young city rat, fond of rock 'n' roll and Hershey bars. As does *Mrs. Frisby*, this book contains many small trials and adventures, which then come together in a grave crisis—here, ecological disaster and threatened destruction of the rats' home when humans build a dam to turn Thorn Valley into a recreation area. Conly has completely mastered the bucolic tone of the first book, adding humor with Racso's classroom antics, city slicker attitudes, and crush on the disdainful Isabella. Much of Racso's mischief is a mask of bravado, covering both his feelings in inferiority around the other rats, and a shameful secret: Racso's father is Jenner, leader of the rats who left the new community. Characterizations all around are more detailed than in O'Brien's book, which really should be read first. Short, fast-paced chapters make this an excellent classroom read-aloud.

201   **Conrad**, Pamela. *Prairie Songs*. Harper, 1985. Library ed. ISBN 0-06-021337-X; Trade ed. ISBN 0-06-021336-1. 176p. Library ed. $10.89; Trade ed. $11.50.

6-8   The setting is the Nebraska prairie, the time is the turn of the century, the narrator Louisa, older child of a family living in a sod house. Louisa is thrilled when a doctor and his wife, the Berrymans, come from New York to be their neighbors; she's happy that they'll have a doctor, but she's even more thrilled by Mrs. Berryman's beauty, her fragility, and the collection of books she uses to teach Louisa and her younger brother Lester, shy and uncommunicative. What happens to Mrs. Berryman is tragic: her child is still-born, she becomes emotionally unstable, she dies of cold when she wanders off into the bitter prairie winter. As an antiphonal song to this elegy, there is Louisa's love for the open panorama of the prairie country, the vast skies of summer, the beauty of prairie flowers. The settlers' reaction to local Indians may be historically accurate, but for today's readers it will seem biased; save for that, this is a touching and effective story, with a strong characterization and a spare, dramatic story line. It is not didactic, but there is a lesson that Louisa learns, as she reacts to the pathos of her neighbor's unhappiness and death: she has been caustic in prodding her brother to speak, participate, and achieve; what she has learned is that to force another human being into a mold is fraught with potential for tragedy.

202   **Conrad**, Pam. *Stonewords*. Harper, 1990. Library ed. ISBN 0-06-021316-7; Trade ed. ISBN 0-06-021315-9. 130p. Library ed. $12.89; Trade ed. $12.95.

5-9   Zoe's grandparents think that Zoe Louise is an imaginary friend, but
*   the truth is far more unsettling. Zoe first meets her namesake when her grandfather refurbishes an old playhouse. "'*This is mine*,' said a little voice, like a voice coming down a tube." Zoe Louise lived in Zoe's house a century ago, and her ghost has returned to solve a terrible mystery. Contemporary children's book ghosts have, on the whole, become a rather friendly breed; Conrad here restores the full treatment, giving us a ghost both lonely and horrific: "Her eyes turned up to mine, her dry, transparent eyes with the barest flicker of life, her awful eyes held to her face with the thinnest cobwebs of lids. 'Come back,' she whispered and behind her dry, cracked lips were gray and terrible small teeth." The supernatural and time-travel elements of the book are viscerally convincing, and the desperate neediness of both girls is fierce and real. The disquieting ending is in the richest

gothic tradition, resolving one mystery only to reveal another even more frightening. This is a very scary book.

203   **Cooney**, Barbara. *Island Boy*; written and illus. by Barbara Cooney. Viking, 1988. ISBN 0-670-81749-X. 32p. $14.95.

5-8 yrs.   Like Cooney's *Miss Rumphius*, this picture book tells a life story against a landscape of the New England coast. Tibbetts Island is named after the man who settled it, and the text describes the homesteader's arrival, the farm he established with his wife and twelve children, and their son Matthias' return after several years as a seaman. Eventually Matthias' children leave the island and urge him to sell it to developers, but a grandson comes back to continue the family traditions before old Matthias drowns in a storm. The island is really the main character here, a small, rounded, green shape set into horizontals of sea blue or gray. Against this backdrop, the people, the gulls, the animals, and even the starkly rectangular white houses appear small and distant except for a few interior close-ups of family activity. Like the endpapers that map a craggy coast, the watercolor paintings trace the ways of people whose lives were hard but who clung stubbornly to the rocks ringing their birthplace.

204   **Cooney**, Caroline B. *Don't Blame the Music.* Pacer/Putnam, 1986. ISBN 0-448-47778-5. 172p. $13.95.

7-9   Although her relationships with friends and her involvement in school affairs are important to the narrator, Susan, her life during the period covered by this story is dominated by Ashley. Twenty-five, the sister who had been Susan's loving protector has come home after a failed career as a rock singer. Bitter, sullen, and destructive, Ash spoils personal and family property, is viciously insulting to Susan and their parents, and is clearly in desperate need of therapy. The weakest aspect of the book is that it takes so long for her parents to suggest it, tolerating her expressed hate with what seems weakness rather than patience. Meanwhile Susan is learning to cope with an arrogant (rather stereotypical) girl rival, to see the true nature of each of the boys she likes, to understand the reasons for Ashley's aggression and hostility. This has well-defined characters and it explores the ramifications of a familial situation in which there is one member so abrasive that there is stress in all parts of the lives of others. This is not as impressive in pace or development as Cooney's previous book, particularly because of the long period of the acceptance of Ashley's excesses, but it touches on issues important to adolescent development, and it certainly has dramatic moments.

205   **Cooney**, Nancy Evans. *Donald Says Thumbs Down*; illus. by Maxie Chambliss. Putnam, 1987. ISBN 0-399-21373-2. 28p. $11.95.

K-2   This is not only a good book for children about thumb sucking, it also
sets a fine example for parents of small children who worry about it.
Donald is embarrassed when, at school, his method of seeking solace
makes other children laugh. His mother is reassuring: he'll stop when
he's ready; his father tells Donald not to worry about it. Both parents
praise him for accomplishments that indicate he's learning new skills
and they are supportive when Donald makes an effort to stop thumb-
sucking completely. And he does, not easily but by his own volition
and efforts. The illustrations are informal, uncluttered, and bright.
Bravo, Donald; bravo, author.

206   **Cooper**, Ilene. *Choosing Sides*. Morrow, 1990. ISBN 0-688-07934-2.
218p. (The Kids from Kennedy Middle School). $12.95.

4-6   Jonathan's tall for a sixth-grader, and he's eager to try out for the
middle school basketball team. Even as his abilities improve,
Jonathan slowly realizes he doesn't enjoy basketball, while at the same
time he struggles with a topic for an English assignment—a paper on a
moral dilemma. Of course, the reader recognizes Jonathan's dilemma
immediately, but Cooper makes certain there's no easy solution. She
gradually adds more and more layers to the problem—pressure from
Jonathan's athletic and macho father, Jonathan's frustration at not
having time to read, his embarrassment at a newly discovered interest
in classical music. Meanwhile, Jonathan goes to his first dance, steals
a dirty magazine from a barber shop, and teeters between confidence
and mortification in several funny scenes. During a dance lesson from
Robin, his romantic interest, Jonathan suddenly remembers the mole
next to his ear: "he started imagining how the mole must look from
close up. Big and brown, like a mud pie. It was probably making Robin
sick." Deftly combining the humor and pain of early adolescence, this
book does just what a series book should—makes you want to read the
next one.

207   **Cooper**, Susan, ad. *The Selkie Girl*; illus. by Warwick Hutton.
McElderry, 1986. ISBN 0-689-50390-3. 30p. $12.95

K-2   The selkie legend has many variants around the Irish and Scottish
coastal regions. Cooper's retelling, and Gerstein's *The Seal Mother*
both personalize this animal-bride tale and, to some extent, temper its
essential sadness. Cooper's is the less childlike, both in the writing
style and in the tone of watercolor paintings that illustrate it. The text
relates the story of Donallan, a lonely fisherman who falls in love with
a beautiful seal maiden and, on the advice of an old island man,
catches her by stealing her seal skin so she cannot return to the sea.
They have five children, and one day the youngest discovers the skin,
releasing his mother to slip away into the waves after a tender
goodbye and a promise to return each year "on the seventh day of the

highest tides of spring." The prose is rhythmic, the pictures cool and blue-hued, with loose shapes and pages bled to give a sense of boundlessness. The selkie appears naked with her sisters in the first spread, but discreetly so, all the better to contrast with her primly confined form as she stares longingly to sea with her first child. The seascapes and shore scenes are light-filled, vintage Hutton.

208   **Corcoran**, Barbara. *I Am the Universe*. Atheneum, 1986. ISBN 0-689-31208-3. 136p. $12.95.

5-8   A daunting title for an engaging story about a thirteen-year-old girl who, in the space of a few weeks, is confronted with too much: Kit's mother's frequent, agonizing headaches have been diagnosed as symptoms of a brain tumor, compounding and magnifying Kit's usual problems with school and family, and her growing awareness of herself as a writer. This is a lot for an author, much less a thirteen-year-old, to handle, but Corcoran weaves the various plot strands with ease, and Kit's slightly caustic—though heartfelt—narration keeps the tone light. There are a few mis-steps (Kit being picked up by the cops for egg-throwing) where the characters act like psychological profiles, but on the whole Kit and her family—especially her eccentrically gifted little brother —are warmly and carefully drawn. Give this one to Anastasia Krupnik fans who are looking for something a little "older."

209   **Cormier**, Robert. *Beyond the Chocolate War*. Knopf, 1985. Library ed. ISBN 0-394-97343-7; Trade ed. ISBN 0-394-87343-2. 288p. Library ed. $11.99; Trade ed. $11.95.

7-10   As he did in *The Chocolate War*, Cormier explores the motivations and the consequences, like a viscous ripple effect, of the combination of evil and power. Archie, leader of the Vigils, the secret society that dominates a Catholic high school for boys, is a senior now and has chosen his successor, a less subtle and more openly vindictive sophomore. Several of the Vigils rebel against Archie in this powerful sequel, but only Archie wins. This has diversity within the framework of Trinity High, with the despair and resentment of several students perceptively detailed and tied together by the inexorable momentum of events. Some readers may find the story depressingly somber; for others it may have the cathartic effect of Greek tragedy, evoking pity and fear.

210   **Cosner**, Shaaron. *War Nurses*. Walker, 1988. Library ed. ISBN 0-8027-6828-8; Trade ed. ISBN 0-8027-6826-1. 106p. illus. with photographs. Library ed. $17.85; Trade ed. $16.95.

5-9   A sometimes tragic but always fascinating subject receives competent summary coverage here with chapters on the role of nurses in the Civil War, the Crimean War, the Spanish-American War, World Wars I and II, Korea, and Vietnam. The text is factual but not dry; the black-and-white photographs, many historical, are revealing. Background information is livened by quotes from letters (no sources cited) and occasionally fictionalized stories about individuals who pioneered the field, from Clara Barton and Florence Nightingale to contemporary women who have crusaded for recognition of nurses' status as veterans. The history of war weapons, of medical developments in dealing with them, and of women's determination to help heal the wounds inflicted on male battlefields all suggest further areas for study and issues for discussion. Unfortunately, there's no bibliography. The index will help students doing reports, while browsers will get caught up in the herstory.

211   Cowing, Sheila. *Searches in the American Desert*; illus. with photographs and maps by Walter S. Cowing. McElderry, 1989. ISBN 0-689-50469-1. 177p. $14.95.

7-
*
The organizing principle guiding the wealth of detail in this book demonstrates the singular virtues of the well-chosen approach. Cowing's subject is the American Southwest, her perspective is historical, her theme is pilgrimage. Taking in turn the searches for gold, souls, freedom, history, and other Grails both real and imagined, Cowing shows the lure of the impossible landscape to be irresistible. The Spaniards came for treasure, the Mormons found the natural hostility of the Great Basin preferable to the persecution they suffered in the East, Robert Oppenheimer needed a secret place to develop the atom bomb. For all of them, Native American inhabitants provided both historical and contemporary evidence that life could be found and made. The doggedness of some of the quests is staggering: it took several explorers almost seventy-five years to determine that there was no river that led to the Pacific through the southwest. Beginning in 1904, Los Angeles fought for forty years to take water from Owen Valley, a controversy that still simmers today. While other books provide an ecological awareness of the desert's natural inhabitants, this one provokes a new look at ourselves—unwelcome but tenacious intruders.

212   Cresswell, Helen. *Bagthorpes Liberated: Being the Seventh Part of the Bagthorpe Saga*. Macmillan, 1989. ISBN 0-02-725441-0. 186p. $13.95.

6-9   The unquenchable Bagthorpes set off yet another cycle of chaos upon their return from a holiday in Wales (*Bagthorpes Abroad*, and *Bagthorpes Haunted*). A tramp has occupied their house; bottles of milk, the delivery of which they've forgotten to cancel, line the driveway. Lethally charming little Daisy pours the curdled milk into the goldfish pond, the tramp dispenses with Mr. Bagthorpe's best

Scotch, and Mrs. Fosdyke gives up housekeeping on account of her nerves, frayed beyond repair by the Bagthorpes' disasters and her conviction that she's prime target for a mass murderer. There's a loose narrative thread of Mrs. Bagthorpe's trying to organize the family into a non-sexist distribution of labor, but, as usual, the strength of the humor depends on a spontaneous combustion of incidents sparked by the irascible personalities of everyone concerned. Although there's no question where it's all headed, the tit-for-tat dialogue and biting authorial observations magnify this situation comedy with a kind of suspense that keeps upping the ante for fans of the series—whatever can happen next?

213   **Crew,** Linda. *Children of the River.* Delacorte, 1989. ISBN 0-440-50122-9. 213p. $14.95.

7-12   A long-favorite plot of both writers and readers is here given an absorbing contemporary context. Sundara has a crush on the local football hero, Jonathan, who is interested in her as well, but her aunt and uncle don't approve. With her aunt and uncle, 13-year-old Sundara escaped from Cambodia at the beginning of the Khmer Rouge terror. Now, four years later, she has no idea if her parents and sister are alive and still carries the guilt of having Aunt Soka's baby die while in her care on the packed and hysterical refugee boat. "They made me throw her into the water." Even in Oregon, Soka is determined to bring Sundara up as a proper Cambodian girl (no dates, and an eventually arranged marriage with a Cambodian boy) and, while encouraging Sundara's determination to become a doctor, is afraid and unable to show her niece love. Except for the idealization of Jonathan as a sensitive, always-there hero, the story is neither sentimental nor sensational: both the horror and the romance are real. This first novel is notable for its strong storytelling and thorough characterization. While teens will enjoy the romance, it's the relationship between Sundara and her aunt that is most involving, both as a dramatic family portrait and as a picture of "new Americans" who know they will never see their home again.

214   **Cross,** Gillian. *Chartbreaker.* Holiday House, 1987. ISBN 0-8234-0647-4. 175p. $12.95.

8-10   First published in England as *Chartbreak*, this is a remarkably effective first-person novel that combines, in a believable success story, the appeals of the entertainment business and of problems shared by many adolescents. Janis is big, homely, and angry, and she has stormed out of the house after a quarrel with her mother and Mum's boyfriend. Alone in a cafe, she defiantly boasts of her singing to the members of a combo; they are so impressed that they subsequently invite Janis to join them. She "borrows," and later repays, her mother's money, and runs off. From there on, it's a vivid description of the grueling task of breaking into the big time (they do, as the title indicates), and the story of the group's climb is nicely balanced by the smoothly integrated story of the relationships between Janis and the men in the group (no sex) and by the poignant disruption of the relationship between Janis and her Mum. No glamorizing here, but a story of hard work; the characterization has depth and consistency, and the narrative flow is enlivened rather than broken by interpolated letters, newspaper articles, and song lyrics.

215   Cross, Gillian. *The Dark behind the Curtain.* Dell, 1988. Paper ed. ISBN 0-440-20207-8. 199p. Paper ed. $2.95.

7-10   Faced by the principal with a choice of being turned over to the police or joining the school play, petty thief and general malcontent Jackus chooses to be in the play. It's *Sweeney Todd,* starring his friend (maybe) Marshall as the demonic barber. When trouble begins— spilled paint, stolen props and valuables—Jackus seems to be the culprit. He knows better, but who would believe the real story? No one else seems to hear the whispering, no one else saw the tiny footprint in the paint . . . . Like the ghosts of miserable street orphans who haunt the production, Jackus is a scruffy outsider; like Sweeney, popular Marshall hides a razor beneath his charm. *Sweeney Todd* is a very scary play and this is a very scary thriller, with ample menace provided by both the living and the dead. Reprinted from a book originally published in Britain in 1982.

216   Cross, Gillian. *Roscoe's Leap.* Holiday House, 1987. ISBN 0-8234-0669-5. 160p. $12.95.

6-9   First published in England, this is a spellbinder. The setting, an
*   isolated, decaying mansion that spans a stream, is Gothic, romantic, mysterious. Why is the children's mother, Mrs. Roscoe, so tense that her son and daughter, (Hannah and Stephen, 15 and 12) are afraid of her? Why does Doug, who takes care of old Uncle Ernest, in the other half of the house, never cross over to visit the children although it is clear that he cares for them? Finally, why is Stephen so terrified by the childhood encounter with an automaton that he blocks the memory? The arrival of a student who is working on a thesis about the ancestor who built the house is a catalyst for unravelling the mystery. This has pace and suspense, a nicely crafted plot, and distinctive characterization and style.

217   Crossley-Holland, Kevin. *Axe-Age, Wolf-Age: A Selection from the Norse Myths;* illus. by Hannah Firmin. Andre Deutsch/Elsevier-Dutton, 1986. ISBN 0-233-97688-4. 175p. $11.95.

7-10   In a retelling of the cycle of Norse mythology first published in his *The Norse Myths*, Crossley-Holland relied, he states in a prefatory note, on two 12th century sources, the *Elder Edda* and the *Prose Edda* of Snorri Sturluson. The storytelling quality is notable, giving humor and narrative flow to the granite characters and forceful drama of the Nordic legends. A glossary (chiefly names of people and places) is provided; the rigid naiveté of the woodcut illustrations is appropriate for the text but not always in agreement with it — a reference to the first human beings emerging out of the primeval ooze under Ymir's left armpit is contradicted by the picture that shows this happening under the right armpit, for example.

218   **Crossley-Holland**, Kevin. *British Folk Tales: New Versions.* Orchard/Watts, 1987. ISBN 0-531-05733-X. 382p. illus. $22.95.

4-
 *   In both range and depth, this is a rich collection of 55 British folktales adapted from widely varied sources which the author has cited in careful, if idiosyncratic, end notes. While some of the titles sound familiar, the versions here may not seem so. The satisfyingly rhythmic "Frog Prince"is distinctly different from Grimm #1. "King of the Cats"appears in monologue form, and "The Small-Tooth Dog,"a variant of "Beauty and the Beast,"has acquired a modern setting. The author is intimate with this lore, and some of his innovations render the tales more immediate. A few, however, seem slightly discon-certing. Casting "The Sea-Woman"(about a Selkie) as a tale within a tale, for instance, distracts more than it adds. Yet Crossley Holland has a strong sense of selection and consistent respect for motif. His most vivid writing adheres closely to the basic shape of the tales. In many cases, as he himself says, "the best thing a reteller can do is 'translate' the dialect into modern English and keep well out of the way." The bookmaking is worthy of the text: handsome print on fine, creamy paper with discretely miniature, skillful scratch-board drawings opening each chapter (the illustrator remains mysteriously unidentified). In its revealing and revitalizing of the traditional, this makes a long-lasting contribution to readers and storytellers alike.

219   **Crouch**, Marcus, ad. *Ivan: Stories of Old Russia*; illus. by Bob Dewar. Oxford, 1989. ISBN 0-19-274135-7. 80p. (Oxford Myths and Legends). $15.95.

4-6   Ivan may be a noodlehead or a trickster or a bold hero; in Russian folklore there are myriad Ivan stories and, in this appealing new compilation, they are retold with wit and a strong sense of the oral tradition. The illustrations, both those in color and those in black and white, echo the comic quality of the retellings, more suave than stark, yet starkly dramatic in visual effectiveness. Lovers of the genre, young or old, will recognize familiar tales (Baba Yaga intercedes in "Three

Brides for Three Brothers") and enjoy Slavic variants of others, as in "Ivan Gets It Wrong," an entertaining companion to "Epaminondas."

220   **Crutcher**, Chris. *Stotan!* Greenwillow, 1986. ISBN 0-688-05715-2. 183p. $10.25.

8-12   In journal form, Walker Dupree recounts the week-long marathon that forever bonds his team of four high school swimmers under the tough direction of their Korean coach. Each of the boys develops emotionally as well as physically through the rigorous testing for strength, endurance, and commitment. Nortie exorcises the ghost of his brother, driven to suicide by their abusive father, and leaves home himself. The narrator sorts out his relationships with two girl friends and eventually, his calling as a writer. Lionel, living alone since his parents' death in an accident, supports rambunctious Jeff through what turns out to be a terminal illness. A subplot involving the boys' fight against local Neo-Nazi activists provides some immediate action, while the various characters' conflicts tighten the middle and ending. The pace lags through the story's introductions; nevertheless, this is a searching sports novel, with a tone varying from macho-tough to sensitive.

221   **Curry**, Jane Louise. *Back in the Beforetime: Tales of the California Indians*; retold by Jane Louise Curry; illus. by James Watts. McElderry, 1987. ISBN 0-689-50410-1. 134p. $11.95.

4-6   Drawing from lore of various California Indian tribes, Curry arranges 22 stories into a cycle of creation myths featuring Coyote, the trickster who contrived that "the animal people had sunshine by day and the moon at night, fire to warm them and to cook with, and salmon and pine nuts in season." His last venture, making a man, begins the period of Aftertime, when, as Old Man Above warns, "no longer will your folk be both animals and people, with the powers of both. No longer will any among you be shape-shifters and workers of magic. You will be animals only, and only Man will have the powers of speech and spirit." These stories of Beforetime, meanwhile, are alive with the mischief, malice, and magic that allowed the clever to survive. Coyote is, as often as not, defeated by his own wiles, as when he tries to fool Badger out of a deer and ends up eating acorns for dinner. Yet by hook or crook, he does manage to win his way, as in his recruiting the animals to steal pine nuts from the Mountain Bluebirds. Like Moses' Israelites, the animal people complain and sometimes despise Coyote, but he is indominable even to the day of his last tricks on Dog. Curry's words are well-turned, the stories brief and often humorous; this is a cohesive, readable collection for introducing young readers to Native American mythology.

222   **Cushman**, Kathleen. *Circus Dreams: The Making of a Circus Artist*;
by Kathleen Cushman and Montana Miller; illus. with photographs by
Michael Carroll. Joy Street/Little, 1990. ISBN 0-316-16561-1. 90p. $15.95.

6-10   This account of eighteen-year-old Montana Miller's training as a
  *   trapeze artist at the National Center for Circus Arts at Châlons-sur-
Marne, France, stands out as unusually honest in a literature that
tends to glamorize career immersion. Montana's pain as she trains for
her specialty is due to physical strain, lack of confidence, and a sense
of isolation (she's the only American in an intensive program). At one
point, she decides to leave after the year is over, but a final performance convinces her to continue, and an afterword reports her first
job with a troupe touring Europe. Diary-like, the year's work is
segmented by date—between one and four entries per month—but is
related in third person rather than first, so that Montana's activities
benefit from an observer's perspective. The black-and-white action
shots are beautifully incorporated into the text, a complex task with so
much interplay between graphics and description of routines. The
strength, exhaustion, and vulnerability reflected in Montana's stocky
body and expressive face, her struggle with timing, and her successful
trapeze flights are all vividly portrayed here. This is a real find for kids
who have longed to join the circus, or who just love to go, or who harbor
other "crazy" dreams of their own. And for adults who remember
those states of mind.

223   **Dahl**, Roald. *Esio Trot*; illus. by Quentin Blake. Viking, 1990. ISBN 0-
670-83451-3. 64p. $14.95.

2-4   This is Dahl in a mellow mood, just as funny as he usually is but not as
tart. Blake's illustrations, with few but telling flyaway lines, reflect the
breezy, amicable mood of the text in a preposterous (but not
impossible) love story. Mr. Hoppy is too shy to disclose his love to the
charming widow, Mrs. Silver, whose balcony is just below his. Knowing
that she dotes on her pet tortoise, Alfie, but worries because Alfie
doesn't grow, Mr. Hoppy gives Mrs. Silver a secret formula (the words
are written backward and should delight readers) for growth.
Meanwhile he fills his apartment with tortoises of all sizes and runs in
substitutes for Alfie. Mrs. Silver, harmlessly duped and delighted,
invites her mentor down for a closer look, and the besotted Mr. Hoppy
proposes and is accepted. It isn't often that a love story offers appeal
to primary grades readers, but this one should prove diverting.

224   **Dahl**, Roald. *Matilda*; illus. by Quentin Blake. Viking, 1988. ISBN 0-
670-82439-9. 240p. $13.95.

4-8   Viola Swamp, *eat my dust*. When it comes to the ingenious torture of
small schoolchildren, James Marshall's evil Swamp hasn't got a patch
on Dahl's Miss Trunchbull, school principal: "What a bunch of

nauseating little warts you are . . . It makes me vomit to think that I am going to have to put up with a load of garbage like you in my school for the next six years." Super-bright Matilda, who read *Great Expectations* at age four, just bides her time, until she discovers Miss Trunchbull's evil control over the beloved first-grade teacher, Miss Honey. Time for action. Reading Dahl can be a bit like being held by the neck and shrieked at in the face, but here, as in his best books, the rude humor is tempered with a poignant understanding of outsiders like Miss Honey and Matilda, a determined heroine not above some nasty tricks of her own, delivered upon the entirely deserving, like her parents. "To tell the truth, I doubt they would have noticed had she crawled into the house with a broken leg." Sweet Miss Honey probably wouldn't, but you ought to try reading this aloud, that is, if your local Trunchbull is safely out of earshot.

225   **Dallas-Smith**, Peter. *Trumpets in Grumpetland;* illus. by Peter Cross. Random House, 1985. Library ed. ISBN 0-394-97028-4; Trade ed. ISBN 0-394-87028-X. 30p. Library ed. $8.99; Trade ed. $8.95.

2-4   In a sequel to *Trouble for Trumpets*, there is conflict again between the amicable Trumpets who live in sunshine and peace, and the dour Grumpets, most of whom have evil intentions, or worse. Worse here, certainly, as Grumpet Havoc steers his ship, a Flying Grumpicat, toward the happy party of friends who are traveling on the ground below. He is, oh joy, foiled in this dastardly attempt. As with the first book, the story is enjoyable but the illustrations are irresistible, being lovely, lavish, and hilariously funny, even for readers who don't get every British reference, like the Northern Line map on the tube.

226   **Daly**, Niki. *Not So Fast Songololo;* written and illus. by Niki Daly. Atheneum/McElderry, 1986. ISBN 0-689-50367-9. 32p. $11.95.

4-6 yrs.   A warm story of a black South African child's trip to town with is grandmother is full of the old woman's patient rhythms and the boy's natural poking gait as he kicks a can or gazes into shop windows. The relationship between them is a touching one of trust and love, and it is no surprise when Grandmother Malusi invests in a new pair of red sneakers (called "tackies" in the book) to replace Gogo's tattered ones. Gogo's simple gratitude leads his grandmother to the concluding joke, that if she had red shoes with white stripes, maybe she could walk as fast as he. The watercolor paintings in mottled patterns of brown, blue, and red offer a rich portraiture of the two main characters: Malusi a heavy old woman immensely strong and kind, Gogo a skinny dreamer with the world a place of wonder to him (though there are pictorial hints of the oppression surrounding him). This is a carefully simple, evocative story that will appeal universally but is all the more special for its personal reflection of a foreign setting.

227   **Danziger**, Paula. *It's an Aardvark-Eat-Turtle World.* Delacorte, 1985. ISBN 0-385-29371-2. 132p. $13.95.

6-9   In *The Divorce Express*, Phoebe was the narrator, and her perceptive story of two broken families ended with an alliance between her father and the mother of her best friend Rosie. In this sequel it's Rosie who tells the story, equally perceptive and just as lively. There's friction between Phoebe and Mindy (Rosie's mother) and it's a difficult adjustment for everyone. Rosie's disappointed, because she had hoped her new sister would continue to be her best friend. There are some problems because Mindy and Jim (Phoebe's father) are not married. There are further problems when Phoebe resents, while they're on a trip together, the fact that Rosie spends time with other people. Eventually, after an estrangement, Phoebe decides that she'll accept counseling and stay with Mindy and Jim and Rosie rather than her mother and stepfather. Rosie is open throughout about the fact that her father's black and her mother's white, indeed, she's proud of her double heritage; only once in the story is there an unpleasant incident, when a bigoted stranger yells at her to stay with her "own kind." Fortunately, the boy she's with responds for both of them "We are the same kind—human." This has moments of sweetness to balance some tartness, an honest approach to problems, a lively and natural writing style, and strong, consistent characterization.

228   **Davidson**, Alan. *The Bewitching of Alison Allbright.* Viking, 1989. ISBN 0-670-82015-6. 157p. $11.95.

5-8   Be careful what you wish for . . . . Morosely discontented Alison
  *   Allbright evidently never heard this particular piece of advice, and the elegant, friendly, rich Mrs. Considine seems to be the answer to many prayers. Lonely for her own daughter "away at school in Switzerland," Mrs. Considine gives Alison everything she wants: clothes, status, admiration. But even the besotted Alison realizes something is odd when Mrs. Considine begins to call her "Camilla," her own daughter's name. "I wouldn't even tell your family about the game we play. It's just a whim of mine." Related in a cool, sinister tone, this novel has an irresistible combination of dream indulgence and unsettling nightmare, perhaps most clearly demonstrated in the scene where Alison/Camilla "savours" her own memorial service, kindly arranged by Mrs. Considine after Alison has supposedly drowned in the lake. While it is a contemporary realistic story, old fairy tale motifs abound: Mrs. Considine is a scary, wicked witch, but complicated in her ambivalence toward the daughter she re-creates; Alison is a trans- formed princess who finds her castle becoming a prison. This is the

kind of instantly appealing novel you won't want to booktalk without multiple copies on hand.

229   **Davis**, Jenny. *Good-Bye and Keep Cold*. Orchard/Watts, 1987. Library ed. ISBN 0-531-08315-2; Trade ed. ISBN 0-531-05715-1. 210p. Library ed. $12.99; Trade ed. $12.95.

7-10   Written in retrospect by Edda, now 22, this is a well-sustained family story, mature and often moving, that focuses on Edda's mother, tragically widowed by a mine accident. Edda, 8 at the time, adjusts both to Mama's going to work and to her being courted by Henry John (gentle, kind, forever guilt-ridden because he had accidentally caused the mine disaster). What makes this first novel impressive is the delicate balance Davis keeps between the immediacy of personal involvement and the detachment that makes it possible (convincingly) for Edda to react to her mother's off/on relationship with Henry John, yet see them both with maturity. Good style, good characters, a good read.

230   **Davis**, Jenny. *Sex Education*. Orchard/Watts, 1988. Library ed. ISBN 0-531-08356-X; Trade ed. ISBN 0-531-05756-9. 150p. Library ed. $13.99; Trade ed. $13.95.

7-10   Powerful. This is a story told by sixteen-year-old Olivia; it is framed by a preface that explains that she is in a mental hospital, writing at her psychiatrist's behest, and it closes with an epilogue that promises recovery. Olivia's illness is a reaction to the death of David, the classmate she has come to love when they act as partners in a sex education class project. They do not become lovers, but Olivia learns from David what loving means, and both of them have learned from their project how intricate love and sex are, and how terrible it can be when they go wrong. The project: finding a person to care about. David and Olivia choose a pregnant, shy new neighbor whose husband is oddly hostile. Both a touching story of an abused wife and a tender story of young love, this is deftly structured, nicely paced, and smoothly written, with strongly delineated characters and thematic depths that give color and substance.

231   **Day**, Alexandra. *Carl Goes Shopping*; written and illus. by Alexandra Day. Farrar, 1989. ISBN 0-374-31110-2. 32p. $9.95.

4-6 yrs.   Wordless except for the first and last pages ("I have to go upstairs to
  *   get Aunt Martha's curtains. Take good care of the baby, Carl. . . . Good dog, Carl!"), this is an entertaining picture narrative in which a large black dog plays nanny. The setting is a department store, where the baby rides on Carl's back—up the elevator, into the toy department, over to the picture-book display, through the hats and gloves, for a rest on the rugs, to the food counter, and finally, after opening all the pet

shop cages, back beside the buggy in time to assume a patiently-
waiting expression. The plot is clearly revealed by the pantomime,
which is not always the case in wordless picturebooks. The illustrations
are thick paint on gray-blue paper, and the fluid drafting of both
human and animal against smoothly textured backgrounds focuses
the main characters with magnetic precision. Straightfaced details
and closely portrayed expressions lend humor to a wishful fantasy that
will storytell well with small children.

232   **Day**, Edward C. *John Tabor's Ride*; illus. by Dirk Zimmer. Knopf, 1989.
Library ed. ISBN 0-394-98577-X; Trade ed. ISBN 0-394-88577-5. 30p.
Library ed. $13.99; Trade ed. $12.95.

5-8 yrs.   "He complained about the wind. He complained about the hot sun.
He complained about the smell from boiling down the blubber."
Young John Tabor is not a happy sailor, and his whining brings
comeuppance from an odd little ancient mariner, who appears on the
whaler one moonlight evening ("I've come for ye, John Tabor") to take
John where he wants to go: back home to Cape Cod and Taborstown.
Via whale. It's a bumpy, *fast* trip, and, once there, the whale, roaring
"like a hurricane through a fleet of fishing boats" takes a chastened
John right back to his ship. Tall tale and mythic drama sail together
here in a "true" story (adapted from J. Ross Browne's *Etchings of a
Whaling Cruise*) that's a great read-aloud. While Zimmer's paintings
have a primarily comic tone, his behemoth is fierce and dark, a
monumental crosshatched presence that overwhelms the landscape
and gives depth to what is actually a very unsettling tale.

233   **De Gerez**, Toni, ad. *Louhi, Witch of North Farm*; ad. from Finland's
epic poem, the *Kalevala* by Toni De Gerez; illus. by Barbara Cooney.
Viking, 1986. ISBN 0-670-80556-4. 28p. $12.95

5-7 yrs.   In a tale adapted from Finland's epic, the *Kalevala*, the wicked witch
    *   Louhi steals the sun and moon from the branches where they are
listening to Vainamoinen play his magical music. When the earth is
plunged into darkness, Vainamoinen goes to his friend, the black-
smith Seppo, who eventually frightens Louhi (spying on him in the
shape of a bird) with the chains he is forging "to wrap around the
skinny gray neck of a certain Witch!" Louhi's release of the sun and
moon in the concluding double page spreads is typical of Cooney's
smoothly blended artwork throughout the book. The landscapes are
spacious. with rounded shapes contrasted against flat horizons. Gray-
blue tones dominate the outdoor snow scenes; warm browns, the
wooden interiors. The mythic-sized struggle at the core of the story
gets dignified treatment here in both text and graphics, but there is
also an immediate, familiar quality about the epic figures.

234   de Regniers, Beatrice Schenk and others, comp. *Sing a Song of Popcorn: Every Child's Book of Poems*. Scholastic, 1988. ISBN 0-590-40645-0. 142p. illus. $16.95.

K-5   The purpose of the original title, *Poems Children Will Sit Still For* (1969), was the provision of material for classroom teachers, and contained selections that were for reading aloud as as well as those that could be enjoyed by independent readers. For the present, oversized edition, 22 new poems have been added to the 106 of the original. The selections are grouped under nine headings (usually subject or genre), and each section is illustrated by a winner of the Caldecott Medal. Suffice it to say that Marcia Brown, Leo and Diane Dillon, Richard Egielski, Trina Schart Hyman, Arnold Lobel, Maurice Sendak, Marc Simont, and Margot Zemach have done work that is varied, polished, often funny, or beautiful. A pleasant book, still a useful if conservative anthology, this has title, author, and first line indexes, and brief notes on the illustrators.

235   DeArmond, Dale, ad. *The Seal Oil Lamp*; ad. and illus. by Dale DeArmond. Sierra Club/Little, 1988. ISBN 0-316-17786-5. 32p. $13.95.

2-5   Beautifully designed and illustrated, this is the moving story of seven-year-old Allugua, who must be left to die, according to the laws of his people, because his blindness would make him a burden to the village. The kindness he has shown to a freezing mouse saves him, however, because Mouse Woman comes with bits of food and water, while the seal oil lamp his mother has left behind miraculously continues to burn till his people return. By that time, Allugua has learned stories and a powerful hunting song from Mouse Woman, and he is accepted back into the village after he kills his first whale. The life-and-death struggle, the meeting of real and mythical realms, and the strong but unintrusive narrative voice make this traditional tale a gripping one. Moreover, the bookmaking, which includes thick white paper, blue-gray print, and starkly forceful black-and-white woodcuts, has been carefully considered to support a strong text. It's too bad there are no source notes, although there is a brief glossary. The respect for nature emphasized here will make the book ideal for reading aloud in conjunction with environmental awareness discussions or study units focusing on native Alaskan groups.

236   DeClements, Barthe. *6th Grade Can Really Kill You*. Viking, 1985. ISBN 0-670-80656-0. 146p. $11.95.

5-7   Some of the characters from earlier DeClements books will be familiar to her readers, in a story that amply compensates for its uneven pace by the natural quality of the relationships and the dialogue in the classroom environment and by the insight gained through the first person treatment of a learning disability. "Bad

Helen" is what they call her, and here she is still playing pranks in her frustration at no being able to read. Tests have shown that Helen has the intelligence to do the work; her overprotective mother refuses to give permission for special training because she does not want her daughter labelled "dumb." Helen's father is wiser, and he takes matters into his own hands, leading to a realistically optimistic feeling, as Helen works with teachers trained in special education, that she'll improve. A serious subject is not handled so seriously that the story is marred.

237   **DeFelice**, Cynthia D., ad. *The Dancing Skeleton*; illus. by Robert Andrew Parker. Macmillan, 1989. ISBN 0-02-726452-1. 32p. $13.95.

5-8 yrs.   Unloved in life and unmourned in death, Aaron Kelly got up out of his
  *   coffin and walked home ("I don't feel dead. I feel fine!"), refusing to go back until he feels dead. Even when he begins to dry up, with nothing left but his skeleton, Aaron just keeps rocking in his chair, old bones clicking and clacking. "His widow did her best to ignore him, but it wasn't easy with all the racket he made." But one night the widow's suitor, a fiddler, comes to call, and Aaron decides to dance . . . . This macabre, but mostly funny, story (adapted from John Bennett's "Daid Aaron II") is a great read-aloud, with bone-popping sound effects, including a showstopping opportunity for some knuckle-cracking. Parker's pen-and-watercolor illustrations, minimally lined for maximum effect, provide the perfect sober-sided companion, portraying the stubborn-jawed Aaron, his long-suffering widow, and the daunted suitor as an unlikely love triangle. One feels that Aaron Kelly, eventually buried but hardly rested, did his widow a favor.

238   **DeFord**, Deborah H. *An Enemy Among Them;* by Deborah H. DeFord and Harry S. Stout. Houghton, 1987. ISBN 0-395-44239-7. 203p. $13.95.

6-9   In a story set in Pennsylvania during the Revolutionary War, the authors use a theme, the "beloved enemy" romance, that will be familiar to readers of historical fiction. Margaret's devotion to her soldier brother is tested when she learns that the Hessian who is helping her father (Christian had been a prisoner of war, a German mercenary) is the man whose bayonet had caused her brother's mortal wound. Christian eventually becomes a Patriot convert and enlists with General Wayne's forces. The change in Christian is plausible, as is the change of attitude among the members of Margaret's German-American family. Some of the incidents are overly dramatized or sentimentalized, but on the whole this is good historical fiction, bringing a period and an event to life and showing a spectrum of behavior on both sides of the struggle.

239   **Dekkers**, Midas. *Arctic Adventure*. Orchard/Watts, 1987. Library ed. ISBN 0-531-08304-7; Trade ed. ISBN 0-531-05704-6. 165p. Library ed. $12.99; Trade ed. $12.95.

6-9   Although this adventure story carries a strong Greenpeace message, it is the narrative that dominates the book. First published in Holland, then translated by Jan Michael for the English edition that carried the title *Whale Lake*, this is the story of two Dutch brothers who go on an exploratory expedition in the Arctic; Adrian is an archeologist and a member of Greenpeace, Menno is his adolescent sibling who becomes committed to the cause and who learns to love the whale they find in a salt lake when they are cast away on an island. There is a dramatic confrontation between a whaler and a Greenpeace rescue boat, so that there is plenty of action and excitement as well as some cogent arguments against animal destruction and for other Greenpeace causes.

240   **Demi**. *A Chinese Zoo: Fables and Proverbs*; illus. by Demi. Harcourt, 1987. ISBN 0-15-217510-5. 28p. $14.95.

5-8 yrs.   Set against a background of impressive but gracefully restrained paintings, these fables have been smoothly abbreviated with morals written in Chinese calligraphy beside the English. The dominant image is a fan-shaped frame arching the double-page spreads, each in a different hue, where delicately stylized animals dramatize the stories. Some will be familiar, as in the tale of the blind mice who feel different parts of the elephant and so arrive at different conclusions about his total appearance. Others will be less so—the struggle between a crane and a clam that are both captured by a fisherman because neither will let the other go ("In the face of disaster, don't waste time arguing"). Although the effect of both art and proverb is quiet and has a mature appeal, each selection is brief enough to hold younger children though a read-aloud/discussion session of several stories at one time. Even middle-grade children who are studying fables can be drawn into this picture book if they are challenged to consider the textual variants here and the graphic concepts of Oriental art represented by Demi's studied work.

241   **Demi**. *Demi's Count the Animals 1, 2, 3*; written and illus. by Demi. Grosset, 1986. ISBN 0-448-18980-1. 47p. $9.95.

2-5 yrs.
*   Here's a counting book that is an effective teaching tool, with clear correlation between words, digits, and pictures and with attractive illustrations of animals. Some of the paintings (chiefly bright pastel colors) are ornamented (elephants in two-color print design) while others are realistic. The numbers go from one to twenty, and Demi has added two ways to count to one hundred. A sample of the text: "1 ONE How many rhinos/on the run?/It's easy to see/there's only one. Count

one rhinoceros." Color, humor, and the appeals of rhyme, rhythm, and a parade of animals equal a winner.

242   dePaola, Tomie. *The Art Lesson*; written and illus. by Tomie dePaola. Putnam, 1989. ISBN 0-399-21688-X. 30p. $13.95.

5-8 yrs.   Budding artist Tommy knows from his grown-up cousins that art's two main credos are "don't copy" and "practice, practice, practice." It's a real blow, then, when Tommy finally gets to first grade and a real art teacher, that she tells the children to *copy* the Pilgrim she's drawn on the board, and allows them only one piece of paper. Tommy goes on strike, but an agreeable compromise is struck, and Tommy goes on drawing, "and he still does," with the last illustration showing a gray-haired Tommy (Tomie?) surrounded by familiar dePaola motifs. While the illustrations hold few surprises, the story has the kind of specificity that characterizes the best dePaola texts, such as *Nana Upstairs and Nana Downstairs*. Here, for example, is kindergarten art time: "It wasn't much fun. The paint was awful and the paper got all wrinkly . . . If it was windy when Tommy carried his picture home, the paint blew right off the paper." And Miss Landers' announcement that everyone must use SCHOOL CRAYONS will strike a chord of remembered dismay in anyone who has ever treasured the Crayola box of sixty-four.

243   Deuker, Carl. *On the Devil's Court.* Joy Street/Little, 1989. ISBN 0-316-13147-1. 252p. $13.95.

7-12   The summer before his senior year, 17-year-old Joe Faust moves to Seattle because of his father's scientific work. Hoping to enter a public school with a good basketball team, Joe gets into trouble with one of the players and is sent to a private school, where he seems to lose his touch during team tryouts. While practicing on a deserted court one night after a class discussion on Dr. Faustus, Joe thinks he would give anything for a full season of powerful playing. Eerily, he has it. Everything that was going wrong starts to go right—games, grades, friendships. But his troubled relationship with his father seems to be the price, and when Dr. Faust has a heart attack, Joe is haunted by the idea that he has indeed sold his soul to the devil. This is a rare sports novel, with complex plot and characterization as well as gripping game play. Deuker is careful not to use easy outs: the local bully is as unpredictably moral in a game as he is immoral on the street; Joe's father works to change his workaholic ways but still can't resist pushing Joe toward Stanford instead of a smaller college where he's been offered a basketball scholarship. Their confrontations are realistic but never overdone, and Joe's mother is well played as the mediator who determinedly maintains her identity as an artist.

244   **Dewey**, Ariane. *Gib Morgan, Oilman*; written and illus. by Ariane
            Dewey. Greenwillow, 1987. Library ed. ISBN 0-688-06567-8; Trade ed.
            ISBN 0-688-06566-X. 48p. Library ed. $11.88; Trade ed. $11.75.

2-4   "'There ain't no place I can't drill.'" Gib Morgan was an oil drilling
            superman. He could fix anything, build anything, and could even
            smell the oil underground. With his twenty-two yard horse Torpedo
            (who had three forward speeds and could run in reverse), Gib could
            get from Pennsylvania to Kansas to Louisiana and back in time for
            dinner—"It sure beat taking the train." When Gib built a rig so high
            he needed hinges to let the moon pass, he thoughtfully added
            bunkhouses on the way up—it took a man fourteen days to climb.
            Tales don't come much taller than these, and Dewey's colorful, naive
            paintings take all the nonsense literally. Even non-readers will gape at
            Gib's fifty-foot square pancake griddle, greased by boys on bacon
            skates, flapjacks flipped by girls with snow shovels.

245   **Dickinson**, Peter. *Eva*. Delacorte, 1989. ISBN 0-385-50129-6. 216p.
            $14.95.

7-12   Daughter of a prominent primatologist, 13-year-old Eva has grown up
  *   around chimps, "and now she was one herself. Okay." Her body
            destroyed in a car accident, Eva's "neuron memory" has been
            transplanted into the body of a chimpanzee named Kelly. Where is
            Kelly now, Eva wonders, and Dickinson uses this question to frame
            both narrative and thematic impetus in a dramatic science fiction
            story about an experiment that may or may not have gone wrong. Able
            to talk with humans via an electronic gizmo, grooming and chattering
            with the chimps, Eva becomes a controlled, contract-bound celebrity
            in an overpopulated world obsessed with 3-D television and chimps,
            who, living in zoos and research enclosures, are almost the only wild
            animals left. Both theme and plot will be familiar to SF movie fans, but
            Dickinson's story of Eva's transformation is never melodramatic, and
            his theme of the rights of animals is understated, allowing the chimps'
            behavior to speak for itself. His literal anthropomorphism of
            Eva/Kelly, in fact, serves not to show us how alike the animals are to
            ourselves, but how different. "Looked at with human eyes, thought
            about with a human mind, felt with human emotions, [a picture of the
            chimps] almost cried aloud . . . Uh-uh, thought Eva. People. They'll
            never understand." But perhaps it is because we are people that the
            last scene is so moving: a dying Eva, who has been living wild with the
            escaped chimps for years, gives her voice box back to the humans.

246   **Dickinson**, Peter. *Healer*. Delacorte, 1985. ISBN 0-385-29372-0. 192p.
            $14.95.

6-9   Dickinson is here, as he has been in earlier fantasy and adventure
            novels, superb at blending the realistic and the occult. His characters

are distinct, drawn with depth, never one-dimensional, whether they tilt toward heroism or villainy. In this absorbing story, a child of ten is The Healer, the core of an institution in which there are elaborate procedures and ritual. The child (no glamourie here, she's pudgy and pale and named Pinkie Proudfoot) seems to be healing sick people: is her power genuine or is the whole operation a fraud? Barry, sixteen, who wants to rescue Pinkie, whom he'd known when she was six, manages to get a job at the institution and he does get Pinkie away to her grandfather—but there's a dramatic reversal that is a powerful ending to a highly original story.

247   **Dijs**, Carla. *Big and Small: A Pop-Up Pal Book of Opposites*; ISBN 0-448-09075-9; *How Many?: A Pop-Up Pal Counting Book*; ISBN 0-448-09076-7. Each book: written and illus. by Carla Dijs. Grosset, 1989. 10p. (Pop-Up Pals). $7.95.

2-5 yrs.   Watch the hands, they tell the story. In this pair of early concept books, pop-up child-sized hands are used, effectively, to reinforce principles of counting and opposites. For "up" (in *Big and Small*), a little girl points to a bird: "The bird is up." For "down," her hands reach towards a bright green turtle. Two "noisy" hands bang pot lids; a girl puts forefinger to lip for "quiet." *How Many?* counts animals, from "one friendly guinea pig" to "ten little goldfish," and for each, the appropriate number of fingers pop up. The illustrations are mass-market simple, with easily identified shapes and an ethnic mix of children. The pop-up parts seem sturdy, but, if broken, can be easily fixed with glue. Two thumbs up.

248   **Doherty**, Berlie. *Granny Was a Buffer Girl*. Orchard/Watts, 1988. Library ed. ISBN 0-531-08354-3; Trade ed. ISBN 0-531-05754-2. 128p. Library ed. $13.99; Trade ed. $13.95.

6-9   In a beautifully crafted story that has won the Carnegie Award, the
*   matrix for memories of an extended English family is given by Jess, about to go to France for a university year abroad. The family gathering (three generations) introduces characters, and the ensuing separate segments are woven into a cohesive if varied single fabric. This is a testament to family love, it is a piece of social history, and it is a fascinating read that involves the reader in making connections among the roundly depicted characters. Good pace, good style. Good awarding.

249   **Doherty**, Berlie. *White Peak Farm*. Orchard, 1990. Library ed. ISBN 0-531-08467-1; Trade ed. ISBN 0-531-05867-0. 102p. Library ed. $12.99; Trade ed. $12.95.

6-9
*

First published in England in 1984 and written for the BBC, this is an account by adolescent Jeannie of the strong bonds and major events in the life of her family, living in comparative isolation on their Derbyshire farm. Although the chapters are episodic (perhaps because of the radio broadcasting format) they are solidly linked, so that there is an overall pattern that accommodates the changes in this family's life. Older sister Kathleen marries the son of a family enemy; brother Martin wants to leave and study art, prompting his father to brutally ruin one of Martin's pictures: "If this is what you think of my farm, then this is what I think of your painting." Both children eventually return. What is strong in these cunningly crafted stories is the sense of place, the love of their land that binds the members of the family almost as much as does their love for each other.

250   **Donnelly**, Judy. *The* Titanic *Lost . . . and Found*; illus. by Keith Kohler. Random, 1987. Library ed. ISBN 0-394-98669-5; Paper ed. ISBN 0-394-88669-0. 45p. (Step into Reading). Library ed. $5.99; Paper ed. $2.95.

K-3

This easy-to-read nonfiction, a rare combination of genres, is part of a graded series intended for beginning readers' home use. It tells in a straightforward but involving style how the ship set sail and capsized, with a chapter on the locating of its hull in 1985. All of the books in the series have competent wash drawings in full color, ranging appropriately in style from jovial to dramatic. Informative, fun, and good practice material.

251   **Dorros**, Arthur. *Ant Cities*; written and illus. by Arthur Dorros. Crowell, 1987. Library ed. ISBN 0-690-04570-0; Trade ed. ISBN 0-690-04568-9. 30p. (Let's-Read-and-Find-Out Science). Library ed. $11.89; Trade ed. $11.50.

2-4

Using harvester ants as a basic example, Dorros shows how the insects build tunnels with rooms for different functions and how workers, queens, and males have distinct roles in the ant hill. Along the way, the author works in details of food and reproduction, ending with descriptions of other kinds of ants and suggestions for ways to observe them (including instructions for making an ant farm). The text is simple without becoming choppy, the full-color illustrations are inviting as well as informative. Another successful addition to a series that is varied in scope and authorship but consistent in quality.

252   **Dowden**, Anne Ophelia. *The Clover and the Bee: A Book of Pollination*; written and illus. by Anne Ophelia Dowden. Crowell, 1990. Library ed. ISBN 0-690-04679-0; Trade ed. ISBN 0-690-04677-4. 90p. Library ed. $17.89; Trade ed. $17.95.

4-

"All flowers, large or small, dull or spectacular, exist for one purpose only—to make new plants." Dowden conveys a sense of wonder and delight in this well-organized, generously illustrated volume. In the first section, she lays the necessary groundwork, describing the parts of the flower and the role of pollen. Her clear explanations are enhanced by abundant visual examples that emphasize the variety of plant life. A second section, devoted to pollinators, includes such lesser known ones as beetles and bats. Finally, Dowden explores the process of pollination itself, going from the simple (saucer and bell flowers) to the complex (closed and trap flowers). Also covered are wind and water pollination and such exclusive partnerships as the yucca cactus and the Spanish bayonet moth. Dowden's descriptions are entertaining and dramatic: "Closed flowers do not always gently guide visitors to nectar. Some of them are almost sinister, with traps that lure victims and then hold them captive until pollination is assured." She shows that the flower can be an active participant in the process: "Sometimes orchid flowers subject their pollinators to very rough treatment, firing pollinia at them like bullets, or tumbling them about in the blossoms." Typical of the book's precision and detail are the two indexes (one general and the other for specific plants and pollinators). Dowden concludes her book with a warning: "The lost habitat of one small butterfly may be the signal that a whole network of plants and animals has been destroyed." The meticulous drawings and paintings, double-spaced text and wide margins make this a very accessible resource.

253   **Downie**, Mary Alice, comp. *The New Wind Has Wings: Poems from Canada;* comp. by Mary Alice Downie and Barbara Robertson; illus. by Elizabeth Cleaver. Oxford/Merrimack, 1985. ISBN 0-19-540431-9. 112p. $11.95.

4-7   In this new edition of a prize-winning Canadian children's book, the illustrations have the same kind of variety and vitality as the first book, and indeed some of the pictures are the same. This is true also of the poems: there have been some deletions and some additions, but many of the selections from the original (1968) publication, *The Wind Has Wings*, are included. This is still (or again) a fine anthology of Canadian poetry, and an index of the poets is provided.

254   **Dragonwagon**, Crescent. *Home Place;* illus. by Jerry Pinkney. Macmillan, 1990. ISBN 0-02-733190-3. 32p. $14.95.

2-4   Walking through the woods, a red-haired narrator discovers the ruins of a house and imagines a black family who might have lived there. "A chimney, made of stone, . . . a round blue glass marble, a nail. A horseshoe and a piece of plate. A small yellow bottle. A china doll's arm." From these she projects the lives of a boy and girl, husband and wife, uncle and grandparents, a clan eventually disbanded when its members die or move away: "still, whether anyone sees, or not, whether anyone listens, or not, the daffodils come up, to trumpet their good news forever and forever." Dragonwagon's text is evocative, and Pinkney's graphics are intensely atmospheric here. Even the endpapers simulate peeling wallpaper. In one picture that recalls images from Toni Morrison's *Beloved*, a woman seems to step through time as she passes from sunlight to shadow through a doorway. Always at home with nature spreads, the artist has quickened his portraiture with more graceful lines and planes; the family dinner makes a powerful scene. In spite of its picture-book format, this richly illustrated prose poem is better suited to independent readers beginning to develop a sophisticated sense of time. The words and art together will have an impact on children realizing their own ancestral past as part of history.

255   **Du Bois**, William Pene. *Gentleman Bear*; written and illus. by William Pene Du Bois. Farrar, 1985. ISBN 0-374-32533-2. 73p. $14.95.

4-6   A story about several generations in a noble English family focuses on the youngest heir's life, from his birth in 1916 to an incident in 1985. The hero is Sir Billy Browne-Browne, and his gentleman teddy bear is Bayard, who was acquired by Sir Billy when he was four. Bayard goes with Billy to boarding school, is present when Billy wins a third-place medal at the 1936 Olympic games, flies with Billy during World War II and becomes internationally famous. The paintings are distinctly Pene Du Bois: clean composition, bright, clear colors that are never brash, fidelity of detail and humor of concept. The story presents one problem: who are the appropriate readers for a tale that is told with vitality and humor, has many sophisticated or latent references, and is about a teddy bear? What it's really about is the English upper class, odd but staunch in the author's affectionate, teasing viewpoint.

256   **Dubanevich**, Arlene. *Pig William*; written and illus. by Arlene Dubanevich. Bradbury, 1985. ISBN 0-02-733200-4. 28p. $12.95.

3-5 yrs.   This book is silly, in the best sense of the word. Pig William is one of those chronic dawdlers, dubbed "turkey toe" by his brothers but undaunted in his pursuit of stalling. He chases butterflies, makes faces in the mirror, paints his body, submerges in the tub, tells stories to fish, and misses the bus to the picnic in Porky Park. Never mind; he and the fish set up a game of catch in the back yard, the others return home after a brief rainstorm closes out the picnic, and Pig William wins the day with his unquenchable sense of play. The pictures elaborate Pig William's distractions; flat pen-and-ink drawings filled with exuberant colors of yellow, purple, red, mint green, and turquoise are often laid out in comic format (the text is entirely ballooned dialogue) but completely without clutter. In fact there is a strong sense of design and pattern throughout. Details such as William's rainbow colored coonskin cap and his fish, which resembles nothing more than a pink baby Jaws, are as imaginative as William. Every child will recognize something of him or herself here.

257   **Duder**, Tessa. *Jellybean*. Viking, 1986. ISBN 0-670-81235-8. 112p $9.95.

5-8   Geraldine, nicknamed Jellybean, lives with her mother and her mother's cello, very often in conflict with the latter. Concerts, rehearsals, and trio work crowd out their time together and often leave Geraldine in the company of various babysitters. The story begins one night when the sitter fails to show up and Geraldine must accompany her mother to a restaurant where she is scheduled to perform. There appears a stranger who sits at Geraldine's table, seems to know her already, and shows up again at an orchestra rehearsal. Geraldine first suspects he is her father, but it turns out he is an old friend of her mother's come to renew their courtship and his own musical career. In the meantime, he wrests from Geraldine her secret ambition to be a conductor and proves to be the friend she needs so desperately to relieve her loneliness. The writing here is beautifully crafted ("the harpist is already in her seat, dropping icicles of sound into the silence"), the characters are closely portrayed, the scenes intensely played. Particularly vivid are the passages of Geraldine experiencing certain pieces of music, as in the section where she listens to the Nutcracker Suite from her hiding place in a corner of the orchestra pit. Although the setting is Auckland, New Zealand, the novel has immediate appeal by virtue of its depth and development.

258   **Duder**, Tessa. *In Lane Three, Alex Archer*. Houghton, 1989. ISBN 0-395-50927-0. 176p. $13.95.

7-10   Alexandra, the narrator, is fifteen, and as a serious contender for the New Zealand swim team she hopes to take part in the 1960 Olympics. The author (a winner of an Empire Games silver medal) gives just enough detail about training to give the story color, but not so much that it swamps the narrative. Despite the handicap of very small print, this is a very readable story: the convincing first-person voice gives immediacy, the main thread of the plot (the rivalry between Alex and another swimmer) is balanced by a tender love story and warm family relations, and the writing has both cohesion and momentum.

259   **Dunlop**, Eileen. *Clementina*. Holiday House, 1987. ISBN 0-8234-0642-3. 156p. $12.95.

6-9   First published in Great Britain, this is a novel in which the realistic and the supernatural are deftly blended and in which the consistency of viewpoint, establishment of setting, and interplay of characters are impressive. Daisy, the protagonist, is thirteen when she goes with her best friend Bridget Graham to spend a month in a Scottish vacation community. Mrs. Graham has invited another guest, Clementina, an older girl from a Children's Home. The events of the past seem, to a frightened Daisy, to be influencing a path toward tragedy that is a repetition of the tragic history of a local family. Question: is Clementina a reincarnation of an 18th century girl of the same name? Despite some moments of lagging, the tension and suspense carry the story along admirably.

260   **Dunlop**, Eileen. *The House on the Hill*. Holiday House, 1987. ISBN 0-8234-0658-X. 147p. $12.95.

5-7
*
While his mother was taking a nursing course in London, Philip was sent (sulking) to stay with elderly great aunt Jane in Glasgow. He didn't expect to like Jane or his cousin Susan, also staying with their great aunt. Dunlop is without peer as a writer whose blending of realism and fantasy is seamlessly smooth. The mysterious light in an empty room is the first clue the children have of a strange secret in the old house, and the development of that mystery emerges against a background of fine characterization, strong but subtle changes in relationships, and a logical ending for both the fantasy theme and the real-life matrix.

261   **Dunrea**, Olivier. *Deep Down Underground*; written and illus. by Olivier Dunrea. Macmillan, 1989. ISBN 0-02-732861-9. 32p. $13.95.

4-6 yrs.   "Deep down underground / 1 wee moudiewort digs and digs," setting up a rhythmic counting-rhyme cumulation of 2 earthworms, 3 beetles, 4 caterpillars, 5 spiders, 6 toads, 7 mice, 8 garter snakes, 9 sow bugs, and 10 ants. These creatures variously patter and chatter, burrow and scrape, scooch and scrunch, scurry and scamper, wriggle and wrangle, etc., until they are STOPPED (backwards, one by one) when the moudiewort (Scottish for mole) sneezes. Dunrea has infiltrated the underground with all the things children love to look for, from bones and fossils to odd rocks, arrowheads, and lost objects that will be fun to find and identify along with the numbering game. Especially appealing to linger over with small groups or in a one-on-one session, this will open the doorway to environmental discussion as well as reinforcing basic arithmetic concepts. The watercolor illustrations, inventively designed with bright-hued creatures against an earth-tone background, manage to repeat motifs without becoming boring. It's a spacious maze under those roots—children will want to tunnel right down there and look around.

262   **Durell**, Ann, comp. *The Diane Goode Book of American Folk Tales & Songs*; illus. by Diane Goode. Dutton, 1989. ISBN 0-525-44458-0. 64p. $14.95.

2-6   A first-rate collection to look at, listen to, and learn, this features seven
       favorite songs for which you can never remember all the words and
       nine fine-tuned traditional stories from various parts of the U.S. Davy
       Crockett, the knee-high Man (Black American), Coyote (Pueblo), the
       twist-mouth family (New England), the greedy wife (Puerto Rico), and
       three girls with journeycakes (Appalachia) make an appearance in the
       stories, which range in tone from down-home funny to suspenseful.
       Yankee Doodle, Buffalo Gal, Billy Boy, Clementine, and others star in
       the songs, which are accompanied by melody lines and full verses.
       The folklore is not watered down, and storytellers will be glad to find in
       "The Coyote and the Bear" a variant of the Jack tale "How Bobtail
       Beat the Devil," in "The Talking Mule" a variant of the talking potato
       or turnip, and other cross-cultural motifs. Diane Goode's illustrations
       on every page are polished in drafting and composition. She relies,
       appropriately, on earth tones, with fine crosshatch for texture and
       shading. Her characters are cleverly caricatured without becoming
       slapstick, and the bordered book design is decorative without
       becoming exaggerated. A prime pick for family or elementary-grade
       entertainment.

263   **Edwards**, Pat. *Little John and Plutie*. Houghton, 1988. ISBN 0-395-
       48223-2. 172p. $13.95.

4-6   In a story set in the rural South in 1897, Little John (age ten) moves,
       with his angry mother, to town to live with Gran. Daddy had gotten
       drunk and lost all the money he'd taken to Memphis so he could buy
       mules. That was how Little John met Plutie, two years older and black
       and bright, Little John's first real friend. The stories of the friendship
       and of John's family are smoothly fused, and Edwards writes percep-
       tively of racial conflict, of prejudice on both sides, and of the integrity
       and compassion that could, at times, supersede prejudice, even in the
       South, even in 1897. The characterization is strong, shaped by dialogue
       as well as exposition, the ending credible: Plutie gets in trouble, Daddy
       lends a hand, John loves them both.

264   **Ehlert**, Lois. *Eating the Alphabet: Fruits and Vegetables from A to Z;*
       written and illus. by Lois Ehlert. Harcourt, 1989. ISBN 0-15-224435-2.
       32p. $13.95.

4-6 yrs. A delicious way to practise letters, identify foods, and experience
       colors, this picture book begins "Apple to Zucchini, / come take a
       look. / Start eating your way/ through this alphabet book." The
       illustrations and book design are tantalizing, from endpapers that
       feature miniature rows of fruit and vegetable icons, to a title page with
       a funny face made of fruits and vegetables, to spacious spreads
       overflowing with both the common and the unusual: "A a" shows
       apricots, artichokes, avocados, asparagi, and apples. Endive, fig,

Indian corn, jalapeno, jicama, kiwifruit, kohlrabi, kumquat, leek, mango, papaya, persimmon, pomegranate, quince, radicchio, rutabaga, star fruit, swiss chard, ugli fruit, vegetable marrow, and xigua all make surprise appearances amidst familiar bananas, cabbages, potatoes, and strawberries. All letters and words are presented in both upper and lower case. There are a few pictures that may defy identification: the cauliflower is too stylized to be realistic, and the huckleberries look just like the blueberries, but the total aesthetic effect is so satisfying as to make these minor quibbles indeed. A glossary of fruits and vegetables in the book gives pronunciation and botanical information on each. A fabulous advertisement for natural foods as well as for appetizing words.

265   Ehlert, Lois. *Feathers for Lunch*; written and illus. by Lois Ehlert. Harcourt, 1990. ISBN 0-15-230550-5. 34p. $13.95.

4-7 yrs.   At least as far as cats are concerned, this one's just as tasty as the illustrator's *Growing Vegetable Soup* and *Eating the Alphabet* . The cat's on the loose ("his food in a can is tame and mild, so he's gone out for something wild"), stalking through a gorgeous garden of collage-and-paint flowers to catch the robin, blue jay, house wren, etc., that live there. Picture books rarely acknowledge so bluntly the predatory instinct, although most kids will be relieved to find that in this story, "cats can't fly and they can't soar, and birds know what their wings are for." Like the flowers, Ehlert's birds are vividly stylized with no loss to the accuracy of their depiction—according to an author's note, all the birds are pictured life-sized. Page design is bold, clean, and witty, and kids will enjoy the printed sound effects ("O-KA-LEE O-KA-LEE") as much as they will like finding the cat amidst the camouflage. A picture glossary of "the lunch that got away" is appended. Yummy.

266   Ehrlich, Amy, ad. *Random House Book of Fairy Tales*; illus. by Diane Goode. Random House, 1985. Library ed. ISBN 0-394-95693-1; Trade ed. ISBN 0-394-85693-7. 208p. Library ed. $14.99; Trade ed. $14.95.

3-6   Ehrlich has chosen nineteen tales, primarily from the Grimm, Perrault, and Andersen collections, capably retelling some of the most familiar fairy tales is a direct and simple style. The book is profusely illustrated, with full color and black and white alternating in double-page spreads. The color is soft, usually pastel, and blends comic and romantic details deftly; the black and white pictures are even softer, with an almost hazy look, gray-toned and never sharp in line.

267   Ehrlich, Amy. *The Story of Hanukkah*; illus. by Ori Sherman. Dial, 1989. Library ed. ISBN 0-8037-0616-2; Trade ed. ISBN 0-8037-0615-4. 26p. Library ed. $14.89; Trade ed. $14.95.

5-8 yrs.   A notable Hanukkah picture book combines cohesive storytelling with distinguished art. Ori Sherman's work is characterized by a collage effect of strongly colored shapes and patterns, often stylized with Jewish and Middle Eastern motifs. The effect is monumental enough to support but not overwhelm the account of the Maccabee revolt and the miracle of light for the rededicated temple. Neither didactic nor condescending, this companion to *The Four Questions* by Lynne Schwartz and Ori Sherman maintains aesthetic respect for a traditional celebration.

268   **Ehrlich**, Amy. *Where It Stops, Nobody Knows.* Dial, 1988. ISBN 0-8037-0575-1. 212p. $14.95.

6-9   Nina is the narrator, a young adolescent who is increasingly puzzled by her mother's behavior. Why do the two of them keep moving from one town to another, back and forth across the country? Why is Nina told not to let any friends know where she is after each move? Then there's the $16,000 Joyce has hidden—stolen, she says—which may be an explanation for their repeated flights. And then the suspicion that Joyce is not her mother's real name. Ehrlich does a fine job of building suspense and adding clues, and she's equally adept at portraying the intricacies of the relationship between Joyce and Nina, especially as trust is eroded but never love. Thus the poignant ending is believable, for Nina has then joined the parents from whom "Joyce" had kidnapped her (in the hospital, when she was a three-day-old infant) and Nina visits her in prison. Trenchant and touching.

269   **Elkington**, John. *Going Green: A Kid's Handbook to Saving the Planet*; by John Elkington and others; illus. by Tony Ross. Tilden/Puffin, 1990. Paper ed. ISBN 0-14-034597-3. 111p. Paper ed. $8.95.

3-6   A readable handbook is divided into sections that explain major environmental problems, suggest procedures for a "green audit" to see what each reader can do at home or school, describe A-to-Z ideas, and list useful books and organizations for more information. The authors strike a good balance between realistic discussion and encouraging advice. Their insistence that each individual has the power to decide and do something ("Refuse, Reuse, and Recycle") about the serious pollution problems delineated in the text will inspire young readers not only to new awareness, but also to meaningful practices, even on a small scale—switching from juice boxes to thermos bottles, for instance. Ross' abundant, full-color cartoons are funny without being condescending. Lively, accessible, and practical, this should be required reading for children and adults together.

270   **Ellis**, Sarah. *A Family Project.* McElderry, 1988. ISBN 0-689-51444-6. 137p. $11.95.

6-8   Eleven-year-old Jessica does a school project in preparation for the coming of her new baby sister, whom she and her two older brothers anticipate and welcome with enthusiasm. Jessica, in fact, has a special touch with baby Lucie, and she is shattered when Lucie is a victim of crib death. This is a story of a family—already changed by the oldest son's departure and stressed by the second son's rebellious adolescence—pulling through a crisis that traumatizes the mother to the point where she can hardly function. Although Jessica's point of view is consistently maintained, each complex character develops in a different way, which makes the novel an ambitious one. There are a few points when the mother's rigidity is perhaps overemphasized (she often talks in capital letters), and the tenant downstairs seems one character too many. In general, however, the cast is subtly portrayed, especially the rebellious brother, and there are some memorable scenes that will touch young readers with a realization of the resilience that is crucial in a loving family.

271   **Ellis**, Sarah. *Next-Door Neighbors.* McElderry, 1990. ISBN 0-689-50495-0. 160p. $13.95.

4-7   It's 1957, and Peggy's family has just moved from the country to Vancouver, where her father has been named minister in a local church. Peggy is twelve (although her behavior and thinking sometimes seem like those of a younger child) and painfully self-conscious; her brave but misbegotten attempt to make friends at school results in ostracism. "Nobody really looked at Peggy. They all just moved in and began to whisper." She does find friendship with two unlikely neighbors: George, a younger boy whose family immigrated from Russia; and Sing, the gardener and "houseboy" of Mrs. Manning, whose good manners barely manage to disguise a cold and bigoted heart. "The thing is that Sing's room is in the basement. Mrs. Manning has a bolt on the door going down there from the kitchen. She locks it at night." The theme of prejudicial scapegoating is confidently woven into an essentially optimistic school-and-family story, with neither characterization nor plot succumbing to didacticism. Plenty of gentle humor, an open and inviting style, and a young heroine both exasperating and admirable recommend this to a wide audience.

272   **Ernst**, Lisa Campbell. *Ginger Jumps*; written and illus. by Lisa Campbell Ernst. Bradbury, 1990. ISBN 0-02-733565-8. 34p. $14.95.

4-8 yrs.   While Ginger the circus dog enjoys performing, what she really wants is a family "with a little girl who had time to play with someone who loves her." Ginger hopes that being in the spotlight for a scary new stunt will find her a family, but her fear of heights keeps her grounded. Top dog Prunella takes her place: "'I'm the only star of this show,' she said, smirking. 'No mutt will ever take my place.'" But Ginger finally manages her leap of faith—right into the arms of the perfect little girl. From the first double-page spread of a lonely, underfoot Ginger to the last of girl and dog united, this is a classic orphan tale, its sentimentality checked by the festive setting and Ginger's own forthrightness, as she selflessly replaces a nonplussed Prunella in the (sabotaged) stunt: "Dashing for the steps, Ginger knocked her aside." Accented with glowing yellow highlights, the large-scale painting are drawn from perspectives both dog's-eye and dizzying. Ginger herself is small, round, and dauntless.

273   **Ernst**, Lisa Campbell, illus. *Up to Ten and Down Again.* Lothrop, 1986. Library ed. ISBN 0-688-04542-1; Trade ed. ISBN 0-688-04541-3. 38p. Library ed. $10.88; Trade ed. $10.25.

2-5 yrs.   There's always room for one more, when a counting book fulfills almost every requirement as a teaching tool. Here a pair of adults and a group of children go on a picnic, play with dogs, get caught in a rainstorm; the tale begins with a single duck who watches all the activity and then as ten clouds appear watches the countdown scurry. The colors in the framed pictures are a bit sugary, but young children should enjoy the situation, the constant action, and the cumulation while they correlate the digits with the countable objects in each double-page spread.

274   **Esbensen**, Barbara Juster. *Great Northern Diver: The Loon*; illus. by Mary Barrett Brown. Little, 1990. ISBN 0-316-24954-8. [32p]. $14.95.

5-8 yrs.   A prime readaloud to accompany storytelling sessions featuring Native American legends or a film showing of *The Loon's Necklace*, this is a smooth natural history narrative in picture book format. Handsome paintings dramatize a text describing the loon's biannual migrations, striking plumage, eerie calls, and territorial, flight, breeding, and feeding patterns. Both author and artist walk the fine line between aesthetics and information: in spite of her lyrical style, Esbensen never tips the factual balance by becoming self-indulgently poetic, and Brown satisfies viewers with eye-catching landscapes that maintain accuracy of botanical and avian detail. The brief opening free verse and the concluding depiction of a snow-filled nest at night are examples of inspired nonfiction for the young.

275   **Esbensen**, Barbara Juster. *Words with Wrinkled Knees: Animal Poems*; illus. by John Stadler. Crowell, 1986. Library ed. ISBN 0-690-04505-0; Trade ed. ISBN 0-690-04504-2. 44p. Library ed. $11.89; Trade ed. $11.95.

2-5   A witty collection of 21 poems wordplays on the sounds of each
subject's name, as in the title lines about "ELEPHANT/ He must have
invented it/ himself. This is a lumbering/ gray word the ears of it / are
huge and flap like loose/ wings a word with/ wrinkled knees and toes/
like boxing gloves." Many of the verses manage to be as meaningful a
comment on language as on creatures. "If/ there is anything/ dead/
in these lines/ CROW/ will pick its bones/ clean." On a sense level,
these poems will appeal to children the way narrative poetry does; on
a sensory level, the sound, imagery, and tonal variation hold appeal:
"Splat! The word lands wet/ and squat/ upon the page FROG." The
black and white drawings are sometimes as inventive as the poems, as
in the snake slithering through the "s" keys of the typewriter, the
shadowy wolf, or the black silhouetted crow; but they sometimes seem
flat or awkward, as in the elephant's charge or the human figure in the
giraffe picture. Overall, though, this is a verbal treat with visual
highlights.

276   **Etra**, Jonathan. *Aliens for Breakfast*; by Jonathan Etra and Stephanie
Spinner; illus. by Steve Björkman. Random House, 1988. Library ed.
ISBN 0-394-92093-7; Paper ed. ISBN 0-394-82093-2. 64p. (Stepping
Stone Books). Library ed. $5.99; Paper ed. $1.95.

3-5   Perfect, smiling Dorf "was cool." But what the rest of the class,
*   excepting Richard Bickerstaff, doesn't know is that Dorf is an *alien*,
specifically, a Drane. "Space trash. Mean. Very mean. When the
Dranes see a planet they like they move in. Before the natives know it,
their minds are mush." Richard knows all this because Aric, a
Ganoobian member of the Interspace Brigade ("Our goal: to wipe out
cosmic trouble-makers") has popped up one morning in Richard's
bowl of Alien Crisp. This appears to have been written by people who
spent more Saturday mornings in front of the TV than was really good
for them, but the book is a thoroughly off-the-wall delight, crammed
with one-liners ("bye-bye, biosphere") and pseudo-sick humor. It
features a spectacular demise for Dorf: "'I hate to lose! I hope you
flunk math and history! I hope you fail science and art and social
studies and English and gym!' Then he blew up." Few transitional
readers have such wit to exploit the comic potential of the short
sentence; material and delivery both have enormous appeal.
Björkman's nutty and plentiful sketches are a definite plus.

277   **Evitts**, William J. *Captive Bodies, Free Spirits: The Story of Southern
Slavery.* Messner, 1985. ISBN 0-671-54094-7. 144p. $9.79.

6-9   This history of black slavery in the southern U.S. strikes a good
balance between individual stories and examination of the general
picture of conditions and laws. The opener is a harrowing escape tale,
and indeed, the book stresses throughout how determined were the

efforts of blacks to gain their freedom, or failing that, to resist domination by "a contest of wills." Various aspects of the slave trade, the enforced work patterns, the systematic destruction of family units, runaways, revolts, the work of white abolitionists, and blacks' fighting in the Civil War get evenhanded treatment in a readable format punctuated by historical drawings and photographs.

278   Evslin, Bernard. *Jason and the Argonauts;* illus. by Bert Dodson. Morrow, 1986. ISBN 0-688-06245-8. 165p. $13.00.

7-12   With tautly ironic style, Evslin details the story of Jason's adventures: the infant prince's escape from a murderous uncle who killed his father to become king; the young man's emergence from a boyhood on the island of Cythera under protection of Venus; and the hero's voyage of maturation to obtain the Golden Fleece and regain his rightful throne. Ekion, son of Hermes, tells the story, and most of it centers on the quest of the Argo and its crew of champions. Pollux' combat with brutal king Amycus is memorable, as is Jason's marriage to Medea and escape from the giant serpent guarding the Fleece. A vivid voyage for students interested in mythology, classics, or sturdy adventure.

279   Farber, Norma, ed. *These Small Stones;* ed. by Norma Farber and Myra Cohn Livingston. Harper, 1987. Library ed. ISBN 0-06-024014-8; Trade ed. ISBN 0-06-024013-X. 84p. Library ed. $11.89; Trade ed. $11.95.

4-6   An imaginative idea with innate child appeal has benefitted from two
 *   dedicated poets' simmering of selections over several years. These are 60 poems about small things "In my Hand," "On the Ground," "In the Air," "Outside," "On the Table," or as "A Piece of It All." The organization is arbitrary: the first section treats of marbles (Valerie Worth), matches (X.J. Kennedy), and jumping beans (Mary Ann Hoberman); the second sings of sandpipers (Charlotte Zolotow) and beach stones (Lilian Moore); the third celebrates fireflies (Elizabeth Madox Roberts), mosquitoes (Jose Emilio Pacheco), etc. What lifts the anthology above the average is the number of poems with that ineffable quality of verbal surprise that arrests a reader and sends him or her back again for an immediate second reading. There is also a thoughtful balance in tone, technique, and cultural context. Several poets are represented at their simplest but best: Lillian Morrison in "Burning Bright," Julia Cunningham in "Little Bird," and Livingston herself in "Math Class." Her afterword discusses the development of the work before Norma Farber's death. Children who "study the lives on a leaf" will find a kindred voice in Theodore Roethke's description or, again, in Pablo Neruda's assertion, "Fleas interest me so much.... "

280   **Faville**, Barry. *Stanley's Aquarium*. Oxford, 1990. ISBN 0-19-558197-0.
152p. $14.95.

9-
*

In this unusual and introspective horror story from New Zealand,
narrator Robyn Kemp takes a job mowing lawns for Mr. and Mrs.
Stanley Swinton and finds the eccentric Mr. Swinton devoted to his
collection of piranhas ("'I always like the blood to drain out of the
meat' he said. 'It helps to liven up the feeding ritual'"). Stanley says
he's been selectively breeding the "pug-nosed Draculas with fins"—
Robyn's term—to produce predatory fish who can exist in the cold
waters of the local and tourist-ridden lake. Robyn's resemblance to
Stanley's lost daughter leads the old man to become obsessed with
her (to the point of a pathetic—and insufficiently explained—physical
overture) as well, whereupon the plot takes several surprising and
threatening twists and progresses with sinister tranquility to its
ominous end. The action here is psychological, not physical; the book
starts slowly and unfolds with a measured but relentless pace through
the narration of its wary and humorous young protagonist. This is a
highly literate (and literary—Coleridge's "Kubla Khan" figures
prominently), atmospheric novel that should appeal not only to horror
fans ready for a more Hitchcockian approach, but also to serious
readers in general.

281   **Fenton**, Edward. *The Morning of the Gods*. Delacorte, 1987. ISBN 0-
385-29550-2. 184p. $14.95.

6-8

The time is the 1970's, when Greece was ruled by a tyrannical junta;
the setting is the small village where Carla Lewis, 12, has come for a
long stay with her great-aunt and great-uncle, Tiggie (Antigone) and
Theo, who had raised her orphaned mother. Adjusting to her mother's
recent death, Carla emotionally embraces all the things her mother
had told her about. This would stand up as a story about family
relationships and adaptability, but Fenton gives the reader far more.
Incorporated into the picture of village life are subtle (and some
deliberately less subtle) comments on the political situation and the
dangers to those who work against it. Boldly, but believably, Carla
helps save a poet who is a national hero from the military. Another
dimension is added by the linking of many of the characters to figures
in the Greek Pantheon. It's been a long time between Fenton books,
and this is worth the waiting.

282   **Fields**, Julia. *The Green Lion of Zion Street*; illus. by Jerry Pinkney.
McElderry, 1988. ISBN 0-689-50414-4. 27p. $13.95.

K-3

In her first book for children, poet Julia Fields uses the voice of a child
to reflect the feelings of a group of children towards the majesty and
mystery of a sculptured lion. The lines, which use some of the idioms
of Black speech, are impressionistic, vividly expressing the children's

pleasure in using their imaginations as well as in working up a pleasurable fright in a safe situation. Occasionally, the power and impact of the writing flag to admit a flat word or phrase, but for the most part this is a bright poetic narrative. Pinkney's paintings are deft: children huddled against the cold penetration of a foggy morning, the lion looming blank-eyed and massive in the gray day.

283   Fine, Anne. *Alias Madame Doubtfire.* Little, 1988. ISBN 0-316-28313-4. 199p. $12.95.

5-
*

Novels about divorce for children are rarely funny; here's one that will have readers laughing from the first page. Lydia, Christopher, and little Natalie have arrived, for their regular Tuesday tea with Dad, carrying yet another letter from Mom ("'Aha!' he cried. 'Another missive from the Poisoned Pen. How *is* your mother, anyway?'") which, as usual, says she'll have to cut the children's next visit short, and which, also as usual, the children have already opened and read. "It came under their general heading of self-defense." Mom (Miranda) has also decided to employ an after-school housekeeper; in the hope of seeing more of his children, Dad (Daniel), a usually out-of-work actor, manages to get the job—by getting up in drag as the magnificent and sublimely capable dowager Madame Doubtfire. The kids catch on quick and are at first gleeful for Daniel's company and the harmless (they think) deception, but then comes a remarkable scene when Miranda, believing she has a friendly ear, spills all her anger at Daniel to Madame. The children join in, at first playfully, and then with barely disguised malice aim their own darts at the helpless target. While Daniel gets most of the good lines ("'Fractions are useful,' Daniel told his son. 'Nobody ever gets all they want out of life.'") it gradually becomes apparent that this wit is also his weakness, a carelessness that can hurt his children. Miranda, at first seeming a cold career woman, is equally revealed as a mother who works terribly hard at her job and family. This novel is a special combination of high humor and genuine pain (the first often expressing the second), showing, ironically and perfectly, in this "broken home" the bonds of shared history and love that keep a family together.

284   Fine, Anne. *My War with Goggle-Eyes.* Joy Street/Little, 1989. ISBN 0-316-28314-2. 166p. $13.95.

5-9   Anne Fine writes some of the funniest—and truest—family fight scenes to be found. Kitty's room is a bit, well, disorganized. Or, as mother's boyfriend Gerald (nicknamed Goggle-eyes by Kitty for the way he looks at mother's legs) prefers, the room is *disgusting*. "He put his foot in it right there. It was quite clear from the expression on Mum's face that, for the moment, she had heard enough from Gerald Faulkner about his views on natty housekeeping." But Gerald is tenacious, pointing out to Mum that her defence of Kitty is "utter baloney," and soon Mum is completely taken in. "'Take care, Gerald,' she giggled. 'Mind what you say! You'll end up in terrible trouble with Kitty.'" That's just one skirmish in an on-going war; perhaps even more pointed is the scene where staunch conservative Gerald accompanies Kitty, little sister Judith, and Mum to an anti-nuclear demonstration witnessed only by the police ("It's not as easy as you might think to get arrested") and some sheep. Contemptuous of their politics as he is, Gerald nevertheless takes Kitty and Jude home when Mum is arrested, and Kitty finds herself beginning to love him. In a benignly barbed family comedy peppered with Hepburn-and-Tracy repartee, readers will empathize with Kitty's step-by-step acceptance of Gerald while at the same time finding this self-described "boring" man magnetically charming from the start.

285   Finkelstein, Norman H. *The Other 1492: Jewish Settlement in the New World*. Scribner's, 1989. ISBN 0-684-18913-5. 100p. illus. with photographs. $12.95.

7-12   This history of Sephardic Jews and Marranos offers a counterview to the lionization of Ferdinand and Isabella's support for Columbus. The year 1492 marked not only the "new world" exploration that was financed heavily by Jewish backers, but also the expulsion of Jews from Spain after five centuries of cultural absorption. Finkelstein's accounts of mob persecution, forced conversion, and Inquisition tragedies are carefully researched and never overdramatic, though the stories of chief figures such as Torquemada and Abravanel are more involving than fiction. The writing is clear, smooth, and well-organized. After a thorough background occupying half the book, the author concentrates on Spanish Jews' determined efforts to settle Brazil as well as North America. With so many books currently emphasizing the fate of Ashkenazis around World War II, this offers more unusual perspective on the Jewish role in a major movement of world history. Accompanied by a solid bibliography of books and articles, the text is illustrated with historical engravings and paintings.

286   Fischer-Nagel, Heiderose. *Inside the Burrow: The Life of the Golden Hamster*; written and illus. with photographs by Heiderose and Andreas Fischer-Nagel. Carolrhoda, 1986. ISBN 0-87614-286-2. 43p. $12.95.

2-4   Like the Fischer-Nagel team's other books on animals, this examination of the Golden Hamster combines brilliantly clear color photography with an impersonal, informational text. The closeups are particularly intriguing because so many of the hamster's activities are out of sight in its burrow, exposed here for views of sleeping, storage, and "bathroom" areas, all connected by tunnels. The birth sequence is absorbing in pictorial clarity, as are the scenes following the growth and development of the offspring. Other facts include background on general behavior patterns of the species and tips on pet care.

287   **Fisher**, Leonard Everett. *Ellis Island: Gateway to the New World*. Holiday House, 1986. ISBN 0-8234-0612-1. 64p. (illus. with photographs). $12.95.

5-7   Profusely illustrated with photographs and with the author-artist's handsome scratchboard drawings, this is a detailed history of the island in Upper New York Bay that eventually came to be called Ellis Island. it served for many years as the entry point for immigrants, and it is this aspect that Fisher stresses, describing the laws that affected immigrants and the procedures that were used to screen and process them. Always a fine artist and a dependably accurate writer, Fisher serves here, as he has done in many of the earlier books about facets of American life, as a social historian. A map and an index are included.

288   **Fisher**, Leonard Everett. *The Great Wall of China;* written and illus. by Leonard Everett Fisher. Macmillan, 1986. ISBN 0-02-735220-X. 31p. $11.95.

3-5   This is a big story for small children to absorb, but Fisher has done his
*   best to scale the text down to a primary-level student's grasp of time and place, channeling the real impact through monumentally scaled paintings in shades of black, white, and gray. These are page-filling, boldly textured pictures that do not stint on the drama and hardship that went into the making of Ch'in Shih Huang Ti's great wall, built with forced labor to keep out Mongol invaders. The emperor's merciless determination is reflected through the suffering of the masses of workers affected by it, including the "whining son" whom he scorns. A front map shows the location and length of the wall, and a concluding note summarizes the later history of the wall and gives translations of the Chinese characters edging each page spread. Especially effective for children who have had some supplementary background study of China.

289   **Fisher**, Leonard Everett. *Pyramid of the Sun, Pyramid of the Moon;* written and illus. by Leonard Everett Fisher. Macmillan, 1988. ISBN 0-02-735300-1. 32p. $13.95.

4-6   In a format similar to that of *The Great Wall of China* and *The Tower of London*, Fisher continues an effective series with a history of the Teotihuacan pyramids in the Valley of Mexico. While the text describes the sequential cultures of the Toltecs, Chichimecs, and Aztecs, shadowy paintings in black, white, and gray—punctuated with brick-red symbols—depict events and ceremonies of monumental

grandeur. The book has an abstract quality, which is just as well for
dealing with the cruelties that marked the Aztec sacrifice of prisoners
and the Spaniards' destruction of Montezuma's city, Tenochtitlan. A
dramatic, well-designed introduction.

290   **Fisher**, Leonard Everett, ad. *Theseus and the Minotaur;* ad. and illus.
by Leonard Everett Fisher. Holiday House, 1988. ISBN 0-8234-0703-9.
32p. $14.95.

5-8 yrs.   Fisher's paintings, styled in monumental proportions, somber colors,
and simple compositions, are well suited to a Greek tale of heroic
deeds and death. A map traces Theseus' journeys from Troezen to
Athens to Knossos to Naxos and back, after which each double spread
focuses on a crucial scene. Suspense is built by shadowy textures
glinting with occasional flashes of thick white light: Theseus' sword,
Aegus' beard, the bones of the Minotaur's victims, the monster's
horns, the moon above the ship. Fisher has also done a careful job of
selecting and consolidating various versions, for which he cites
sources in the beginning. An impressive meeting of myth and picture
book.

291   **Fisher**, Leonard Everett. *The Wailing Wall;* written and illus. by
Leonard Everett Fisher. Macmillan, 1989. ISBN 0-02-735310-9. 32p.
$14.95.

2-4   In a format similar to *The Great Wall of China* and others in this
series, Fisher gives a trenchant account of the 4,000-year history of the
site sacred to Jews because of Abraham's covenant, the Tabernacle,
the First Temple, and the Second Temple, of which the Wailing Wall
is a western section. A chronology (1900 B.C.-1967 A.D.) and map at the
beginning of the book outline time and place, while the black-and-
white, rough-stroked paintings project massive shifts of history—
usually violent, in battles for possession of the area. The war between
Moslems and Jews is compacted into a kind of afterword ("More
About the Wailing Wall"), an understandable way to avoid
controversy and to maintain perspective on the ancient reaches of the
story. With characteristic ingenuity of design, Fisher has displayed
symbols on each page to represent Jewish, Babylonian, Persian,
Greek, Roman, Christian, and Islamic dominance. A solid addition to
a landmark series.

292   **Fleischman**, Paul. *Coming-and-Going Men;* illus. by Randy Gaul.
Harper, 1985. Library ed. ISBN 0-06-021884-3; Trade ed. ISBN 0-06-
021883-5. 147p. Library ed. $10.89; Trade ed. $11.50.

6-9   In four linked stories, a procession of traveling men (salesmen or
showmen) visits the small town of New Canaan, Vermont; each is
profoundly affected by his encounters there and some make a deep

impression on at least one of the residents. The subtle humor, the
extravagance that is not quite exaggeration, and the sharp eye for
human foibles that Fleischman has shown in other books are in a
flourishing state here, particularly in the first story, in which the
silhouette cutter Mr. Snype is also hunting for the Devil as he travels,
knowing that Satan casts no shadow from which a silhouette could be
cut. At the same time, the young girl spotted by Snype as the essence
of honesty and goodness becomes increasingly sure that Mr. Snype is
Satan. Period details (the year is 1800) are convincing, the language
and the concepts of the characters are appropriate for the time and
place, and the writing style is honed and polished in a book that is
enjoyable almost as much for its style as for its story.

293   **Fleischman**, Paul. *I Am Phoenix: Poems for Two Voices*; illus. by Ken
Nutt. Harper, 1985. Library ed. ISBN 0-06-021882-7; Trade ed. ISBN 0-
06-021881-9. 51p. Library ed. $10.89; Trade ed. $11.50.

6-   Devotés of the almost lost art of choral reading should be among the
first to appreciate this collection of poems designed for reading aloud
by two voices. Printed in script form, the selections, all of which are
about birds, have a cadenced pace and dignified flow; their combination of imaginative imagery and realistic detail is echoed by the
combination of stylized fantasy and representational drawings in the
black and white pictures, all soft line and strong nuance. An exciting
book.

294   **Fleischman**, Paul. *Joyful Noise: Poems for Two Voices*; illus. by Eric
Beddows. Harper, 1988. Library ed. ISBN 0-06-021853-3; Trade ed.
ISBN 0-06-021852-5. 44p. Library ed. $11.89; Trade ed. $11.95.

4-6   A companion volume to *I Am Phoenix*, this includes 14 poems for two
voices. All of the poems focus on insects, their movements, voices,
appearance, and metaphoric significance. One of the best is "Digger
Wasp," narrated by the female as she digs a protective nest for the
young she will never see (my young will/ know me well./ When they
care/ for their own children"). There's lots of humor: a book louse
begins, "I was born in a / fine old edition of Schiller." "Whirligig
Beetles" has the same frenetic quality as the bugs' movements, which
are also captured by pencil drawings swirling around the page. Some
of the poems make better use of two voices than others; in "Honey-
bees," for instance, there is an amusing back-and-forth between a
worker and a queen which ends in a simultaneous chant, "Truly, a
bee's is the/ worst (best)/ of all lives." The poems are of necessity
simple on the page, but the sound effects are playful and the dual
voice form is a natural for sociable children who want to share the
joyful noise of reading aloud.

295   Fleischman, Paul. *Saturnalia*. Zolotow/Harper, 1990. Library ed.
ISBN 0-06-021913-0; Trade ed. ISBN 0-06-021912-2. 128p. Library ed.
$12.89; Trade ed. $12.95.

7-10   A wicked humor informs this stern tale set in the "tombstone-cracking
cold" of colonial Boston. William, the printer Charles Currie's brilliant
fourteen-year-old apprentice, is an Indian, and thus a thorn in the side
of Mr. Baggot, local tithing-man, zealot, and sneak. In fact, Mr. Baggot
regards the entire Currie family with suspicion: although assured that
the family does not celebrate the "reeking" holiday of Christmas,
Baggot has heard they indulge in the far more pagan festivity of
Saturnalia, the day on which masters and servants trade places.
Several sets of masters and servants people the story, with pratfalls
provided by the wigmaker Mr. Hogwood and his conceited
manservant Malcolm, both courting ladies and disaster. While
William has a good situation, he still searches for his Narraganset
family, finally finding his great-uncle and a cousin living in abusive
slavery. The writing here is dense and complex, but the antique styling
has a read-aloud rhythm that complements the steady storytelling.

296   Fleischman, Sid. *The Midnight Horse*; illus. by Peter Sis. Greenwillow,
1990. ISBN 0-688-09441-4. 84p. $12.95.

4-6   Every ingredient appropriate to a fantasy adventure with Gothic
overtones and a romantic base has been included by the author. An
orphan boy, a charming heroine (about to be bilked out of her
heritage by a curmudgeon who also is prepared to cheat the orphan),
a rascal, and a ghost who is also a magician. How this remains credible
is a mystery, the solution of which can be attributed only to Fleischman's gift for keeping derring-do in proportion and leavening
melodrama with humor. Touch, the orphan, is instrumental in spotting
a thief, saving his inheritance and Miss Sally's, outwitting nasty Judge
Wigglesworth, and avoiding the orphanage. Fast-paced fun.

297   Fleischman, Sid. *The Scarebird*; illus. by Peter Sis. Greenwillow, 1988.
Library ed. ISBN 0-688-07318-2; Trade ed. ISBN 0-688-07317-4. 30p.
Library ed. $11.95; Trade ed. $11.88.

5-8 yrs.   Lonesome John protects his isolated fields with a scarecrow that has,
*   initially, only arms and legs ("if that's not the most fearsome sight I
ever saw, it'll do"). But the creature bothers him, so he adds a head
and various articles of clothing as the weather dictates. The more
human it looks, the more he talks to it, even to the point of a one-sided
game of checkers. Enter Sam, an orphan seeking work. In folk-
loristically rhythmic style, the clothes come off the scarecrow one by
one as Sam has need of them until, by and by, John and Sam are
friends and the scarecrow stands alone with its shadow. The shadow,
not mentioned in the text, is a graphic addition and a strong sample of

Sis' art, which echoes the lean prose with austerely textured brush
strokes. Reds dominate the beginning and ending, while the central
portion of the story is illustrated in corn-field green and sky blue, all of
which emphasizes the circular action. In a period of thin picture
books, this has much to teach about the substance of stories and the
complement of illustration. Some young listeners will look for a last
line after the suspended question that serves as ending ("Do you play
checkers?"), but the pictorial conclusion should satisfy them.

298   **Fleischman**, Sid. *The Whipping Boy;* illus. by Peter Sis. Greenwillow,
       1986. ISBN 0-688-06216-4. 89p. $11.75.

4-6   A round tale of adventure and humor, this follows the fortunes of
       Prince Horace (better known as Prince Brat) and his whipping boy,
       Jemmy, who has received all the hard knocks for the prince's mischief.
       When Horace decides to run away from boring palace life, he also
       decides that he requires Jemmy's assistance in carrying his lunch
       basket. The two are shortly apprehended by scoundrels, who kidnap
       them and place Jemmy in a tight spot between their greedy demands
       of the king and the king's assumption that Jemmy is the kidnapper. To
       make a short story shorter, Jemmy's knowledge of the city sewers
       comes in handy, and Horace's change of heart is highly satisfying.
       There's not a moment's lag in pace, and the stock characters, from
       Hold-Your-Nose Billy to Betsy's dancing bear Petunia, have enough
       inventive twists to project a lively air to it all. A top-notch read-aloud.

299   **Flournoy**, Valerie. *The Patchwork Quilt;* illus. by Jerry Pinkney. Dial,
       1985. Library ed. ISBN 0-8037-0098-9; Trade ed. ISBN 0-8037-0097-0.
       32p. Library ed. $10.89; Trade ed. $10.95.

K-3   At first it was only Tanya who was interested in helping Grandma
       make a new quilt, but soon Mama took part and, after Grandma
       became ill, Tanya's brother helped. They all enjoyed seeing familiar
       bits of material in the quilt, but Tanya loved it best; when the quilt was
       done and Grandma was well again, it was possible to add the finishing
       touch: stitched in a corner was "For Tanya from your Mama and
       Grandma." A quiet story, gently expressive of an attractive, com-
       fortably middle-class black family.

300   **Folsom**, Michael. *The Macmillan Book of How Things Work;* by
       Michael Folsom and Marcia Folsom; illus. by Brad Hamann.
       Macmillan, 1987. Trade ed. ISBN 0-02-735360-5; Paper ed. ISBN 0-689-
       71139-5. 77p. Trade ed. $15.95; Paper ed. $8.95.

4-7   A much more effective approach than most technological overviews of
       this sort, the Folsoms' presentation is well-organized to answer the
       questions either burning or lurking in most children's minds about
       how television, telephones, and other common electrical or electronic

mechanisms work. The explanations are selectively simplified and clear, as are the labelled color drawings and diagrams in their uncluttered, two-column format. An extensive table of contents directs students looking for specific material: the section "At Home," for instance, includes electrical system (generator, switch, circuit, fuse and circuit breaker, meter), water system (reservoir, storage tank, water treatment, sewer system), etc. Business, transportation, musical, and medical machines are also covered. Two indexes, one to the illustrations and one to the text, offer further help in accessing information, but browsers just may get caught by their own curiosity to take in the whole book.

301   **Forsyth**, Adrian. *Journey through a Tropical Jungle*. Simon, 1989. ISBN 0-671-66262-7. 80p. illus. with photographs by the author and others. $14.95.

5-8   Forsyth, a Canadian naturalist, takes readers along for a ramble through the Monteverde Cloud Forest Reserve in Costa Rica. His organization of material is casual, combining anecdotes about plant life, animals, and weather as he encountered them. For example, while investigating the crooks and crannies of a strangler tree, Forsyth "jumped back when a big mother scorpion came scuttling out with her stinger tail held up in the air." Thrills and chills are amply balanced with hard information, and the loose organization has a synergistic effect, showing how each member of the environment affects the others: quetzals eat avocados, spit out the seeds, start new avocado plants. Forsyth is also gently insistent about the role the tropical forests play in our own lives. "If you've eaten a chocolate bar, you've eaten a bit of a tropical forest tree." Color photographs are many, well-keyed to the text, but arranged in a somewhat placid layout.

302   **Fowler**, Zinita. *The Last Innocent Summer*. Texas Christian University, 1990. Paper ed. ISBN 0-87565-045-7. 145p. (Chaparral Books). Paper ed. $11.95.

6-9
*   Skeeter, the ten-year-old narrator, tells the story of a murder that rocked the small Texas town in which she lived, and of how her family's involvement changed their lives in that troubled summer of 1931. The suspected killer is a prostitute, and the victims her two young daughters. Arsenic poisoning is suspected, and Skeeter's father, a chemist, is asked to help with the autopsy. From this sad situation, Skeeter learns that lawyers can be dishonest, that mothers can fail to love their children, and that children don't always love their mothers. Fowler's deftly crafted story has depth and pace and a picture of a community that may remind some readers of Harper Lee's *To Kill a Mockingbird*.

303   Fox, Paula. *Lily and the Lost Boy*. Orchard/Watts, 1987. Library ed.
          ISBN 0-531-08320-9; Trade ed. ISBN 0-531-05720-8. 149p. Library ed.
          $12.99; Trade ed. $12.95.

6-9   Although there are three children central to Fox's new novel, the real
          heartbeat of the story is the Greek island where they are visiting for
          the summer. Each character—and especially the island—takes shape
          in the reader's mind through indelible scenes and sensory descrip-
          tion. Lily is nearly twelve and the smartest of the lot, an observant,
          sharp-tongued girl wary of the reckless young stranger, Jack, who
          diverts her fourteen-year-old brother's attention and who ultimately
          plays out a role in a classic tragedy. Jack has been rejected by his
          mother and neglected by his father. It is inevitable, from foreboding
          hints in the text, that he will cause grief—as it turns out, the death of a
          Greek child with a close, loving family. The irony here is clear and
          striking, and the role of the protagonist, Lily, an interesting one in
          relationship to the boys' friendship. It is Lily who ultimately perceives
          and retrieves Jack from self-destructive isolation. As is her wont, Fox
          presents readers with a book that sustains thought with subtleties of
          tone and meaning. The dynamics of characterization also sustain
          attention, as does the close rendering of atmosphere: at one point, Lily
          tries to recapture a melody "like a little silver bird flashing in the
          woods; it vanished when you tried to fix it with your eyes." Along with
          the American cast here, readers will be transported to another place,
          with another sense of time.

304   Fox, Paula. *The Moonlight Man*. Bradbury, 1986. ISBN 0-02-735480-6.
          179p. $12.95.

7-10   Few writers see with such microsurgical precision the complex and
 *   interrelated strands of a human relationship; fewer still can incor-
          porate their vision into memorable characters within a story that
          unfolds with the spare inevitability of a structure as natural as a crystal
          or a flower. In its depiction of the growing and intricate understanding
          between a teenage girl and the father she has known so little, this is
          reminiscent of Paul Fleischman's *Rear-View Mirrors*. Catherine Ames
          is not the narrator, however, and this is a more balanced book than it
          would be were she the voice of the story, because it makes it possible
          for the author to maintain an objectivity that would be false on the
          part of a girl who feels anguish because of the way she is being
          manipulated by an alcoholic and irresponsible charmer. Readers who
          appreciate the bittersweet quality of the father-child relationship in
          Blowfish Live in the Sea will see the same quality in this new approach
          to the ambivalence of a painful love.

305   Fox, Paula. *The Village By the Sea*. Orchard/Watts, 1988. Library ed. ISBN 0-531-08388-8; Trade ed. ISBN 0-531-05788-7. 147p. Library ed. $13.99; Trade ed. $13.95.

5-8
 *
An intensive portrait of three characters reverberates with insights that emerge from a child's involvement with her game. Emma must stay with her aunt and uncle while her father has heart surgery and her mother attends him. Adding to her concern about her father is the stress of hostile remarks from Aunt Bea, an ex-alcoholic who is obsessed by old family jealousies: " . . . she has a habit of resentment. It's a kind of addiction, too, like brandy." This grip of hatred causes Aunt Bea to destroy the miniature village which Emma and a friend have spent many days creating from flotsam they find on the shore. Bea's fury seems contagious, and Emma barely overcomes, with the help of her uncle, a violent urge for vengeance in the larger context of the two adults' village by the sea. More than ever, Fox's style is compressed without seeming dense, each scene and image allowed space for clean effect. Although the emotional layering is sophisticated, the viewpoint is unfalteringly that of the child. The novel is easy to read and complex to consider, an encounter that moves the reader from Gothic narrative suspense to compassionate illumination of the dark in human nature.

306   **Fradon**, Dana. *Harold the Herald: A Book about Heraldry*; written and illus. by Dana Fradon. Dutton, 1990. ISBN 0-525-44634-6. 40p. $14.95.

3-5
In this follow-up to *Sir Dana: A Knight*, Sir Dana (a talking suit of armor) comes to Miss Quincy's class to talk about his 14th-century friend Harold, herald to Prince Lionel. While Harold was responsible for all kinds of activities (organizing jousts, writing wills for knights, delivering proclamations and love letters), the emphasis here is on the herald's responsibility as record-keeper of the coats of arms: their origins, etiquette, meanings, and design. Sir Dana is a sometimes annoying narrator ("Ho! I but jest") yet he conveys a great deal of information about heraldry, its language, its colors (such as gules, azure, sable, and vert), patterns (ermine and vair), shapes (fess, chevron, saltire, lozenge, etc.), and animal symbols ("A man with a dog on his shield would be loyal, would never desert his master, and would willingly die for him"). The examples are clearly drawn and colored, and easily copied. Accompanying cartoon illustrations are often silly but keep the format open and inviting. New horizons for graffiti artists.

307   **Frank**, Rudolf. *No Hero for the Kaiser*; tr. from the German by Patricia Crampton. Lothrop, 1986. ISBN 0-688-06093-5. 222p. $13.00.

7-10
Effective both as historical fiction and a historical document, this German anti-war novel, published in 1931 by a World War I veteran,

was publicly burned by Nazi officials in 1933 for its indictment of militarism. The story centers on a young Polish boy, Jan, whose mother is dead and whose father has been conscripted to fight the Germans. Jan's remaining family member is killed at the outset, and he is adopted by an invading German artillery unit. Jan grows to love the men and saves them several times with his knowledge of the countryside and uncanny instinct for spotting danger. The bitter devastation on the Eastern front is superseded only by the trench warfare on the West after the gunners are forced to retreat from Russian territory to fight in France. Jan's experiences disillusion him as to the chauvinistic platitudes fostered by any government, and he runs away the day the Kaiser is to award him citizenship and military honors. The action here is solid, the style often witty despite the depressing situation, and the characterization of the men down-to-earth and distinctive (one of them describes Jan's beloved dog as "a cross between a mudpie and a bedside rug." These elements more than support the occasional thematic intrusions of humanitarian philosophy.

308   Freedman, Russell. *Buffalo Hunt.* Holiday House, 1988. ISBN 0-8234-0702-0. 52p. illus. with photographs. $16.95.

5-8   After an introduction to the role of the buffalo in Native American lore
*   and life-style, the author describes preparations for a Plains Indian hunt, techniques for approaching and attacking a herd, and the women's work of using everything "from the brains to the tail." Finally, he discusses the appearance of repeating rifles, bounty hunting, and railroad sports shooting as death knells. "The days of the buffalo hunters had faded like a dream," to be kept alive in legend alone. Freedman has hit his stride in terms of selection, style, and illustration: the color reproductions of historical art work form a stunning complement to the carefully researched, graceful presentation of information. The paintings of George Catlin, Charles Russell, Karl Bodmer, and others, including a robe by a Crow artist, speak in moving visual terms of a lost culture and the environment upon which it was based. A book brilliantly designed in all aspects.

309   Freedman, Russell. *Cowboys of the Wild West.* Houghton/Clarion, 1985. ISBN 0-89919-301-3. 102p. illus. with photographs. $14.95.

5-9   Historical photographs and a well researched text leave no doubt about the hardships behind the romantic mystique of cowpunching. In a style and format similar to *Children of the Wild West*, Freedman describes the herders' duties on the open range roundups and trail rides, their ranch and line-camp life, the clothes and equipment dictated by their work, and the economic necessities that defined the job in its heyday, from the 1860s to the 1890s. There is plenty of information, inherently colorful without glamorization, and it makes good reading. Here's a chance to swap some stereotypes for the truly amazing facts.

310   **Freedman**, Russell. *Franklin Delano Roosevelt*. Clarion, 1990. ISBN 0-89919-379-X. 200p. illus. with photographs. $16.95.

7-
*   Profusely illustrated with photographs, this is a biography that is outstanding for its candor and objectivity as well as for the smooth integration of personal and political details into a coherent portrait of the man and of the major events that affected his political life. An impressive list of sources attests to Freedman's research; the index has been carefully compiled; a list of places to visit is included. The book should be of interest to adult as well as young adult students of history, and it gives with remarkable clarity assessments of such major events as World War II, the Great Depression, the New Deal, and the changes in social services established during Roosevelt's long tenure in the White House.

311   **Freedman**, Russell. *Indian Chiefs*. Holiday House, 1987. ISBN 0-8234-0625-3. 150p. illus. and with photographs. $15.95.

7-12
*   These six biographical essays on Red Cloud, Satanta, Quanah Parker, Washakie, Joseph, and Sitting Bull form a gripping historical portrayal of Native American resistance to whites' taking their western lands. The story is a tragic one, and this is a moving account. Yet it also shows glimpses of the humor with which the Indians sometimes lightened their own load. The Nez Perce, for instance, while fleeing from the army in 1877, "paced themselves to stay two days ahead of Howard. They began to call him 'General Day-After-Tomorrow.'" Freedman has selected leaders who showed superlative courage and wisdom in the face of a doom that most of them foresaw as inevitable. Without becoming repetitive, he gives a sense of the trail of broken treaties, encroachments, and reprisals that ended an ancient way of life. The perspective in the first and last chapters, framed by Sitting Bull's inauguration as Sioux chief in the 1860s and his murder two weeks before the Wounded Knee Massacre in 1890, gives readers a general context from which the individual stories will emerge to make an unforgettable impression. The writing, selection of historical photographs, bookmaking, and subject combine to make this an exceptional piece of nonfiction. A bibliography, Index, and list of photographic sources conclude the book.

312   **Freedman**, Russell. *Lincoln: A Photobiography*. Houghton/Clarion, 1987. ISBN 0-89919-380-3. 150p. illus. with photographs. $15.95.

5-9
*
With confident ease of selection, Freedman has made his way through some of the quantities of documentary research on Lincoln to shape a clear account of his personal and political life. Unlike many photodocumentaries, the text is as substantial as the pictorial content. Both are vivid and revealing of the times as well as the man. Some shots from the battlefield render the Civil War more immediate than any words could, but the thematic explanations of political shifts and social attitudes toward slavery are essential in understanding the context of the war. This is a carefully conceived and designed book. Following the closing chapter on Lincoln's assassination is "A Lincoln Sampler"from his speeches and writing, a section on relevant historic sites open to the public, a bibliographic note on sources, and an index. Students who come to this for reports may find themselves browsing through the whole thing.

313   **French**, Fiona. *Snow White in New York;* written and illus. by Fiona French. Oxford, 1986. ISBN 0-19-279808-1. 32p. $11.95.

3-4
Snow White, in this Art Deco spoof of the traditional tale, is a Kewpie-doll blonde, and her newly-acquired stepmother is a slinky brunette Theda Bara. Angry at what she sees in the *Mirror* (the *New York Mirror*) praising Snow White, the villainous stepmother tells a bodyguard to kill Snow White. The rest of the plot is adapted in similar style: S.W. is taken in by 7 jazz musicians when the hit man lets her go; her sleep is caused by a poisoned cherry put into her cocktail, her recovery (cherry dislodged when a coffin-bearer stumbles) leads to marriage when a handsome society reporter smiles at her awakening. This sophisticated picture book may not be appreciated by very young children, but independent readers (who do not need the very large print that's used) should enjoy as much of the joke as they can comprehend. Distributed in 1987 in this country, the book won the 1986 Kate Greenaway Award in Great Britain, and the illustrations are indeed distinctive, with geometric abstractions, handsome use of silhouettes, and intriguing complexities of perspective and color used as backgrounds for the svelte, elongated figures in John Held style.

314   **Friedman**, Ina R. *The Other Victims: First-Person Stories of Non-Jews Persecuted by the Nazis.* Houghton, 1990. ISBN 0-395-50212-8. 214p. $14.95.

7-12
Thirteen narrators relate their experiences during the Holocaust, when they were imprisoned in labor or concentration camps as being degenerates, enemies of the Nazi state, pollutants of the Aryan race, or simply occupants of territories conquered for German "living space." Friedman, author of *Escape or Die: True Stories of Young People Who Survived the Holocaust*, has researched the history of these 5 million doomed offenders and interviewed a few who survived.

Her brief chapter introductions provide background for accounts by a Gypsy, a Catholic priest, a Jehovah's Witness, a deaf girl sterilized because of her disability, a Jew married to a Christian doctor, two dissident students, Czech and Polish resistance fighters, and two Dutchmen captured for slave labor. Although some historical context is provided for persecution of blacks and homosexuals, a lack of living witnesses is cited for including no personal accounts. The preface acknowledges sources, some personal, some archival, while a concluding list suggests other children's and young adult books on the subject. Well organized and edited, the tales are harrowing, though they all end happily, often with escape or immigration to America and highly successful careers. Friedman points out that these were the lucky ones, and her book serves as a much-needed reminder that the Nazi nightmare extended far beyond Europe's Jewish population.

315   Fritz, Jean. *China Homecoming;* illus. with photographs by Michael Fritz. Putnam, 1985. ISBN 0-399-21182-9. 143p. $12.95.

6-   As admirers of *Homesick: My Own Story* will know, Jean Fritz lived in China until she was thirteen; in this companion volume she describes her return to Hankou, her home town, four decades later. Although she no longer spoke as fluently, she still spoke Chinese. This is, therefore, a record of a very personal search for roots and memories. It is also a rarely candid and objective picture of contemporary China. As both kinds of story it is wonderfully vivid, often touching, and it is written with a practiced grace and narrative flow.

316   Fritz, Jean. *China's Long March: 6,000 Miles of Danger.* Putnam, 1988. ISBN 0-399-21512-3. 113p. $14.95.

7-   Although the author's intended audience is young people, this
  *   account of the long, dogged march of the Chinese Red Army in 1934 and 1935 compares favorably with some of the best adult books on the subject. Because Fritz is adept at gauging her intended audience, and because most of her material is based on interviews with survivors, the writing has an easy flow and an immediacy that make the ordeal vivid and personal. Jean Fritz loves the country where she spent most of her childhood, and her book is a felicitous blend of sympathetic under- standing and an objective assessment of historical events.

317   Fritz, Jean. *The Great Little Madison.* Putnam, 1989. ISBN 0-399- 21768-1. 160p.]illus. $15.95.

6-9   Reproductions of portraits and prints are included in a biography that
  *   is invested with Jean Fritz's ability to bring a character to life without depending on the excesses of either adulation or pejorative criticism. Small, soft-spoken, and by nature diffident, James Madison found it difficult to speak in the midst of controversy, but his zeal and his

convictions in the struggle between Republicans and Federalists gave him confidence, and his successes brought him to the presidency. Fritz has given a vivid picture of the man and an equally vivid picture of the problems—especially the internal dissension—that faced the leaders of the new nation in the formative years after the appearance of the Declaration of Independence and the turmoil of the several decades that followed the ratification of the Constitution. Notes by the author and a bibliography are appended.

318　　**Fritz**, Jean. *Make Way for Sam Houston*; illus. by Elise Primavera. Putnam, 1986. Trade ed. ISBN 0-399-21303-1; Paper ed. ISBN 0-399-21304-X. 109p. Trade ed. $12.95; Paper ed. $4.95.

6-9　　A canny politician, a successful military leader, an articulate and loquacious extrovert, Sam Houston was devoted, in his public life, to fair treatment for Indians, to the founding and preservation of Texas, and to preventing civil war in the United States. Fritz never fails to give him credit for achievements that contributed to improving any of those causes, but she never makes him a likable man, perhaps intentionally. Her research is always dependable, and is evidenced here by the notes and list of sources that precede the index. There are infrequent lapses in style ("At the time Americans argued if there should even be a war. . . .") but on the whole the writing is expectably competent if a bit heavy, and the pace and structure of the biography are good.

319　　**Fritz**, Jean. *Shh! We're Writing the Constitution*; illus. by Tomie dePaola. Putnam, 1987. Trade ed. ISBN 0-399-21403-8; Paper ed. ISBN 0-399-21404-6. 58p. Trade ed. $12.95; Paper ed. $5.95.

4-7　　In this year of the bicentennial celebration of the signing of a
＊　　hammered-out constitution, there have been many books published. None is better than this lively, detailed, and authoritative description of the conflict among delegates to the "Grand Convention" in Philadelphia, the issues, the people, the compromises, and the resolution and ratification. In addition to the appended Constitution are notes by the author, who has distinguished herself (again) by making a landmark event an exciting story.

320　　**Furlong**, Monica. *Wise Child*. Knopf, 1987. Library ed. ISBN 0-394-99105-2; Trade ed. ISBN 0-394-89105-8. 228p. Library ed. $12.99; Trade ed. $11.95.

6-8　　Set in Britain in "very early Christian times," according to jacket copy, this is a long effective meshing of reality and fantasy, as told by a nine-year-old waif (called Wise Child) who is nine when she begins her story. Deserted by her mother, longing for her seafaring father, Wise Child is taken in by a woman who is an outcast, Juniper. A sorceress and healer, Juniper is tolerated in their Scottish village—until bad times bring accusations of her evildoing. By the time Wise Child is old enough to know and love Juniper, her vicious mother tries to take her daughter away from the one person who has loved and protected her. This is the author's first novel for children; her readers will surely hope it is not her last. First published in England, the story is impressive both for its style and its structure, and the characterizations and relationships are as capably handled as the period details. The jacket art, by Leo and Diane Dillon, is a gravely beautiful painting in medieval mood.

321   **Gabhart**, Ann. *Discovery at Coyote Point*. Avon, 1989. Paper ed. ISBN 0-380-75497-5. 164p. Paper ed. $2.75.

5-8   Sent to stay at his grandparents' farm for a year while his mother works in Mexico, Ance, a twelve-year-old city kid, begins to question the circumstances of his father's death five years before. His dad had disappeared while on a walk in the wilderness near the farm, and while Ance's mother is sure he was killed in an accident, both grandparents seem to believe their son Russell still lives: Grandfather believes Russell ran away; Grandmother insists he has amnesia and will return. "I read about that happening to this man just the other day in one of my magazines." The novel isn't a mystery so much as it is an exploration of the family's attempts to come to terms with the absence of a man they loved. Grandfather, bitter and afraid, keeps himself aloof from Ance; Grandmother, longing for Russell, calls him Rusty; and Ance wanders daily through the wilderness, befriending a coyote and learning what his father loved. The growing bond between Ance and his sad grandparents is convincingly developed through a skillful use of dialogue and plot, and the eventual revelation of his father's fate is cathartic without being melodramatic. Never a tear-jerker, this simple story comes honestly to its considerable emotional effects.

322   **Gardner**, Robert. *Science and Sports*. Watts, 1988. ISBN 0-531-10593-8. 112p. illus. with photographs. (Venture Books). $11.90.

7-10   A teacher of physical science and a coach for his school's football and baseball teams, Gardner is well-qualified to write a text that uses various aspects of sports to illustrate basic principles of physics. Gardner shows how the construction of cycling tracks, the size or shape of pieces of sports equipment, the importance of momentum for a long hit in baseball, the way a swimmer may shave his head or a skier bend her knees relate to what is known about gravity, speed, collision, rotation, or the exertion of force. A final chapter entitled "Food, Energy and Health" gives, briefly, facts about the human body and the ways in which it obtains and uses energy. A short bibliography, most of which is relevant (*Sports Riddles?*) precedes the index;

photographs and diagrams are, for the most part, informative and are well-correlated with textual references.

323   **Garfield**, Leon. *The December Rose.* Viking Kestrel, 1987. ISBN 0-670-81054-1. 203p. $12.95.

6-9   The colorful cant, the idiom and dialect of the London poor, and the Dickensian type-casting make this an adventure story that creates a lively picture of Victorian times—on the seamier side. The ragamuffin sweep who's called "Barnacle" for his ability to cling as he climbs, is a filthy child, a biter and a liar and a thief. He runs away with a stolen locket, is hunted by a dour police inspector, and is taken in by a bargee, Tom Gosling, who has a Heart of Gold. There are two plots: one is the predictable redemption of Barnacle, the other is a wild concoction of international intrigue, espionage, treason, and murder, in which both Barnacle and his mentor become involved and endangered. There are a few instances of ethnic slurs that may be found offensive by some readers (". . . Chinese reach-me-downs, still inhabited by slant-eyed moths," and "Mr. Levy... with a fluttering, anxious manner, like a Hebrew moth in a church"), but Garfield fans will enjoy the usual combination of salty dialogue, broad humor, and plot and characterization that are deliberately overdone.

324   **Garfield**, Leon. *The Empty Sleeve.* Delacorte, 1988. ISBN 0-440-50049-4. 205p. $14.95.

6-8   A master of plotting and style, Garfield uses a combination of ingredients that will be familiar to his fans: Dickensian dialogue, settings that are reminiscent of Thomas Hardy's openings, and a heady mixture of suspense, danger, and adventure in a structure that has intricate shifts and turns. The title refers to a spectre that haunts one of a pair of twins, Peter, who has been sent to London as an apprentice. Peter has been troublesome, his twin Paul angelic to a fault. Garfield makes it clear just what that fault is, in a picaresque story of the 18th century that has a judicious balance of realism and fantasy.

325   **Garfield**, Leon. *The Wedding Ghost*; illus. by Charles Keeping. Oxford/Salem House, 1987. ISBN 0-19-279229-4. 62p. $11.95.

7-   Haunting in both art and narrative, this sophisticated modern elaboration on "Sleeping Beauty" will appeal to adults as much as it will to precocious juvenile readers. It opens with the shower of a young couple, Jack and Gillian, to be wed the following Sunday. Jack's old nurse is not invited, but an anonymous gift—an old map—arrives addressed to Jack, who becomes obsessed with following it. Along city streets enshrouded with fog, down a river, through a dense forest full of human bones, Jack makes his way to a castle and kisses the sleeping woman awake; but his marriage to the princess superimposes on his wedding to Gillian, and he is left married to both the homely real and the romantic ideal. Keeping's black pen-and-wash drawings are mysterious and sinister, projecting the power of Garfield's densely packed writing with a relentless force of their own. The book is deceptively formatted in the size of a large picture book. Illusions of time, allusions to literature, and some terrifying graphic images make it a supernatural tour de force for an audience with a taste for the Gothic.

326   **Garfield**, Leon. *Young Nick and Jubilee*; illus. by Ted Lewin. Delacorte, 1989. ISBN 0-385-29777-7. 134p. $13.95.

5-7   Orphaned siblings (Nick is ten, Jubilee nine) live precariously in 18th century London, and, through the offices of Mr. Owen (a thief) are accepted as scholars at a charity school. The arrangement benefits the children and Owen, whom they mendaciously claim as their father. It is almost inevitable that a tenderness enters the relationship and fosters affection between Owen and the children. Garfield is a colorful writer, skilled at creating atmosphere and introducing period details. The style is robust and humorous, the weakness being in the use of poor grammar in exposition: "His face, his hair, and his fine blue coat was a ruin of dirt and stinking fish slime," or "There weren't no boozing nor cursing . . ." or "Next night there was mutton chops on the table. And that weren't all!" What this does is to make the use of such language less effective in dialogue (where it is appropriate) because it serves to surfeit rather than set off by contrast.

327   **Garner**, Alan. *A Bag of Moonshine*; illus. by Patrick James Lynch. Delacorte, 1986. ISBN 0-385-29517-0. 144p. $16.95.

4-6   Twenty-two stories from England and Wales offer entertaining variants of some well-known tales. "The Three Gowks" follows the same pattern as "The Three Sillies"; "Harry-Cap and the Three Brothers," of "The Lad Who Went to The North Wind"; "Billy Bowker's Mowing Match," of "How Bobtail Beat the Devil." There's a changeling tale, "Hom Bridson," and "Belenay of the Lake," a version of the legend Susan Cooper adapted in *The Silver Cow*. The mood varies from humorous to eerie, but almost all the tales are terse, powerful, and rhythmically told; the dialect is strong but generally accessible. Storytellers will recognize "Mr. Vinegar" but discover some new treasures, such as "The Grey Goat," full of enchanting suspense. The illustrations in color and black-and-white have a nineteenth century air sometimes reminiscent of Rackham.

328   **Garner**, Alan. *Alan Garner's Book of British Fairy Tales;* illus. by Derek Collard. Collins/Delacorte, 1985. ISBN 0-385-29425-5. 160p. $16.95.

4-6   Garner's adaptations of twenty-one British tales are fluent in the best
*   sense of the oral tradition, rich and varied in style, as effective for reading alone or aloud as they are for the storyteller. They are based on solid sources, all of which are provided at the back of the book, and they are a nice mixture of less familiar tales with others as well-known as "Molly Whuppie" or "The Black Bull of Norroway." Collard provides a title page for each story, with an intricately designed border around a central picture; the use of black, white, greys, and browns gives these decorations (they are not really illustrations) a look of stylized restraint. This is a distinguished anthology.

329   **Garrigue**, Sheila. *The Eternal Spring of Mr. Ito.* Bradbury, 1985. ISBN 0-02-737300-2. 163p. $11.95.

4-6   After almost a decade, a sequel to *All the Children Were Sent Away*
*   continues the story of an English child who has come to stay with a Canadian aunt and uncle for the duration of World War II. The story is more serious and cohesive than its predecessor. Here, with the bombing of Pearl Harbor and Hong Kong, there is a wave of hysterical anti-Japanese prejudice and persecution. Sara, the protagonist, is dismayed by the way her uncle's family treats wise, gentle Mr. Ito (the gardener who had saved her uncle's life when they served together during the first World War), and she secretly pays a visit to the Ito family in their bleak, crowded internment camp. Sara's concern and her sensible compassion do effect a change in the attitude and behavior of her family in a story that is dramatic, convincing, and touching as a narrative and quite powerful as an indictment of war and the hysterical prejudice war can generate.

330   **Gauch**, Patricia Lee. *Christina Katerina and the Time She Quit the Family;* illus. by Elise Primavera. Putnam, 1987. ISBN 0-399-21408-9. 32p. $12.95.

5-7 yrs.   The third and best of several picture books about a feisty young character, this features a text true to the vicissitudes of child behavior along with watercolor scenes of authentic family chaos. Feeling nagged and put upon, Christina changes her name and defines her own autonomous areas of the house. Her mother wisely supports this separation, helps label the dividing lines, and waves goodbye. Needless to say, Christina, alias Agnes, eats junk, wreaks messy havoc, wears mismatched clothes, and stays up late. And needless to say, she begins to suffer the consequences—it's a real feat to tuck yourself in at night. Fortunately, her mother invites her back into the family for some chocolate cake and storytelling, and Christina rejoins them ". . .

because Christina liked doing what she pleased, and that's exactly what pleased her just then." The issue of control is of inexhaustible interest to young children, and this girl's carefree abandon in rebelling will be as entertaining as her return to the fold is satisfying. The art kicks up its heels as well, reveling in spirited depictions of anarchic clutter with ironically controlled line and color.

331   **Geller**, Mark. *What I Heard.* Harper, 1987. Library ed. ISBN 0-06-022161-5; Trade ed. ISBN 0-06-022160-7. 115p. Library ed. $11.89; Trade ed. $11.50.

5-9
*

A story that is at once terse, easy to read, and grippingly developed begins with brief scenes quicksketching the contrasting families of the 12-year-old narrator, Michael, and his friend Tannenbaum. It is clear that Michael's father is distracted, and Michael finds out the reason when he eavesdrops on a phone conversation: his father is having an affair. Michael's reaction is intense and suspenseful. He tries to tell his mother but can't; he tries to get Tannenbaum to make a threatening call to his father's girlfriend but ends up confronting his father himself. After a climactic scene in which Michael's mother guesses something is wrong, Michael disappears until late and takes the rap for upsetting the family with general adolescent irresponsibility. Michael's mother never knows, Michael's father breaks off the affair, and Michael is stuck trying to understand and forgive a father who has suddenly been exposed in a state of weakness and remorse. The triumph of the book is the peace Michael makes with his father. The boy's vulnerability, desperation, anger, and forgiveness are equally convincing. This is a masterpiece of mini-scenes and dialogue, both of which seem casually natural but are in fact intensely revealing. The phone chat between Michael's father and his lover, the way Michael talks to Tannenbaum (which captures the humor of junior high banter without becoming glib), the brief appearances of Michael's mother all reveal secondary characters who are nice people with limitations—just like the rest of us. Moreover, this does justice to both the child's pain and the adult's perspective. Michael's family survives to become a happier one; there are no absolute solutions except a love that can bend in the wind. There is no preaching here, either, but some insightful, accurate perceptions into the human family. The implications of Michael's own guilt for breaking the rules of privacy are hinted but never directly addressed. Large print and simple vocabulary will make these complexities particularly accessible for discussion among readers who can't handle higher reading levels.

332   **George**, Jean Craighead. *On the Far Side of the Mountain*; written and illus. by Jean Craighead George. Dutton, 1990. ISBN 0-525-44563-3. 170p. $13.95.

5-7   After thirty years, a sequel to the still-popular *My Side of the Mountain* is told convincingly by Sam Gribley, now an adolescent and still living in contented solitude on his mountain. Now, however, his young sister Alice lives nearby in her own tree-house; she, too, has learned how to be independent in the wilderness, and she shares Sam's concern for living creatures. There are two themes here: for one, there is the quest, as Sam and a friend follow Alice's trail when she leaves a message to say she's going off on her own; second, there is Sam's desperate effort to retrieve his pet falcon after he learns that the man who has her is not the conservation officer he claimed to be when he took Sam's bird. There is, therefore, a doubling of suspense, and there is always the threat of danger. However, the story would be intriguing to many readers even without these appeals, since it again demonstrates the vast knowledge of wilderness-living-lore that was in the first book.

333   **George**, Jean Craighead. *One Day in the Prairie*; illus by Bob Marstall. Crowell, 1986. Library ed. ISBN 0-690-04566-2; Trade ed. ISBN 0-690-04565-6. 42p. Library ed. $11.89; Trade ed. $11.95.

4-6   Black and white drawings, accurately detailed and nicely incorporated into the page layout, add visual appeal to an authoritative and informative continuous text. George uses a narrative framework to carry the description of a single day on a prairie wildlife refuge in Oklahoma. The text is given drama by the inclusion of a tornado and is given focus by the description of the actions and reflections of a boy who is an amateur photographer. Most of the material is about the animals of the prairie (including some like the buffalo and the longhorn steer that are, as threatened species, protected), but other aspects of the prairie ecology are included. George achieves an amazing concentration of facts without being either tedious or turgid. An index and a bibliography are supplied.

334   **George**, Jean Craighead. *Water Sky*; written and illus. by Jean Craighead George. Harper, 1987. Library ed. ISBN 0-06-022199-2; Trade ed. ISBN 0-06-022198-4. 212p. Library ed. $11.89; Trade ed. $11.95.

6-9   As she has done before, Jean George combines her considerable skills as naturalist and as narrator to produce a story in which the setting and the nature lore are as strong as the story but do not overwhelm it. Because his father had so enjoyed his own stay, when young, with an Eskimo family, he has sent Lincoln to Alaska. Caught up in the beauty of Eskimo culture, the excitement of whale hunting (Eskimo style) and a first shy love affair, Lincoln almost forgets that he is determined to find the beloved uncle who had disappeared in the vicinity. The characters are strong, the plot is smoothly developed, and the setting vividly drawn in a novel imbued with understanding and respect for the rich traditions of Eskimo life.

335   **Gerrard**, Roy. *Mik's Mammoth*; written and illus. by Roy Gerrard. Farrar, 1990. ISBN 0-374-31891-3. 32p. $13.95.

5-8 yrs.
*
Like Gerrard's other picture books, this casts a humorous light on history, or, in this case, prehistory. And, like *Rosie and the Rustlers*, it has lots of child appeal, as the abandoned young hero Mik rescues a baby mammoth from the snow, walls the front of his cave, heats it with fire, gathers and grows food, fends off a dangerous bear, catches fish, decorates the cave walls with paintings, and finally becomes a hero by saving his returning tribe from pursuing marauders—with a little help from his large pet. "The moral is that little chaps/ May overcome life's handicaps,/ And, with some effort, they perhaps/ Can triumph in the end./ For Mik won through on brains and wit,/ Though fortunate, I must admit,/ To have one priceless benefit—/ A mammoth for a friend." Of course it's the art that turns all these narrative conventions of outcast turned survivor turned rescuer into something special, for Gerrard's signature watercolor paintings show increasing versatility. Though the perspectives are as arresting as ever, the art relies less on exaggerated contrast between squat figures and looming landscapes and more on clever drafting, texture, and color blends. The icy environs of a virginal winter vie with spring greens and furry browns in a captivating sequence of spreads. Pair this with the other perfect prehistoric farce of the season, Yorinks and Egielski's *Ugh*.

336   **Gerrard**, Roy. *Rosie and the Rustlers*; written and illus. by Roy Gerrard. Farrar, 1989. ISBN 0-374-36345-5. 32p. $12.95.

4-8 yrs.
"Where the mountains meet the prairie, where the men are wild and hairy / There's a little ranch where Rosie Jones is boss. / It's a place that's neat and cozy, and the boys employed by Rosie / Work extremely hard, to stop her getting cross." With this balladic kick-off, Gerrard launches another historic spoof illustrated with his signature wit. When Rosie's hearty crew leaves the ranch unprotected to visit their Cherokee friends, Greasy Ben's outlaw band steals the herd. The subsequent chase scene leads Rosie, her boys, and the viewer through some spectacular Western scenery, a perfect showcase for the artist's favorite play with contrasting perspectives—diminutive, tall-hatted humans against cacti or dazzling bluffs. Both the patterned landscapes and detailed portraits make this one of Gerrard's best, while the verses, syllabically crowded and sometimes hokey as they are, will round up young listeners by the dozen.

337   **Gerrard**, Roy. *Sir Cedric Rides Again*; written and illus by Roy Gerrard. Farrar, 1986. ISBN 374-36961-5. 32p. $11.95.

K-3   The corpulent, balding little knight of *Sir Cedric* rides off for "a change and a rest" accompanied by his patient wife, his hoydenish daughter Edwina, her weedy suiter, timid Hubert, and a sizeable corps of retainers. They sail to France from England, and "one night at nine," after days of weary walking, they reach Palestine. Naturally they are set on by the infidel oafs of Abdul the Heavy; naturally Hubert becomes an instant hero, rescuing Edwina and her mother from the toils of Abdul, and just as naturally love conquers all. This is lively, witty narrative poetry, and the paintings are of comparably high quality: romantic (just a bit tongue in cheek) landscapes, handsome ornamental details, and fine use of color in effective compostions. Great fun, and the humor of Gerrard's tale may attract older readers as well as the read-aloud audience.

338   Gerstein, Mordecai. *The Mountains of Tibet;* written and illus. by Mordecai Gerstein. Harper, 1987. Library ed. ISBN 0-06-022149-6; Trade ed. ISBN 0-06-022144-5. 23p. Library ed. $11.89; Trade ed. $11.95.

5-7 yrs.   A Tibetan boy grows up dreaming of sights beyond the mountains, "cities and oceans, and people of other races,"but he ages and dies before he can see them. Given a choice of reincarnation among myriad possibilities of time and situation, he takes the same place and parents, though this time he is born a girl. This is an unusual theme for Western picture books, and it could both broaden young listeners' awareness and at the same time underscore their love for the familiar. Gerstein's full-color illustrations, which are framed in small squares at the start, expand into circles that symbolize galactic reaches and global variety of animals and peoples, then retract into the reality of choices. He has proved to have a deft touch with both mythology (*Tales of Pan*) and folklore (*The Seal Mother*), maintaining a light simplicity in his art and adaptations without sacrificing central patterns.

339   Gerstein, Mordicai, ad. *The Seal Mother;* ad. and illus. by Mordicai Gerstein.. Dial, 1986. Library ed. ISBN 0-8037-0303-1; Trade ed. ISBN 0-8037-0302-3. 32p. Library ed. $10.89; Trade ed. $10.95.

K-2   Gerstein's selkie tale is a visual and textual contrast to Cooper and Hutton's. In this version, an old man tells the story of the fisherman who falls in love with a selkie, steals her skin, marries her, and has one son, Andrew. After the seven years she has promised bondage, she begs to return to the sea, but the fisherman has hidden her skin, and only when Andrew finds it can she regain her seal form. When she does, she takes Andrew on an underwater journey to meet his seal family and visits him on land whenever he sings for her. The ending entails a Midsummer's Eve celebration of humans and seals together. The watercolor paintings here are dominated by a deeper blue than

Hutton's with less statuesque, almost dancing shapes within square framed compositions. The story is more simply phrased and reassuring in its conclusion. Both versions work well when read aloud to children. Cooper's has somewhat more dignity and Gerstein's more animation.

340   **Gerstein**, Mordicai. *Tales of Pan;* written and illus. by Mordicai Gerstein. Harper, 1986. Library ed. ISBN 0-06-021997-1; Trade ed. ISBN 0-06-021996-3. 63p. Library ed. $12.89; Trade ed. $12.95.

5-8 yrs.   With a light and lively tone suited to Pan's more innocently mischievous moments, Gerstein adapts 13 Greek myths centered on his escapes, including his invention of panic, his music contest with Apollo, and his part in King Midas' acquiring donkey ears. A foreword sets the storytelling scene by neatly summarizing, in two pages, Pan's place in the family of gods, who "lived on top of Mount Olympus, under great craggy clouds that looked like whipped cream." Pan's dedication to noise and naughty confusion will immediately appeal to children, and Gerstein has successfully joined the stories with thematic characteristics and references such as Pan's "panic yell," which is important to several episodes. The art is as frothy as the text, with pastel and swirling soft line work weaving in and out of the text or sometimes covering the pages. This is a natural readaloud, an entertaining introduction to mythology for the very young, and an extension of the imaginary world into the real. The last two pages show Zeus' family in contemporary attire, sitting for their photograph, while Pan sneaks off with his pipes into Central Park. "YAAAAHHOOOOO-YIPPEEEYIPPEEEYAAAAAHOOOOOO!"

341   **Gherman**, Beverly. *Agnes de Mille: Dancing Off the Earth.* Atheneum, 1990. ISBN 0-689-31441-8. 138p. $13.95.

6-10   Chapter notes and a bibliography indicate the research done by the author on the life of one of this country's outstanding dancers and choreographers. With no parental support, with a late start in beginning the study of ballet, and with the knowledge that she did not have "the ideal ballet body," Agnes de Mille persisted, practiced, and worked until a stroke ended her ability to dance. Anecdotes drawn from de Mille's own books and articles provide lively color and intimate details, so that this biography presents a perceptive picture of an artist struggling to gain self-confidence as well as acclaim. The text is cohesive, coherent, and flowing despite some awkward phrases.

342   **Gibbons**, Gail. *Catch the Wind: All About Kites;* written and illus. by Gail Gibbons. Little, 1989. ISBN 0-316-30955-9. 32p. $12.95.

5-8 yrs.   This is the kind of topic best suited to Gibbons' style, with a manageable amount of information to simplify into a serviceable story and color cartoon art. Katie and Sam bring their savings to Ike's Kite Shop to choose their entries in a kite festival. While they're looking around, Gibbons explains a bit of history ("Chinese flew the very first kites more than three thousand years ago") and depicts the use of kites for science experiments, including Ben Franklin's proof of electricity, the Wright Brothers' aeronautic work with box kites, and the National Weather Service's maintenance of kite stations for forecasts from 1898 to 1933. Basic kite shapes, parts, and principles of flight are also covered before Katie and Sam make their selection and join the festival. Instructions for making a flat kite, launching it, and bringing it down round off the presentation, which includes safety tips. A breeze for first flyers.

343   **Gibbons**, Gail. *From Path to Highway: The Story of the Boston Post Road;* written and illus. by Gail Gibbons. Crowell, 1986. Library ed. ISBN 0-690-04514-X; Trade ed. ISBN 0-690-04513-1. 31p. Library ed. $11.89; Trade ed. $11.95.

1-3   In an interesting departure from her usual books, Gail Gibbons describes the evolution of the three post roads between Boston and New York. Beginning with the Indian trails, she shows the important role the roads played in the developing New England colonies. Modes of transportation change—from foot to horse to wagons and stage-coaches, trains, and *"Honk! Toot!* It's 1920 and the road is busy again. The automobile is here." Gibbons gives the story human interest with descriptions of individuals who traveled the roads, including Sarah Knight, who rode her horse along the southern route in 1704 and composed a clever quatrain upon her return: ". . . Over great rocks and many stones/God has presarv'd from fracter'd bones." The clear, factual, and deliberate text is matched by completely charming illustrations. With gentle lines and bright colors, Gibbons shows both individual scenes filled with detail, and map-like spreads of the region in different times and seasons, often using the naive perspective characteristic of folk landscape painting. A wonderful introduction to roads, transportation, history, progress.

344   **Gibbons**, Gail. *Sunken Treasure;* written and illus. by Gail Gibbons. Crowell, 1988. Library ed. ISBN 0-690-04736-3; Trade ed. ISBN 0-690-04734-7. 32p. Library ed. $12.89; Trade ed. $12.95.

2-4   With wash drawings that avoid some of the glitzier cartoon effects in her prodigiously serial nonfiction picturebooks, Gibbons shows the fate of the Spanish galleon *Atocha* and its epic modern-day recovery. This is a story that has been well told with photographs in George Sullivan's *Treasure Hunt,* but the challenge of condensing and illustrating the facts in a briefer format is well met here. The hardship and tragedy that dogged Mel Fisher's enterprise, including his son's death, have been omitted for an outline of the techniques of searching and raising the treasure. Similarly, the archeological preservation of the wreck is indicated without reference to the conflicts that still surround the artifacts. For youngsters eager to investigate tales of hidden treasure, this is as good an introduction as any available for the age group.

345   Giblin, James Cross. *From Hand to Mouth: Or, How We Invented Knives, Forks, Spoons, and Chopsticks & the Table Manners To Go With Them.* Crowell, 1987. Library ed. ISBN 0-690-04662-6; Trade ed. ISBN 0-690-04660-X. 86p. illus. and with photographs. Library ed. $11.89; Trade ed. $11.95.

4-6   An informed and informative historical survey of eating utensils suggests the social context for changes such as the introduction of the fork, the rounding of knife tips, and the decline of Asian children's dexterity in wielding chopsticks. This is one of those books that stimulates observations about everyday patterns and gives a long view on their development. The style is clearcut and the book design lively, with arresting photographic reproductions and spacious format. A 3-page bibliography includes both adult and juvenile (asterisked) books, and the index is thorough. The return of contemporary Americans to eating fast food with fingers casts a thought-provoking perspective on historical cycles.

346   Giblin, James Cross. *Let There Be Light: A Book about Windows.* Crowell, 1988. Library ed. ISBN 0-690-04695-2; Trade ed. ISBN 0-690-04693-6. 162p. illus. with photographs. Library ed. $14.89; Trade ed. $14.95.

5-9   Including "curiosity" as well as light and air among the reasons people put holes in their dwellings, Giblin's historical survey of windows covers a good 12,000 years and an equally impressive span of cultures. Details of glass and papermaking are thorough, and there is a smooth blend of technological and architectural developments. As was true of the author's *From Hand to Mouth*, social commentary runs fluently throughout: why Moslems constructed windows that allowed one to see out but not in; the differences between cultures that built windows facing a courtyard and those that built them facing the outside. This is as much a history of how people live as it is a history of windows, and Giblin's impeccable research shines through.

347   Giblin, James Cross. *The Truth About Santa Claus.* Crowell, 1985. Library ed. ISBN 0-690-04484-4. Trade ed. ISBN 0-690-044383-6. 96p. illus. Library ed. $10.89; Trade ed. $11.50.

3-5   Doing his usual job of research and well-organized presentation, Giblin describes the various truths, legends, and accretions that evolved or (like the Clement Moore poem) were grafted to produce the characteristics of the Santa Claus figure familiar today, sleigh, reindeer octet, red suit, and all. Reproductions of paintings and cartoons, as well as photographs, illustrate both the diverse European legends and the contemporary Santa Claus figure. A bibliography adds to the usefulness of a book that not only gives information about Santa Claus (Kris Kringle, Father Christmas, the Christ-kindl, and other gift-bringers as well) but also gives an interesting picture of the ways in which customs arise, fuse, change, are diffused only to change again.

348   **Gilbert**, Sara. *Get Help: Solving the Problems in Your Life*; illus. by Ellen Friedman. Morrow, 1989. ISBN 0-688-08010-3. 144p. $12.95.

6-10   No judging, no patronizing, no soothing: this is a tremendously useful, wide ranging, and well-organized compendium of organizations and groups that offer either direct help, or access to further help or information, on problems that range from abuse or addiction to running away or legal rights. The writing is crisp and clear; the foreword explains how the book is arranged, what the significance of included or omitted material is, that all sources cited are either free or low-cost help for adolescents, and how entries were compiled and coded. A sample of the format is that of "Education and Scholarships," which begins with general facts, a list of sources (annotated and including addresses and telephone numbers) under "Contact," tips on telephone approaches, a "Get help" section and a more detailed "More help" section. A final section provides backup material, such as what to do if you dial an 800 number and it's out of service, or how to get help if you are deaf or disabled, or where to call (often a hotline) if there is an emergency. Just what has been needed, this gives readers information about more than 100 national organizations, tells readers what to expect from them, and how best to benefit from the help they provide.

349   **Gilmore**, Kate. *Enter Three Witches*. Houghton, 1990. ISBN 0-395-50213-6. 210p. $13.95.

6-9   This is a deft merging of reality and fantasy, as sixteen-year-old Bren, accepting the fact that his mother and grandmother are witches, tries desperately to keep the fact from the girl with whom he's fallen in love. Erika is a dancer, playing one of the witches in *Macbeth*, and Bren is working (frantically) on the play's lighting. The third witch is black, also a member of the household, and there's an extra surprise-witch introduced in a humorous last twist. A yeasty mix of mounting a play, enjoying the New York scene, falling in love, and coping with an irrepressible family, this is good fun, with a writing style that sports an excellent ear for dialogue.

350   **Ginsburg**, Mirra, ad. *The Chinese Mirror*; illus. by Margot Zemach. Harcourt, 1988. ISBN 0-15-200420-3. 32p. $14.95.

K-3   Watercolor illustrations, more spare of line than is most of Zemach's work, are "inspired by the paintings of two eighteenth-century Korean genre painters, Sin Yun-bok and Kim Hong-do," an endpaper note states. The soft colors and sly humor of the pictures echo the quiet tone and humor of Ginsburg's retelling of a Korean folktale. When a villager returns from China with a strange object that mimics his actions (nobody knows what it is: a mirror) the members of his family take turns looking at the piece of glass. The wife is jealous because she sees a picture of a pretty young woman, her mother-in-law is confused because the "picture" is that of an older woman, while the father-in-law is even more baffled, because the picture isn't that of a woman at all. No moral here, unless it is that things aren't what they seem, but the message to the reader is one children appreciate: you are smart enough to understand although the characters in the story are not. Nicely done.

351   **Girard**, Linda Walvoord. *We Adopted You, Benjamin Koo*; illus. by Linda Shute. Whitman, 1989. ISBN 0-8075-8694-3. 32p. $10.50.

3-5   Age nine, Benjamin Koo Andrews talks about his life, both what he's been told (abandoned ten days after his birth, left on the steps of a Korean orphanage, adopted by an American couple and taken to the United States) and what he has experienced: a loving extended family, the advent of a baby sister, also adopted (this time from Brazil) and the realization that his appearance is accepted casually by many but received with varying degrees of hostility by a few. It might seem ambitious to tackle in one short book such major themes as adjustment to adoption, cultural adaptability, sibling relationships, and prejudice. Girard handles this with aplomb, and makes Ben's voice both childlike and convincing. Perhaps because it eschews both cuteness and sentimentality, the story is touching without being maudlin, and its tone is direct and candid rather than being overburdened with Message.

352   **Glassman**, Bruce. *The Crash of '29 and the New Deal*. Silver Burdett, 1986. Trade ed. ISBN 0-382-06831-9; Paper ed. ISBN 0-382-06978-1. 62p. (Turning Points in American History) Trade ed. $13.96; Paper ed. $5.95.

5-7   This pithy introduction to the causes and effects of the Great Depression gives a surprising amount of perspective within its limited confines. The Wall Street panic of October 24, 1929, is vividly detailed, along with a solid explanation of the financial speculation and tenuous economic situation that led to the collapse. A background on contemporary federal policies and political philosophies clarifies some of Hoover's action (and nonaction) and underscores the radical innovation of Roosevelt's reform programs. A first-rate look at a complex decade illustrated with large, well-selected black and white photographs.

353   **Glenn**, Mel. *Play-by-Play.* Houghton/Clarion, 1986. ISBN 0-89919-392-7. 126p. $11.95.

3-5   This is a sports story and it does have some game descriptions, but—despite the title—the book is not a series of game sequences precariously held together by thin threads of plot. It's a robust story about a boy who feels that he is average, has ups and downs in his family relationships, and an even more see-saw record of best-friendship. Jeremy is in fourth grade, he's the narrator, and he always feels eclipsed by best friend Lloyd, a superior athlete and vocal about it. When excited, Lloyd is derisive about Jeremy's performance, and Lloyd is usually excited during a game. All this comes to a head when a new gym teacher introduces the class to soccer. The boys learn that girls can be good players and good sports, Lloyd learns to restrain himself, and Jeremy learns to be tolerant in a story that has good pace and balance, and that is convincing as the product of a fourth-grader.

354   **Goble**, Paul. *Death of the Iron Horse*; written and illus. by Paul Goble. Bradbury, 1987. ISBN 0-02-737830-6. 28p. $12.95.

5-8 yrs.   A fine example of pictorial history recounts the only incident when Indians wrecked a train—a Union Pacific freight derailed by Cheyennes on August 7, 1867. The brief introduction dispels the movie myth that trainwrecking was a constant Native American activity and sets the stage for the story, which begins with a Cheyenne prophet's dream of whites stripping the earth and covering it with iron bands. The ensuing settlers' and soldiers' destruction bears the dream out; when several villages are burned and scouts bring word of an Iron Horse threatening their camp, a group of warriers determines to destroy it. Their raid has both humorous and tragic aspects: they derail the train without realizing quite how they've done it, leave several of the crew dead, and raid the shipment of many products that have been withheld or sold too dearly to them by traders. They keep the coins for decoration and throw away the paper money, galloping wildly across the plain with bolts of cloth streaming behind them in a game long remembered by their people. Their triumph, of course, is shortlived, and the last picture makes a telling statement with an Amtrak train speeding across a littered landscape surmounted by fighter jets. Goble's art is all the better for a new infusion of non-folkloric subject matter. The landscapes here are stunning, one double-page spread green with a stippling of locomotive smoke rising among the trees, the next dawn gray with silhouetted shapes of the war party facing a white circle of light from the engine. The angles of the wrecked cars are echoed in the body of the dead crewman, while later, the flowing cloth flies as wildly as the warriors' excitement. A different view of history, socially and aesthetically.

355   **Goble**, Paul. *Her Seven Brothers*; written and illus. by Paul Goble. Bradbury, 1988. ISBN 0-02-737960-4. 27p. $13.95.

5-7 yrs.   After his foray into historical legend with *The Death of the Iron Horse*, Goble has returned to a Cheyenne myth about the creation of the Big Dipper. The story tells of a girl skilled in embroidering deer and buffalo skin clothes with porcupine quills. In tune with the spirit world and language of the animals, she makes clothes for seven brothers, journeys to their tipi, and happily sets up housekeeping as their sister. When a buffalo chief demands her in marriage and she refuses, the eight young people must escape a vengeful stampede by climbing a tree into the sky, where they become the stars of the Big Dipper. Goble's full-color illustrations are consistent with the style that has shaped his other ten books, showcasing landscape compositions punctuated by Native American motifs and harmonic nature imagery. It is much to his credit that he gives complete references for the story sources from which he adapts the text and that he describes the setting, with a note on artistic techniques used to reflect it.

356   **Goble**, Paul, ad. *Iktomi and the Boulder: A Plains Indian Story*; retold and illus. by Paul Goble. Orchard/Watts, 1988. Library ed. ISBN 0-531-08360-8; Trade ed. ISBN 0-531-05760-7. 30p. Library ed. $13.99; Trade ed. $13.95.

5-7 yrs.
*   This is just what the doctor ordered for Paul Goble: a change of tone from stories of dignified weight to a trickster tale adapted and illustrated with mischief. Iktomi is so vain that he struts off toward the next village in his best clothes and blanket. When the sun shines too hot, he gives the blanket to a boulder; but when the rain falls he takes it back, infuriating the boulder so that it rolls after him and pins him down. Finally, Iktomi tricks some bats into destroying the rock, after which he sets off again, battered-looking but jaunty as ever. The basic story is in large black print, the narrator's periodic remarks to the audience in gray italics, and the trickster's comments ("That rock has a terrible temper") in small print in the midst of the pictures. These are simply composed against lots of white space that allows a smooth, amusing blend of diverse design and color elements. The picture of Iktomi completely enveloped in his isolated, tent-shaped blanket with rain and lightning aiming at its peak is particularly funny, as are his lies to the bats ("He said that you sleep upside-down because you don't know your 'up side' from your 'down side.'") The last depiction of Iktomi, showing one leg in traditional garb and the other in an athletic sock to go with his baseball cap, steps the story right into modern

times. With source and background notes and an attention-grabbing cover that portrays Iktomi upside down under the rock ("Help!"), this is a coup.

357   **Goble**, Paul, ad. *Iktomi and the Ducks: A Plains Indian Story*; ad. and illus. by Paul Goble. Jackson/Orchard, 1990. Library ed. ISBN 0-531-08483-3; Trade ed. ISBN 0-531-05883-2. 32p. Library Ed. $14.99; Trade ed. $14.95.

5-8 yrs.   "There goes that white guy, Paul Goble, telling another story about me. . . . My attorney will Sioux," says Iktomi. This picture book, even more than the first two in the series, reveals the artist as trickster. Here Iktomi starts out looking for his horse to ride in a dress parade. On the trail ("who could possibly ride such a wild horse?"), Iktomi spies some ducks and coaxes them to dance with their eyes closed, bopping them on the head and cooking them on a fire, his every move watched by Coyote. As usual, Iktomi proves his own undoing and loses out on the ducks. Never mind: "I never liked roast duck—too greasy—bad for my cholesterol level." The special effects—a runaway horse, a shadowy coyote, some ridiculous ducks, two sinister trees that trap Iktomi between creaking branches—are based on a witty use of silhouettes. Other visual jokes include leaf patterns that echo the ducks' tracks, associating the catcher with the caught. Rhythmic shapes keep every page action-packed, and the varied typefaces allow several levels of narration to proceed simultaneously, ending with that time-honored cliffhanger, "what do you think he will get up to next?"

358   **Goodall**, Jane. *My Life with the Chimpanzees*. Pocket Books, 1988. Paper ed. ISBN 0-671-66095-0. 124p. illus. with photographs. Paper ed. $2.75.

3-6   "What would it be like to live with the animals?" is a perennial childhood question—and it was Jane Goodall's, who describes in this autobiography her early passion for Lofting's *Doctor Doolittle* books. In describing her childhood and first thoughts of vocation, Goodall seems uneasy writing for a young audience (whom she addresses as "you") and is occasionally patronizing. In discussing Konrad Lorenz's work with geese, for example, she writes "They fall in love, marry, and stay together until one of them dies." Her account loses awkwardness when she tells of arriving in Kenya to work with Louis Leakey, and beginning her own research with the chimpanzees in Gombe. David Greybeard, Goliath, Flo and her children are all here, and may be familiar to children from Goodall's TV specials. Always using anecdotes from her work, Goodall cites the importance of close observation, detailed record-keeping, and patience, concluding with a passionate chapter explaining the importance of the humane treatment of animals.

359   **Goor**, Ron. *Insect Metamorphosis: From Egg to Adult*; written and illus. with photographs by Ron and Nancy Goor. Atheneum, 1990. ISBN 0-689-31445-0. 32p. $13.95

2-5   Brilliant color close-ups document the development of several species representative of complete and incomplete metamorphosis. The four stages of the first (egg, larva, pupa, adult) and three stages of the second (egg, nymph, adult) get well-defined explanations through examples of monarch butterflies, hickory horned devil caterpillars, mourning cloak butterflies, cecropia moths, mosquitoes, paper wasps, braconid wasps, praying mantids, dragonflies, and cicadas. Although each insect has characteristic variations, the repetition of molting and other patterns of change will help readers (this could also be read aloud to a young audience) absorb the rhythmic cycles. Clear and concisely thorough.

360   **Gordon**, Ruth, ed. *Under All Silences: Shades of Love.* Harper, 1987. Library ed. ISBN 0-06-022155-0; Trade ed. ISBN 0-06-022154-2. 78p. Library ed. $12.89; Trade ed. $12.95.

9-
*   Rich but never heavy, this collection of 66 love poems offers a taste of Maya Angelou, Adrienne Rich, Kenneth Rexroth, e e cummings, Kenneth Patchen, Amy Lowell, and a range of others, including many translations from non-Western cultures and/or earlier times. Although varied in mood from the gently affectionate to the passionately sexual, the poems share an intimate I-thou tone that will involve young readers immediately, whether they are browsing or making their way through the carefully juxtaposed selections. A few choices— Yeats' irresistible "Song of Wandering Aengus," for instance—are well known, but many are not popularly anthologized, and the expressions of love common to contemporary, ancient Egyptian, or Medieval Japanese poets make a striking statement about emotions that young people of today share with those in other periods and places. More informal than McCullough's *Love Is Like the Lion's Tooth*, this is an intensely personal but generally moving anthology.

361   **Gordon**, Sheila. *Waiting for the Rain: A Novel of South Africa.* Orchard/Watts, 1987. Library ed. ISBN 0-531-08326-8; Trade ed. ISBN 0-531-05726-7. 212p. Library ed. $12.99; Trade ed. $12.95.

8-   Whenever Frikkie had come to visit his aunt and uncle on the farm, he had played with Tengo. Black and white, best friends, the two accepted their roles, young master and young servant. That is the beginning of the story, in which Tengo, sensitive and intellectually curious, grows up to learn what apartheid means, while stolid Frikkie accepts the Boer philosophy as he accepts his mediocrity as a student and his diligence as a soldier. Inevitably, there is a meeting, and a bitter confrontation helps Tengo decide that he will fight for freedom but follow a path of non-violence. Despite a slow pace, this is a dramatic novel and a strong indictment of the regime as well as a convincing picture of one man's growing awareness and involvement.

362   **Graeber**, Charlotte Towner. *Fudge*; illus. by Cheryl Harness. Lothrop, 1987. ISBN 0-688-06735-2. 123p. $11.75.

3-5   A natural for third and fourth graders, this recounts a major event in nine-year-old Chad's life: the acquisition and training of his first dog. His parents agree only conditionally that he can have one of the new puppies that his babysitter's dog has whelped. Chad's mother is pregnant with twins and unable to manage any additional work; Chad must prove he can take complete responsibility for Fudge, as he names the Labrador retriever. Chad's parents are the firm type, which adds to the suspense, and readers will be rooting for him to remember each of Fudge's meals and to clean up after every mess. The family relationships are warmly portrayed, both Chad's and his babysitter's, Mrs. Garcia, along with her husband and children. There's a real sense of neighborhood and a subplot involving a playmate whose parents are not as understanding but who nevertheless come through in the end. The black-and-white drawings are occasionally stiff but mostly homey, with well-varied textural contrasts. Easy to read, easy to enjoy.

363   **Graham**, Bob. *Crusher Is Coming!* written and illus. by Bob Graham. Viking, 1988. ISBN 0-670-82081-4. 26p. $11.95.

4-7 yrs.   A deft hand and a sense of humor make Graham's lively line and wash drawings enjoyable in themselves and a fine foil for the deliberate blandness of a story told entirely in dialogue. The set-up: a boy is pleased but nervous at the impending visit by his school's football hero. Pete reminds his mother to call the visitor "Crusher," not to give him a kiss when he and Crusher come home, and above all to keep baby sister Claire out of his room. The development: Crusher, although politely responsive to doing whatever Pete suggests, is obviously smitten by the baby and happily plays with her. The denouement: after Crusher leaves, Pete gives Claire a piggyback ride just as his hero did. Clever, funny, and touching without being saccharine.

364   **Graham**, Thomas. *Mr. Bear's Chair*; written and illus. by Thomas Graham. Dutton, 1987. ISBN 0-525-44300-2. 31p. $10.95.

3-6 yrs.   Spacious, double-spread oil paintings with one or two lines per page
   *   tell the story of Mr. Bear, who fixes pancakes for Mrs. Bear only to see her crash to the floor when her chair breaks. The rest of the book follows his satisfyingly methodical construction of a new chair, from felling a tree to weaving the cane seat. Equally satisfying is the deliciously predictable crash that follows when Mr. Bear sits down to supper, breaking his chair, and sets off into the sunset with his toolbox

again. This combines slapstick elements of humor with warm affection between the characters and satisfaction over making something useful. The story is planed down to a clean minimum. The art, without investing too much in detail, packs everything into facial expressions and physical poses: Mrs. Bear putting on her dress or ruefully rubbing her bottom, Mr. Bear concentrating on his project, the cat peering around the doorway after the commotion. The colors are smoothly modulated, the textures smooth and thick, the figures varied in size for interesting perspective. A winner for the younger listener, one on one or in a group.

365   **Gray**, Nigel. *A Balloon for Grandad*; illus. by Jane Ray. Orchard, 1988. Library ed. ISBN 0-531-08355-1; Trade ed. ISBN 0-531-05755-0. 30p. Library ed. $13.99; Trade ed. $13.95.

4-7 yrs.
  *
A picture book with plot, poetic writing, psychological reassurance, natural ethnic representation, and exceptional art, this uses particularized details to focus on an experience of general concern among children. Sam's balloon has blown out the back door, and as his father holds him close, they have that throat-catching experience of watching a beloved object fly high . . . and away. Dad comforts Sam by describing an imaginary journey "high over the sparkling blue-green sea where silver fish leap from the waves; high over the hot yellow sand of the desert where scorpions, and spitting spiders, and sidewinder snakes hide from the heat" to Grandad Abdulla's. "And sandgrouse will peck at it . . . and falcons will fall on it, and hawks will fly after it, and vultures with their big hooky beaks and their sharp talons will tear at it, but the dry desert wind will help it to dodge and weave and nothing will harm it." Of course, when Grandad Abdulla receives the balloon he immediately perceives it as a message from Sam "to show that, although he's so far away, he's thinking of me." Associating the loss of a toy with separation from a dear family member brings this story very close to home, and those common sadnesses are brilliantly lightened by Chagallian art lending child-like perspective to the landscapes—both physical and emotional—that are crossed here. The sudden, almost cubist contrasts of shape and color in the illustrations reflect the jerky flight of the balloon, which is also captured in the rhythms of the prose. The book design itself is filled with complex patterns balanced by enough free-floating space to save the images from clutter. For Everychild.

366   **Greene**, Constance C. *Isabelle and Little Orphan Frannie*. Viking, 1988. ISBN 0-670-82266-3. 131p. $11.95.

3-5   Isabelle, the indomitable fifth-grader who gravitates toward trouble because she is inventive, ebullient, thoughtless, and determined, is back; she's as lively, appealing, and amusing as in earlier books. This time she takes eight-year-old Frannie on, having learned that Frannie can't read. A peripatetic waif, Frannie declares she is "a norphan," and in a way she is, her mother having come to stay with her friend because, as Frannie (calculatedly pitiful) explains, her old daddy died and her Mom is looking for a new one. The lessons don't go well, but after Frannie moves on, Isabelle gets a postcard: "I go to scool now. I can read some. Your a good teach." So the story ends with Isabelle happy, her project accomplished. There's no question of condescending charity, Frannie being a tough little character who knows how to get what she wants. As is usual in Greene's stories, the perceptive affection that pervades the book is balanced by light, bright humor, especially in the dialogue. This has some deliciously entertaining classroom scenes.

367   **Greene**, Constance C. *Just Plain Al.* Viking, 1986. ISBN 0-670-81250-1. 132p. $11.95.

5-8   A fifth book about Al (Alexandra) is again narrated by her best friend, who remains nameless. Al, approaching her 14th, feels that she needs a new nickname. Maybe Zandi? As in the earlier books, this is a witty account of the friendship, the family relationships, and the young teen concerns of two lively and engaging characters. The narrative is convincing as the product of a twelve-year-old, the style is yeasty, and the Manhattan background is used to stimulating effect. Strong characters, the two girls remain recognizable as their earlier selves, and both develop and mature as time marches on.

368   **Greenfield**, Eloise. *Under the Sunday Tree*; illus. by Amos Ferguson. Harper, 1988. Library ed. ISBN 0-06-022257-3; Trade ed. ISBN 0-06-022254-9. 39p. Library ed. $12.89; Trade ed. $12.95.

2-5   A more symbiotic collaboration than most picture poetry books, this makes it hard to tell where poem leaves off and picture begins. Greenfield gives voice to portraits: "pineapples, pumpkins, chickens, we/ carry more than the things you see/ we also carry history." Through cool planes of green and blue, Ferguson creates a peaceful ocean shore that makes visible Greenfield's "place I know/ where children go to find/ their deepest feelings." Sometimes contemplative, often funny ("It takes more than a wish/ to catch a fish") the poems glide and bounce with rhythmic effects echoed in the bold paintings, which are naively drawn and iconographic, and formally patterned with two-dimensional perspectives. For "The Brave Ones" ("We hear the bell clanging/ we come in a hurry/ we come with our ladders and hoses/ our hoses") Ferguson paints a stylized house afire, its straight lines surrounded by bomb-like blobs of smoke and a wreath of flame around the chimney, all capturing the danger and excitement of the poem. "The Sailboat Race" sounds and looks ready to rush off the page. The last poem is a marvelously festive toast from both poet and illustrator: "let's lift our punch/ to the bunch/ (that's us) . . . this toast we'll repeat/ each time we meet/ and now, my friends—/ let's eat". Crisply designed, with poem and painting on facing pages, the collection is supposed to be "an affectionate portrait of life in the Bahamas," but given the breadth of vision contained herein, the book extends far beyond the Caribbean.

369   **Greenwald**, Sheila. *Rosy's Romance*; written and illus. by Sheila Greenwald. Joy Street/Little, 1989. ISBN 0-316-32704-2. 106p. $12.95.

4-6   Inspired by their new obsession with teen romance series like *Sugerwater High* and *Sakrinhill Quints*, Rosy and Hermione decide to turn Rosy's rather bohemian older sisters into real *teens*. As Hermione says of Anitra and Pippa, "they may be teens, but the Sakrinhill Quints wouldn't let them through the door." Thus is born Project Romance, as Rosy and Hermione scheme to get the sisters "dates and crushes and parties and . . ." to the prom, "the most exciting thing of all." Paperback daydreams and romantic reality collide most entertainingly here, and Project Romance becomes an apt mix of slapstick and send-up while Rosie's own romance (complete with an anonymous love note) begins without any machinations at all. Rosie and Hermione are engaging as always, and Anitra and Pippa prove themselves to be a pair of really good sports.

370   **Grifalconi**, Ann. *The Village of Round and Square Houses*; written and illus. by Ann Grifalconi. Little, 1986. ISBN 0-316-32862-6. 31p. $14.95.

4-7 yrs.
*
An exceptional blend of scene setting, story-telling, and complementary illustration opens with a narrator recollecting her isolated but happy childhood in the west African village of Tos. Here the men live in square houses, the women in round ones, and after a lively description of a typical evening meal together, the narrator recalls the story of how the hut arrangement began, as told by her grandmother. This complex framework of a tale within a generational flashback evolves smoothly, and the actual story is a dramatic one involving an erupting volcano (Mother Naka), some climactic poetical passages, rhythmic sound effects, and rich scenarios of cultural peace and prosperity, with a bit of universal philosophizing thrown in ("each one has a place to be apart, and a time to be together. . . . "). The art is beautifully modulated in color and textural effects, with striking organic patterns and natural sweeps of line. The sharp explosion sequence gives way to ashy gray/brown monotones after Mother Naka's eruption, swinging slowly back into earth colors and finally normally intense everyday hues. An involving experience for children and adults alike.

371   **Griffith**, Helen V. *Georgia Music*; illus by James Stevenson.
Greenwillow, 1986. Library ed. ISBN 0-688-06072-2; Trade ed. 0-688-
06071-4. 22p. Library ed. $11.88; Trade ed. $11.75.

K-3   A solitary old man incorporates his granddaughter into his gardening
*   routine when her mother leaves her in Georgia for a long summer
visit. In the morning the two hoe together, in the afternoon they
snooze, in the evening Grandaddy plays the mouth organ "for the
crickets and the grasshoppers." The two get along just fine, sharing
quiet little jokes over a "sassy old bird" that mocks them from a fence
post. But when the girl comes back to visit the next summer,
Granddaddy is ill; they bring him back to Baltimore, where he pines
for his cabin until the girl finally learns to play "Georgia music" to him
on the harmonica, even the sounds of the "sassy old bird." This is a
precise, poignant short story delicately enhanced by Stevenson's
watercolor portraits of the two main characters set into homey,
impressionistic rural scenes. Both art and narrative are low-key, letting
the understated warmth of a relationship between two nontalkers
emerge in quiet, strong harmony. Despite the picture-book format,
the story, read aloud, will appeal to older children as well.

372   **Griffith**, Helen V. *Grandaddy's Place*; illus. by James Stevenson.
Greenwillow, 1987. Library ed. ISBN 0-688-06254-7; Trade ed. ISBN 0-
688-06253-9. 38p. Library ed. $11.88; Trade ed. $11.75.

K-3   Janetta has never met her grandfather, and while she enjoys riding the
*   train with her mother, she is nervous about farm animals, noises of
wild creatures, and other aspects of farm life. Grandaddy doesn't push
it: his overtures are subtle, his treatment of Janetta's fears is casual,
and his storytelling irresistible. Soon Janetta's mother is shaking her
head with rueful affection and saying "One of you is as bad as the
other" as her father and daughter find themselves in rapport. No
sentimentality here, but there's sweetness and warmth and humor in
a story nicely told and just as nicely illustrated.

373   **Grimm**, Jakob Ludwig Karl. *The Fox and the Cat: Kevin Crossley-
Holland's Animal Tales from Grimm*; ad. by Kevin Crossley-Holland;
illus. by Susan Varley. Lothrop, 1986. ISBN 0-688-04636-3. 55p. $13.00.

3-5   Both this book and the one illustrated by Postma, reviewed below, are
worth purchasing wherever there is a well-used collection of fairy tales.
Crossley-Holland's eleven selections will suit a younger age group,
since most of the animal tales are brief and action-packed. These are
also smoothly translated, with a fillip of humor in the choice of words
"You shabby-whisker-licker, you spotted idiot, you poor scrounger and
mouse-hunter, have you gone out of your mind?"). The watercolor
paintings, some full-page and others smaller oval insets that relieve
the text, are full of vitality and fine-line wit. The picture of a horse

dragging a lion along by its back legs, which are firmly tied to the horse's tail, is typically lively. Children will enjoy reading this as well as hearing it read aloud.

374   **Grimm**, Jakob Ludwig Karl. *Red Riding Hood;* retold and illus. by James Marshall. Dial, 1987. Library ed. ISBN 0-8037-0345-7; Trade ed. ISBN 0-8037-0344-9. 32p. Library ed. $10.89; Trade ed. $10.95.

4-8 yrs.   Some people are born to be funny; James Marshall can't help himself.
  *   Fortunately. Here he extends his high humor to a Perrault/Grimm tale with a serious past. Sticking to the basic plot formula, he reduces the text to the minimum, with a few choice bits of dialogue ("It is I, your delicious—er—darling granddaughter," says the wolf, and later, "I'm so wicked... *So* wicked"). Most of the high jinks are pictorial, however, and played out against some of the boldest color compositions the artist has done. When the wolf comes to the door, we are treated with a view of Granny's feet, replaced, ominously enough, by a pair of gray clawed paws when Red Riding Hood knocks on the door. On the last page, as proof that R.R.H. keeps her promise never to speak to another stranger, she spurns the overtures of a large green crocodile. Marshall's version may be counterproductive to the moral; however, this is one wolf not to be missed.

375   **Grimm**, Jakob Ludwig Karl. *Rumpelstiltskin;* illus. by Paul O. Zelinsky. Dutton, 1986. ISBN 0-525-44265-0. 37p. $12.95

4-8 yrs.   Oil paintings rich in Italian Renaissance style, setting, and costume
  *   unfold the Grimms' second-edition—and most familiar—version of this strange tale of greed compounded and, finally, confounded. Most of the colors are highlighted or dominated by variants of gold except for the sudden darkness of a servant's escapade into the night-time world of Rumpelstilskin's fiery chant revealing his name. The characters here are preeminently graceful, from the beautiful miller's daughter to her cold, elegant king and the spidery little man who demands her first child in payment for spinning straw into gold. Zelinsky has caught the human complexity represented in fairy tales and layered it visually into an absorbing book. A note on the story is appended.

376   **Grimm**, Jakob Ludwig Karl. *The Twelve Dancing Princesses and Other Tales from Grimm;* illus. by Lidia Postma. Dial, 1986. ISBN 0-8037-0237-X. 100p. $14.95.

4-6   The fourteen stories here are longer and more sophisticated than those in the Grimm collection by Crossley-Holland, reviewed above, but they represent an appealing mix of old favorites like "Cinderella" and less common ones, such as "The Nixie of the Mill Pond." These have been slightly adapted, but not seriously tampered with.

"Cinderella" alters the rhymes, for instance, but with full respect for literal meanings. Most extraordinary are Postma's haunting illustrations, which range from impressionistic to precise in style without seeming to break continuity. Most often, the muted colors and eerie compositions are meant to suggest rather than define, a provocative quality that is well-matched with the imaginative depth of the tales.

377   **Grimm**, Jakob Ludwig Karl. *The Water of Life*; ad. by Barbara Rogasky; illus. by Trina Schart Hyman. Holiday House, 1986. ISBN 0-8234-0552-4. 39p. $14.95.

K-3   One of the Grimms' more somber stories gets dark treatment in Hyman's accompanying paintings, with medieval trappings and Christian symbols woven thematically through the book as graphic motifs. The tale is one of betrayal, as three sons search for the water of life to cure their father, and the older two, motivated only by greed and ambition, deceive and plot against the youngest. Rogasky has made a few adaptations in the long text, which is close to Ralph Manheim's translation. Hyman's portraiture of the characters casts a personal light on the archetypes with chilling effect, heightening, at the same time, the strange details of the story, as in the realistic depiction of a dining hall filled with enchanted princes (including a Christ figure). The princess whose marriage to the hero creates a happy ending seems more enchantress than the stock heroine and quite secondary to the male conflicts at the heart of the tale. This is strong stuff, with brooding colors, austere gray frames, and a slightly spooky convergence of real, religious and superstitious worlds.

378   **Grimm**, Wilhelm. *Dear Mili: An Old Tale*; tr. by Ralph Manheim; illus. by Maurice Sendak. Farrar, 1988. ISBN 0-374-31762-3. 40p. $16.95.

3-5   Since the discovery, in 1983, of a previously unknown tale (found in a letter and presumably an original story) by Wilhelm Grimm, and the subsequent announcement that a translated version would be illustrated by Maurice Sendak, there has been excited anticipation of its publication. This information is included in the jacket but not within the book itself, nor is a source note provided. The art exceeds informed expectation, as Sendak again responds with sensitivity to a tale that is sentimental, somber, and devout, a Gothic fragment that is given beauty by the gravity and tenderness of the pictures. Sent into the woods by her mother because a war is moving closer to them, a little girl takes her refuge with an old man who is kind and who sends her home on the third day with a rosebud. He is Saint Joseph, who says "Never fear. When this rose blooms, you will be with me again." The child goes home to find her three days have actually been thirty years. After a blissful reunion, mother and child sleep; in the morning neighbors find them dead, St Joseph's rose lying between them. The soft pastels, the intricacies of the foliage, and the depiction of the child's guardian angel as another charming little girl, make the book visually memorable.

379   **Guy**, Rosa. *The Ups and Downs of Carl Davis III.* Delacorte, 1989. ISBN 0-440-50138-5. 113p. $13.95.

5-8   As Carl quickly makes clear in the letters that comprise this novel, he's out of place in the South Carolina town where his parents have sent him to visit Grandma (and to get himself straightened out). Rosa Guy uses the correspondence capably in developing conflicts and characters, especially the protagonist's transition from irrefutably obnoxious to refutably obnoxious. It's only the tone that sometimes seems forced too far—Carl's self-conscious intellectualism, for instance, or Grandma's lecturing Carl's prejudiced teacher and classmates on African-American history. The relationship between Carl and a neighboring boy who's using drugs is realistic, as is Carl's sadness over his New York friend who has died of an overdose. On balance, this is a bitter-sweet book that's refreshingly frank about being black, being proud, and saying it out loud.

380   **Gwynne**, Fred. *Pondlarker*; written and illus. by Fred Gwynne. Simon, 1990. ISBN 0-671-70846-5. 32p. $13.95.

K-3   In witty corroboration of the influence of books, here's the tale of a frog, Pondlarker, who was convinced by the story his mother read again and again that his mission was to kiss a princess and become a prince. His parents had a heart-to-heart talk with him, but Pondlarker continued to dress like a prince and hunt for a princess. And one day, at last, he saw a sign: "Princess, 4 miles." The denouement is unexpected, funny, and logical if quirky—this is in the category of yes-I-CAN-stand-to-read-it-aloud-yet-again. The illustrations have a vernal freshness of color, line, and action that intensifies the story's vitality.

381   **Haas**, Dorothy. *The Secret Life of Dilly McBean.* Bradbury, 1986. ISBN 0-02-738200-1. 202p. $12.95.

5-7   "Dilly McBean was being raised by a bank. And Dilly McBean was magnetic." Thus Haas bravely sets out with the two most preposterous tenets of the book and then makes a pretty convincing case for both of them. The Commercial Chemical and Corn Trust and Savings Bank has done a credible job of educating Dilly since he was orphaned at an early age, but nobody has paid enough personal attention to him to realize his extraordinary gift of magnetism; except for the odd occasion when he's forgotten to control his powers, he has kept the promise of secrecy he made as a tiny tot to his father. Now, suddenly, two scientists have shown up, one situating him in a friendly little town far from his old boarding school, and the other suggesting that she help him explore what he can do beyond picking up paper clips with his bare fingers. Dilly also picks up a dog and some good friends for the first time—in fact, in the nick of time to thwart his being kidnapped by a mad scientist determined to computerize the future. This has all the elements of a James Bond spoof, but the characterization is sound, the style often amusing, the fantasy details and plot twists carefully worked out, the ending open yet satisfying. In sum, an inventive popular pick.

382   **Haas**, Jessie. *The Sixth Sense: And Other Stories.* Greenwillow, 1988. ISBN 0-688-08129-0. 180p. $11.95.

7-12   Nine short stories develop the relationship between humans and animals in a collection that weaves together several sets of characters who meet and affect each others' lives: an old woman and her grand-niece, the former grieved by the death of her cat and the latter by conflict with her father; a boy and his determination to become a horseman; another boy who saves a greyhound from routine extermination after a disappointing race; a girl who finds unexpected serenity, in the midst of tensions over her parents' divorce, on a goat farm. The voices are variously first and third person, the narratives tightly crafted to focus on a perceptual turning point in an adolescent's life. The "pets" are individualized without losing their creature traits. Respect for animals is, in fact, the theme of the collection. Although some of the plots are more strongly structured than others— "Tanglewood," for instance, deftly telescopes a complex family transition while the title story seems to meander a bit— these make a real contribution to the short story genre, being both resonant and readable.

383   **Hackwell**, W. John. *Digging to the Past: Excavations in Ancient Lands*; written and illus. by W. John Hackwell. Scribner, 1986. ISBN 0-684-18692-6. 50p. $13.95.

6-9   Capably illustrated by the author, who is both an artist and a doctoral student in the field of archeology, this is a carefully detailed description of the division of labor and the step-by-step procedures in the work of members of an expedition. Hackwell's style of writing is dry, but it is both clear and authoritative, so that the work of the archeologist is comprehensible and its importance firmly stated. A one-page index is appended.

384   **Hadithi**, Mwenye. *Crafty Chameleon*; illus. by Adrienne Kennaway. Little, 1987. ISBN 0-316-33723-4. 30p. $12.95.

4-6 yrs.   A tale that may be familiar to storytellers as "How Brother Rabbit Fooled the Whale and the Elephant" is played out here with a different set of characters. The trickster is a chameleon, and the bullies are a leopard and a crocodile. The latter torments Chameleon until he challenges them to a tug of war and fools them into pulling against each other instead of him. The vividly hued, strongly patterned paintings offer close perspectives from which the animals seem to leap out at the viewer against their African landscapes. A striking selection for group presentations.

385   **Hahn**, Mary Downing. *Following the Mystery Man*. Clarion, 1988. ISBN 0-89919-680-2. 180p. $12.95.

6-10   Madigan is so enchanted by the handsome stranger who rents a room in her grandmother's house that she fantasizes he's the father she's never known. By the time she lets herself recognize suspicious signs that he's a thief, she's followed him too far—and becomes victim of a kidnapping. This is a novel that scores high on several counts: it's a solid first-person narrative, a tightly plotted thriller, and a vivid character portrayal of the antagonist as well as the protagonist. Clint James has a tangible charisma, and his complexity along with Madigan's vulnerability is clearly realized against the backdrop of a small-town setting. Readers will be waiting in line.

386   **Hahn**, Mary Downing. *Wait Till Helen Comes: A Ghost Story*. Houghton/Clarion, 1986. ISBN 0-89919-453-2. 184p. $12.95.

5-8   "'Helen Elizabeth Harper,' she whispered. 'My friend and your enemy.' " No one in the family but 12-year-old Molly believes that Helen is more than Heather's imaginary playmate. Ever since their parents married, 7-year-old Heather has made life miserable for Molly and her brother Michael. Now her whining, sulking, and lying have taken a dark turn, as she threatens the others with retribution from the ghostly Helen. This junior gothic is genuinely scary, complete with dark secrets from the past, unsettled graves, and a very real ghost. The family relations, heightened and intensified by the supernatural goings-on, are real too: the squabbling among step-siblings, and a pair of artist/bohemian parents who don't pay quite enough attention to their children ("Oh, for heaven's sake, Michael! You're ten years old. Act like it!). Although the ending has a pat psychological twist, it is still satisfying. Hahn writes with an easy, practiced style, building suspense naturally and effectively. Spooky and alluring cover art will attract readers, and they won't be disappointed.

387   **Halam**, Ann. *The Daymaker*. Orchard/Watts, 1987. Library ed. ISBN 0-531-08310-1; Trade ed. ISBN 0-531-05710-0. 173p. Library ed. $11.99; Trade ed. $11.95.

6-10   In a far-future society where magic has replaced technology, 10-year-old Zanne is sent away to Covenant school, where she learns to control and deepen the magic-making skills inherited from her mother. Magic comes easily to Zanne; always a headstrong girl, she is fascinated instead by stories of the old days before magic and the Covenant: "Couldn't people move mountains without magic?" After discovering a hidden cache of forgotten machines, Zanne becomes determined to find the fabled (and forbidden) Daymaker, which can make machines run without magic. Halam's prose is stately and often powerful, and while the story is slowed down with explorations of the moral intricacies of magic and technology, this material is fresh and thought-provoking, and adds a dimension to the world-building often slighted in fantasy fiction. The ending indicates the possibility of a sequel; it would be most welcome.

388   **Halam**, Ann. *Transformations*. Orchard/Watts, 1988. Library ed. ISBN 0-531-08366-7; Trade ed. ISBN 0-531-05766-6. 246p. Library ed. $13.99; Trade ed. $13.95.

6-12
*
In this sequel to *The Daymaker* , Zanne of Garth, now a covener, has been sent to investigate the troubled community of Minith, infected with the bad magic of a maker, an ancient machine relic of the long-dead technological world. While a prologue sets the scene, a reading of the first book is necessary to appreciate fully Halam's intricate fantasy world. The Minithers are a gloomy, hardworking people who have twisted the magical Covenant: "the plain and simple agreement to do no harm to the world, which had somehow become for Siri a monster. Yes, that was the only word. A monster, with teeth and claws." Siri is a young girl Zanne hopes to save from the terrible secret Minith is keeping. Darker and scarier than the first book, this is also more intensely focused, with a tremendous Gothic climax. Magical doings are kept to the necessary, characterization is complex and vivid, and readers of spooky-children books will enjoy this as much as will fantasy fans.

389   **Haldane**, Suzanne. *Painting Faces*. Dutton, 1988. ISBN 0-525-44408-4. 32p. illus. with photographs by Suzanne Haldane and others. $13.95.

4-6   Full-page color photographs depict face painting by various cultures —from East Asian to African and Native American—for ritual, dance, drama, and other purposes. With brief informational background and step-by-step instructions, these models serve as suggestions for contemporary children's face painting, also shown in a creative array of traditional and free-form designs. Many young readers will be content to browse through the pictures rather than spend time on the text. Even so, the book will open up connections to other times and

societies as well as stimulate a popular activity. Warnings about skin
allergies are included.

390   Hall, Barbara. *Dixie Storms*. Harcourt, 1990. ISBN 0-15-223825-5. 197p.
$15.95.

7-10   This seamless novel of family encounter is set on a Virginia tobacco
*   farm threatened by drought. Fourteen-year-old Dutch Peyton is the
narrator, and she's faced with a sudden visit from a beautiful city
cousin whose parents are getting divorced. At the same time, Dutch's
father seems overwhelmed by financial difficulties; her older brother
nurses permanent anger toward the wife who left him; the nephew
she's trying to help raise is becoming imprinted by his father's anger;
and her love for a local boy isn't prospering. Dutch's nervous aunt is
no substitute for the loving mother who died when Dutch was born,
nor for the gentle sister-in-law who left. These complexities emerge
through richly developed scenes in which Dutch learns her own
strength and weakness along with an acceptance of others'
unresolvable differences. The setting is vividly detailed and the
dialogue naturally tuned to each character ("I'm sorry I called you
ugly, ugly," says nine-year-old Bodean). The tension of human conflict
and empty rainclouds offers a suspense roundly capped by a Dixie
storm. This is a promising pick for readers who have enjoyed Sue Ellen
Bridgers' fiction.

391   Hall, Donald, ed. *The Oxford Book of Children's Verse in America*.
Oxford, 1985. ISBN 0-19-503439-9. 319p. $18.95

All   This should prove to be of great interest to readers of poetry, teachers
ages   of poetry, students of the history of children's literature, and those who
are fascinated by Americana. Hall includes examples of the kind of
poetry that is indigenous and has been offered to children from the
days of the stern injunctions of Puritan didacticism to the light verse or
polished imagery of the major contemporary children's poets. The
arrangement is chronological by birth dates, the range of material is
unusual, the end papers informative. Particularly valuable is Hall's
preface, which is almost a mini-history of children's poetry in America,
and which makes it clear that the book has been compiled to show
what American children were reading,even if the poems have not
stood the test of time. The indexes (one of authors and the other of
first lines and titles) are preceded by a section of notes on the poets
whose work has been included.

392   Hall, Lynn. *The Giver*. Scribner, 1985. ISBN 684-18312-9. 128p. $11.95.

7-10   This is Lynn Hall at her best, in a story that is poignant and potent, a
story of love that is wise and altruistic. Mary is not interested in the
boys she knows, finding them callow; she is convinced that her feeling

for her teacher, middle-aged Mr. Flicker, is more than a crush. He, too, feels affection but is aware that it would ruin Mary's life and might well end his career. He does love her, and he treats her love with respect and dignity, gently telling her that she must find someone her age. In a brief epilogue after Mary is married years later, she sees Mr. Flicker at a homecoming dance and thanks him. Other facets of Mary's life (particularly her familial relationships) give balance to a story written with insight and craft.

393   **Hall**, Lynn. *A Killing Freeze.* Morrow, 1988. ISBN 0-688-07867-2. 124p. $11.95.

6-9   Adolescent Clarie, the narrator, is perfectly happy with her quiet life in a small Minnesota town and with her loving friendship with Dad, who'd raised her from infancy when her mother decamped. The big event of the year for them is a winter carnival that Dad runs and that makes a big difference in his snowmobile business. The carnival and the community are drastically affected by the murder of an elderly woman who has been Clarie's close friend. Then, second shock, a prime suspect is murdered; only when his killer is identified does it become clear that the first "murder" was a freak accident. This has the plausible structure and suspense that are touchstones for good mystery writing, and the well-defined characterizations and relationships give it substance. Because it is written with directness and simplicity, it should appeal to reluctant readers.

394   **Hamilton**, Virginia. *Anthony Burns: The Defeat and Triumph of a Fugitive Slave.* Knopf, 1988. Library ed. ISBN 0-394-98185-5; Trade ed. ISBN 0-394-88185-0. 193p. Library ed. $12.99; Trade ed. $11.95.

7-12   Hamilton has done a masterly job of melding historical fact with fictional characterization to the enhancement of both. This is the gripping story of a slave who, after escaping to Boston, is recaptured by his southern master and returned to Virginia by the power of the Fugitive Slave Act. It is also the story of abolitionists' attempts to resist the law, a judge's fateful decision, and a black minister's determined and finally successful efforts to buy Burns' freedom. One of Hamilton's most remarkable capabilities is her revelation of the present through glimpses of the past. Here she alternates between the tense courtroom or crowd scenes and Burns' recollections of his youth. Without too much psychological speculation, this device shows the reader what slavery was like, for Burns, for his family, for his friends. It is ironic but understandable that he escapes the cruelties of current reality through remembrance of suffering survived. The past is familiar and finished; the future, unknown and all the more terrifying. Although Burns' worst fears come true when he is punished in a prison camp for runaways, he is bought back and freed, realizing his dream to be an educated minister before his death at age 28. Hamilton's afterword makes careful distinctions between documented facts and educated guesswork; she also includes selections from the Fugitive Slave Act of 1850 and a valuable bibliography of primary and secondary sources.

395   **Hamilton**, Virginia. *Cousins*. Philomel, 1990. ISBN 0-399-22164-6. 125p. $14.95.

5-8
*

Hamilton is back in her fictional element here, realizing a relationship between two characters who live out—to a bitter end—the tensions between their own mothers. Cammy and Patty Ann are jealous cousins, the first strong-minded and fiercely loyal to her dying grandmother, the second beautiful and perfectly mannered on what seems, at first, a superficial level. With the girls' older brothers as sometimes defiant foils, this is a complex family drama, briefly developed through some unforgettable scenes: Cammy visiting a nursing home to comfort Gram, Cammy caught in a rainstorm and sheltering in her aunt's home, Cammy discovering that Patty Ann's unemployed brother drinks too much, and, finally, Cammy watching tragedy unfold at a summer-camp outing. By the conclusion, she has been reconciled to an acceptance of death, as well as, on a happier note, to the father she had lost through divorce. A poor relation, Elodie, is introduced too late in the story to be as completely developed as Cammy and Patty Ann, but her role as pawn between the two primary characters is nevertheless effective. Like Marion Dane Bauer's *On My Honor*, this is a powerful portrayal of guilt and emotional survival.

396   **Hamilton**, Virginia, ad. *In the Beginning: Creation Stories from Around the World*; illus. by Barry Moser. Harcourt, 1988. ISBN 0-15-238740-4. 161p. $18.95.

5-9

The adaptation of 25 diverse creation myths is an ambitious undertaking, and this book succeeds in that it brings the stories together for comparative reading and suggests powerful metaphors, both in printed and graphical statements. Hamilton has ranged across African, Asian, South and North American, Mediteranean, Australian, and European cultures for source material and rendered the retellings with her customary intelligence, though not with the rhythmic familiarity that characterized *The People Could Fly*. There remain two problems. First, the brief notes after each tale are often descriptive recaps that do not include specific titles of origin, except, ironically, for the Biblical stories that most young readers will know. Second, those stories with which the adapter seems most familiar get the most extensive treatment, as in the near fictionalization of Pandora. A few drawbacks are inherent in the format. Many of these tales belong to longer cycles, and here involvement is frustratingly limited: twice we get hints of Prometheus' fate, for instance, but never learn what it is. Several of the tales are confusing out of context of cultural annotation, as in the Aboriginal "Bandicoots Come From His Body: Karora the Creator," but that is a problem beyond the scope of this collection. An afterword explains some of the basic types of creation myth and includes a three-page bibliography. Moser's paintings are powerful, in some cases relying on suggestion, as in the mystical blue oval for "Bursting from the Hen's Egg: Phan Ku the Creator" and in others fostering the comedy of strict detail, as in the profile of Warm Dog, duped by the Russian Altaic devil Ulgen. There are few juvenile collections against which to measure this—Penelope Farmer's *Beginnings: Creation Myths of the World* (*BCCB*: 11/79) is out of print; the book is badly needed and handsomely done.

397   **Hamilton**, Virginia. *The People Could Fly: American Black Folk Tales*; illus. by Leo and Diane Dillon. Knopf, 1985. ISBN 0-394-86925-7. 178p. $12.95.

4-6   Prefatory comments and notes that follow each selection give added
*   interest to an eminent author's retellings of folk tales from several sources. Some, like those with European roots, have been adapted and changed, as folk literature always is, by the ethos and the needs of black Americans; some spring directly from the time of slavery or were African tales adapted by the slaves to express their fears or joys, their relationship to the dominant whites, their yearning for freedom. Readers will recognize some of the characters: the ubiquitous Brer (or Bruh) Rabbit, John who wooed the Devil's daughter, and Wiley, whose Mama outwits the hairy man. Virginia Hamilton's prose has a singing quality, wonderful in its color and cadence. Like the felicitous blend of realism and fantasy in the writing, the illustrations, handsome pictures by the Dillons, evoke an aura of magic-in-life. The forty illustrations have both strength and softness; they are as effective in composition as they are in use of color. In sum, a book that is lovely to look at and as good a source of storytelling as it is to read aloud or alone.

398   **Hamilton**, Virginia. *A White Romance*. Philomel, 1987. ISBN 0-399-21213-2. 191p. $13.95.

9-12   Through her running partner, Didi, Talley Barbour gets involved with a charismatic drug dealer named David and with Didi's boyfriend, an addict called Roady. This is the story of two couples, vividly character-ized both as individuals and as a self-made "family" with dynamics shifting according to the needs and demands of each. The emotional, sexual, and racial tensions are honestly drawn as these four, all from broken homes, try to ease their loneliness with some kind of caring company. Even villainous David, who manipulates Talley into an affair and then dumps her when she's courted by a "straight" black athlete, Victor, shows a vulnerable spot for his old buddy Roady. Roady's decision to give up drugs is welcome if a bit mystifying in origin— Victor's relationship with Talley is a more credibly developed resolution. The action here is internal except for a few memorable scenes, one set in a high school hall lined with lockers, another at a rock concert; yet Talley's journey from child to adult makes an absorbing first-person narrative that will touch contemporary young readers.

399   **Hansen**, Joyce. *Out From This Place*. Walker, 1988. Library ed. ISBN 0-8027-6817-2; Trade ed. ISBN 0-8027-6816-4. 135p. Library ed. $14.85; Trade ed. $13.95.

6-9   In a sequel to *Which Way Freedom?*, Hansen focuses on Easter, the girl that Obi (black hero of the first book) left behind him. Like Obi, Easter is determined, after her escape from bondage, to find and keep freedom. A tenacious and resourceful adolescent, she joins those recently emancipated Sea Islands workers who rebel when the government denies them promised land. Always hunting for Obi, Easter at last decides she will leave the South, go North to train as a teacher, and hope that her path and Obi's will cross. At the close, there is a strong hint, in an epilogue, that that may happen: "No matter how long it took, he would find her."

400   **Hansen**, Joyce. *Which Way Freedom?* Walker, 1986. Library ed. ISBN 0-8027-6636-6; Trade ed. ISBN 0-8027-6623-4. 120p. (Walker's American History Series for Young People) Library ed. $12.85; Trade ed. $12.95.

6-9   In a strong historical novel, Joyce Hansen describes the way in which one young black man, Obi, struggles over a period of three years (1861-1864) politically and ideologically toward the goal of being a free man. Hoping to find the mother he doesn't remember, reluctant to leave the few people who are almost family, Obi is determined to get away from his master, and he does so in a way that is exciting and believable. Obi (he spurns the surname of his owner, and eventually chooses a new last name) eventually joins a Union regiment and is one of the few to escape from the bloody battle at Fort Pillow, Tennessee. Hansen has made Obi real, emphasizing his tenacity and courage by showing it rather than declaring him a cardboard hero. He is himself, but he also exemplifies the commitment of all those who fought to be free, just as he illustrates the contributions made by many black soldiers in the Civil War.

401   **Hansen**, Joyce. *Yellow Bird and Me*. Houghton/Clarion, 1986. ISBN 0-89919-335-8. 155p. $12.95.

4-6   In a sequel to *The Gift-Giver*, its gentle hero, Amir, is still missed by his friend Doris, the narrator, who is black and bright. Doris is in sixth grade, and so is Yellow Bird, who clowns in the class and irritates Doris by asking for her help with his lesson preparation. Two plot threads are capably meshed; one is the mounting of a play in which Bird is given the lead thanks to an astute visiting playwright/director, and the other is the fact that Doris realizes that Bird is intelligent but has a learning disability. The author, a teacher, paints a hard picture of her fictional counterpart, who refuses for too long to recognize the fact that Bird is handicapped, even when Doris points it out. However, her characterization is certainly believable, and the children are depicted with insight and their personalities and changing relationship developed logically and positively.

402   **Hansen**, Rosanna. *My First Book of Space*; written by Rosanna Hansen and Robert A. Bell; developed in conjunction with NASA. Messner, 1986. Library ed. ISBN 0-671-60621-2; Trade ed. ISBN 0-671-60262-4. 41p. illus with photographs. Library ed. $11.79; Trade ed. $7.95.

2-5   On a par with Seymour Simon's individual volumes about the moon and various planets, this compacts a great deal of material covering the solar system generally, in simple, clear, and often comparative terms. The oversize format is spacious enough to accommodate impressively large color photographs and paintings offsetting factually condensed blocks of text. The diagrams and total organization, with sections clearly marked for browsing or specific reports, make this an excellent introduction.

403   **Harlan**, Judith. *Hispanic Voters: A Voice in American Politics*. Watts, 1988. ISBN 0-531-10586-5. 112p. illus. with photographs. $12.90.

7-12   While "Hispanic Voters" is probably a too-limiting misnomer, this is a solid introduction to Hispanic immigration, assimilation, and participation in the U.S. political structure. Harlan covers immigration reform laws, bilingual education and the "English-only" movement, and political and union organizing, providing, along the way, capsule portraits of Hispanic leaders such as Cesar Chavez and Henry Cisneros. Her discussion is comprehensive and controlled, synthesizing institutional, cultural and demographic forces to explain the current political impact of the various Hispanic communities and showing their divisions as well as unity. Unfortunately, source citation is incomplete, and the six-book bibliography includes no books published after 1983.

404   **Harris**, Joel Chandler. *Jump On Over!: The Adventures of Brer Rabbit and His Family*; ad. by Van Dyke Parks; illus. by Barry Moser. Harcourt, 1989. ISBN 0-15-241354-5. 48p. $15.95.

4-6
*

How can you lose? Brer Rabbit has perennial appeal and Barry Moser just gets better and better (see also the collections *Jump!*. and *Jump Again!*). Here are five more stories: "How Brer Rabbit Frightened His Neighbors," "Brer Rabbit and Brer Bear," "Why Brer Wolf Didn't Eat the Little Rabs," "Another Story about the Little Rabs," and "Brer Fox Gets Out-Foxed." Just for the record, Brer Rabbit frightens his neighbors by wearing the tin coffee pot, cups, and plates he has bought for his family. He fools Brer Fox by enticing Brer Bear into a goober-patch trap for a dollar a minute. He tricks Brer Wolf into chasing Brer Fox by persuading the former that the latter's blood tastes like molasses. He comes home to find that even his children have, with the helpful advice of a friendly bird, outfoxed Brer Fox. And he persuades Brer Fox that a team of horses has sunk into quicksand by judiciously planting a few tails. No child can resist such a trickster, and no adult can resist Moser's sly portraits, with their varied perspectives, uncanny draftsmanship, and sparely detailed southern settings. Parks' adaptations are looser and more comfortably idiomatic this time around; music to his song "Home" is appended.

405   **Harris**, Joel Chandler. *The Tales of Uncle Remus: The Adventures of Brer Rabbit*; retold by Julius Lester; illus. by Jerry Pinkney. Dial, 1987. Library ed. ISBN 0-8037-0272-8; Trade ed. ISBN 0-8037-0271-X. 151p. Library ed. $14.89; Trade ed. $15.00.

5-
*

This adaptation of 48 Brer Rabbit stories fulfills all the promise of his intelligent, balanced foreword and of storyteller Augusta Baker's introductory endorsement. In terms of quantity and quality, it's also the most substantial collection of the several, drawn from Joel Chandler Harris' versions, that have been published lately. It is the work of a writer familiar with the methodology of folkloric and historical research but also with the techniques of flavoring fiction. Lester himself makes wry narrative asides that punctuate but don't intrude on the stories the way the "Uncle Remus" framework did. The animals' dialogue is spontaneously current without forbidding barriers of dialect—adhering, meanwhile, to the bantering tone of the older source and retaining some of the best lines or chants (the rhythmic repartee between Son Riley Rabbit, Riley and Aunt Mammy-Bammy Big-Money or Biggedy Dicky Big-Bag in "Brer Rabbit's Luck" is a perfect example). The characters are never cutsied up but delivered with original, full-bodied flavor. This integrity of treatment of course involves a range of trickery, some humorous, some violent, in the symbolic mode of fairy tales from the Grimms and other cultural traditions. There are also lines of rich observation: "Brer Rabbit wondered. He wondered and he wondered, and the more he wondered, the more he didn't know." Almost all the stories are subversively supportive of the smaller animals against the larger. Storytellers as well as young readers will delight in getting their hands on accessible versions of "How Brer Rabbit Became a Scary Monster," "Brer Rabbit Eats the Butter," and many more. Pinkney's illustrations—black-and-white drawings with occasional double-page spreads in full color—are well drafted, fresh, and funny though not so wickedly witty as Barry Moser's in *Jump: The Adventures of Brer Rabbit* (adapted by Van Dyke Parks and Malcolm Jones. Other Uncle Remus collections adapted by Lester include *Further Tales of Uncle Remus* and *More Tales of Uncle Remus*.

406   **Harvey**, Brett. *Cassie's Journey: Going West in the 1860's*; illus. by Deborah Kogan Ray. Holiday House, 1988. ISBN 0-8234-0684-9. 36p. $12.95.

2-4   Like the author and illustrator's *My Prairie Year* , this is based on actual accounts of wagon-train journeys westward in the mid-19th century; this book, too, is illustrated by deft, soft, pencil drawings that convey both mood and setting effectively with an economical use of line. Cassie, whose name we learn late in the story (it is used on the jacket flap) writes in diary form, although the absence of dates or other devices to separate parts of the continuous text may not make this immediately clear to readers. On the whole, an ingenuous, at times vivid, description of some of the vicissitudes of going west.

407   **Harvey**, Brett. *My Prairie Christmas*; illus. by Deborah Kogan Ray. Holiday House, 1990. ISBN 0-8234-0827-2. 32p. $14.95.

3-5   In a companion volume to *My Prairie Year*, the narrator is again nine-year-old Elenore Plaisted, the author's grandmother. The place is the Dakota Territory, the time is the turn of the century, and the children are, with their mother, hoping that the blizzard won't keep Papa from getting back in time for Christmas. The modest plot has suspense, as the family anxiously waits. It has the appeal of the Christmas setting and it has unobtrusively incorporated period details as Mama and the children prepare homemade gifts and food, and brave the snow to chop down a small tree. The author avoids sentimentality but imbues her story with a gentle affection, and this quality is reflected in the soft pastel drawings.

408   **Harvey**, Brett. *My Prairie Year: Based on the Diary of Elenore Plaisted*; illus by Deborah Kogan Ray. Holiday House, 1986. ISBN 0-8234-0604-0. 39p. $11.95.

3-5   Soft pencil drawings, spacious and often dramatic, illustrate a story that is descriptive rather than narrative, is simply written, and is based on the notes made by the author's grandmother, Elenore Plaisted. Elenore was nine when her family came to the isolated house in the vast, open spaces of the Dakota Territory. It was 1889, and the rest of the family came by train to join Daddy, who had gone ahead to build their house. Elenore describes daily tasks, seasonal events, and occasional dramatic natural disasters in a way that is immediate and vivid. This is an attractive book and an informative one; it should be interesting to readers curious about frontier life.

409   **Haskins**, James. *Black Music in America: A History through Its People*. Crowell, 1987. Library ed. ISBN 0-690-04462-3; Trade ed. ISBN 0-690-04460-7. 198p. illus. with photographs. Library ed. $12.89; Trade ed. $12.95.

7-10   Beginning with the slaves who brought with them nothing but their chains and their songs, Haskins traces the dual developments of black musicians who performed in white classical styles and black creators of spirituals, ragtime, blues, jazz, gospel, and soul music. The text alternates between passages giving historical perspective and biographical sketches of great musicians, from Elizabeth Taylor Greenfield, a successful operatic soprano in the 1850s, to Wynton Marsalis, a brilliant trumpet soloist on the 1980s jazz scene. Haskins strikes a comfortable balance between general information and specific facts. He gives enough flavor of leading personalities and trends to point young readers toward more in-depth sources, or better still, some listening experiences. Unfortunately, a discography is not included, but there's a bibliography organized by books, articles, and archival sources.

410   **Haskins**, James. *Shirley Temple Black: Actress to Ambassador*; illus. by Donna Ruff. Viking, 1988. ISBN 0-670-81957-3. 58p. (Women of Our Time). $10.95.

4-6   It is unlikely that even the most sophisticated young heart can be hardened against Temple's films of *Heidi* and *A Little Princess*; this biography shows the sometimes painful real story behind the dimpled melodrama. Temple began her film career in the sleazy "Baby Burlesks" (the kind of films, as Haskins points out, that the grown-up Shirley Temple would crusade against as exploitative) but her star took off after *Stand Up and Cheer*, and she had a phenomenal, though relatively brief, reign as "America's Sweetheart" until 1940. "As a teenager, Shirley didn't have much luck getting more roles. She was not pretty enough to attract movie audiences." Haskins is no sob-sister, and his account is candid in discussing the actress' trials and triumphs. He does a good job of placing Temple within historical context—through her relationship with black actor Bill "Bojangles" Robinson, her status as a symbol of better times for Depression audiences, and, more recently, in her role as savvy politican and ambassador. An effective counter to fan magazine hype and an illuminating portrait of young Hollywood.

411   **Hastings**, Selina, ad. *Sir Gawain and the Loathly Lady*; illus. by Juan
Wijngaard. Walker, 1985. ISBN 0-688-05823-X. 26p. $13.00.

4-6   In stately prose, Hastings retells one of the Arthurian legends, the tale
 *   of a hideous woman who saves the king's life but demands as
payment that he provide one of his knights as her husband. Devoted
Gawain volunteers, and it will probably not surprise even those
readers who are not familiar with this particular tale that on the
wedding night, the bride changes to a radiant beauty. This one has just
about everything. It embodies loyalty, courtesy, honor, peril (and
escape) and romance. It is illustrated with handsome pictures
elaborately framed and bordered in the style of medieval manuscripts. Wijngaard, who moved from South America to England, is
surely destined to become an illustrator of major import.

412   **Haugaar**d, Erik Christian. *Prince Boghole*; illus. by Julie Downing.
Macmillan, 1987. ISBN 0-02-743440-0. 31p. $12.95.

5-8 yrs.   An original fairy tale cleverly blends archetypal devices into a new
story about a Medieval Irish king's seeking a husband for his
daughter, Orla. After inviting haughty princes from Leinster and
Ulster, King Desmond finds himself more comfortable with a humble
prince from a poor northwestern kingdom; the lad's name is Brian,
and he joins the suitors in a test of seeking the most wonderful bird in
the world. After a year, each brings back a bird characteristic of his
own traits: one, a fierce-eyed eagle; another, a beady-eyed peacock;
and Brian, a nightingale that fills the air with music and wins Princess
Orla. The writing here has a subtle grace that hues to folkloric grain
without becoming selfconscious ("Although a year is long, it is soon
gone"). The structure is neat, with a resounding end: "The nightingale
flew away . . . . But that didn't bother Prince Brian, for he came from
the west country, and there they like to do the singing themselves."
The king and his daughter are a vivid pair generally matched by the
full-color illustrations, although here and there the drawing seems
stiffer than the proficient design and coloration. The attention to detail
in castle and cast and the sense of humor pervading both text and art
(King Desmond's patched socks go well with his homey disposition)
make this a jovial addition to picture book fairy tale collections.

413   **Hautzig**, Esther. *Make It Special: Cards, Decorations, and Party
Favors for Holidays and Other Celebrations*; illus. by Martha Weston.
Macmillan, 1986. ISBN 0-02-743370-6. 86p. $11.95.

4-6   Most of the projects suggested in this how-to book require materials
that are easily obtainable and that are free or inexpensive. Hautzig's
premise is that home-made decorations are festive and provide
enjoyment for hosts and guests. The author gives a list of tools and
materials needed for each project; she adds general suggestions to

those specific to each, and reminds readers that they can adapt and invent, as well as follow instructions. The material is adequately organized, with chapters on such subjects as table decorations or party favors. The illustrations are useful for the most part, although on some pages there are step-by-step diagrams that are cluttered.

414   Havill, Juanita. *Jamaica Tag-Along*; illus. by Anne Sibley O'Brien. Houghton, 1989. ISBN 0-395-49602-0. 32p. $13.95.

4-6 yrs.   In a situation to which every younger sibling can relate, Jamaica follows her brother Ossie to the park and tries to join his game of basketball but is told not to tag along. Stung by the rejection, Jamaica spurns little Berto's attempt to help her build a sand castle, then stops herself and teaches him how to help her. Together, they create such an exciting project that eventually Ossie wants to join them after his game. It's a pleasant conclusion, and the importance of kindness to lesser mortals is clearly stressed. Unfortunately, there's another message, as well, that boys play ball and girls take care of little children. However, that's the way life is in the park. The scenario is realistic and the black and Hispanic cast, portrayed in friendly, effective watercolors, will win the attention of young listeners, who may remember the appealing main character from *Jamaica's Find*.

415   Hawks, Robert. *This Stranger, My Father*. Houghton, 1988. ISBN 0-395-44089-0. 226p. $13.95.

7-10   What threatens, in the first few pages, to be another teen-girl-school-boyfriend story changes, cleverly and shockingly, to a strong novel of suspense. Freshmen Patty Meely and her best friend Kimmers, waiting after school one day for Patty's father to pick them up, are discussing Patty's Mark-or-Larry boyfriend problem. Dad soon arrives—and is immediately surrounded by three gray sedans and a team of federal agents: "They stuck their pistols in the back of his neck." Dad is arrested, Patty taken away to be interrogated, where she learns (although the agents believe she's known all along) that her real name is Patricia Pelling and that her father escaped twenty years ago from prison, where he was being held on an espionage conviction. After terrifying confrontations with the agents and a seedy foster family, Patty runs away and joins her father, who has escaped (again) as well. In character and theme this bears resemblance to LeCarré's *The Little Drummer Girl*, as Patty slowly recognizes the amorality of her father and gradually becomes his accomplice, reluctantly learning elusion, deceit, cynicism, and the many paradoxes in her father's character. Hawks handles complex questions of morality and identity ("I *was* Karen Peterson. I had a driver's license to prove it") with smooth craft, allowing them to inform but not overwhelm a terrific thriller.

416   **Hayes**, Sarah. *Eat Up, Gemma*; illus. by Jan Ormerod. Lothrop, 1988. ISBN 0-688-08149-5. 24p. $13.00.

4-7 yrs.   After wreaking holiday havoc in *Happy Christmas, Gemma*, baby Gemma now doesn't want to "eat up," instead joyfully throwing any proffered food to the floor, or to the dog, or banging it to bits with her toy hammer. Big brother finds the solution when he sees Gemma, at church, mesmerized by the fruit decorations on the lady's hat in front of her. One inverted bowl, a couple of bananas, some grapes . . . A familiar situation handled easily if superficially, this combines the appeals of infant destructiveness and big brother know-how. While facial expressions tend toward the cute, the full-color illustrations (and nice-sized type) are set neatly within lots of white space, and are framed with fruit-festooned endpapers juicy enough to make the pickiest eater salivate. The book is a British production, Gemma and her family are black, but this is a cozy any family/anywhere kind of story.

417   **Hayes**, Sarah. *Happy Christmas Gemma*; illus. by Jan Ormerod. Lothrop, 1986. ISBN 0-688-06508-2. 27p. $13.00.

2-5 yrs.   Ormerod's paintings (realistic in detail, spacious, bright, and soft in palette) add humor and vitality to a simply written text in which the speaker is a small black child in a three generation family. Gemma, his little sister, is celebrating her first Christmas, chiefly by enjoyable messiness and minor destruction. It is the narrator's bland account of events that, in contrast to the depredations of Gemma, give the story humor. First published in Great Britain, this story of a middle-class Jamaican family should have a universal holiday appeal.

418   **Haynes**, Mary. *Catch the Sea.* Bradbury, 1989. ISBN 0-02-743451-6. 172p. $12.95.

5-8   When her artist father goes to New York for an important exhibition of his work, Lily, who's supposed to be busy starting eighth grade, is left to guard their summer cottage and their secret: Dad is supposed to be working on some "dumb-and-ugly" seascapes for a wealthy patron, and he's not. During the week he's gone, Lily fends off the patron, makes a friend of a woman, an astronomer, in a neighboring cottage, and begins a tentative exploration of her own creativity. Haynes' writing is simple and clear, confidently blending thematic questions—"You're sure you're not an artist?"—with the emotional palette of Lily's life: her loving but distracted father, and her mother, far away and famous in Paris. Lily's evasions of the forbidding patron, Mrs. Phipps, add humor and suspense, and the characters, like the sea Lily works so hard to paint, revealingly change in the shifting light.

419   Hayward, Linda. *All Stuck Up*; illus. by Normand Chartier. Random House, 1990. Library ed. ISBN 0-679-90216-3; Paper ed. ISBN 0-679-80216-9. 32p. (Step into Reading Books). Library ed. $6.99; Paper ed. $2.95.

K-2   Brer Rabbit's been stuck in this situation by a thousand storytellers and hasn't died yet. Not even as brief a treatment as this can kill the tale of the trickster tricked—Brer Fox conned into letting go the victim he's trapped with a tarbaby (here homogenized to "some mighty sticky stuff"). About fifty sentences all told, with one or two per gracefully color-cartooned page, this is reduced to the most basic motifs, but it does respect the ones it keeps. It will be a book to hand to kids who clamor for a version they can read for themselves after story hour. Tell them to fill in their own details, and be sure to point their parents or significant other read-alouders toward wittier versions by Julius Lester, Van Dyke Parks, and Virginia Hamilton.

420   Härtling, Peter. *Crutches*; tr. from the German by Elizabeth D. Crawford. Lothrop, 1988. ISBN 0-688-07991-1. 173p. $12.00.

5-8   The place is Austria, and the time is 1945. His father has been killed in the war, he's been separated from his mother on a transport, and his Aunt Wanda is dead. With no one to turn to, Thomas attaches himself to a one-legged man, Crutches, who feeds the boy, cares for him, and, hardest of all, eventually lets him go when they locate his mother. There are three portraits here: the boy, the man, and the face of war. The author has achieved concentrated strength by particularizing each of these. Though sometimes the context goes unexplained, the incidents are vivid enough to make the story cohesive. When Thomas and Crutches "organize" some piglets from the countryside, for instance, the tension of crossing check-points and the breakdown of the trailer on bombed-out roads speaks for itself. Other elements are somewhat more mysterious—the survival of a beautiful Jewish woman with a luxury apartment in which Crutches and Thomas take shelter until their return to Germany. Most impressive is the characterization of Crutches, an embittered, anti-Hitlerian ex-soldier who tries to protect his battered heart from further incursions but who cannot resist getting involved. The translator has worked effectively to capture Härtling's trenchant style without becoming choppy, and readers will get involved in spite of the fact that this is less about the dangers of defeat than about its drudgeries.

421   Härtling, Peter. *Old John*; tr. from the German by Elizabeth D. Crawford. Lothrop, 1990. ISBN 0-688-08734-3. 120p. $11.95.

5-8   As honest as the author's Batchelder Award-winning book, *Crutches*, but more cohesive in narration, this recounts the moving in, adjustment, and eventual decline of Laura and Jacob Schirmer's grandfather, Old John. The central focus on an individualistic family renders each member distinctive and yet reserves central place for the group as a whole: "Everything new or out of the ordinary had to be discussed in detail from every angle and usually at top volume as well." This dynamic is especially touching at the point when a decision must be made about whether to bring Old John home from the hospital after a stroke, even if it means living day by day with his dying. Most impressive, however, is the helter-skelter humor that dominates the book, from Old John's idiosyncrasies (including a pair of triangular swimming trunks) to his December romance with a village teacher. The tone is outspoken, the portrayal affectionate, and the viewpoint true to a child's perceptions.

422   **Hearne**, Betsy. *Eli's Ghost*; illus. by Ron Himler. McElderry, 1987. ISBN 0-689-50420-9. 104p. $10.95.

4-7   When Eli Wilson finds out his mother may still be alive, he runs away to search for her in a swamp where his father has forbidden him to go. He's not alone for long. Two friends, Lily and Tater, trail him with a pack of dogs, and the town sheriff is determined to find him. Neither party catches up before he nearly drowns in a whirlpool. Close to death, Eli releases his own ghost, who, in the doppelgänger tradition, turns out to be the reverse side of Eli's serious nature. For Eli Wilson, his mother and friends, and even some citizens of his small, southern town, life will never be the same. Suspense, the supernatural, and humor are effectively blended in this story of a boy's hunt for a home . . . and a home for a haunt.

423   **Hearne**, Betsy. *Love Lines: Poetry in Person*. McElderry, 1987. ISBN 0-689-50437-3. 68p. $7.95.

9-   A collection of 59 lyric poems about love explores the joys of discovery, the riches of relationships, and the sorrows of loss. Hearne meditates on romantic love, family love, and friendship, saying in her introduction, "Love poetry can be benevolent or bitter, sweet or strong or sad. Whatever the texture, there is no better net of words to catch the complexities of loving."

424   **Hedderick**, Mairi. *Katie Morag and the Two Grandmothers*; written and illus. by Mairi Hederick. Little, 1986. ISBN 0-316-35400-7. 30p. $10.95.

K-3   It's the light touch in the writing, a mood reflected in humorous line-and-wash drawings, that makes the story of the folk of a Scottish island engaging. Grannie Mainland (a "wee dazzler") comes for a visit at the time of the annual fair; she's coiffed, perfumed, and modishly clad. Katie's other grandmother, Grannie Island, is not enamored of her opposite number. Grannie Island wears pants and boots as she does farm chores and prepares to enter her sheep in competition at the fair. Mainland Grannie never knows that all her toiletries have been used to clean and prettify the sheep. The bland, direct style of the narration sets off the mild malice of the ploy, and the humor is implicit rather than stressed.

425   **Heide**, Florence Parry. *Tales for the Perfect Child;* illus. by Victoria Chess. Lothrop, 1985. Library ed. ISBN 0-688-03893-X; Trade ed. ISBN 0-688-03892-1. 67p. Library ed. $12.88; Trade ed. $13.00.

3-5   Seven very short stories are written in so direct and simple a style that they can be used for children in the primary grades as well as for the middle grades, but it is the latter group that should respond the more appreciatively to the bland, sly humor that is Heide at her best. The amicably ghoulish illustrations are just right for the tales of a procession of children who are sloppy, lazy, deceitful, parent-manipulative, self-indulgent, and iron-willed in avoiding cleanliness, responsibility, and other conforming traits. The style is nicely honed, and while the author's tongue may be in her cheek, the fact that her protagonists prevail over fate and mothers will undoubtedly win readers.

426   **Heintze**, Carl. *Medical Ethics.* Watts, 1987. ISBN 0-531-10414-1. 118p. illus. with photographs. $11.90.

7-   Writing on a topic that has always been complex but that has had increasingly controversial aspects as medical technology, new drugs and changing procedures bring further debate, an experienced science writer does a good job in discussing today's medical-legal-moral issues. Heintze provides historical background, defining ethics and medical ethics and explaining how some facets change while others do not; he then moves on to chapters that deal with such topics as euthanasia, organ transplants, and artificial insemination. His attitude is non-judgmental, his material capably written and carefully organized, his tone calm and impartial. Good coverage of important issues provides substantial information. End papers include chapter notes, a bibliography, an index, and replication of the Hippocratic Oath and the Helsinki Declaration.

427   **Helgadóttir**, Gudrún. *Flumbra: An Icelandic Folktale;* tr. from the Icelandic by Christopher Sanders; illus by Brian Pilkington. Carolrhoda, 1986. ISBN 0-87614-243-9. 27p. $12.95.

K-3   In a story resonant with some ancient elements, an ugly giantess
  *   courts a lazy giant and delivers eight sons, each as revolting to the world as he is beautiful to his mother. She nurses them (in a bare-breasted pose) till milk runs down the mountainside and finally sets out to show them off to their distant father. But the way is long and the

children dawdling. the sun rises and turns them all to stones—stones that no child should fear despite their intimidating size and shape. Details of the Icelandic landscape are vivid in these paintings, intriguing in their effects of spatterbrush contrasted with smooth textures, of rounded shapes with rough edges. It is a story of mythic dimension, out of time but also intimately poignant, and, not coincidentally, explanatory of some natural catastrophes ranging from earthquakes and volcanoes to landslides.

428   **Heller**, Ruth. *Kites Sail High: A Book about Verbs*; written and illus. by Ruth Heller. Grosset, 1988. ISBN 0-448-10480-6. 43p. $10.95.

2-4   With the same verve she brought to *Chickens Aren't the Only Ones*, Heller romps through an explanation of verbs. The verses are saved from a forced quality by their interaction with the exuberantly varied illustrations. Against the verso of a dramatic stage backdrop appears one stanza, "The INDICATIVE MOOD just states a fact," and across a visual pause to the recto facing it, "We ACT." The following spread shows an underseascape: "The SUBJUNCTIVE MOOD expresses a wish . . . or uses the words 'as though' or 'if.' If I WERE a fish, as though that COULD BE, I'd SWIM in a beautiful tropical sea." One brilliant array of chocolate candies displayed close up lures young readers through the following information: "The IMPERATIVE MOOD makes a request. Please TAKE just one . . . and LEAVE the rest." Graphic pace and word play make this an ingenious lesson that no classroom grammarian should miss.

429   **Heller**, Ruth. *Merry-Go-Round: A Book About Nouns*; written and illus. by Ruth Heller. Grosset, 1990. ISBN 0-448-40085-5. 43p. $13.95.

2-4   "Nouns name a person, place or thing, a damsel, a forest, a dragon, a king. These nouns are all common, and they're very nice, but proper nouns are more precise. King Arthur is this person." After a graphic display of examples in her characteristically lavish double spreads, Heller goes on to versify the distinctions between abstract, concrete, compound, and collective nouns, adding rules for the singular, plural, possessive, and determiner as well. The artist's skill at juggling color and pattern in eye-catching designs makes up for the awkward drafting of faces; animals and objects outweigh humans here, anyway, and the book will prove just as useful as Heller's others on words (*Kites Sail High*) and on biological concepts (*Chickens Aren't the Only Ones*).

430   **Hendershot**, Judith. *In Coal Country*; illus. by Thomas B. Allen. Knopf, 1987. Library ed. ISBN 0-394-98190-1; Trade ed. ISBN 0-394-88190-7. 36p. Library ed. $13.99; Trade ed. $13.95.

5-8 yrs.   A well-wrought complement of first-person narrative and evocative
art describes the lives of an Ohio coal mining family during the
Depression. The text, framed in a square of colored paper that
matches the background of the facing full-page pastel illustration, is
spare but telling. Papa "was always covered with grime and dirt, but I
could see the whites of his eyes smiling at me." The picture here is
rendered vivid not only by the color contrast but also by an imaginative detail: the child narrator, running to meet her father, is brightly
reflected in the miner's mirror crowning his begrimed hat. Other
illustrations, all set against and dominated by subtle earth tones, have
a similar delicacy of conception, rendered poignant by the bleak
setting of a coal mining town. The memories, too, are light in the midst
of hard labor and poverty. The seventy-five children who live in the
Company Row of ten houses gleefully play "king of the mountain" on
dirt and gob piles. In mood, this is reminiscent of Rylant's *When I
Was Young in the Mountains,* and the two picture books would make
good companions for discussion of America's past.

431   **Hendry**, Frances Mary. *Quest for a Maid.* Farrar, 1990. ISBN 0-374-
36162-2. 288p. $13.95.

6-9   In a deft blending of fantasy and historical fiction, Hendry tells the
*   story of Meg, who begins with "When I was nine years old, I hid under
a table and heard my sister kill a king." This is loosely based on the
violent events that followed the death of Alexander III of Scotland
near the end of the 13th century. Meg suspects a much-loved older
sister of using sorcery to achieve regicide, and she is torn between that
love and loyalty to the crown in the person of the young Norwegian
princess who is the rightful heir. Fast-paced, dramatic, colorful in its
historical details, and written with control of style and characterization,
this strong story is preceded by an author's note that draws a distinction between the fact and the fiction that follows.

432   **Henkes**, Kevin. *Grandpa and Bo;* written and illus. by Kevin Henkes.
Greenwillow, 1986. Library ed. ISBN 0-688-04957-5; Trade ed. ISBN 0-
688-04956-7. 29p. Library ed. $11.88; Trade ed. $11.75.

K-2   Soft drawings, grays on cream paper, with some black lines, are neatly
framed and face pages on which the type is set off by ample space.
The story of a small boy's summer spent with a beloved grandfather
on a farm (where Grandpa seems to live alone but have all his time
free) is low-keyed and gentle. This won't have the appeal of action or
humor, but it's a pleasant book about a relationship and a situation,
and the read-aloud audience should enjoy the way Grandpa names
flora and fauna, and the way he and Bo celebrate Christmas on a
summer night to make up for being apart on the holiday.

433   **Henkes**, Kevin. *Jessica*; written and illus. by Kevin Henkes. Greenwillow, 1989. Library ed. ISBN 0-688-07830-3; Trade ed. ISBN 0-688-07829-X. 24p. Library ed. $11.88; Trade ed. $11.95.

4-7 yrs.   Henkes' latest dauntless heroine is Ruthie, a little girl whose best friend is Jessica. "There is no Jessica," say Ruthie's parents (in big boldface type), but Ruthie stands firm by her imaginary friend, even taking her along to the first day of kindergarten where a surprising— yet inevitable—new friend is found. Jessica may be invisible, but there's nothing unreal about the strong friendship Ruthie shares with her, vignettes of which are pictured in tiny, tidy, line-and-watercolor illustrations scattered cleanly and cleverly among the text. This is an exceptionally well designed picture book, with a witty use of white space and an imaginative variety of type and line placement. For example, the line "And if Ruthie was glad, Jessica felt exactly the same" tootles out of Ruthie's horn as she blithely marches through a meadow of wildflowers. Henke's felicitous prose makes this a prime pick for reading aloud to kids and their significant others, invisible or not.

434   **Henkes**, Kevin. *A Weekend with Wendell*; written and illus. by Kevin Henkes. Greenwillow, 1986. Library ed. ISBN 0-688-06326-8; Trade ed. ISBN 0-688-06325-X. 30p. Library ed. $11.88; Trade ed. $11.75.

4-7 yrs.   This story of mischievous mouse-boy Wendell, parked over the weekend with mouse-girl Sophie's parents while his own are out of town, sounds as if the author has been eavesdropping on children at play. "So they played house and Wendell made the rules. He was the father, the mother, and the five children. Sophie was the dog . . . . When they pretended they worked in a bakery, Wendell was the baker and Sophie was a sweet roll." Wendell doesn't get any easier to live with; he leaves Sophie's crayons on the porch to melt, fingerpaints with peanut butter and jelly, and gives Sophie a new hairdo with shaving cream. Finally the silent Sophie fights back with a hose, and the two make friends—just before Sophie's relieved parents call him in to go home. The soft, neatly framed watercolors complement the funny text with the characters' expressive faces and postures, extending the story without overwhelming it. This is a hilarious read-aloud and could prove a turning point in the life of a bossy child—or a mousy one.

435   **Hess**, Lilo. *Secrets in the Meadow*; written and illus. with photographs by Lilo Hess. Scribner, 1986. ISBN 0-684-18525-3. 64p. $13.95.

4-6   With graceful style and scientific attention to detail, Hess catalogues the wildlife of a meadow, including deer, rabbits, mice , and other mammals, but with special emphasis on bugs and insects. The characteristics of many of the latter will have natural appeal for the intended age group, which will relish descriptions of the ambush bug sucking its victims dry, the stink bug spraying its surroundings, or the click bug snapping straight up into the air from its back. Black-and-white photographs are clear and involving. After one's submergence in the text, the conclusion comes as a shock when surveyors invade the area for work on a housing development. Hess' last page of questions ("Where will all the animals go?") gives readers pause for serious environmental thought. A glossary and index are appended.

436   **Hest**, Amy. *The Purple Coat*; illus. by Amy Schwartz. Four Winds, 1986. ISBN 0-02-743640-3. 28p. $12.95.

4-6 yrs.   In what is clearly a yearly ritual, Gabrielle and her mother take a train to the city so that Gabrielle can be fitted for a new coat in Grampa's tailoring shop. This time, though, Gabrielle demands purple instead of the conservative navy blue that has always been chosen for her. Mama says no, but while she is out shopping, Grampa creates a compromise, a reversible coat of navy and purple, reminding Mama on her return that she once demanded (and got) a tangerine dress in her childhood. The loving family dynamics are clearly reflected in the writing as Grandpa passes on his wisdom to Gabby ("Once in a while it's good to try something new"). The illustrations, however, project the relationship even more strongly, as the two homely figures echo each other's stances, positions, and expressions. Appropriate in a story about fabric, there is much attention to texture and pattern in the art, with clothing a palpable presence in all the figures and a focus of contrast or coordination with the surroundings. A rich observance of childhood experience.

437   **Heuck**, Sigrid. *The Hideout*; tr. by Rika Lesser. Dutton, 1988. ISBN 0-525-44343-6. 183p. $12.95.

6-9   A trenchant novel about two Jewish children who are separated from their parents in the last days of World War II Germany. Rebecca's memory, even of her last name, has been blasted away in a bombing raid, after which she is found crying near the ruins of a house. Although Nazi authorities are suspicious, they assign her to an orphanage, where she suffers cruel taunts from other children who call her "Gypsy Child." Nearby, she discovers Samuel hiding out in a corn field, and his imaginative stories create a fantasy world that allows them brief respites from hunger and the artillery terrors of the advancing front. He also makes her a cornhusk doll, and her attachment to it is the most poignant and well-developed aspect of the book. The fantasy seems almost to intrude on the immediately suspenseful realism, but it plays out the children's capability to cope through powers of imagination. The telescoped ending is half fairytale, half fable: Rebecca's parents "were found in a camp. They adopted Sami and emigrated. They searched for a country where there would be no war, a country with everlasting peace." The most powerful element here is the depiction of fateful quirks in a war-stricken dictatorship: with a stupid prank, one of the orphans betrays the very woman who has protected her. Indeed, the author's portrayal of children's confused responses to war are the heartbeat of the book.

438   **Hewitt**, Kathryn, ad. *The Three Sillies;* ad. and illus. by Kathryn Hewitt. Harcourt, 1986. ISBN 0-15-286855-0. 28p. $12.95.

5-8 yrs.   A traditional—and immanently tellable—fools tale gets fresh visual treatment by the artist who gave Noah's voyage such a hilarious interpretation in *Two By Two: The Untold Story*. The characters here are porcine, which lends their foolish actions an even more ridiculous air. When the farmer's daughter goes to the cellar to draw cider for the gentleman courting her and spies an ax stuck in the rafters and weeps for their future children should the ax fall on their heads, she's joined by her portly parents and eventually by the suitor, who swears to journey till he finds three creatures sillier than they are. Of course, he finds them, and in the process, makes a bit of a fool of himself in one of Hewitt's sly graphic jokes (the suitor leans against some wet paint and returns to marry his sweetheart with streaks of yellow all down his back). The smooth, earth-toned watercolors in variously bordered miniature scenes or designs are filled with amusing details of the sights observed by the pseudo-sophisticated pig on his travels; children and adults alike will smile along the way.

439   **Highwater**, Jamake. *The Ceremony of Innocence*. Harper, 1985. Library ed. ISBN 0-06-022302-2; Trade ed. ISBN 0-06-022301-4. 192p. Library ed. $10.89; Trade ed. $11.50.

8-   This sequel to *Legend Days* continues the story of Amana, alienated from her people and isolated by bereavement as a young woman. Here she is befriended by half-breed Amalia, and it is to Amalia that she turns again when her white lover leaves her, unaware that she is pregnant. For many years Amana longs for her own people, the Blood, but she stays in the town where she has a job and where her child, Jemima, is brought up in Amalia's home, a brothel in which Amana and Jemima live apart. Amana longs for her child, then for her grandchildren to carry on the tradition of their people, but they are taken from her. Tradition lies in the legends of the life of this one old woman, whose youth was filled with vigor and promise, whose days of greatness are over, who seems to symbolize her people—their only hope, like hers, lying in those young people who may fight to preserve the dignity and beauty of another way of life. This is a powerful novel, written with controlled strength and emotion, clear in its vision.

440   **Highwater**, Jamake. *Eyes of Darkness*. Lothrop, 1985. ISBN 0-688-41993-3. 189p. $13.00.

7-   This begins, dramatically, with the agonized ambivalence of a Native American who sees the carnage at Wounded Knee and is in despair. Alexander East is his name, he is a medical doctor, and he has already had many occasions on which he felt sharp cultural conflict. The story then moves back to tell of his childhood and youth and college years. He was the boy Hakadah, brought up by a loving grandmother to love his people (the Santee) and their way of life, to respect tradition, and to so live that he garner love and respect himself. In many ways, the white man and his culture impinge on the life of Hadakah and his people; he works earnestly to gain knowledge, but he cannot avoid knowing the bitter facts of injustice. The central, major part of the story is stately in pace and vividly detailed, a tribute to the good life of the People of the Plains, a sympathetic picture of an Indian boy's growth and acculturation that is often touching. The frame of reality of the (then) present is harsh, the contrast between the two a reflection of one man's sadness because he must forget the past and live with the cruel change that has come. The boy Hadakah who became the young man Yesa who became Dr. East is a memorable character, and Highwater gives depth and immediacy by writing from the sad hero's point of view.

441   **Hill**, Kirkpatrick. *Toughboy and Sister*. McElderry, 1990. ISBN 0-689-50506-X. 121p. $12.95.

4-7   Toughboy and Sister are apprehensive when their father leaves them
*   alone at a remote fishing cabin while he goes back to the village to drink. This is their first uneasy taste of managing on their own, and their relief at his return soon turns to despair when Daddy dies in an alcoholic stupor. Far from their Athabascan Indian village and their friends, the two orphans learn to fish and cook and protect themselves, all the while growing to appreciate the other's unexpected gifts. Toughboy is eleven, Sister eight, and their alliance is brave and real, captured in Hill's plainspoken prose: "When they were grown-up, they could do anything they wanted to do. That was good to think about when you were just a kid and you were going to have to do something you didn't want to do at all." Their survival story is straightforwardly rendered and elementally satisfying, its realism developed through the clear details of living in the Alaskan wilderness. A bear scare adds excitement, and eventual rescue by an old neighbor, Natasha, promises the children a well-deserved new family. Strongly and simply told, this is an ideal story for readers too young for the survival adventures of Gary Paulsen and Jean George.

442   **Hilton**, Suzanne. *The World of Young Tom Jefferson;* illus. by
       William Sauts Bock. Walker, 1986. Library ed. ISBN 0-8027-6622-6;
       Trade ed. ISBN 0-8027-6621-8. 92p. Library ed. $13.85; Trade ed. $13.95.

6-8   In a biography that is fictionalized with restraint and written with
       polish and authority, Hilton focuses on Jefferson's childhood and his
       years as a young college student, although the final chapter gives a
       compressed account of his life and work as an adult. Despite the fact
       that Jefferson never emerges as a vibrant character, the text shows
       how childhood events and attitudes foreshadowed his later philo-
       sophy. One of the strong points of the book is the way the author
       brings in, at appropriate moments, a wealth of pertinent information
       about such subjects as medicine or education of the period. A
       chronology, an index, and a list headed, "Whatever Happened To
       . . . ?" are provided.

443   **Hinton**, S. E. *Taming the Star Runner.* Delacorte, 1988. ISBN 0-440-
       50058-3. 166p. $14.95.

6-9   After a brief stay in a juvenile hall, sixteen-year-old Travis is sent to
       stay on his uncle Ken's ranch. Ken is preoccupied with his impending
       divorce and how it will affect his relationship with his small son, but
       he's kind to Travis. Certainly it's better than being at home with his
       mother and his abusive stepfather. Hinton, whose perceptive
       interpretation of the young person who is isolated has brought
       deserved recognition, here uses two aspects of Travis' life to show his
       interests and his ambivalence: one is the fact that his manuscript for a
       novel has been accepted, a work in which he is articulate in a way that
       he is not in person; second, his relationship with the people who work
       or ride at a riding school run by Casey, whom he comes to love and
       whom he admires because of her courage and her independence.
       There's a lot about horses here (Star Runner is Casey's horse), and the
       book will probably appeal most to those readers who are also horse
       lovers, but Hinton's fans are legion, and this is far from a formula
       horse story; it has depth, pattern, perception, and a communicable
       empathy for its protagonist.

444   **Hirsch**, Marilyn, ad. *Joseph Who Loved the Sabbath;* illus. by Devis
       Grebu. Viking, 1986. ISBN 0-670-81194-7. 28p. $10.95.

4-7 yrs.   A Jewish folktale contrasts a poor man, Joseph, who buys only the best
       for celebrating the Sabbath, to the rich landowner, Sorab, who sneers
       at Joseph's wasting his hard-won wages on such nonsense. When
       Sorab is visited by a dream warning him that Joseph will inherit
       everything he has, he sells his lands, buys a ruby, and sets out on a
       voyage. But in a twist of fate common as a folk motif, he is lost at sea
       and the ruby swallowed by a fish that Joseph subsequently buys for his
       Sabbath meal. Thus Joseph buys all of Sorab's lands with the ruby and

celebrates the Sabbath ever more bountifully. The angular watercolor paintings that accompany this compact retelling are stylized in design and composition, with Middle Eastern details of setting and costume. Brief notes on the story and the celebration of the Sabbath are added. A good choice for contrasting folkloric variants for story hours with a Jewish theme.

445   **Hirschfelder**, Arlene. *Happily May I Walk: American Indians and Alaska Natives Today.* Scribner, 1986. ISBN 0-684-18624-1. 152p. illus. with photographs. $12.95.

5-9   This comprehensive reportage of native American groups is well-researched and up-to-date in content but suffers from repetition ("It is difficult for non-Indians to learn Indian languages" and, one paragraph later, "It is possible but extremely difficult for non-Indians to learn an Indian language"). Tribal governments, reservations, languages, religion, education, history, and culture get detailed attention that sometimes breaks down into dry organization, as in the catalogue-like chapters on arts and sports figures. Nevertheless, the discussions of Indian treatment at the hands of the U.S. government is a sympathetic one, and students working on reports will find the facts and figures they need here, along with black-and-white photographs, a good bibliography, and an index.

446   **Hirschi**, Ron. *What Is a Bird?* Library ed. ISBN 0-8027-6721-4; Trade ed. ISBN 0-8027-6720-6. *Where Do Birds Live?* Library ed. ISBN 0-8027-6723-0; Trade ed. ISBN 0-8027-6722-2. 32p. Each book: illus. with photographs by Galen Burrell. Walker, 1987. 32p. Library ed. $11.85; Trade ed. $10.95.

3-5 yrs.   Two filmic, fast-moving photodocumentaries qualify as introductions to bird life for the younger listener. With a poetic text of a few words per page, the double-spread color photographs, sometimes inset with smaller contrasting photos, capture sensuous impressions of feathers, flight, or floating. In a few cases, the images interfere with the information: "Birds are eggs, waiting", for instance, may have to be explained or rephrased to avoid confusion. If the books err on the side of aesthetic appeal, however, they still give the audience a better sense of bird life than a volume of prosaic detail. The photographs are vivid and arranged for arresting contrasts, as in the pictures showing Dark-eyed Juncos and Northern Pintail ducks against snowy backgrounds, followed by a Curve-billed Thrasher in a summer desert setting. For each book, an afterword identifies the birds in every picture, including, in the second title, descriptive notes.

447   **Hirst**, Robin. *My Place in Space*; by Robin and Sally Hirst; illus. by Roland Harvey and Joe Levine. Orchard, 1990. Library ed. ISBN 0-531-

08459-0; Trade ed. ISBN 0-531-05859-X. 40p. Library ed. $13.99; Trade ed. $13.95.

1-3   Weird little drawings of a small Australian town serve as foreground for dramatic paintings of the universe—all illustrating exactly where Henry Wilson and his sister Rosie live. Just like wise-guy kids who put interminable return addresses on their envelopes, Henry tells the bus driver about Gumbridge, Australia, the southern hemisphere, Earth, the solar system, the solar neighborhood, the Orion Arm, the Milky Way . . . "'Most of space is just that—space,' added Henry, trying to relieve the driver's puzzled look." Children will appreciate this cosmological cumulation, which satisfies a need for order, predictability, and egocentricity. The science is sound, presented in enough detail to be interesting but with enough simplicity to be recalled and repeated aloud. Illustrations effectively combine two techniques (and artists) to convey the context of a bustling, down-to-earth earth (complete with several funny dramas that run from page to page) in a dizzying photorealistic firmament of planets, stars, and supergalaxies. It all begins to look like home.

448   **Hiscock**, Bruce. *Tundra, the Arctic Land;* written and illus. by Bruce Hiscock. Atheneum, 1986. ISBN 0-689-31219-0. 135p. $13.95.

5-8   A storehouse of information, this blends natural history background on the Tundra with the author's observations as he travels on a three-week camping trip in the brief Arctic summer. Trees, plants, birds, insects, animals, and even various peoples have all related in a delicate ecological balance for centuries until some recent upheavals due to the discovery and exploitation of oil and mineral deposits. Hiscock describes this ecological balance with particular attention to the specific details of surviving conditions of extreme, unrelieved cold. One truck rut over the tundra, for instance, can cause uneven melting of the permafrost and create serious erosion of the land around it, affecting plant and animal life in a chain reaction. The style is smooth, as is the organization; the treatment, both scientific and personal; the approach, encompassing. The black-and-white illustrations and overall book design are strikingly handsome, the bibliography (juvenile books are marked), useful.

449   **Ho**, Minfong. *Rice without Rain.* Lothrop, 1990. ISBN 0-688-06355-1. 236p. $12.95.

7-
 *   Jinda and her family are suspicious of the university students from Bangkok who have come to "learn" in the drought-stricken northern village of Maekung. Their leader, Ned, is earnest, charismatic, and handsome, winning Jinda's heart and, eventually, the trust of the villagers. Ned convinces them to give just a third, not half, of their precious rice to the landlord. This resistance puts Jinda's father in

prison and takes Jinda to Bangkok, where she is caught up in the student protest movement. A foreword explains the political situation in Thailand in the mid-70's, providing a useful context for a story that succeeds dramatically on its own terms. Jinda regards herself as an ordinary village girl, in love with a revolutionary but suspicious of the visitors' slogans. "She couldn't help thinking that Maekung had just been a vacation for them. Now that the vacation was over, it was time for the good little students to go back to school." While Ned's commitment to the cause is paramount, he confesses to Jinda that "sometimes it's easier to talk like a book than a person." Their love story is inevitably fused with the political events of their country, a balance that disallows excesses of romantic melodrama or earnest didacticism. The events are painful, violent, and graphically portrayed, especially in the climactic terror of a rally in which there is a brutal massacre of students by the military. The conclusion, in which both Jinda and Ned find their futures, is sad but honest.

450   **Hoban**, Tana, illus. *1, 2, 3;* illus. with photographs by Tana Hoban. Greenwillow, 1985. ISBN 0-688-02579-X. *What Is It?;* illus. with photographs by Tana Hoban. Greenwillow, 1985. ISBN 0-588-02577-3. Both books have 10 pages and are $3.95.

1-2 yrs.   In small, square books with heavy board pages, Hoban uses excellent color photographs of simple, familiar objects against a clean background. Each page in the number book carries, in addition to the picture, the digit, the word for the digit, and the corresponding number of dots, well-spaced devices to ramify concepts. Pictures are paired on facing pages in *What Is It?*: a sock and a shoe, a bib and a drinking mug, a spoon and a bowl of cereal, etc. A delight to look at, these are enjoyable as well as effective teaching tools.

451   **Hoban**, Tana, illus. *Is It Larger? Is It Smaller?;* illus. with photographs by Tana Hoban. Greenwillow, 1985. Library ed. ISBN 0-688-04028-4; Trade ed. ISBN 0-688-0402706. 29p.. Library ed. $11.88; Trade ed. $11.75.

2-5 yrs.   Unsurpassed for her use of color photography in concept books, Hoban here presents a series of pictures in which there are sets of large and small objects that show contrasting size. Most of the photographs show items so clearly (a large and small goldfish in an aquarium; big beads and small ones) that the pair is immediately identifiable; occasionally (a child holding a rabbit) children may wonder what the big-small comparison is (ears, in this case) but it's always there, and the moment of searching may add a bit of game element.

452   **Hoban**, Tana. *Red, Blue, Yellow Shoe;* illus. and with photographs by Tana Hoban. Greenwillow, 1986. 11p. $3.95.

1-3 yrs.   With her customary clarity of concept and precision of photographic composition, Hoban has created a board book to equal *1,2,3 (A First Book of Numbers)* and her other concept books for the youngest child. Each page contains one object, a familiar and attractively presented one, with a large dot in the featured color and the name of the object in large block print. Green is represented by a handsome maple leaf, gray by a feather in shades from light to dark, and black by an appealing but not sentimentalized kitten. The book itself is easy to handle, with rounded edges, and will serve for use in identifying the objects as well as the colors. Sturdy in every respect.

453   **Hoban**, Tana, illus. *Shapes, Shapes, Shapes;* illus. with photographs by Tana Hoban. Greenwillow, 1986. Library ed. ISBN 0-688-05833-7; Trade ed. ISBN 0-688-05832-9. 30p. Library ed. $11.88; Trade ed. $11.75.

3-5 yrs.   There are many picture books about shapes, including Hoban's own *Shapes and Things* (silhouettes of familiar objects), but most of those that introduce geometric forms to young children focus on the few that are simplest: square, circle, etc. Here in a wordless book with handsome color photographs that are preceded by a page on which shapes are identified appear both the familiar and the less familiar, such as a parallelogram or star or hexagon. This is as useful as it is attractive.

454   **Hodges**, Margaret, ad. *The Kitchen Knight;* illus. by Trina Schart Hyman. Holiday House, 1990. ISBN 0-8234-0787-X. 32p. $14.95.

3-5
 *
Margaret Hodges, experienced in adapting classics such as *Saint George and the Dragon*, which was excerpted from Spenser's *Faerie Queene* and also illustrated by Trina Schart Hyman, has made a resounding version of this medieval tale from Malory's *Le Morte D'Arthur*. The kitchen knight is really King Arthur's nephew in humble disguise, come to win his spurs by challenging every strong knight that comes down the pike—the black one, the blue one, and, finally, the red one. The beautiful Linesse, whose sister Linette first scorned the kitchen knight's ragged appearance, is his prize, but she's imprisoned in a tower. Ours not to question the royal rules of chivalry, though constant testing by physical thumps does seem increasingly archaic from this distance. However, Hyman's paintings confer great dignity on the whole affair. Her portraiture is stronger than ever. The monolithic weight of war horses, armor, shields, and battlefield morality is balanced by graceful lines and a sly glint in the expressions of the outspoken Linette. The borders here are appropriately plain, with the graphic narrative furthered, instead, by miniature insets that detail action happening somewhere other than in the full-page scenes. This frame within a frame composition achieves a kind of "meanwhile" storytelling effect appropriate to the tale within a tale.

An effective introduction to Arthurian legend for elementary and even junior high or high school students.

455   Hoff, Syd. *Mrs. Brice's Mice*; written and illus. by Syd Hoff. Harper, 1988. Library ed. ISBN 0-06-022452-5; Trade ed. ISBN 0-06-022451-7. 32p. Library ed. $9.89; Trade ed. $8.95 check this.

4-6 yrs.   Mrs. Brice has twenty-four mice; well, twenty-five, but the last, "one very small mouse," is always intent on distinguishing himself from the rest. Twenty-four mice sleep on the bed with Mrs. Brice (in an arrangement reminiscent of *Madeline*); one very small mouse sleeps on the alarm clock "in case he wanted to know what time it was." His distinction comes in handy when, while on a walk, the mice meet a cat, and while twelve run this way and twelve that way, the one little mouse runs this way *and* that, wearing out the cat and saving them all. The simple, gracefully repetitive text and bright cartoon drawings will make a preschool hero of the clever little mouse.

456   **Hogrogian**, Nonny. *The Cat Who Loved To Sing*; written and illus. by Nonny Hogrogian. Knopf, 1988. Library ed. ISBN 0-394-99004-8; Trade ed. ISBN 0-394-89004-3. 26p. Library ed. $13.99; Trade ed. $12.95.

3-5 yrs.   Hogrogian's wash drawings provide a traditional setting for this Armenian cumulative song-tale about a cat which, in return for a loaf of bread, gives the thorn in its foot to a woman to use as a needle. The cat then swaps the bread for a chicken, the chicken for yarn, the yarn for a coat, the coat for a dog, the dog for a sheep, and the sheep for a shepherd's mandolin, which will accompany the cat's singing forevermore. The words and music of the cat's song conclude the book, which is designed with woodsy endpapers that extend the verdant scenery of the cat's capers. The fused effects of the backgrounds contrast nicely with the pencilled lines texturing the cat's fur for a gentle effect to which young listeners will respond by quickly picking up the chant.

457   **Holman**, Felice. *The Song in My Head*; illus. by Jim Spanfeller. Scribner, 1985. ISBN 0-684-18295-5. 62p. $12.95.

3-6   Holman's whimsy never becomes cloying or her imagery obscure in this new collection of poems, mostly light and mostly lyrical. Some see life from a child's viewpoint ("Friend," "When I am President") and some ("Cardinals," "Oriental Poppy," or the title poem) have a broader scope. Like any collection of good poetry, this can be read aloud to younger children and enjoyed by adults. The format is spacious and the illustrations, some abstract and some representational, are finely detailed, the black and white softened by stippling.

458   **Hooker**, Ruth. *Matthew the Cowboy*; illus. by Cat Bowman Smith. Whitman, 1990. ISBN 0-8075-4999-1. 32p. $12.95.

4-6 yrs.   "A cowboy suit! Just what I've always wanted." Six-year-old Matthew is pleased with his birthday present, immediately going outside—and out West—to be a cowboy. He gets some "jingle, jangle, jingle" spurs at the general store; finds a beautiful white horse, Silver, on the plain; and meets cowboy Rocky, who enlists Matthew's help in roundin' up some cattle rustlers. This pokerfaced fantasy is a deft presentation of wish-fulfillment at its most sublime, and the watercolor cartoon illustrations have lots of appealing energy, especially in the sequence where Matthew—"Ya-a-a-*ah*!"—confronts Bad Bart. Little boys, of course, will love this, but liberated parents will be pleased that Matthew's cowboy friends are a multiethnic mix, and include a ponytailed woman, Tex. At the end, Matthew hangs up his spurs, bids a tearful goodbye to Silver, and goes in for dinner. "'How about some grub?' his mother asked." Home on the range.

459   **Hooks**, William H. *The Ballad of Belle Dorcas*; illus. by Brian Pinkney. Knopf, 1990. Library ed. ISBN 0-394-94645-6; Trade ed. ISBN 0-394-84645-1. 40p. Library ed. $14.99; Trade ed. $13.95.

2-5   "Belle Dorcas was free issue, her daddy being a white master, her mama being his house slave." But though Belle has papers, she falls in love with a slave named Joshua, whom a new master plans to sell. Granny Lizard's conjure bag turns Joshua into a cedar tree by day, a man by night; even when the tree is chopped down to make a smokehouse, Joshua is resurrected from the cedar shingles nightly until Belle Dorcas ages and dies, leaving "two young cedar trees . . . growing side by side." An episodic legend depending on magic to resolve each threat, this combines the haunting motif of a lover transformed with a tragic historical drama. The author's note cites an oral tale from his Carolina coast childhood as the only source and gives information on Gullah conjure tales as well as on the "free" offspring of slave masters and slave women. Pinkney's full-color scratchboard illustrations swirl white lines against black backgrounds in a contrast that naturally highlights the secrecy and danger of the action. The visual effect is one of muted suspense, a tone especially appropriate for the misty past recreated here. Although this is a picture book in appearance, it's actually better suited for reading aloud to elementary students who have some historical sense in which to fit the complex elements of fantasy and reality.

460   **Hooks**, William H. *The Three Little Pigs and the Fox*; illus. by S. D. Schindler. Macmillan, 1989. ISBN 0-02-744431-7. 32p. $13.95.

4-7 yrs.   With a perfect storytelling balance of invention and convention,
   *   Hooks relates an Appalachian variant of The Three Little Pigs that is
            subtly contemporized without leaving behind elemental tradition. Our
            hero is "a tiny little girl runt named Hamlet," who has no trouble
            retaining her mother's three basic rules of life: " . . . watch out for that
            mean, tricky old drooly-mouth fox . . . build yourself a safe, strong
            house out of rocks . . . come home to see your mama every single
            Sunday." Hamlet's gluttonous older brothers fail on all counts ("That's
            a lot to remember"), but the runty female fools the fox with an old ploy
            ("'Are the dogs getting closer?' the fox mumbled from inside the
            churn. 'What dogs?' asked baby Hamlet.") and brings her brothers
            home for a Sunday of snorting and eating to their hearts' content. The
            satisfyingly patterned repetitions are spiced by well-timed surprises
            ("'Oh, shut up,' said mean, tricky old drooly-mouth fox"). With an ear
            for colloquial wit and an eye on the family dynamic that sends these
            characters on their journey of maturation, Hooks has found a perfect
            fit in Schindler's watercolor scenes. Drafted with ease of proportion,
            colored with rural blends, and elegantly underplayed in expression,
            the animals are fresh and funny without being self-conscious. Pair this
            one with James Marshall's funny cartoon version and/or Jon
            Scieszka's wolf's-eye view in *The True Story of the Three Little Pigs* .

461   **Hooper**, Patricia. *A Bundle of Beasts*; illus. by Mark Steele.
            Houghton, 1987. ISBN 0-395-44259-1. 52p. $12.95.

4-6   Exceptionally ingenious wordplay distinguishes these 25 poems,
   *   unified by archaic names for groups of animals, as in a *drift* of hogs, a
            leap of leopards, or a *watch* of nightingales. Musically, the verse sings
            with the kind of lilting, spontaneous rhythms that Silverstein and
            Prelutsky manage so easily, and the tone is humorous as well. Yet
            these poems are more unusual in their verbal banter without ever
            abandoning an accessible simplicity of concept, and they make
            shrewd fun of animal—and human—life through their ostensible
            nonsense. Most of the poems extend to a double spread, illustrated by
            vigorous gray line-and-wash drawings, and the reader is always glad to
            find more than one page. There's usually a narrative thread, too, as in
            "A *Route* of Wolves," which begins, "The wolves lay down in the
            grass./ They said, 'We are making a road!/ When the rabbits come
            by,/ How still we shall lie!' / And the moon in the melon tree glowed."
            There follow six funny but suspenseful stanzas in which the rabbits,
            who are searching for raspberry buns, discover through various
            sensations that they are running along a route of wolves ("But they ran
            when they noticed its nose!"). An author's note on the origin of the
            terms and a list of suggested readings for discovering others conclude
            this original combination of craft and cunning. Choice verse for a
            browse, a class-read-aloud, or a language arts program.

462   **Hoover**, H. M. *Orvis*. Viking Kestrel, 1987. ISBN 0-670-81117-3. 185p. $12.95.

5-8   The time is the distant future, the setting an Earth that is only partially settled, since most Terran descendants have lived for generations in space ships or space colonies. Toby is attending an Earth school and is unhappy because her domineering grandmother has decided to transfer her to a school on Mars. With a younger friend, Thaddeus, and the highly intelligent old robot Orvis, she decides to visit the great-grandmother who lives near Lake Erie and whom she's never seen. Thus begins the journey that turns into danger and disaster, as the children and Orvis set off but are trapped by hijackers and abandoned in the wilderness. It is Orvis who is the hero, rescuing the children repeatedly before they reach the haven of Great-grand-mother's home. Hoover is deft and consistent in her creation of a not-so-brave new world; her characters are solidly defined by their words and actions, and she maintains a brisk pace while subtly incorporating some thoughtful comments on human behavior.

463   **Hopkins**, Lee Bennett, comp. *Dinosaurs*; poems selected by Lee Bennet Hopkins; illus. by Murray Tinkelman. Harcourt, 1987. ISBN 0-15-223495-0. 40p. $14.95.

3-6   The combination of poetry and dinosaurs is inspired, considering how much the popular subject will dispel aversion to a literary form that sometimes puts young readers off. Hopkins has also gone out of his way to select some new names for this anthology in addition to veterans such as Lillian Moore, Valerie Worth, and Myra Cohn Livingston. The tone is varied, with some poignant reflections on "The Last Dinosaur" (Victoria Day Najjar) as well as humorous rhymes contrasting the present with the past ("It's much more pleasant/To know/That he's/The one who isn't" —Margaret Hillert). A full-page, pen-and-ink, shadowy hatch drawing faces each of the 14 poems, some of which are reprinted from collections and some of which seem to appear here for the first time. Teachers will make a grab for this if students haven't already done so.

464   **Hopkins**, Lee Bennett, comp. *More Surprises*; illus. by Megan Lloyd. Harper, 1987. Library ed. ISBN 0-06-022605-6; Trade ed. ISBN 0-06-022604-8. 58p. (I Can Read). Library ed. $10.89; Trade ed. $9.95.

1-3   Continuing one of his best ideas—anthologizing poetry into an easy-to-read format—Hopkins includes 35 selections by Karla Kuskin, Mary Ann Hoberman, Jack Prelutsky, N.M. Bodecker, and others who display a knack for simple, entertaining rhymes. The rhythmic repetition, humor, and narrative quality of pieces like "If You Ever Meet A Whale" (anonymous) or "My Nose" (Dorothy Aldis) make them natural practice material. Although these are not difficult to find elsewhere, their appearance here is convenient and reinforces teachers' using more creative approaches to reading by exercising skills on inventive language and imaginative literature.

465   Horejs, Vít. *Pig and Bear*; illus. by Friso Henstra. Four Winds, 1989. ISBN 0-02-744421-X. 40p. $11.95.

1-3   Sometimes Pig and Bear sound more like two very shaggy dogs: "A mosquito *inside* a room, for instance, is much fiercer and treacher-ouser than he can ever be *outside*. Now, it is very important to find out exactly when an outsect becomes an insect. I am deeply convinced that at this *in-between* moment, the very small beings are harmless, while it is hard to catch an outsect and almost impossible to outsmart an insect." So says Pig, in the course of what could have been the simple procedure of shutting the door. Pig is clever, talkative, and prickly; Bear is slow but steady, and a loving friend. Witness his idea, for example, of opening a *pawshop*: "a place where animals went when they didn't feel so good . . . and a big warm paw patted them. Or just held them. Tight." Unlikely in the way best-friendships often are, this duo seems all the stronger for its quirks and tics. The book includes four conversational adventures between the two friends, all char-acterized by circuitous wit and tender loyalty. Henstra's spaciously set ink drawings capture both fun and friendship.

466   Horenstein, Henry. *Sam Goes Trucking*; written and illus. with photographs by Henry Horenstein. Houghton, 1989. ISBN 0-395-44313-X. 40p. $14.95.

4-7 yrs.   Sam is going trucking with his dad in their Mack model R-600. They enjoy an early breakfast, head for the terminal, check the truck and hitch the trailer to the cab, fill the tank with diesel fuel, pick up a load of fish, and deliver it, with the requisite lunch break for burgers and fries at Cindy's Truck Stop. Kids will find out there's more than one meaning for the words reefer (a refrigerator trailor), smokey (a state trooper), log (a record of how far and where the truck goes), and white-line fever (road fatigue). Best of all is the affectionate relationship between a boy and his father, who's known as "Big Stuff" on the CB. Although the well reproduced and formatted color photographs base this solidly in the real world, the idealized experience will seem a dream/fantasy for most boys. A photodocumentary with sure appeal for young browsers.

467   Horvath, Polly. *No More Cornflakes*. Farrar, 1990. ISBN 0-374-35530-4. 134p. $12.95.

4-6   "Since Mom has been pregnant, she's been scarfing up the old cornflakes like nobody's business . . . She concentrated so hard on those cornflakes it was like she and they were one," says ten-year-old

Hortense, who is horrified by the thought of a baby sibling and feels left behind by everyone she knows. Her older sister has formed a family-excluding (or at least Hortense-excluding) bond with friends her own age, her mother and father spend an embarrassing amount of time publicly pretending to be rabbits, and even her normally compliant friend Doris has had the temerity to take ballet lessons *without Hortense.* She tries to make a soul-mate of her crisp Aunt Kate, a professional writer and fellow resident of the Hemple house, but finds her a demanding if stimulating figure ("If there's one thing I can't stand," says Aunt Kate to a wounded Hortense, "it's people emoting all over the place"). Eventually Hortense finds a friend in formerly alarming Virginia Vermeulen ("I thought she was a walk on the wild side, but here she was sounding like the voice of reason"), with whom she has more in common than with wimpy Doris, and she finally greets the birth of brother Max with delight and acceptance, stating "I don't think our family will fall apart just because it keeps changing." Hortense is the Midwest's answer to Anastasia Krupnik— witty, sophisticated and literate, with her uncertainty and occasional loneliness apparent beneath the self-confidence of her narration. Characterization is deft throughout, with Aunt Kate a particular standout: delightfully free from any climactic sentimental thaw, she tolerates Hortense only because Hortense has proved herself sufficiently civilized to be interesting. This is a funny, flowing, sharply observed portrait of family life.

468   **Hotze**, Sollace. *A Circle Unbroken.* Clarion, 1988. ISBN 0-89919-733-7. 202p. $13.95.

6-9   Rachel Porter, seventeen, had been living happily in the Sioux community to which she had been brought as a captive in 1838; now, in 1845, she is forcibly taken back to her widowed father and finds it hard to adjust to another life-style and its strictures. In this first novel, Hotze makes a convincing case for Rachel's decision to go back to her Sioux family and the way of life she had enjoyed; the reluctant agreement of her stern father is less convincing, given his bias against the "hea- then" who had taken three members of his family. The writing style is adequate, as is the structure of the book and the characterization; the narrative is weakened by its slow pace.

469   **Houghton**, Eric. *Walter's Magic Wand*; illus. by Denise Teasdale. Orchard, 1990. Library ed. ISBN 0-531-08451-5; Trade ed. ISBN 0-531- 05851-4. 26p. Library ed. $13.99; Trade ed. $13.95.

4-8 yrs.   In this *Jumanji,* jr., Walter's magic wand creates satisfying upheaval at the library. Tapping a book called *Tigers* turns the place into a jungle, *Pirates* run amok, *Oceans* . . .well, get the mop. It's just another day for the fearless librarian: "When the pirates waved their swords and shouted bloodcurdling threats, the librarian shot pencils at them with a rubber band and drove them away." The twin themes of books-as-adventure and librarian-as-friend are disarmingly presented, and the bright, catastrophe-laden paintings are large and clear enough for a first-visit storyhour.

470   Houston, James. *The Falcon Bow: An Arctic Legend*. McElderry, 1986. ISBN 0-689-50411-X. 92p. $12.95.

5-8   This sequel to *The White Archer* brings the young Inuit, Kungo, back to the island of his aging adoptive parents only to be summoned after a season to seek his sister, now married to a hunter among inland Indians. The coastal Inuit believe that the inlanders have cut off their supply of caribou; the inlanders believe the Inuit have built weirs to hold back the fish. Both groups are starving and on the verge of hostilities when Kungo makes his journey and reconciles the two peoples just as, somewhat luckily, the caribou that were scattered by tundra fires return and the fish begin their run. The real tension here evolves from humans fighting the forces of nature rather than each other. Several scenes of Kungo in danger from thin ice or storms are gripping, while the resolution of the suspicious hunters seems a foregone conclusion after one brief confrontation. Readers of the previous book will have had the benefit of built-up expectations based on previous characterizations and situations. Those who come to this book first can still enjoy the details of survival among native peoples in a harsh country.

471   Howard, Ellen. *Gillyflower*. Atheneum, 1986. 106p. $11.95.

6-10   With her parents' marriage under stress from her father's jobless depression and her mother's evening shift at the hospital, Gilly suffers an unbearable load of responsibility for her beloved younger sister, Honey, and guilt over her father's insistent sexual molestation. Isolated in a protective fantasy world, she finally makes contact with a healthy family that moves next door and confesses her situation to her mother, mostly out of fear for her little sister. This is a highly concentrated novel, with characters clearly delineated within the limitations of the problem and scenes that communicate Gilly's relentless burden. Her relationship with schoolmate Mary Rose is handled delicately, as the troubled new friendship evolves in fits and starts according to Gilly's home situation. Relevant without becoming a case study, Gilly's story is developed sensitively and crafted capably.

472   Howard, Ellen. *Sister*. Karl/Atheneum, 1990. ISBN 0-689-31653-4. 148p. $12.95.

5-7   While *Sister* follows *Edith, Herself*, it is set earlier (1886) and is also based on events in the lives of the author's ancestors. Edith has not yet been born in this story of Alena, her oldest sister. Alena yearns to stay in school and is encouraged by her teacher to think that she might get a scholarship to go to Normal School. Her hopes are dashed by the fact that her mother, brooding over the death of a newborn daughter, needs Alena's help at home. Alena is also stunned by grief, having felt close to the baby she had delivered because Father was away. Characterization is strong and consistent; Howard gives a convincing picture of the busy life of an Illinois farm family as well as a touching picture of the relationships among its members. The writing style is strong and flowing, and Howard manages to instill excitement and momentum into the drama of everyday life.

473   **Howe**, James. *There's a Monster Under My Bed*; illus. by David Rose. Atheneum, 1986. ISBN 0-689-31178-8. 32p. $11.95.

4-7 yrs.   Spacious paintings with a spooky perspective reflect the tone of this first-person narrative about a little boy, Simon, confronting his first bedtime without a nightlight. Typically, his imagination soars from one monster under the bed to two ("They're fighting . . . over who gets to eat me") to a whole crowd, all generously depicted in tasteful, only suggestively grotesque detail. "Goodbye, Mom! Goodbye Dad! Goodbye Glen Oaks Elementary! Goodbye, Mrs Grover! I'm sorry I put that dead fish in your drawer last week." However, before Simon finishes his last rites, he discovers a flashlight his mother has left beside the bed, takes courage in hand, and peers at . . . his little brother, hiding under Simon's bed from the monsters under his own. Simon reassures Alex ("There's no such tings as monsters. Don't be a baby"), and the two settle in together for the night. There's plenty of natural child's point of view here, simply phrased and authentic. The text is paced with both suspense and humor; the art heightens both, with a judicious balance of fantasy figures and stark backgrounds.

474   **Howker**, Janni. *Badger on the Barge and Other Stories*. Greenwillow, 1985. ISBN 0-688-04215-5. 208p. $10.25.

6-10
*   In each of the five long stories in this first book by an impressive new British writer, there is a special relationship between a child and an elderly person whose role is minor but whose influence is a major one. Howker writes with sensitivity; her ear for dialogue is excellent, her settings and characters equally colorful. Different as the stories are, they are alike in the high quality of craftsmanship they display.

475   **Howker**, Janni. *Isaac Campion*. Morrow, 1987. ISBN 0-688-06658-5. 85p. $10.25.

7-   An old man, Isaac Campion, recalls the spring of 1901, when his elder brother Dan is killed in a bizarre accident and he must take over as helper to his bitter, hard-handed father. Old Samuel Campion is a horse dealer, but the dominant passion in his life is hatred for a neighbor whose son makes the dare that cost Dan Campion's life. This is partly the story of that destructive feud, partly a view of a place and period when most aspects of country living were unrelentingly difficult and often cruel. It is also the portrait of a child who finally frees himself from his father's abuse. The writing is dense, the dialect difficult, but the fictional crafting will reward readers who can appreciate the careful development of character and scene that has typified Howker's other award-winning work, *Badger on the Barge* and *The Nature of the Beast* .

476   **Howker**, Janni. *The Nature of the Beast.* Greenwillow, 1985. ISBN 0-688-04233-3. 138p. $10.25.

6-9   It takes an artist to effectively combine a story about the grim effects on a small English town when its major industry closes, and a taut adventure tale about a mysterious creature that is preying on the livestock of local farmers. Howker is, then, an artist, for through her narrator, Billy, she does blend the two themes and at the same time depict, with insight and sympathy, the love Billy has for the father and grandfather with whom he lives. There is suspense in Billy's hunt for the marauding beast, and a surprise in the conclusion of the story after he finds it. One of the additional appeals of the book is that the author uses local dialect judiciously, so that it colors the narrative but does not, for American readers, obscure it.

477   **Hoyt-Goldsmith**, Diane. *Totem Pole*; illus. with photographs by Lawrence Migdale. Holiday House, 1990. ISBN 0-8234-0809-4. 32p. $14.95.

3-5   Color photographs liberally illustrate a first-person text narrated by David, whose father is a skilled carver. They are members of the Eagle Clan of the Tsimshian tribe; David's mother has been adopted into the Eagle Clan although she is of European descent. David describes the way his father carves a new totem pole, pointing out the traditions associated both with the making of the pole and with the intricate ceremony of raising it and celebrating its installation. The writing is simple and direct, the tone of pride is strong, the information is not often found in books for children, and the book is imbued with cultural dignity and a sense of the value of the extended family and community. A glossary and an index make the contents accessible.

478   **Hudson**, Jan. *Sweetgrass*. Philomel, 1989. ISBN 0-399-21721-5. 159p. $13.95.

6-9   An extensive bibliography attests to the careful research that is so unobtrusively incorporated into this impressive first novel. Hudson's protagonist/narrator is a Blackfoot girl of fifteen, Sweetgrass, who worries about being so old (younger girls have become wives) and not yet wed, and is even more concerned that she be promised to the young warrior she loves, Eagle-Sun. Will he want her? Will he have enough horses (the status symbol, in their tribe) to be accepted by her father if he does ask? Will her father's wife, Almost-Mother, pronounce Sweetgrass responsible enough to be a wife? In a flowing text that has conviction and immediacy, Hudson depicts life on the western Canadian prairie in the 19th century as the Blackfoot people struggled with natural disasters, encountered the white settlers, fought other tribes, observed traditional rituals, and succcumbed to the terrible ravages of smallpox. What brings this book past its documentary interest is the strongly individual characterization, expressed in both exposition and dialogue.

479   **Hughes**, Dean. *Family Pose*. Atheneum, 1989. ISBN 0-689-31396-9. 192p. $13.95.

5-10   As fully realized as an adult novel but with appeal for junior high and
*   high school readers, this portrays a night-shift hotel crew's becoming family for an orphaned runaway. David's foster homes have so damaged him that Paul, the middle-aged bellboy who sneaks him into a room and feeds him, has to work hard to win his trust. The desk clerk, the telephone operator, and the cocktail waitress unite to offer him the affection and respect he craves, but each of them is a loner for different—and complex—reasons. Whether anyone will undertake responsibility for him, or whether they will shuffle him back into an impassive system, remains in question until the last satisfying but never sentimental page. The detailed setting, the subtle observation of each character, and the realistic development of a life crisis make this a high point in young adult fiction.

480   **Hughes**, Shirley. *Angel Mae: A Tale of Trotter Street*; written and illus. by Shirley Hughes. Lothrop, 1989. Library ed. ISBN 0-688-08539-3; Trade ed. ISBN 0-688-08538-5. 26p. Library ed. $12.88; Trade ed. $12.95.

4-6 yrs.   Shirley Hughes has an unerring instinct for avoiding sentimentality,
*   and she manages to make this story of an English child's participation in a Christmas play, and her adjustment to a new baby, touching and funny and true—but never sugary. One way this is accomplished is through the illustrations, which are comic and cozy; Mae, a happy participant in the play, is a bit chubby, is not pretty, and wears glasses. A bit apprehensive about being dethroned, Mae is disappointed when Mum goes into labor just before the Christmas play but Grandma is there, Dad comes from the hospital, and Mae surmounts a minor dramatic crisis (falling off her chair). The picture of Mae, whining at the foot of the stairs as her pregnant Mum toils up to the third floor, will be recognized with amusement by both parents and children.

481   **Hughes**, Shirley. *The Big Alfie and Annie Rose Storybook*; written and illus. by Shirley Hughes. Lothrop, 1989. Library ed. ISBN 0-688-07673-4; Trade ed. ISBN 0-688-07672-6. [64p]. Library ed. $14.88; Trade ed. $15.00.

K-2   It is possible that the reader-aloud will enjoy the stories and pictures in this appealing collection just as much as those to whom it is read. Shirley Hughes has always drawn people's faces and bodies with a happy combination of anatomical accuracy and fond humor. Here Alfie and his baby sister engage in activities that have a universal appeal; the setting is English, but children everywhere have small adventures like those of Alfie and Annie Rose, make small advances in growing and understanding, enjoy grandparents and birthdays, and perhaps get a bit jealous when a sibling seems to prefer one's friend to oneself. Hughes has a writing style that's as direct and ingenuous as her child characters.

482   **Hughes**, Shirley. *An Evening at Alfie's*; written and illus. by Shirley Hughes. Lothrop, 1985. Library ed. ISBN 0-688-04123-X; Trade ed. ISBN 0-688-04133-1. 29p. Library ed. $9.88; Trade ed. $9.25.

K-2   His fans will be delighted to see another Alfie story, and well they might. The fidelity and warmth in the pictures are a bonus; the base is fine draughtsmanship. The open, ingenuous look of the characters' faces is matched by the cheerful directness of the story. Like other Alfie tales, this deals with an ordinary household incident (a water pipe bursts). The babysitter calls her mother and then her father to cope. Alfie's baby sister weeps in her crib and Alfie has a fine time, enjoying the excitement and the puddles. By the time Mom and Dad come home, the water's turned off, the children are dry and cozy, and the sitter's family (neighbors) have taken care of everything. All very reassuring: things may go wrong, but those in charge can handle it; they don't panic and they are kind.

483   **Hughes**, Shirley. *Here Comes Charlie Moon*; written and illus. by Shirley Hughes. Lothrop, 1986. ISBN 0-688-06401-9. 143p. $10.25.

3-5   This vacation adventure story, which takes place in a British resort town that has seen better days, is as insubstantial as a French farce or a wave of sea-spray, but it's just as funny as the former and as refreshing as the latter. Visiting his Auntie Jean, Charlie (who appears, in the deft sketches that top each page, to be about ten) becomes involved with some ex-show-biz characters, what appears to be a compounding of crimes, and the start of a romance that blossoms into marriage for two of the ex-performers, and generally has a spirited visit during which he proves his honesty, valor, and good nature. Brisk, wholesome, diverting.

484   **Hughes**, Shirley. *Out and About;* written and illus. by Shirley Hughes. Lothrop, 1988. Library ed. ISBN 0-688-07691-2; Trade ed. ISBN 0-688-07690-4. 46p. Library ed. $12.88; Trade ed. $13.00.

3-5 yrs.   Eighteen simple, cheery rhymes are surrounded with illustrations that
  *   will sweep youngsters through the four seasons. Starting in spring, there are several paeans to rainy days and mud play. Summer celebrates picnics in the park and at the beach; autumn, the wind and harvest fruits. The best verses come with winter, one about being sick, another about a bonfire: "Fire is a dragon/ (Better beware),/ Dangerous and beautiful/ (Better take care)./ Puffing out smoke/ As soon as it's lit,/ Licking up leaves,/ Crackle and spit!" The children who romp through these non-stop family scenes are rosy, cared-for, active, and enthusiastically messy. Hughes' drawing is always good, but the composition and coloration here mark some of her most cohesive book design and art work.

485   **Hughes**, Ted. *The Iron Giant: A Story in Five Nights;* illus. by Dirk Zimmer. Harper, 1988. Library ed. ISBN 0-06-022639-0; Trade ed. ISBN 0-06-0022638-2. 58p. Library ed. $11.89; Trade ed. $11.95.

2-4   Resonant in style and robust in essence, these five stories have stood the test of twenty years since their first publication for a fresh reappearance with Dirk Zimmer's powerful pen-and-ink drawings. Each story presents a monumentally scaled threat, first *by* the Iron Giant to the human world, and then, after they're reconciled, *to* the Iron Giant *and* the human world by a space-bat-angel-dragon from a star in the constellation of Orion. The fullness and mythical overtones of these stories make many a contemporary picture book pale by contrast. The Iron Giant has a pathos like that of the Golem and other monsters, and the boy Hogarth, who first traps and then befriends him, has the folktale appeal of a typical unlikely small-guy hero. For great sound effects, from rhythmic repetition to onomatopoeia, read this one aloud—you'll have the Gobot and Transformer crowd entranced.

486   **Hunter**, Mollie. *Cat, Herself.* Harper, 1986. Library ed. ISBN 0-06-022635-8; Trade ed. ISBN 0-06-022634-X. 278p. Library ed. $11.89; Trade ed. $12.50.

6-9   Catriona is a child of a tinker family, one of the close-knit families of Scottish "Travellers" who live by being migrant laborers, tinkers, poachers. Cat loves their life, travelling through the countryside with horses and wagons, learning to live off the land, adhering to the old-fashioned morals and mores of her culture within a modern society. The book has two themes: one is the treatment of such itinerant peoples in Scotland, and how prejudice is giving way to understanding and respect for a different way of life. The other is Cat's coming of age:

learning new skills, taking charge of the birth of a brother, falling in love, reconciling her love and her fierce conviction that she will not be a chattel like other travellers' wives, but maintain independence after marriage and always be Cat herself. Hunter does a fine job of telling the story of Cat's rites of passage and her fusing of traditional patterns and new ideas. The characters and their dialogue have depth and vitality, and the narrative flow of the story never sags.

487   **Hunter**, Mollie. *The Mermaid Summer.* Harper, 1988. Library ed. ISBN 0-06-022628-5; Trade ed. ISBN 0-06-022627-7. Library ed. $12.89; Trade ed. $12.95.

4-6
*
As she did in her masterly story, *The Wicked One*, Hunter combines fiction and legend to the enhancement of both. The heroine here is young Anna Anderson, who faces down a temperamental mermaid to save her fishing village from the vain creature's fierce whims and to bring her grandfather home from an exile forced by the same mermaid. Each character is briefly but vividly drawn, the two principal females in living color (sea-green eyes, hair of red). A clever plot makes folkloristic use of gifts for rescue: a comb, a mirror, a conch shell, a knife, a length of silk—each fits into the pattern of resolution foretold by a witch-like herb woman. There are even, in the end, three wishes, each one granted in a most satisfying way. With alluring cover art to send it on its way, this is briskly paced for reading aloud or alone.

488   **Hurd**, Thacher, ad. *The Pea Patch Jig*; ad. and illus. by Thacher Hurd. Crown, 1986. ISBN 0-517-5607-X. 33p. $10.95.

3-6 yrs.   Baby Mouse can't resist trouble. She takes a nap in a head of lettuce—the head Farmer Clem plans to chop for his salad. Tempted by the invitingly round tomatoes, Baby climbs into the plant and kicks them, "SPLAT!!!" on the ground—and onto Grandfather Mouse's head. But it's Baby's mischief (and her pea-shooter) that saves the family from a marauding fox. Bright, jazzy shapes and colors complement this sprightly ode to vegetables, which concludes with a joyous hoe-down in the moonlight, the mice dressed up as vegetables, Baby as a bright green pea.

489   **Hurwitz**, Johanna. *Class Clown*; illus. by Sheila Hamanaka. Morrow, 1987. ISBN 0-688-06723-9. 98p. $11.75.

3-5   Lucas Cott is one of those not-always-endearing characters who seems to appear in every class: the wise-cracker, the cut-up, the kid who reacts too fast for his own control system to censor. Hurwitz has done a good job of developing her protagonist's personality, situation, motivations, and, ultimately, change for the better through the graces of a third-grade teacher who cares—and persists. Lucas' rivalry with a bright classmate, Cricket, slowly turns into a friendship after she dares him to keep quiet one whole day and he succeeds. His younger twin brothers turn into friends as he proves himself both playmate and helpmate (in one especially telling scene, he throws a series of wrestling holds on them to keep them still in the barber shop chairs). Most of all, he gains confidence by appearing in the class play, a mini-circus that was his idea, not as a clown but as a substitute ringmaster (the real ringmaster's last-minute tonsillitis is a bit too fortuitous). The author has a knack for catching the exuberance and anxieties of this age group in light, selectively detailed fiction. It's no mean feat.

490   **Hurwitz**, Johanna. *Hurray for Ali Baba Bernstein*; illus. by Gail Owens. Morrow, 1989. Library ed. ISBN 0-688-08242-4; Trade ed. ISBN 0-688-08241-6. 112p. Library ed. $11.88; Trade ed. $11.95.

3-5   Like *The Adventures of Ali Baba Bernstein*, this features entertaining episodes that are mildly humorous and child-appealing for kids who still find reading itself a challenge. Ali Baba is a likable character who has nicknamed himself to avoid confusion with the many other Davids in his class. His energetic imagination further evidences itself in the way he solves his everyday problems—or cases, as he prefers to call them. Unraveling the mystery of the fat man in the apartment upstairs, Ali Baba makes him a running partner. (Ali Baba discovered running when he went A.W.O.L. from a class field trip and raced home to get a library card he had forgotten to bring to school.) He turns a boring shopping trip with is mother into a visit with royalty when he interprets all the signs literally: the Underwear King, the Egg Roll King, the Donut King, The Sweater Palace, and Burger King. "Ali Baba Meets Santa Claus," "Ali Baba on His Own," and "Ali Baba and the Mystery of the Missing Circus Tickets" are all palatable sit-com chapters at a comfortable reading level.

491   **Hurwitz**, Johanna. *Russell and Elisa*; illus. by Lillian Hoban. Morrow, 1989. Library ed. ISBN 0-688-08793-0; Trade ed. ISBN 0-688-08792-2. 88p. Library ed. $11.88; Trade ed. $11.95.

2-4   In this latest addition to an amiable series, Russell shares the limelight with three-year old Elisa. She finds it hard to impress an older brother and is pleased when Russell deigns to participate in her new game of playing barber with a friend's hair: "Annie held very still, and Russell cut some of her hair. Cutting hair was much more fun than cutting paper, he thought." Russell is less enthused about having his sister tag along to his first ball game, especially since she insists on bringing Airmail, her doll. Elisa's attachment to Airmail allows her to venture bravely under the dining room table during her parents' dinner party in order to retrieve her doll. Unfortunately, she falls asleep, waiting for the adults to leave, and wakes up alone, in the dark, and terrified. The situational humor is akin to Beverly Cleary's, though lacking some of her sparkle. Hurwitz excels in conveying the young child's point of view without any condescension. The moments of laughter in this family story ring true, and Hoban's gentle pencil sketches will encourage newly independent readers. Short chapters and straight-ahead storytelling also make this ideal for reading aloud.

492   **Hurwitz**, Johanna. *Yellow Blue Jay;* illus. by Donald Carrick. Morrow, 1986. ISBN 0-688-06078-1. 112p. $10.25.

3-4   Jay Koota is a pudgy archconservative: he likes school, model airplanes, and orderly control in life; he doesn't like swimming, over-exertion, creepy-crawly things, and irregularities of any kind, especially in meals. Thus a family vacation in Vermont with two other children he doesn't know raises apprehensions, which, it turns out, are sometimes justified but more often overcome. By his return to New York, Jay has climbed a mountain, captured a bat singlehanded, cooked shishkabob, made a new friend, floated on his back, dropped a few pounds, and picked up some confidence. The point of view here is all. Hurwitz has a keen sense of an 8-year-old's fears and insecurities, revealed in natural dialogue and action. The scope is carefully limited for maximum characterization in minimum space.

493   **Hutchins**, Hazel J. *The Three and Many Wishes of Jason Reid;* illus. by Julie Tennent. Viking, 1988. ISBN 0-670-82155-1. 81p. $9.95.

3-5   With a bright tone and winning characters, this plays the old tale of three wishes for an irresistible new angle. Eleven-year-old outfielder Jason Reid has read all those stories about the downfall of greedy wishers, so he's not entirely unprepared when Quicksilver, an Elster of the Third Order, appears on top of a garbage can and offers him three wishes. Jason asks for a baseball glove that will catch anything, a grant of immunity from surprise or questioning about the glove and three more wishes. The rest of the book details Jason and his friend Penny's juggling of wishes to include something more generous than small, personal-type acquisitions, and in the end . . . . Well, it wouldn't be fair to tell the end, but it's ecological, suspenseful, and convincing. The pen-and-ink drawings are competent but lack the natural grace of the writing. A first novel carefully crafted for transitional readers: home run!

494   **Hutchins**, Pat. *The Doorbell Rang;* written and illus. by Pat Hutchins. Greenwillow, 1986. Library ed. ISBN 0-688-05252-5; Trade ed. ISBN 0-688-05251-1. 22p.. Library ed. $11.88; Trade ed. $11.75.

3-5 yrs.   Watercolors that are busy but not overcrowded, bright but not brash, and repetitive but not boring, illustrate a story that has good structure, problem/solution, and a light style. It also sneaks in some basic mathematical precepts, as more and more children are invited to

share a dozen cookies. Each time the bell rings, the individual portion
diminishes; each time the anticipatory praise is countered with "No
one makes cookies like Grandma," and it is Grandma herself who
appears at the end, bearing so many cookies that the children are
heartened. Then, in a typical Hutchins twist, the doorbell rings
again. . . .

495   **Hutchins**, Pat. *The Very Worst Monster;* written and illus. by Pat
Hutchins. Greenwillow, 1985. Library ed. ISBN 0-688-04011-X; Trade
ed. ISBN 0-688-04010-X. 27p.. Library ed. $11.88; Trade ed. $11.75.

K-2   Given Hutchins' light touch and humor, the appeal of the subject, and
the combining of two sure-fire ideas (sibling dethronement and the
worst-is-the-best) this could hardly fail to be amusing and popular.
Bright, imaginative pictures, featuring monsters with strong family
resemblances illustrate the sprightly text in which Hazel is jealous of a
new-born baby brother. Everybody coos at him, gloating over how bad
he is, how loudly he growls, how strong his fangs are. Hazel mutters to
herself that she's bad, too, and growls even louder. Alas for her ego,
little Billy wins a baby contest by trying to eat the judge: "Worst
Monster Baby in the World." Hazel tries to lose Billy, frighten him,
and give him away. Nothing works. Her parents, horrified, say "You
gave your own baby brother away! You must be the Worst Monster in
the World!" "I told you I was," Hazel points out, and confesses that
the family who had taken Billy had given him back. Yeasty fun.

496   **Hutton**, Warwick, ad. *Beauty and the Beast;* ad and illus. by Warwick
Hutton. Atheneum, 1985. ISBN 0-689-50316-4. 30p. $11.95.

K-3   In a picture book version of a classic tale, Hutton retells the story of
the beast whose true form (a young and handsome prince) reappears
when Beauty declares her love, engendered by his kindness and
patience and love. The watercolor illustrations are rich and imaginative, with settings that have a Moorish influence and a beast who is
like a giant cat, ugly of face, walking like a man. Hutton is particularly
good at using light and shadow to establish mood.

497   **Hutton**, Warwick, ad. *Theseus and the Minotaur;* ad. and illus. by
Warwick Hutton. McElderry, 1989. ISBN 0-689-50473-X. 32p. $13.95.

5-8 yrs.   Although the story of Theseus may seem too epically proportioned for
a picture-book format, it has been accorded dignified, if simplified,
treatment in company of Leonard Everett Fisher's brooding art and
now Hutton's light-and-shadowed watercolors. In scenes that seem
frozen from a mythical stage drama, Theseus volunteers to replace
one of the young people sent as forced tribute to the Cretan Labyrinth,
wins Ariadne's admiration, fights the Minotaur, escapes with his fellow
victims, abandons Ariadne on Naxos, and causes the death of his

father Aegeus by forgetting to swap the black sail for the white. Although the human figures here are sometimes stiffly posed, especially in the dance of Dionysus, Hutton's pen-and-wash seascapes set a grand scale for heroic deeds and haunting human frailties. The dark interior of Minos' palace and the blazing white of the Mediterannean coast make brilliant contrasts naturally suited to Hutton's chiaroscuro effects, which have characterized a distinguished series of classical stories.

498   **Hyde**, Margaret Oldroyd. *Cancer in the Young: A Sense of Hope;* by Margaret Oldroyd Hyde and Lawrence E. Hyde. Westminster, 1985. ISBN 0-664-32722-2. 90p. $8.95..

6-   An informative book, sober but not grim, in which the arrangement of material is logical and sequential, and the coverage broad, this has the usual careful accuracy of other Hyde books. The text discusses types of cancers, treatments, the increasingly positive statistics for remission and cure, the known causes and the theories of causal factors of cancer, and some of the ways in which young cancer patients are helped to adjust to their illness or ways in which they comment on it. In addition to an index and a glossary, end papers include a list of camps (for cancer patients, including some that accept siblings), a bibliography, and a list of organizations that can provide further information.

499   **Irwin**, Hadley. *Abby, My Love.* Atheneum, 1985. ISBN 0-689-50323-7. 168p. $11.95.

7-10   Chip begins his story when he is listening to Abby deliver the valedictory address at her high school graduation; a year older than she, Chip had been in love with Abby since she was twelve. They have a durable relationship, but Chip has always been baffled by Abby's moods, her withdrawal, the apparent inconsistency of her affection. He's aware that her father is very protective, but he doesn't see what most readers may suspect: that Abby's father is abnormally propri- etary or even that she is the victim of sexual abuse. For that is the case, and Abby finally tells Chip when she reaches a point of desperation. From that point, events move logically to a solution, and the book ends with a more secure Abby able at last to be an adolescent in love. Irwin handles the situation with delicacy and dignity, and her characters and their relationship are developed with depth and consistency.

500   **Isaacson**, Philip M. *Round Buildings, Square Buildings, & Buildings that Wiggle Like a Fish;* written and illus. with photographs by Philip M. Isaacson. Knopf, 1988. Library ed. ISBN 0-394-99382-9; Trade ed. ISBN 0-394-89382-4. 121p. Library ed. $16.99; Trade ed. $14.95.

6-12
*

An aficionado of fine buildings, Isaacson has undertaken the daring task of teaching readers to observe three-dimensional structures through the two-dimensional medium of a book. The format is crucial here: beautifully composed and reproduced color photographs are numbered for reference in the text, which describes almost poetically the effects of contrasting architectural elements, styles, shapes, materials, and functions. There is no effort to convey systematic historical information. In fact, it is only in an appended list that one can find background information on the 93 international buildings featured here, from the 17th century Taj Mahal through houses, palaces, barns, and offices to an early 20th-century church in Wimauma, Florida. The emphasis is entirely on visual literacy, with stunning examples such as the facing pictures of two light-filled ceilings, Michaelangelo's dome at St. Peter's and the fan vaulting at King's College Chapel. For those few textual passages separated from the pictures to which they refer, the numbers act as guides. The writing is lyrical without abandoning fact, and the photographic perspectives are arresting. An enticement for high school art students as well as an eye-opener for younger readers.

501

Isadora, Rachel. *I See*; written and illus. by Rachel Isadora. Greenwillow, 1985. Library ed. ISBN 0-688-04060-8; Trade ed. ISBN 0-688-04059-4. 29p. Library ed. $11.88; Trade ed. $11.75.

1-3 yrs.

A companion volume to the author-artist's *I Hear* has the same soft lines, subdued colors, and controlled composition as the other book. This, too, depicts familiar activities that a very young child can recognize: the small girl in the illustrations is interested in herself, her toys, her food, the world immediately around her. The text is brief, direct, simple.

502

Isenbart, Hans-Heinrich. *Birth of a Foal*; illus. with photographs by Thomas David. Carolrhoda, 1986. ISBN 0-87614-239-0. 43p. $12.95.

K-3

With a very clear focus and organization, this has color photographs that are even more striking than were the fine black-and-white ones for Isenbart's *A Foal is Born*, published in 1976 and now out of print. After a fairly detailed opening summary of the equine reproductive cycle, the narrative is simplified to descriptions of a foal's birth and early life, with careful note of facts such as nighttime births relating to safety in the wild. Diagrams of the development of the fetus and passage through the birth canal, along with a glossary, conclude a well-designed book. Excellent coverage.

503

Ivimey, John W. *The Complete Story of the Three Blind Mice*; illus. by Victoria Chess. Joy Street/Little, 1990. ISBN 0-316-13867-3. 32p. $13.95.

K-2   How did they get that way? Ivimey's verse tells: "Three Small Mice.
Three Small Mice. Pined for some fun. Pined for some fun." The Small
Mice leave home ("and all the luggage they took was a comb"), beg
for food from the Farmer ("Three Starved Mice. Three Starved Mice"),
and get chased into the brambles by the farmer's wife. "Three blind
mice . . . ." This *pourquoi* gloss on an old rhyme was written at the turn
of the century, and Chess clearly relishes its gruesome charm. The
characters—all mice—are tidily placed in a cozy vernal setting that
would be picturesque were the Farmer's Wife's eyes somewhat less
malevolent. And as for the Three, blinded—no, you never have seen
such a sight in your life.

504   **Jacobs**, Paul Samuel. *Born Into Light.* Scholastic, 1988. ISBN 0-590-
40710-4. 146p. $12.95.

6-10   Just before sunrise on a spring morning in 1913, ten-year-old Roger
*   Westwood sees an intense burst of light in the woods near his house,
and soon after, a wild naked boy comes running into the yard. Easily
tamed by the gentleness of Roger's sister Charlotte, Benjamin (as they
name him) becomes a member of the family, astounding them with
his quick learning and growth, and his ingenuous kindness. In a war
game with the other boys, Benjamin says "I would never hurt your
kind." The family soon acquires another child of that morning, Nell,
beautiful and strange like Benjamin, but, also like him, easily tired
and growing old too quickly. "They will be like meteors, bright and full
of light, but quick expiring," says Roger's doctor father, who has some
idea of the differentness of Benjamin and Nell. The story of the two
and the others like them is related seventy years later by Roger, whose
voice is etched from the beginning with a quiet, measured sadness
that allows horror but no sensationalism to intrude on what readers
will only gradually realize is a science fantasy story. Like Ray Bradbury
but without his nostalgia, Jacobs writes of ordinary people whose lives
are changed through contact with ultimately unknowable aliens,
distant relations who "one day, sooner than we would like, will all be
taken from us."

505   **Jaffrey**, Madhur. *Seasons of Splendour: Tales, Myths, and Legends of
India;* illus. by Michael Foreman. Atheneum, 1985. ISBN 0-689-31141-
9. 123p. $15.95.

5-8   An intriguing collection that contrasts strongly with Thompson's
retelling of the Rama tales (reviewed below). Although there are a few
overlaps, Jaffrey includes folktales and family stories in addition to
accounts of Rama, Krishna, and other mythical characters. She has
also framed her stories with personal recollections of how she heard
them, organizing them into seasonal cycles according to festival. The
stories themselves are rousing, with births, deaths, heroics, and

treachery undiluted. The narrative is informal and easy to read. Foreman's paintings reveal more of his own demonic vision than of traditional images. Although tantalizing for adult storytellers, this will require either a gifted young reader or one especially interested in Hindu lore and culture. It's a natural selection for schools and libraries with large Indian populations.

506   **Janeczko**, Paul B., comp. *Going Over to Your Place: Poems for Each Other.* Bradbury, 1987. ISBN 0-02-747670-7. 159p. $13.95.

8-   An ample and varied collection of contemporary poetry explores
*   human relationships in their diversity of mood and involvement. Some, like Richard Shelton's "My Love," treat of intimacy; others, like Henry Treece's "Conquerors," of the connection among strangers—in this case, soldiers finding the body of a child. The many poets represented include Nikki Giovanni, Ted Kooser, Jim Wayne Miller, Mark Strand, and Elizabeth Jennings. The 132 poems are well balanced, with notes of the humor as well as the tragedy that commonly touch everyday life. Janeczko has the energy and resources to find poems that are not frequently anthologized, and he clusters them so that transitions are smooth between selections. There is an accessible tone consistent with Janesczko's other books, although on the whole this one seems less intense, more wide-ranging, and sometimes more adult in focus.

507   **Janeczko**, Paul B., comp. *Pocket Poems: Selected for a Journey.* Bradbury, 1985. ISBN 0-02-747820-3. 138p. Paper. $8.95.

6-   An anthologist of growing reputation, Janeczko has selected for this
*   small volume (fine for journeys, indeed, but certainly not just for them) poems that have variety of structure and style and mood but rather remarkable consistency of quality. None is more than sixteen lines long; there are over a hundred poems by almost a hundred modern American poets, some of whom are noteworthy newcomers while others are as well-known as Howard Nemerov, Maya Angelou, Galway Kinnell, and Ogden Nash.

508   **Janeczko**, Paul B., comp. *The Music of What Happens: Poems That Tell Stories.* Orchard/Watts, 1988. Library ed. ISBN 0-531-08357-8; Trade ed. ISBN 0-531-05757-7. 188p. Library ed. $14.99; Trade ed. $14.95.

7-   A book that demonstrates the rich potential for originality in
*   anthologizing, this features 75 untraditional narrative poems deeply reflective of the events they relate. Most are long contemporary selections in free verse reverberating with internal rhythms and rhyme. Subjects are sustained through intertwined imagery and language patterns that underscore taut or richly surprising endings. "The White Rose: Sophie Scholl 1921-1943" by Erika Mumford—as

compressed a biographical comment on victims of World War II as any—is deeply moving, as is the next selection, "Tending the Garden" by Eric Pankey. Together they chronicle the experience of a doomed German resistance fighter, a French prisoner of war, and a Jewish girl gassed by the Nazis. Balancing the tragic stories are lighter moments of buoyant humor and incidents of everyday familiarity caught unawares, as in Michael Pettit's piquant "Driving Lesson." Janeczko has played these poems like a piano, combining themes, tones, and even sounds for a true composition that will take young readers beyond the usual dose of Henry Wadsworth Longfellow or Rudyard Kipling.

509   **Janeczko**, Paul B., comp. *This Delicious Day: 65 Poems* . Orchard/Watts, 1987. Library ed. ISBN 0-531-08324-1; Trade ed. ISBN 0-531-05724-0. 82p. Library ed. $11.99; Trade ed. $11.95.

5-7   "Meals for the eye... meals for the ear... meals for the tongue... meals for the mind—any and all of the 65 poems presented here—and, yes, of course you may come back for seconds!" An inviting anthology, from the jacket copy quoted above to the last poem by Arnold Adoff, called "Past," a fresh mixture of imagery centering on time and food: "But I know that tomorrow/ morning/ I'll wake up/ empty, and hungry for that/ next/ bite/ of my new/ day." For younger readers than Janeczko's previous books have targeted, this brings together a lively assortment of brief poems by Richard Snyder, ("O I have Dined on This Delicious Day"), X.J. Kennedy ("The Cat Who Aspired to Higher Things"), Dennis Lee ("Alligator Pie"), William Stafford ("Rover"), and many others. Once again, Janeczko has shown characteristic sensitivity to mixing the known and the unknown, to coordinating styles and subjects into a smooth flow. The general tone is light and lively, varying from the abruptly humorous (Jim Daniels' "Blubber Lips") to the softly descriptive (Gary Soto's "Stars"). Children who enjoy dipping their fingers into poetry will find here a tasty buffet of structured and free verse.

510   **Jenkins**, Lyll Becerra de. *The Honorable Prison.* Lodestar, 1988. ISBN 0-525-67238-9. 199p. $13.95.

9-   Much more than a political indictment of dictatorship, this is a
*   powerful novel about the characters victimized by it. Seventeen-year-old Marta Maldonado is the narrator, and her story unfolds with terrifying inevitability as she and her family are rounded up and imprisoned because of her father's journalistic criticism of a South American military regime. Marta's voice is clear and observant of the details that accompany the family's isolation and starvation as her father lies dying of tuberculosis and she, her brother, and her mother fight for survival. Even without the rape and torture that accompany

many arrests, some of the scenes are excruciating: the killing of the brother's pet chicken forecasts the murders of several sympathetic campesinos who try to help them. There is also a moment of passion, as Marta is briefly attracted to a local youth whose uncle betrays them. And there is humor, the staple of their survival. The controlled structure of the writing is such that even the reader falls into the rhythm of the children's weekly outings to the market early on, and then into the time-effacing apathy that possesses them as hunger sets in. In place of the sensationalized shortcuts that might have created a temporary shock effect, Jenkins opts for a much more effective, journalistic patience. The General is finally overthrown, but not before the family—and the reader—have been forever altered. Although this is fiction developed at an adult level, it will hold young adults in a relentless grip and inject their thinking with new social awareness.

511   Jin Xuqi. *The Giant Panda*; by Jin Xuqi and Markus Kappler; tr. by Noel Simon. Putnam, 1986. ISBN 0-399-21389-9. 46p. illus. with photographs. $12.95.

5-7   Fine color photographs illustrate a book first published in Switzerland and fluidly, if occasionally repetitively, translated. This should take its place with other substantial books about the giant panda, since style and translation are smooth, coverage and organization are excellent, and accurate information provided in the text is augmented by full captions for photographs. In additon to facts about habits and habitat, the authors describe the successful efforts being made to protect and foster the animal that is so appealing in this book, as it is in zoos in or outside of China.

512   Johnson, Angela. *Tell Me A Story, Mama;* illus. by David Soman. Orchard, 1989. Library ed. ISBN 0-531-08394-2; Trade ed. ISBN 0-531-05794-1. 32p. Library ed. $13.99; Trade ed. $13.95.

5-7 yrs.   Bedtime serves as the setting for a mother-daughter conversation in which the child requests a story and then proceeds to remind her mother of all the details. This is more a friendly family history than a story, however, and the similarity between the child and her mother as a child, as well as between the mother and the grandmother as a younger woman, may confuse young listeners ("which one said that?") unless the adult reader can simulate two distinctive voices with natural ease. The realistic watercolor paintings are dominated by warm browns and are spaciously formatted, if occasionally posed. A modest but welcome addition to the decreasing number of books centering on the experience of black characters.

513   Johnson, Annabel. *Prisoner of PSI;* by Annabel and Edgar Johnson. Atheneum, 1985. ISBN 0-689-31132-X. 149p. $12.95.

7-10   When, in the year 2000, Emory Morgan, a television psychic, announces that Libya is building a missile that will be aimed at Cairo, investigation proves he's right. In reprisal, Emory is kidnapped by Libyan terrorists. Several of his closest friends, some of whom also have extrasensory powers, come to his aid, but their hopes are pinned on the son, now seventeen, who had run away some years before; Tristan Morgan could communicate telepathically with his father. This is a well-plotted and briskly paced adventure story, with colorful characters, the appeals of danger and a love story (girl whose father had been killed by terrorists wants to help but sneers at ESP) and a satisfying resumption of rapport between Emory and the son who finally realizes that he's not just being used for his occult ability but that he's deeply loved.

514   Johnson, Sylvia A. *Wolf Pack: Tracking Wolves in the Wild*; written by Sylvia A. Johnson and Alice Aamodt. Lerner, 1985. ISBN 0-8225-1577-6. 95p. illus. with photographs. $12.95.

5-9   An articulate introduction to Canis lupis discusses characteristics of the species, habits of the pack, and various ways in which wolves communicate, mark territory, and hunt. Concluding chapters expose false images of the wolf in human lore and detail modern methods of tracking and observation. Scientific without being pedantic, this is full of engrossing, well-selected information and color photos of wolves in the wild, with occasional diagrams and historic reproductions. A glossary and index will help researching students, but most will find themselves reading the text straight through.

515   Johnston, Ginny. *Andy Bear: A Polar Cub Grows Up at the Zoo*; written by Ginny Johnston and Judy Cutchins; illus. with photographs by Constance Noble. Morrow, 1985. Library ed. ISBN 0-688-05628-8; Trade ed. ISBN 0-688-05627-X. 56p. Library ed. $12.88; Trade ed. $13.00.

3-5   Photographs of good quality illustrate a description of the first year of a zoo-born polar bear cub. In danger of being killed by his sire, the infant bear was rescued by one of the zookeepers, who took him home and became his substitute mother. Very much dependent on his keeper for security, Andy had to be gently led to each new stage of growing independence; at first he lived at home with the keeper, Constance Noble, and by the end of the year was finally ready to live alone in a separate accommodation at the Atlanta Zoo. The style is straightforward, the tone crisp, the subject appealing.

516   Johnston, Ginny. *Scaly Babies: Reptiles Growing Up*; by Ginny Johnston and Judy Cutchins. Morrow, 1988. Library ed. ISBN 0-688-07306-9; Trade ed. ISBN 0-688-07305-0. 40p. illus. with photographs. Library ed. $12.88; Trade ed. $12.95.

3-5   Exceptionally well written and illustrated with striking color photographs, this is also ecologically centered. Environment is inherent to
the conceptualization and organization as well as being the emphasis
of a concluding summary. In describing each creature's life cycle and
characteristics, the authors consider its place in a natural habitat and
food chain. The sections on snakes, lizards, crocodilians, and turtles
include lively descriptions and immediate detail ("The Gila monster
drags the lifeless body under a rock and munches it"). Stereotyped
human reactions to reptiles are effectively countered with intriguing
graphic and textual information. The bold, potentially distracting book
design actually works for smooth coordination of print and pictures;
glossary and index are included.

517   **Jonas**, Ann. *The Trek;* written and illus. by Ann Jonas. Greenwillow,
1985. Library ed. ISBN 0-688-04800-5; Trade ed. ISBN 0-688-04799-8.
30p. Library ed. $11.88; Trade ed. $11.75.

4-6 yrs.   The game aspect of the carefully controlled watercolor art work is the
drawing card here. A young girl walks to school imagining she's
negotiating a dangerous jungle; it's up to the reader to find and
identify all the animals she sees lurking on a lawn, along a fence, in a
grove of trees, or popping out of a fruit stand. The last two pages
picture and identify all the creatures camouflaged in the illustrations,
and many a viewer will be forced to flip back for further investigation
of a hiding place. Thin, but playful and certainly handsome.. Who
could've imagined a hippo emerging from five watermelons?

518   **Jones**, Diana Wynne. *Eight Days of Luke.* Greenwillow, 1988. ISBN 0-
688-08006-5. 150p. $11.95.

7-12   Briefer and simpler than many of Jones' fantasies, this early novel
*   (now published for the first time in the U.S.) involves two family
disputes: between David and assorted relatives who don't really want
him around, and among the Norse gods, who very much want their
errant son "Luke" to come back to the family fold. David and Luke
meet when David unwittingly frees the other boy from a supernatural
prison while trying out some curses on his family. David at first thinks
that Luke is some kind of friendly genie, until others, like the one-eyed
"Mr. Wedding" and the menacing gardner "Mr. Chew" come along
and reveal that Luke has hidden something of great importance that
they want returned. The mythological and contemporary worlds
collide in unexpected, usually humorous ways (Siegfried in a video
game parlor), but at the same time Jones maintains the dignity of the
mythic quest: the search for Thor's hammer. Both gods and humans
are complicated characters; particularly well drawn is Mr. Wedding
(Wotan), feared and loved by his sons Siegfried and Loki, and a figure
of painful ambivalence for David as well. Loki (Luke) has become

David's friend, but fatherless David has come to respect Wotan as well, and "it came home to David that Luke and Mr. Wedding were going to be on opposite sides, when that final battle came." An afterword explains the mythological background.

519   Jones, Diana Wynne. *Howl's Moving Castle.* Greenwillow, 1986. ISBN 0-688-06233-4. 212p. $10.25.

6-9   This has a more deliberate pace than most of the author's earlier books, but it has the same ebullient writing style and yeasty humor, and the same kind of whole, rounded conception of a fantasy world as have distinguished its predecessors. It is unusual in that the protagonist, Sophie, spends most of the long story as a woman of ninety, because she is under a spell cast by a wicked witch. The witch pits her powers against those of the wizard Howl, into whose (literally) moving castle Sophie enters to find a home and learn the truth about Howl. Reputed to suck the souls from young girls, Howl proves to be only a woman-charmer. It will come as a surprise to few readers that, after chapters of adventure, magic, danger, and other facets of sturm-und-drang, all curses and spells are removed and Sophie and Howell (Howl) discover themselves to be in love. Meanwhile, all readers have been able to have a romp. A funny book.

520   Jones, Diana Wynne. *The Lives of Christopher Chant.* Greenwillow, 1988. ISBN 0-688-07806-0. 230p. $11.95.

5-7   A decade ago, in *Charmed Life*, Jones introduced a wonderfully fresh fantasy world—or, rather, a series of divergent worlds simultaneous in time—in which two children of the Chant family took it for granted that part of their education was the study and perfection of witchcraft. Christopher Chant is their ancestor, this new story being set many years before *Charmed Life*. Here Christopher is a boy, quickly learning through a series of deftly-structured adventures how great his power is, and slowly adjusting to the fact that he has been chosen as the next Chrestomanci, the arch-magician of a wholly-conceived fantasy world that is firmly rooted in realism and is leavened with wry humor.

521   Jones, Diana Wynne. *Warlock at the Wheel and Other Stories.* Greenwillow, 1985. ISBN 0-688-04305-4. 160p. $10.25.

5-8   Although not every tale in this book of short stories is equally strong structurally or equally effective as a fantasy, the collection as a whole is of superior quality and, like the author's novels, has fresh, new concepts and plots. In the title story, a hapless wizard who has stolen a car is in abject misery because of the small child, large dog, and vocal automatic controls the vehicle contains. There's a story about a robot, another about a strange creature like a giant mantis that emerges from its stick-chrysalis, and—one of the most deft—the story of another time and world, "Dragon Reserve. Home Eight."

522   **Joosse**, Barbara M. *Better with Two;* illus. by Catherine Stock. Harper, 1988. Library ed. ISBN 0-06-023077-0; Trade ed. ISBN 0-06-023076-2. 32p. Library ed. $11.89; Trade ed. $11.95.

5-7 yrs.   Every day Laura watches Mrs. Brady and her dog Max follow a punctilious routine, including walks ("slowly, because Max is very old"), *elevenses* ("Max has perfect manners. . . . He never spills a drop of tea nor leaves a crumb of biscuit"), and rocking or sometimes singing on the porch swing ("Max likes 'I've Been Working on the Railroad' best"). Then Max dies. Laura tries to cheer up her elderly neighbor with small gifts, but it is only Laura's company for tea that finally lightens Mrs. Brady's sadness. Softly washed drawings create a hushed, even expectant mood for the interchange that resolves the story. This has a quiet, distant quality but makes an appropriate companion for Hans Wilhelm's livelier *I'll Always Love You* and other tender tales of lost pets.

523   **Joyce**, William. *George Shrinks;* written and illus. by William Joyce. Harper, 1985. Library ed. ISBN 0-06-023071-1; Trade ed. ISBN 0-06-023070-3. 30p. Library ed. $9.89; Trade ed. $10.50.

K-2   Although he uses a lighter palette, the composition and the feeling of solidity of objects is very much like those in Richard Egielski's pictures. This is a fantasy about a person shrinking to tiny size, a procedure that has intrigued readers since Alice tried the bottle that said: "Drink Me." Here there is more contrast in size between the diminutive protagonist, George, and his surroundings than in the Burgess book, and a story in which the text consists of a bland parental note that is humorous in contrast to the wild action of the pictures. Example: "Take out the garbage and play quietly," is illustrated by two pictures: in the first a tiny George has harnessed his infant brother to a wagon in which there's a pail of garbage—the baby is crawling and George is riding him. In the second picture George is standing on the baby's head as they both frighten a cat into jumping into the air. This palatable nonsense has a particularly nice integration of text and pictures.

524   **Jukes**, Mavis. *Blackberries in the Dark;* illus. by Thomas B. Allen. Knopf, 1985. Library ed. ISBN 0-394-97599-5; Trade ed. 0-394-87599-0. 44p. Library ed. $10.99; Trade ed. $10.95.

2-4   Like Jukes' first two award-winning books, this resonates with personalities unveiled in everyday situations that are more important than they seem on the surface. Nine-year-old Austin gets off the plane for his yearly visit with his grandparents feeling awkward. A neighbor has driven his grandmother to meet him, but Grandpa's recent death leaves both her and Austin without a mainstay. Nothing in the house seems right either. Austin breaks the beads on the antique doll his grandmother has recovered from the attic; going inside the barn reduces him to tears. Then his grandmother sends him off blackberry picking, and suddenly, comically, shows up in Grandfather's fishing gear. The two of them begin to rebuild a relationship bridging Grandpa's loss, letting the first trout of the season go as was the old man's wont. Back home, Austin restrings the beads for the doll that symbolizes Gram's loneliness, and Gram gives him Grandpa's fishing knife. Knowingly crafted with the small details that sustain meaning, this is a rich comment on life, death, and renewal. Soft pencil drawings suggest scenes without overwhelming the simple narrative.

525   Juster, Norman. *As: A Surfeit of Similes*; illus by David Small. Morrow, 1989. Library ed. ISBN 0-688-08140-1; Trade ed. ISBN 0-688-08139-8. 80p. Library ed. $9.88; Trade ed. $9.95.

3-6   Clever drawings that are scratchy, often cross-hatched, animated and amusing, illustrate a series of similes-in-verse that are interrupted a few times by dialogue. Although there is an occasional note of aspersion or contrivance ("As drunk as a sailor," or "As queer as a duck") most of the figures of speech are familiar ("As blind as a bat," "As fresh as a daisy") or, less often, are poetic: "Elusive as tunes," for example. The repetitive form produces deja vu reading, but the book should indelibly imprint the simile in readers' minds; it is more often funny than forced, and the appeals of rhyme and metric lilt make it easy to remember verses and likely that they will be quoted.

526   Kalman, Maira. *Sayonara, Mrs. Kackleman*; written and illus. by Maira Kalman. Viking, 1989. ISBN 0-670-82945-5. 32p. $14.95.

K-3   With the same visual verve she brought to the daring but ill-conceived *Hey Willy, Look at the Pyramids*, Kalman here disciplines her considerable talent to the demands of a story. After seeing a performance of *The Mikado*, Alexander wants to go to Japan, and big sister Lulu, anticipating a piano lesson with the "dreaded Mrs. Kackleman," figures this is a good time to get out of town. So off they go ("Bring back presents," say the parents) on a whirlwind tour, visiting a Japanese school and hotel, taking the bullet train, and experiencing a Zen garden. "The quiet was so quiet that the quiet filled the air." Surrealistic twinges are everywhere in both pictures and text: a haiku-reciting frog, shoes for dinner, "a beautiful movie star named Fujiko" who throws a party for an intriguing collection of clowns and clones. The visual whimsy is consistently amusing, but several of the compositions lack strong focus. This is post-modern with a vengeance, yet it's grounded by a sensible (but funny) story, and the bond between Lulu and Alexander is a loving core. Dreams and reality collide in witty ways, and underneath all the zaniness is a true and affectionate portrait of Japan.

527   **Kandoian**, Ellen. *Under the Sun;* written and illus. by Ellen Kandoian. Dodd, 1987. ISBN 0-396-09059-1. 32p. $11.95.

3-5 yrs.   A child's common question serves to take young listeners around the world and demonstrate a science concept at the same time. "Where does the sun go when I go to bed?" asks Molly, and her mother replies that "it goes to the Mississippi River where a little boy watches it set from his houseboat," and then across the U.S. and the ocean to Japan, China, the Mongolian Desert, and Eastern Russia, where a little boy lies wondering the same thing just as Molly is about to wake up. An afterword suggests demonstrating the principle with a globe or ball and flashlight. The sunny, pen-and-wash illustrations never overload the concept, but gently tie it together with simply composed pictures of children and animals unified by the same phenomenon. In fact, the stress on commonality makes this a logical addition to recent booklists on world peace. A multi-purpose book for nursery school or family discussion.

528   **Kaye**, Geraldine. *Comfort Herself;* illus. by Jennifer Northway. Andre Deutsch, 1985. ISBN 0-223-97614-0. 160p. $10.95.

5-7   A story set in England and Ghana opens with pathetic impact (in the dramatic sense) as Comfort's mother is killed in a London street accident. Comfort is a young adolescent, and although she has encountered bias, she is happy that she is black like her father, Mante. Mante is now in Ghana, remarried. Comfort, sent to live with her English mother's parents in a small town, longs to be with her father, writes him, and is sent for. In Ghana she is coolly welcomed by her stepmother and, although it is clear her father loves her, is shunted off to the country to stay with her other grandmother. It is Comfort herself who makes the decision between her two worlds at the end of an unusually perceptive story about cultural conflict. It is not conflict between black and white that troubles Comfort, although her situation causes some problems, but conflict between a society that gives her opportunity as a female and one that limits her because of her sex, both in education and independence. An admirable heroine, Comfort wins over both of her grandmothers, each of whom has felt uncomfortable at the start with Comfort's mixed parentage; it is probable that readers may also better understand how little difference skin-color makes in a person's ability and self-esteem.

529   **Keller**, Beverly. *Desdemona—Twelve Going on Desperate.* Lothrop, 1986. ISBN 0-688-06076-5. 153p. $10.25.

5-8   Readers who chuckled over Keller's *No Beasts! No Children!* will
        welcome back this family, who, with no mother and no money,
        manage to survive a range of scrapes with their verve intact. This time,
        the landlord's brother is threatening to turn Desdemona's house into
        an expensive high-rise condo. Generating from this basic threat is a
        series of non-stop, bitingly funny episodes. At one point, Desdemona
        washes her hair from a shampoo bottle which the twins have used to
        save some leftover floor varnish—and has to live with an excrutiatingly
        short haircut. At another, the twins find it necessary to relocate the
        inhabitants of their broken ant farm. And later on, Desdemona dis-
        covers, while catering the landlord's mayoral party, that she has fed
        truffles to the dog and spread dogfood on the canapes being
        consumed by the guests. Keller has a gift for connecting absurd
        characters, themes, and situations with a logical certainty that builds
        into farce. Her style is unforced and even her villains familiarly
        human. A family comedian in the tradition of Helen Cresswell.

530   **Kellogg**, Steven, ad. *Pecos Bill*; ad. and illus. by Steven Kellogg.
        Morrow , 1986. Library ed. ISBN 0-688-05872-8; Trade ed. ISBN 0-688-
        05861-X. 39p. Library ed. $12.88; Trade ed. $13.00.

K-2   Like Kellogg's *Paul Bunyan*, this combines visual farce with verbal
        exaggeration to provide a graphic rendition of an American tall tale.
        Adapted here into one simple story line are episodes of Bill's adoption
        by coyotes, his taming of a giant rattlesnake and a critter "that was
        part grizzly, part puma, part gorilla and part tarantula," his trans-
        formation of the Hell's Gulch Gang into Texas ranch hands, capture of
        the wonder horse Lightning, development of short-legged steers for
        steep slopes, and courtship of Slewfoot Sue. Although there's a lot
        going on in these pictures, they're not cluttered; both the gradations of
        color and the page design smooth the lines of continuous action and
        tumult of humorous detail. Kellogg's portrayal of Pecos Bill as a
        perpetual boy will appeal to children. The retelling is a smooth
        adaptation for introducing young listeners to longer versions to
        accompany storytelling sessions centered around tall-tale heroes.

531   **Kemp**, Gene. *Jason Bodger and the Priory Ghost*. Faber, 1986. ISBN 0-
        571-13645-1. 140p. $12.95.

5-7   Kemp sets the tone with the very first sentence, long and funny, and
        just on the verge of slapstick. This broad humor is used deftly to pull
        together, throughout the book, the realistic and fanciful elements that
        are at first separate and then merge as tough Jason, the despair of
        timid teachers, becomes cowed by, and finally cooperates with, a
        medieval ghost. Kemp tells the story of Mathilda de Chetwynde in her
        real life, tells the story of Jason and the ghost that only he sees (many
        centuries after Mathilda's death), and brings the two together in a

final romping finish to a book in which the author uses exaggeration
and repetition in exposition to good effect. There's quite a bit of idiom
and vocabulary that are distinctly British, but both are usually made
clear by the context in which they're used.

532   **Kendall**, Carol, ad. *The Wedding of the Rat Family*; illus. by James
Watts. McElderry, 1988. ISBN 0-689-50450-0. 32p. $13.95.

K-3   This decorously ornamented retelling of a Chinese folktale concerns
the ambitious marriage plans that a highborn rat couple (who,
between their teeth, refer to each other as "My Precious" and "My
Beloved") have for their youngest daughter. Power and Influence are
what matter, so Precious tells Beloved to go ask the Sun—but the sun
insists he is less powerful than Black Cloud, who refers Beloved to
Wind, who gives way to (the Great) Wall, who complains that rats are
eating him away. Who, then has more Power and Influence than Rat?
Cat, who is more than happy to oblige: "the cat family were well
pleased with the prospect of enfolding the rat family into their own
lives." A cautionary tale enlivened with considerable wit is illustrated
with delicately small-scale paintings of the rats in opulent dress; the
larger paintings of Sun, etc. have a cartoon quality that is awkward but
energetic.

533   **Kennedy**, Richard. *Amy's Eyes*; illus. by Richard Egielski. Harper,
1985. Library ed. ISBN 0-06-023220-X; Trade ed. ISBN 0-06-023219-6.
437p. Library ed. $13.89; Trade ed. $13.50.

4-6   This is, in brief, the story of a girl who turns into a doll (and back again)
and a doll that turns into a man, and the eventful voyage they take in
search of gold, facing mutiny and pirate pursuit. Kennedy does a fairly
good job of spinning this out to several hundred pages, but he slows
his own story by long digressions (a page and a half about figureheads,
for example, when the figurehead of the ship is mentioned) and some
vocabulary that seems to put a burden on the readers who will be the
primary audience. Left at an orphanage by her sailor father, Amy is
thrilled when the sailor doll left with her comes to life and becomes a
ship's captain; unfortunately she spends most of the exciting voyage
as a doll. The crew consists of animals that were once toys and that
have been brought to life by the captain, who considers Amy his sister.
There's an evil woman on board, a frog who is in love with her, a
mutinous duck, and a Golden Man who comes out of the sea (Amy's
long-lost father) and conflict with the yo-ho-ho pirate Goldnose, and a
treasure, et cetera and occasionally it seems ad infinitum. The title
reference is to the fact that Amy, while a doll, is sentient and can see
but not talk or move; unfortunately her eyes are cut out, and they go
overboard and are swallowed by a fish, where they continue observing
while in the fish and after they are eaten by an albatross and saved by

a black healer called Mama Dah-Dah and eventually returned to Amy, who is now a girl again. This has some engaging concepts, a great deal of droll and often sophisticated humor, and passages of fine writing, but it is long, complex, and occasionally precious, which may mean that die-hard fantasy lovers who are also proficient readers will be the most appreciative audience.

534   **Kennedy**, X. J. *Brats;* illus. by James Watts. McElderry, 1986. ISBN 0-689-50392-X. 42p. $11.95.

2-4   Forty-two brief verses, mostly rhymed quatrains, celebrate or denigrate the actions of mischievous children, many of whom meet fearful fates. These are bright, tight, and inventive, with plenty of playground chanting potential: "On his motorbike Lars stands/ Roaring past us— 'Look! no hands!'/ Soon with vacant handle bars/ Back the bike roars. Look, no Lars!" Word choices are simple, with reliance on inventive situations, as when one young brat drenches the T.V. set to find out whether "flash floods/ Turn soap opera to suds." Another imp, Sue, sticks a pig to the ceiling with Elmer's Glue. ("Uncle, gawking, spilled his cup./ 'Wow!' he cried. 'Has pork gone up!'"). A few of the selections have a slightly grisly ring (specifically, in the case of Louise, who sneaks up on a snoozing bear), but it's all done in high humor, as are the slapstick black-and-white drawings that illustrate the spacious pages. Neatly crafted poetry that will be highly popular as well.

535   **Kennedy**, X. J. *Fresh Brats*; illus. by James Watts. McElderry, 1990. ISBN 0-689-50499-3. 48p. $12.95.

3-5   This gallery of poetic mischief-makers features the ghoulish, gross, or catastrophic humor that children love most in the middle grades. It's hard to select favorite examples—students will be popping these poems at each other like spitballs: "To the bottom of his drink/ Dad beholds an earthworm sink./ For her bio project, May/ Must have used the ice-cube tray." Often the straightforward joke ends with a twist, as in the case of "jealous would-be-actor Jay," who sabotages the Yuletide play with marbles, only to end up in a cast different from the kind he envied. These irrepressibly rhymed verses make an irresistible introduction for reluctant readers as well for enthusiastic listeners. To be illustrated with black-and-white drawings by the same artist who livened up the preceding volume, *Brats*.

536   **Kerr**, M. E. *Fell.* Harper, 1987. Library ed. ISBN 0-06-023268-4; Trade ed. ISBN 0-06-023267-6. 165p. Library ed. $11.89; Trade ed. $11.95.

7-12
*   While still occupied with the questions of privilege and class that mark all her Seaville novels, Kerr here adds an unusual dimension of mystery. Seventeen-year-old John Fell is smarting over his treatment at the hands of Helen Keating (friend to Skye Pennington of *Gentle-*

hands) when he receives a curious offer: wealthy Woodrow Pingree will pay Fell twenty thousand dollars to attend his exclusive alma mater under his son's name—the real Ping, Jr., under Fell's name, will go to a "country club" school in Switzerland. It's all too complicated to go into here, for what Kerr has written is a subtle variation on the detective story, carefully dropping clues from the beginning, but clues to what?—we don't know what crime has been committed, much less by whom, but we know there are secrets, and we are intrigued. Fell seems to be the kind of detective who bumbles his way into trouble—as when he happens upon a body on the last page, promising another adventure. We can't wait.

537   **Kerr, M. E.** *I Stay Near You.* Harper, 1985. Library ed. ISBN 0-06-023105-X; Trade ed. ISBN 0-06-023104-1. 182p. Library ed. $10.89; Trade ed. $11.50.

7-10   In three linked long stories Kerr tells of three generations of a family in a small town. First the story of an intense love affair between Mildred Cone, poor and proud and beautiful, and the son of the town's richest family, a story that ends with Mildred's marriage to another man who knows that she is pregnant and that her lover has been killed in military action. The story has been told by Mildred's friend, while the second story, in third person, is about Mildred's son Vincent, who is bereft when the girl he loves marries another man, and who eventually learns who his real father was. Last, in first person, Vincent's troubled son, who yearns to be close to his father, especially after his mother dies, and who is aware that Vincent, a drug-hooked pop star, puts his son low on the list of life's priorities. This is both tough and tender, a trenchant and moving novel that has color, variety, compassion, and percipience—Kerr at her best.

538   **Kerr, M. E.** *Night Kites.* Harper, 1986. Library ed. ISBN 0-06-023254-4; Trade ed. ISBN 0-06-023253-6. 216p. Library ed. $10.89; Trade ed. $11.50.

8-12   "Pete says night kites are different, they don't think about the dark." Seventeen-year-old Erick remembers his older brother's illuminated kite, flying in the darkness, when he meets Nikki, Seaville's local bad girl, who is also his best friend Jack's new girlfriend. Nikki's definitely night kite material; in a school filled with preppies, she dresses like Madonna, is into "dark, flawed passions," and calmly lures Erick away from his more conventional girlfriend Dill. Having alienated all his friends, Erick has only Nikki when Pete comes home and reveals he has AIDS. While the two stories are essentially separate (necessarily because Erick has been forbidden to tell anyone about his brother), they combine in escalating thematic force to the end, when Nikki dumps Erick, who learns the truth of his father's favorite chestnut:

"Family is first." Kerr has insight, but no easy sympathies for her characters: Nikki is a heartless poseuse; Erick, rather a pushover; Pete is promiscuous, unable to fall in love. The most sympathetic portraits are of Erick's parents, as they each take a different, fumbling way of handling Pete's homosexuality and disease. The celebrated Kerr wit is subdued here, and is in fact missed in some of the slower, aimless passages of the book. But the overall tone of melancholy—from the title image to Erick watching Nikki with a new boyfriend—seems absolutely right for what is most likely the saddest book Kerr has written.

539   Kesey, Ken. *Little Tricker the Squirrel Meets Big Double the Bear*; illus. by Barry Moser. Viking, 1990. ISBN 0-670-81136-X. 32p. $14.95.

5-9 yrs.   "Don't tell me you're the *only* youngsters never heard tell of the time
    *   the bear came to Topple's Bottom? He was a huge high-country bear and not only huge but *horrible* huge. And hairy, and hateful, and *hungry*! Why he almost ate up the *entire Bottom* before Tricker finally cut him down to size, just you listen and see if he didn't. . . ." And listen kids will, to this language that plays like Carl Sandburg's and doesn't fool around when it comes to plot. Folktale elements emerge without seeming either self-conscious or precious. After Big Double eats a couple of little ground animals, just to whet his appetite, he finds himself eye to eye with Tricker the tree squirrel, who admits to being impressed: "you may have been a little short-changed in the thinking department but when it comes to running, jumping, and climbing you got double portions." In addition to music and wit in the words, which will sustain repeated read-aloud sessions, there's wild satire and more action than usual (without loss of control) in the masterful watercolors with which Barry Moser portrays this archetypal cast. Lots of writers and painters who have concentrated their artistry on adults can't switch to children without loud tonal flaws, but Kesey and Moser have proved the exception. Like the hazelnuts ripening in the tree below Tricker's "cottonwood high rise," this picture book is *"just about per*fect!"

540   Kessler, Ethel. *Stan the Hot Dog Man*; written and illus. by Ethel and Leonard Kessler. Harper, 1990. Library ed. ISBN 0-06-023280-3; Trade ed. ISBN 0-06-023279-X. 64p. (I Can Read Books). Library ed. $10.95; Trade ed. $10.89.

5-8 yrs.   Sixty-five-year-old Stan's retired from the bakery, but he's not ready to retire, and his flashy red and blue hot dog truck is all set to go. Stan is a kindly hot dog man, selling his dogs two for one when he discovers a customer can't afford the four his family needs; and Stan's a lifesaver as well, taking in a bus driver and her charges when all are stranded in a blizzard. While the plot lacks momentum, this easy-reader has an appealing focus (food) and a real-life drama that new readers will find comfortable. It's nice, too, to have an easy-reader protagonist who is neither young nor green.

541   **Kessler**, Leonard. *Old Turtle's Soccer Team*; written and illus. by Leonard Kessler. Greenwillow, 1988. Library ed. ISBN 0-688-07158-9; Trade ed. ISBN 0-688-07157-0. 48p. Library ed. $11.88; Trade ed. $11.95.

1-2   Beginning independent readers of both sexes should welcome a story about a unisex sport that has become increasingly popular. The characters are animals (appealing) who make silly mistakes (very appealing) but who win their first game against another team (also v.a.). Cartoon-style illustrations are bright and not too busy, the division of the text into five "chapters" flatters readers who like their books to have the same structure as those for older children, and there's just enough information about the game to be appropriate for the audience. Print is large, leading is adequate, and vocabulary is controlled but not stilted.

542   **Khalsa**, Dayal Kaur. *Tales of a Gambling Grandma*. Potter/Crown, 1986. ISBN 0-517-56137-9. 32p. $10.95.

K-3   Her grandmother, the narrator reports, escaped the Cossacks and came to America when she was three, "hidden in a hay cart all across the wide, slate-green Atlantic Ocean. At least, that's how she told the story to me." That's the signal for the audience for this picture book to understand how Grandma airily stretches the truth. Grandma is indeed a gambler (she'd been trained by a card shark and was not above marking the deck) and while some adults may feel dubious about presenting such an image, most young children will respond positively to Grandma's inventive mood, to her love for her grandchild, and to the fun they had together. The writing is direct and simple, the paintings effectively composed.

543   **Kidd**, Ronald. *Second Fiddle: A Sizzle and Splat Mystery*. Lodestar, 1988. ISBN 0-525-67252-4. 167p. $12.95.

6-9   In a sequel to *Sizzle and Splat*, the narrator is again Sizzle (Prudence Szyznowski) who plays trumpet in a youth orchestra and who again embarks on a detective venture with her pal, tuba player Splat (Arthur Hadley Reavis Pauling III). This time it's a mystery about a series of pranks that culminates in the burning of a Stradivarius violin. Like the first book, this has a structure too fraught with incidents to be quite credible, but it has wit and humor in dialogue, some lively characters, and an enjoyably comfortable familiarity with classical music.

544   **Kimmel**, Eric A. *Anansi and the Moss-Covered Rock*; illus. by Janet Stevens. Holiday House, 1988. ISBN 0-8234-0689. 32p. $13.95.

4-7 yrs.   Exuding humor from every printed pore, this combines Stevens'
            knack for drawing funny animals with Kimmel's sense of rhythmic
            storytelling. Anansi finds a magic rock that puts to sleep anyone
            nearby who happens to remark, "isn't this a strange moss-covered
            rock." After falling unconscious several times himself ("KPOM!"),
            Anansi uses the rock to knock out the other animals, raiding their
            carefully hoarded food stores. Finally the trickster gets a taste of his
            own medicine when Little Bush Deer, who has been spying on the
            whole scenario, turns the tables on Anansi. Stevens has cleverly
            avoided cartooning the spider's face and opted instead for empha-
            sizing his very expressive set of eight black legs. The stylized
            exaggeration of words and pictures is just wry enough to avoid
            cuteness and maintain the mischief of a true trickster tale.

545   **Kimmel**, Eric A. *The Chanukkah Guest*; illus. by Giora Carmi. Holiday
        House, 1990. ISBN 0-8234-0788-8. 32p. $14.95.

4-7 yrs.   Holiday story hours will benefit from this gentle spoof (text first
            published in *Cricket* magazine) in which an old woman mistakes a
            bear for the rabbi she expects to visit on the first night of Chanukkah.
            "Bubba Brayna was ninety-seven years old and did not hear or see as
            well as she used to, but she still made the best potato pancakes in the
            village." Thus it is that she serves up a grand meal after playing
            dreidel with the bear, and sends him off with the gift of a warm red
            scarf before the real guests arrive. Younger listeners especially will
            enjoy the joke, which offers possibilities for dramatic exaggeration in
            sharing aloud. Full-color illustrations, dominated by the golden-brown
            hues of the bear's fur, the latkes, and the rabbi's beard, are broadly
            humorous. The third and lightest of Kimmel's Chanukkah romps.

546   **Kimmel**, Eric. *Hershel and the Hanukkah Goblins*; illus. by Trina
        Schart Hyman. Holiday House, 1989. ISBN 0-8234-0769-1. 32p. $14.95.

5-8 yrs.   Billed as an original story, this is built with familiar folk motifs in
            Jewish traditional garb. Hershel agrees to spend eight nights of
            Hanukkah in a haunted old synagogue to rid the village of goblins. He
            fools the first, tiny goblin by crushing a hardboiled egg that looks like a
            rock; the second, larger goblin by tempting him with a bottle of pickles
            into which the greedy goblin stuffs his hand and gets stuck; and the
            third, by a clever gambling ruse with the dreidel. We don't find out
            exactly how Hershel survives the other four devilish visitors, but the
            eighth night brings the frightful King of Goblins, whom Hershel tricks
            into lighting the candles himself by pretending it's too dark to see.
            Thus the spell is broken and the spirit of Hanukkah triumphs. Well,
            after all, the Maccabees must have used a few tricks of their own—
            there are only so many ways to outmaneuver an opponent. This will
            provide relief from the boring, candy-coated read-alouds that so often

comprise holiday fare and will fit companionably with haunted castle variants. Hyman is at her best with windswept landscapes, dark interiors, close portraiture, and imaginatively wicked creatures. Both art and history are charged with energy.

547   **King-Smith**, Dick. *Ace, the Very Important Pig*; illus. by Lynette Hemmant. Crown, 1990. Library ed. ISBN 0-517-57833-6; Trade ed. ISBN 0-517-57832-8. 134p. Library ed. $13.99; Trade ed. $12.95.

4-6   Creating a fictitious pig as distinctive as Babe in King-Smith's *Babe, the Gallant Pig*, which won England's 1984 Guardian award, is a challenge, but Ace manages to garner a place of his own. He's saved from the market by an extraordinary intelligence that allows him to understand human speech from birth. Gaining access to Farmer Tubbs' television set, Ace eventually educates himself and ends up on the BBC, after a memorable visit to the village pub. Ace's companions—a goat, a cat, and a Corgi—are also well-realized characters, and fans of the author's other animal fantasies will find this one just as realistically detailed and casually humorous. A comic British companion to *Charlotte's Web*.

548   **King-Smith**, Dick. *The Fox Busters*; illus. by Jon Miller. Delacorte, 1988. ISBN 0-440-50064-8. 117p. $13.95.

5-7   In a saga of Chanticleerian proportions with a feminist twist, this
 *   relates the defeat of some determined foxes by three heroic pullets. With characteristically witty dispatch, King-Smith establishes the world of the barnyard and individualizes the principal animals in the heat of action. The opening scene is an ambush of chicks by a fox hidden in the water trough, and the pace mounts from there as Ransome, Sims, and Jefferies (named for a plow) are hatched, develop their genetically enhanced flying and scheming powers, and fend off fox raids forever. Their heat tolerance training in an abandoned greenhouse for the purpose of dropping hardboiled eggs—laid mid-air at terrific speeds and aimed with the skill of constant target practice—on attackers' heads is only one detail of an inventive arsenal. This is life-or-death stuff, with feathers flying and even a moment of poignancy as the courageous but somewhat slow-witted cock Massey-Harris (after the tractor) meets a noble end. Imaginative fare for reading aloud with Chaucer's tale and other chicken-fox fables.

549   **King-Smith**, Dick. *Harry's Mad*; illus. by Jill Bennett. Crown, 1987. ISBN 0-517-56254-5. 123p. $9.95.

4-6   Harry, when he heard that a great-uncle in America had left him a prize possession, did a lot of fantasizing about what it could be. He never expected a parrot, nor was he pleased with his inheritance. That is, he wasn't pleased until he learned that Madison, the parrot, could talk—not "Pretty Polly," but talk as humans did. The removal of Madison by a frustrated burglar and the complex mishaps that ensue before the reunion of Harry and his Mad are lively, funny, fast-paced, and adroitly told. King-Smith is a master of word-play, and his deft comic writing is multilevel.

550   King-Smith, Dick. *Sophie's Snail*; illus. by Claire Minter-Kemp. Delacorte, 1989. ISBN 0-385-29824-2. 68p. $11.95.

3-5   King-Smith has conceived a four-year-old heroine who is amusing and endearing without being the slightest bit winsome or cute. Independent readers can read this with no embarrassment, because the style is sophisticated in the true sense and because there is a tart humor throughout the episodic chapters that describe small but important events in the life of Sophie, her family, her snail and other pets (wood lice, for example), and those others fortunate (or, at times, unfortunate) enough to move into the restricted ambit of a four-year-old's life. Delightful.

551   Kismaric, Carole, ad. *The Rumor of Pavel and Paali: A Ukrainian Folktale*; illus. by Charles Mikolaycak. Harper, 1988. Library ed. ISBN 0-06-023278-1; Trade ed. ISBN 0-06-023277-3. 32p. Library ed. $13.89; Trade ed. $13.95.

3-5   "Which is the better way to live, by doing good or by doing evil?" That's the pivotal question posed in this Ukrainian folktale (no source given), both for the plot and the theme. To resolve a wager, twin brothers (one good, one wicked) pose this question to three men, who all agree that evil seems to get one farther in the world. Paali, the good, loses all his possessions and eventually his eyes to Pavel, but all (and virtue) are eventually restored, with the wicked Pavel turned into an evil spirit. Mikolaycak's handsome paintings are vigorously colored, intensified by black outlining, and brightly patterned, including the margins of the text, sometimes resulting in a gorgeous but over-whelming confusion. This is controlled somewhat by placing text blocks over some of the action, which both relieves the eye and provides visual suspense. As in some previous books, the artist solidifies light and liquid; silly in a picture of a gushing fountain, dramatic in the sweeps of flames and evil spirits.

552   Kitchen, Bert. *Animal Numbers*; written and illus. by Bert Kitchen. Dial, 1987. ISBN 0-8037-0459-3. 24p. $11.95.

3-5 yrs.   Like his *Animal Alphabet* , Kitchen's large-scale paintings are marvelously effective, with his animals twined about, or perched on, or contained within, the large digits that are set off by white space on the oversize pages. The numbers go from one to ten, then come 15, 25, 50,

75, and 100. The final page has facts about each animal, giving its name, which is not on the original page; this emphasizes the fact that it's a counting book but may prove frustrating to some children, who may wonder what animals 6 and 7 are (shrew and opossum).

553   **Kitzinger**, Sheila. *Being Born*; illus. with photographs by Lennart Nilsson. Grosset, 1986. ISBN 0-448-18990-9. 64p. $14.95.

2-4   A social anthropologist who specializes in childbirth education,
*   Kitzinger addresses her simply written text to the reader, describing the nine months of gestation in terms of an experience every reader has had; "Once you were in a small, dark place inside your mother's body," the book begins. Conception is described succinctly and accurately, but the focus is on the changes that take place in the mother's body and on the recurrent miracle of the changes in utero from a ball of cells to an infant ready to breathe independently. The text is authoritative and the photographic illustrations are stunning: full color, usually highly magnified, almost all depicting the embryo in the womb. This is medical photography at its best, and the oversize pages are used brilliantly to display pictures in a layout with spacious dignity.

554   **Klein**, Norma. *Going Backwards*. Scholastic, 1986. ISBN 0-590-40328-1. 182p. $12.95.

7-10   Norma Klein's novels are always candid, occasionally humorous, often provocative, and clearly written in the belief that children ought to have exposure to those problems they encounter (personally or vicariously) in real life. Here, although some minor themes are interwoven, she gives a vivid picture of a family's reaction to the deterioration of personality caused by Alzheimer's disease, to the conflict for the adolescent narrator between his emergent sexuality and his self deprecating shyness, and to the intricacy of familial relations that extend, within Charles Goldberg's family, to the black housekeeper. The end of the story seems rushed by compression, but it is a story with good style and pace, convincing characterization and dialogue, and issues of interest to young adults.

555   **Klein**, Norma. *My Life as a Body*. Knopf, 1987. Library ed. ISBN 0-394-99051-X; Trade ed. ISBN 0-394-89051-5. 247p. Library ed. $13.99; Trade ed. $12.95.

8-10   Augie is a senior at a small, progressive private high school in Manhattan, and she's far from enthralled when the school counselor asks her to tutor a new student, Sam, who has suffered physical and mental damage because of an accident. Sam is confined to a wheelchair, and Augie is uncomfortable and self-conscious at first; as Sam improves, the two begin to talk, become friends, and eventually become lovers.

They are found in flagrante delicto by Sam's mother. Time, parental censure, and separation (Augie goes to the Rhode Island School of Design) bring a painful rift—and in time this pain also passes. This is a subtle and sophisticated novel, believably told by Augie, four-letter words included. It deals perceptively with romantic and physical love felt for (and by) a person who is handicapped, but has wider implications for all young people who suffer adolescent pangs of indecision, ambivalence, and inadequacy. Klein's portrayal of Sam's parents (protective, acquisitive, critical) and of Augie's (gentle, tolerant, intellectually absorbed) are particularly sharp. Good style, good characterization, interesting theme, and natural dialogue are strong points in a perceptive story, and they compensate nicely for an uneven development of plot.

556   Klein, Norma. *Older Men.* Dial, 1987. ISBN 0-8037-0178-0. 226p. $15.95.

9-12   Sixteen-year-old Elise is the sole object of her father's lavish affections. The psychological isolation of Elise's mother, June, becomes physical when Elise's father arranges for a hospitalization from which June cannot release herself. This is the story of Elise's discovery that her father has no use for women who grow up, including his first wife, his stepdaughter, his second wife, his mother-in-law, and, as soon as Elise begins to establish independence, his daughter. Indeed, the book ends with a scene of his courting another woman with a little girl. The writing here is capable and smooth, the characters clearly delineated. At times the focus seems unrelieved, but the situation is solidly established if psychologically obvious. The sexual scenes between Elise and her father's stepson by a first marriage are both explicit and integral to the plot.

557   Klein, Robin. *Came Back to Show You I Could Fly.* Viking, 1990. ISBN 0-670-82901-3. 189p. $11.95.

5-9   Seymour is a timorous eleven-year-old boy whose mother has stowed him with a bossy family friend for the summer holidays; Angie is a wild older teenager with a tattoo and black fingernail polish; they meet when Seymour runs into Angie's yard while escaping from a gang of bullies. Long before Seymour allows himself to figure it out, readers will understand that Angie has a serious drug problem. She lies to Seymour (and convinces herself in the process) about her past, her family, her daily visits to a remote clinic. Seymour's faith in his friend, even when he sees her shoplifting, or when she asks him to lie to her landlady, is believable, as is his gradually developing backbone, grown at Angie's impetuous insistence. Tough encounters, such as when Angie takes Seymour along for a visit to her family, are confidently placed amid scenes of the two sharing fantasies and adventures in the city. By an Australian writer celebrated for her deftly popular touch, this is occasionally didactic (with a happily hopeful ending), but engagingly written, offering a pair of protagonists readers will be pleased to meet. Winner of the Australian Children's Book of the year Award.

558   **Klein**, Robin. *Hating Alison Ashley*. Viking Kestrel, 1987. ISBN 0-670-80864-4. 182p. $11.95.

4-6   A world class liar to rival Cleaver's Ellen Grae, Erica is used to being an academic star (as well as the class braggart and hypochondriac) and she's put out when the new girl in sixth grade, Alison, turns out to be an A student as well as being a very pretty clotheshorse. To add insult to injury, Alison's clothes are in impeccable taste. Erica, the narrator, lives with her family in a noisy, slapdash environment. This very funny, very astute story brings the two girls together with such compassion and wit that it doesn't matter a whit that the rapprochement has been inevitable from the start. First published in Australia, this is a gem of a school-and-camp story.

559   **Kleitsch**, Christel. *A Time to Be Brave;* by Christel Kleitsch and Paul Stephens. Annick Press/Firefly, 1985. ISBN 0-920303-26-9; Paper ed. ISBN 0-920303-27-7. 61p. illus. with photographs. Trade ed. $5.95; Paper ed. $2.95.

4-6   A simple but dramatic story is told by eleven-year-old Tafia, who lives with her grandmother, father, and brother in a house in a small "reserve," an Ojibway community in Ontario. Based on a film, this is illustrated with some of the frames, several of which are dark and fuzzy. This is a much better job of translating film to print than most such efforts; the style of writing is convincingly like a child's and the first person format gives immediacy and warmth to a text that describes how the family lives, what their problems and pleasures are, and in what ways they reconcile traditional Indian life and the white culture that impinges upon it. The story has an exciting (and believable) ending in which Tafia's courage in a crisis helps her to get over some of her fears and insecurity about herself.

560   **Klingsheim**, Trygve B. *Julius;* illus. with photographs by A. Jakobsen. Delacorte, 1987. ISBN 0-385-29611-8. 60p. $11.95.

5-7 yrs.   There's no other word for it: Julius is cute. And that's the zoo officials' problem when the newborn chimpanzee is rejected by his mother. They have to raise him in a loving home without becoming too attached to him or letting him think he's a real human child. It's tricky, but the director and the doctor take turns so that neither of their families will monopolize his affections. This is a photodocumentary of Julius' adoption, development, and triumphant return to his own kind

on Monkey Island at the Kristiansand Zoo in Norway. The color
photography is well-reproduced and entertaining, the account
strengthened by a basic theme of respect for animal life.

561   **Knudson,** R. R., comp. *American Sports Poems*; comp. and ed. by R.
R. Knudson and May Swenson. Orchard/Watts, 1988. Library ed.
ISBN 0-531-08353-5; Trade ed. ISBN 0-531-05753-4. 238p. Library ed.
$14.99; Trade ed. $14.95.

6-12   America's gym teachers should be convinced that this collection is a
*   terrific read-aloud alternative to rainy day health and hygiene movies.
What is initially most impressive about the poems is their tremendous variety in subject, form, tone and length (The shortest: "They all
must fall/ In the round I call."—Muhammad Ali). Beginning with
poetic tributes to sports greats like Babe Ruth, Vince Lombardi and
Joan Benoit, this anthology moves through baseball ("Sometimes ball
gets hit/ (pow) when bat/ meets it,/ and sails/ to a place/ where mitt/
has to quit/ in disgrace."—May Swenson) football, soccer, hockey,
basketball, swimming, skating . . . and throughout there is a
concreteness to the images and a welcome lack of sports-as-
metaphor-for-life that make the poems enjoyable on a literal level as
well as providing the depth that only specificity can give. With more
than 150 selections that include Updike, Sexton and Nemerov (as well
as Runyon, Nash, and Cole Porter), this is an all-star lineup. Notes on
the poems and poets, title and author index, and a valuable subject
index are included.

562   **Knutson,** Barbara, ad. *How the Guinea Fowl Got Her Spots: A Swahili
Tale of Friendship*; ad. and illus. by Barbara Knutson. Carolrhoda,
1990. ISBN 0-87614-416-4. 32p. $12.95.

3-6 yrs.   An East African pourquoi tale holds great appeal for very young
*   listeners because it is unabashedly brief, literally illustrated, and
reassuring as to the rewards of friendship. "Guinea Fowl was a little
bird, but she had a big friend. And that was Cow. They liked to go to
the great green hills where Cow could eat grass and Nganga could
scratch for seeds and crunch grasshoppers. And they would both keep
an eye out for Lion." Twice Nganga risks her small life for Cow, who
thanks her by spattering spots of white milk across her feathers to
confuse Lion and camouflage the future guinea fowls of the world.
With ink and watercolor on scratchboard, Knutson treats line, pattern,
and composition sparingly. Her understated, angular figures emerge
powerfully from spacious white backgrounds. Technically ingenious in
design, strikingly simple in effect.

563   **Koertge,** Ron. *The Arizona Kid*. Joy Street/Little, 1988. ISBN 0-316-
50101-8. 228p. $14.95.

7-10   Sounds like a great summer. Midwesterner Billy is going to spend it
with his uncle in Tucson, working with a horse trainer, and hopefully
pursuing his First Time. But Uncle Wes is gay, the work harder and
dirtier than Billy expects, and Cara Mae not exactly friendly. "'Get
bent,' she said." Of course, it does turn out to be a great summer,
though not without complications, including a coupla mean ol'
varmints who want Billy and Cara out of the way. Wes is not one of
those stereotyped gay uncles who crop up far too often in YA books,
the regular-guy type who "just happens" to be gay. Tall and gorgeous
and kind, Wes is also fanatically neat (he has his underwear pressed)
and, more seriously, occasionally despairing, watching his friends die
of AIDS and worrying about his own chances. He also, another first for
the genre, actually has (safe) sex, and instructs Billy about the
importance of condoms. The other characters are drawn with an equal
specificity that includes both humor and depth: Cara Mae is neither
nervous filly nor racetrack floozie, but rather a combination of real
and pretended arrogance ("Man, I'd love to sit on a million dollars
and tell it to go fast,") and understated vulnerability. More relaxed
and even funnier than Koertge's previous novel, *Where the Kissing
Never Stops*, this is perfect for growing-up fans of Betsy Byars.

564   **Koertge**, Ron. *Where the Kissing Never Stops*. Atlantic, 1986. ISBN 0-
87113-125-0. 217p. $14.95.

9-12   "God, I thought about sex a lot." And, seventeen-year-old Walker's
preoccupation is not helped one bit when his mother announces that
she has a new job, as an "exotic dancer," and she starts "Tonight. The
snake got sick and Eve can't do very much without a snake." Walker is
doubly mortified that his mother actually enjoys stripping, and he
works hard to make sure his new girlfriend Rachel does not discover
the family secret. There has been a slew of sentimental books and
movies for teens about macho, horny boys who, with the help of an
understanding girlfriend, learn to stop hiding their feelings, but this
very funny novel never falls into that trap. Both tender feelings and
exasperating pig-headedness are generously distributed among all
the characters here, and Koertge honestly explores a range of
sexuality, from Walker and best friend Sully's self-conscious jokes
about breasts, to beautifully vulnerable lovemaking between Walker
and Rachel.

565   **Konigsburg**, E. L. *Up from Jericho Tel*. Atheneum, 1986. ISBN 0-689-
31194-X. 178p. $12.95.

4-6
*   Whether she is writing a realistic or a fanciful story, Konigsburg
always provides fresh ideas, tart wit and humor, and memorable
characters. As for style, she is a natural and gifted storyteller. Here she
gives a firmly matter-of-fact matrix for a fantasy about two children,

Malcolm and Jeanmarie (each an assertive and articulate character) who find that Jericho Tel, their secret place, is a doorway to another world—and to an imposed but fascinating quest. And who is the imposer? Children may not recognize the loving spoof of Tallulah Bankhead, but they'll enjoy this salty character, drawn as a chain-smoking ghost named Tallulah who sends the children on missions that bring them into theatrical circles. This is a lively, clever, and very funny book. When reproached for smoking, Tallulah says, "When I want health advice, darling, I'll haunt the Mayo Clinic." She also says, "The difference between going to school and getting an education is the difference between picking an apple and eating it."

566   **Korschunow**, Irina. *Adam Draws Himself a Dragon*; tr. from the German by James Skofield; illus. by Mary Rahn. Harper, 1986. Library ed. ISBN 0-06-023252-8; Trade ed. ISBN 0-06-023249-8. 57p. Library ed. $9.89; Trade ed. $9.95.

1-4   A double rarity, this is an entertaining novel for primary graders and a translated book that easily transcends cultural differences. Adam is a misfit already in his first year of school: he's fat, insecure, and fast locking into patterns of incompetence in skills of all kinds. Then there emerges, from his despondent twig-drawings on the ground, a tiny black dragon who is a failure at the things that dragons are supposed to do—for starters, he has only one head instead of three, a serious disadvantage in breathing out variously colored fire. As the dragon lives with Adam and tries out human activities, Adam gets encourage-ment and practice in writing, somersaults, etc., and the dragon eats most of his chocolate. By the time the dragon says goodbye, Adam has lost weight, defied a bully, and made a human friend. There are numerous inventive twists on an old theme here, yet the style never leaves the required confines of simplicity. The vivid incidents and friendship keep the book from becoming didactic, and its warm, intimate tone gets further assistance from fine, softly toned pencil drawings set in a well designed format that is spacious but not babyish. A book that young readers could pursue independently after hearing the first chapter read aloud.

567   **Korschunow**, Irina. *Small Fur Is Getting Bigger*; tr. from the German by James Skofield; illus. by Reinhard Michl. Harper, 1990. Library ed. ISBN 0-06-023290-0; Trade ed. ISBN 0-06-023289-7. 67p. Library ed. $14.89; Trade ed. $14.95.

5-8 yrs.   Small Fur may be getting bigger, but he's scared of Uncle Ned, who has come for his annual visit. Uncle Ned bullies and berates Small Fur ("You're a sissy"), and when his (equally intimidated) mother won't take his side, Small Fur runs away. In a hair-raising scene, Small Fur is almost lured into the swamp by a gurgle-girl, but is saved by rumored-witch Trulla, who enchants Small Fur with his own self-confidence. Fiercer than the first book, this one builds on a strong realization of the fear and resentment children feel in the presence of a bullying grown-up. While the atmosphere is sometimes scary, young listeners will probably enjoy the shivers, and they will certainly appreciate Small Fur's rebellious backtalk ("No!") and recognize its justice. Children who heard the first story, *Small Fur,* a couple of years ago might be able to read this one on their own; both readers and lookers-on will empathize with Michl's Sendakian drawings that show a very bossy Uncle Ned and an even more threatening gurgle-girl. In both text and pictures, Small Fur is a very sturdy hero.

568   **Krementz**, Jill. *The Fun of Cooking;* written and illus. with photographs by Jill Krementz. Knopf, 1985. ISBN 0-394-54808-6. 121p. $14.95.

5-9   There are almost two hundred photographs in this oversize book, and they are up to the usual Krementz standard. They bear out the concept of the title, for nineteen boys and girls (ages six to sixteen) share, through informational interviews that include tips, techniques, and details of recipes, the special dishes that they enjoy making. Ingredients, utensils, and instructions are carefully listed, and the text is preceded by some safety rules and helpful hints. The pages stay open but do not lie perfectly flat, but it's a minor weakness in a cookbook that is explicit and attractive, and that may entice readers, because they are addressed by their peers, into culinary experiments.

569   **Krementz**, Jill. *A Visit to Washington, D.C.;* written and illus. with photographs by Jill Krementz. Scholastic, 1987. ISBN 0-590-40582-9. 44p. $13.95.

1-3   Endpapers add to the usefulness of this introductory guide to Washington by providing maps that clearly indicate all sites mentioned in the text. The color photographs are of excellent quality, and the scenes commented on by the six-year-old protagonist are ones that would interest a child (not the furnishings of the White House, but the joys of the Discovery Room at the National Museum of Natural History) and, while there are some parts of Matt's monologue that are tinged with brochure-like provision of facts, most of the text is casually conversational.

570   **Krensky**, Stephen. *Lionel at Large;* illus. by Susanna Natti. Dial, 1986. Library ed. ISBN 0-8037-0241-8; Trade ed. ISBN 0-8037-0240-X. 54p. Library ed. $8.89; Trade ed. $8.95.

1-2   Five simply written stories for the beginning independent reader are illustrated by full-color drawings, line-and-wash, that have a cheerful vitality and humor. Each story is a modest anecdote about Lionel: a visit to the doctor, a confrontation with the necessity of eating vegetables, a nervous hunt for an older sister's pet snake . . . in other words, experiences similar to those most children have. There's a quiet humor in the writing, so that readers can enjoy the joke while they are empathizing with Lionel's problems and with his success in overcoming or tolerating them.

571   **Kroll**, Steven. *Gone Fishing*; illus. by Harvey Stevenson. Crown, 1990. Library ed. ISBN 0-517-57590-6; Trade ed. ISBN 0-517-57589-2. 48p. Library ed. $13.99; Trade ed. $12.95.

5-7 yrs.   Eight brief episodes—each of about two pages of print per story facing full-page wash drawings—recount Willie's release from school, departure for the family beach house, preparation of the boat, and all-day fishing trip. This is an idyllic venture, including a dog named Boris and a father who calls his son Sport and hugs him when they lose the catch of the day. It's not total wish fulfillment, because they never do hook the big porgy Willy hopes for, but there's always tomorrow, and young listeners will fantasize themselves right alongside Willie on the bay. The full-color illustrations are well drafted, especially striking in the scene where a flashlight outlines a deer at night. This is low-key vacation fare that will appeal especially to the pole-and-bait set, for whom not enough picture books are tailored.

572   **Kronenwetter**, Michael. *Taking a Stand against Human Rights Abuses*. Watts, 1990. ISBN 0-531-10921-6. 144p. illus. with photographs. (Taking a Stand). $13.40.

7-
*   Working from the principle that "although human rights are ours by nature, they need to be fought for and protected by law and tradition," Kronenwetter has created an unsensationalized, rational, and compelling book that lives up to its title, not only telling readers why they should take their stand but also arming them for the fight. Basic enough to educate the innocent but comprehensive enough to enlighten the informed, the work includes a history of the idea of human rights, an even-handed discussion of why and where they are abused (including allied countries and enemies, left- and right-wing regimes, and not sparing the U.S. itself), and an overview of past and current fights against human rights abuses. Even more impressive is the full one-third (plus appendices) of the text devoted to explaining what the reader can do. Never patronizing or preaching, the book enumerates small steps and large: how to join or even form a human rights organization; how to write a foreign official or U.S. politician (and how it can be effective even when the writer is not of voting age); how to cope with the necessary expenses and possible failures. Despite its serious topic, the book is highly readable, peppered with anecdotes and showing no sign of the excessive earnestness that can infect this

kind of endeavor. Endnotes, appendices (including the U.N. Declaration of Human Rights, instructions and format for writing letters to editors and officials, and a directory of leading human rights organizations), and an index are included.

573   **Kudlinski**, Kathleen V. *Hero Over Here*; illus. by Bert Dodson. Viking, 1990. ISBN 0-670-83050-X. 56p. (Once Upon America). $11.95.

4-6   Set in 1918, this is the story of a boy of ten who copes with the illness of his mother and his sister during the influenza epidemic of 1918. His father and brother are at the front, so there's only Theodore to take care of his kin. The war ends, father comes home, and Theodore is surprised when his parents talk about him as though he were a hero. Heroes were "Over There," fighting—but readers learn that there were heroes over here too. What Theodore does is believable. His story has pace and flow despite its brevity, and it gives a vivid picture of the depredations of the "Spanish flu." Like Zibby Oneal's *A Long Way to Go* , this is an entry in the "Once Upon America" series, brief stories designed to introduce to younger readers the concept that ordinary people and the events of their lives are as much a part of history as wars or rulers or explorers.

574   **Kudlinski**, Kathleen V. *Juliette Gordon Low: America's First Girl Scout;* illus. by Sheila Hamanaka. Viking, 1988. ISBN 0-670-82208-6. 64p. (Women of Our Time). $10.95.

3-5   Although there are traces of adulatory writing, the author has—as she did in her biography of Rachel Carson—done a good job of pulling together facts about her subject, providing information about Low's role as founder of the Girl Scout movement as well as giving a picture of her as a person, and noting, in the closing pages, how the research was done. The author's note is as simply written as the book itself, and is equally brief and clear. Kudlinski shows how a child of wealth became a post-Civil War Southern belle, a socialite who was expected to be nothing but decorative and gentle, then a childless widow whose energy and affection for children led her to establish an organization that gave girls the freedom to be active and the chance to be responsible, both unusual opportunities.

575   **Kudlinski**, Kathleen V. *Rachel Carson: Pioneer of Ecology;* illus. by Ted Lewin. Viking Kestrel, 1988. ISBN 0-670-81488-1. 55p. (Women of Our Time). $10.95.

5-7   When different authors contribute to a series of uniform excellence, some credit surely belongs to the series editor. Most, of course, to the author, and here Kudlinski has provided a model of brief biography. The tone is appreciative rather than reverential, the balance between Carson's personal and professional lives is nicely maintained, amd the writing is clear, direct, and informative. A pioneer environmentalist, Carson was also an elegant writer, and her biographer informs readers of both those facts as well as of the subject's integrity. An appended note provides information on Kudlinski's research methods.

576   **Kuklin**, Susan. *Fighting Back: What Some People Are Doing about AIDS;* written and illus. with photographs by Susan Kuklin. Putnam, 1989. ISBN 0-399-21621-9. 110p. $13.95.

7-   While there have been many commendable books for teens about
 *   AIDS, its causes, symptoms and prevention, this is the first one to tell—with candor and detail—what it is like to live with the disease. Susan Kuklin spent nine months working with a team of volunteers from the Gay Men's Health Crisis organization in New York. These volunteers (straight, gay, young and old) are "buddies," helping people with AIDS with shopping, cooking, cleaning, talking and listening. More than anything, one sees from Kuklin's account that there is no strict division between the helpers and the helped (called "clients"); instead, there is reciprocal attention and friendship among people sharing a common concern. Some of the buddies have AIDS themselves; one straight buddy, Kachin, is thinking about having the AIDS test because she wants to have children someday. "Take someone with you when you are tested," says her client Michael. "Don't go alone." Perhaps surprisingly, there is plenty of humor in this book. Manuel wants a wild haircut before he dies, so while his mother wails in dismay, friend Stephen gives him a bright orange Mohawk. Sister Kathleen, a Franciscan nun, gives safe-sex lectures and demonstrations. "Oh, I use a banana. It's the second best model." Stories weave in and out: brave, funny, irritated and angry, sad but never mawkish, and the book closes with Kachin and Michael's inspiring visit to the AIDS quilt on display during the march on Washington for gay and lesbian rights. Kuklin's organization of material is fluid and fluent, her black-and-white photographs give faces to the voices, and, wisely, she lets her subjects speak for themselves. Says one buddy, relieved and surprised that his AIDS test was negative: "My interest in AIDS hasn't changed. I used to think, that's me. Now I look at these young kids and think, why should it be them?" (Note: this book should not be confused with Sabra Holbrook's ill-conceived *Fighting Back: The Struggle for Gay Rights*).

577   **Kuklin**, Susan. *Taking My Cat to the Vet;* written and illus. with photographs by Susan Kuklin. Bradbury, 1988. ISBN 0-02-751233-9. 32p. $12.95.

2-3   In a companion to *Taking My Dog to the Vet*, young Ben tells readers about taking his cat Willa, adopted as a kitten from the A.S.P.C.A., to the veterinarian for a standard checkup. The vet, a woman, explains her way through the examination, testing Willa's eyes and ears, taking her temperature, trimming her nails, and giving her shots. The dialogue rarely strains to be informative, and the large color photographs are well composed and businesslike. The author/photographer steers clear of sentimentality, gives listeners a preview of procedures that can be intimidating if not scary, and lists suggestions for a successful visit to the vet, including tips for preparation, waiting room, exam room, and return home. Too bad the cat can't read them.

578   Kuklin, Susan. *Thinking Big: The Story of a Young Dwarf;* written and illus. with photographs by Susan Kuklin. Lothrop, 1986. Library ed. ISBN 0-688-05827-2; Trade ed. ISBN 0-688-05826-4. 43p. Library ed. $10.88; Trade ed. $10.25.

2-4   A photodocumentary essay focuses on eight-year-old Jaime Osborn and her family, who belong to Little People of America because Jaime is a dwarf. "Think Big" is the organization's motto. The writing is straightforward, the tone matter-of-fact and candid; the book explains how dwarfs differ from midgets and how Jaime copes with clothes that are too big, chairs that are too high, stairs that are too steep. She's a lively child who faces problems with cheerful honesty, and the account shows how important the support of a loving family is. An epilogue explains the genetic cause and discusses Jaime's physical problems in the past and the future, and possible social problems she may have during the teen years, as most adolescent dwarfs do. This does a good job of providing information simply; it should help readers understand that having a disability doesn't make another child different in any but a physical sense.

579   Kurelek, William. *They Sought a New World: The Story of European Immigration to North America;* written and illus. by William Kurelek; additional text by Margaret S. Engelhart. Tundra, 1985. ISBN 0-88776-172-0. 45p. $14.95.

5-   In a posthumous publication, some of the text and all of the paintings are by the late, great Canadian artist whose work records the courage of immigrants to North America as well as the work they did and the settings in which they labored. Some of the pictures have never before been published; others are from earlier Kurelek books, particularly *The Polish Canadians*. Engelhart's writing is direct and informative; comments by Kurelek are shown in italics. The paintings are vivid and varied, some showing details of people working or if interior scenes, but the most impressive are those outdoor scenes that reflect the wide skies, the changing colors of the seasons, the vastness of the land.

580   Kuskin, Karla. *Jerusalem, Shining Still*; illus. by David Frampton. Harper, 1987. Library ed. ISBN 0-06-023549-7; Trade ed. ISBN 0-06-023548-9. 27p. Library ed. $12.89; Trade ed. $12.95.

3-5   In rhythmic prose that occasionally breaks into verse, Kuskin impresses readers with the age and vicissitudes of a city holy to many religions. Her thematic emphasis of the stones—their construction, destruction, and reconstruction—becomes a symbolic reflection of the comings and goings of conquerers, which she reinforces with a kind of litany. "You have not forgotten that after the Babylonians came from Babylonia, the Greeks came and then the Romans, those worshippers of Gods and omens. Then the Persians came in troops, Moslems followed, groups and groups, the Fatimid Egyptian forces, Seljuk Turks on foot and horses. After that the Crusaders, Saladin and more Molsems, the Mamelukes and the Ottoman Turks all came to stay, for a while, and went away." Frampton's full-color woodcuts have their own rhythmic patterns of linear development—Jerusalem particularly seems to lend itself to this medium. There is one confusing transition from an introductory note on time that seems to direct the reader back to the city's beginning but in fact leads to a description of contemporary Jerusalem. Overall, however, this is a strongly evocative, handsomely illustrated presentation.

581   Kuskin, Karla. *Something Sleeping in the Hall*; written and illus. by Karla Kuskin. Harper, 1985. Library ed. ISBN 0-06-023634-5; Trade ed. ISBN 0-06-023633-7. 62p. (An I Can Read Book.) Library ed. $9.89; Trade ed. $8.95.

2-5 yrs.   There are no titles, no spacing separating a series of poems about animals, only the turns of some pages. The selections are brief, humorous, sometimes whimsical, and all child-centered. They are spaciously laid out and illustrated with three-color drawings that reflect the briskness and humor of the poetry. This collection doesn't have the depth or variety that Kuskin has shown in other collections, but it's just right for the very young child.

582   Kuskin, Karla. *The Dallas Titans Get Ready for Bed*; illus. by Marc Simont. Harper, 1986. Library ed. ISBN 0-06-023563-2; Trade ed. ISBN 0-06-023562-4. 32p. Library ed. $11.89; Trade ed. $11.95.

K-3   Even more fun than the pair's *The Philharmonic Gets Dressed*, this
*   reverses the process, taking the Dallas Titans football team off the field, into the locker room and shower, and finally home to bed. As forty-five players undress, Kuskin and Simont reveal an enormous amount of information about the game and gear, providing at the same time a sophisticated counting book: "Ten men wear silky gloves. These make it easier to hold onto the ball with sweaty hands. Four of them wear just one glove. Twelve of the gloves land on the floor. One

flies into a laundry bin. Three are lost forever." Several small dramas
are also going on, and readers can get involved in looking for Number
Fifty-Three Zelinka's little brother, and the coach's lucky hat. Kuskin's
text throughout is a poetic, energetic romp, and Simon's robust
pictures of the big, round players (in the shower they look like "small
wet whales") and the glorious upheaval of the locker room are a
perfect match.

583   Lacey, Elizabeth. *The Complete Frog: A Guide for the Very Young
Naturalist*; illus. by Christopher Santoro. Lothrop, 1989. Library ed.
ISBN 0-688-08018-9; Trade ed. ISBN 0-688-08017-0. 72p. Library ed.
$11.88; Trade ed. $11.95.

4-6
 *   The title hints at the gentle humor and stylistic flair that distinguish
this top-flight science writing. The text conveys an astonishing amount
of information with easy but never off-hand informality: "the list of
things a frog will eat is very long. Longer still is the list of things that
will eat frogs." She encourages observation: "one of the things you
notice first about a frog is that pair of big eyes on top of its head, one at
each side. This may look odd to you, but it is very useful to the frog."
She addresses readers with an awareness of their limitations ("for
those of us who do not have an x-ray machine handy . . .") but never
diminishes the information with tonal condescension on the subjects
of anatomy, adaptations to habitat, or characteristics: "sometimes it
may 'play dead,' which is not playing at all, for when severely frightened a frog can 'faint' into a state where it looks quite dead." The
respect for creature comfort is obvious, including warnings not to
handle a frog with insect repellent-covered hands because of
chemical damage to its skin; the list of rules "gives the animal its best
chance to survive the adventure of having met you." There are also
practical tips: "Never pursue a frog into the water. It will head for the
deepest place, and you have no way of knowing just how deep that
may be or what else is out there. If you are dealing with a frog in a big
puddle, it may try to hide by burrowing into the soft bottom. If you go
after it you are going to get terribly muddy. You may not mind, but
whoever does your laundry may be annoyed." From far-out Guinness-
type facts such as the size contrast of African Goliath frogs (over 30",
more than 7 pounds) and Cuban arrow frogs (less than 1/8" long at
hatching from its parent's single egg) to a feel for the marvels of
"frogness" and its place in myth and history, Lacey relates environmental phenomena to the lives of children: "the future of both [frogs
and the natural world] depends on your continuing curiosity as well as
your continuing care." The book has been quietly but lovingly
designed, mostly with abundant, careful black-and-white drawings but
with one section including color to convey the unusual markings of
"odd fellows." In a period of nonfiction marked by photographic

displays that sometimes dwarf textual content, this is an intelligently balanced book.

584   **Laird**, Christa. *Shadow of the Wall*. Greenwillow, 1990. ISBN 0-688-09336-1. 144p. $12.95.

6-9   An inevitably heartbreaking book about the last days of the Warsaw Ghetto focuses on the experiences of Misha, living with his two sisters in Janusz Korczak's orphanage. The disintegration of living conditions is apparent as Misha's foraging activities become futile in sustaining his tubercular mother, who dies soon after her baby is smuggled across the wall to a gentile family. Misha watches his remaining sister marched away by the Nazis to a death camp on August 6, 1942, soon after he joins the partisan resistance, which effects his escape from the ghetto through a sewer. This is a smoothly written and gripping World War II novel, with the historical figures well integrated into a fictional cast of characters. Although there's an occasional slip in point of view from Misha to Korczak, and the doctor is presented unreservedly as a saint, Laird's realization of both personalities commands the reader's attention and carries the plot beyond purposive research to the realm of anguished experience. A postscript provides factual background on Korczak, and an acknowledgment suggests several biographies. The story itself serves as bearable context for any young person exploring the important question of how the Holocaust could have happened.

585   **Laird**, Elizabeth. *The Road to Bethlehem: An Ethiopian Nativity*. Henry Holt, 1987. ISBN 0-8050-0539-0. 32p. illus. $12.95.

2-4   Adapted from Ethiopian nativity stories and illustrated with paintings from 18th-century illuminated manuscripts, this will serve as an art history resource as well as a Christmas book. The text weaves familiar New Testament motifs with popular legends and miracles into a cohesive narrative. When Mary escapes to Egypt with the baby Jesus, she cures many illnesses: "The dumb spoke, the lame ran, the deaf heard and the blind could see." The radiant paintings project much of the book's impact and are more vividly reproduced than those in Laird's book about St. Tekla Haymanot in *The Miracle Child: A Story from Ethiopia*. Each picture, captioned with helpful commentary, is intense in color and beautifully balanced with rhythmic shapes and traditional patterns.

586   **Langstaff**, John, comp. *What a Morning!: The Christmas Story in Black Spirituals* by John Langstaff and John Andrew Ross; illus. by Ashley Bryan. McElderry, 1987. ISBN 0-689-50422-5. 24p. $12.95.

4-8 yrs.   A series of five Black spirituals, alternating with illustrated Bible verses, unfolds the story of Jesus' birth: "My Lord, What a Morning";

"Mary Had a Baby"; "Go, Tell It On the Mountain"; "Sister Mary Had-a But One Child"; and "Behold That Star." The music for each song includes piano and guitar accompaniments, and Langstaff has added a note about spirituals, with suggestions for singing or playing the songs. Bryan's paintings of a Black nativity feature bold, almost glaring color contrasts and geometric designs with African motifs in clothing and setting. The art sometimes seems crowded, but this is a striking production that will prove a standby for adults working with children during Christmas celebrations.

587   **Langton**, Jane, ad. *The Hedgehog Boy: A Latvian Folktale;* illus. by Ilse Plume. Harper, 1985. Library ed. ISBN 0-06-023697-3; Trade ed. ISBN 0-06-023696-5. 38p. Library ed. $11.89; Trade ed. $11.95.

K-3   Soft and bright, paintings in the European folk tradition, romantic pictures with geometric borders, illustrate a tale that combines two familiar motifs: the animal-mate, and the child that is magically given to a childless couple. Here the child proves to be prickly-skinned (not depicted in the illustrations) and he demands the king's youngest daughter as payment for showing the monarch the way home. On their wedding night the princess sees that her groom has taken off a prickly coat of fur, burns it, and nurses back to health the husband who is now a handsome young man. Langton tells the story with a sense of drama, a sense of humor, and a fine narrative flow.

588   **Larrick**, Nancy, comp. *Cats Are Cats;* illus. by Ed Young. Philomel, 1988. ISBN 0-399-21517-4. 80p. $17.95.

4-6   With twice as many selections as appeared in Livingston's *Cat Poems* and only a few cases of duplication ("The Open Door" by Elizabeth Coatsworth, "Cat" by Eleanor Farjeon, "The Song of the Jellicles" by T.S. Eliot, and "The Cat Heard the Cat-Bird" by John Ciardi), this anthology is a worthwhile investment for ever-ready fans of the feline. Where Trina Schart Hyman's illustrations for the earlier book were humorously literal, Ed Young's are suggestive dark shapes on brown paper. The effect is of one of images shadowing the 42 poems, which include favorites such as Karla Kuskin, Eve Merriam, Lilian Moore, and Valerie Worth, along with others of renown in children's literature. This is a solid selection with striking art, the latter especially notable for varied textures and perspectives that catch the reader by surprise as often as do the verbal nuances.

589   **Larrick**, Nancy, comp. *Mice Are Nice;* illus. by Ed Young. Philomel, 1990. ISBN 0-399-21495-X. 48p. $15.95.

4-6   Moving down the food chain from *Cats Are Cats*, Larrick and Young here showcase twenty-six poems featuring the lowly mouse. Poets represented are generally familiar names with proven child appeal—

John Ciardi, Valerie Worth, A. A. Milne, and so forth—and the well-chosen poems range from those contemplating mice ("Mice/ Find places/ In places"), to those through which mice merely scurry ("Calico Ban/ The Little Mice ran,/ To be ready in time for tea"), to nursery rhymes ("Six little mice sat down to spin"). Young's illustrations, soft pastel and charcoal in a range of warm browns (on white paper this time), extend as well as illustrate the poems, conveying the mouse's delicate charm (although cats appear with enlivening frequency) in a way that may soften sternly practical readers as well as delight those enamored of small creatures.

590   Lasker, Joe. *A Tournament of Knights*; written and illus. by Joe Lasker. Crowell, 1986. Library ed. ISBN 0-690-04542-5; Trade ed. ISBN 0-690-04541-7. 32p. Library ed. $12.89; Trade ed. $12.95.

1-3   In a book as well-illustrated as his *Merry Ever After: The Story of Two Medieval Weddings* but of more general interest to children, Lasker describes a medieval tournament, from the pronouncement and tent raisings, to the gathering of knights and testing of noble-born in melee and joust. Lasker makes it clear that these duels were violent and costly—often the loser became a prisoner who had to ransom his horse, arms, and armor, perhaps even land. The story here is of a young lord who must defend his father's barony against an experienced knight errant; in the end, the older man loses because of the sun's heating his suit of armor as much as his young opponent's skill. The story is heavily weighted as a vehicle for information, but it serves its purpose, and the watercolor paintings are bright-hued and action-packed. An apt companion to Aliki's *Medieval Feast*, this gives brief but vivid insight into an imagination stirring aspect of history.

591   Lasky, Kathryn. *Pageant*. Four Winds , 1986. ISBN 0-02-751720-9. 221p. $12.95.

8-12   In this complex portrayal of an upper-middle class Indianapolis family, Lasky has returned to the sure voice she found in *The Night Journey*. Simply but cleverly constructed around four years of the Jewish protagonist's experience in a conservative, private high school, the novel begins each of its sections with a scene from rehearsals for an annual Christmas pageant that Sarah Benjamin sees from her view as a principal-appointed "shepherd" slumbering with a few other dark-haired renegades like herself. Tumbling out of these increasingly ridiculous situations are school parodies, successfully constructed and extended jokes, mini- and maxi-crises, rich dialogues, and the drama of a loving nuclear family subjected to the pressures of the sixties, along with the more perennial stress of growing up and/or older. Only the ending, despite its evocation of the immediacy with which most Americans felt Kennedy's assassination, betrays some impatience on the author's part, as she compresses her heroine's resolution and telescopes her future. The balance of the book is toward wit, vivid development, and characterization equally piercing of adolescents and adults. Because she has preferred the particular to the general— even unto the frustration of explaining one's father's work to a blind date if one's father is a proctologist—Lasky has given us a clear sighting on the New Frontier decade.

592   Lasky, Kathryn. *Dinosaur Dig;* illus. with photographs by Christopher G. Knight. Morrow, 1990. Library ed. ISBN 0-688-08575-X; Trade ed. ISBN 0-688-08574-1. 64p. Library ed. $13.88; Trade ed. $13.95.

5-7   A full-color photodocumentary takes young readers to the Montana Badlands for a fossil hunt with paleontologist Keith Rigby. Lasky and Knight bring their own children along on this educational jaunt, and the discomforts of camping in a windstorm and hiking in 106-degree weather become as clearly apparent as the excitement of digging up *Triceratops* bones from the Cretaceous Period. There are plenty of scientific facts here, but the main emphasis is on various aspects of an exploratory expedition. With its personal, detailed approach, this is a primetime book for family sharing or kicking off field trips.

593   Lauber, Patricia. *The News About Dinosaurs.* Bradbury, 1989. ISBN 0-02-754520-2. 48p. illus. $14.95.

3-5   A new angle on presenting information about dinosaurs is getting harder to conceive as more books feed into the maw of children's bottomless appetites for the subject. Here Lauber's emphasis is on discoveries that have dispelled traditional misconceptions such as the idea that dinosaurs resembled reptiles in living alone (many banded together in herds, packs, or pairs) or in not caring for their young (at least some dinosaurs guarded nests of eggs and babies). The text explains ("the news is . . . ") the study of footprints and bones as showing that dinosaurs walked upright easily, that some traveled with their young encircled by adults, that birds developed from dinosaurs, and that a collision with meteorites, as much as a cooling earth, may have accounted for the creatures' extinction. Abundant full-color illustrations, many by paleontologically trained artists, suggest models of various species' appearance and behavior. A pronunciation guide begins the book, and an index ends it. More informal in tone than Sattler's *Tyrannosaurus Rex and Its Kin,* this focuses on science as a historical and ongoing investigation.

594   Lauber, Patricia. *Tales Mummies Tell.* Crowell, 1985. Library ed. ISBN 0-690-04389-0; Trade ed. ISBN 0-690-04388-0. 118p. Library ed. $11.89; Trade ed. $11.95.

4-7   Although not a lengthy text, this is more comprehensive than most
books about mummies, since it deals with more kinds of mummification than that practiced by the Egyptians, the subject of most
books. Lauber describes the various ways, intentional or accidental,
that animals and human beings have become mummies, and she
discusses the various ways (carbon-14 dating, x-rays, analysis of body
tissue and stomach contents) that scientists use to establish facts
about the individual or the culture or changes over the centuries.
Clearly written and well-organized, this is an informative and
eminently readable text.

595   **Lauber**, Patricia. *Volcano: The Eruption and Healing of Mount St.
Helens.* Bradbury, 1986. ISBN 0-02-754500-8. 60p. illus. with
photographs. $14.95.

4-7   As dynamic as it is informative, this recounts the sequence of
*   developments in Mount St. Helens' eruption with a smoothly
energetic style that makes the facts flow cohesively. Even more
important to the intelligent conception of the book is Lauber's
devotion of half the space to the ecological recovery of plant and
animal life in an area that appeared totally decimated. Color
photographs of the highest quality, along with key diagrams and
maps, are a major part of the book's impact. The balance of informational details and larger scientific concepts marks this as an
exceptional sample of natural history narrative.

596   **Lauber,** Patricia. *Voyagers from Space: Meteors and Meteorites;* illus.
by Mike Eagle and with photographs. Crowell, 1989. Library ed. ISBN
0-690-04634-0; Trade ed. ISBN 0-690-04632-4. 74p. Library ed. $14.89;
Trade ed. $14.95.

4-7   Capably organized, written, and illustrated with color photographs and
diagrams, this describes the formation and orbit of meteroids, as well
as their collision with Earth and other planets. Lauber's explanation of
the meteorite theory of dinosaur extinction exemplifies her clarity of
style, and there are other intriguing mysteries described here, too,
including the Tunguska Event of 1908, when an explosion over
northern Asia gutted an entire forest. This is an immensely complex
subject, and young readers could have used a glossary to keep straight
the distinctions between meteors, meteorites, meteoroids, asteroids,
comets, and other galactic goodies. They're all clearly defined in the
text, however, so this is a quibble about an otherwise effective
presentation. With a list of six juvenile books suggested for further
reading, an index, and a spaciously designed format.

597   **Lawlor**, Laurie. *Daniel Boone;* illus. by Bert Dodson and with
photographs. Whitman, 1989. ISBN 0-8075-1462-4. 160p. $10.50.

5-9   Relying mainly on primary sources such as the letters and documents
*   collected by nineteenth-century Boone scholar Lyman Draper, Lawlor
         has written a riveting account of an American folk hero. This is a case
         in which the real story is more interesting than the cultural myth, and
         the author has taken advantage of the adventure in Boone's life to
         detail a vivid characterization. Lawlor is so enthusiastic about her
         subject that she often extends an account with footnotes, which are
         thoughtfully included at the bottom of each page for impatient young
         readers and which often include intriguing historical vignettes (the
         tale behind the term "Quaker," for instance) as well as explanations of
         terms and sources. The cruelty of the war between settlers and Indians
         is unflinchingly exposed. Boone's first son was tortured to death by
         Shawnee, as witnessed by a slave who escaped the attack; another son
         was killed in battle, a daughter kidnapped, and Boone himself often
         captured or nearly killed. The author takes care to remind readers of
         concurrent atrocities committed by whites against Indians. In fact, the
         text begins by openly addressing the problem: "Daniel Boone would
         not wish to be remembered as a rip-roaring Indian fighter. Upon
         reading a particularly bloody acount of his life, he once complained,
         'This book represents me as a wonderful man who killed a lot of
         Indians. I don't believe the one has much to do with the other.'"
         Financially plagued with bad luck, self-destructively restless,
         affectionate but often neglectful of his long-suffering wife (she bore
         one child to Boone's brother, who took care of her during one of
         Boone's twenty-month absences), Boone nevertheless emerges, on
         balance, as a man whose physical and moral stature, augmented by
         an irrepressible sense of humor, made him memorable in the eyes of
         Indians as well as whites. With a chronology, bibliography, index, and
         gallery of historical pictures along with black-and-white drawings
         throughout the book, this is as solidly researched and dynamic as
         children's biography should be.

598   **Lawlor**, Laurie. *Second-Grade Dog*; illus. by Gioia Fiammenghi.
         Whitman, 1990. ISBN 0-8075-7280-2. 40p. $12.95.

5-8 yrs. One of those happy hits with built-in child appeal, this is homely
         fantasy about a lonely dog that decides to attend school for the
         company it might provide. Treated royally by his middle-aged owners,
         Bones nevertheless tires of tearing up toilet paper, so he disguises
         himself in shirt, shorts, sneakers, and backpack and joins the morning
         student crowd. Bones is as successful in the classroom as he is on the
         playground until a finicky fire marshal observes that he's a dog and
         sends him home—accompanied by a troop of rebellious classmates
         who promise to visit him after school next day. Exuberant pencil and
         paint illustrations cartoon the action with compositional flair, extend-
         ing the spoof on grown-ups in general and officials in particular with
         colorful aplomb.

599   **Lawrence**, Louise. *Children of the Dust*; Harper, 1985. Library ed.
ISBN 0-06-023739-2. Trade ed. ISBN 0-06-023738-4. 192p. Library ed.
$12.89; Trade ed. $12.50.

7-10   In a story about an England that has suffered multiple atom bomb
attacks, Lawrence envisions, with acid clarity, what life will be like for
bomb victims who survive the blast but eventually die from its effect,
and for the succeeding generations who may have inherited genetic
mutation. The novel is divided into three parts: in the first, Sarah sees
all of the members of her family die save a small sister, Catherine,
whom she takes to a safe house before going back to face her own
death; Catherine is a mature woman living in a rebuilt rural
community in the second part of the book, and she meets a young
half-sister (their father, away from home at the time of the bombing,
had been living in an underground military establishment and had--
being sure that none of his family had survived--remarried); in the
third part, the son of that younger sister comes back to the farm
settlement from the underground base that has been dependent on
technology and that has failed, while the outdoor community has
thrived. This third generation of the family, Simon, is horrified that
most of the young people he meets are white-eyed and covered with a
fine furry down--and then he realizes that they are strong and capable,
the hope of the new world, while he is the weakling and the misfit. A
gripping story, this has pace and contrast, a strong story line, a smooth
meshing of realistic base and fantasy projections.

600   **Lawson**, Don. *The Abraham Lincoln Brigade: Americans Fighting
Fascism in the Spanish Civil War*. Crowell, 1989. Library ed. ISBN 0-
690-04699-5; Trade ed. ISBN 0-690-04697-9. 160p. illus. with
photographs. Library ed. $11.89; Trade ed. $11.95.

7-10   Lawson gives good background material about Spain's role in the
European community, its decline as a sea power, the loss of colonial
lands that contributed to the establishment of a republican
government, and the subsequent seizure of military and political
power by General Franco. Comparatively few young people today
know the details of the military involvement in behalf of the Loyalists
(against Franco's Rebels and the Fascist countries that gave him
massive support) by volunteers from the United States. Called the
Abraham Lincoln Brigade, many of these young men—and some
women—saw the war as a rehearsal for a second world war; they were
aware that there was no support at home because the U.S.
government was suspicious of the help the Loyalists got from the
U.S.S.R. For some readers, there may be too-detailed accounts of
individual battles, but Lawson does convey the idealism, the courage,
the desperation of brigade members. He describes some of their
leaders, particularly Captain Bob Merriman; he makes it clear that

there were other international brigades who served in the war that was won by Franco and that led to the establishment of a fascist government in Spain. Lots of action, lots of drama, lots of history. Lawson is a careful researcher, a capable writer, and an observer who strives for impartiality. A closing note suggests other sources of information, including several adult books about the Spanish Civil War.

601   Lawson, John. *If Pigs Could Fly*. Houghton, 1989. ISBN 0-395-50928-9. 136p. $13.95.

6-9   Once upon a time, John Lawson wrote two subtle, fanciful, evocative books: *You Better Come Home with Me* and *The Spring Rider*. Now, after a twenty-year silence, he has produced another engaging story, this time a very funny piece set at the time of the War of 1812. Readers may believe historical details at their own risk; it is highly improbable, for example, that a Scottish regiment was defeated because bees attacked the men under their kilts. The hero, Morgan James, is a Billy Budd type who is so innocent and modest that he doesn't even understand that his lady love is inviting his advances. There are some historical characters and some invented ones (a feisty girl of ten will appeal to readers) and brisk action and an effervescent style in this highly original story.

602   Le Guin, Ursula K. *Catwings*; illus. by S. D. Schindler. Orchard/Watts, 1988. Library ed. ISBN 0-531-08359-4; Trade ed. ISBN 0-531-05759-3. 40p. Library ed. $10.99; Trade ed. $10.95.

3-5
*   A more unlikely premise than four cat characters with wings could not be found, so Le Guin's developing it into a credible and even capti- vating fantasy deserves all the more credit. Thelma, Roger, James, and Harriet have been well brought up. Their mother can only speculate on *why* they were born with wings, but she takes care of them as best she can in a bad neighborhood and bids them fly when the time comes. Their adventurous flight eventually lands them safely with two country children who feed them and vow to protect them with secrecy. Le Guin's adroit writing style, the well-observed feline detail, the thematic concern for natural victims of human environment, and the gentle humor make this a prime choice for reading aloud, although one would not want children to miss the fine-line hatch drawings that further project the satisfying sense of reality.

603   Le Guin, Ursula K. *Catwings Return*; illus. by S. D. Schindler. Orchard, 1989. Library ed. ISBN 0-531-08403-5; Trade ed. ISBN 0-531-05803-4. 49p. Library ed. $10.99; Trade ed. $10.95.

4-6   Although the startling ingenuity of winged felines is necessarily diminished by a second appearance, this is still a story that qualifies as heartwarming without becoming maudlin. Secure in their barnloft with access through the pigeonholes, two of the four cats in *Catwings* decide to visit their mother, Mrs. Jane, in the city. They find the old neighborhood under attack by wrecking balls and barely rescue Mrs. Jane's last kitten, winged and black, before saying good-bye to their aging mother, who has been adopted by a benefactor. Schindler's pen-and-wash drawings are as precisely delicate as Le Guin's writing style. A neatly formatted book that will appeal mightily to cat (and series) lovers.

604   **Le Guin**, Ursula K. *Tehanu: The Last Book of Earthsea*.
Karl/Atheneum, 1990. ISBN 0-689-31595-3. 226p. $15.95.

6-10   In spite of references to *The Tombs of Atuan* and other episodes in Le Guin's high fantasy series, the last book stands on its own with the development of a new heroine. The hope of the future lies in Tehanu, a child traumatized by abuse, deformed by fire, and saved by an aging Tenar's loving care. This is Tenar's story, too, and she is reunited with Ged in spite of his lost power and of threats from sorcerers hostile to women. Male misuse of power is an overt theme, and the villains here are vicious and unremitting in their misogynous violence. Since wizardry is on the way out—there's no archmage to replace Ged—it's not clear how Tehanu will develop her defensive powers unless she can count on timely appearances by the dragon Kalessin, a magnificent character but a deus ex machina nonetheless. Readers who have thrived on the Earthsea chronicles will no doubt extend this happy ending with explanations of their own shaping. A life-or-death plot and strong realization of the main cast sustain the book, despite representational secondary figures and occasional theorizing, for the ultimate effect of a solidly imagined world.

605   **Lee**, Dennis. *Jelly Belly*; illus. by Juan Wijngaard.
Bedrick/Blackie/Harper, 1985. Trade ed. ISBN 0-911745-94-7; Paper ed. ISBN 0-87226-001-1. 60p. Trade ed. $12.95; Paper ed. $7.95.

2-5 yrs.   Softly colored paintings, occasionally touched with the sort of precision that is reminiscent of Pene du Bois, but more often rounded or misty, illustrate the rhymes of one of Canada's leading poets for children. Most of the selections are lilting, breezy, brief, and comic. A few are lyric, a few seem to mimic Mother Goose verses, and a few— including the title poem—are just a bit gross. There are rhymes that are just right for games or rope-skipping; there are some Canadian references, but they are nicely worked in so that children in the United States can enjoy them (chiefly place names) for their sound. And there are some fingerplay rhymes for infants. A refreshing collection, much of which may be enjoyed by independent readers in the primary grades.

606   **Lerner,** Carol. *Dumb Cane and Daffodils: Poisonous Plants in the House and Garden;* written and illus. by Carol Lerner. Morrow, 1990. Library ed. ISBN 0-688-08796-5; Trade ed. ISBN 0-688-08791-4. 32p. Library ed. $13.88; Trade ed. $13.95.

4-6   Like her companion volume *Moonseed and Mistletoe: A Book of Poisonous Plants,* this overview of common shrubs, climbers, vegetables, and decorative plants with poisonous properties is handsomely illustrated. Lerner's detailed botanical drawings and paintings are the real highlight of the book, though descriptions of the plants and explanations of their effects on humans, especially children and house pets, are capably written. Young readers will be surprised to find some of our most attractive garden flowers— narcissus and lily-of-the-valley among them—included as troublemakers, along with common house plants such as philodendron: "Their leaves—and sometimes other plant parts as well—contain sharp crystals. If the plant is chewed or eaten, these crystals cut into the mouth and throat like hundreds of burning spears. The tongue, mouth, and throat swell, sometimes so badly that it becomes impossible to breathe." This will leave kids with a healthy respect for knowing what flora to look at and leave alone.

607   **Lerner,** Carol. *Moonseed and Mistletoe: A Book of Poisonous Wild Plants;* written and illus. by Carol Lerner. Morrow, 1988. Library ed. ISBN 0-688-07308-5; Trade ed. ISBN 0-688-07307-7. 28p. Library ed. $12.88; Trade ed. $12.95.

4-6
*   A book that will intrigue children as well as benefit them, this describes and illustrates various types of poisonous plants: those poisonous to the skin; others with poisonous berries, leaves, flowers, or roots; some poisonous bushes and trees. The text is an interesting mixture of description, instruction, and commentary. The gummy juice of poison ivy, for instance, "is so strong that the amount on a pinhead can give a rash to five hundred people. And it has a long life: scientists got skin rashes from touching a dry plant sample that was one hundred years old." The book is handsomely formatted, with each page framed in a green design and illustrated with either black-and-white detail drawings or meticulous full-page paintings of the specimens discussed, which include hemlock, mountain laurel, mistletoe, and many others.

608   **Lester,** Julius, ad. *How Many Spots Does a Leopard Have?: and Other Tales;* illus. by David Shannon. Scholastic, 1989. ISBN 0-590-41973-0. 80p. $13.95.

4-6   "I have fitted the story to my mouth and tongue," says Lester in an author's note, but he takes care to disclose what changes he has made and what sources he has used in selecting these twelve uncommon stories. Most are African—from the Efik-Ibibio, Xosa, Basuto, Fan, Mende, Hausa, Masai, and Ngoni peoples—and a number are pourquoi tales or myths. Two are Jewish, and one combines variants from African and Jewish lore. Lester is practised at adaptation, respecting core elements while rejuvenating details with his own unobtrusive but distinctive style. Storytellers will consider this a valuable resource, and independent young readers will find the text accessible as well. Shannon's deep-toned paintings are powerfully imaginative, poignant to match the tone of "The Woman and the Tree Children," humorous for "Tug-of-War," scary for "The Monster Who Swallowed Everything," mythic for "Why the Sun and Moon Live in the Sky," full of motion for "Why Dogs Chase Cats" and "Why Monkeys Live in Trees," surrealistic for "What Is The Most Important Part of the Body?" Overall, the book is a strong foil for the classic European fairy tale collections that are flooding the market.

609   **Levin**, Betty. *Brother Moose*. Greenwillow, 1990. ISBN 0-688-09266-7. 224p. $12.95.

6-8   Although an appended author's note indicates that this historical novel is set late in the nineteenth century, readers will gather clues from period details rather than the provision of a date. However, clues are amply provided amply, and information about the farming out of homeless children (in the note) serves as substitute for the provision of reference sources. Two such children, capable Nell and retarded Louisa, are, through a chain of circumstances, taken in charge by Joe, a Native American, and his grandson Peter. Together they travel from Canada to Maine and face the natural dangers of the wilderness so that Nell can reach a foster mother who, she hopes, will also take Louisa in. There are moments of contrivance, and there is some uneven pacing, but the combination of the vivid descriptions of the arduous journey, the protective compassion that Nell and Joe feel for Louisa, the development of friendship between Nell and Peter, and above all the depiction of Joe (a man whose charity, common sense, and sensitivity should make readers forgive, as Nell does, the fact that he had killed a man who was responsible for his son's death) as a believably heroic figure, outweigh the minor flaws.

610   **Levine**, Ellen. *I Hate English!*; illus. by Steve Björkman. Scholastic, 1989. ISBN 0-590-42305-3. 32p. $12.95.

2-3   The author, who has served on the board of directors of Manhattan's Chinatown Planning Council, shows quite clearly how a newcomer from Hong Kong resents and resists using the English language. As do most children, Mei Mei picks up a second language quickly and can understand English. She just doesn't want to use it—until a friendly, understanding teacher leads her, through laughter, to acceptance. A bit pat, perhaps, but the tone is light, the telling pleasantly styled, the line-and-wash pictures animated (although the faces are not well drawn), the solution believable, and the ending nicely nonpartisan: "And to this day Mei Mei talks in Chinese and English whenever she wants."

611   **Levinson,** Nancy Smiler. *Christopher Columbus: Voyager to the Unknown.* Lodestar, 1990. ISBN 0-525-67292-3. 118p. illus. with photographs. $15.95.

5-9   Almost every schoolchild knows that Columbus "discovered" America. Few know anything about his three later voyages to the New World, that he was sent back to Spain in chains after being found unfit to run the new colony, or that he was marooned on Jamaica for over a year during his final voyage. Levinson's highly readable account provides a sympathetic but balanced view of the explorer: though he was a great navigator, Columbus was a poor governor, and he never abandoned his belief that he had reached the East Indies. Levinson also presents the darker side of history, pointing out that Columbus departed for America on the same day that the last Jews were expelled from Spain and that he was in some ways responsible for the beginning of slavery in the New World. Historical imprints, maps, and occasional excerpts from Columbus' log and letters provide a sense of immediacy: "From sunset to daybreak [we] labored much with the wind and the very high sea and tempest." The book contains an index but no footnotes. Included are a chronology of events and the full text of several historical documents, such as the ship's lists of the *Pinta,* the *Nina,* and the *Santa Maria.* The location of Columbus' first landing in the New World and that of his final resting place are both still unknown; by discussing these and other controversies, Levinson shows us that history is not just a series of dates and places, but an ongoing investigation.

612   **Levinson,** Nancy Smiler. *Clara and the Bookwagon;* illus. by Carolyn Croll. Harper, 1988. Library ed. ISBN 0-06-023838-0; Trade ed. ISBN 0-06-023837-2. 64p. (I Can Read). Library ed. $10.89; Trade ed. $9.95.

1-3   This is one of those books you want to put in every six-year-old's hands—personable, easy-to-read historical fiction about a period when books were hard to get and reading was a privilege. The oldest of three children, Clara works alongside her parents. "There were no schools for farm children" (here a date would have been helpful, though it's provided in the afterword as 1905). On a rare trip to town, she looks longingly at the general store's "book station" but is forbidden by her father: "Books are for rich people. Farm people like us do not have time to read." Finally he is persuaded otherwise by a pioneer librarian in the first travelling bookwagon, and Clara gets her chance at learning to read. The story builds naturally in several episodes, and the style is contained without becoming contrived. The full-color illustrations are somewhat doll-like, with the flavor more of a Pennsylvania Dutch than a Maryland setting, but the rounded shapes and blended tones are comfortable to look at. A good follow-up to Carol Purdy's *Least of All.*

613   **Levinson**, Riki. *Watch the Stars Come Out*; illus. by Diane Goode. Dutton, 1985. ISBN 0-525-44205-7. 28p. $12.95.

5-7 yrs.   Fine-textured, color-pencil art evokes times past and remembered here by a grandmother telling the story of her own mother's immigration to America, with only her 10-year-old brother to watch over her after an old lady supposed to do so dies on the boat. After a strenuous 23-day voyage and a disconcerting health inspection, the two children are met by their family for a joyous reunion, trolley ride, and homecoming, whereupon Mama washes them, feeds them, and tucks them in for the first time after their long separation. Although the story within a story framework is somewhat confusing, the narrative is simple and understated. The illustrations harbor intense hues filtered by a subdued blending of lines and framed by soft, buff paper. Especially appropriate as accompaniment to a book like Rylant's *When I Was Young in the Mountains* (also illustrated by Goode) for discussions of family background and ethnic heritage.

614   **Levitin**, Sonia. *The Return.* Atheneum, 1987. ISBN 0-689-31309-8. 213p. $12.95.

6-9   In a docunovel of a Jewish Ethiopian family's flight to Israel, Levitin focuses on an orphan, Desta, whose older brother, Joas, persuades her to leave the village where hunger and political recriminations constantly threaten their lives. Joas is killed almost immediately, and Desta must safeguard her younger sister across the Ethiopian-Sudan border, where another in their party, Dan (Desta's betrothed), is shot. The horrors of starvation and disease in the Sudanese refugee camp and the dangers of Operation Moses, a secret Israeli airlift of Ethiopian Jews (called Falashas in their country), end for Desta when she arrives safely in Gan Tikva and is reunited, somewhat unrealistically, with Dan. The information packed in this culture-within-a-culture saga sometimes overwhelms the character development; the cast seems ultimately to tell the story of a whole people. Still, that story is a moving one, and thus the book leaves a strong impression. One hopes that any sequel will show some of the difficulties that Ethiopian Jews have had in adjusting to resettlement in what they perceived as the Promised Land.

615   **Levoy**, Myron. *Pictures of Adam*. Harper, 1986. Library ed. ISBN 0-06-
       023829-1; Trade ed. ISBN 0-06-023828-3. 218p. Library ed. $12.89; Trade
       ed. $12.95.

6-9   When Adam was transferred from a class for special students to Lisa's
       science class, she felt sorry for him, since other people made it clear
       that they thought he was weird. They don't even know what Lisa finds
       out when she makes overtures of friendship: Adam insists that he has
       come from another planet, even showing Lisa a buried "space
       capsule." This touching and unusual story is told by Lisa, who falls in
       love with Adam, gets to know his mother and sister when she takes
       pictures of their ramshackle home for a photojournalism contest, and
       is upset both by her mother's dislike of Adam and by some of his
       behavior, which seems borderline psychotic. Knowing that he has
       been a victim of severe abuse (from a long-gone father) Lisa is torn
       between anger at some antisocial behavior, exasperation at Adam's
       insistence that he is not of Earth, not his mother's child, and her strong
       love and sympathy. Lisa finally forces Adam to admit the truth. The
       story ends on a realistically hopeful note; it has the same poignant
       quality as the author's *Alan and Naomi*. Lisa's voice is convincing in
       this percipient and touching story that has depth of characterization
       and competent writing style.

616   **Lewin**, Ted. *Tiger Trek*; written and illus. by Ted Lewin. Macmillan,
       1990. ISBN 0-02-757381-8. 34p. $14.95.

5-8 yrs. In a misty early-morning scene, several trekkers mounted on
       elephants set out through an Indian jungle, observing wild dogs,
       monkeys, deer, and a tiger hunting to feed her cubs. Lewin's dignified
       watercolors blend the big cat into undergrowth and even into the
       shadowy "ruins of an ancient palace where a maharajah once lived."
       Beside a lake, as a peacock screams dramatically across a double
       spread, the tiger kills a chital fawn—"in a few days she must hunt
       again. She may not be so lucky the next time, but today she and her
       family will eat." Lewin wisely relies on the inherent natural drama of
       the scenes, underplaying each with camera-like objectivity while
       focusing the compositions with subtle painterly perspective. This is an
       expedition on which few children could expect to go; they'll relish the
       experience of a picture book safari.

617   **Lewis**, J. Patrick. *A Hippopotamusn't*; illus. by Victoria Chess. Dial,
       1990. Library ed. ISBN 0-8037-0519-0; Trade ed. ISBN 0-8037-0518-2.
       40p. Trade ed. $12.95; Library ed. $12.89.

4-8 yrs. Playful, clever, and, above all, freshly worded, Lewis' thirty-five rhymes
   *   would be a read-aloud bonanza even without the artistic wit of Chess'
       picture-book setting. The subjects are animals' and birds' distinctive
       features, including "that redheaded woodpecker,/ redwooded

headpecker,/ rockheaded woodpoker's head." The flamingo poem is shaped into a figure like the bird's, and the camel poem offers an unforgettable way to distinguish the one-humped Dromedary from the two-humped Bactrian (just turn over the initial letters). There's a wolf that howls the moon home, robins that play tug-of-worm, a culture-defying vulture that eats with his toes, and the title hippopotamusn't flossing his hippopotamolars. This is all grist for the illustrator's signature mischief; Chess has a knack for depicting silly, beady-eyed creatures, humans included, as in the picture of an old woman watched by her chop-licking cat as she consumes her oyster stew: "There's a squishy/ Fishy critter/ Swishing in my/ Oyster stew./ Tell me, Oyster,/ Mister? Sister?/ Girl or Boyster?/ Which are you?" Bon appetit.

618   **Lewis**, Richard, ad. *In the Night, Still Dark*; illus. by Ed Young. Atheneum, 1988. ISBN 0-689-31310-1. 32p. $13.95.

2-4   The poetic text is an abridgement of a Hawaiian creation chant. It moves from the void of nothingness ("Darkness of the sun, darkness of the night, nothing but night") through the birth of plant and animal forms to the emergence of the first people. "Here on the ocean's edge, Here in the damp forest, Here in the cold mountains, People spread over the land. People were here, And so it was: DAY." All of the pages have minimal text and, against dark backgrounds, swirling impressionistic forms of living things. When people come, the dark night is broken by a rosy light on the horizon. The last double-page spread shows the dawn. A lovely fragment for reader alone, reader-aloud, or storyteller, this will surely appeal to a larger audience than the grades 2-4 for whom the combination of format and vocabulary makes it most appropriate; it can be read aloud to younger children and studied by adults interested in comparative mythology. A closing note from Lewis indicates that the book was based on a shorter version of the whole chant (The Kumulipo) that appeared in Maria Leach's *In the Beginning: Creation Myths Around the World*.

619   **Lexau**, Joan M. *Don't Be My Valentine*; illus. by Syd Hoff. Harper, 1985. Library ed. ISBN 0-06-023873-9; Trade ed. ISBN 0-06-023872-0. 60p. (An I Can Read Book) Library ed. $9.89; Trade ed. $8.95.

1-2   With a holiday motif, a classroom setting, an interracial cast, and a bit more plot than is found in most books for beginning independent readers, this should have marked audience appeal. Sam is irritated by the repeated efforts of Amy Lou (who sits at the desk in front of him) to give unwanted help and advice. Since the class is engaged in making valentines, Sam makes a cutting remark in the one for Amy Lou. The consequent confusion when he mislays the valentine and it gets delivered to the teacher is mildly amusing, and primary-grade readers should recognize the realism of the easily flammable relationships within the group dynamics of the classroom.

620   **Lindbergh**, Reeve. *Johnny Appleseed*; illus. by Kathy Jakobsen. Joy Street/Little, 1990. ISBN 0-316-52618-5. 36p. $14.95.

5-8 yrs.   Elaborately detailed folk paintings provide a rich complement to Lindbergh's plain-spoken poem about Johnny Appleseed: "The man who planted apple trees/ Once stood here on this land,/ A sack of seeds upon his back/ A Bible in his hand." Told from the point of view of Hannah, a little frontier girl whose family was visited by the gentle sower, the poem has the sturdy rhythm of sampler verse and is appropriately bordered by quilt squares containing small vignettes from Johnny Appleseed's travels. The poem ends with a now elderly Hannah, "her own trees grown so tall," meeting him once more: "He said farewell and traveled on/ And did not come again,/ But in this orchard, sharp and sweet,/ His apples still remain." Dominated by alluring blue tones, Jakobsen's idealized paintings of colonial America are cozy and balanced, with scenes of home, woodland, and river that appear both comfortable and exotic. The pictures are filled with small particulars that will hold a child's eye, and the steady measures of the verse invite reading aloud and along. A useful historical note about John Chapman, the real Johnny Appleseed, is appended.

621   **Lindgren**, Barbro. *The Wild Baby Gets a Puppy*; ad. by Jack Prelutsky; illus. by Eva Eriksson. Greenwillow, 1988. Library ed. ISBN 0-688-06712-3; Trade ed. ISBN 0-688-06711-5. 28p. Library ed. $11.88; Trade ed. $11.95.

K-2   A third book about the adventurous baby of *The Wild Baby* and *The Wild Baby Goes to Sea* has come from Sweden, fantastically conceived by Lindgren, illustrated with bravado and an echoing humor by Eriksson, and adapted by Prelutsky into bouncing, lilting verse. Here Baby Ben is disappointed at getting a toy dog when he'd been expecting a real one for his birthday, but in the magic of the night the puppy, Rags, comes alive—and the two, joined by Ben's toys, go off on a flight that is varied and joyful. Pure nonsense and great fun.

622   **Lisle**, Janet Taylor. *Sirens and Spies*. Bradbury, 1985. ISBN 0-02-759150-6. 169p. $11.95.

7-10   Elsie is thirteen, her sister Mary two years older; both have been violin students, and Mary cannot understand why Elsie (much more talented than any other of Miss Fitch's pupils) had quit so abruptly and sold her instrument. Romantic, ebullient, mysterious, the elder Miss Fitch is injured in her home, seemingly the victim of an intruder. Is it the alcoholic Jimmy Dee who secretly listens each night when Miss Fitch plays her violin? If so, why? And why is Elsie so angry at the teacher she used to love? In a deft unfolding of laminated revelations, Mary and Elsie learn about the past of Miss Fitch when she returns from the hospital; it is a dramatic and tragic story, and it brings into sharp focus the differences in the two sisters' approach to the relationship and their different degrees of understanding. This is a truly sophisticated book, not in the superficial sense, not because Miss Fitch proves to have been the mother of a child born in France during the war and fathered by a German soldier, but because of the compassion and the tolerance evoked in two adolescent girls and perhaps echoed by readers.

623   **Lisle**, Janet Taylor. *Afternoon of the Elves*. Orchard, 1989. Library ed. ISBN 0-531-08437-X; Trade ed. ISBN 0-531-05837-92. 122p. Library ed. $12.99; Trade ed. $12.95.

5-7   Nine-year-old Hillary has a happy home, all the material possessions she wants, and plenty of friends at school. Eleven-year-old Sara-Kate is an outcast, thin, poorly dressed, with failing grades, a decrepit house, and a weedy yard adjoining Hillary's neat garden. But Sara-Kate has an elf village, and with it she hooks Hillary into a friendship that thrives on elf stories but suffers from Sara-Kate's stormy moods and prickly pride. It is for Hillary to discover that Sara-Kate alone is caring for a mother who is mentally ill, penniless, and unable to provide the most basic physical or emotional necessities. It is Sara-Kate who teaches Hillary to "go slowly and quietly, and look deep." This is a carefully developed story focused on two childen who influence each other in realistic, subtle stages. The ending is ambiguous: whether Sara-Kate will be crushed or cared for by the authorities who separate her from her mother, whether Hillary was being trusted or used by the older girl, are both unanswered questions. What's certain is that a petted child has seen a wilder side, that a potentially smug individual—and perhaps the young reader as well—has been sensitized to life beneath surface appearances.

624   **Little**, Jean. *Hey World, Here I Am!*; illus. by Sue Truesdell. Harper, 1989. Library ed. ISBN 0-06-024006-7; Trade ed. ISBN 0-06-023989-1. 89p. Library ed. $10.89; Trade ed. $10.95.

4-7   Nice. Very nice. The voice is that of Kate (*Look Through My Window* and *Kate*, which introduced the girl whose exploration of self was both sensible and tender) and thoughts and memories are expressed in a series of poems and brief anecdotes. They are wonderfully vivid and each is complete in itself, but what is most impressive about them is that they do two things simultaneously (and do them both well): they reveal Kate as an individual and they speak for all adolescents who are sensible and sensitive and intelligent. Scratchy line and wash pictures, black and white, have the humor of cartoon art.

625   Little, Jean. *Little by Little: A Writer's Education.* Viking, 1988. ISBN 0-670-81649-3. 233p. illus. with photographs. $11.95

5-9   Written with direct simplicity, candid about small childhood sins, and touching in the descriptions of being an outsider, of struggling as a young writer, and of the loving relationship with her friend-and-critic father, this autobiography describes Jean Little's life (up to the time of her first accepted children's book) with the integrity and momentum that have characterized her fiction. This should appeal to readers because of its unsentimental forthrightness about the author's visual handicap, because of her triumph over this handicap, and because of the fact that her books are loved.

626   Little, Jean. *Lost and Found;* illus. by Leoung O'Young. Viking, 1986. ISBN 0-670-80835-0. 82p. $9.95.

3-5   Basically, this is an old plot: child meets/loves/loses a pet . . . and finds another to love. Lucy, who has just moved to a new town, finds comfort in the stray dog that she keeps; with a new friend who likes to play detective, Lucy tries to find the dog's former owners—hoping they'll never turn up. They do. The story, which ends with Lucy choosing another dog from an animal shelter, is quiet rather than dramatic, but it is given depth and warmth by the direct style and affectionate aura that are found in so many of Jean Little's books; simple structurally, the story engages the sympathy of the reader.

627   Little, Jean. *Mama's Going to Buy You a Mockingbird.* Viking, 1985. ISBN 0-670-80346-4. 213p. $11.95.

5-8   One of Canada's most distinguished writers of children's books here presents a moving story about the adjustment that Jeremy and his mother and sister make to his young father's death. The operation had told them it was cancer, and the progress of the disease had been swift; the pain of his loss was so intense that Jeremy decided it was better to forget than remember Dad. If he could. In the course of his bereavement, Jeremy reaches out to make a new friend and finds that it helps; he also comes to realize that his grief will be assuaged if he shares it and if he does what he can to console his mother. The story has depth and insight, and it ends on a convincingly positive note. Little has good command of the elements of her writing, so that there is a smooth narrative flow and enough balance of subplots to highlight, rather than compete with, the thrust of the story line.

628   Lively, Penelope. *A House Inside Out;* illus. by David Parkins. Dutton, 1987. ISBN 0-525-44332-0. 127p. $12.95.

4-6   With crisp wit Lively has written 11 short stories about the "five humans, thirty-nine animals and several thousand insects"that inhabit the Dixons' house at 54 Pavilion Road. The main characters are imaginatively developed: Willie, the white terrier; Sam, a foolhardy mouse; Nat, an uncommon pillbug; and a pugilistic spider. The humans serve as amusing props. Point of view accounts for much of the humor, both in style ("'It's not me that's underfoot,' Willie would grumble, 'it's you who are overdog'") and in plot. Willie is so childlike in his susceptibility to trouble that young readers will hold their breaths with suspense and sympathy as he digs for a nonexistent bone that a hostile cat has assured him is buried in the forbidden rose garden. Lively's postscript inviting children to consider the inside-out of their own houses is irresistible on top of such inventive storytelling.

629   **Lively**, Penelope. *Uninvited Ghosts and Other Stories;* illus. by John Lawrence. Dutton, 1985. ISBN 0-525-44165-4. 120p. $10.95.

4-6
*
Nobody, but nobody does a better job of combining ludicrous situations with a bland, straightforward style than Penelope Lively. Whether it's an extraterrestrial visitor or a cloyingly chummy family of ghosts, the fantasy characters nestle into their realistic matrices. The eight tales in this collection, three of which have been previously published, are varied in subject and concept but united in being written with polish, humor, and grace and in having sound structure and a lively pace.

630   **Livingston**, Myra Cohn, comp. *If the Owl Calls Again: A Collection of Owl Poems;* illus. by Antonio Frasconi. McElderry, 1990. ISBN 0-689-50501-9. 114p. $13.95.

6-10
*
Lest you shy away from what appears to be a specialized topic, come and read. Owls have attracted great poets (of greatly varied cultures), whose range of emotion in capturing these birds with words will surprise many a reader. Livingston's introduction evokes the owl's mythical resonance, and her list of contents forms a rhythmic incantation of its own—"Owls in the Light, Owls in Flight, Owls to Delight, Owls of Night, Owls to Fright." Frasconi's arresting black-and-white woodcuts further the total effect of an elegant piece of bookmaking. However, it is the poems themselves that lure one on, from haunting Native American chants ("The owl feathers sing in the air") to funny verses by David McCord (especially "The Hitchhiker"), X. J. Kennedy, John Gardner, Jack Prelutsky, Lewis Carroll, and even Sir Walter Scott, who rarely cracked a smile in print. Some of the poems are, of course, hushed, including Livingston's own ("If you seek answers/ you will find them/ trembling/ on the ground"), or summon the mouse's point of view ("where the smallest letters/ cower in the dark" as Esbensen writes). The poets range from Shakespeare to the little-known but sharp-sighted Clarice Short. Whether the selections

are conceptually sophisticated, as is the piece from Julia Fields'
"Alabama" or simple folk rhymes, they are accessible in style. The
subject lends itself to sonorous effects, and if there seem a few too
many *to-wit-to-woos* on a straight readthrough, browsers won't be
struck by it. In fact, this is made to order for reading aloud; teachers
take note, and start with the translation of Robert Desnos' playful
lines, all ending in long *u* sounds.

631   **Livingston**, Myra Cohn, comp. *Thanksgiving Poems;* illus. by Stephen
Gammell. Holiday House, 1985. ISBN 0-8234-0570-2. 28p. $12.95.

K-3   In this holiday anthology there are two Native American songs of
praise and a few other traditional selections; like earlier books
(*Christmas Poems, Easter Poems*) in a distinguished compiler's series,
this consists chiefly of selections written for the book by notable
contemporary writers of poetry for children: McCord, Merriam,
Holman, Kennedy, Starbird, and others. The two-color illustrations
have a soft, melting quality that is given contrast by precision of line
on some pages, so that the pictures have a range in technique and
mood that matches the poems they illustrate.

632   **Livingston**, Myra Cohn. *There Was a Place and Other Poems.*
McElderry, 1988. ISBN 0-689-50464-0. 40p. $9.95.

4-6   Thirty-two poems expand on the theme of families faced with death,
divorce, or remarriage. The viewpoint is consistently that of the child,
which is the strength of the collection. The poetics are as simple as the
voice, fleeting rhymed narratives of changing houses, conflicts
between mothers and fathers, empty places at the table, the occasional triumph of a kind new stepparent, yearning for better times
past or future. A few poems project more complex form and imagery;
indeed, the underlying meaning of "Mt. St. Helens," as it fits into the
emotional context of the collection, may escape readers entirely. In
general, however, this reads like a cadenced collective diary of
contemporary children saddened by loss.

633   **Livingston**, Myra Cohn. *Up in the Air;* illus. by Leonard Everett
Fisher. Holiday House, 1989. ISBN 0-8234-0736-5. 32p. $14.95.

5-8 yrs.   This sonorous celebration of airplane travel will enhance any child's
*   excitement over flying and make the adult reader rethink what may
have become routine. In quick-paced tetrameter of three rhyming
lines per page, the passenger prepares ("Good-bye to the airport!
Good-bye to the ground!/ My seatbelt is buckled tightly around./ The
airplane is full of a roaring sound") and soars ("Off to the blue of the
highest sky,/ A thin curl of clouds passes us by./ Ruffled clouds
chasing us, up we fly"). An exuberant, lilting narrative poem simply
structured within the framework of a journey, this describes changing

"pictures" out the window and the final thump-down ("Faster and faster and faster we race./ Good-bye to sky and good-bye to space./ Hello to Earth in another place"). In suggesting rather than defining patterns of landscape, Fisher's characteristically expressionistic paintings extend the poetic imagery without intruding on it. Younger than the author and artist's *Sky Songs* series, this is a poetic prerequisite for a child's first flight.

634   **Livingston**, Myra Cohn. *Worlds I Know and Other Poems;* illus. by Tim Arnold. Atheneum, 1985. ISBN 0-689-50332-6. 59p. $12.95.

4-6   Small black-and-white drawings, nicely placed and nicely expressive of the poems they illustrate, are a modest addition to the appeal of a new collection by a noted anthologist and poet for children. Not every poem contains sharp imagery or vivid phrasing, but many do; Livingston has firm control of form, but it is her ability to see the world from a child's viewpoint and to make the familiar seem fresh that gives her work its distinction. Here there is often a focus on the past, especially on the extended family, that makes the continuity of family life a dominant theme.

635   **Liyi**, He, tr. *The Spring of Butterflies and Other Folktales of China's Minority Peoples;* ed. by Neil Philip; illus. by Pan Aiqing and Li Zhao. Lothrop, 1986. ISBN 0-688-06192-3. 144p. $13.00.

5-9   Prefatory material gives information about He Liyi, a Chinese English teacher whose translations of folktales of minority peoples living in China have been capably adapted by Philip, who explains that he left untouched some flavorful phrasing. The book was first published in England; here and there thare are idioms that obtrude: "straight as a die", for example, or "a real out-and-out dragon." On the whole, the stories (from such ethnic groups as Thai, Naxi, Tibetan, and Kazak) flow smoothly, and they are highly moral and very romantic, reflecting such familiar concepts as punishment for a greedy sibling who envies a brother's wealth, or a magical favor done by an animal which has been kindly treated, or such concepts as are stressed in Asian cultures: filial duty and reverence for old people. Notes on sources give information about the tales, the tellers, and occasionally about other versions.

636   **Lloyd**, David, ad. *The Ridiculous Story of Gammer Gurton's Needle;* illus. by Charlotte Voake. Potter, 1987. ISBN 0-517-56513-7. 48p. $13.95.

K-3   Comic wash drawings have a lighter line than Margot Zemach's but have the same kind of robust peasant humor, and very appropriate it is for the adaptation of one of the early classics of English theater. The lively pictures echo the biff-bam pratfall humor of a farce in which a clever rogue, Diccon the Bedlam, sets Gammer Gurton and several other neighbors to brawling and shouting about a lost (or stolen, Diccon says) needle while he himself takes advantage of the turmoil to eat and drink their provender. Hallowed by time, perhaps, but this has the pop culture appeal of a comic book.

637   **Lobel**, Anita. *Alison's Zinnia*; written and illus. by Anita Lobel. Greenwillow, 1990. Library ed. ISBN 0-688-08866-X; Trade ed. ISBN 0-688-08865-1. 32p. Library ed. $12.88; Trade ed. $14.95.

4-6 yrs.
*
An unusual alphabet book incorporates reinforcement of individual letters into a dazzling display of floral painting as Lobel links girls' names, flowers, and verbs in a chain of floral gifts. Each page has a painting, below which is a line of type, below which is a large letter and a smaller strip of painting across the bottom of the page. The text reads: "Alison acquired an Amaryllis for Beryl. Beryl bought a Begonia for Crystal. Crystal cut a Chrysanthemum for Dawn. Dawn dug a Daffodil for Emily. . . ." The alphabet-set will enjoy the continuous-loop ending, as Zena zeroes in on a Zinnia for Alison.

638   **Lobel**, Arnold. *Whiskers and Rhymes;* written and illus. by Arnold Lobel. Greenwillow, 1985. Library ed. ISBN 0-688-03836-0; Trade ed. ISBN 0-688-03835-2. 48p. Library ed. $12.88; Trade ed. $13.00.

3-6 yrs.
Lobel's rhymes for the nursery set are lilting, brief, comic, often nonsensical, occasionally related to a Mother Goose rhyme ("Orson Porson/Pudding and pie. . ." or "My London Bridge/Has just one task/It has to stand/That's all I ask. . ."). They have that fun-to-say/easy-to-memorize quality that creates a devoted read-aloud audience. There are clever pictures, softly tinted and drawn with panache, on every page, and the layout of illustrations and poems on the pages has been done to make both communications maximally effective.

639   **Lomas Garza**, Carmen. *Family Pictures/Cuadros de Familia*; written by Carmen Lomas Garza and Harriet Rohmer; Spanish text by Rosalma Zubizarreta; illus. by Carmen Lomas Garza. Children's Book Press, 1990. ISBN 0-89239-050-6. 32p. $12.95.

5-8 yrs.
Not a picture book, this is instead an album of paintings accompanied by explanatory captions. Drawn from the artist's memories of growing up in a small Texas town, the paintings are naïvely styled, straight-forward depictions of what life was like in her Hispanic community: celebrating a birthday, picking cactus, making tamales, going to church. This would be nostalgic but for the specificity of the images and memories: "This is my grandparents' backyard. My grandmother is killing a chicken for dinner. My grandfather is in the chicken coop trying to catch another chicken. Later, my family will sit down to eat Sunday dinner—chicken soup." The painting shows grandmother

calmly breaking a chicken's neck while one surprised child spills his snowcone. Another shows people playing "cakewalk," a musical-chairs game "to raise money to send Mexican Americans to the university." The paintings are filled with small patterns and details, with each leaf and blade of grass sharply defined. The flat perspective iconographically places the activities on a two-dimensional plane that gives each scene a formalized dignity. This is an honest portrayal of a culture rarely seen in children's books, and (more important as far as children are concerned) every page offers a lot to look at. The text is in both English and Spanish.

640   **Lowry, Lois.** *Anastasia Has the Answers.* Houghton, 1986. ISBN 0-395-41795-3. 123p. $12.95.

4-7   "Anastasia Krupnik, 13, aspiring journalist," despairs of ever mastering rope-climbing, a worry compounded by her crush on glamorous gym teacher Ms. Willoughby. Her continued attempts and setbacks (even her *mother* can climb a rope, for pete's sake) provide a casual but suspenseful narrative line which still allows plenty of room for other antics. There's matchmaking for next-door neighbor Gertrude Stein (*and* Ms. Willoughby, *and* friend Daphne's mother—all with the same man, her recently widowed Uncle George). There are problems with her English teacher—"The test on *Johnny Tremain* was grim." Anastasia hates *Johnny Tremain,* why can't they study *Gone With the Wind*? Sam is again an embarrassment, as he insists on playing funeral for Uncle George: "He laid the G.I. Joe on the kitchen floor, covered it with a paper napkin, and smoothed it with his hand. 'Goodbye, dead Aunt Rose,' Sam said." While some books in this series suffer from occasional desultory plotting and too-broad humor (although they are always entertaining), this one recaptures the freshness and heart of the earliest volumes, and Sam is rapidly assuming the position of the most off-the-wall scene-stealer since Ramona.

641   **Lowry, Lois.** *Anastasia's Chosen Career.* Houghton, 1987. ISBN 0-395-42506-9. 142p. $12.95.

5-8   Anastasia's at it again, having evolved a plan to remedy her thirteen-year-old lack of grace and poise. The plan has three parts: 1) Anastasia will get her composition on "my chosen career" written during winter vacation 2) by interviewing a bookstore owner in downtown Boston 3) while satisfying her real purpose of taking a modeling course at Studio Charmante. Naturally, Anastasia does all three, in addition to making a lively new friend who turns out to have the modeling potential that Anastasia realizes will never be her own lot. Along the way, there are numerous funny scenes involving the odd assortment of teenagers who turn up in response to the modeling school ad, and a more serious episode involving one of them. Actually, Lowry cannot get Anastasia on a bus without some hilarious bits, so the seedy modeling school offers lots of possibilities along with its natural appeal to the target audience of readers. Anastasia may not have glamor, but she's never at a loss for presence.

642   **Lowry**, Lois. *Rabble Starkey*. Houghton, 1987. ISBN 0-395-43607-9. 192p. $12.95.

5-8   Parable Starkey and her mother, Sweet Hosanna, move into the Bigelows' house to take charge of the children after Mrs. Bigelow's hospitalization for mental illness. That suits Rabble just fine; Veronica Bigelow is her best friend in sixth grade, little Gunther Bigelow is her favorite kid, and Mr. Bigelow is both wise and generous. In fact Rabble begins to feel this is the family she never had, until Mrs. Bigelow's recovery forces her to confront and accept change as courageously as Sweet-Ho has in taking on a college education to become a teacher. This is a novel complicated by many factors. Mrs. Bigelow's nervous breakdown is wrenchingly depicted in a scene in which she tries first to nurse and then to baptize her four-year-old son, nearly drowning him in a stream. Rabble's memories of the grandmother who raised her and who has recently died are poignant. Sweet-Ho, married and pregnant in eighth grade and deserted shortly thereafter, is subtly characterized as a loving parent (as is Mr. Bigelow) but also as an independent, growing person. Rabble and Veronica's relationships with each other, with the cranky old neighbor they try to help, and with a delinquent boy down the street are well developed in a smooth first-person narrative that quietly takes on class as well as individual differences. In the end, Lowry has managed to portray a large, diverse cast by carefully and consistently focusing the point of view as one of a maturing observer.

643   **Lowry**, Lois. *Switcharound*. Houghton, 1985. ISBN 0-395-39536-4. 118p. $10.95.

4-6   Whether or not readers remember siblings J.P. and Caroline (*The One Hundredth Thing About Caroline*), they should enjoy this story of the united front the two achieve when faced with what seems to them not just adversity but catastrophe. Their father, remarried and now also the father of a boy of six, Poochie, and twin female infants, has decided after some years of ignoring them, to have J.P. and Caroline visit for the summer. They don't want to leave New York to come to Des Moines and they certainly don't want to spend the summer as Dad has planned: babysitting for Caroline (babies bore her) while her stepmother takes a course, and baseball coaching of Poochie's team for J.P., who hates baseball. There is a bit too convenient an all-ends-tied final chapter, but the strong characterization, the humorous style and yeasty dialogue, and the change and development (including some shaking of stereotypical sex roles) in the two main characters give the story both substance and appeal.

644   **Lowry**, Lois. *Your Move, J. P.* Houghton, 1990. ISBN 0-395-53639-1. [108p]. 122p. $13.95.

5-8   "James Priestley Tate, age twelve, had an overwhelming urge for the first time in his life, to use deodorant" in this third book about J. P. and his sister Caroline. J. P.'s sudden fascination with personal hygiene is sparked by his crush on Angela Galsworthy, newly arrived at his private school from London, England. Suddenly, J. P. finds chess (his former passion) a bore, starts walking into walls, tripping over his own feet, and confiding in a total stranger. It *must* be love! Anxious to sustain Angela's interest, J. P. tells her that he is suffering from triple framosis, a rare but fatal disease. Angela believes him and J. P. is stuck with his lie. Lowry's brand of comic realism combines a keen sense of the absurd with a sympathetic understanding of early adolescent angst. This fast-paced plot contains only one implausible element: J. P.'s conversation with a stranger in the park who acts as his conscience and sounding board. J. P.'s ardency makes him seem a cousin to Byars' Bingo Brown. Like Byars, Lowry articulates her hapless hero's thoughts in words more witty than he could imagine (or appreciate); at the same time she keeps the narrative and dialogue spontaneous, natural, and humorous.

645   **Lyttle**, Richard B. *Il Duce: The Rise and Fall of Benito Mussolini.* Atheneum, 1987. ISBN 0-689-31213-X. $13.95.

7-
*   A masterfully written biography, this has the absorbing quality of fiction grounded in the meticulous attention to detail required of historical research. In tone, Lyttle has achieved a nonjudgmental approach that allows him (and readers) a close look at a complex character. He lets the political context speak for itself, and a gripping story it tells. In pacing the narrative, the author slows down to an hour-by-hour account during crises in Mussolini's life, and the effect is to intensify the reader's involvement while still providing more relaxed lulls for informational background. This is particularly noticeable during the events leading up to the end of World War II and Mussolini's death, but important incidents during his takeover of the Italian government and his relationship with Hitler are also dramatically presented without compromise of fact. The text is well balanced in presenting the various periods, aspects, and contradictions of Mussolini's life, both personal and political. One could wish for source notes, but in general, the book is an achievement by any standards of biographical writing.

646   **Mabinogion**. *Tales from the Mabinogion;* tr. by Gwyn Thomas and
Kevin Crossley-Holland; illus. by Margaret Jones. Overlook Press,
1985. ISBN 0-87951-978-7. 82p. $14.95.

5-8   A distinguished interpreter of folklore, Crossley-Holland worked with
Gwyn Thomas, professor of Welsh, to produce this new version of the
four major parts, called "Branches," of the larger (eleven) tales that
constitute the Mabinogion, a collection of medieval fantasy tales. The
illustrations, romantic and conventional, are—although not imi-
tative—reminiscent of the grave solidity of Pyle and the gnarled line of
Rackham. One picture shows a nude woman; generally, they are
primly decorous. The four branches (the core of the Mabinogion) are
linked; the translation is fluent, the dialogue nicely balanced between
language easily comprehensible to today's readers, and the mood of
ancient magic that pervades the tales. Fans of such fantasy writers as
Lloyd Alexander and Alan Garner will be prepared for the many
Welsh names; for others, a glossary is provided.

647   **Macaulay**, David. *Black and White;* written and illus. by David
Macaulay. Houghton, 1990. ISBN 0-395-52151-3. 32p. $14.95.

3-5   There *is* something new under the sun, and David Macaulay is just
the person to reveal it. In a book with a strong game element that
invites sustained reader involvement, the title page bears a warning
that begins "This book appears to contain a number of stories that do
not necessarily occur at the same time. Then again . . ." What the
ingenious author/artist has done is to quarter the pages, with each
location assigned a separate story, each illustrated in a different style
and palette. One quarter follows a child's train trip, another shows
people waiting at a small station, a third is about a family in which the
parents are either busy or silly, and the fourth is about some rambling
Holstein cows. Gradually, humorously, the stories overlap—a sophisticated concept, and clever execution.

648   **Macaulay**, David. *The Way Things Work;* written and illus. by David
Macaulay. Houghton, 1988. ISBN 0-395-42857-2. 384p. $24.95.

6-
*   Having explained the major mysteries of architectural history, the
Audacious Author here undertakes to explain everything else. This
giant reference/browsing book is organized into four parts: the
mechanics of movement, harnessing the elements, working with
waves, and electricity and automation. Concluding sections provide
brief background on major discoveries or inventions, plus definitions
of technical terms. With a clarity built by consistently proceeding
from the simple to the complex, Macaulay depicts the principles and
mechanics of machinery. These are frequently injected with diverting
stories about a wooly mammoth, reports reputedly written by an
ancient explorer/inventor who makes ridiculous deductions from

observing the creature's actions and interactions. The stories are neither cute nor distracting but serve to lighten both the condensed factual information and the gravity of scientific assumptions. A lubricant of urbane wit reduces the friction of resisting minds. Readers young and old will find out what they always wondered about the workings of modern technology, from zippers to transmitters. The more sophisticated will pick up the continuous visual jokes—the Mammoth Tabernacle Choir that demonstrates principles of sound waves and music, for instance, or the Trojan Mammoth, an anonymous nuclear gift with chilling implications. The full-color drawings, diagrams, and book design that allows them to energize the pages without overwhelming them amount to a coup of instructive art. When molecular theory, aerodynamics, and the microchip are demonstrated so clearly, it seems unfair to quibble, but there is the occasional gap between knowledgeable writer and ignorant reviewer. One example is the description of inertia, which omits the role momentum plays (if any) in the operation of a potter's wheel. However, in light of what Macaulay has accomplished here, the occasional caveat flickers out. This is a work of mammoth imagination, energy, and humor. It justifies every critic's belief that information and entertainment are not mutually exclusive—good nonfiction is storytelling at its best.

649   **Macaulay,** David. *Why the Chicken Crossed the Road;* written and illus. by David Macaulay. Houghton, 1987. ISBN 0-395-44241-9. 30p. $13.95.

5-8 yrs.
     *

Macaulay romps through the answer to why the chicken crossed the road in a spoof on cause-and-effect disasters. The chicken startles some cows, who stampede over an ancient bridge, which collapses onto a passing train (specifically, the dining car—"Who ordered their beef rare?"), which allows a thief to escape. Further catastrophes lead to the capture of Desperate Dan, which leads to a luncheon honoring the brave young hero, who orders chicken, which is why .... Macaulay's illustrations are thick with paint and humor. He has an eye for cartoon detail: the tuft of a cow's tail parted by a lady's nose, a pair of hoofs and an udder appearing simultaneously through the train ceiling, a cow grabbing a bite of lettuce from a man's fork on her cataclysmic descent. Blocky shapes and strong colors build a solid case for this nonsensical string of incidents. The narrative is sophisticated enough to appeal to the older picture book fans who will get the most out of the derisive pokes. "Left to their own devices, the Anderson twins turned to science and substantially enlarged the bathroom. Stunned by the explosion, Clarella Sweet conducted a surprise inspection of Mel Tooms' garbage truck." This is accompanied by a fireburst that sends an innocent passerby flying into fishheads and orange peels. Whereas the artist's *Baaa* was satire for the special reader or adult, here's fun for all.

650   MacDonald, Suse. *Alphabatics*; illus. by Suse MacDonald. Bradbury, 1987. ISBN 0-02-761520-0. 52p. $15.95.

3-6 yrs.   The illustrator uses big, bold letters and big, bold pictures to achieve the impact of poster art in this inventive alphabet book that reflects her interest in letterforms. On each verso page are the paired upper and lower case letters, then some frames in which the letter changes shape to become a visual foreshadowing of a part of the picture (with label) that is on the recto page. For example, the circle of a Q opens, in four stages, and spreads to echo the wingspread of the quail on the opposite page. An intriguing presentation that may encourage the observer's powers of observation but that does not interfere with the book's function, this is effective and attractive.

651   MacLachlan, Patricia. *The Facts and Fictions of Minna Pratt*. Harper, 1988. Library ed. ISBN 0-06-024117-9; Trade ed. ISBN 0-06-024114-4. 136p. Library ed. $11.89; Trade ed. $11.70.

4-7
 *   Minna is eleven, her beloved brother a year younger; their father is a psychologist, their mother a writer, contentedly disorganized. A devoted member of a string quartet, Minna produces excellent tone on her cello, but has not yet achieved a vibrato. Few writers could do what MacLachlan does: she makes Minna's quest pulse with humor and suspense enough to attract readers who do not share Minna's passion for Mozart, or her devotion to practice sessions for a quartet competition. Smoothly blended into this theme are Minna's concerns about the peculiarities of her parents (especially as they compare to the very proper parents of Lucas, the viola player she loves) and developing tolerance of her own shortcomings. The intellectual and musical atmosphere are not gauged for popular appeal, but the author's style and humor, her lively dialogue, and her wonderfully vivid characters should attract and hold even those readers who have never before considered writing imaginary letters, as Minna does to her hero, Wolfgang Amadeus Mozart. "Dear WA Mozart," one letter begins, "You probably don't know me . . ."

652   MacLachlan, Patricia. *Sarah, Plain and Tall*. Harper, 1985. Library ed. ISBN 0-06-024102-0; Trade ed. ISBN 0-06-024101-2. 58p. Library ed. $8.89; Trade ed. $8.95.

3-5
 *   Anna, the narrator, has been running the family's modest prairie home since her mother died giving birth to Caleb; both of them are excited when their father says he has been corresponding with a woman in Maine who may become his bride. Sarah, who writes of herself as "plain and tall," comes west for a month's trial and the two

children try in every way to make her love them as they instantly love her. So this is a love story, but a most unusual one, and it is told with distinction, in a style that is imbued with lyricism although it is simple prose. The structure is spare and strong, the characters firmly established.

653   Maestro, Betsy. *A More Perfect Union: The Story of Our Constitution;* illus. by Guilio Maestro. Lothrop, 1987. Library ed. ISBN 0-688-06840-5; Trade ed. ISBN 0-688-06839-1. 48p. Library ed. $12.88; Trade ed. $13.00.

2-4   In undertaking the difficult task of simplifying the Consititutional Convention of 1787 into picture-book format, the Maestros have succeeded in producing a smooth, informationally balanced text and some impressive double-page spreads, though the closeup figures are stiff and awkward. Beginning with a map and description of the states' disunity, they focus on the delegates' arrival in Philadelphia, the ensuing debates, the compromises made and principles agreed on, and the finalizing of the document that was ratified the following year. A five-page appendix summarizes the articles of the constitution, names the signers, gives a table of important dates, offers some interesting notes, and lists the amendments. Since Jean Fritz' *Shh! We're Writing the Constitution* is for a slightly older audience, this will be most useful as the earliest introduction available to the Constitution.

654   Maestro, Betsy. *The Story of the Statue of Liberty;* written and illus. by Betsy and Giulio Maestro. Lothrop, 1986. Library ed. ISBN 0-688-05774-8; Trade ed. ISBN 0-688-05773-X. 40p. Library ed. $12.88; Trade ed. $13.00.

5-8 yrs.   Far and away the most attractive of the spate of books celebrating the centennial of the Statue of Liberty, this unfolds the story in a simple, read-aloud text set into panoramic watercolor spreads that are striking enough for use with classes or groups of children. The opening aerial view of Liberty Island encircled with sea and ships makes a breathtaking introduction, and the monumental scale of the statue is clearly conveyed in oversize drawings as the building history progresses, climaxing in a night scene in which the lady is lit up with fireworks. Several concluding pages give additional information: a table of dates, dimensions of the statue, important people in its construction, and notes on repairs. From one flag-centered endpaper to another, this is a well-designed book.

655   Mahy, Margaret. *17 Kings and 42 Elephants;* illus. by Patricia MacCarthy. Dial, 1987. ISBN 0-8037-0458-5. 24p. $10.95.

3-5 yrs.   "Seventeen kings on forty-two elephants/ Going on a journey through a wild wet night,/ Baggy ears like big umbrellaphants,/ Little eyes a-gleaming in the jungle light." Thus begins a musical nonsense rhyme with the combined appeal of rhythmic word play and large-scale watercolor illustrations of a wild animal parade. It's a perfect read-aloud for toddler picture-book sessions, with only two lines of text to each page and with dramatically visible art that features white-outlined shapes against vividly contrasted colors. The effects are patchy close up but striking at a distance. The compositions reflect the fun of the text: in the spread illustrating hippopotami, three are facing viewers and one is—dare we call it—mooning them with its perfectly huge bottom centered by a smallish, dangling tail. A rump . . . I mean, romp.

656   **Mahy**, Margaret. *The Catalogue of the Universe.*
            Atheneum/McElderry, 1986. ISBN 0-689-50391-1. 185p. $11.95.

7-12   Just before her graduation from high school, Angela May acts on her
 *   burning desire to find and confront her father, whom her mother describes as having been the love affair of her life but a married man with family, and therefore inaccessible. What Angela discovers is a hard, cold man who never cared for either her mother or herself except in the stories her mother has fabricated to make her feel wanted. What Angela also finds in the course of her search, however, is deepening friendship with a warm, intelligent classmate, Tycho, whose plain looks are just the opposite of her father's elegance. Despite the title, this abandons the fantasy mode of Mahy's previous work, but not the sensual currents of romance. Angela's relationship with her mother and Tycho's complex family dynamics are sensitively developed. The plot, though lacking the desperate urgency of *The Changeover*, is immediate and well-paced, with an auto accident forming a dramatic climax and with a satisfying resolution in the main characters' affections matured.

657   **Mahy**, Margaret. *The Great Piratical Rumbustification & The
            Librarian and the Robbers*; illus by Quentin Blake. Godine, 1986. ISBN
            0-87923-629-9. 57p. $11.95.

3-6   Mahy seems able to flex her wit at almost any level, from picture book
 *   to young adult novel, and these two middle-grade short stories are no exception. The first introduces the Terrapin family just as the parents, desperate to go out to an important dinner, call the sitting agency and end up with an ex-pirate to take care of their three sons for the evening. ("At last," think the children, "a baby-sitter worthy of us—we deserve him, and he deserves us—what could be fairer than that!") While Mr. and Mrs. Terrapin suffer through an interminable soup course, the pirate is organizing a huge party, which encompasses the entire neighborhood, all the ex-pirates in the city, and, eventually, Mr. and Mrs. Terrapin. The second story is an equally hilarious account of

a band of robbers kidnapping a librarian, who gives them all a case of Raging Measles, converts them to literature, and marries their leader. These are splendid read-alouds, but listeners should not miss Quentin Blake's exuberantly ridiculous, black-and-white cartoons, which tumble across the pages with much the same verve as Mahy's text—a matchless combo of child-like irreverence.

658   Mahy, Margaret. *Jam: A True Story;* illus. by Helen Craig. Atlantic, 1986. ISBN 0-87113-048-3. 24p. $12.95.

4-6 yrs.   As she did so well in *The Boy Who Was Followed Home,* Mahy builds an absurd situation out of the most ordinary details. After Mrs. Castle gets a job as an atomic scientist, her husband proves super-effective at keeping house, so much so that in his spare time he takes to making jam from the plums off their tree. His enthusiasm gets a little out of hand as jam overflows every jar in the house, appears in every conceivable form, meal and snack, makes the whole family fat, and begins to haunt everyone's dreams and fantasies. Although "Mr. Castle's jam proved very useful, for as well as being delicious, it stopped leaks," the family is relieved to see it gone at last . . . just before the first plum of the new season falls ripe to the ground. The spoof on housekeeping, the sex-role reversal, and the sweet theme itself combine for a gay romp that's roundly reflected in the bustling, pen-and-wash pictures. The characters' antics are well cartooned and the colors judiciously dominated by sticky red.

659   Mahy, Margaret. *Memory.* McElderry, 1988. ISBN 0-689-50446-2. 278p. $13.95.

8-12   On the fifth anniversary of his sister Janine's death from a fall, drunken nineteen-year-old Jonny Dart, "swollen with apparitions," is wandering the streets of the city. He meets a bedraggled but charming old woman named Sophie, who seems to mistake him for someone else ("It's lovely to have you here. There's no one quite like one of your own, is there!") and takes him to her home, a decrepit building with an enormous purple water tap affixed to the front, courtesy of Sophie's late husband, a plumber. The house is filled with junk and cats and memories—all belonging and carefully placed, but in the wrong places: cheese in the soap dish, soap in the sugar bowl, "a crazy stumbling contraption made up of strange things fitted together." Almost despite himself, Jonny moves in, helping Sophie to shop and bathe, teasing her about mistaking him for an old beau; sorting through her memories and, in the process, making peace with some of his own. While occasionally thematically overstated and psychologically obvious, this is strong, direct storytelling, told from Jonny's point of view: perceptive but not pompous, with an edge of self-mockery that adds a poignant note to the narrative. Sophie's confusion (revealed to be Alzheimer's disease) is skillfully portrayed, containing its own wit and dignity and "longing to be busy and useful" that becomes clear and moving to Jonny and readers as the story progresses to a warming conclusion.

660   **Manson**, Christopher. *Two Travelers*; written and illus. by Christopher Manson. Holt, 1990. ISBN 0-8050-1214-1. 32p. $14.95.

5-7 yrs.   The two unlikely travelers celebrated here are a Jewish envoy from Charlemagne to the caliph of Baghdad and an elephant sent back as a gift in token of peace. Isaac and Abulabaz are not sure of each other at first, but after crossing an ocean, a desert, and a mountain range, they have become such fast friends that Abulabaz pines in Isaac's absence until Charlemagne makes him the imperial elephant keeper. "The story . . . is mostly true," says an author's note, but the picture-book version does leave a lot of questions dangling. What, for instance, does Abulabaz eat on the trip? Elephants consume 150 to 500 pounds of hay or foliage a day, but there's not a wisp or leaf in sight. The adults here express themselves like children and the elephant thinks like a human, but for all that, the robust color-pencil illus-trations are jolly good fun. Their energetic composition combined with a humorous text and unusual historical setting tips the balance toward broad appeal.

661   **Marek**, Margot. *Different, Not Dumb*; illus. with photographs by Barbara Kirk. Watts, 1985. ISBN 0-531-04722-9. 30p. $8.90.

2-3   Large print, a clear type-face, and plenty of white space make this appropriate for primary grade readers, whether they are reading at grade level or, like the protagonist, experiencing a learning disability. Mike's in second grade and has no trouble with arithmetic but is in the bottom group in reading. Already self-conscious about it, Mike feels even worse when he's sent to a special class in remedial reading. However, the individualized attention and another technique than that used in his regular classroom do the trick. Mike makes progress; he even helps a better reader solve a problem (identifying the word on a box that's fallen off a truck: "Explosives"). The ending is a bit concocted, but the problem is real, the solution believable, the book encouraging to the child who shares Mike's problem, and the facts (a child can be slow though intelligent; children acquire different skills at different rates) illuminating enough to help other children under-stand. The photographs are of excellent quality and seldom seem as though the subjects had posed.

662   **Marie de France**. *Proud Knight, Fair Lady: The Twelve Laïs of Marie de France*; tr. by Naomi Lewis; illus. by Angela Barrett. Viking, 1989. ISBN 0-670-82656-1. 100p. $19.95.

7-   After an introduction to the twelfth-century writer Marie de France, Naomi Lewis delivers graceful prose translations of twelve stories revolving around chivalrous love and fealty. The formal narrative quickly becomes a familiar voice, and the events are laced with fairy tale magic, legendry, and medieval adventure. Lovers tryst, undertake challenges, change shape, die heartbroken, or triumph depending on their destiny and the heart with which they meet it. Junior high and high school readers who have outgrown fairy tales but enjoy Robin McKinley's work will revel in these, and students of the Middle Ages will find in the tales an immediacy of detail that lends perspective on the high culture of the period. The pictures, both full-page and illuminated miniatures, are drawn, colored, and composed with exquisite restraint.

663   **Marino**, Jan. *Eighty-Eight Steps to September*. Little, 1989. ISBN 0-316-54620-8. 154p. $13.95.

5-8
*   Amy has the usual sibling tensions with her brother Robbie, and in the book's opening these center on their love for a puppy that Amy acquires to replace a dog too big for their new home. The focus soon shifts, however, to Robbie's illness—he is diagnosed as having leukemia and taken to the hospital. Amy feels increasingly abandoned as her parents leave her in the charge of an unsym-pathetic babysitter in order to stay with him. What keeps this from being just another tearjerker is the singular voice of the narrator, the authentic details of a family in stress, and the smooth development and natural incorporation of secondary situations. Amy has a deep friendship with an Italian girl. She fights with classmates, is affectionate with a babysitter who "rescues" her, takes loving responsibility for the puppy, and, ultimately, for her brother. A fine balance of the ordinary and the heroic.

664   **Mark**, Jan. *Fun*; illus. by Michael Foreman. Viking, 1988. ISBN 0-670-82457-7. 28p. $11.95.

4-6 yrs.   Line and wash drawings that are simply composed but appealingly animated illustrate a story of parent-child relations and the reversal of stereotypical roles. The story, too, is simply composed and should warm the collective hearts of those members of the read-aloud audience who, like James, patiently endure entertainment devised by adults based on what *they* enjoy. Mom and Dad like being noisy and active. James likes to sit still and watch things. A cloud. A caterpillar. Eventually James learns of a place where he can do things his way and not stop Mom's fun, in a modest but innovative tale that uses exaggeration to make its point—but just enough. A nice pairing of talents here.

665   **Mark**, Jan. *Trouble Half-Way;* illus. by David Parkins. Atheneum, 1986. ISBN 0-689-31210-5. 129p. $11.95.

4-6   Amy is a worrier, and her new stepfather, Richard, had said, "You don't meet trouble half-way, you go and knock on the door . . ." When Mum was called away to help in a family crisis, Amy was left with Richard, with whom she felt uncomfortable; when he insisted that she come with him (he was a van driver and had to go to another part of England), Amy was angry as well as worried. The author adroitly creates a well-paced story out of a familiar situation and a modest journey, and the change and growth in Amy and in her reluctant respect and affection for Richard are both interesting and credible. The structure of the story is stripped, the style and characterization substantial and smooth.

666   **Marrin**, Albert. *Aztecs and Spaniards: Cortes and the Conquest of Mexico.* Atheneum, 1986. ISBN 0-689-31176-1. 212p. $12.95.

7-   As dramatic as fiction but well-grounded in fact, this account of the clash between Aztecs under Montezuma and conquistadors under Cortes gives vivid cultural background on each group, fine portraits of the leaders involved, and a well-organized tour through the action-packed events. Marrin includes telling quotes from observers and writers of the sixteenth century; his own style is readable, even in detailed battle descriptions, and his balanced perspective and respect for each side are clearly an asset. The unfamiliar names have pronunciation guides in parentheses after each one is introduced. A list of books for further reading is appended. An excellent resource for any study of Central American history or in conjunction with research into parallel developments in the U.S.

667   **Marrin**, Albert. *The War for Independence: The Story of the American Revolution.* Atheneum, 1988. ISBN 0-689-31390-X. illus. with photographs. 276p. $15.95.

7-   A spirited and thoughtful account of the American Revolution (next to Vietnam, the country's longest war) bridges the period between the years described in two earlier books by Marrin, *Struggle for a Continent: The French and Indian Wars* and *1812: The War Nobody Won.* Profusely illustrated by prints, paintings, and maps, the text is notable both for its style and its depth. There are many books about the War for Independence; this one links the events to the people who effected (and were affected by) them, so that motivation and causation are smoothly incorporated to heighten narrative impact and to increase readers' understanding—rather than stuff them with names and dates. A sizeable bibliography is provided.

668   **Marshak**, Samuel. *The Pup Grew Up!*; tr. by Richard Pevear; illus. by
Vladimir Radunsky. Holt, 1989. ISBN 0-8050-0952-3. 32p. $13.95.

K-3   First published in the Soviet Union in 1926, this narrative poem has
been capably translated and has been newly illustrated by Radunsky
in a style that was popular at the time of original publication. It's silly
and funny, it takes a poke at officialdom, and it uses repetition in a
way that the read-aloud audience enjoys, usually to the point of
participation. Boarding a train with a list of luggage that begins with a
pan and a divan and concludes with "a tiny Pekingese," a woman
complains at the end of the journey that what she has is a huge Great
Dane. (The officials having noticed that the tiny dog was left behind,
have brought in a stray as substitute.) The owner is aghast; the officials
blandly suggest that the pup grew up. That doesn't make a convincing
end to the story, but it does make an amusing one, and plausibility is
not meant to be the strong point of this picture book, nonsensical
exaggeration is. The pictures are deftly comic, reminiscent of the work
of Miroslav Sasek in the use of line and color, although Radunsky's
paintings are more subtle.

669   **Marshall**, Edward. *Four on the Shore*; illus. by James Marshall. Dial,
1985. Library ed. ISBN 0-8037-0142-X; Trade ed. ISBN 0-8037-0155-1.
46p. Library ed. $8.89; Trade ed. $8.95.

1-2   Stories within a story make this appropriate for the beginning
independent reader because of the brevity of segments; the
vocabulary is undemanding, the print large and set off by ample
space. Three children who find Willie, younger brother of one of them,
an adhesive nuisance, decide to vie in telling stories that will frighten
little Willie when he follows them about. He staunchly declares that
their stories aren't scary, that he can do better—and he does. they
claim they're not scared, but they vehemently reject Willie's offer to
tell another story. The tales (including Willie's) are slight, the appeal
being in the concept rather than the execution of the story line; the
exaggeration and humor of the line and wash drawings add to the
book's potential for popularity.

670   **Marshall**, James. *The Cut-ups Cut Loose*; written and illus. by James
Marshall. Viking Kestrel, 1987. ISBN 0-670-80740-0. 30p. $11.95.

1-3   While he's probably best known for the bland, "what, me worry?"
effrontery of his illustrations, Marshall's ear for the quirks and cliches
of the American language has always been an important contribution
to his peculiar sense for what is funny. Those two, Spud and Joe, "a
couple of *real* cut-ups," are back, and eager for the first day of school,
"the biggest challenge of all." But also returning is the boys' chief
nemesis, school principal Lamar J. Spurgle, and even though Spud
and Joe promise to be on their best behavior "for the rest of their

lives," the cut-ups just can't help themselves. "Unfortunately, some habits are hard to break." Marshall's esay handling of simultaneous deadpan drollery and outrageousness is unique, demonstrated especially well here by the boys' friend, "that nice Mary Frances Hooley," and her benefactress, Sister Aloysius, who takes on Spurgle with practiced ease: "Shame on you." As Mary Frances says, "Nobody messes with Big Al."

671   **Marshall**, James. *Fox Be Nimble*; written and illus. by James Marshall. Dial, 1990. Library ed. ISBN 0-8037-0671-4; Trade ed. ISBN 0-8037-0760-6. 48p. Library ed. $9.89; Trade ed. $9.95.

K-3   Fox be nimble, Fox be quick—but not quick enough to keep from falling over his feet. He does make the TV news by playing rock star (while the kids he's supposed to be babysitting float away on balloons) and he tries to follow them (and gets stranded on a high-diving board). He even absorbs a little bravery from his sister and, best of all, proves himself capable of showing off in style with a cheerleading baton. He is, as usual, one of the liveliest leaders of the easy-to-read pack, and near enough to the foibles of all of us to appeal doubly to children too often confronted with placid little animals at this stage of the reading game. Marshall's full-color illustrations keep up with his characters, an appealingly off-the-cuff cast.

672   **Marshall**, James. *George and Martha Round and Round*; written and illus. by James Marshall. Houghton, 1988. ISBN 0-395-46763-2. 47p. $13.95.

5-8 yrs.   Forever fresh and funny, George and Martha survive five more tests of friendship when he gives her an annoying cuckoo clock or challenges her to use her imagination on an uncomfortable boat ride; when she criticizes his art work, has to sleep with her own scary story, or forgives (but does not forget) a surprise dousing by hose. Marshall's sense of the ridiculous permeates spare watercolor compositions such as Martha's presentation of a picture with only slightly more paint than her own substantial body has been spattered with in the process of creation. And there are always the details: the waterlily on George's head after his spill in the pond neatly parodies the tulip behind Martha's almost nonexistent ear; Martha's goosebumps coordinate with the dots on the patchwork quilt. Reliably engaging of young listeners' or early readers' humor.

673   **Marshall**, James, ad. *The Three Little Pigs*; ad. and illus. by James Marshall. Dial, 1989. Library ed. ISBN 0-8037-0594-8; Trade ed. ISBN 0-8037-0591-3. 32p. Library ed. $11.89; Trade ed. $11.95.

4-6 yrs.   The allure of James Marshall's folktale picture book series lies in his coupling of traditional (well, more or less) texts with off-the-wall cartoon characters that kids can chortle over while nestling secure in the folds of familiar plot. Marshall, who proved he could execute a masterly wolf in *Red Riding Hood* and who has had practice with beady-eyed pigs as well, here produces a brick house of Victorian proportions that properly foils the lean and hungry and not-too-bright villain. This wolf, like the pigs he has eaten, gets consumed in the end. Perhaps the porcine brothers' jovial appearance on stage, across the front and back covers of the book, will convince young listeners that the demise of two of them was all an act or, better yet, a spoof.

674   **Marshall,** James. *Three Up a Tree*; written and illus by James Marshall. Dial, 1986. Library ed. 0-8037-0329-5; Trade ed. 0-8037-0328-7. 43p. (Dial Easy-to-Read). Library ed. $8.89; Trade ed. $8.95.

1-3
*
Marshall is at his best in this funny beginning reader that incorporates the trio familiar from *Three By the Sea*, plus two of his recent favorite characters, a chicken and a fox, *plus* everychild's favorite green monster. These appear variously in a story-within-a-story pattern with ebulliently silly pictures and lines: says a hungry fox sidling up to a disguised hen waiting with her groceries for a bus, "I can smell that you're having chicken tonight." And she, seeking to dissuade him from coming to dinner, explains that she will cook it "in sour chocolate milk with lots of pickles and rotten eggs. . . ." "It sounds delicious," says the fox. A treat for students struggling from one word to the next.

675   **Martin,** Bill. *The Ghost-Eye Tree*; written by Bill Martin and John Archambault; illus. by Ted Rand. Holt, 1985. ISBN 0-03-005632-2. 30p. $11.95.

K-3
*
A top-notch hair-raiser that will do for any old night of the year but will really spike a Halloween story hour. It's poetry, too, the kind that reaches out to grab you. The narrator remembers one autumn eve when his mother asked him and his sister "to take the road/to the end of town/to get a bucket of milk." His problem is dread of a haunted old oak tree. Both his fears and his old hat draw teasing from his big sister, until, lugging their milk home, she sees the oak ghost, too. They both run pellmell home, and, in a touching finale, his sister courageously retrieves the hat he has dropped. This is very real in capturing both the siblings' tit-for-tat talking and childhood terrors in general. The language and sound patterns beg for oral presentation, and the watercolor paintings for group viewing. They give full play to light/dark contrasts, the yellows and white startling against black shapes and deep-blue skies. The focus of the compositions is arresting, too, with faces central to shadowy backgrounds. Evocative for adults and immediate for children.

676   **Martin**, Bill. *Knots on a Counting Rope;* by Bill Martin and John Archambault; illus. by Ted Rand. Henry Holt, 1987. ISBN 0-8050-0571-4. 32p. $12.95.

5-8 yrs.   A dialogue between an old man and his grandson, Boy-Strength-of-Blue-Horses, relates, in chant-like rhythms, the story of the latter's birth on a stormy night, his weakness, his naming after the horses to which he made his first physical response, his growth, and his success at horse racing. Subtly, in the course of the storytelling, readers learn that the boy is blind and that Grandfather has gently guided him to self-sufficiency in crossing "the dark mountains . . . always around us." It is a moving narrative, and the watercolor paintings that build from nighttime shadows to daylight colors echo the boy's development. A last dark scene harkening back to his fear ends with the Grandfather's fire-bright words, "You will never be alone, Boy. My love will always surround you . . . with the strength of blue horses." The southwestern landscapes are vivid, the Native American portraits strong, and the disability perceptively dealt with. This will speak to any child's need for family connection and confidence, and will be especially effective dramatized by two voices reading aloud.

677   **Martin**, C.L.G. *The Dragon Nanny;* illus. by Robert Rayevsky. Macmillan, 1988. ISBN 0-02-762440-4. 29p. $14.95.

K-2   Visually dominated by Rayevsky's drawings of dragon scales and the soft, cool colors given contrast by touches of a rich red, this is an engaging first effort by Martin. Her heroine is a durable, spunky, heart-of-gold Nanny, deemed by the king to be too old to stay on in the royal nursery. Nanny takes on the job of caring for two juvenile dragons. Unable to teach them to breathe fire, she invents a way to simulate that achievement in order to satisfy their mother, the monstrous Dragonia. A surprise ending (but not an illogical one) brings peace and amity to both the dragon family and the royal family. Crisply told and nicely structured.

678   **Martin**, Eva. *Tales of the Far North;* illus. by Laszlo Gal. Dial, 1986. ISBN 0-8037-0319-8. 112p. $12.95.

4-7   Twelve tales, retold from both the French and English traditions of Canadian lore, include variants of several Grimm and Perrault stories, along with a version of "Beauty and the Beast." Although selections such as "The Three Golden Hairs" and "Little Golden Sun and Little Golden Star" will seem familiar, there are new twists in all of them, especially the sense of vast and threatening wilderness areas. One hero figures in three tales, "Ti-Jean and the Unicorn," "Ti-Jean Brings Home the Moon" (a variant of "Jack the Giant-Killer"), and "Ti-Jean and the White Cat." The narrative style is smooth without self-conscious embellishment, the structural elements respected throughout the adaptations. One, "St. Nicholas and the Children," is especially chilling in its depiction of a wicked butcher "who worked with the local giant. The giant hunted and killed game for the butcher to sell in his shop and in return the butcher pickled little children as a delicacy for the giant to eat." Needless to say, it is the villains who get pickled in the end. Laszlo Gal's full-page illustrations create a mythic mini-world for each story, preserving the sense of time past with full-color scenes framed by narrow black-and-white drawings. A lively source for both children and storytellers.

679   **Martin**, Katherine. *Night Riding*. Knopf, 1989. Library ed. ISBN 0-679-90064-0; Trade ed. 0-679-80064-6. 197p. Library ed. $13.99; Trade ed. $12.95.

5-8
*

An ably written, sometimes gripping first novel is vividly set in rural Tennessee, where eleven-year-old Prin must cope with her father's hospitalization for tuberculosis, her mother's unexpected pregnancy, and the resulting family stress and financial strain, not to mention concern about new "white trash" neighbors named Hammond. Mr. Hammond's violence toward his illegitimately pregnant 15-year-old and his sexual threats toward Prin escalate to a climactic scene one night when Prin rides the horses she and her father have cared for together. Except for the archvillain, each character is three-dimensional, with scenes evolving naturally from dynamics of interaction and internal development. The dialogue is subtly tuned and the treatment of incest honestly but delicately handled, always from a young protagonist's viewpoint without didactic intrusion. The fictional details and plot as a whole authentically reflect the customs and values of the 1950s in the conservative south, to which Martin is especially true in depicting the secrecy surrounding unsanctioned or even marital sex.

680   **Martin**, Rafe. *Foolish Rabbit's Big Mistake*; illus. by Ed Young. Putnam, 1985. ISBN 0-399-21178-0. 30p. $13.95.

4-6 yrs.
*

A gem for reading aloud to story groups because of its dramatic illustrations and simple text, this is an interesting Jataka variant of Chicken Little's assumption that the sky is falling when it's only an acorn. Here, Foolish Rabbit hears an apple crashing behind him and runs away to tell all the other animals that the earth is breaking up. They all panic in turn until Lion leaps down to put a stop to their nonsense. At this point in the illustration begins one of the great all-time series of double-page spreads: the first is Lion's huge paw spread mammothly wide, with yellow fur and white claws gleaming; the second spotlights Lion's stern snout and glowing eyes, and the third, his BIG RED ROAR as he turns Foolish Rabbit back to check the source of everyone's fears. In fact, all of the art is striking and unusual for Young's delicate styling. Both the pages and shapes are oversize, with colors shocking in intensity, yet carefully controlled for emphasis. In one spread, the angry animals are represented as dark shadows against a deep pink ground. At the happy ending, the colors mellow and blend. Action-packed.

681   **Matas**, Carol. *Code Name Kris*. Scribner's, 1990. ISBN 0-684-19208-X. 152p. $12.95.

7-10   In a sequel to *Lisa's War*, a story of the rescue operation mounted by Danish citizens to save Danish Jews from a Nazi roundup, it is Jesper (code name Kris) who is the narrator. Jesper has continued working as a member of the resistance; he thinks often of Lisa, now safely in Sweden, and of her brother Stefan, who had been his best friend. The story is told as a flashback, as Jesper, now imprisoned, recalls his underground struggle, describing with terrible clarity the German treatment of the Danes and the courageous persistence of the resistance fighters. Matas maintains Jesper's point of view, and does not overwhelm his own dramatic story with background details, so that the book is strong in its narrative quality despite its documentary aspects.

682   **Matas**, Carol. *Lisa's War*. Scribner, 1989. ISBN 0-684-19010-9. 128p. $12.95.

7-10   Lisa, who tells the story, is a young adolescent whose older brother Stefan becomes a member of the Danish resistance to the occupying Nazi forces. The time is 1940, the setting is Copenhagen, and Lisa's family is endangered as are all Danish Jews. Lisa insists on doing her share in the resistance and frets because her cousin Erik and his parents refuse to see, or admit, that the Germans are a threat to all Jews and those who sympathize with them or help them. The story, told smoothly, with good pace, structure, and suspense, ends with the mass evacuation of Danish Jews to Sweden, an effort in which hundreds of non-Jewish Danes participated.

683   **Matsubara**, Hisako. *Cranes at Dusk;* tr. from the German by Leila Vennewitz. Dial, 1985. ISBN 0-385-27858-6. 253p. $15.95.

7-
  *   Capably translated from the original German, this is a stunning novel about a child's divided allegiance between parents locked in a permanent cold war, about her efforts to understand her changing world, and about her compassion and courage. Saya is ten, the daughter of a nonconformist Shinto priest and a rigid, narrow-minded woman who sees her husband as her enemy. The setting is Kyoto in 1945, when the people of Saya's neighborhood are stunned by their country's defeat and apprehensive about the advent of the American troops. Published originally as an adult book, this should be attractive

to young adult readers as well, exploring as it does the complexities of familial relationships, the ambivalencies that confront children, and the marvelous adaptability of the young. Matsubara writes with clarity and perception; her characters are drawn with depth and strength; and her setting, vividly established, is made an integral part of her story.

684   Matthews, Downs. *Polar Bear Cubs;* illus. with photographs by Dan Guravich. Simon, 1989. ISBN 0-671-6675-2. 25p. $12.95.

5-8 yrs.
*   A stunning match of color photography and clean writing, this follows a polar bear from her winter hibernation through the birth, care, and training of her cubs over a period of two years. The irresistible subjects will absorb young listeners and lure independent readers as well, and the text is simple enough, without any condescension, to be read aloud or alone. Information about the North Pole emanates naturally from the central focus, and the tone is one of respect for both the animals and the environment. Guravich's close-ups speak of long, cold vigils and an uncanny command of technology to capture creature habit and characteristics, including some unusually humorous poses. From one frozen Arctic endpaper to the other, this is picture book nonfiction at its best. Children who enjoyed Cutchins and Johnston's fine photodocumentary *Andy Bear: A Polar Cub Grows Up At the Zoo* should have a chance to see cubs in their natural habitat. Let's hope the weak binding holds up to the hard use.

685   Mattingley, Christobel. *The Angel with a Mouth Organ;* illus. by Astra Lacis. Holiday House, 1986. ISBN 0-8234-0593-1. 30p. $12.95.

3-5
*   Of several recent picture books about war, this has the strongest story and clearest child's perspective. It follows a refugee family from the first bombing of their village through a long march, seven moves, and their last camp, where the narrator and her older sister and mother wait hopefully for Father's return. The years are telescoped into several moving incidents: the loss of a neighbor's baby, the death of Grandma, the rounding up of Father and other male civilians to replace soldiers shot down in the road, the children's endless search for food, shelter, and coal. The narrator recalls moments of beauty—a pattern of frost crystals, the song of a cuckoo—as well as the toll her experiences take on her childhood. Characterizations are adeptly suggested through brief scenes, as when the narrator's sister angrily smashes a chubby plaster baby in its creche and the narrator replaces it with her one-armed doll. The father's return is a triumph of family warmth. Vivid pen-and-wash illustrations surround the text, giving it a sensitive immediacy; artist Lacis manages to express the family's circle of strength and sense of play amidst the devastation around them. Without diluting the truth, her pastel colors and delicate

hatching soften it to the tone of a manageable memory. Although basically a story for elementary-grade readers, this could also be shared aloud with second graders or younger children with one-on-one discussion.

686   **Mayer**, Marianna, ad. *Aladdin and the Enchanted Lamp;* illus. by Gerald McDermott. Macmillan, 1985. ISBN 0-02-765360-9. 81p. $15.95.

4-6   This adaptation extends the story with detail, dialogue, and lavishly colored full-page paintings. The basic elements remain intact, although Aladdin is more consistently heroic (in most versions, he's portrayed as a ne'er-do-well at first), and there's a novelist's attention to consistency and motivation: Aladdin is chosen for his ancestry rather than at random, for instance; and the sorcerer himself, rather than his younger brother, appears for revenge at the end. Descriptions are graceful and the romance delicate. The illustrations, bordered with middle eastern motifs, combine stylized shapes with some realistic detail against stipple-textured backgrounds. Warmer in artistic and narrative tone than Leonard Lubin's *Aladdin* (1982), this is a well-patterned version, both textually and graphically, that will appeal especially to children versed in fairy tales.

687   **Mayer**, Marianna. *The Little Jewel Box;* illus. by Margot Tomes. Dial, 1986. Library ed. ISBN 0-8037-0149-7; Trade ed. ISBN 0-8037-0148-9. 29p. Library ed. $10.89; Trade ed. $10.95.

4-7 yrs.   Based on folkloric patterns with the reverse twist of a heroine proving her mettle and winning a husband, this unfolds the tale of Isabel, who seeks her fortune and finds it with the help of a magic box and the hindrance of her mother's inadvertently baking her a bad luck cake. This last is a bit contrived, but on the whole, the story is well conceived, sustained, and styled. Tomes' illustrations show more artistic growth than any of her other recent work, however fine that has been. Here she has broadened her range to include some stunning landscape compositions, skillful graphic characterizations, deepened colors, and distinctive line work. If the hawk does on occasion look like a cross between a pigeon and a parrot, it nevertheless has a lot of expression, as do the other creatures in the animal-helper roles and the three funny little men who reluctantly leave their napping in the magic box to build or move castles at a moment's notice. Sturdy storytelling in art and text.

688   **Mayne**, William. *Antar and the Eagles.* Delacorte, 1990. ISBN 0-385-29977-X. 166p. $13.95.

5-8   Strong, suspenseful storytelling married to a confident use of folkloric
*   motifs makes this one of Mayne's most accessible fantasies. Climbing for the second time ("he remembered, too, that he was going to be

very frightened") to the steeple of the church, six-year-old Antar is taken by an eagle to help rescue a very special baby: the embryonic Great Eagle, asleep in a golden egg, captive to a King. His eagle taskmasters harsh but just, Antar learns to live in their mountain eyrie, to communicate in squawks and bows and pecks, and, finally, to fly. The scenes of Antar's abduction and forced march to the eagle home are tense and exciting; his evolving respect for his captors is credibly developed. And while the eagle clan has a fierce nobility, they aren't above pranks, tricks or general disagreeableness. A formidable kitten adds a comic accent. Fantasy fans won't be put off by the tender age of the protagonist, "the child who shall lead them" being a respectable convention in the genre. Less introverted than much of Mayne's fiction, this has a compelling narrative drive with natural, cliff-hanging chapter endings that recommend it for classroom reading aloud. Choose your own adventure.

689   **Mayne**, William. *Drift*. Delacorte, 1986. ISBN 0-385-29446-8. 166p. $14.95.

5-9   Rafe is swept into immediate adventure when the Indian girl Tawena takes him to "go get look at bear. Bear my people father." The two become caught in a fishing shack on the frozen lake, the bear patiently breaking in: "It began to bite the corners of the hut, high up the wall, and right down at the bottom." But in an eerie, not quite supernatural moment, the bear breaks down the door and then is separated from the hut as the ice breaks, bear and hut floating in different directions. Rafe and Tawena land on an inhospitable shore ("Land of bears, all ever bears") and Tawena, sensing the approach of two hostile Indian women, takes Rafe's knife and deserts him. He is captured by the women, journeying with them through the wilderness to, he thinks, a life of slavery. We don't quite know where or when this historical novel is set (there is a reference to fighting the French), but it's a terrific survival story, as Mayne meticulously details the skills Rafe learns to gain the approval of the Indians. There are many instances where Rafe questions the reality around him, particularly during the attack of the "Wendagoo," a shower of branches, animals, and fishes; and his disorientation is heightened by the noncommittal, sometimes contradictory behavior of the Indians: what are they going to do with him? A second section returns to Tawena's adventures after stealing Rafe's knife; this is anticlimactic and a bit jarring. Still, her story is interesting, amplifying and furthering the mystical overtones of the first part.

690   **Mayne**, William. *Gideon Ahoy!* Delacorte, 1989. ISBN 0-440-50126-1. 160p. $13.95.

6-9   Gideon is a deaf, mentally retarded seventeen-year-old undergoing a
 *   transition that provokes one family crisis after another. Mum,
        Grandpa Catt, twin toddlers Mercury and Tansy, and even Dad, who
        rushes in and out of the scene between sailing assignments, are all
        well realized. The viewpoint, however, is twelve-year-old Eva's, and she
        has special insight into the limitations, logic, and language of Gideon.
        His expressions for pleasure ("Dththth"), upset ("Rauh"), hunger
        ("Hyagh"), etc. become familiar to the reader, as does Mayne's use of
        the present participle for Gideon's actions, projecting the boy's
        perpetual state of "now" without sense of past or future. As
        portraiture, this is masterful, and there is suspense in Gideon's
        running away when his job on a canal boat is terminated. The family
        reactions when he lies in a coma from which he may never recover
        make one of the most subtly developed denouements in children's
        literature. Mayne is an experimenter, one of the few who will take a
        chance on unusual techniques of crafting fiction for the young. The
        perspectives he works with here are sometimes acutely on target ("Eva
        wiped the [twins'] mouths with a towel, streaking it blue. Saints, she
        thought. Stains") and sometimes a bit self-conscious ("the little ones
        remembered how whiskers would tickle tummies, and were on the
        table walking them into it, while Mum tried to stow stray legs in night-
        clothes"). Yet any reader with the concentration to adjust to the odd
        twists of associative language—and there's plenty of literal narrative
        to balance them— will be caught up in Gideon's fate and rewarded
        with insights richly written.

691   **Mazer**, Harry. *When the Phone Rang*. Scholastic, 1985. ISBN 0-590-
        32167-6. 181p. $11.95.

6-9   When the phone rang, it was an airlines official to tell Billy, the
        narrator, that his parents had been killed in a crash. There's a younger
        sister, Lori, and an older brother in college, and the children's nearest
        relatives agree that they should be split up. This is the story, per-
        ceptive and focused, of how the three work out a way to live as a family,
        staying together despite the problems of role adjustment and their
        several patterns of reaction to bereavement. Like most of Mazer's
        books, this has a strong narrative flow, characters that are well-
        defined, and a positive conclusion that is sympathetic and believable.

692   **Mazer**, Norma Fox. *After the Rain*. Morrow, 1987. ISBN 0-688-06867-7.
        290p. $11.75.

6-9   Adolescent Rachel has always been a little afraid of Grandpa Izzy, her
        mother's father; sharp-tongued and irritable, the old man seems to
        have no kindness or softness in his nature. After the family learns that
        he has terminal cancer (which Izzy isn't told), Rachel begins to visit
        him and walk with him daily, and by the time he is near the end and

hospitalized, she has come to love him. This is a story all the more moving because Mazer preserves Grandpa's integrity as a character, so that both during his life and after his death, as Rachel adjusts to loss, her grandfather is consistently taciturn and graceless—and the book speaks convincingly to the power of family love that is strong enough to accept this. Some of the text is exposition, some consists of entries in Rachel's journal, and the whole is smoothly fused, balanced in mood by some comic moments and in structure by Rachel's relationships with her peers, her parents, and a much older brother to whom she writes long, revealing letters that are never answered.

693   **Mazer**, Norma Fox. *Silver*. Morrow, 1988. ISBN 0-688-06865-0. 261p. $11.95.

6-9   Mrs. Silver is very happy when she and Sarabeth get a chance to move to the other end of their trailer park; it means a different—richer— school district. Sarabeth isn't so sure, until she meets Grant, a beautiful rich girl who welcomes Sarabeth (anointing her "Silver") into her clique, a coup that Sarabeth pulls off under less than honest pretensions. Mazer doesn't ever resort to the easy or expected in this novel, and it's a particular pleasure to see some rich kids in YA fiction who aren't lonely, bored, and disaffected. Like all kids, however, they have problems, as Silver discovers when new friend Patty reveals she is being sexually abused by her uncle. Even here the novel doesn't become didactic, and Mazer allows the girls and Mrs. Silver to solve the problem themselves, wisely keeping herself out of the way. Neither the lives of the rich nor those of the trailer park residents are romanticized or stereotyped, but are seen honestly through Silver's perspective, which is realistically limited. We never get a full picture, for example, of Mrs. Silver's romance with chimneysweep Leo, just as we never quite find out why Silver's new boyfriend unexpectedly drops her. It's a convincing viewpoint and perspective, more revealing than most so-called first-person YA novels.

694   **McAfee**, Annalena. *Kirsty Knows Best*; illus. by Anthony Browne. Knopf, 1988. Library ed. ISBN 0-394-99478-7; Trade ed. ISBN 0-394-89478-2. 32p. Library ed. $9.99; Trade ed. $8.95

2-4   Kirsty Little is intrepidly uncowed by reality. Taunted by Nora, the school bully, whose mean little mouth is just one of Browne's expert touches (another is the way the menacing echoes of Nora's pigtails pop up on nearly every page), Kirsty imagines, in rhyming couplets, how it really is: "To get round town she does adore her/ Little rickshaw pulled by Nora." Kirsty's father may be unemployed, but Kirsty knows what's really happening in that backyard workshop of his: "Not content with this small operation,/ He's set his heart on world domination." And when Nora tries a little reality therapy ("Your mom's a drudge, your dad's a slob"), Kirsty is pleased to see the bully turn into a toad and to see the toad . . ."EXPLODE!" Browne contrasts precise paintings of dreary reality with the more loosely styled fanciful flights: Nora at the rickshaw appears on a royal blue Chinese plate; Mrs. Little (who is really a torch singer, you see) is a voluptuous diva; and Nora's three-frame transformation into a toad is a warts-and-all triumph. Catharsis for quiet dreamers everywhere.

695   McCaughrean, Geraldine, ad. *El Cid*; illus. by Victor G Ambrus. Oxford, 1989. ISBN 0-19-276077-7. 126p. $17.95.

6-
*

Although the imprint page somehow emerged as information about *Pinocchio*, there is no impact on the text or the illustrations, both of which are magnificent interpretations of the mass of stories about the great Spanish hero, El Cid. Exiled by the weak, vindictive King of Spain, El Cid (Don Rodrigo Diaz de Vivar), who was already a soldier-hero, won new glory for himself and his King in conquering the Moors who held much of the country. The paintings are Ambrus at his best, rich and colorful, delicate in detail and strong in composition, and permeated with humor. The writing has the same qualities, but with even more wit and with the panache that obtains to all those heroes whose stories of greatness are part history, part legend. Kudos all around.

696   McCaughrean, Geraldine. *A Little Lower Than the Angels*. Oxford, 1987. ISBN 0-19-271561-5. 133p. $13.95.

6-8

In a first novel from an experienced adapter and editor, McCaughrean writes a lively and informative tale of medieval England, in those days when the traveling troupes of performers of Mystery and Morality plays offered resented competition for established celebrations in towns and villages. The story concerns an apprentice, Gabriel, who is so cruelly treated that he runs away to join a band of players and becomes the focus of a belief in miracle healing. The plot has color and pace, the characters and dialogue are handled deftly, and the historical details are smoothly incorporated. The structure gives strong form to the informational aspect of a novel that marks an impressive debut.

697   McCaughrean, Geraldine. *Saint George and the Dragon*; illus. by Nicki Palin. Doubleday, 1989. Library ed. ISBN 0-385-26529-8; Trade ed. ISBN 0-385-26528-X. 32p. $13.95.

2-
*

This no-nonsense version of the St. George legend could serve elementary, junior high, and high school students as an introduction to England's patron saint. The dragon here is a rank villain whose father is Evil, whose mother is Darkness, and whose name is Wickedness. It eats dogs, sheep, and finally children until St. George arrives in time to save the princess of the medieval town under attack. The paintings do not flinch from projecting the terror of all who are threatened, from St. George's wild-eyed horse to the Princess Sabra, tied to a stake as dragon's meat after her name is chosen in the lottery to appease the creature's appetite. The red-gold cast of the art suggests blood as well as fire. The anatomical detail and facial expressions are masterfully drafted with robust action and Renaissance stylistic flourishes. Youngsters can sharpen their acumen by comparing this to Trina Schart Hyman's Caldecott-award-winning *St. George and the Dragon*. A note on the story is appended.

698   McClung, Robert M. *Lili: A Giant Panda of Sichuan;* illus. by Irene Brady. Morrow, 1988. Library ed. ISBN 0-688-06943-6; Trade ed. ISBN 0-688-06942-8. 85p. Library ed. $11.88; Trade ed. $11.95

3-5   This story recounts the life of Lili, a giant panda, from her birth in Sichuan to the rescue of her cub by a wildlife official, Chang, from a poacher's trap. Although the amount of description may deter students looking for specific facts, the writing is smooth, as is the blend of information and fictional narrative. Chang's role in Lili's life, beginning with his finding her as a cub and continuing when he saves her from starvation during a relocation program after the bamboo in her area dies, is fortuitous but not incredibly so. There are enough natural crises in the panda's life to give the book pace, and Brady's black-and-white drawings are both well-drafted and attractive. An introduction sets the environmental scene, a final section packs in some history of scientists' knowledge of the animal and its current endangered status, and an annotated bibliography distinguishing adult from juvenile titles suggests books for further reading.

699   McClung, Robert M. *Whitetail;* illus. by Irene Brady. Morrow, 1987. Library ed. ISBN 0-688-06127-3; Trade ed. ISBN 0-688-06126-5. 82p. Library ed. $11.88; Trade ed. $11.75.

4-6   A nature narrative with unusually good balance between storytelling and factual information recounts the life cycle of a male whitetail deer from birth to maturity. The occasional meetings of Star (named for the mark on his forehead) with a boy on a nearby farm lend a human interest element without becoming contrived, and the deer's brushes with death on the highway or during hunting season are typical but suspenseful. At no time is anthropomorphism allowed to impinge on a naturally interesting subject. This is a good read-aloud suggestion for classes that have enjoyed *The Yearling*, a title included in the brief bibliography at the end of the book. Brady's fine-line black-and-white illustrations are patiently detailed, accurate, and alluring, as is the spacious format.

700   **McCully**, Emily Arnold. *Grandmas at the Lake*; written and illus. by
Emily Arnold McCully. Harper, 1990. Library ed. ISBN 0-06-024127-6;
Trade ed. ISBN 0-06-024126-8. 65p. (I Can Read Books). Library ed.
$10.89; Trade ed. $10.95.

1-3   In a sequel to *The Grandma Mix-Up*, Pip's two grandmothers and his
friend Ski are his companions at a lakeside cabin, rented by Grandma
Nan, who has invited Grandma Sal and the boys. The hostess is rigid
and highly organized, while plump Grandma Sal is easy-going. Pip and
Ski get tired of being told what to do by the Grandmas, especially
when the directives contradict each other. They are even more weary
of never being allowed to do anything by themselves. While the
women are napping, the boys go off in a rowboat. At first alarmed, the
grandmothers concede that the boys are doing a good job and come
for a ride, promising to let Pip and Ski play by themselves. The
paintings are bright, casual, and funny in cartoon style; the story is
nicely gauged for the beginning-to-read audience, with appropriate
length and vocabulary. While not outstanding in conception or
development, it should please readers who sympathize with the boys'
desire for independence and enjoy, vicariously, the pleasure of having
achievement recognized.

701   **McDonnell**, Christine. *Friends First*. Viking, 1990. ISBN 0-670-81923-9.
171p. $11.95.

5-8   "His best friend is a girl and he doesn't care what anybody says about
it." So begins Miranda's junior-high essay on her best friend Gus, who
lives upstairs from Miranda and her mother. Gus and Miranda's
friendship is old and solid but now seems threatened from several
directions, including the amorous attentions of Miranda's friend
Catherine towards Gus: "If they started liking each other, who would I
be friends with?" While in many ways this is a cozy friends-and-family
story, rather plotless but appealingly detailed with eighth-grade
authenticity, a darker theme gradually emerges. Soon after a lecture
by the housekeeper about being careful of "how you sit and dress, how
you act," Miranda and Gus are nearly mugged by a gang of boys while
trick-or-treating. Later, shockingly, she is assaulted on her doorstep by
a stranger: "That's when he grabbed me." Gagged and tied-up,
Miranda is soon saved by Gus and his family. The violence here, as in
real life, is intrusive, particularly as it is set against the comfortable
background of Thanksgiving and the school Christmas play. The
attack leaves Miranda afraid of men, including Gus, but a wrap-up
lecture by Mom brings some security (to Miranda if not the reader,
who may be newly alarmed at Mom's discussing the attack as almost-
rape). McDonnell is saying that the world can be a dangerous place,
and, more pointedly, that men can be threatening to women. If the

theme is sometimes effortfully developed, it is nonetheless a brave statement, particularly as occasioned in the junior-high genre.

702   **McIntyre**, Vonda N. *Barbary*. Houghton, 1986. ISBN 0-395-41029-0. 192p. $12.95.

6-9   Winner of several awards for her adult science fiction, the author successfully adapts to a younger audience in this, her first juvenile novel. Her protagonist is an orphan, Barbary, who is hiding her pet cat on the journey to a space station where she will live (after a series of foster homes on Earth) with a man who was her mother's best friend at college and who has a daughter, Heather, of Barbary's age. The journey has suspense, the details of life at the space station are interesting, and the story describes the girls' encounter with the beings of an alien ship. The writing style has vigor and momentum, the characters are capably drawn, the structure and pace of the story are deftly handled.

703   **McKenna**, Colleen O'Shaughnessy. *Eenie, Meanie, Murphy, NO!* Scholastic, 1990. ISBN 0-590-42899-3. 192p. $10.95.

4-6   This fourth entry in a likable series takes Collette to camp, where she encounters First Love (including an entirely innocent but subtextually suggestive scene where he teaches her how to fish) and a mean fellow camper, Peally, who will stop at nothing to get Tommy back. Peally's tricks (decorating Collette's cabin with her underwear, etc.) are deliciously nasty; readers will writhe at her reading of Collette's (stolen) diary out loud at dinner. While Collette does wreak satisfying revenge, Peally remains refreshingly unreformed at the end of the summer and the book. Straight-ahead funny fare for those who don't understand why everybody else thinks *Anastasia Krupnik* so amusing.

704   **McKenzie**, Ellen Kindt. *Stargone John*; illus. by William Low. Holt, 1990. ISBN 0-8050-1451-9. 67p. (Redfeather Books). $13.95.

4-6
*   "Star gone" is a family nickname for quiet, abstracted John, youngest of seven children in a small-town Wisconsin family. The name, though, becomes a taunt when John starts attending the one-room schoolhouse, silently enduring the abuse of an ignorant teacher who insists, to no avail, that John speak and write. "He sat and didn't talk. He sat and didn't read. When Miss Vordig spoke to him he sat. I don't think he heard her. He was star gone, and now and again he got whacked." John is hit and humiliated by the teacher, once even wetting his seat because she refuses to let him get up to go to the outhouse. The story is told by John's older sister and confidante Liza, who herself gets bumped back to the third-grade row for trying to help John survive his first day. Set in an era (probably late nineteenth century) when special children could not be comfortably labelled, this

is a gently perceptive story of a gifted boy's triumph, as John, with the help of friends both real and imaginary, learns that language is *good*. "I knew what that meant. John meant it had to be worth the while." The one-room schoolhouse setting is in itself an interesting portrait, and the classroom dynamics will be familiar—sometimes ruefully so— to contemporary readers. They will especially relish John's response to Miss Vordig's mocking challenge that he "at least write a word" on the blackboard: "JANE IS BAD" neatly writes John, naming a fellow first-grader who has been tormenting him. And could John have known that Jane is also Miss Vordig's first name? The story is both funny and moving, empathetically narrated by John's most staunch defender. The several pencil illustrations have a simple dignity, with an expressive use of light and texture that contributes to the novel's plainspoken appeal.

705   **McKinley**, Robin. *The Outlaws of Sherwood*. Greenwillow, 1988. ISBN 0-688-07178-3. 282p. $12.95.

6-10   Once again, as she did in *Beauty*, McKinley takes a fresh look at a classic, changing some of the events or deviating from standard characterization to gain new dimensions. Her afterword explains her artistic compromise with myth and history, her wish to write a version that is "historically unembarrassing." With a few exceptions, she has done that admirably, creating a story that has pace and substance and style, and that is given nuance and depth by the characterization. The exceptions are in the use of dialogue—occasionally—that sounds too modern: "Her father bought it . . ." (in the sense of believing a lie), or too sophisticated for an unschooled outlaw of the period. Historians may find the concept of Richard the Lionheart offering Marian the post of sheriff of Nottingham odd, but most readers will enjoy the novelty of a Robin whose Sherwood Forest enclave is conceived by others, whose prowess at archery is inferior to that of Marian's, and who reluctantly accepts the sobriquet "Robin of the Hood."

706   **McKissack**, Patricia C. *Flossie and the Fox*; illus. by Rachel Isadora. Dial, 1986. Library ed. ISBN 0-8037-0251-5; Trade ed. ISBN 0-8037-0250-7. 31p. Library ed. $10.89; Trade ed. $10.95.

5-7 yrs.   An orally tuned southern story follows Flossie through the woods with her basket of eggs, which are coveted by a fox whom Flossie refuses to recognize as a predator. "I don't believe you a fox, that's what," she tells the aggressive, and increasingly aggrieved, animal. While Flossie speaks dialect, the fox speaks king's English—and loses the battle of wits with the girl, because she fearlessly pretends not to believe what he is until she reaches safety. In the end, Mr. Fox manages to oturun the hounds, but Flossie delivers her eggs with a cocky grin. The illustrations in brown, gold, green, and russet are literal but flexible, with a black protagonist and a vivid natural world (although the "piney woods" appear to be mostly birches and maple or poplar); they project the action in lively tempo. Just scary enough, this is a rural mini-adventure with folkloric dimensions.

707   **McKissack**, Patricia C. *Mirandy and Brother Wind*; illus. by Jerry Pinkney. Knopf, 1988. Library ed. ISBN 0-394-98765-9; Trade ed. ISBN 0-394-88765-4. 32p. Library ed. $13.99; Trade ed. $12.95.

5-8 yrs.   One of the surest new storytelling voices in picture books has followed
*   up *Flossie and the Fox* with another winner, also drawn from memories of Patricia McKissack's family. Here, Mirandy is sure that she'll win the cake walk if she can catch Brother Wind for her partner, but he eludes all the tricks her friends advise. When she finally does catch him with her own quick wits, she ends up wishing instead for her boyfriend Ezel to overcome his clumsiness. Sure enough, the two children finish first in high style. "When Grandmama Beasley had seen Mirandy and Ezel turning and spinning, moving like shadows in the flickering candlelight, she'd thrown back her head, laughed, and said, 'Them chullin' is dancing with the Wind!'" This narrative gets a high score, too, for plot, pace, and characterization. Mirandy sparkles with energy and determination, while the action dances with its own rhythm. Pinkney's watercolors are splashed with multi-hued, overlapping shapes that fill the pages with patterned ferment, occasionally threatening to overwhelm the story but never quite doing so. The translucent blue, larger-than-life figure of Brother Wind is clothed in the same historical costume as the rest of the southern black cast. Occasionally the portraits seem studied, but the rural settings are lush with laurel and wisteria, aflutter with chickens, and evocative of country communities at their best. A treat to pass on to new generations.

708   **McKissack**, Patricia C. *Nettie Jo's Friends*; illus. by Scott Cook. Knopf, 1989. Library ed. ISBN 0-394-99158-3; Trade ed. ISBN 0-394-89158-9. 32p. Library ed. $13.99; Trade ed. $12.95.

5-7 yrs.   Nettie Jo is trying to stand still for her flower-girl-dress fitting when Mama says that Annie Mae, Nettie Jo's tattered old doll, must have new clothes to go to Cousin Willadeen and Charles Henry's wedding. Unfortunately, nobody in the family has a spare sewing needle. From there, the plot follows a folkloristic pattern of animal helper tales, with Nettie Jo going to a rabbit, a fox, and a panther for help in finding a needle. After she relieves each creature of a problem, all three bring her a needle in an ending that's somewhat more mystical than traditional. Densely textured paintings portray, with sweeping, rounded motion, a pigtailed black child and slyly caricatured animals in an old-fashioned southern setting. The intensification of patterned narrative devices with unexpected artistic depth make this a solid story hour choice for small groups that can gather close to the ruddy, subtly toned illustrations.

709   McLaughlin, Molly. *Earthworms, Dirt and Rotten Leaves: An Exploration in Ecology*; illus. by Robert Shetterly. Atheneum, 1986. ISBN 0-689-31215-6. 86p. $12.95.

4-6
*
An outstanding example of science writing, this uses the common earthworm to teach observation, experimentation, and documentation. The writing is both informal and graceful, the facts are grounded in a context of scientific inquiry. Starting with a "guide to watching worms," the text includes questions to ask and diagrams to augment what cannot be seen through a magnifying glass. All experiments include precautions on the importance of respecting the creature being examined and avoiding actions that might cause it pain or shock. Sections on anatomy and characteristics pay special attention to principles of adaptation and lead into ecological background on food chains. The black-and-white drawings and diagrams are unpretentious but accurate and very helpful. This is a reading experience equivalent to a class with a first-rate, enthusiastic teacher; in fact, McLaughlin is an educator on the staff of The Franklin Institute Science Museum.

710   McMillan, Bruce. *Counting Wildflowers*; written and illus. by photographs by Bruce McMillan. Lothrop, 1986. Library ed. ISBN 0-688-02860-8; Trade ed. ISBN 0-688-02859-4. 26p. Library ed. $11.88; Trade ed. $11.75.

3-6 yrs.   This is a counting book of many uses: (a) it's beautiful to look at (b) there is no mistaking the number of objects in each strikingly composed picture (c) the color-coded circles running between the clear black numerals and the written numbers add color identification possibilities (d) the close-up color photographs are clear and scientifically labelled to serve as a guide to garden/sidewalk variety flowers. Add to this a humorous surprise on the final photo spread, with three chicory flowers captioned "How many?" facing a mass of maiden pinks captioned "Too many to count" (a dare if ever there was one). Afterward comes a listing of the wildflowers' scientific names, their blooming periods, and places to look for them. A bargain for creative learning experiences.

711   McMillan, Bruce. *Growing Colors*; written and illus. with photographs by Bruce McMillan. Lothrop, 1988. Library ed. ISBN 0-688-07845-1; Trade ed. ISBN 0-688-07844-3. 32p. Library ed. $12.88; Trade ed. $12.95.

1-3 yrs.   A luscious-looking book that will help children identify colors and possibly even develop a taste for vitamins in their natural state. Fruits

and vegetables appear dewy fresh in the color photographs that fill
the recto; a facing page features a smaller illustration of the plant
above the word for the color. The word is in huge print matching the
color named, and it's up to the child to say what food is pictured—
raspberries, peas, corn, cantaloupe, etc. A balance of common and
unusual items is considered, and several colors appear twice to
enhance the guessing game. A concluding double spread gives (and
shows) the answers for children learning to read on their own.
Consistently well designed, with a background note on the picture-
taking, this is notably a treat for kids and an example of photography
as an art form in picture books.

712   **McMillan**, Bruce. *One Sun: A Book of Terse Verse*; written and illus.
with photographs by Bruce McMillan. Holiday House, 1990. ISBN 0-
8234-0810-8. 32p. $14.95.

4-7 yrs.   Warning: this book may be contagious and should be considered, at
*   the very least, catching. Well, catchy, anyway. Each of fourteen
rhyming phrases faces a full-page color photo of an engaging boy
playing at the beach. The front cover starts the game (One Sun) and
the back cover (Blue View) extends it. Between them comes a parade:
*Sand Hand, Lone Stone, Snail Trail, Six Sticks, Small Ball, Wet Pet,
Tan Man, Neat Seat, Stuck Truck, Whale Pail, Scoop Group, Round
Mound, Pink Drink,* and *White Kite,* all so naturally pictured that
there's not a trace of cuteness in any of the scenes of play among
children who are Asian, black, and white. They all look suitably wet
and sandy to offset the glamorous unlittered glitter of the ocean front.
One page not only leads you speeding to another, but anyone
listening will keep going after the book is over. Fun won!

713   **McNaughton**, Colin. *Jolly Roger and the Pirates of Abdul the
Skinhead*; written and illus. by Colin McNaughton. Simon, 1988. ISBN
0-671-66843-9. 42p. $14.95.

3-5   Called "Jolly" because he looks so miserable all the time, Roger
decides to live up to his nickname and joins up with pirates, escaping
his mad-for-cleaning Mum and hoping to find his Dad, last seen in an
inn on the Barbary Coast. Abdul the Skinhead and the other pirates of
The Golden Behind are a smelly, stupid lot, even allowing themselves
to be captured (and cleaned up) by Mum, until they're saved by Roger
and the pirates' cook, who has suffered amnesia since a bonk on the
head. Guess who? While weakened by too many annoying asides by
the author, the flip tone suits the spoof, and if one leaves out the
parenthetical cuteness, this will be a lot of fun to read aloud. "I'm
Abdul 'the skinhead'—Hip-hip!/The 'Golden Behind' is my ship . . . ."
The illustrations combine boisterous double-page spreads with
smaller cartoon panels, all reeking with wit and stubble and a satiric

edge that will be enjoyed by kids who think they're too old for picture books.

714   **McNulty**, Faith. *Peeping in the Shell: A Whooping Crane is Hatched*; illus. by Irene Brady. Harper, 1986. Library ed. ISBN 0-06-024135-7; Trade ed. ISBN 0-06-024134-9. 60p. Library ed. $10.89; Trade ed. 10.95.

2-5   A five-part narrative introduces readers to the characteristics and plight of the whooping crane and describes scientists' efforts to save this endangered species. Most of the book focuses on ornithologist George Archibald and his "courtship" of whooping crane Tex, imprinted by a human. After artificial insemination, Tex does lay an egg, whose hatching the author witnesses and describes with immediacy. The long, complex life-and-death struggle to free itself from the shell makes the emergence of the chick a priceless gift, which will impress young readers more than any statistics on the status of disappearing wildlife. Brady's soft pencil drawings, generously distributed throughout an open format, lend grace to the text. A fine read-aloud for primary-grade science units as well as an unusual resource for independent readers.

715   **McPhail**, David. *Emma's Vacation*; written and illus. by David McPhail. Dutton, 1987. ISBN 0-525-44315-0. $7.95.

3-5 yrs.   Gently humorous, soft in line and color, McPhail's watercolor pictures augment a text that is brief, simple, and engaging if not substantial. Emma and her parents (bears) have a few problems (getting lost en route, arriving in the rain) at the start of their holiday, then frenziedly see the sights. Emma suggests that they stay at the cabin, and they have a wonderful time playing and relaxing in the wilderness. The read-aloud audience should enjoy the parental participation (father climbing a tree, mother trying to catch a fish by paw) and identify happily with the sagacity of the cub.

716   **McVitty**, Walter, ad. *Ali Baba and the Forty Thieves*; illus. by Margaret Early. Abrams, 1989. ISBN 0-8109-1888-9. 32p. $14.95.

5-8 yrs.   With smooth storytelling and exquisitely rendered art in the style of
 *   Persian miniatures, this represents the best aspects of the contemporary publishing trend of illustrated classics. Margaret Early's borders around every page of text are technically elaborate but aesthetically restrained in service of spacious double spreads. Similarly, each full-page picture develops multiple design and color motifs with such delicately patterned line work that the most complex compositions effect a unified tone. Those familiar with the Arabian Nights story of the poor man who discovers a cave concealing a robber band's wealth will remember the ferocious elements of the tale as well as the noteworthy intelligence of its real hero, Morgiana. This

rendition neither compromises nor overdramatizes these elements, but incorporates them into an absorbing complement of narrative and graphic image. Honorable mention should also go to the fine reproduction and bookmaking. The answer to that nagging question of "do we really need another edition" is, in this case, a resounding yes.

717   **Meltzer**, Milton. *Ain't Gonna Study War No More: The Story of America's Peace Seekers.* Harper, 1985. Library ed. ISBN 0-06-024200-0; Trade ed. ISBN 0-06-024199-3. 282p. Library ed. $11.89; Trade ed. $12.50.

7-   Meltzer's many fans will get what they have come to expect from him: a serious, thought-provoking, and comprehensive treatise that is based on careful research, is logically organized, and is written in a temperate but forceful style that is built on the author's convictions but is tempered by moderation. There is some preliminary material about peace through recorded history, but the focus is on individuals, organizations, movements, and religious groups that have opposed war in the history of our own country and that have often suffered for their actions or convictions. The book concludes with a chapter in which Meltzer considers the perils of the future and nuclear disarmament. A bibliography is included, as is an extensive relative index.

718   **Meltzer**, Milton, ed. *The American Revolutionaries: A History in their Own Words, 1750-1800.* Crowell, 1987. Library ed. ISBN 0-690-04643-X; Trade ed. ISBN 0-690-04641-3. 210p. illus. with photographs. Library ed. $12.89; Trade ed. $12.95.

6-   Following the format of *The Black Americans: A History in their Own Words* and a similar book about Jewish Americans, Meltzer has assembled a collage of eyewitness accounts, speech and diary excerpts, letters, and other documents for a choronological account of the half century that included the American Revolution. He has been careful to incorporate various points of view and to give a balanced perspective in the narrative with which he pieces together the primary sources. The account of Indian cruelty to white settlers, for instance, is followed by a description of Colonel George Clark's butchery of Indian captives. The voices of women who accompanied the troops and of blacks who fought with the army are both represented, and there are vivid scenes of battle and of its aftermath for wounded and imprisoned soldiers. It is a difficult assignment to combine such diverse elements into a pattern, but after the opening sections, which sometimes seem fragmented, the book gains a momentum and takes on, especially in the parts dealing directly with the war, a cohesive direction. A first-rate student resource, with a note on sources in addition to the citations following every entry.

719   **Meltzer**, Milton. *Benjamin Franklin: The New American*. Watts, 1988. ISBN 0-531-10582-2. 288p. illus. $14.90.

6-
*
Even from so distinguished a social historian as Milton Meltzer, one would not have expected so familiar a subject of biographies as Franklin to enthrall anew. It does; this is certainly one of the author's best biographies, and certainly the best about Franklin written for young people since Thomas Fleming's 1973 *Benjamin Franklin*. Meltzer has used source material (cited in great detail at the close of the text) in a smooth incorporation into exposition and dialogue, themselves nicely balanced. The biography gives adequate attention to background information without obscuring the personality of the biographee or the respectful record of his many interests and achievements. Indexed.

720   **Meltzer**, Milton. *Crime in America*. Morrow, 1990. ISBN 0-688-08513-X. 170p. illus. with photographs. $12.95.

7-
An indefatigable researcher, Meltzer supplies facts and, sketchily, their sources, as well as a brief "Notes on Sources" that precedes the index. The coverage is broad, with separate chapters on different kinds of crime (physical abuse of women and children, white collar crime, crime in government, organized crime, etc.) and with discussions of our system of justice, of the increase in vigilante response, and of the intricacy of such crime-related problems as drugs, gun laws, and violence within the social fabric. A final chapter, "What Can Be Done About It?" examines some of the causes (such conditions as poverty, ignorance, and injustice) and suggests some of the changes (the educational system or the legal system, for example) that might alleviate or reduce crime and violence in the United States. While the writing style is solemn, the material is inherently dramatic—at times inherently lurid, and depressing. An important topic is given thoughtful consideration despite the fact that the magnitude of the problem prohibits extended treatment of its various aspects.

721   **Meltzer**, Milton. *Dorothea Lange: Life Through the Camera*; illus. by Donna Diamond and with photographs by Dorothea Lange. Viking, 1985. ISBN 0-670-28047-X. 57p. (Women of Our Time) $9.95.

5-7
One of the great photographers of our time, Dorothea Lange recorded much of the social history of the United States for several decades, winning recognition as both documentary commentator and artist. Meltzer explains the research on which his longer book, *Dorothea Lange: A Photographer's Life* is based. This shorter volume is smoothly written, although there are occasional comments that could be clarified. Still, the combination of a competent and careful biographer and a fascinating subject make accessible to readers the story of a strong contemporary artist they may not have known.

722   **Meltzer**, Milton. *Rescue: The Story of How Gentiles Saved Jews in the Holocaust.* Harper, 1988. Library ed. ISBN 0-06-024210-8; Trade ed. ISBN 0-06-024209-4. 168p. illus. with photographs. Library ed. $12.89; Trade ed. $12.95.

5-9   One of the first chroniclers of the Holocaust for young readers here takes up the more hopeful side of history—those who helped save Jews from the Nazi's final solution. Relative to those Gentiles who accepted or participated in the persecution of the Jews, the numbers who resisted were small, but their stories are heroic and hair-raising, from isolated individuals like Oskar Schindler to entire villages such as Le Chambon and countries such as Sweden and Belgium. Some rescuers are well known and saved thousands—Raoul Wallenberg, for example; others, unheralded, risked their own families to save one child. Each case, however, implies a question of what the reader would have done in the same circumstances. There is introductory background on anti-Semitism and a concluding discussion of characteristics or beliefs common to the "Righteous Gentiles" honored in archives such as Yad Vashem, but the emphasis is on the accounts themselves, which are often related by witnesses; unfortunately, these lack source citations. An important complement to current books on the Holocaust by Miriam Chaikin and Barbara Rogasky.

723   **Merriam**, Eve. *Fresh Paint*; illus. by David Frampton. Macmillan, 1986. ISBN 0-02-766860-6. 42p. $11.95.

4-7   Some of the best writing Merriam has done surfaces in these 45 poems, which achieve a light, effortless tone with echoes of meaning. The title poem, "Fresh Paint," sets the pace with fresh images of color blended into an invitation: ". . . and look/ how the word DON'T is painted out/ so the sign reads/ touch." "A New Pencil" subtly sketches the portrait of an immigrant grandmother; "Flying for the First Time" catches the thrill of an airplane ride with a comparison to swimming in the sea. Some of these — "New Love," "Skip Rope Rhyme for Our Time" (about junk mail), and "Artichoke"—reach toward an older awareness than the audience implied by the format, which is delicately illustrated with small woodcuts. On the whole, however, the language is simple and ideas lyrical.

724   **Merriam**, Eve. *Halloween A B C*; illus. by Lane Smith. Macmillan, 1987. ISBN 0-02-766870-3. 32p. $14.95.

3-5   The title and format are deceptive here, because this is more sophisticated in poetry and art than the picture book appearance suggests. The verse is well structured and skillful, ranging in tone from satanically sinister to impishly funny. Some lines are thought provoking ("Conceal, conceal,/ peel off and reveal/ the mask that no one detects:/ your face that the mirror reflects"), others entertaining ("a pet that's not the least bit vicious,/ yet finds the neighbors quite nutritious"); most are surprising. The poems are arranged by title alphabetically: "Apple," "Bat," "Crawler," "Demon," "Elf," "Fiend," etc. Each is accompanied by a darkly delicate, surrealistic painting that intensifies the creepy mood considerably. This will disquiet adults and galvanize kids.

725   **Merriam**, Eve. *You Be Good & I'll Be Night: Jump-on-the-Bed Poems*; illus. by Karen Lee Schmidt. Morrow, 1988. Library ed. ISBN 0-688-06743-3; Trade ed. ISBN 0-688-06742-5. 40p. Library ed. $12.88; Trade ed. $12.95.

3-6 yrs.   A romping collection of twenty-eight poems features mostly jump-rope rhythms and chanting rhymes. Many of the verses turn everyday activities into play: "You'll be saucer, / I'll be cup, / piggyback, piggy-back, / pick me up. / You be tree, / I'll be pears, / carry me, carry me / up the stairs. / You be Good, / I'll be Night, / tuck me in, tuck me in / nice and tight." Each poem is accompanied with bouncy watercolor scenes, often including comically incongruous animals—an alligator swinging from the moon ("Swing me till summer, swing me through fall, / I promise I'll never get tired at all") or a rat on the telephone ("Hello, hello, / will you spell your name? / It's R.A.T. / and yours is the same"). Some are quite funny, including the one about Harriet, who "by magic force, / turned herself into a horse." A few are too jingly, but on the whole this is nonsense with flair.

726   **Miller**, Jim Wayne. *Newfound.* Jackson/Orchard, 1989. Library ed. ISBN 0-531-08445-0; Trade ed. ISBN 0-531-05845-X. 213p. Library ed. $13.99; Trade ed. $13.95.

7-10
*   Robert Wells begins his narrative on a Tennessee mountain road after the last day of fifth grade and ends it at the beginning of his freshman year at Berea College. In between come scenes that vividly recreate an Appalachian community without ever rendering it quaint or representative. His parents' divorce, the strain between grand-parents of different socio-economic classes, and the close ties among neighbors at the mercy of natural disasters and stripmining economy form a steady structure. Each member of Robert's extended family is distinctively characterized through linked stories that evoke a setting resonant with rich traditions. We experience the hard work of sharecropping tobacco, only to watch it destroyed by hail; we feel the status of outcast in the transfer from a backwoods to a modernized school. If the direction meanders at times, it's only for the sake of following an interesting side road. Readers will find, by the end, that they have traveled deep into the country and learned something of themselves as well as of those rooted in the region.

727   **Miller**, Luree. *The Black Hat Dances: Two Buddhist Boys in the Himalayas;* illus. with photographs by Marilyn Silverstone. Dodd, 1987. ISBN 0-396-08835-X. 86p. $11.95.

5-6   Since both author and photographer have lived in Asia for many years (Silverstone has become a Buddhist nun in Nepal), this description of the lives of Samdup and Tashi has an authoritative note. The former lives in a monastery and is preparing for the religious life, the latter is a farmer's son. The book gets off to a slow start by presenting facts about Buddhism in the United States, a chapter that also includes anecdotes about individual children in Buddhist families and information about the Buddhist faith—how it began, how it spread, how it is observed. The major part of the text uses the lives of Tashi and Samdup to give a broad picture of life in Sikkim, that part of India where the monastery and the community that supports it are located. Since there is comparatively little material about the subject for younger readers, this will be useful. The writing style is simple and rather flat; the quality of the many photographs is variable. An index and a list of suggested readings are provided.

728   **Miller**, Margaret. *Hot Off the Press!: A Day at the Daily News;* written and illus. with photographs by Margaret Miller. Crown, 1985. ISBN 0-517-5647-2. 45p. $12.95.

4-8   Miller's photodocumentary follows the news coverage of a Thanksgiving Day Parade in New York City from the City Editor's assignment of the story to a Daily News reporter/photographer team through on-the-scene interviews, the rewrite terminal, copy editing, photo desk selection, layout, computer typesetting, laser transmission, letterpress printing, and distribution. Although the use of actual names for persons on the job can be confusing, it does lend vitality to the explanations. The range of work described is astonishing, from manual hand tinting and board composition to the technological phenomenon of the Laser Reader. An eye-opener for young readers whose concept of newspapers may be limited to jokes about black and white and read all over.

729   **Miller**, Margaret. *Who Uses This?;* written and illus. with photographs by Margaret Miller. Greenwillow, 1990. Library ed. ISBN 0-688-08279-3; Trade ed. ISBN 0-688-08278-5. 40p. Library ed. $12.88; Trade ed. $12.95.

2-5 yrs.   Crisp color photographs, simply composed and clearly focused, form the basis for a guessing game about "tools of the trades," which are grouped together on the last page of the book. Opposite the first boldface question "Who uses this?" is pictured a hammer; turn the page to find the answer, "Carpenter," set between a craftsman working on a house and a young girl hammering on a building project.

The choice of objects is imaginative—including a juggling club, football, rolling pin, watering can, leash, baton, scissors, and paintbrush—and the candid shots equally so, with the dogwalker fielding a dozen canines down a city sidewalk and, on the page opposite "Barber," a child cutting her teddy bear's hair. Perhaps the children are a bit squeaky clean (except for one, who has just stepped in paint), but a conscientious ethnic balance and a book design skillfully calculated for group showing as well as one-on-one sharing make this a preschool coup.

730   **Miller**, Marilyn. *The Bridge at Selma.* Silver Burdett, 1985. ISBN 0-382-06826-2. 60p. illus. with photographs. (Turning Points in American History) Library ed. $10.47; Trade ed. $13.96.

6-9   Miller begins her detailed, full, and harrowing account of the first Selma march and takes it to the point of confrontation, ending the chapter with a device that may irritate some readers: "Before finding out what did happen on the Edmund Pettus Bridge that afternoon, let us trace the road that brought the marchers there." Thirty pages later, the action resumes. While the account of suffrage discrimination, persecution of civil rights workers, and legislation in the intervening pages is substantial, the book (also broken by inserts of colored pages that deal with subjects that are pertinent but interruptive and that could have been inserted at the end of the book) loses some of its impact by this separative process. The writing is solid, almost heavy, but the drama of the tragic and compelling events should carry the reader's interest; the book concludes with a brief resume of changes in black voting patterns and power since that day in Selma in 1965.

731   **Mills**, Claudia. *Dynamite Dinah.* Macmillan, 1990. ISBN 0-02-767101-1. 128p. $11.95.

3-6   Ten-year-old Dinah Seabrooke is an irrepressible crowd-pleaser who loves the limelight: she performs a class recitation of Millay's "Renascence" (the longest poem she could find), a dance with the school janitor's mop, and a frolic on the rooftop in the rain. Unfortunately, her new baby brother, whom she had expected to be an audience for her exuberant antics, turns out to be "the world's most useless individual." And when the coveted part of Becky in the class production of *Tom Sawyer* goes not to Dinah but to her best friend Suzanne, Dinah's jealousy causes a rift in their friendship. Dazzling Dinah's relationship with the modest Suzanne is unerringly depicted, as is Dinah's ambivalence about her only occasionally charming new sibling. Mills' heroine is an older Ramona, whose delight in herself is not only understandable but contagious. Even when (temporarily) reformed and abject, she cannot resist self-dramatizing: "And yet Dinah felt somehow sorry for the world, deprived of humorous routines with her hose, denied the opportunity to hear another version of 'Renascence.' . . . She was nicer than she had been before, yes, but undeniably less interesting." The writing is both savvy and sparkling, making Dinah a distinctive and memorable individual with broad appeal.

732   Mills, Judie. *John F. Kennedy*. Watts, 1988. ISBN 0-531-10520-2. 370p. illus. with photographs. $14.90.

7-
 *   A meticulous consolidation of biographical information about John Kennedy is focused thematically on his relationship with his father and older brother, against whom Jack measured himself even after Joe Jr.'s death on a bombing mission during World War II. Jack's lack of academic concentration, chronic ill health, use of the family's wealth and influence, and womanizing are all addressed but shown to have come under control with his maturation as a politician and father. Although some of the detail in the early campaigns seems given equal weight with later, more important developments, the book shouldn't be faulted for its thoroughness. In fact, one would like to learn even more about sisters Jean, Pat, and Eunice (the rebellious Kick died young and Rosemary was mentally disabled), who seem consigned here to unindividualized campaigning in service of the men's ambitions. Ted doesn't get much attention either, but those who most affected Jack's career—Joe Sr. and Jr., Rose, Bobby, and Jackie, along with select aides who were privy to the Hyannis compound early on—are clearly delineated. This is by far the most definitive portrait of Kennedy written for young people and certainly the first biography to have such thorough documentation, including footnotes for factual background as well as quotations. A solid bibliography of books and videos will further assist students researching the complex life and times reflected here.

733   Milne, Lorus J. *A Shovelful of Earth*; written by Lorus J. and Margery Milne; illus. by Margaret La Farge. Henry Holt, 1987. ISBN 0-8050-002-3. 114p. $12.95.

5-7   Although there have been several recent books on soils and their composition (notably *Earthworms, Dirt, and Rotten Leaves: An Exploration in Ecology* by Molly McLaughlin), this is more comprehensive in treating both biological processes and variations of geographical environment. The first half of the book covers plant and animal life by ground layer, and the second touches on special adaptations in evergreen, tropic, desert, Arctic, and alpine regions. The writing is not always smooth (the preface begins with a misplaced modifier), but the text is straightforward and generally well organized by chapter and subsection, with an index for access to specific topics. The fine-line and stipple pen drawings are meticulously accurate as well as attractive. A glossary, bibliography, and list of research questions are appended.

734   **Mitchell**, Barbara. *Shoes for Everyone: A Story About Jan Matzeliger;* illus. by Hetty Mitchell. Carolrhoda, 1986. ISBN 0-87614-290-0. 59p. (Creative Minds) $8.95.

2-4   After the initial reaction to this title (a biography of *who*?), one finds a compelling story of human endeavor. A clear text blessedly allows the extraordinary individual in focus, Jan Matzeliger, born of a white father and black mother in Dutch Guiana, 1852, to emerge without undue exclamatory adulation. A paradoxically brilliant but humble inventor, Matzeliger set out against all odds, including prejudice and hunger, to pursue his singular dream of making a shoe-lasting machine to replace the tedious, time-consuming hand sewing that held up manufacturing processes in his day. With his loneliness relieved only by church affiliations in Philadelphia and Lynn, Massachusetts, Matzeliger starved himself to collect the instruments and scraps of metal needed to experiment, and then saw most of the profits go to the investors who finally backed him after he managed to get a patent. This hero of black history and business enterprise will give readers a glimpse of the uncommon aspects of unknown figures.

735   **Modell**, Frank. *Ice Cream Soup;* written and illus. by Frank Modell. Greenwillow, 1988. Library ed. ISBN 0-688-07771-4; Trade ed. ISBN 0-688-07770-6. 24p. Library ed. $11.88; Trade ed. $11.95.

4-6 yrs.   No birthday party, not this year. Best friends Milton and Marvin hear the same verdict from their mothers, so they decide they'll give themselves a birthday party; they blow up old balloons and make paper hats and send out invitations (dozens, as shown in the illustrations), and try to make their own cake and ice cream. The cake's a sad, sagging mess, the ice cream is soup. Owners of the local bakery and ice cream stores turn away when asked for advice—but they save the well-attended party by showing up with a three-tier cake and a drum of ice cream. An improbable ending, but the read-aloud audience is not likely to object; after all, adults do sometimes come to the rescue. Like other Modell books, this is brisk, bouncy fun, and the cartoon illustrations are impressive for their economy of line. Birthdays, minor disasters, and mission accomplished: those are three strong appeals.

736   **Moerbeek**, Kees. *New at the Zoo: A Mix-and-Match Pop-Up Book;* written and illus. by Kees Moerbeek. Random House, 1989. ISBN 0-679-80076-X. 10p. $7.95.

3-6 yrs. In the spate of paper engineered books that have come out recently,
   *   this scores high for invention, information, and amusement. Five
          animals—a monkey, zebra, hippo, camel, and tiger—open and close
          their mouths at the viewer with lines such as "I like to swing through
          the trees . . . and eat bananas for lunch." For nonreaders, it's a
          guessing game; for beginning readers, the answer is written in
          boldface beside the animal. Then, playing on Chukovsky's discovery
          that a child's first sense of humor involves reversal of known concepts,
          the book is divided horizontally so that the top and bottom half-pages
          can be manipulated to compose nonsensical combinations of picture
          and word—the top of the hippo over the bottom of the tiger, for
          instance, makes a hipger. The figures are simple, the art sprightly, the
          pages sturdy.

737   **Mohr**, Nicholasa. *Going Home*. Dial, 1986. Library ed. ISBN 0-8037-
      0270-1; Trade ed. ISBN 0-8037-0269-8. 192p. Library ed. $11.89; Trade
      ed. $11.95.

4-6   A charming sequel to the author's *Felita*. Now 11, Felita is ecstatic over
      her upcoming trip to Puerto Rico, as well as her first boyfriend, shy
      Vinnie from Colombia. While the upbeat tone never really darkens,
      there are conflicts: Mami's new strictness with Felita, her bossy
      brother Tito, the jealousies of other girls. When Felita gets to Puerto
      Rico she discovers homesickness and meets discrimination from
      some of the other kids, who call her "Nuyorican" and "Gringita." But
      justice is dealt, and Felita is surprised to find that she will miss the
      island and her new friends when she returns to New York. Felita's
      narration is colloquial and exuberant, and Mohr has a particularly
      sharp eye for the friendships (as well as the downright meanness) of
      pre-teen girls. And that Vinnie's a charmer.

738   **Moore**, Emily. *Whose Side Are You On?* Farrar, 1988. ISBN 0-374-
      38409-6. 134p. $11.95.

4-7   Barbra knows she needs tutoring to pass sixth grade math, but why did
      Mrs. Stone have to assign T. J. Brodie the task? "'You and Anthony
      have been in the same class since first grade.' 'And I've always hated
      it. Please, Mrs. Stone.'" Of course Barbra likes T. J. more than she
      suspects, something she discovers when T. J. disappears. This pre-teen
      school story distinguishes itself from the pack in many ways: a warm,
      affectionate tone convincingly voiced in Barbra's narration; a good
      balance of classroom antics and more serious scenes; a black middle-
      class urban setting. Too often these slice-of-life stories turn into
      predictable series, but Barbra, T. J., and friends are an appealing cast
      who deserve at least one more book.

739   **Moore**, Lilian. *I'll Meet You at the Cucumbers;* illus. by Sharon
Wooding. Atheneum, 1988. ISBN 0-689-31243-1. 63p. $12.95.

3-5   One of those rare books that combines quality and appeal (for
transitional readers yet), this is really a fictional development of the
town mouse and the country mouse—with a major thematic
difference. Junius Mouse persuades his bucolic friend Adam to visit
the city and meet Amanda Mouse on her birthday. Several elements
make the trip special for young readers or listeners. One is Moore's
knowledge of children's interests: the details of preparing a birthday
present with a message in riddle form, the delight of Adam's zooming
around in a toy car, the momentary suspense of his sudden dis-
appearance. Then there is Adam's fresh perspective on what he sees:
traffic lights appear as jewels, a bridge seems to be "a great shining
web hanging in the air." With natural grace, Adam's poetic thoughts
appear in verse form throughout the story, but he only realizes he's a
poet during a trip to the children's room of the library. At the end of
the book, Adam has ventured and gained. "Not often does one smell
roasted peanuts. Not every day does one discover that he is a poet . . .
." Now it is Amanda's turn to overcome her fear of the faraway and
find seeds that taste of the sun. A golden read-aloud.

740   **Morimoto**, Junko. *My Hiroshima;* written and illus. by Junko
Morimoto and with photographs. Viking, 1990. ISBN 0-670-83181-6.
32p. $12.95.

2-4   A picture book that inevitably will be compared to Toshi Maruki's
Hiroshima No Pika, this is younger in graphic tone and text. The
narrator describes her pre-war childhood before detailing the events
of August 6, 1945, when she and her family were lucky enough to
survive the blast that destroyed their home and to shelter in a cave.
After witnessing death and devastation all around them, Marimoto,
who was home with a stomach-ache when the bomb fell, visited the
ruins of her school to find "an aluminum lunch box with burnt, black
rice inside. I found the bones of many of my friends." Although this
does not have the power of Maruki's paintings, the full-color
illustrations, varied but spacious page design, and authentic story
combine for a telling effect. A last page gives facts about the bombing
of Hiroshima, and endpapers include historical black-and-white
photographs together with an author's note to parents and teachers.

741   **Morpurgo**, Michael. *King of the Cloud Forests.* Viking, 1988. ISBN 0-
670-82069-5. 146p. $11.95

5-8   Ashley is fourteen when his father, a medical missionary, insists he
leave China and the dangers of the Japanese invasion. Disguised as a
mute Tibetan pilgrim, accompanied by his "father," a wise Chinese
doctor, Ashley makes a dangerous journey to the border where he and

Uncle Sung are separated, and Ashley, near death from starvation and cold, is found by a fabled Yeti tribe. The ape-like creatures call him "Leelee" and seem to revere him as a god, welcoming him into their idyllic community. Improbable never descends to implausible here, even when Ashley eventually returns to England and discovers why the Yeti welcomed him as a long-lost friend. Ashley is a clear-eyed but very real fourteen, Uncle Sung is a convincing father figure, and the Yeti are depicted with dignity and humor. It is unfortunate that, for the most part, the old-fashioned boys' adventure story has been left to the choose-your-own crowd; here's a brief and dramatic novel that may woo reluctant readers back to the fold.

742   **Morrison**, Lillian, comp. *Rhythm Road: Poems to Move To.* Lothrop, 1988. ISBN 0-688-07098-1. 148p. $11.95.

5-10   This anthology of nearly a hundred poems is imaginatively organized into ten sections related to the movements of dancing, riding, water, music, animals, entertainment, sports, work, technology, and mental activity. None of the poems is inaccessible, although there is a considerable difference in levels between a Ruth Krauss poem such as "Duet" and William Carlos Williams' "Illegitimate Things." May Swenson crops up frequently, as does E. E. Cummings. It's a lively collection, with lots of clamorous verse (Poe's "Bells," of course, and Southey's "Cataract of Lodore"), as well as an abundance of concrete poetry which occasionally becomes gimmicky. On the whole, however, there's tonal balance, with a combination of the traditional and the unusual.

743   **Mother Goose.** *Sing a Song of Sixpence;* illus. by Tracey Campbell Pearson. Dial, 1985. Library ed. ISBN 0-8037-0152-7; Trade ed. ISBN 0-8037-0151-9. 22p. Library ed. $10.89; Trade ed. $10.95.

2-5 yrs.   It's the blackbirds that dominate Pearson's ebullient and very funny illustrations for a picture book version of a nursery favorite. The king and queen are buxom, as is their little daughter; all members of the royal family wear spiky little crowns, even the dog, and the line and wash pictures are filled with (but not overfilled with) such comic details as the queen taking her shoes off while she eats bread and honey or the king capsizing in a flurry of blackbirds. Full of vitality, full of fun. Notation for the melody line is provided at the back of the book.

744   **Mother Goose.** *The Orchard Book of Nursery Rhymes;* comp. by Zena Sutherland; illus. by Faith Jaques. Orchard, 1990. ISBN 0-531-05903-0. 88p. $21.95.

3-6 yrs.   This collection of seventy-six favorite and familiar nursery rhymes is illustrated with many full-color paintings "that place the verses in an eighteenth century setting, reflecting the historical period when many of them first appeared in print." A first-line index and notes on the rhymes and illustrations are appended.

745   **Mother Goose.** *The Random House Book of Mother Goose*; comp. and illus. by Arnold Lobel. Random House, 1986. Library ed. ISBN 0-394-86799-8; Trade ed. ISBN 0-394-86799-8. 170p. Library ed. $14.99; Trade ed. $14.95.

3-6 yrs.   A comprehensive collection of 306 nursery rhymes, with beautiful,
    *   endlessly inventive illustrations. Lobel has set his Mother Goose squarely in the past, with the requisite billowing gowns and pastoral vistas, all touched with a joyful flamboyance. Some of the rhymes are illustrated with a single small painting; others share a large illustration—a double-page spread of a gloriously messy kitchen illustrates five rhymes, including "Polly Put the Kettle on" and "Pease Porridge Hot," each text clearly separated but coming together in the picture. Still others are visually narrated through several frames, from a two-frame of "Doctor Foster" (boisterously marching along in the first, "up to his middle" in a puddle in the second) to a very funny "Twelve Days of Christmas," where the smitten suitor becomes gradually overwhelmed by the gifts he is carrying. There are several large paintings for single verses: a moody, double-page vertical for "Wee Willie Winkie," a forest full of herring for "The Man in the Wilderness," and a rolling, dramatic spread for "If All the Seas Were One Sea." The tones are varied—a grotesque "Jack Sprat," a romantically tender "Hush Little Baby"—but the overall vision is unified. From the rhymes of Mother Goose, Lobel has created a world.

746   **Mother Goose.** *Three Little Kittens*; illus by Paul Galdone. Houghton/Clarion, 1986. ISBN 0-89919-426-5. 31p. $13.95.

2-4 yrs.   Galdone's characteristically exuberant pen-and-wash drawings fill these pages with feline faces, first rueful, then joyful, then repentant, and finally excited about the prospects of catching "a rat close by." This is one of those sustained nursery rhymes that initiates youngest listeners into the concentration required for stories, and there's enough dramatic movement and color contrast in the art to hold toddlers' attention. (The cat face on the pie featured on the back cover will not go unnoticed, either.) There are other attractive versions of this verse still in print, including Lorinda Cauley's, but Galdone's style is especially suited to group sessions.

747   **Murphy,** Jill. *Five Minutes' Peace*; written and illus. by Jill Murphy. Putnam, 1986. ISBN 0-399-21354-6. 30p. $9.95.

4-6 yrs.   Inasmuch as children can laugh at themselves and their parents, this will appeal to young listeners; adults will love every minute of it. Mrs.

Large takes one look at her three elephant children wreaking havoc at the breakfast table, makes up a tea tray, and sneaks off to the bathroom for "five minutes' peace." There she is shortly joined by Lester, who plays "Twinkle, Twinkle, Little Star" three and a half times; Laura, who reads four and a half pages of "Little Red Riding Hood"; and the baby, who generously throws all his toys into Mrs. Large's bubble bath. Abandoning the tub to the children, Mrs. Large returns with the newspaper (the children have eaten her breakfast) to the kitchen, where she finally achieves three minutes and forty-five seconds of peace. The fine-grained color pencil drawings are softly textured and funny; and mother elephant's dilemma is a familiar enough one that children may enjoy it even from her perspective.

748   Murphy, Jim. *The Boys' War: Confederate and Union Soldiers Talk About the Civil War.* Clarion, 1990. ISBN 0-89919-893-7. 110p. illus. with photographs. $15.95.

5-9   Just in time to follow up on the interest stirred by the PBS series on the Civil War, this will serve long-term student research needs as well. Various chapters cover young soldiers' enlistment, battle experiences, living conditions, food supplies, medical and sanitary problems, and imprisonment. Drum and bugle corps boys get special attention, since they tended to be the youngest recruits. The author acknowledges that we have no statistics on how many underage boys fought or died in the war, but there were many; and some of their eyewitness accounts, here woven into background explanations, are vivid. Unfortunately, the sources for these are not directly documented, although readers could track a few of them from names cited in the text to names appearing in titles of the bibliography (*Private Elisha Stockwell, Jr. Sees the Civil War*, for instance). Numerous historical photographs, reproduced in sepia and well-placed in the text, add significant impact to the information.

749   Murphy, Jim. *The Call of the Wolves*; illus. by Mark Alan Weatherby. Scholastic, 1989. ISBN 0-590-41941-2. 32p. $13.95.

5-8 yrs.   With an involving text and arresting art, this is a nature narrative that commands attention without ever becoming sentimental or anthropomorphic. A young wolf is separated from his pack during a caribou hunt that is interrupted by illegal hunters shooting from a plane. Trapped, the wolf plunges over a cliff, injures a leg, and labors through a snowstorm in another pack's territory to return home. The story yields plenty of unobtrusive information, and an afterword explains how much modern research contradicts myths of the past. A brief list of important sources for futher information is appended. Because the style is straightforward and the dramatically textured paintings—each a handsome composition unto itself—are so dynamic, this can be read by independent readers older than the picture book listeners for whom it's intended.

750   Myers, Bernice. *Sidney Rella and the Glass Sneaker;* written and illus. by Bernice Myers. Macmillan, 1985. ISBN 0-02-767790-7. 30p. $12.95.

2-4   His parents work, his two tall, burly older brothers are on the football team, and Sidney, small and wistfully compliant, stays home and does all the chores. Sidney yearns to play football too, but his brothers just laugh at the idea. Along comes a wee fairy godfather (with wings and mustache) who bumbles a bit but finally gets the spell right and produces a uniform for Sidney, who gets into the game, makes many touchdowns, reverts to form at dinnertime, and is not accorded his full due until the team's coach comes around to see who can wear the left-behind glass sneaker. Giggles for all, but perhaps a special pleasure for boys who may have felt left out of this classic tale of a dear wish granted. The style is blithe, the cartoon-type drawings comic.

751   Myers, Walter Dean. *Crystal.* Viking Kestrel, 1987. ISBN 0-670-80426-6. 196p. $12.95.

6-9   Black and beautiful, sixteen-year-old Crystal had been spotted during a commercial made at her church, and now she is launched on a career as a model. Her mother is anxious to have Crystal succeed and advises her daughter to expect and accept some disadvantages; her father wants to protect his child's innocence and integrity. It is Crystal herself, however, who decides (partly because of a producer's sexual overtures, partly because of another young model's tragic end, partly because she knows she's missing a social life that's normal in adolescence) to stop modeling. The milieu is convincingly detailed, the characterization and storyline equally believable. Myers writes with an easy narrative flow that smoothly blends plot and nuances in relationships.

752   Myers, Walter Dean. *Fallen Angels.* Scholastic, 1988. ISBN 0-590-40942-5. 309p. $12.95.

8-   Black, seventeen, perceptive and sensitive, Richie (the narrator) has enlisted and been sent to Vietnam; in telling the story of his year of active service, Richie is candid about the horror of killing and the fear of being killed, the fear and bravery and confusion and tragedy of the war. This trenchant novel is about a particular war, but it is an indictment of all war; Myers uses the language of soldiers and he identifies with their concerns. A tough book, a vivid story.

753   Myers, Walter Dean. *Scorpions.* Harper, 1988. Library ed. ISBN 0-06-024365-1; Trade ed. ISBN 0-06-024364-3. 216p. Library ed. $12.89; Trade ed. $12.95.

6-9   Jamal, who is black, and his best friend Tito, Puerto Rican, are not
terribly sophisticated twelve-year-olds when they are confronted with
the "choice" to join a gang, the Scorpions. Jamal's big brother Randy
was the gang's leader until he was imprisoned for murder, and
running crack for the gang seems like the only way to raise money to
pay a lawyer for Randy's appeal. Along with the job comes a gun, a
powerful thing for Jamal, who never actually uses it but finds he
cannot bring himself to get rid of it until the gun finds its way into
Tito's hand. While Tito's grandmother and Jamal's mother and
impish little sister ("Am I cute or what?") provide, as well as they can,
love and support, the Harlem world portrayed here is unsparingly cold
and frightening (the school nurse gives Jamal tranquilizers to keep
him tractable; the two boys pass a park filled with "thrown-away
people") and the barely comforting ending is clearly only a reprieve.
Myer's anti-gang message is strong but not didactic, effectively voiced
through the words and actions of the Scorpions themselves. His
compassion for Tito and Jamal is deep; perhaps the book's signal
achievement is the way it makes us realize how young, in Harlem and
elsewhere, twelve years old really is.

754   **Namioka**, Lensey. *Island of Ogres.* Harper, 1989. Library ed. ISBN 0-
06-024373-2; Trade ed. ISBN 0-06-024372-4. 197p. Library ed. $12.89;
Trade ed. $12.95.

7-10   Another story of medieval Japan (Valley of the Broken Cherry Trees,
Village of the Vampire Cat, and others) that features the courage and
sagacity of the ronin (retired samurai) Zenta and Matsuzo. In this tale
of a power struggle on an island, a third ronin, Kajiro, plays a major
role. There's a bit of a love story, an element of mystery, good
historical details, and rather more depth of characterization than is
usually found in adventure novels. Namioka's style, plot, and pace are
strong.

755   **Nathanson**, Laura. *The Trouble with Wednesdays.* Pacer/Putnam,
1986. ISBN 0-399-21269-8. 176p. $13.95.

5-8   The one thing Becky worried about, when she thought of getting out of
sixth grade and going to junior high next year, was her teeth. She knew
she needed braces; she knew her parents could ill afford them. She
didn't like Dr. Rolfman, the dentist who was her father's cousin, but he
had offered to do the work at cost. And that was the start of Becky's
nightmare, for every Wednesday when the orthodontia was done, Dr.
Rolfman silently, urgently would rub against her, caress her, terrify
her. And every week he became more importunate. This is a first book
and a very impressive one; the author, a pediatrician, has balanced
the theme of sexual abuse with the other aspects of Becky's life, and
has made her fear, guilt, and embarrassment vividly real. This has the

validity of a case history (especially the treatment of the incredulous parents, and of Becky's shamed silence) but none of the bare-bones purposiveness; it's smoothly written and the characterization has depth and consistency.

756   **Naylor**, Phyllis Reynolds. *Alice in Rapture, Sort of.* Atheneum, 1989. ISBN 0-689-31466-3. 166p. $12.95.

5-8   Fans of *The Agony of Alice* will stand in line for this sequel about Alice's dating Patrick during the summer before they start junior high school. The dynamics between Alice and her two best girlfriends, Alice's yearning for her dead mother to help with the ordinary and extraordinary problems of growing up, and her individualistic approach to dating are smoothly blended into a funny, sometimes poignant narrative. Some questions are quickly resolved ("How was I supposed to eat and hold a rose at the same time?"). Others, such as working out a relationship with boys, take longer ("It was comforting in a way to know that I didn't have to squeeze it all into a single summer or all into seventh grade or even do it all in high school"). Naylor has as natural a voice for preadolescent romance from the girl's perspective as Betsy Byars has from the boy's in *Bingo Brown and the Language of Love.* The two make perfect companions for booktalking.

757   **Naylor**, Phyllis Reynolds. *The Keeper.* Atheneum, 1986. ISBN 0-689-31204-0. 212p. $13.95.

7-10
*
During his last year of junior high school, Nick watches his father leave two jobs, become gripped by paranoid delusions, and turn on both Nick and his mother as members of an imagined conspiracy. Although a school counselor and a priest are sympathetic, no one can do anything to get Nick's father committed without proof of insanity, and it is Nick who finally must force his father into a situation that reveals the man's dementia to authorities. The focus on the problem is unrelenting, but the story is grippingly detailed, with characters emerging full-dimensioned rather than being cast into roles of typical reaction (the exception to this is a girl who breaks her date with Nick after his father's hospitalization). Nick's stages of realization, anger, and pain are subtly developed, as are his mother's realistic mixture of strength and limitation and two school friends' genuine affection for Nick.

758   **Nelson**, Theresa. *And One for All.* Orchard, 1989. Library ed. ISBN 0-531-08404-3; Trade ed. ISBN 0-531-05804-2. 182p. Library ed. $12.99; Trade ed. $12.95.

7-12   A moving novel set in the years 1966 to 1968 portrays a family affected by the Vietnam war when their oldest son, Wing, enlists in the marines. The viewpoint is his sister Geraldine's, but each member of the family is vividly realized, including the youngest boy of six and both parents, the father slightly deaf from World War II wounds. It is to the novelist's credit that she concentrates on developing the home front—Wing's long-term school problems, his friendship with a neighboring boy who turns anti-war demonstrator, and the vivid detail of family rituals and dynamics—before building to the inevitable and tragic climax. Plot, dialogue, and setting are effortlessly authentic and never overwhelmed by the theme, which, while compellingly effective, is neither didactic nor dominant over the emotional impact. Smoothly written and easily read, this also manages to challenge assumptions in a thought-provoking probe of the past.

759   **Nelson**, Vaunda Micheaux. *Always Gramma*; illus. by Kimanne Uhler. Putnam, 1988. ISBN 0-399-21542-5. 32p. $13.95.

K-3   There have been, in the last several years, many books designed to inform and comfort the young child whose beloved grandparent has become senile. This story does not use the designation of Alzheimer's disease, but the pattern is there: the first forgetfulness, the disorientation, the irrational behavior and violence that are so hard for a young child to comprehend. Here the child is the speaker, first remembering all the things she and her grandmother did together, then describing the painful disintegration of Gramma's personality, and concluding with a regretful admission that Gramma doesn't know her family any longer, but they all love her, all visit often. Watercolor paintings that are simply composed but that often have a smeared look are adequately integrated with correlating text. This doesn't get sugary, but it has a sweet simplicity that makes it one of the best on its sad subject.

760   **Nerlove**, Miriam. *I Made a Mistake*; written and illus. by Miriam Nerlove. Atheneum, 1985. ISBN 0-689-50327-X. 26p. $10.95.

2-4 yrs.   Nonsense verses based on a jumprope rhyme will tickle youngest listeners, who make so many mistakes but keep trying so hard: "I went to the kitchen to bake a pie, I made a mistake . . . and baked a fly." This unappetizing prospect does not daunt our young heroine, who goes on to walk the dog but ends up leashing a frog, approaches the well to make a wish but instead kisses a fish, etc. Pen and wash illustrations capitalize on the absurd surprises without getting frenetic. This is a good one to read aloud when everything seems to go wrong and everyone needs a dose of humor to counteract the tension.

761   **Newman**, Robert. *The Case of the Murdered Players*. Atheneum, 1985. ISBN 0-689-31155-9. 174p. $11.95.

5-7   In a detective story set in London in the 1890s, one of a series, two young people help Inspector Wyatt of Scotland Yard unravel a mystery about a series of murders of actresses. The young people, Sara and Andrew, are part of a theatrical household (Andrew's mother is a star of the British stage) and Wyatt is engaged to Andrew's mother, so the characters are personally involved. This has a brisk style, sound structure, and good period details. It is given added color by the use of street slang of the period and by behind-the-scenes theatrical details.

762   **Nicholson**, Darrel. *Wild Boars;* illus. with photographs by Craig Blacklock. Carolrhoda, 1987. ISBN 0-87614-308-7. 43p. (Nature Watch). $12.95.

4-6   With the striking color photography and uncondescending coverage typical of the series, this book presents an animal whose intelligence and adaptability are not widely known. The details are surprisingly interesting: the boar's growth of a thick shield of protective skin before seasonal battles for leadership; the piglets' habit of lying side by side, head to toe for close physical contact; the trick a drift (group of boars) will pull in escaping a predator by running in fanlike formation and circling back to surround and attack the pursuer. Characteristics, reproductive cycle, social order, and ecological impact are all considered in a neatly-organized, well-designed text that has a glossary and index.

763   **Nickman**, Steven L. *When Mom and Dad Divorce;* illus. by Diane de Groat. Messner, 1986. Trade ed. ISBN 0-671-60253-9; Paper ed. ISBN 0-671-62878-X. 70p. Trade ed. $9.29; Paper ed. $4.95.

4-7   A pediatrician and psychiatrist, Nickman uses a series of anecdotes as bases for discussions of different aspects of children's coping with divorce and of different kinds of separation situations. Much of the advice he gives is available in other books designed to help boys and girls through difficult situations and to assuage their worry or guilt. Not many other books strike such a good balance between candor and reassurance. The text is specific, addressing such topics as dealing with stepparents and their children, or the child's role and rights if there's a custody battle. Best of all, the text is always child-focused—but calmly so. An index is included.

764   **Nimmo**, Jenny. *The Snow Spider*. Dutton, 1987. ISBN 0-525-44306-1. 136p. $11.95.

4-6   First published in Great Britain, Nimmo's fantasy—smoothly meshed with its realistic matrix—is set in Wales. Gwyn, on his tenth birthday, received odd gifts from his eccentric grandmother, who said it was time to find out if he were a magician. One of the magic elements is a silvery spider whose web holds images, and out of this conjuring appears a pale, silvery girl who seems to be a reincarnation of a sister who died years before. Through Eirlys, the girl in the web, Gwyn's parents are finally able to accept his sister's death, and his father is able to forgive Gwyn's role in that tragedy. Cohesive and compelling, this tautly-structured story has a depth and nuance that never interfere with its clarity.

765   **Nixon**, Joan Lowery. *Fat Chance, Claude;* illus. by Tracey Campbell Pearson. Viking Kestrel, 1987. ISBN 0-670-81459-8. 28p. $10.95.

4-7 yrs.   Backing up a bit from the time frame of *If You Say So, Claude* and *Beats Me, Claude,* this tells the story of Shirley and Claude's childhoods and courtship. Ever the individual, Shirley has an independent disposition that scares away most suitors—the last one runs after he sees her riding a bull—until she sets out for Colorado to pan for gold and finds herself parked next to Claude in the wagon train west. After saving him from a rattlesnake and later staking out the same claim as Claude, she agrees to go partners all the way. This represents endearing characters, adroit writing, and an action-packed feminist pioneer tall tale all at once ("Shirley was born long and lean, with hair the color of prairie dust and a mouth wide enough to hold a couple of smiles at the same time"). To enjoy—north, south, and east as well as west.

766   **Nixon**, Joan Lowery. *Secret, Silent Screams.* Delacorte, 1988. ISBN 0-440-50059-1. 180p. $14.95.

7-10   Mourning the death of her friend Barry, Marti is convinced that the verdict (suicide, the latest of a number of suicides of high school students) is wrong. Several clues do tend to support the idea that Barry took his own life, but Marti is sure she knew him well enough to know it was unlikely; too, the gun had been in Barry's right hand—but he was left-handed. The only adult authority who takes Marti seriously is a young police officer, Karen. Nixon is an old and polished hand at creating suspense and building logical clues into the structure of her stories. The solution is, therefore, achieved credibly while maintaining dramatic impact including Marti's dangerous confrontation with Barry's murderer. Nixon also incorporates information about adolescent suicide without disturbing the story's narrative flow.

767   **Norman**, Howard. *Who-Paddled-Backward-With-Trout;* illus. by Ed Young. Little, 1987. ISBN 0-316-61182-4. 30p. $13.95.

5-7 yrs.   Norman cites his source, an old man of the Swampy Cree Indians in northern Canada, and leaves it to readers to discover the humor in this translated tale about a boy who sets out to find a new name. The joke is on macho quests: Trout-with-Flattened-Nose wishes, after some experimental misnomers, to become Who-Paddles-a-Canoe-Better-Than-Anyone. Instead, after a complicated series of mishaps with some hungry beavers, he's assigned the title name: Who-Paddled-Backward-with-Trout. The story is full of simple but subtle surprises. When the beavers chew one of his paddles into a fish shape, the boy complains "This isn't the trout I'm looking for. Just then the paddle said, 'You're right, I'm not! It leaped off the fishing line and swam away." Or, in the end, "'It's a fine, strong name,' the trout interrupted. 'And you most certainly have earned it!'" Young's black silhouette illustrations form an elegant sequence of shapes without becoming static. The medium itself is well suited to folklore, for it is faceless but expressive. Aside from the aesthetic considerations, children, who are not always as coordinated as they would like to be, will enjoy reading about a character who thematically bumps into things.

768   **Numeroff**, Laura Joffe. *If You Give a Mouse a Cookie*; illus. by Felicia Bond. Harper, 1985. Library ed. ISBN 0-06-024587-9; Trade ed. ISBN 0-06-024586-7. 28p. Library ed. $9.89; Trade ed. $9.95

2-5 yrs.   Children love to indulge in supposition or to ask "What will happen if . . . ?" and here there is a long, satisfying chain of linked and enjoyably nonsensical causes and effects. If you give a mouse a cookie, he'll want milk; if you give him a glass of milk, he'll ask for a straw; if he gets a straw, he'll want a napkin, et cetera. After several rounds of activities (including a great deal of fetching and carrying on the part of an obliging child) the chain comes full circle with another glass of milk, "And chances are if he asks for a glass of milk, he's going to want a cookie to go with it." The illustrations, neatly drawn, spaciously composed, and humorously detailed, extend the story just the way picture book illustrations should.

769   **O'Dell**, Scott. *Black Star, Bright Dawn*. Houghton, 1988. ISBN 0-395-47778-6. 134p. $14.95.

6-9   The Iditarod is the annual Alaskan dog sled race (1,197 miles from Anchorage to Nome) across two mountain ranges and the Yukon River. It is clear that O'Dell has done careful research to achieve such verisimilar details, and just as clear that those details are given dramatic immediacy by being presented in the voice of Bright Dawn, who enters the race to replace her injured father. Through the grueling course of the Iditarod, the Eskimo girl shows tenacity and courage that will involve and engage readers. No, she doesn't win—but she's excitingly close.

770   **O'Dell**, Scott. *My Name Is Not Angelica*. Houghton, 1989. ISBN 0-395-51061-9. 130p. $14.95.

7-10   Raisha is renamed Angelica by the slaveowners who purchase her for their plantation on St. John, an island in the Danish West Indies (now the U.S. Virgin Islands). Both Raisha and her betrothed, Konje, have been captured and sold into slavery by a rival African king, and soon after landing in St. John, Konje escapes to a hidden colony of runaways intent upon revolt. Based upon historical records, Raisha's narration of the conditions and events leading to the tragic rebellion is vivid, intensely conveying the humiliation and torture inflicted upon the slaves (and occasionally by the slaves) and the brutalization of the whites. While events are occasionally telegraphed and character-ization emblematic, this is a fierce story, fairly and urgently told.

771   O'Dell, Scott. *Streams to the River, River to the Sea: A Novel of Sacagawea*. Houghton, 1986. ISBN 0-395-40430-4. 191p. $14.95.

7-10   O'Dell returns here to his most effective voice, a simple first-person narration of historical journey. The story begins with Sacagawea's capture, along with her Shoshone cousin, by Minnetaree warriors. Her adjustment to life with that tribe, escape from a hostile neighboring chief, and marriage to a French trader after her owner's gambling loss all test the courage and strength she will need to survive the hardships of the Lewis and Clark expedition to the Pacific—which she makes with a baby strapped to her back. This is action-packed drama, believably revealed by a stoic heroine who maintains her self-worth despite vagaries of fortune in which she's a pawn of men and natural forces. Although the return eastward telescopes into almost a catalogue of tribes and perils overcome, the book retains its grip on the reader to a fine-honed finish, when Sacagawea abandons her romantic feelings for Clark and returns to her people. An informative and involving choice for American history students and pioneer-adventure readers.

772   O'Dell, Scott. *The Serpent Never Sleeps: A Novel of Jamestown and Pocahontas*; illus. by Ted Lewin. Houghton, 1987. ISBN 0-395-44242-7. 227p. $15.95.

6-9   Although she has been bidden by King James to come to court, Serena Lynn runs off to join the company that is sailing from Plymouth to Jamestown in 1609. The "serpent" of the title is on a ring the king has given Serena, telling her that it will protect her. There are many times that she hopes the ring will do so, as she follows the man she loves to the New World. The dangers and delays of travel, the tragedy of the Jamestown colony, and the story of the Indian princess whom Serena comes to know are told with O'Dell's usual narrative flair, his usual smooth blend of fact and fiction, and his usual ability to bring the past to life.

773   O'Shea, Pat, ad. *Finn MacCool and the Small Men of Deeds;* retold
       by Pat O'Shea; illus. by Stephen Lavis. Holiday House, 1987. ISBN 0-
       8234-0651-2. 88p. $12.95.

4-6   O'Shea has the great Irish gift of stretching small stories into tall ones,
       and the adventures of Finn MacCool offer her a prime opportunity.
       MacCool starts out the book immobilized by a headache, but his
       sarcastic servant shames him into responding to a call for help: a
       giant-king's first two sons have disappeared shortly after birth, and the
       third baby is now threatened by the unknown kidnapper. The real
       heroes here are eight tiny men, each with a special magic power that
       plays a role in retrieving the kidnapped children from the king's evil
       sister, who is a powerful witch. Readers and listeners will enjoy the
       playful inventions ("'I had a headache,' he said. 'I have it here in my
       hands,' the thief said") and humorous exaggeration of fairy tale
       elements ("Keys turned in locks and these keys were then locked in
       caskets. The caskets were locked in their turn, and their keys were put
       into leather purses and brought to the King who hung them about his
       neck"). The tale takes a bit too long to get started but moves well once
       it's under way. Boisterous pen-and-ink hatch drawings with handsome
       Celtic motifs enliven a handsomely designed format.

774   O'Shea, Pat. *The Hounds of the Morrigan.* Holiday House, 1986.
       ISBN 0-8234-0595-8. 469p. $15.95.

5-8   This robust fantasy, despite its length, reads almost effortlessly. Ten-
       year-old Pidge and his little sister Brigit are drawn into a battle
       between two ancient Irish spirits: the Dagda, "God of the earth and
       the life in it," and the Morrigan, "Goddess of Death and Destruction."
       The children's mission is to find and bring to the Dagda a small red
       pebble: it is a crystalized drop of Morrigan's blood, and her power will
       be invincible if she regains it. While the children's travels through the
       fairy world of Tir-na-nog have a predictable rhythm—magic spells and
       animal helpers turn up with monotonous regularity—each episode
       has great drama, and O'Shea's characterizations, many based on Irish
       folklore, are inventive and delightful. There's the earwig who thinks
       he's Napoleon ("Between life and death—zere is but a moment so—
       go for ze noses"), a brave and loving fox, Pidge and Brigit ("five years
       old and five years daft") themselves. What is most remarkable is the
       ease and effectiveness with which O'Shea handles shifts in tone from
       the comic, almost burlesque, to the mythic—the Morrigan and her two
       alter-egos, Macha and Bodbh, cast spells and cause mischief with
       demented hilarity, yet in the final battle for the pebble (a tremendous
       scene) they become awesome, terrible monsters. "Even though the
       battle might go against her; she gloated that she had been its cause.
       She chanted for blood and flecks of foam fell from her lips." The prose

is rather relentlessly ornamented, but the images are always concrete and, like the narrative, have vigorous strength.

775   **Oakley,** Graham. *Henry's Quest*; written and illus. by Graham Oakley. Atheneum, 1986. ISBN 0-689-31172-9. 32p. $12.95.

7-   In order to gain the hand of the Princess Isolde, shepherd Henry goes off at the king's behest to find the magical, long-forgotten substance GASOLINE. Set in a future England where technology has been lost, but its monuments remain, this is a sly comedy that will best appeal to older readers despite the picture book format. Most of the humor is in the intricate paintings, which must be closely examined to get the punchlines to the straight-faced text. "Henry asked the friendly ones about GASOLINE, but not one of them had ever heard of such a thing" — this, asked of a man milking a cow hitched up to a decrepit gas pump. The town where Henry eventually finds GASOLINE is a dystopian delight, with police breaking up demonstrations for "STRONGER BEER," and "MORE 24 HR. DISCOS," and a theater that features "NEW IMPROVED SHAKESPEARE 100% MORE SIZZLE" with an Ophelia water ballet and "King Leer."

776   **Olson,** Arielle North. *The Lighthouse Keeper's Daughter*; illus. by Elaine Wentworth. Little, 1987. ISBN 0-316-65053-6. 30p. $14.95.

5-7 yrs.   Based partly on a famous incident at the Matinicus Rock lighthouse off the coast of Maine in 1856, this tells the story of a young girl who keeps the lights burning during her father's absence throughout several weeks of winter storm. Like the heroine in *Keep the Lights Burning, Abbie*, an easy-to-read version by Peter and Connie Roop, Miranda dashes out to save her chickens from being washed away as waves cover the island. This is a slightly more dramatic version: Miranda is alone, with no sisters to help her and her mother; and she is portrayed as having a yearning for a garden, which she finally grows when grateful fishermen bring her loads of dirt for her seeds. Full-page watercolor paintings emphasize the drama of the heavy seas crashing against the isolated rock. The sweeping seascapes and snug indoor scenes offset the long text and sometimes clarify it, as in the case of a confusing transition from Miranda's memory of arriving on the island to her lamplighting during the storm. Between the illustrations and the narrative action, this historical fiction in picture-book format will stir a reader's imagination.

777   **Oneal,** Zibby. *Grandma Moses: Painter of Rural America*; illus. by Donna Ruff and with paintings by Grandma Roses. Viking, 1986. ISBN 0-670-80664-X. 58p. (Women of Our Time). $9.95.

5-8   Another in an excellent series, Oneal's book, like Meltzer's on Winnie Mandela , gracefully conveys the central focus of the subject's life and work. In this case, the strength and independence of Anna Mary Moses' personality emerge long before the art for which she became famous. Her country childhood and hard life as a farm wife simply set the stage for the serving of a talent that had simmered many years. Oneal's style is graceful and richly spiced with Grandma Moses' own pithy comments. Illustrated with reproductions that exemplify the succinct descriptions of Moses' paintings.

778   **Oneal**, Zibby. *In Summer Light*. Viking, 1985. ISBN 0-670-80784-2. $11.95.

7-9   When she was a little girl, Kate had adored her father, a famous painter; now that she is an adolescent, aware that he is self-centered and that he had dismissed her own ambitions as a painter as trivial, she is not happy at home. Seventeen, she has been sent home from school to recover from mononucleosis, and the only thing that makes her life bearable is Ian, the graduate student who has been hired to catalogue her father's paintings. It is Ian who helps her find her way back to painting, who gives her confidence despite his gentle rejection of her love. There is little drama here or even narrative movement; the strength of the book is in its insight into relationships and how they change, its convincing and consistent characterization, and its fluid style.

779   **Opie**, Iona, comp. *Tail Feathers from Mother Goose*; comp. by Iona and Peter Opie. Little, 1988. ISBN 0-316-65081-1. 126p. illus. $19.95.

3-6 yrs.   Many adults will be as interested as the very young children for whom this unusual compilation has primary appeal. *The* authority on nursery rhymes, Iona Opie explains in her preface that the rhymes in this collection, few of which have been previously published, have been collected by the Opies (or sent to them); some are little-known variants of more familiar verses ("Ride a cock-horse to Coventry Cross/ To see what Emma can buy . . ."). Each verse is illustrated by a different artist (usually in a double-page spread) so that the book has visual variety; among the illustrators are several winners of the Greenaway Award. Most of the artists are British, but the cover art is by Maurice Sendak—who probably can be considered an artist-citizen of the world of children's books. Not all the verses are memorable, but the book is.

780   **Oppenheim**, Joanne. *You Can't Catch Me!*; illus. by Andrew Shachat. Houghton, 1986. ISBN 0-395-41452-0. 31p. $12.95.

2-5 yrs.
*   It's rare to find contemporary verse with a true nursery rhyme ring, but this has it, along with satisfying and original art work. There's a hint of the Gingerbread Man in this fly and his fate; he's obstreperous enough to chant, each time he annoys an animal and then escapes it,

" 'No matter how hard you try/try/try/ you can't catch me!'/ called the pesky / black / fly." After pestering a series of barnyard animals, the fly makes the mistake of resting on a rock—really a turtle that gives him his comeuppance. The paintings are reminiscent of John Burningham but are fresh in their own right, with subtle blendings of mild color giving a spacious look to what is actually a fairly small format. The animals are inventively cartooned, the shapes of the pigs particularly humorous in two compositions of rounded shapes compounded into a series. A+ for graphic and sound effects.

781   **Orr**, Katherine. *My Grandpa and the Sea*; written and illus. by Katherine Orr. Carolrhoda, 1990. ISBN 0-87614-409-1. 32p. $12.95.

4-7 yrs.   Vividly set on a Caribbean island, this story is narrated by young Lila, whose grandpa fishes in a dugout canoe carved from the trunk of a tree. "He had never been to school, but he was very wise. He could read the sea and sky like most of us read books." When big, high-powered boats reduce the fish population too much for Grandpa to pay expenses, he tries to drive a taxi and help Grammy in her bakery, but seems to pine away until an idea for farming sea moss in floating frames takes him back on the water where he belongs. The narrative and dialogue are natural enough to soften the moral, which has a disarmingly open naïveté. Orr's primitivistic paintings depend on oceanic hues brightened with red and yellow; the seascapes, full of sweeping organic shapes, contrast with indoor scenes that bring this black family into close perspective. A childhood vista of loving bonds and natural values.

782   **Oxenbury**, Helen. *All Fall Down*. ISBN 0-689-769040-7. *Clap Hands*. ISBN 0-689-769030-X. *Say Goodnight*. ISBN 0-689-769010-5. *Tickle, Tickle*. ISBN 0-689-769020-2. All four books written and illus. by Helen Oxenbury. Aladdin, 1987. 8p. $4.95.

6-24   One of the first—and still one of the best—creators of board books,
mos.   Oxenbury here goes to a larger size format filled to overflowing with
*   babies of similar plump shape but several colors of skin. The texts lend themselves to rhythmic play with wiggly listeners: "Clap hands, dance and spin, open wide and pop it in, blow a trumpet, bang a drum, wave to Daddy, wave to Mom." The sportive infants are doing just what's described, with funny flourishes: while two obediently "pop it in," the third grabs something from another's plate and the fourth pours his juice over his neighbor's head. There's great general appeal in this series. *Say Goodnight* shows babies being lifted and tossed ("Up, down, up in the sky"), pushed ("swing low, swing high"), bounced ("bumpity, bumpity, hold on tight"), and bedded down ("hush, little babies, say goodnight"). Buoyant action and vital colors against open

white space will keep these moving from hand to mouth and back again.

783   **Oxenbury**, Helen, comp. *The Helen Oxenbury Nursery Story Book;* comp. and illus. by Helen Oxenbury. Knopf, 1985. Library ed. ISBN 0-394-97519-7; Trade ed. ISBN 0-394-87519-2. 69p. Library ed. $12.99; Trade ed. $12.95.

4-6 yrs.   More humorous but less refined in both illustration and text than *The Baby's Story Book* by Chorao (above), this also features brief, favorite folk tales, from the "Three Billy Goats" to "The Little Red Hen." Here the versions are slightly longer, but the retellings are down to earth: Cock and Mouse declare "I won't," like a stubborn child, instead of "Not I," like a fabled figure. The page design is less elegant but more spacious, with half-page, full-page and double-page action-packed watercolors, some of which are quite funny. Both collections would serve preschoolers well for bedtime reading.

784   **Oxenbury**, Helen. *I Can.* ISBN 0-394-87482-X. *I Hear.* ISBN 0-394-87481-1. *I See.* ISBN 0-394-87479-X. *I Touch.* ISBN 0-394-87480-3. All books are written and illus. by Helen Oxenbury; Random House, 1986; 12p. $2.95.

8-24   Many a board book has come down the pike since Oxenbury's first
mos.   series (*Family*, etc.) in 1981. She's still one of the best in terms of maintaining simple concepts, lively art, and action generated from object. In *I Touch,* for instance, a picture of a ball is followed by a toddler rolling on it in characteristic play; the tattered blanket blowing dry on the wash line is followed by the pajama-clad child holding it, sucking a thumb with eyes closed in a bliss of softness. *I Hear* has a child clapping hands over ears beside a furiously barking dog, listening to grandfather's watch, and soothing a screaming baby sibling. *I Can* demonstrates typical movements, including stamping, falling, and stretching; and *I See* gently reminds little ones that flowers can be gazed on at ground level without being uprooted, and that a frog and a friend are wondrous sights. Good pickings for parent-sharing with the youngest.

785   **Parish**, Peggy. *Merry Christmas, Amelia Bedelia;* illus. by Lynn Sweat. Greenwillow, 1986. Library ed. ISBN 0-688-06102-8; Trade ed. ISBN 0-688-06101-X. 61p. Library ed. $10.88; Trade ed. $10.25.

1-3   You would think Mrs. Rogers would know by now not to tell Amelia Bedelia to trim the tree or stuff the stockings. Just as well, though, as children can't get enough of the literal-minded maid and will laugh themselves silly at the shorn tree ("Maybe it was too fat") and the stockings stuffed with turkey dressing and "hung" so the fireplace resembles a gallows. And, although the "date" cake seems a little funny, Amelia Bedelia's spice cake tastes just fine, sending everyone (especially Aunt Myra, who reveres Amelia's mistakes as pure poetry) back for seconds. Sweat's full-color paintings nicely give the punchline to the dead-pan text.

786   **Parish**, Peggy. *Scruffy;* illus. by Kelly Oechsli. Harper, 1988. Library ed. ISBN 0-06-024660-X; Trade ed. ISBN 0-06-024659-6. 64p. (I Can Read). Library ed. $10.89; Trade ed. $9.95.

1-2   In a modest way, this is an exemplary story for the beginning independent reader: vocabulary controlled (but not rigidly), story line sturdy, plot not taxing, subject appealing, print large, and pages uncluttered. It also gives some information about getting and caring for a pet, it advocates consideration for animals, and it tells the story of a child who gets just what he's wanted for his birthday, a kitten. Line and wash drawings are a bit repetitive, but they have vitality and humor, and they're nicely integrated with the text on almost every page.

787   **Park**, Barbara. *My Mother Got Married (And Other Disasters)*. Knopf, 1989. Library ed. ISBN 0-394-92149-6; Trade ed. ISBN 0-394-82149-1. 138p. Library ed. $11.99; Trade ed. $10.95.

4-6   Park has consistently shown an ability to shed humorous light on potentially dreary situations. In this sequel to *Don't Make Me Smile*, Charles' unhappiness about his parents' divorce and about being "displaced" by stepfather Ben (and Ben's teenage daughter and preschool son) makes him a prime candidate for a surprisingly fresh treatment of a common theme. Although the protagonist's first-person voice is entertaining, his selfishness is candidly realistic. At one point he ruminates about having to share a room with five-year-old Thomas: "Sharing is not normal. . . . The only time lions like to share is when they're already finished eating. And to me, that's not sharing. That's full." Later he refuses to feel flattered that Thomas follows him around: "It would be like wading through a swamp and coming out with a leech on your leg. You would never really feel proud that you're the one it picked." The author has a way of introducing information naturally. In describing his best friend, Charles talks about how his "mother says it's getting hard to tell us apart. This is funny only if you know Martin is black." The plot is hardly noticeable among the family interactions. Charles denies adjusting to the new situation even after Ben's quiet understanding brings them closer. But he does accept it, and comes close to admonishing readers (many of whom will have known similar situations) to do the same.

788   **Parker**, Nancy Winslow. *The United Nations from A to Z;* written and illus. by Nancy Winslow Parker. Dodd, 1985. Trade ed. ISBN 0-396-

08663-2; Paper ed. ISBN 0-396-08738-8. 73p. Trade ed. $11.95; Paper ed. $4.95.

4-6   Created specifically for browsing ("Do NOT read this book from the beginning to the end in one sitting"), this collection of one-page descriptive reports is like a mini-encyclopedia of U.N. history and activities. The author has not confined herself to one entry per alphabetical letter (U has 23), but has tried to incorporate a broad range of information within well-marked and illustrated sections. Flags, maps, lists of members, and organizational diagrams extend the tongue-in-cheek cartoon drawing on every page. Random fact finders who delight in curiosities will enjoy the FAO food testing projects that include Breaded and Fried Peruvian Guinea Pigs and Roasted Nigerian Giant Rat a la Safari (these rodents offer several advantages: "They eat scraps, multiply at astonishing rates, and need no refrigeration as they are one-meal size"). An unusual approach for the young researcher.

789   **Parnall**, Peter. *Feet!;* written and illus. by Peter Parnall. Macmillan, 1988. ISBN 0-02-770110-7. 32p. $13.95.

3-6 yrs.   With elegant drafting and witty composition, Parnall creates a concept book that will invite young children to observe and identify the feet in each of these 15 double spreads. While the title page shows contrasting types (clawed, toed, hoofed), most of the pictures concentrate on one. The line "I like BIG feet," for instance, is accompanied by a close-up drawing of the elephant's foot with a distant miniature of the animal in its environment. Others included are the armadillo ("LONG-TOED SCALY feet"), the bear ("HAIRY" feet), the pelican ("WEBBED" feet), etc., ending with humans and a note identifying all the creatures. The game-puzzle quality of the book is no less effective for Parnall's spare illustration, in pen and ink with highlights of yellow, blue, and green.

790   **Pascoe**, Elaine. *Racial Prejudice.* Watts, 1985. ISBN 0-531-10057-X. 118p. illus. with photographs. $10.90.

7-10   An unusually clear, well-focused presentation balances discussion of general prejudicial patterns with specific history of the groups that have been discriminated against in the U.S. The most substantial examination is of Blacks, beginning with colonization and continuing with the economics and social forces of slavery, reconstruction, Jim Crow laws, and the Civil Rights movement. Native Americans, Asians, and Hispanics all get an attentive survey as to their differences and similarities in responding to deeply rooted racial prejudice. A thought-provoking summary and a bibliographic essay conclude the book.

791   **Patent**, Dorothy Hinshaw. *Babies!* Holiday House, 1988. ISBN 0-8234-0685-7. 37p. illus. with photographs. $14.95.

4-7 yrs.   Illustrated with lots of informative color photographs of beautiful babies, this is an easy to read guide for younger children to the stages of infant development. Patent combines factual information ("Young babies are more interested in looking at patterns than in seeing solid colors") reassurance ("It may alarm you when the tiny body jerks with a hiccup but it doesn't bother the baby") and practical advice ("You have to be sure nothing dangerous can be reached from anywhere on the floor") in a smooth and simple text that will give older children a welcome sense of involvment with and responsibility for a new arrival.

792   **Patent**, Dorothy Hinshaw. *How Smart Are Animals?* Harcourt, 1990. ISBN 0-15-236770-5. 208p. illus. with photographs. $16.95.

7-12   Patent's discussion of kinds, degrees, and definitions of intelligence in animals is scrupulously paralleled by an analysis of the scientific methodologies used by animal researchers. She describes both laboratory experiments and ethological observation of insects, birds, and mammals, persistently reminding readers that all species are adapted to their own circumstances. "Since the lives of animals are so different from ours, we can't apply human standards to them. We must develop different ideas of what animal intelligence might be." The experiments described are intriguing, and include both familiar projects, such as Patterson's work with Koko the gorilla, and some lesser-known ones, such as Pepperberg's teaching shapes and colors to Alex the parrot. "When he doesn't want to continue a series of experiments he says 'No,' and gets a rest from working." Some of the recounting is overly-detailed (and could use clarifying illustrations), but Patent always provides a careful commentary on what each experiment proves and what remains speculation. A lot depends, she suggests, on what we mean by intelligence, illuminating not only the ways animals think, but the way humans think about animals and about themselves. Notes, glossary, bibliography and index are all included.

793   **Patent**, Dorothy Hinshaw. *Quarter Horses;* illus. with photographs by William Munoz and others. Holiday House, 1985. ISBN 0-8234-0573-7. 91p. $12.95.

4-7   Young equestrians will appreciate Patent's clear focus and crisp style, along with the black-and-white photographs of quarter horses in action. The text covers the development of this uniquely American horse, the breeding into ranch, racing, and rodeo stock, and the physical characteristics that lend themselves to cutting cattle, straight-track running, and competitions. There are lists of places to write for more information, publications of interest, a glossary, and an index.

794   **Patent**, Dorothy Hinshaw. *Thoroughbred Horses.* Holiday House, 1985. ISBN 0-8234-0558-3. 86p. illus. with photographs. $12.95.

4-7   Dependably thorough and lucid in her writing, Patent here gives broad but fully detailed coverage to the topic of Thoroughbred horses. Her text includes a discussion of founding sires and blood lines; descriptions of breeding, training, and racing; Thoroughbreds used for participation in events or exhibitions other than racing; and other breeds that have been improved by introducing Thoroughbred strains. The writing style is crisp, and the book should prove interesting to the general reader as well as to horse-lovers. A bibliography, glossary, and index are included; the book is profusely illustrated by photographs, many of which are action shots.

795   **Patent**, Dorothy Hinshaw. *Wheat: The Golden Harvest;* illus. with photographs by William Munoz. Dodd, 1987. ISBN 0-396-08781-7. 61p. $12.95.

4-6   Photographs of excellent quality (some in color, and some in black-and-white) illustrate a text that is typical of Patent's writing: crisp style, logical organization, no padding. She describes the plant and its parts, explaining which parts are used for which food products; she discusses the different kinds of wheat, how wheat is grown and harvested, and how wheat products are processed into foods. A glossary and an index are appended.

796   **Patent**, Dorothy Hinshaw. *Where the Wild Horses Roam;* illus. with photographs by William Muñoz. Clarion, 1989. ISBN 0-89919-507-5. 72p. $15.95.

5-7   While there is adequate background here on the characteristics of wild horses and their herd structure, the real emphasis is on protecting them without over-grazing the environment in which they reproduce so prolifically. Patent is objective in presenting arguments by ranchers, who say the horses threaten their livestock, and organizations (listed, with addresses, at the end of the book) that work against destruction of the animals. The handsome color photographs, including stunning western landscapes, will hook horse lovers, and the indexed text provides students with smoothly written information for reports.

797   **Patent**, Dorothy Hinshaw. *The Whooping Crane: A Comeback Story;* illus. with photographs by William Muñoz. Clarion, 1988. ISBN 0-89919-455-9. 88p. $14.95.

4-6   There's inherent drama in examining a bird that has come close to extinction; from a world population of 21 in 1941, the number of whooping cranes has grown to almost 200. Patent turns a practiced hand to describing the bird's life cycle and characteristics, as well as the complex rescue efforts of scientists who have resorted to various environmental and breeding experiments to rebuild dwindling flocks. The color photographs capture the beauty of the bird, while the black-and-white photos extend the information in pictures of incubating eggs or of chicks getting weighed and sprayed with protective antibiotic. A natural pick for ecology reports.

798   **Paterson**, Katherine. *Come Sing, Jimmy Jo*. Lodestar, 1985. ISBN 0-525-67167. 197p. $12.95.

6-9   This is a story of country music, of family bonding and friction, and above all of the realignment of perspectives for eleven-year-old Jimmy Jo. His real name is James, and he is uncomfortable with the "Jimmy Jo" his mother (who has also decided she'll be known as Keri Su rather than Olive) has decided should be his professional name. He joins the family singing group, and his sweet singing brings them more fame than they've ever had. It also brings publicity, and with his new prominence James is a target for fans, and for a man who insists he's James' real father. What James learns to accept is the fact that the man's telling the truth and that the loving man he's always called his father is still the one he loves. He even understands why Olive never told him, understands why the family circle must hold fast. This is a tender, touching story of familial love that prevails over the petty jealousies and abrasions of family life and the tensions of professional differences. Paterson creates strong characters and convincing dialogue, so that her story is effective even to those to whom the heavy emphasis on country music strikes no sympathetic chord.

799   **Paterson**, Katherine. *The Tale of the Mandarin Ducks*; illus. by Leo and Diane Dillon. Lodestar, 1990. ISBN 0-525-67283-4. 40p. $14.95.

5-8 yrs.   Great artists keep growing. The Dillons show more depth of line, color,
*   and style than ever before in this original blending of Japanese art (ukiyo-e), art deco, and picture book illustration. Watercolor and pastel paintings envelop, without overwhelming, the text of a story about a pair of mandarin ducks, whose separation ultimately leads to a happy ending. A cruel lord captures the male for its plumage and then punishes the samurai whom he believes to be responsible for releasing the bird to return to its mate. The samurai refuses to betray the kitchen maid who really opened the cage and, reduced to the status of servant, falls in love with the kindhearted woman. The two are saved from a death sentence by the magical intercession of two imperial messengers, who lead the lovers to a snug hut in the woods before turning into a pair of mandarin ducks. Paterson's adaptation of a Japanese folktale (no sources given) is as graceful as the figures so skillfully drawn by the Dillons. The life-and-death drama is concluded

with an unobtrusive moral: "Yasuko and Shozo...had many children who gave them much happiness—and a little trouble. But as they had learned years before, trouble can always be borne when it is shared." The Dillons' loving visual development of these two characters, curved together with flowing outlines, says even more than words can.

800   **Patterson**, Francine. *Koko's Kitten;* illus. with photographs by Ronald H. Cohn. Scholastic, 1985. ISBN 0-590-33811-0. 29p. $9.95.

4-6   For over fourteen years Koko, a gorilla, has lived at the Gorilla Foundation, where she has learned to communicate through the American Sign Language. She had signed, when asked what she wanted for a gift, that she wanted a cat; offered a choice of three, the gorilla chose a tabby kitten. Photographs show even more than the text with what love and gentleness Koko treated her pet, whom she named "All Ball," and they are most appealing in the contrast between the huge black anthropoid and the tiny kitten nestling so trustingly in her arms or riding on her back. Although this has interest for all readers, the combination of the subject, the clear writing style and the excellent photographs should be especially attractive to animal lovers.

801   **Paulsen**, Gary. *Dogsong*. Bradbury, 1985. ISBN 0-02-770180-8. 177p. $11.95.

7-10   Russel is fourteen, an Eskimo who is not happy with the snowmobile society, and he follows his father's suggestion and talks to the very old man of the tribe, Oogruk. Thus it is that Russel starts off on a long journey, by dogsled, to face the icy wilderness on his own, developing survival techniques and making a journey of self-discovery that is parallel to his trek. He achieves a feeling of unity not only with his dogs and with nature but with the old way of life, in which each individual had and was a song. Although more lyrical and intro- spective, this is reminiscent of James Houston's ability to capture the atmosphere of barren desolation. The sparely structured narrative is broken twice: once by Russel's encounter with a young, pregnant woman who has come into the wilderness to expiate her feelings of guilt, and several times by dream sequences in which an earlier, other Russel fights the woolly mammoth. Slow-moving, but effective in its starkness and intensity.

802   **Paulsen**, Gary. *Hatchet*. Bradbury, 1987. ISBN 0-02-770130-1. 195p. $12.95.

6-9   En route to visit his father for the first time after his parents' divorce, thirteen-year-old Brian is alone in the Canadian wilderness after the pilot of the small plane dies of a heart attack and the plane crashes into a lake. This is a story of survival, and it has good pace, suspense, and convincing details of Brian's ingenuity and growing self-confidence. It is weakened by stylistic flaws (speaking of a coil of wire, "it sprung into a three foot long antenna") and by the melodramatic treatment of "The Secret," the fact that Brian had seen his mother, prior to the divorce, kiss a man whom she later "continued to see," as explained in an epilogue after Brian's rescue; but as a story of boy-against-nature, it's deftly conceived and developed.

803   **Paulsen**, Gary. *The Winter Room.* Jackson/Orchard, 1989. Library ed. ISBN 0-531-08439-6; Trade ed. 0-531-05839-5. 103p. Library ed. $11.99; Trade ed. $11.95.

5-8   After an offputting preface ("If books could have more, give more, be more, show more . . .") this settles into a quietly engaging portrait, set in the recent penny-candy past, of a farm family in northern Minnesota as seen by the younger son Eldon. The boy's observations are sparely matter-of-fact, whether about the details of planting and plowing, or the slaughter of a steer. "It's one of those things I wish I didn't watch but I do." While this seems at first to be a collection of anecdotes organized around the progression of the farm calendar, Paulsen subtly builds a conflict that becomes apparent in the last brief chapters, forceful and well-prepared. Characterizations are similarly realized, with details about Eldon's brother Wayne, for example, casually building to a telling moment. Lyrical and only occasionally sentimental, the prose is clean, clear, and deceptively simple.

804   **Paulsen**, Gary. *Woodsong.* Bradbury, 1990. ISBN 0-02-770221-9. 132p. $12.95.

7-   The autobiographical stories Paulsen tells here are as gripping and well told as anything he's ever cast into fiction. They rely on observations of a wild Minnesota setting, the dogs he ran in preparation for the Iditarod, and the race itself. The theme of respect for animal nature as it is rather than as it is sentimentally or clinically projected emerges as a natural theme, and Paulsen considers his own human ignorance with a perspective of humor, even humility. His passion for sledding leads to the centering of details through a straightforward narrative without stylistic distractions. Kids who have enjoyed his novels will see this as a natural extension—may, in fact, find here a clearer voice. Unquestionably, they will meet some memorable canine characters and the challenge of Alaska's unyielding winter. The individuality—and sometimes violence—of the dogs who lead their human and probably save his life make for strong reading.

805   **Pearce**, Philippa. *Emily's Own Elephant*; illus. by John Lawrence. Greenwillow, 1988. Library ed. ISBN 0-688-07679-3; Trade ed. ISBN 0-688-07678-5. 32p. Library ed. $11.88; Trade ed. $11.95.

5-8 yrs.   This might be entitled "The Perfect Plan," so idyllic a scenario does it unfold. Emily's family is possessed of a large meadow with trees, a shed, and a river running alongside. Her father is forever threatening to pull down the shed and trees, but during a visit to the zoo, Emily finds the perfect use for all of it—a miniature elephant in need of a home. Of course the elephant will have to have its friend, the monkey, and central heating, which Dad obligingly agrees to install in his spare time. All of this is neatly unfolded in four brief chapters of a picture book illustrated with congenial pen-and-wash spreads. There's a good deal of humor embroidering the realistic elements on to the more far-fetched. The description of the elephant's arrival and the celebratory picnic with plum cake, sugar biscuits, and chocolate is delivered with straight-faced aplomb. The amusing tone is reflected in the art—one picture, for instance, shows the elephant in its cozy shed (no muck in *this* stall!) with pink curtains, blanket, and umbrella. Wishful thinking at its best.

806   **Pearce**, Philippa. *Lion at School and Other Stories;* illus. by Caroline Sharpe. Greenwillow, 1986. ISBN 0-688-05996-1. 122p. $10.25.

2-4   Nine stories, originally written for radio and published as part of the BBC Listening and Reading series, concentrate on the small back-waters of humble perception: a dim-witted horse who finally finds a friend in his own image; a little boy who tames the nightmare on his grandfather's stairs; a girl who finds adventure in the corridors behind a tearoom. Pearce's delicacy of detail leaves one with the impression that she has lifted the rug off children's lives and peeked under to see how they really think and feel. There's neither swashbuckling action nor self-occupied introversion here, but some acute observations of young characters' typical blending of imagination and reality.

807   **Pearce**, Philippa. *Who's Afraid? And Other Strange Stories.* Greenwillow, 1987. ISBN 0-688-06895-2. 152p. $10.25.

5-9   Young people's taste for ghost stories has been more than gratified lately with several epicurean collections from Aidan Chambers, Joan Aiken, and now Philippa Pearce, eleven of whose stories are gathered here with a tonal range from scary to sympathetic. Pearce's strong sense of place permeates each story, whether it takes place in a basement apartment converted from an old mansion in which, long ago, the cook's son poisoned a pudding with hate ("A Christmas Pudding Improves with Keeping"); or in a field in which an ancient grove of trees stymies the destructive intentions of a greedy heir ("The Hirn"). The protagonists—mostly children—are as vivid as the ghosts that haunt them. Little Joe's fear of his cousin in "Who's Afraid?" is palpable, and his rescue by a 100-year-old greatgrandmother leaves a memorable impression. The last story, "The Yellow Ball," is ingenious and warmly satisfying as two children bring together the ghosts of a dog and its ball. Sure selections for reading aloud or alone.

808   **Peck**, Richard. *Blossom Culp and the Sleep of Death*. Delacorte, 1986. ISBN 0-385-29433-6. 185p. $14.95.

5-9   As fresh and funny as any in the series, this follows the valiant attempts of an unlikely Sensitive, high school freshman Blossom Culp, to settle an Egyptian princess, mummified but very restless in spirit, back in the midst of her rightful splendor. Much against his will, Alexander Armsworth finds himself involved again, assigned to an ancient Egypt project by the formidable new suffragette history teacher, who tackles the Daughters of the American Revolution head-on. The Princess seems convincingly capable of carrying out her curses, and Blossom's wayward Mama is always a treat, as is the pre-World War I cast of small town characters. The plot elements are perfectly spliced, the pace carefully metered, the style tongue-in-cheek. A well-crafted, extrasensory mystery with mischievous scenes of high appeal.

809   **Peck**, Richard. *Remembering the Good Times*. Delacorte, 1985. ISBN 0-385-29396-8. 181p. $14.95.

7-10
*
Although Buck tells the story, it belongs just as much to Kate and Trav; their three-way friendship has been solid since they were all twelve. This is written in retrospect, four years later, as Buck remembers what they meant to each other, the good and bad times they had, and the despair that he and Kate felt when Trav, driven by his search for perfection, his compulsion to achieve, hanged himself. Why hadn't they seen the signs, why hadn't they been able to save Trav? In the end, it is old Polly Prior, Kate's great-grandmother, who soothes them at the memorial service the school holds for Trav. Polly's a wonderfully vivid character, but she's no exception; all Peck's characters are fully developed. This is a sad book but not a morbid one, and it's written with insight and a saving humor.

810   **Peck**, Sylvia. *Seal Child*. Morrow, 1989. ISBN 0-688--8682-9. 200p. $12.95.

4-7   A variation of the selkie motif that has been featured in several picture books (Susan Cooper, Mordicai Gerstein, Jane Yolen) and fictionalized by Carolyn Sloane in *The Sea Child* and Mollie Hunter in *A Stranger Came Ashore*, this holds its own as the only version set in the U.S., a vividly recreated stretch of Maine coast. It is also the only one that involves friendship rather than the more traditional romance. Molly is a lonely sixth-grader who finds, during summer vacation, the skinned body of a seal, with its pup crying nearby. Soon afterwards, an old neighboring woman takes in a strange girl, Meara, who seems ignorant of many things, who never gets cold, and who refuses to swim in the sea. Molly and Meara become close, in spite of Molly's jealousy of her own little brother Douglas, who claims Meara's devoted attention. Then, in a climactic scene, Meara must make a choice to save Molly at the cost of their human friendship. This is subtly developed, building mystery by focusing on the main characters rather than the obvious ploy of exploiting the seal hunters as a threat. At the same time, the story is easy to read, and Molly's devotion to her Labrador retriever makes it an appealing dog story. A theme song has the music notation, and Parker's black ink and gray wash pictures, together with a gray reflection shadowing each chapter heading, contribute to handsome bookmaking that underscores the story's exploration of the doppelgänger.

811   **Peet**, Bill. *Bill Peet: An Autobiography;* written and illus. by Bill Peet. Houghton, 1989. ISBN 0-395-50932-7. 190p. $16.95.

3-6   At a time when it seems that too many illustrators don't draw very well, it's refreshing to have this album full of expert cartooning. Bill Peet's reminiscences of his childhood and career as an artist are accompanied by dozens of drawings, scenes both from his work and from his life. The textual tone is observant rather than nostalgic, and Peet is candid about his difficult childhood with a neglectful father, and about the ups and downs of his tenure at the Disney studios and relationship with the autocratic Walt. While almost all of the drawings are new with this book, Peet recreates many of his sketches for *101 Dalmatians, The Sword in the Stone,* and *The Jungle Book,* revealing his mastery of humorous movement, an animated quality that served him well in his second career as an illustrator. The writing here isn't as strong as the pictures and the book is too long, but Peet's many fans will enjoy this generous self-assessment.

812   **Perl**, Lila. *Blue Monday and Friday the Thirteenth: The Stories Behind the Days of the Week;* illus. by Erika Weihs. Houghton/Clarion, 1986. ISBN 0-89919-327-7. 96p. $12.95.

5-7   Clearly intrigued by her subject, Perl in turn interests readers with a neatly spliced account of the mythologies, linguistic histories, and customs that have contributed to naming our days of the week. The cumbersome Roman system (imagine Caesar's being stabbed on the "twelfth day before the calends" instead of the ides of March), the derivation of Christians' "Easter" from an Anglo-Saxon goddess of spring, the fear of the number thirteen (triskaidekaphobia), Saturn's eating his children as a metaphor of time creating and destroying life on earth, the tradition of dusting on Thursdays before vacuum cleaners eased household air pollution—all these tidbits will enrich browsers as well as inform them. Young researchers will find out the surprising complexity behind everyday schedules and may be spurred to think about deeper cultural concepts of time as well. Competently researched and written, the book is also cleverly designed, with more than a hint of humor in the handsome black-and-white illustrations, which combine scratchboard and woodblock effects.

813   **Perl**, Lisa. *Mummies, Tombs, and Treasure: Secrets of Ancient Egypt*; illus. by Erika Weihs. Houghton/Clarion, 1987. ISBN 0-89919-407-9. 120p. illus. and with photographs. $14.95.

5-8   The subject of mummies is endlessly fascinating, and although there are other good juvenile books on the subject (*Tales Mummies Tell* by Patricia Lauber, *Wrapped for Eternity* by Eileen Pace), there's always room for one more in a collection children use for history reports or personal browsing. Here, Perl incorporates a good deal of information on burial customs, religious beliefs, and historical background along with specifics of the mummification process and the archeological finds that have kept the study of the dead a dynamic one. Without getting too wordy, Perl has included specifics: examination of bone development by X-rays, for instance, documents the average life-span of the short-statured ancient Egyptians to be about 40, but King Ramses lived to the age of 90 and was six feet tall. The discovery of Tutankhamen's tomb is recounted in some detail, and well-formatted photographs, maps, and drawings in black and white add considerably to the factual descriptions. A bibliography of adult and juvenile books is included, along with an index.

814   **Perrault**, Charles. *Cinderella*; ad. by Barbara Karlin; illus. by James Marshall. Little, 1989. ISBN 0-316-54654-2. 32p. $12.95.

5-8 yrs.   No one could accuse James Marshall's recent renditions of can't-miss tales (*Red Riding Hood, Goldilocks*) of being no more than the coffee table variants that currently crowd the shelves. And neither are they parodic—his Cinderella is funny, but never at the expense of the tale. Karlin's retelling is simple (sometimes too simple, as when she neglects to get the stepmother out of the house on ball night) and she favors a sweet ending (the forgiven stepsisters marry lords of the court) rather than the more vengeful —if satisfying—traditional conclusion. But she leaves the humor to Mr. Marshall, who paints the stepsisters and mother as smug, overfed kewpies (and never has this trio looked more related), the prince as a handsome dolt (our first sight of him shows only his feet, hanging off the edge of a hammock while his father ponders his greatest desire—to get the dolt married) and Cinderella herself as a lovable, generously proportioned frump. You kind of wonder what she and the prince see in each other, but it's clear from the bedroom-eyed exchange on the last page that they definitely see something.

815   **Perrault**, Charles. *Puss in Boots*; tr. by Malcolm Arthur; illus. by Fred Marcellino. Di Capua/Farrar, 1990. ISBN 0-374-36160-6. 32p. $14.95.

5-8 yrs.   Dramatic perspectives characterize Marcellino's full-color illustrations for Perrault's fairy tale, beginning with cover art dedicated to a full-page close-up of a ruddy cat's face—title, author, and illustrator appear on the back cover. Bronze endpapers, large taupe typeface, varied picture formats, and sudden changes of view all contribute to the look-at-me tone of the book design. While the drafting in the human faces is sometimes bland—purposely, no doubt—the creatures and the scenes in which they appear are wittily lined, with postures and patterns emphasized by contrasting hues. Best of all are the unexpected visual details: the snake's tail trailing from a covered dish being carried to the Ogre, for instance, or two mice pointing to the portrait of Puss, who "became a great lord and gave up chasing mice, except just once in a while, for the fun of it."

816   **Pevear**, Richard, ad. *Mister Cat-and-a-Half*; illus. by Robert Rayevsky. Macmillan, 1986. ISBN 0-02-773910-4. 29p. $12.95.

K-2   From Ukrainian folklore, this has the elements of wit, logic, and repetition that signal an eminently tellable story. A stray cat who gains a reputaton as a fierce mouser turns lazy but gets lucky as well. Mistress Fox of the forest marries him, spreads word of his appetite and strength, and scares the wolf, boar, bear, and hare into providing a feast, at which the cat mistakes the boar's tail for a mouse and sets off a train of events that send the larger animals tumbling over each other to escape. The witty illustrations, with fine lines and earth tones set off by plenty of white space, avoid any hint of cartoon cuteness in favor of a robust respect for the archetypal animal characters.

817   **Philip**, Neil, comp. *A New Treasury of Poetry*; illus. by John Lawrence. Stewart, Tabori & Chang, 1990. ISBN 1-55670-145-4. 256p. $25.00.

5-   Anthologies tell the anthologist's story, and Philip's story is coherently
*   told. With an eloquent introduction and eight cohesive but not restrictive sections, these 285 poems add to each other like kaleidoscopic designs. What a pleasure to move from A. E. Housman's "blue remembered hills" to Edward Lear's "beautiful pea-green boat"—two impossible worlds realized with brilliant imagery. In addition, Philip's book has handsome wood engravings that decorate the pages without overwhelming the poetry—something graphically akin to the vocal expression of a poem subtly read aloud. Indexed by author, title, and first line, this represents a high-caliber cross-section of the Anglo-American poetic tradition.

818   **Philip**, Neil. *The Tale of Sir Gawain*; illus. by Charles Keeping. Philomel, 1987. ISBN 0-399-21488-7. 100p. $11.95.

6-9   Old and ill, Sir Gawain lies wounded outside the French castle to which
*   Sir Lancelot had fled, and he tells his young squire old tales of courage
       and treachery, of the Holy Grail, of courtship and magic and betrayal.
       The pen-and-ink drawings are starkly dramatic and handsome,
       echoing the boldness and drama of the story. Gawain's narration is,
       appropriately, that of an elderly person—he is garrulous, colloquial,
       articulate, heartsick at the breach with his best friend and the
       disintegration of the Round Table company. Philip has linked
       episodes and characters in the Arthurian cycle in a way that clarifies
       loyalties and relationships.

819   **Phipson**, Joan. *Hit and Run*. Atheneum, 1985. ISBN 0-689-50362-8.
       123p. $9.95.

7-10   In a wonderfully gravid preface, a police officer (Constable Sutton) in
       an Australian town sees two boys who, while competing, inadvertently
       hit a car window. Sutton knows that it is the son of wealthy, angry Mr.
       Fleming who's done the damage but another lad is blamed. The story
       then begins. By now the two boys are sixteen, and Roland Fleming is
       arrogant, sure that he can do whatever he wants, and sure that he can
       get away with it when he knocks over a baby in a pram while driving a
       stolen car. Most of the story, taut in its suspense and tight in its
       structure, takes place in the countryside where Roland is hiding and
       Sutton is hunting him. The chase becomes a moral crisis when Sutton
       is injured and young Roland must decide whether to flee and save
       himself or go for help and face the consequences of his theft, the
       damage to the car, and most of all the injury that may have been done
       (neither he nor Sutton know how the child is) to the baby. Phipson is a
       fine craftsman, and here her technical skill is rivalled by the percip-
       ience of the intricacies of the character of a confused adolescent and
       the relationship with his pursuer, both influenced by the stress of a
       crisis situation.

820   **Pierce**, Meredith Ann. *The Pearl of the Soul of the World*. Joy
       Street/Little, 1990. ISBN 0-316-70743-0. 243p. $15.95.

7-10   In the third volume of the Darkangel trilogy, Pierce again achieves a
       triumph of style and concept over the drawbacks of convoluted
       intricacy and, to a lesser extent, the occasional bit of recapitulation. To
       save the world from her evil rival, Aeriel must penetrate the strong-
       hold of the witch and outwit her through magic—and, in the end,
       Aeriel must choose between her own good and that of the world. The
       intrepid protagonist is a truly heroic figure, and her role in the struggle
       for good against the forces of evil is both credible and exciting within
       the parameters of an imaginative and forceful high fantasy.

821   **Pierce**, Tamora. *The Woman Who Rides Like a Man*. Atheneum, 1986. ISBN 0-689-31117-6. 253p. $14.95.

7-10   In a third tale about Alanna, who had masqueraded as a boy to learn the skills of knighthood, the doughty young knight and magician goes through several trials to prove herself worthy of becoming shaman of a desert tribe. She is adopted by the gruff old courtier who had been her teacher, she ends her love affair with Prince Jonathan, she becomes mistress of the leader of the city's thieves, and she goes off on another adventure. This is good fantasy in its pace and richness, although the characters, particularly Alanna, amass experiences rather than gain depth. The combination of the chivalric role of the protagonist and the intricate magic powers possessed by her and others should have a strong appeal to fantasy buffs.

822   **Pilling**, Ann. *Henry's Leg*; illus. by Rowan Clifford. Viking Kestrel, 1985. ISBN 0-670-80720-6. 153p. $10.95.

5-7   First published in England and winner of the Guardian Award for children's fiction, this is a lively and well-structured suspense story. His father had left them, and Henry was living alone with his mother in a large, rambling house, in which Henry's room was a junk museum. A new item in his collection is the leg of a fashion manne-quin, which it soon becomes clear is desperately wanted by some local thugs, who eventually steal it. Henry's sure it is related to a jewelry store robbery, but it takes the help of an adult cousin and the right combination of persistence and luck for the mystery to besolved, not without danger to Henry, This has good pace, strong characters and dialogue, and a believably happy ending.

823   **Pinkwater**, Jill. *Buffalo Brenda*. Macmillan, 1989. ISBN 0-02-774641-3. 203p. $13.95.

7-10   "Do you think we do these weird things because we're nerds looking for attention?" Here's the rare YA novel that manages to portray sympathetic characters while poking gentle fun at them at the same time. Brenda Tuna and India Ink Teidlebaum (children of 60's parents) want to be rebels, but approval keeps getting in their way. After getting detention for some rabble-rousing articles in the school paper, Brenda and India not only find the detention room packed with supporters, they make friends with the local hoods, Slick and the Boys. An exposé on the cafeteria food ("BLACK BEAUTY BURGERS SERVED TO STUDENTS!") causes an all-school walkout, memorial service and . . . barbecue, sponsored by the PTA. "There were hamburgers and hot dogs and sausages. Everyone ate heartily." When the girls start a school booster club as a front for, well, never mind, they are amazed to see it turn into a *real* booster club, with even Slick and the Boys going all-out for school spirit. Satiric but never mean, this takes on the high-school world of cliques, adult authority, and peer pressure ("Let's vote. I'll go along with the majority if the vote is secret") with a warm wit that lets us know that Jill Pinkwater is one writer who's not afraid of her audience.

824   Pitt, Nancy. *Beyond the High White Wall*. Scribner, 1986. ISBN 0-684-18663-2. 135p. $12.95.

6-8   The narrator, a 13-year-old Ukrainian Jewish girl named Libby, witnesses the murder of a peasant by the overseer of a nearby estate. Although there is a loose plot building toward the overseer's burning her family's house and forcing them to realize that far-off America holds more promising prospects than their provincial home town, the strongest aspects of the book are its 1903 setting and the depiction of a family on the verge of upheaval. Several episodes, including the protagonists entertainment of a mysterious gypsy-like group of wandering Serbian ex-aristocrats and the violent death of the overseer himself, seem more like vivid short stories than integral parts of a novel. Yet the smooth writing is a binding force, the tone of personal memoir convincing, and the sense of history as individual experience indelibly conveyed.

825   Polacco, Patricia. *Babushka's Doll*; written and illus. by Patricia Polacco. Simon, 1990. ISBN 0-671-68343-8. 34p. $14.95.

K-2   Bright and vigorous, Polacco's line and wash pictures are nicely composed, set off by plenty of white space, and carefully placed to echo the humor and warmth of the story. A Russian child, Natasha, comes to visit her grandmother and is selfishly demanding. When Natasha wants food or attention, she wants it immediately. Left alone for a time, Natasha plays with Babushka's doll; the doll comes to life and is even more selfish and imperative than Natasha, so that by the time Babushka returns (and the doll becomes mute) Natasha understands why her grandmother had played with the doll only once. Once is enough! As for Natasha, she "turned out to be quite nice after all," the story ends. Lightly and effectively told, an amusing story has a message conveyed by humor, not by preaching.

826   Polacco, Patricia. *Thunder Cake*; written and illus. by Patricia Polacco. Philomel, 1990. ISBN 0-399-22231-6. 32p. $14.95.

5-8 yrs. In a picture book that will appeal mightily to any child who has quaked at the sounds of a thunderstorm, Polacco illustrates a first-person narrative about a little girl's experience on her grandmother's farm in Michigan. A Russian immigrant, Baboushka placates her granddaughter's fears by baking a "Thunder Cake" that requires the two of them to gather ingredients to the count of the approaching booms: ". . . you got eggs from mean old Nellie Peck Hen, you got milk from old

Kick Cow, you went through Tangleweed Woods to the dry shed, you climbed the trellis in the barnyard. . . . only a very brave person could have done all them things." The art features an array of earth tones in sweeping compositions that use organic shapes and patterns inventively. The figures occasionally strike a coy pose, but Polacco relies less on her signature use of pencilled faces against luminous color, and the result is a better blend. A recipe for Grandma's Thunder Cake is appended for young listeners who want to crawl out from under the bed and try it.

827   **Pollack**, Pamela, comp. *The Random House Book of Humor for Children*; illus. by Paul O. Zelinsky. Random House, 1988. Library ed. ISBN 0-394-98049-2; Trade ed. ISBN 0-394-88049-8. 311p. Library ed. $14.99; Trade ed. $14.95.

3-6   Compiled with discernment, this oversize anthology is illustrated by
*   soft pencil drawings that often have grotesque elements in their comic appeal. Pollack has used excerpts and stories that are of high quality, that stand alone, and that offer a range of some of the best humorous writing in mostly contemporary fiction from writers such as Beverly Cleary, Sid Fleischman, and Louise Fitzhugh (Twain and Kipling and T.H. White also fit in nicely). This will appeal primarily to middle grades readers but because of the inclusion of such writers as Shirley Jackson and Garrison Keillor, it will reach an older audience as well. It is to laugh.

828   **Pope**, Joyce. *Kenneth Lilly's Animals*; illus. by Kenneth Lilly. Lothrop, 1988. ISBN 0-688-07696-3. 93p. $16.95.

4-6   The subtitle not included on the title page, "a portfolio of paintings," makes an accurate description of this handsome browsing item, easily accessed for report purposes by an index and list of "facts and figures" about each animal. The book is divided into types of environment—hot forests, cool forests, seas and rivers, grasslands, deserts, and mountains—with typical representatives of species common to each. The first section, for instance, is introduced by a brief geographical summary followed by a page each devoted to gorillas, okapi, tigers, gibbons, orangutans, slender loris, spotted cuscus, scarlet macaws, chimpanzees, and Indian elephants. The meticulously executed closeup paintings are well-designed to cross the page gracefully from one animal to the next, and in most cases a baby or family group is shown, along with an inset global diagram showing where the animals live in the wild. Although there is no organizational continuity in the order of the animals' appearance, the very breadth of selection gives an impressive sense of variety, environmental adaptation, and understanding of the need for conservation. Pope's descriptions of each animal, while limited to an encyclopedic shorthand, give a surprising number of factual tidbits (giraffe babies land with a thump when they're born to their tall upright mothers, camels intake the moisture from their own breaths through a channel running from nose to lips, the harvest mouse's nest grows taller with the plants from which it's made, young male zebras have a close bond with their fathers). Some of the illustrations will be familiar to Lilly fans—the jack rabbit, road runner, orangutan, walrus, harvest mouse, and others, for instance, were included in a board book series for younger children. However the scope and design of this volume make it an especially handsome reference selection.

829   **Pople**, Maureen. *A Nugget of Gold*. Holt, 1989. ISBN 0-8050-0984-1. 183p. $13.95.

7-9   In alternate chapters, Sally and Ann speak in an intriguing novel set in Australia. Sally, visiting her family's friends, the Coopers, has been sent away because of marital tension. She finds a nugget, with an inset diamond and the words "Ann Bird Jem ever" engraved on it. Ann Bird, who had lived in the same place Sally does, but over a century earlier, tells her own story of privation, struggle, and romance as a settler. This is not time-shift, but an alternation of contemporary and historical fiction; each segment is nicely developed, and it is through Sally's curiosity that readers learn the end of Ann's story. There is, therefore, some mystery to spice the adroit structuring of the double plot; solid characterization, a smooth style with natural dialogue, and logical linkages that contribute to readablility.

830   **Pople**, Maureen. *The Other Side of the Family*. Holt, 1988. ISBN 0-8050-0758-X. 167p. $13.95.

6-9   Kate, the fifteen-year-old narrator, had been sent to Australia to stay with her mother's parents because she would thus escape the bombing in England during World War II. Because there are Japanese submarines in Sydney harbor, the grandparents decide Kate would be safer living inland with her other grandmother. Kate is apprehensive, having heard that Grandmother Tucker is a dour, taciturn woman who is wealthy and who wants nothing to do with her son or his family. This is a story of personal growth and adjustment, so that it has universal qualities in addition to the highly personal account of Kate's maturation as she learns not to judge others by reputation or appearances. Grandma proves to be a feisty woman who does housecleaning for others, not rich at all, and she and Kate become fast friends. The writing style is light and polished, the characters and relationships are drawn with depth and firmness, and the setting is nicely established—as are period details and issues—without being punched.

831   **Porte**, Barbara Ann. *Harry's Mom*; illus. by Yossi Abolafia.
Greenwillow, 1985. Library ed. ISBN 0-688-04818-8; Trade ed. ISBN 0-688-04817-X. 51p. (Read-Alone) Library ed. $10.88; Trade ed. $10.25.

1-3   The author has proved herself adept at investing simply presented
situations with emotional substance—here, both humor and sadness.
The opening line is a grabber: "I, Harry, am an orphan." Harry has
found himself defined in the dictionary, technically, as "a person
without a mother or father, or both," and it causes him some pain. His
father the dentist wisely pays attention and reminds Harry of the
caring people in his life: a father, aunt, and four grandparents. In the
end, Harry is able to write a composition identifying with both parents.
Although the theme is serious, the dialogue is natural and light. Harry
interrupts his father's work saying, "But this is important." "To Ms.
Miller," says his father, "so is her molar." The mother's adventurous
activities as a sports reporter are also an inventive touch. Bright
cartoons give the text a spacious, friendly aura but fall short of its
depth.

832   **Porte**, Barbara Ann. *Ruthann and Her Pig*; illus. by Suçie Stevenson.
Jackson/Orchard, 1989. Library ed. ISBN 0-531-08425-6; Trade ed.
ISBN 0-531-05825-5. 84p. Library ed. $14.99; Trade ed. $14.95.

3-5   A fresh and innovative present-tense narrative recounts the doings of
*   farm girl Ruthann and her pet pig, which sports several names,
including Ernestine and Franciswerner, before Ruthann settles on
Henry Brown. The cast gets introduced in practiced storytelling
patterns: the italicized words "Here comes Ruthann and her pig"—
neatly set off in the text with illustrated footprints—start a parade that
periodically grows ("Here comes Ruthann and her pig and her cat and
her dog and her cousin Frank") and changes ("Here comes Frank's
mother and father in their station wagon") like a smoothly revolving
stage. Through a series of episodes and letters, Ruthann and her
cousin develop a friendship, Grandma finds long-lost immigrant
Grandpa, Frank gets the pet he craves despite all allergies, and the
parents of the two children emerge as real characters kept where
children like to keep them, in a secure, low-profile background. The
full-color cartoon drawings are light without being cute, and the book
design is broken up for a user-friendly look without being obtrusively
easy. Distinctively done and lots of fun to read out loud.

833   **Poulin**, Stephane. *Ah! Belle Cité!/A Beautiful City ABC*; written and
illus. by Stephane Poulin. Tundra Books/University of Toronto Press,
1985. ISBN 0-88776-175-5. 30p. $11.95.

4-6 yrs.   This is a bilingual alphabet book, but it is much more than an ABC
device; it's a nice way to introduce or induce an interest in a second
language, it's a love letter to Montreal, and it's a representational

delight to the eye. The clearly blocked masses and sharp colors of the compositions are evocative and inventively detailed. On the inside margin of each page, next to the painting, are upper and lower case letters and the French and English words: "antiquaire, antique dealer; balcon, balcony; caleche, carriage." Occasionally the word is the same in both language, a fact that can serve as a springboard for discussion of how words travel. Notes about Montreal are appended.

834   **Powzyk**, Joyce. *Tracking Wild Chimpanzees;* written and illus. by Joyce Powzyk. Lothrop, 1988. Library ed. ISBN 0-688-06734-4; Trade ed. ISBN 0-688-06733-6. 32p. Library ed. $13.88; Trade ed. $12.95.

4-7   The author/artist has illustrated a diary describing her trek through the Kibira Park forest in Burundi, Central Africa. There are six chapters detailing her arrival, observations of wildlife on the trail, and departure, all during the rainy season. Every page is partially or fully illustrated with watercolor paintings of flora and fauna referred to in the text. Although the volume's size and appearance suggest a picture book audience, this is in fact research material for older elementary-grade readers, with information that is personalized by experience and objectified by ecological themes. There's a map and a chart ("vertical distribution of primate species"), along with an animal index and glossary.

835   **Prelutsky**, Jack, comp. *Read-Aloud Rhymes for the Very Young;* illus. by Marc Brown. Knopf, 1986. Library ed. ISBN 0-394-97218-X; Trade ed. ISBN 0-394-87218-5. 98p. Library ed. $14.99; Trade ed. $13.95.

1-4 yrs.   More than 200 verses cover every conceivable aspect of child life in this oversize picture-book poetry collection. Almost all the selections are bouncy, with popular names like Dennis Lee, Clyde Watson, Gwendolyn Brooks, Karla Kuskin, William Cole, and Prelutsky himself featured generously. The poems are clustered around a subject — the beach, birthdays, cats, etc. — but they are not rigidly forced into categories. The art is in full color and full of fun. Brown's double-spread page designs incorporate the text with fluidity and humor, often creating story scenes around a theme, as in the snowball fight and skating/sledding activities with which he surrounds Sendak's "January," McCord's "Snowman," Kuskin's "Snow," and others on the page. There's something to everyone's taste here, from Lewis Carroll's "Twinkle, Twinkle, Little Bat" to Jane Taylor's "Twinkle, Twinkle, Little Star." Parents and teachers who want to pick out even a page or two per day will find range and contrast, as in the nighttime page including Beatrice Schenk de Regniers' lyrical "Night Comes," Marchette Chute's "Sleeping Outdoors," and Elizabeth Madox Roberts' "Firefly." Contemporary nursery rhymes for all seasons.

836   **Prelutsky**, Jack. *Ride a Purple Pelican*; illus. by Garth Williams. Greenwillow, 1986. ISBN 0-688-04031-4. 59p. $13.00.

2-6 yrs.   Almost every one of these bouncy rhymes hosts a reference to a city or region in America, and each is faced with a stunning, full-page illustration that blends, with strong colors and spaces, a sense of the real and unreal. "Two robins from Charlotte/ set out on a stream,/ they rowed to Savannah/ for peaches and cream, the peaches were sweet,/ so those two little birds/ remained in Savannah/ for seconds and thirds." The picture features two portly avians systematically stuffing themselves in a purple rowboat tied to a blade of grass. Some of the poems have a tongue-twister element, which will add to the fun, and almost always there's the child's-eye view: "When Molly Day wears yellow clothes,/ finches flutter by her toes, . . . /but when she wears her suit of gray,/ no one follows Molly Day." The art, too, sports a variety of tone, from two dancing pigs kicking up their heels in Arkansas to sad Mr. Pennington Poe, whose array of rusty trucks might dot the snowy landscape of any rural slum. In modes of the silly (Timmy Tatt with his watermelon hat) or the sublime (a white cloud swan over Saskatchewan), this combo of veteran illustrator and seasoned rhymster will have youngsters chanting aloud with parents and teachers.

837   **Pringle**, Laurence. *The Animal Rights Controversy*. Harcourt, 1989. ISBN 0-15-203559-1. 103p. illus. and with photographs. $16.95.

7-10   Pringle has done an even better job than usual at explaining and assessing the arguments on all sides of a controversial issue. While animal rights concerns may seem to many to be very much an issue of the 1980's, Pringle traces their history back to the 18th century and the writings of Humphrey Primatt and philosopher Jeremy Bentham: "The question is not, Can they *reason?* nor Can they *talk?* but, *Can they suffer?*" Much of the discussion about contemporary problems is based on the writings of Peter Singer and Tom Regan, whose work Pringle cogently and fairly introduces. Whether describing the procedures of "factory farming" or Draize testing, Pringle is never sensational, making this book both a sensible witness and an effective counterpoint to overheated propaganda. The lack of footnotes is unfortunate, particularly in the face of controversial and/or ludicrous quotes ("a spokesperson for the veal industry said that the calves are chained in these small enclosures so they can have 'privacy'"); a reading list and index are appended. Black-and-white photographs illustrate the points without sensationalizing them.

838   **Pringle**, Laurence P. *Animals at Play*. Harcourt, 1985. ISBN 0-15-203554-0. 72p. illus. with photographs. $12.95.

4-7   A sensitively written and designed book, this introduces the patterns
           and functions of play in canines, felines, primates, a few other
           representative mammals and birds, and humans. Various types of
           play (object, social, locomotor) and playful moves or signals (the bow,
           rush, leap-leap, and open-mouth expression of dogs, for instance)
           become clear both through descriptions and black-and-white photo-
           graphs well placed to illustrate them. Many examples will bring young
           readers to a sudden understanding of their own pets' familiar moves,
           allowing a vivid glimpse into more general habits of the animal world.
           Technical terms are discretely italicized, and a list of books and
           articles for further reading is appended, along with an index.
           Readable and immediate.

839   **Pringle**, Laurence P. *Nuclear War: From Hiroshima to Nuclear
           Winter.* Enslow, 1985. ISBN 0-89490-106-0. 121p. illus. with
           photographs. $11.95.

7-12   Pringle has built an iron-clad and disturbing case for the physical,
           social, economic, and ecological devastation that would follow a
           nuclear war. Beginning with a scientific look at early experiments with
           fission, he shows how military use of nuclear energy led to the
           bombing of Hiroshima, the arms race, and ongoing stockpiling of
           weapons. Statistics of casualties and estimates of destruction get
           careful consideration here, with frequent quotes from studies by
           doctors, ecologists, and economists. A final chapter on nuclear winter
           concludes the report, which, though admittedly anti-nuclear, does air
           and analyze more optimistic views. Grim but necessary information
           for discussion and student research, illustrated with black-and-white
           photographs. A glossary, strong bibliography, and index are
           appended.

840   **Pringle**, Laurence. *Rain of Troubles: The Science and Politics of Acid
           Rain.* Macmillan, 1988. ISBN 0-02-77537-0. 121p. $12.95.

5-9   Pringle systematically defines and describes acid rain, with its effects
           on lakes, watersheds, flora, fauna, cities, and humans. In giving
           examples and experts' opinions, he walks the fine line between
           presenting the pressure of the problem and some perspective on it.
           Concluding chapters elaborate on the economics and politics
           militating for or against remedies suggested in a previous section. An
           up-to-date bibliography includes plenty of accessible articles for
           researching students. Indexed and to be illustrated with black-and-
           white photographs, drawings, and maps, this is thorough, scientific,
           and crystal clear.

841   **Procházková**, Iva. *The Season of Secret Wishes*; tr. by Elizabeth D.
           Crawford. Lothrop, 1989. ISBN 0-688-08735-3. 213p. $12.95.

6-8   In a story that has vitality and immediacy (qualities that are preserved by the translator) eleven-year-old Kapka describes the events and people of a springtime when her family has just moved to a new neighborhood in Prague. Her father is an artist whose work has been rejected by the authorities, and it is Kapka and her new friends (all ages) who help mount a street show of Papa's sculpture. This is not a bitter indictment, but a soft impeachment, of an authoritarian regime. Structure, style, and characterization are sturdy, there is humor in incidents and dialogue, and the story gives a vivid picture of the interesting differences between life in Czechoslovakia and in the United States while reaffirming the universality of young people's needs, interests, and concerns.

842   **Provensen**, Alice. *The Buck Stops Here: The Presidents of the United States*; written and illus. by Alice Provensen. Harper, 1990. Library ed. ISBN 0-06-024787-8; Trade ed. ISBN 0-06-024786-X. 64p. Library ed. $17.89; Trade ed. $17.95.

3-6   From Washington ("First and foremost, Washington/ Our best beloved President One") through Bush ("And now George Bush is Forty-one./ Good luck to him and all to come"), this presidential pageant offers lots to look at. Each president is given a mnemonic couplet or quatrain, and most are afforded full- or double-page spreads that include a portrait cleverly surrounded by smaller pictures, slogans, maps, and symbols that give some historical context. Harry Truman sits at a desk littered with papers referring to NATO, the UN, Potsdam and Korea; behind him bursts the atomic bomb while the twin suns of Germany and Japan set out of sight. Kennedy's picture ("Thirty-five, Kennedy, young John F.,/ One more President shot to death") is carried aloft by a crowd that also displays signs about Cuba, the Peace Corps, civil rights, and the Test Ban Treaty. The visual tone of the ink-and-watercolor illustrations is pure Americana, evoking old campaign posters and cigar boxes, and the flat perspectives of Colonial painting. While the pictures are filled with stories and details and words, the designs are well-balanced, clean, and uncrowded. The total effect is disarmingly light (Carter in a peach orchard, Reagan on a marquee) and wittily informative (philatelist FDR surrounded by stamps that picture highlights of his tenure). Appended notes explain most of the visual and textual references.

843   **Provensen**, Alice. *Shaker Lane*; written and illus. by Alice and Martin Provensen. Viking Kestrel, 1987. ISBN 0-670-81568-3. 30p. $14.95.

K-3   "The people who lived on Shaker Lane took things easy," and when the ramshackle world of Norbert and Charlene La Rose and the Whipple boys and Bobbie Lee Peach is disturbed by the threat of eminent domain for a reservoir, the neighbors leave as laconically as they lived. As Virgil Oates puts it, "Can't swim." It's always autumn in the Provensens' paintings of this quiet rural drama, with the browns and russets of land and sky providing a comfortable background for the rickety houses and piled-up yards of Shaker Lane's inhabitants. There's plenty of wry humor here, and the whole has a tone of inevitability rather than tragedy—even the painting of the new reservoir rising over the tops of the deserted houses is quietly beautiful. A cool spring green intrudes with the spread depicting the modern subdivision on newly christened "Reservoir Road," but Shaker Lane gets the last word in the person of Old Man Van Sloop, now living on a houseboat. "I like the water."

844   **Pullman**, Philip. *The Ruby in the Smoke*. Knopf, 1987. Library ed. ISBN 0-394-98826-4; Trade ed. ISBN 0-394-88826-X. Library ed. $11.99; Trade ed. $11.95.

8-   What an opening: "her name was Sally Lockhart; and within fifteen minutes, she was going to kill a man." Sixteen-year-old Sally doesn't kill him with the pistol in her handbag; he dies of shock when Sally mentions the other legacy from her recently, mysteriously dead father—a cryptic note with the words "The Seven Blessings." And so begins a non-stop Victorian thriller, complete with an ancient curse, a fabled gem, betrayal in the Sepoy Wars and on the China Sea, the thrall of an opium dream, and, in the person of the malevolent Mrs. Holland, a villainess to rival *Sweeney Todd*'s Mrs. Lovett. While the pastiche is word-perfect, it's never played for laughs. Pullman shows us an 1870s London of squalor and darkness, and the final confrontation between Sally and Mrs. Holland on deserted London Bridge is bleak, revealing ever more terrifying secrets.

845   **Pullman**, Philip. *Shadow in the North*. Knopf, 1988. Library ed. ISBN 0-394-99453-1; Trade ed. ISBN 0-394-89453-7. 331p. Library ed. $13.99; Trade ed. $12.95.

8-
*   In this sequel to *Ruby in the Smoke* Sally Lockhart, now twenty-two, has set herself up as a financial consultant, helping, among others, elderly Miss Walsh invest a small legacy. Anglo-Baltic, the company in which Miss Walsh invested her £3000, has collapsed under mysterious, and deadly, circumstances. Sally promises to investigate, walking fearlessly ("'You warned me about what, exactly? Let's be clear about it, Mr. Bellman. What exactly must I stop doing, and what exactly will you do if I don't?'") into a shadowy world, "more than a little devilish," which includes such disparate elements as a master magician, a murder in Russia, a beautiful, doomed heiress, and a terrifying war machine reaped from all the technological cunning of the late nineteenth century. As he did in *Ruby in the Smoke*, Pullman weaves all this together in a way that makes moral as well as narrative

sense, constantly shocking readers who have too-rosy expectations of what a neo-Victorian thriller should be. Pullman also excels at the anticlimactic climax (remember Sally casually tossing the ruby in the Thames): when Sally finally recovers the £3000, it is hardly a triumph, for her whole world has been destroyed to obtain it.

846   **Purdy**, Carol. *Iva Dunnit and the Big Wind;* illus. by Steven Kellogg. Dial, 1985. Library ed. ISBN 0-8037-0184-5; Trade ed. ISBN 0-8037-0183-7. 31p. Library ed. $12.89; Trade ed. $12.95.

K-3   A tall tale with a strong heroine and "six fine children . . . that knows how to stay put" opens with the family successfully fending off fire, wolves, and a horse thief. The Big Wind brings a peck of trouble, though. The children are snug but the chickens unsheltered ("There ain't no critter dumber than a chicken"). In rescuing her four best layers, Iva Dunnit loses her petticoats and literally holds the roof on till the kids come and save *her*. There's nonstop action in the illustrations, with swirling sweeps of the wind zipping along each composition and a funny slant on family and fowl alike. Kellogg's sunset colors make the prairie a striking setting for a tongue-in-cheek pioneer story with built-in child appeal.

847   **Purdy**, Carol. *Least of All;* illus. by Tim Arnold. McElderry, 1987. ISBN 0-689-50404-7. 26p. $11.95.

5-8 yrs.   A model match of story and illustration, this tells the story of six-year-
*   old Raven Hannah, the youngest in a Vermont farm family of six children. All the others are boys, constantly busy with chores that Raven Hannah is not strong enough to do, until she discovers that she can churn the creamy milk into butter. While she's doing that lonely job, she teaches herself to read — the first in her family to do so — by studying the Bible. "People can be strong in differing ways," says Grandmama, and Raven Hannah teaches the rest of the family to read during the long, cold winter. The story is understated but warm, with subtly focused details of a close family in earlier, harder times; when the child's parents are moved by her reading, readers will be touched as well. The watercolor art, too, is small and spare but rich in tonal blends, with strikingly simple compositions appropriate to the country setting. A satisfying portion of Americana that will appeal to children's tastes in its sympathetic depiction of the smallest person's importance.

848   **Ra**, Carol F., comp. *Trot, Trot to Boston: Play Rhymes for Baby;* illus. by Catherine Stock. Lothrop, 1987. Library ed. ISBN 0-688-06191-5; Trade ed. ISBN 0-688-06190-7. 32p. Library ed. $11.88; Trade ed. $11.75.

6 mos.- This collection of mostly familiar action rhymes includes both verses
2 yrs.   and directions, the latter conveniently printed in small italic type at
         the bottom of each page. There are rhymes for jiggling ("To Market-
         To-Market"), tickling ("This Little Piggy"), face and hands ("Here Sits
         the Lord Mayor," "Pat-a-Cake"). Stock's full-color illustrations and
         decorations have a springtime flavor, with rollicking scenes of
         cavorting animals, and a few tender portraits of babies and mothers
         (and one Grandpa) enjoying the rhymes.

849   **Rappaport**, Doreen, ed. *American Women: Their Lives in Their*
         Words. Crowell, 1990. Library ed. ISBN 0-690-04817-3; Trade ed. ISBN
         0-690-04819-X. 318p. illus. with photographs. Library ed. $16.89; Trade
         ed. $16.95.

9-   The material in this collection is arranged by thematic sections
*   ("Settling the West," "Work and Politics," "Race and Ethnicity," etc.)
         introduced by and interspersed with the editor's competent historical,
         cultural, and biographical commentary. The voices gathered here
         (approximately sixty women in all) are rich and diverse: the old and
         young, wealthy and poor, joyful and grief-stricken are all heard from,
         and eras from the Colonial to the contemporary represented. Sources
         range from the famous (Anne Bradstreet has a poem included) to the
         anonymous (a turn-of-the-century Chinese woman tells of her sale
         into American prostitution), and well-known pieces such as Sojourner
         Truth's "Ain't I a Woman" speech appear alongside the lesser or
         even completely unknown, such as an understated, moving, and
         previously unpublished account of the nineteenth-century courtship
         of a well-bred Spanish-American girl. Even those who approach the
         book only as a tool for research will find themselves engrossed in the
         stories—don't miss Jacqueline Cochran's cocky account of female
         World War II pilots testing planes the men were afraid to fly. Black-
         and-white photographs (too often undated) appear throughout the
         text; source notes, a further bibliography, and an index are provided.

850   **Rappaport**, Doreen. *The Boston Coffee Party;* illus. by Emily Arnold
         McCully. Harper, 1988. Library ed. ISBN 0-06-024825-4; Trade ed.
         ISBN 0-06-024824-6. 64p. $10.89.

1-3   A small segment of Revolutionary War history (cited, in an author's
         note, is an excerpt from a letter written by Abigail Adams) is used as
         the basis for a simply written piece of fiction for beginning inde-
         pendent readers. A greedy Boston merchant, hoarding coffee so he
         can raise the price, is set upon by a group of angry women who force
         him to surrender his keys and then help themselves to coffee beans.
         The author begins by focusing on two small sisters who report the
         merchant's behavior and set off the spark for the women's action. This
         is just right for the intended audience, since it's easy to read, has

action, punishes avarice, and doesn't give more historical background than a young child can absorb.

851   **Ray**, Deborah Kogan. *My Daddy Was a Soldier: A World War II Story*; written and illus. by Deborah Kogan Ray. Holiday House, 1990. ISBN 0-8234-0795-0. 40p. $12.95.

2-4   Soft pencil drawings extend a quiet text that describes what life was like for one child and her mother in the last two years of World War II. Daddy was somewhere in the Pacific theater, Mama had a job as a welder, everybody coped with food shortages, lack of gasoline, occasional blackouts, and—worst of all—the loneliness and fear when a family member was in the armed forces. This is more a log of wartime than a story, but it is a very effective account, simply written and focused on those facets of everyday life that would concern children of the same age as the child narrator.

852   **Raymond**, Patrick. *Daniel and Esther*. McElderry, 1990. ISBN 0-689-50504-3. 160p. $14.95.

9-   At the experimental British boarding school of Dartington in the years
*   preceding World War II, two teenagers fall in love, only to be swept apart by forces more powerful than their own internal adolescent drama. Esther is a beautiful Viennese refugee whose cool reserve finally gives way before Daniel's intense, creatively chaotic nature. Daniel tells the story in 1939, three years after it began, and his narrative fully realizes a complex world in which he finds his calling as a composer only to hear that the man who inspired him has been killed fighting Fascists in Spain. So, too, Daniel loses Esther just as the two of them have established a close bond—she is sent to rejoin her parents in Europe, and he is summoned by his American father. To focus on Daniel's immediate emotional deprivation, Raymond has set the narration before the Holocaust, leaving the implications of Esther's fate and of Daniel's eventual reactions to the reader's imagination. These characters and their peers come alive through vivid scenes that hold one with a strength of detail and of mood that recalls the bitter-sweet reflection dominating *A Separate Peace*.

853   **Rayner**, Mary. *Mrs. Pig Gets Cross: And Other Stories*; written and illus. by Mary Rayner. Dutton, 1987. ISBN 0-525-44280-4. 64p. $11.95.

5-8 yrs.   Instead of stretching one story thin, which is a picture-book trend
*   these days, Rayner has packed seven hilarious short stories into a collection about the pig family. With ten children, there's a rich field to mine: William's mischief gets a special feature ("Wicked William"), as does Benjamin's bad day ("Lettuce Is Too Flat") and another of Garth's close calls with Mrs. Wolf ("Bathtime for Garth Pig"). "Piglets and Pancakes" settles, once and for all, the question of

whether boys or girls are stronger and should do prescribed chores. Surprising things grow in "The Potato Patch," and toys that are left out by a tired Mrs. Pig stymie a fox burglar in "Mrs. Pig Gets Cross." After all of the piglets slip into their parents' bed one night, in "Father Pig Sleeps On,"Mr. and Mrs. Pig take refuge in the deserted bunks. These are very much family read-aloud stories, true to the humorous experiences of everyday life and embellished with imaginative flourishes of phrase and watercolor illustration. The behavior and dynamics of the siblings are graphically detailed: an older sister's convincing a cranky toddler to do something by suggesting that he not do it, for example, or the youngest eating the pancake he's supposed to flip in a race, or two brothers planting the week's supply of bananas in the garden. Young listeners and adult readers will both recognize themselves here, and be all the better for sharing the spectacle.

854   **Reeder**, Carolyn. *Shades of Gray*. Macmillan, 1989. ISBN 0-02-775810-9. 152p. $12.95.

5-7   His father and brother had been killed by the Yankees; his two sisters had died of typhoid and his mother of grief. Mama had left instructions that twelve-year-old Will should stay with her sister in the Virginia countryside. It is very hard for Will to accept his uncle, Jed, who had refused to fight for the South; many of Jed's neighbors also feel that he is at best a coward, at worst a traitor to the South. In an excellent first novel, Reeder develops, believably, a change in Will's attitude as he comes to realize that neutrality is not treason and that it has taken enormous courage for Uncle Jed to stand firm in his pacific conviction. Minor plot threads (Will's adjustment to rural life, his relationships with the local boys and his affection for his cousin Meg) provide changes of tone and tempo in a novel that has, despite an uneven pace, both momentum and nuance.

855   **Reid**, Margarette S. *The Button Box*; illus. by Sarah Chamberlain. Dutton, 1990. ISBN 0-525-44590-0. 24p. $12.95.

4-6 yrs.   In a first-person narrative with which many children will identify— enviously—a boy describes playing with his grandmother's button box. Sorting through this round treasure chest, he imagines the buttons as belonging to elegant costumes, rough and ready clothes, uniforms, and assorted other garments that are depicted, paper-doll-fashion, in the full-color illustrations. He makes patterns according to size and color, plays guessing games with Grandma, makes a button hum along a twisted string, and learns what buttons are made of: seashells, sand (via glass), wood, horns, etc. "When it's time to put the buttons back, I pretend I'm very rich, counting all my gold. I like to feel the buttons then, the bumpy and the smooth. I like the way they sound—clickety tappety—falling through my fingers, one by one, into the box." Rich, indeed, and an inventively varied page design incorporates art featuring the same neat, satisfyingly rounded shapes as the subject. A one-page history of buttons concludes the story, which will send children straight to the nearest caretaker with a request for their own button box. Simple toys are best, and when they're done as well as this, simple books as well.

856   **Rettich**, Margret. *Suleiman the Elephant*; written and illus by Margret Rettich; tr. from the German by Elizabeth D. Crawford. Lothrop, 1986. Library ed. ISBN 0-688-05742-X; Trade ed. ISBN 0-688-05741-1. 31p. Library ed. $11.88; Trade ed. $11.75.

2-4   A sophisticated picture book relates the betrothal and marriage of Prince Maximilian from Austria and Princess Maria in Spain, where the king of Portugal presents the couple with an elephant that impresses Max far more than Maria does. After the wedding, the three travel with their retinue through Italy and Austria to Vienna, with attention riveted on the elephant all the way. The creature survives the Alps, barely, and Max and Maria become friendly enough to produce, eventually, 16 children. There is quite a bit of humor in the text ("This animal is an elephant," says the king of Portugal. "He comes from India, which belongs to me. The elephant belongs to you"). The illustrations, in muted colors against a gray parchment background, are tumultuous with tastefully cartooned historical detail and humorous action: Max probably didn't fall off his horse the first time he saw the elephant, as pictured here, but a page of notes at the end does establish the facts of the episode ("This is what really happened"), which are lively enough to support most of the story with only a little festoon of exaggeration.

857   **Reuter**, Bjarne. *Buster's World*; tr. by Anthea Bell. Dutton, 1989. ISBN 0-525-44475-0. 112p. $12.95.

4-7   Buster Oregon Mortensen, son of a charming but useless street magician, is the delightfully amoral anti-hero of this Danish import. Buster's lame sister Ingeborg is having trouble with a big bully, so Buster, busy, hands her a stone. "Throw it at him." The bully then goes for Buster, and their unending circle of revenge becomes the thread that leads Buster from triumph to mishap to trouble to romance. While there's plenty of entertaining slapstick mayhem here, Buster's loyalty to Ingeborg and their muddled family, and his affection for a street that smells of lilac and for a girl who lives there occasion an inviting synthesis of pathos and humor. Getting ready for his first date, Buster says, "I put Dad's deodorant under my left arm and Mom's under my right arm." Buster has inherited his Dad's silver tongue as well as his way with a magic trick, and the combination should prove irresistible for fans of Roald Dahl *and* Betsy Byars.

858   **Ride**, Sally. *To Space and Back*; by Sally Ride and Susan Okie. Lothrop, 1986. ISBN 0-688-06159-1. 96p. illus. with photographs. $14.95.

3-6   An engrossing account of a space journey, from blastoff to landing, gives intimate, you-are-there details of adjusting to weightlessness, preparing and eating meals, going to the bathroom, sleeping, washing, dressing, and working on scientific projects or upkeep technology on board the shuttle. Ride gives plenty of examples from her own experience, but keeps the focus generalized enough to be broadly informative. Large-size color photographs by her and other astronauts are abundant and commanding; they range in tone, with crew members sleeping side by side—one right side up, the other upside down—or maneuvering outside the shuttle in jetpacks, or playing with their floating food. A personal approach to what too often seems too far away, this will inspire young readers with the heights of adventure to which an interest in science can take ordinary people like themselves.

859   **Rinaldi**, Ann. *The Last Silk Dress*. Holiday House, 1988. ISBN 0-8234-0690-3. 348p. $12.95.

7-10   Susan is fourteen, as ardent a supporter of the Confederate cause as were other citizens of Richmond at the time of the Civil War. She adores her father; despairs of ever pleasing the mother who unac-countably calls her a "Yankee brat"; confides in Rhody, the black housekeeper; wonders why there has been a breach between her parents and her older brother Lucien; and conceives the idea of asking women to donate their silk dresses so that the Cause can have an observation balloon as the Yankees do. Rinaldi does a good job of interweaving these elements, a modest love story, and historical details. Although the writing has some flaws (chiefly in the uneven use of phonetically-manifested dialect) it is on the whole stylistically competent, with good pace and momentum, smooth integration of fact and fiction, consistent characterization (including tyrannical behavior by Lucien), and a particularly strong development of the theme. What Rinaldi is concerned with is the relationship between white slave-owners and their abuse and exploitation of black slaves. Susan discovers that her adored father is not her natural father; she is a scorned "Yankee brat" because her mother (emotionally disturbed after the death of a child) had an affair with a Yankee to take revenge on her husband because he fathered a child by a slave. As Susan learns about the prevalence of the latter practice in Southern society, she becomes heartsick and angry. That so serious a theme is adequately treated but does not overbalance the narrative is very impressive. A prefatory note gives information about those parts of the book that are based on fact; a bibliography provides access to the author's sources.

860   **Riordan**, James, comp. *The Woman in the Moon and Other Tales of Forgotten Heroines;* illus. by Angela Barrett. Dial, 1985. Library ed. ISBN 0-8037-0196-9; Trade ed. ISBN 0-8037-0194-2. 86p. Library ed. $11.89; Trade ed. $11.95.

4-6   Strength, justice, mercy, and wisdom make these heroines the exception to the fairy and folk tale females so often appearing in anthologies for children's consumption. Thirteen stories from as many parts of the world, including Asia, Africa, and Europe, celebrate a Tartar warrior woman, a Lapland survivor, an Irish giantess, a Vietnamese healer. The humbler their origins, the smarter they must be to survive. This collection will not only prove successful in combating sex stereotyping but also stirs listeners with its adventurous plots and often poetic, sometimes humorous retellings. A find, either for storytellers or for children, who will find the text manageable and the pen-and-ink hatch drawings forceful. A selective bibliography includes the best of the few similar anthologies along with some adult books analyzing sexism in juvenile literature.

861   **Robertson**, Keith. *Henry Reed's Think Tank.* Viking, 1986. ISBN 0-670-80968-3. 180p. $11.95.

4-7   It's been sixteen years since Henry's last appearance, but aside from a few contemporary touches (word processors, cordless telephones) things haven't changed much in Grover's Corner. Henry and best friend Midge handle all kinds of problems with their summer think tank: a girl's too-small allowance, a pair of twins whose mother serves nothing but health food, an unathletic boy who needs to convince his competitive father that he is good at something. Their solutions are always ingenious and are accompanied by much mayhem and slapstick along the way. Henry's narration is as brisk and self-confident as ever, and Midge just as agile at keeping her bossy friend in his place.

862   **Robinson**, Barbara. *My Brother Louis Measures Worms; and other Louis Stories.* Harper, 1988. Library ed. ISBN 0-06-025083-6; Trade ed. ISBN 0-06-025082-8. 149p. Library ed. $11.89; Trade ed. $11.95.

4-6   Mary Elizabeth Lawson, age eleven, is the narrator of a series of short stories about her family, particularly her precocious (believably precocious) younger brother, her perennially-flustered mother, and her perennially-baffled father, who knows that all his wife's relatives are peculiar and expects the worst. And the worst occurs, in amusing tales that are told in high style; the bland matter-of-fact comments by the narrator are a fine contrast to the more sophisticated dialogue and to the excesses of Mother's clan. Well, there's also Father's sister. . . . It's a romp, it's a great family story, it's a good choice for reading aloud as well as alone.

863   **Robinson**, Margaret A. *A Woman of Her Tribe*. Scribner's, 1990.
ISBN 0-684-19223-3. 160p. $13.95.

7-10   Annette, half Nootka Indian, has grown up in her late father's village
on the wild west side of Vancouver Island, but she and her mother
move to the city of Victoria when Annette wins a scholarship to the
very English St. John's Academy. Although most aspects of her new
life seem alien to Annette ("*Hurry up*. It was not a Nootka idea, not a
Nootka expression, not Nootka in any way at all"), she makes friends
with lively Ukrainian-Canadian Katie and develops an interest in art
and anthropology, subjects through which she can express and
explore her Nootka culture. On returning to the village for the
holidays, she finds she has drifted apart from her Nootka friends and
realizes she must decide how the Nootka and white traditions will
shape her life. This is a beautifully balanced book about the importance of heritage, maturity, and individual integrity; neither side of
Annette's background is romanticized, and the Native American
characters, for once unstereotyped, are as well-delineated as the
others. The author has a refreshing faith in her readers and in her
strong young heroine, and she condescends to neither, succinctly
conveying emotional dynamics and history in apparently small
moments. May Robinson soon follow this sensitive and well-crafted
first YA novel with others.

864   **Robinson**, Nancy K. *Oh Honestly, Angela!* Scholastic, 1985. ISBN 0-
590-32983-9. 114p. $9.95.

2-4   A lively, episodic story takes the unusual tack of depicting three
friendly siblings of 5, 11, and 13 without losing its target audience. The
tone is funny and the time Christmassy as Angela, Tina, and
Nathaniel cope with their mother's jury duty, their father's absence
(on a concert tour) and their collective determination to sponsor an
orphan. There are particulars here that could only be based in reality,
so true are they to the condition of childhood, as when Tina dutifully
orders the least expensive thing in a fancy French restaurant and
must then make her way determinedly through a plate of eels in green
sauce. These are nice kids, and the point of sharing is well made in
short chapters tailored for holiday reading aloud.

865   **Rochman**, Hazel, comp. *Somehow Tenderness Survives: Stories of
Southern Africa*. Harper, 1988. Library ed. ISBN 0-06-025023-2; Trade
ed. ISBN 0-06-025022-4. 142p. Library ed. $12.89; Trade ed. $12.95.

7-   Ten short stories by southern African writers including Nadine
Gordimer, Mark Mathabane, Peter Abrahams, Dan Jacobson, and
Doris Lessing confront the tragic reality of apartheid. Although
originally written for adults, these stories will have a special appeal for
adolescents: one is about a black boy forced to apologize to an unjust

white man; another concerns a black girl whose can only find privacy in a public toilet. All of them show strength amidst terrible circumstances.

866   **Rodowsky**, Colby F. *Julie's Daughter*. Farrar, 1985. ISBN 0-374-33963-5. 231p. $12.95.

7-10   This is a story successfully told by three people; the dying elderly artist Harper Tegges, her next-door neighbor Julie, and Julie's daughter Slug. When she was seventeen and unmarried, Julie had left her baby and run away from her mother's home. Now her mother has died and Slug and Julie are together for the first time, equally awkward in the new relationship. It is partly through the care of Harper (who has been brought home after cancer surgery to be taken care of by a panel of neighbors so that she may die in her own bed) that the mother and daughter are slowly, painfully brought together. The situation is subtly and convincingly developed, in a book that is carefully structured and adroitly developed so that the reader sees, as Slug and Julie see, that individuals act--and react--in complex ways to the stresses in their lives.

867   **Rogasky**, Barbara. *Smoke and Ashes: The Story of the Holocaust*. Holiday House, 1988. ISBN 0-8234-0697-0. 187p. illus. with photographs. $16.95.

7-12
*
A carefully researched history of the Holocaust details the Nazi operations calculated to solve "the Jewish problem" with slave labor and death camps. With Meltzer's *Never to Forget: The Jews of the Holocaust* and Chaikin's *A Nightmare in History: The Holocaust 1933-1945*, this makes a kind of trilogy. Meltzer's book is strongest on quoting primary sources, Chaikin's for chronological clarity, and Rogasky's for intensely focused factual information. *Smoke and Ashes* gives, for instance, the average caloric content for Jewish food rations in the ghetto. It lists the major figures tried for war crimes and their sentences, which were often light or reduced. It systematically catalogues those individuals and governments who resisted the Nazis with help for the Jews. It includes a section (which seems misplaced between chapters on rescuers and survivors) on other "holocausts," including the destruction of various Native American peoples by whites in this country, Armenians by Turks, and Cambodians by the Khmer Rouge. Its descriptions of the Nazi camps are probably the most specific, realistic, and thus horrifying of any in children's literature. In these, Rogasky's reporting is most effective. In the political analyses, her moral outrage is occasionally redundant; in the case of U.S. and British reactions, for instance, the facts speak loudest and clearest when unaccompanied by editorial commentary or rhetorical questions. On balance, however, this is a wrenching and

thoroughly supported picture of the Holocaust, with historical photographs that document the horror more graphically than words. A partial list of sources is divided into eyewitness accounts and references.

868   **Rogers**, Fred. *Going on an Airplane;* Trade ed. ISBN 0-399-21635-9; Paper ed. ISBN 0-399-21633-2. *Going to the Dentist;* Trade ed. ISBN 0-399-21636-7; Paper ed. ISBN 0-399-21634-0. Each book: illus. with photographs by Jim Judkis. Putnam, 1989. 28p. (First Experiences). Trade ed. $12.95; Paper ed. $5.95.

3-6 yrs.   Would that all the world were as safe and gentle as Fred Rogers' Neighborhood, but in these books he demonstrates what comfort can be had in two potentially scary places: in the air and *in the chair*. Both books, illustrated with clear and friendly photographs, infuse facts about flying and dental visits with radiant benevolence; both assure toddlers that not only are grownups there to help, but that they often share similar experiences: "Everyone who goes to the dentist wears a bib—even grownups!" Mister Rogers knows what we're all afraid of— "*dials* and *instruments* tell . . . how much fuel the airplane has and which way to go even when the airplane's in the clouds"—and capably calms us down.

869   **Rogers**, Fred. *Going to the Hospital;* illus. with photographs by Jim Judkis. Putnam, 1988. Library ed. ISBN 0-399-21503-4; Paper ed. ISBN 0-399-21530-1. 30p. (First Experiences). Library ed. $12.95; Paper ed. $5.95.

3-6 yrs.   Color photographs of children, having their first hospital experiences add a corroborative note to the simple, direct text that is addressed to children. The author's style is just right for this level of informational book: reassuring yet candid, matter-of-fact about those aspects of hospitalization that may be frightening or painful, yet not in itself alarming. Seeing, in this book, some of the equipment or procedures (even something as simple as a face-mask) can facilitate acceptance of the inevitable. Not the only good introduction to hospitalization, this is surely one of the better ones.

870   **Rogers**, Fred. *When a Pet Dies;* illus. with photographs by Jim Judkis. Putnam, 1988. Library ed. ISBN 0-399-21504-2; Paper ed. ISBN 0-399-21529-8. 30p. (First Experiences). Library ed. $12.95; Paper ed. $5.95.

2-5 yrs.   Like the books above, this has color photographs of good quality, although here they do not serve to augment informational aspects of the text; in fact some are rather cute or look posed. However, they show children those emotions of grief and anger and loneliness that are a part of bereavement. Rogers doesn't deny the pain, but he does make it clear that time will alleviate sadness, that there will be happy memories, and that there may be, in time, another pet to want and love. This is both a sensitive and sensible first book about death.

871   **Rogers**, Jean. *Runaway Mittens;* illus. by Rie Munoz. Greenwillow, 1988. Library ed. ISBN 0-688-07054-X; Trade ed. ISBN 0-688-07053-1. 22p. Library ed. $11.88; Trade ed. $11.95.

3-5 yrs.   The snowy spaces of the Alaskan settings are vividly evoked in the deftly stylized paintings of the artist (both she and Jean Rogers are Alaskan) with their textured skies and rosy-cheeked people. The story, however, could be set anywhere, since it deals with two themes familiar to most children: the perversity of objects that are repeatedly mislaid, and a love for animals. The story line is not substantial, but it has an easy flow, a mild humor, and an appealing ending as little Pica, who has many times lost his mittens, decides he can do without them when he finds they are under a litter of new-born puppies.

872   **Rogers**, Jean. *The Secret Moose;* illus. by Jim Fowler. Greenwillow, 1985. Library ed. ISBN 0-688-04249-X; Trade ed. ISBN 0-688-04248-1. 58p. Library ed. $9.88; Trade ed. $9.75.

3-5   Softly shaded black and white drawings, realistically detailed, are attractive in themselves and also echo the gentle quality of the text. The story of a small boy who finds and feeds a wounded wild animal is written with simplicity and restraint; Gerald doesn't tell his sister or parents that he has seen a moose, but when he investigates its tracks and finds the animal motionless and injured, he comes every day to feed it (carefully, at a distance, by using a rake) and then watches, enthralled, when he finds the moose has just given birth. He makes no move toward the moose and calf, they leave after the moose is recovered, and he never tells anyone. He observes safety measures even while he cares for and enjoys his secret moose, and from this young Gerald gets his modest pleasure. No great drama here, no unbelievable taming of a wild creature; what Rogers does is capture the feeling of Gerald's protective love and sense of wonder and communicate them to the reader.

873   **Rosen**, Billi. *Andi's War.* Dutton, 1989. ISBN 0-525-44473-4. 139p. $13.95.

6-9   Andi and her brother Paul live with their grandmother while their parents, both Communist guerrillas in the Greek Civil War, battle the Monarchists for control of the country after World War II. Andi is a fierce eleven-year-old, unafraid of bullets or the local bully, but Paul is younger and vulnerable. It is he whom the Monarchists sacrifice to lure Andi's mother into a death trap. The writer is not always in control of this intense story, but the telling smooths out as the plot develops, and the situation becomes vivid and real, with strong characterizations of each villager, a palpable sense of danger, and unforgettable family scenes of love and stress. Victims, witnesses, and even intimates of violence, the children here reflect the conflicts that have raged around them all their lives. The scenario is haunted with mythology, from Andi's mother, Cassandra, to the local police chief, whom Andi calls Cyclops. In many respects, this is a classic tragedy, beginning with a folktale and entwined with proverbs incorporated into everyday dialogue. An apt choice to follow Alki Zei's *Wildcat Under Glass* and *Petros' War*, which depict the occupation of Greece before and during WWII.

874   **Rosen**, Michael, ad. *We're Going on a Bear Hunt*; illus. by Helen Oxenbury. McElderry, 1989. ISBN 0-689-50476-4. 33p. $14.95.

3-6 yrs.   "Bear Hunt" is a time-honored story hour stretch, but whoever thought you needed pictures? However, this oversized picture book is a natural step from Oxenbury's board book series of baby rhymes (*All Fall Down*, etc.). Double-page spreads in pencil of a family outing ("We're not scared") alternate with full-color surprises for the sound effects ("Stumble trip! Stumble trip! Stumble trip!") with both pictures and text big and emphatic enough for the noisiest crowd. After the close encounter ("IT'S A BEAR!!!!"), Dad and the kids make a breathless return through the elements to the security of a big pink comforter, and while they're *"not going on a bear hunt again"* your audience won't be able to wait.

875   **Rosenberg**, Maxine B. *Finding a Way: Living with Exceptional Brothers and Sisters*; illus. with photographs by George Ancona. Lothrop, 1988. Library ed. ISBN 0-688-06874-X; Trade ed. ISBN 0-688-06873-1. 48p. Library ed. $11.88; Trade ed. $11.95.

2-4   In this companion volume to *My Friend Leslie: The Story of a Handicapped Child*, photographs of good quality show the children of three families in which one child (in one case, two) in the family suffers from a chronic illness or an orthopedic handicap. With a calm tone, in a clear and direct style, and with the authority of professional experience, Rosenberg writes about what it is like to be the brother or sister of a child who has a special physical problem; covered here are diabetes, asthma, and spina bifida. What is most valuable in her writing is the objectivity with which she approaches the fact that the sibling who is not disabled also has problems of acceptance and adjustment; a second strength is the recurrent emphasis on the positive, both in the coverage of sibling relationships and in the demonstration of the fact that, disabled or not, children have similar needs and interests.

876   **Rosenberg**, Maxine B. *Living in Two Worlds*; illus. with photographs
by George Ancona. Lothrop, 1986. Library ed. ISBN 0-688-06279-2;
Trade ed. ISBN 0-688-06278-4. 44p. Library ed. $10.88; Trade ed. $10.25.

1-4   The focus of this photodocumentary is on children of biracial parents,
the features they inherit from their respective genetic pools, the
sometimes awkward position this puts them in socially, the strengths
represented by the diversity of their worlds. Several families are
spotlighted, including racial mixes of white, black, Chinese, and Asian
Indian, along with Jewish and Christian heritages. The photographs
are candid and friendly, as is the text, in which occasional quotes show
the children as fairly comfortable with the polarities in their lives. A
good selection for family and class discussion.

877   **Rosofsky**, Iris. *Miriam*. Harper, 1988. Library ed. ISBN 0-06-024854-8;
Trade ed. ISBN 0-06-024853-X. 188p. Library ed. $11.89; Trade ed.
$11.95.

7-10   This creditable and credible first novel details a New York orthodox
Jewish childhood sharply remembered and vividly communicated.
The narrator is Miriam, who begins her story with a remembrance of
her brother Moshe's *briss* and ends it with her mourning his death
from pneumonia shortly after his bar mitzvah. In between comes the
family drama of her parents' determined resistance to assimilation,
their preferential treatment of frail, scholarly Moshe, Papa's
humiliating exposure by his partner for stealing food from the store,
and the tension between Mama and a brother-in-law who has always
loved her. Miriam's loneliness is palpable as she is separated first
from her brother, then her cousin, and finally from the society from
which she is alienated because of her background. The survival of her
self-confidence despite rejection on many sides depends solely on an
independent intelligence and gleanings of encouragement from an
English teacher. Her first job working in a book store leads to the
conclusion, which shows both her strength of resolve and her
uncertainty about the future as she contemplates Moshe's grave. The
descriptions here are vivid enough to give a full flavor of traditional
Jewish life, but also to transcend that context for a more universal
understanding of the pain of growing up. The child's perspective on
those around her ("They were mostly grown-ups who knew who they
were and what they wanted and how to get it") is in ironic contrast to
evidence that will convince readers of how bewildered most of those
adults are.

878   **Ross**, Tony. *Lazy Jack*; written and illus. by Tony Ross. Dial, 1986. ISBN
0-8037-0275-2. 26p. $11.95.

4-6 yrs.   Ross' spacious watercolors add narrative twists of their own to this
traditional tale from Joseph Jacobs' *English Fairy Tales*. A milkmaid

misses the pail, for instance, as she gawks at Jack pouring from a giant pitcher on his back; the tails of various species trail out of a sausage grinder as Jack heedlessly turns the crank. After each job, he ruins the day's payment by bringing it home the way his mother advised him to carry the previous day's reward—a jug of milk poured into his pocket where he should have carried yesterday's gold coin; a cheese melting on his head where he should have carried the jug of milk, etc. The tale is tongue-in-cheek, the art absurd, the overall effect a super-silly read-aloud and perfect accompaniment for the popular southern variant, "Epaminondas."

879   Ross, Tony. *Mrs. Goat and Her Seven Little Kids*; written and illus. by Tony Ross. Atheneum, 1990. ISBN 0-689-31624-0. 28p. $13.95.

4-7 yrs.   Although he has retained the basic plot of this old folktale, Ross updates the scenes with spoofy graphics that depict Mrs. Goat's children generating chaos with skateboard, toy tank, soccer ball, and other clutter while she sets off to the supermarket. The Hungry Wolf gets a music teacher to help him disguise his voice ("If you don't, I'll bite your beak off"), an artist to paint his paw to resemble a hoof ("Do a good job of it, and I won't bite your nose off"), and a dentist to cut off his telltale tail. When the kids finally open the door, they're all gobbled up except the youngest, who crawls from the coal bucket to tell Big Mother Goat, who in turn butts the napping wolf so hard that her kids shoot out of his mouth. The watercolor illustrations shift the story from a symbolic to a literal level, opening up an array of humorous possibilities that diffuse the suspense of stranger danger. The kids, for instance, evoke less sympathy when we can see the villain's obvious ploys—how could anyone be silly enough to mistake those painted claws for a hoof?—but the littlest goat's spunky suspicions restore a semi-heroic point of view and provide a happy ending.

880   Rostkowski, Margaret I. *After the Dancing Days*. Harper, 1986. Library ed. ISBN 0-06-025078-X; Trade ed. ISBN 0-06-025077-1. 217p. Library ed. $13.89; Trade ed. $13.95.

5-8   Against her mother's explicit instructions, 13-year-old Annie Metcalf has been visiting the hospital for wounded veterans where her physician father works, and where she has become friends with Andrew, a young, bitter vet disfigured by mustard gas in France. Set in a small town outside Kansas City just after World War One, this first novel successfully depicts the ambivalence Americans felt toward the returning wounded. "I don't know but it would have been better if they had died in Europe. And so awful to look at," says Annie's Sunday school teacher, a feeling echoed by Annie's mother, who lost her beloved brother Paul and many friends, and who now wants only to put the whole tragedy behind her. The conflict between mother and daughter is central, and if Annie seems a bit too neatly on the side of the angels, her mother is drawn with insight and complexity. Mrs. Metcalf's eventual coming-around (she gives a piano recital at the hospital) may be a sentimental ending, but it is a satisfying one, and the telling throughout is simple and warm.

881   **Roth-Hano**, Renée. *Touch Wood: A Girlhood in Occupied France*. Four Winds, 1988. ISBN 0-02-777340-X. 297p. $13.95.

5-9   Starting on August 22, 1940, this long novel in diary format tells the experiences of a pre-adolescent Jewish girl in occupied France. Renée Roth's family has fled from Alsace to find safety in Paris, but the Nazi restrictions and round-ups force her parents to send their three daughters to a convent in Normandy, where they're lonely but cared for in relative comfort until caught in the bombing that fronts the Allied invasion. Many of the chatty entries describe Renée's interactions with her sisters, friends, and the nuns in charge. The last entry, Friday, September 1, 1943, finds them reunited in Paris, with news that their grandmother, aunt, uncle, and cousins in France have survived. The extensively developed scenes and characterization have more flavor of fiction than of first-person witness, but the tone is gentler than that of many autobiographical novels of the period and may thus reach young readers unready for more historically horrific accounts.

882   **Rounds**, Glen. *I Know An Old Lady Who Swallowed a Fly*; illus. by Glen Rounds. Holiday House, 1990. ISBN 0-8234-0814-0. 32p. $14.95.

3-7 yrs.   Like his inimitable *Old MacDonald*, the old lady who swallowed a
  *   fly encounters a slew of oddball animals who are as distinctly unappetizing as they're supposed to be in order to gross out the primary audience. The fly looks like a cross between a World War II fighter plane and a guerilla helicopter, the spider projects phantas-magoric proportions, the bird resembles a plucked chicken with clipped wings, the cat is something you wouldn't want to meet in any alley, the dog is alarmingly angular, the goat has red eyes, the horse is reminiscent of a German tank, and the old lady effectively lays to rest any unnerved sympathy youngsters might have as to her bizarre plight. These humorously head-on images are all contained within heavy black lines filled with colored chalk, set against plenty of white space, and accompanied by large black print for sing-along sessions. The whole tone heartily offsets a current trend of glamorized folklore. No music, but who needs it?

883   **Rounds**, Glen. *Old MacDonald Had a Farm*; illus. by Glen Rounds. Holiday House, 1989. ISBN 0-8234-0739-X. 32p. $14.95.

1-6 yrs. This animal gallery features vintage Glen Rounds humor in the
*   drafting of each creature's anatomy, pose, and expression. From hefty
          black outline and richly textured color are formed an irresistibly
          ridiculous assortment of cows, roosters, sheep, dogs, turkeys, horse,
          ducks, cats, hens, crows, geese, guinea hens, and . . . what's this, a
          skunk? Kids will love singing the surprise ending—"With a PEE-YOO
          here,/ And a PEE-YOO there,/ Here a PEE-YOO, there a PEE-YOO,/
          Everywhere a PEE-YOO"—and examining the somewhat rotund
          skunk sniffing a can of sardines. Youngest participants can use the
          book for identification (each messy animal is neatly labelled); older
          preschoolers can practise reading the **BOLDFACE WORDS**. Music
          is appended. Suitable for framing and, mainly, laughing.

884   **Ruby**, Lois. *Pig-Out Inn.* Houghton, 1987. ISBN 0-395-42714-2. 171p.
          $12.95.

5-9   Set a peripatetic pacifist (who wanted to name her daughter Dove-of-
*   Peace, but settled on Dovi) down in a Kansas truck stop, throw in a
          colorful cook and a (perhaps) abandoned, wisecracking nine-year-old,
          and you could have trouble; but Ruby deftly avoids cheap stereotypes
          or sentiment to tell a warm and funny story. Fourteen-year-old Dovi is
          the narrator, who, ruefully but forbearingly, follows her mother to her
          latest venture (Dad has stayed in Wichita to insure the family's
          solvency), where they are soon confronted with Tag, left at the diner by
          her trucker father, C.W. Tag manages to endear himself to everyone
          by being a total nuisance, and all are dismayed when Tag's mother
          shows up to claim him—Tag was taken by C.W. in a custody battle.
          There are no villains here, just Tag's and Dovi's families trying hard to
          find solutions in the best interests of both parents and children.

885   **Russell**, Jean, ed. *Supernatural Stories: 13 Tales of the Unexpected.*
          Orchard/Watts, 1987. Library ed. ISBN 0-531-08323-3; Trade ed. ISBN
          0-531-05723-2. 156p. Library ed. $11.99; Trade ed. $11.95.

5-7   An anthology of eerie tales, all first published in Great Britain,
          includes a few tedious stories, but for the most part the selections
          range from good to stunningly good. Ghosts abound, but other
          manifestations of the occult are also evident, and some of the best of
          the tales are by such eminent writers as Vivien Alcock, Adele Geras,
          Joan Aiken, Dick King-Smith, and Jan Mark.

886   **Ryder**, Joanne. *Inside Turtle's Shell and Other Poems of the Field*;
          illus. by Susan Bonners. Macmillan, 1985. 84-833. ISBN 0-02-778010-4.
          56p. $10.95.

2-5   Soft black and white drawings, almost misty yet highly textural,
          illustrate a book of poetry that speaks of the small creatures of pond
          and meadow. Like the drawings, the poems have a quiet tenderness

and empathy that are reminiscent of the work of Carmen de Gasztold. Most of the poems are brief, some almost as compressed as haiku; most have delicate imagery; all are evocative.

887   **Rylant**, Cynthia. *All I See*; illus. by Peter Catalanotto. Orchard, 1988. Library ed. ISBN 0-531-08377-2; Trade ed. ISBN 0-531-05777-1. 32p. Library ed. $14.99; Trade ed. $14.95.

5-8 yrs.   Generously scaled photo-realistic watercolor paintings project the story of a shy boy, Charlie, who, while summering by a lake, becomes fascinated with the work of a painter named Gregory. Secretly watching Gregory paint and hum Beethoven's Fifth symphony to his white cat, Charlie eventually communicates by canvas, leaving first a picture and then messages before coming out into the open for lessons, a gift of paints, and friendship. Gregory's individual quirks (he only paints whales—"it is all I see") form a characterization that emerges naturally as part of a larger story about the visionary space needed to create. It's a theme which all children, boxed in as they are by structured requirements, can fit to their own creative needs. "Charlie, too, looked out across the water, and he knew Gregory's whales were there somewhere. He also knew that something was waiting for him, waiting to be seen and to be painted." The art is oddly literal to accompany a story that consciously suggests more than it states, but the verbal and visual images are both warm and expansive so that the spirit of neither is violated.

888   **Rylant**, Cynthia. *A Blue-Eyed Daisy*. Bradbury, 1985. ISBN 0-02-777960-2. 99p. $9.95.

5-7   Like many realistic novels, this describes a year in a child's life; unlike many, it is written with enough grace and nuance and momentum to compensate amply for lack of a story line. Ellie is eleven, youngest of five girls. She wishes her father didn't drink but understands his frustration, since an accident caused an injury serious enough to prevent his return to the coal mine and to keep him from hunting. It is a bond between them when they acquire a hunting dog, since the older girls aren't interested. Those are two of the most important aspects of Ellie's life; she also acquires a best friend during the year, gets her first kiss (and is surprised to see that she enjoys it) and adjusts to the fact that some of the events in her life will be sad ones. And she turns twelve, looking back over the year with pleasure at how full life has been.

889   **Rylant**, Cynthia. *Henry and Mudge and the Happy Cat*; illus. by Suçie Stevenson. Bradbury, 1990. ISBN 0-02-778008-2. 48p. $11.95.

K-3
*

It's hard to keep a series fresh, especially at the easy-to-read level, but this may be the best Henry and Mudge book since the first two. The important new addition to a two-star cast is a cat with "a saggy belly, skinny legs, and fur that looked like mashed prunes." ("'Are you sure it's a kitty?' said Henry's father.") This benighted stray falls in love with Mudge, however, and Mudge loves it ("but Mudge also likes turkey gizzards," says Henry's father). Posters at first fail to produce the owner ("'Don't put the cat's picture on them,' said Henry's father, 'or we'll have that cat forever'") until one day a policeman shows up looking for his lost cat, which he describes as looking "something like mashed prunes." Bingo! But it's hard to let a friend go, though a present of thirty giant dog bones and a gold police badge eases the pain. Stevenson's affectionate illustrations win again, too, with confident, full-color depictions of this ludicrous family, especially mashed in a couch cuddle dominated by huge Mudge and the shabby cat.

890   **Rylant**, Cynthia. *Henry and Mudge: The First Book of Their Adventures*; illus. by Suçie Stevenson. Bradbury, 1987. ISBN 0-02-778001-5. 36p. $10.95.

1-3
*

These easy-to-read mini-stories offer a perfect medium for Rylant's style of poetic compression and repetition mixed with sensitive selection of detail. They also have some warmly funny, down-to-earth child appeal that is boosted by clean watercolor cartoons featuring an enormous, comical dog named Mudge ("he weighed one hundred eighty pounds, he stood three feet tall, and he drooled"). The friendship between Mudge and his young owner, Henry, has its ups, as in the reunion after the two get lost from each other in the first book; and its downs, as in the moment when Mudge eats the flower Henry has waited so long to pick, in *Puddle Trouble*. The latter book is most lively, with a triumphant scene of Henry's father joining the boy and dog in an oceanic mud puddle and, later, an exciting climax in which Mudge defends a nestful of kittens (named Venus, Earth, Mars, Jupiter, and Saturn—"Henry loved planets, too"). With a series in the works, this duo has a dynamic future.

891   **Rylant**, Cynthia. *The Relatives Came*; illus. by Stephen Gammell. Bradbury, 1985. ISBN 0-02-777220-9. 31p. $12.95.

K-2

Gammell's exuberant, exaggerated color pencil drawings add to the warmth and cheerfulness of the text. Although Rylant's story is thin in plot (relatives come, hug and eat and sleep and work and play, they go) it is robust in every other way: it speaks vividly of the love in an extended family, it speaks humorously of the makeshift arrangements in a crowded household, and it speaks wistfully of the relative pleasures of the familiar scene and the change of scene.

892   **Sachar**, Louis. *There's a Boy in the Girls' Bathroom*. Knopf, 1987.
Library ed. ISBN 0-394-98570-2; Trade ed. ISBN 0-394-88570-8. 193p.
Library ed. $11.99; Trade ed. $11.95.

5-7   Bradley Chalkers is the quintessential class outcast, and he makes
sure that no one gets near enough to change his status; when he's sure
of failure, there's no risk of being unable to succeed. Then a new boy
arrives who weathers Bradley's obnoxious front, and a school counselor breaks the rejection cycle by convincing him that she finds him
interesting and intelligent. Slowly Bradley works his way toward
normal—if individualistic—behavior, which is almost immediately
threatened by the counselor's leaving. This is a funny book, not in the
flip way implied by the title, but in the slightly sad sense that touches
all true comedy. Neither Bradley's family nor the school authorities
are cast into a villainous role; they are simply unable to deal with a boy
who is his own worst enemy. Bradley's retreat into friendship with his
ceramic animals is touching, as are many of the scenes of his mishaps
and misdemeanors. Readers will cheer during his triumphant
attendance of a girl's birthday party (he is in fifth grade and has not
been invited to a party since he sat on someone's birthday cake
several years ago) because the author has managed to show both
Bradley's point of view and the reasons for his classmates' low
expectations of him. Sachar has also imbued everyday details of
school life, such as a book report, with the kind of weight they carry for
children. The personality of the counselor is occasionally overdrawn,
along with a few parent reactions against her in a farcical example of
PTA-type meetings; but those notes of exaggeration fit in with the
absurdist, catch-22 tone of the whole book.

893   **Sachs**, Marilyn. *Almost Fifteen*. Dutton, 1987. ISBN 0-525-44285-5.
135p. $10.95.

7-10   A warm, funny portrayal of Imogen Rogers, who is contending with
allergies, a height of five feet ten, a family who won't work for a living,
heavy demands on her time as a babysitter (she's gifted with
children), and a crush on an older man in the apartment upstairs.
Sachs allows none of these problems to get too heavy, nor, on the other
hand, does she exaggerate for slapstick effect. Instead, she juggles a
handful of kind and quirky characters in an upbeat pattern of
dynamics. Dialogue, double-talk, daydreams, and quick-sketch
scenes enliven this first-person narrative by a protagonist whose
intelligent observations lead her to some honest conclusions about
who she is and what to expect from her friends and family.

894   **Sachs**, Marilyn. *Baby Sister*. Dutton, 1986. ISBN 0-525-44213-8. 147p.
$12.95.

7-10   Penny, the narrator, is a high school sophomore; her sister Cass is a
senior, a flamboyant and self-confident girl who is sought after by
boys, given a scholarship by Harvard, and doted on by her parents.
Penny, in contrast, is prim, conforming, has no ambition, few friends,
and poor grades. Penny adores the handsome Gary, who adores Cass.
When Cass goes to college, Penny—who loves Cass and lives
vicariously through her—must find a new way of life, a new relationship with Cass and Gary, an establishment of herself as more than just
"Baby Sister," as Gary calls her. The use of first person achieves
intimacy and immediacy, and there are variant viewpoints through
Cass's letter and diary entries as well as through dialogue. The story
has good pace and flow, the characterization has depth, and the
concept of a protagonist who has limitations and accepts them (Penny
makes a career of sewing) should appeal to readers.

895   **Sachs**, Marilyn. *Fran Ellen's House*. Dutton, 1987. ISBN 0-525-44345-2.
97p. $11.95.

4-6   After a 16-year gap, a sequel to *The Bears' House* continues the story
of Fran Ellen, who—with her brother and sisters—had tried to cope
with their father's desertion and their mother's mental illness. Now
mother and children, who have for over a year been living in separate
foster homes, are reunited. Mama has had therapy, and Fletcher is
now old enough to have a part-time job. Fran Ellen's problem is Flora,
the three-year-old who had been her charge and her dearest love;
Flora weeps for her foster family and Mama is constantly irritated by
her. Fran Ellen, the narrator, is heartsick when the social worker
agrees to send Flora back to her foster family, and she's especially
angry at Felice (age seven) because Flora loved her instead of Fran
Ellen. Woven throughout is the rehabilitation of the old bears' house,
a dollhouse with a family of toy bears, a theme supported by italicized
dialogue that is Fran Ellen's fantasy/therapy. What Sachs does here is
show, deftly and believably, the changing attitude of Fran Ellen as she
first grudgingly permits Felice to share her play and then comes to
love her and to accept the loss of Flora. Very effective, very moving.

896   **Sacks**, Margaret. *Beyond Safe Boundaries*. Lodestar, 1989. ISBN 0-
525-67281-8. 160p. $13.95.

7-10   Elizabeth Levin, the narrator, describes some of the changes in her life
beginning with the arrival of her new stepmother (instantly loved by
little Elizabeth, deeply resented by her older sister Evie) at their South
African home. The story is set late in the 1950s and in the early 1960s,
and it is both a story of the universal perils and concerns of adolescence and the story of a child who, coming from a careful and
conservative Jewish family, learns from her own experiences and from
Evie, who has become an idealistic activist in the fight against

oppressive government policies. Elizabeth, developing a rising anger as she knows more about the excesses of apartheid, sadly concludes—after Evie is smuggled out of the country—that some day she too will leave to seek a better life. The author, who came to this country from South Africa, writes with perception and candor about the relationships between races and classes, but she has written a convincingly personal story without allowing the message to overwhelm the book.

897   **Sakai**, Kimiko. *Sachiko Means Happiness*; illus. by Tomie Arai. Children's Book Press, 1990. ISBN 0-89239-065-4. 32p. $12.95.

3-5   The natural egocentricity of children often contributes to their resentment and grief when a beloved grandparent no longer knows them. Here the child (and the narrator) is Sachiko, named for her grandmother. She describes the change in Grandma, her resentment when Grandma doesn't know her, her anger when Grandma says she is five years old and wants to go home to her mother. They go for a walk, and young Sachiko (who looks to be about ten or eleven, and sounds that age) realizes that this is still the person she loves; tenderly, she invites her "friend" to come home with her and stay. This picture of a victim of Alzheimer's Disease and of a child's reaction is particularly affecting because it is in first person and told with simplicity and directness. The family heritage is Asian, but the situation is of universal interest. The fact that the story deals with rather complex emotions and a mature response indicates a discrepancy between the reader who will understand the nuances and the picture book audience for which it seems intended. The full-page crayon drawings are bright but repetitive; the print is large, with space below and an ornamental floral panel to the side.

898   **Sampson**, Fay. *A Free Man on Sunday*. Gollancz/David & Charles, 1989. ISBN 0-575-04114-5. 138p. $17.95.

6-8   Restricted to public paths in the Derbyshire hills, walking clubs ("ramblers") of townspeople rebelled, in 1932, against the restrictions imposed by local landowners. There was a massive protest (the "Mass Trepass") that resulted in some arrests but that led, eventually, to the establishment, in 1949, of the National Parks and Access to the Countryside Act. The protagonist here is Edith Ramsden, whose father looked forward to his Sunday rambles and who was part of the resistance movement. Sampson has done a fine job of integrating fiction and history, giving the story color and pace and structure, defining an issue but never letting it become more important than the narrative.

899   **San Souci**, Robert D. *The Boy and the Ghost*; illus. by J. Brian Pinkney. Simon, 1989. ISBN 0-671-67176-6. 32p. $13.95.

5–8 yrs. Many librarians will recognize in this southern black tale a variant of "The Tinker and the Ghost," included among Ruth Sawyer's favorite Spanish stories in *The Way of the Storyteller*. San Souci has a full note on his own sources and has adapted turn-of-the-century story fragments from the *Journal of American Folk-Lore* with a natural ease that sits well in a picture-book medium, including the low-key dialect. J. Brian Pinkney's watercolors have a style of wash over sketch-work not unlike that of his father, the notable Jerry Pinkney, to whom he will inevitably be compared. However, Brian's human figures and faces have a distinctive grace and versatility. His subtly hued scenes maintain a spacious simplicity of composition that makes his first book a choice one for group read-alouds.

900   **San Souci**, Robert D., ad. *The Talking Eggs: A Folktale from the American South*; illus. by Jerry Pinkney. Dial, 1989. Library ed. ISBN 0-8037-0620-0; Trade ed. ISBN 0-8037-0619-7. 32p. Library ed. $12.89; Trade ed. $12.95.

5–7 yrs. A Creole folktale about a widow and her two daughters, who "lived on
  *   a farm so poor, it looked like the tail end of bad luck," combines elements of Cinderella with distinctively southern black lore. The youngest child, abused by her mother and sister, helps an old woman who rewards her with magic eggs that produce gold and jewels. When the evil sister seeks the same old woman and disobeys her, the eggs give forth snakes, toads, and vermin. It's a strong story well told, and Pinkney's elaborate watercolor scenes play it to the hilt. The two-headed cow with corkscrew horns and a mulish bray, the multi-colored, many-legged chickens that whistle like mockingbirds, and the old woman who removes her head to comb her hair are haunting images of magic, both verbally and visually. In spite of occasional stiffness in drafting of human faces and figures, there is an eerie quality to these scenes that will electrify storytelling or picture-book sharing sessions.

901   **San Souci**, Robert D., ad. *The White Cat*; illus. by Gennady Spirin. Orchard, 1990. Library ed. ISBN 0-531-08409-4; Trade ed. ISBN 0-531-05809-3. 32p. Library ed. $15.99; Trade ed. $15.95.

3–5   An elaborate marriage of story and art celebrates the French fairy tale tradition. San Souci's text is based on Madame D'Aulnoy's 1698 literary tale, which in turn draws on a folktale in which a king sends his three sons on three tests to decide their inheritance. The youngest son produces, at the end of the first year, the tiniest dog and, at the end of the second year, the finest linen—both with the help of a magical white cat who becomes his human bride when he breaks a spell bewitching her. Golden-toned paintings embellished with fine detail depict scenes of courtly grandeur. The artist has played subtly with contrasts of scale, using skillful miniaturizations to demonstrate that the smallest can be the most elegant. The formal tone of pictorial gentility never lessens the impact, serving instead to lend a distance characteristic of fairy tale frames. The text is long and the art sophisticated for preschool picture book audiences, but this will appeal to young romance and fantasy fans in elementary school and perhaps even in junior high.

902   **Sanders**, Scott Russell. *The Engineer of Beasts*. Orchard/Watts, 1988. Library ed. ISBN 0-531-08383-7; Trade ed. ISBN 0-531-05783-6. 258p. Library ed. $14.99; Trade ed. $14.95.

7-10   In this not-too-far-future fantasy, scrappy orphan Mooch (spiritual sister to Aiken's Dido Twite) is more than a match for old Orlando, who runs a menagerie of mechanical beasts in New Boston, a bubble-domed city off the coast of Cape Cod. Worming her way into his heart (and into the mouth of his mechanical lion) Mooch changes the zoo, trying as hard as she can to restore to the ersatz animals the dignity their fabled ancestors once knew. "There's more wildness in my left little toe than in your whole kitchy-koo zoo." Meanwhile, Orlando's friends Humphrey and Grace have plans of their own for New Boston; they've been secretly filling one of its hollow plastic mountains with all the trash the citizenry believes has been safely "recycled" in the bowels of the city. While Sanders' dystopia will be a familiar one to science fiction fans, he manages to invest it with the inevitability that assures credibility, and readers will share Mooch's exhilaration when she escapes the "Enclosure." Sanders' handling of tension and suspense is variable: the scene where Grace and Humphrey blow up the trash-filled mountain almost slips by unnoticed. But for the most part there is strong storytelling at work here, and easily managed shifts between the satiric and heroic, especially well personified in Mooch, whose mechanical tinkering leads her to a vision quest and new name.

903   **Sandin**, Joan. *The Long Way Westward*; written and illus. by Joan Sandin. Harper, 1989. Library ed. ISBN 0-06-025207-3; Trade ed. ISBN 0-06-025206-5. 64p. (I Can Read Books). Library ed. $10.89; Trade ed. $10.95.

1-3   Large print and spacious layout facilitate independent reading in this well-paced account of the travels of a Swedish family who go from New York City to a small town in Minnesota, helped along their way by members of the Svea Society and other Swedish-American residents. A concluding author's note points out that in the "hunger years" of 1868 and 1869, more than 50,000 Swedish emigrants came to the United States. For beginning readers who enjoy the dignity of "chapter" books, there are four chapters in a story that is nicely calculated to suit the audience in its length, its vocabulary, and its simple coverage of unfamiliar historical details.

904   **Sanfield**, Steve. *The Adventures of High John the Conqueror*; illus. by John Ward. Orchard, 1989. Library ed. ISBN 0-531-08407-8; Trade ed. ISBN 0-531-05807-7. 132p. Library ed. $12.99; Trade ed. $12.95.

4-6   High John the Conqueror has captured storytellers' imaginations as a trickster equal to Brer Rabbit in his exploits but much more threatening, in the form of a superhuman, to white masters or bosses. The 16 stories show many aspects of black slaves' talents in fooling their owners, and several will be familiar from other cultures. "John Wins a Bet," for instance, is a neat variant of the Jack tale "How Bobtail Beat the Devil." These are capably styled ("when it came to his stomach, the important thing was to keep it full"), with a note about the folklore and an excellent five-page bibliography of story sources and books about slavery, including both adult and children's books. The use of words like "Massa" is clearly ironic in context, and the brief, simply styled tales make good reading for elementary school students as well as a reference for storytellers. Illustrated in black and white.

905   **Sanfield**, Steve. *A Natural Man: The True Story of John Henry*; illus. by Peter J. Thornton. Godine, 1986. ISBN 0-87923-630-2. 43p. $13.95.

4-6   In subtly rhythmic prose, Sanfield retells the legend of John Henry, from childhood (33 pounds at birth, with a voice that raised the roof) through his various youthful feats, to his work as a steel driver on the railroads. The final scene of John Henry racing the steam drill to his death is well focused and moving, with a momentum punctuated by sound effects: "chugga-chugga-chugga-chugga" for the machine, "Take this hammer (Wham!)/ Carry it to the Captain (Wham!)" for the man. Music for the song, along with 12 of its many verses, is included at the end of the book, which is beautifully designed with handsome typeface and a thin frame around each page of text and each full-page picture. The illustrations are softly textured pencil drawings with refined shading and contrast. The black hero is larger than life, yet humanly expressive in context of the ordinary folk surrounding him. In both art and narrative, this is a durable edition worthy of the folk tradition it reflects.

906   **Sattler**, Helen Roney. *The Book of Eagles*; illus. by Jean Day Zallinger. Lothrop, 1989. Library ed. ISBN 0-688-07022-1; Trade ed. ISBN 0-688-07021-3. 64p. Library ed. $14.88; Trade ed. $14.95.

5-   Profusely and meticulously illustrated by detailed paintings that can
*   be used for identification, this is impressive both as a reference book and as a text that communicates the author's enthusiasm, concern, and knowledge. Sattler discusses differences and similarities among

the major types of eagles, describes their habitats, and examines the ways in which eagles hunt, court, nest, and grow from nestlings to magnificent fliers and hunters. One chapter ("Humans: Friends or Foes?") considers both the ways in which humans have decimated or threatened some species, and the ways in which other humans have established protective or breeding programs to maintain genera and species. Appended material increases the book's reference use: a list of all known eagles, by groups and genera, a superb glossary that shows each bird and adds a small picture of the underside (in flight) and provides both a map and a descriptive text, a list of books for further reading, and a relative index. As is true of most good reference books, this may be useful to readers younger than the target audience.

907   **Sattler,** Helen Roney. *Giraffes, the Sentinels of the Savannas*; illus. by Christopher Santoro. Lothrop, 1990. Library ed. ISBN 0-688-08285-8; Trade ed. ISBN 0-688-08284-X. 80p. Library ed. $14.88; Trade ed. $14.95.

4-6   In a text that is logically arranged and clearly written, Sattler presents a range of information that has both breadth and depth. She describes species (including some that are now extinct), their habits and habitats, and the behavior that has led to giraffes being called the "gentle giants" of the animal world. Although there is an occasional need for definition ("ruminant" is used several times before it is obliquely explained), the text is almost always comprehensible and is as admirable for its accuracy as for its narrative quality. Sattler includes a discussion of the dwindling numbers of giraffes (decimated by a loss of available territory and, to a lesser extent, by hunters who are desperately seeking food). Profusely illustrated with nicely detailed drawings, the book closes with a glossary of giraffes (like the text and its illustrations, this includes extinct species) and a chart and classification system as well as a bibliography and a relative index.

908   **Sattler,** Helen Roney. *Pterosaurs, the Flying Reptiles*; illus. by Christopher Santoro. Lothrop, 1985. Library ed. ISBN 0-688-03996-0; Trade ed. ISBN 0-688-03995-2. 45p. Library ed. $12.88; Trade ed. $13.00.

4-6   An oversize book gives the illustrator opportunity for sweeping views of the many varieties of "flying reptiles" that Sattler discusses in a well-organized, continuous text. The artist may have made his pterosaurs inventively colorful, but the paintings are carefully detailed and labelled. The author, in discussing species, gives salient information: size, habitat, and habits or flight patterns to the extent that scientists have been able to determine such facts. The subject is one that fascinates many children, the writing style is crisp and authoritative, and the text encourages or may foster a scientific attitude by its clear discrimination between fact and conjecture.

909   **Sattler**, Helen Roney. *Tyrannosaurus Rex and Its Kin: The Mesozoic Monsters*; illus. by Joyce Powzyk. Lothrop, 1989. Library ed. ISBN 0-688-07748-X; Trade ed. ISBN 0-688-07747-1. 48p. Library ed. $13.88; Trade ed. $14.95.

4-6   Sattler is fast becoming the lexicographer of dinosaurs, with *Baby Dinosaurs, Pterosaurs, Dinosaurs of North America*, and *The Illustrated Dinosaur Dictionary* already to her credit. Here she describes the large variety of carnosaurs that roamed the world between 200 and 65 million years ago. Generously scaled, labelled watercolor illustrations will attract young browsers, who seem to gulp down names such as *Carcharodontosaurus* and *Yangchuanosaurus shangyouensis* while finding ordinary words quite indigestible (a pronunciation guide and index to the dinosaurs does appear at the end of the book). A helpful map and a time chart augment the catalogue-style text, which is especially careful to mention how complete are the skeletal remains upon which scientists base their conjectures about an animal's appearance and characteristics. A brief bibliography suggests eight titles for further reading.

910   **Say**, Allen. *El Chino*; written and illus. by Allen Say. Houghton, 1990. ISBN 0-395-52023-1. 32p. $14.95.

2-4   Billy Wong grew up in Nogales, Arizona, the fourth of six children of a
*   Chinese immigrant grocer. All Billy wants to be is a basketball player, an ambition at which his siblings laugh. "Who's heard of a Chinese athlete?" Billy never even got to play in college ("I was too short") and defers his dream for a job as a highway engineer. The illustrations through this point in the story have been formally framed and monochromatic, like a series of photos in an album. The six children jostle stiffly together for a portrait; a picture of a framed photograph in an empty hall filled with cold light is a memorial to Billy's father, who died when Billy was ten. On the opposite page is a shot of Billy in action on the basketball court, a picture that looks like it's taken from the high school yearbook. Billy escapes his dull job with a vacation in Europe, and a visit to a bullfight is a revelation. It brings the first flash of color to Say's illustrations. Billy gets himself a room in a boarding-house, some Spanish clothes ("In the mirror I looked like a fine Spanish gentleman"), and directions to the nearest bullfighting school. He sends telegrams to his boss and mother. "Very sorry and please forgive, I am not coming home." He does well in matador school, and while he's tall enough, there is another problem: not that Billy is Chinese, but that he is not Spanish. Then the epiphany: "A Spanish matador? What had I been thinking all this time? I'm Chinese!" And Billy transforms himself from a Chinese in a Spanish suit, his face obscured by the brim of his cap, to *El Chino*, an un-abashed Chinese bullfighter in a Chinese costume. "It was as if I were

seeing myself for the first time. I looked like a *real* Chinese. And as I stared in the mirror, a strange feeling came over me. I felt powerful." The triumph is severalfold in this vivid portrait of a dream made true. Billy is a hero in the simplest of ways, and Say's eloquent paintings are entirely on a realistic plane, filled with ordinary, beautiful sunlight.

911   **Say**, Allen. *The Lost Lake*; written and illus. by Allen Say. Houghton, 1989. ISBN 0-395-50933-5. 32p. $14.95.

3-5   Luke, the narrator, has come to spend the summer with his father, but Dad is a silent man and a busy one, so much of the time Luke is alone and bored. He's all the more excited, then, when Dad proposes a camping trip during which they will go to the isolated spot, "Lost Lake," Dad had discovered with *his* father. The lake, it turns out, has become a popular place, and Dad rather grimly hikes on, looking for privacy—and, eventually, finding it in a place that Luke loves instantly. "It really seemed as if Dad and I were alone in the world," the story ends, "I liked it just fine." The text has a static quality, since it is low-keyed and little happens; it explores a relationship, but not deeply, and it speaks with conviction of the pleasure of solitude and the beauty father and son find in their own "lost" lake. The latter is expressed more by the paintings than the text, however; the spacious composition and restrained use of color are effective, as are the intimate scenes of an Asian-American father and son. Both indoor and outdoor scenes are vivid in their establishment of weather or time of day by quality of light.

912   **Scarboro**, Elizabeth. *The Secret Language of the SB*. Viking, 1990. ISBN 0-670-83087-9. 120p. $11.95.

4-7   Adam enjoys being an only child. Thus, he doesn't take kindly to the news that Susan, a Taiwanese orphan and temporary charge of his social worker mother, is coming to live with them for an unspecified period of time. For one thing, he questions his mother's motives: "This was probably just an excuse so she could take care of a girl. Maybe she wanted a daughter all along." Much to his relief, Adam finds that Susan is no smirking parent pleaser, but a terrific soccer player, a talented artist, and best of all, a kindred spirit who knows how to keep a secret. Before they get to the secret sharing stage, Scarboro takes her characters through a series of low-key, trust-building encounters. She convincingly portrays the growing chemistry between them, which, though not as intense, is similar to that of Jess and Leslie in Paterson's *Bridge to Terabithia*. Susan's secret, a paralyzing fear of reading out loud in class, and Adam's reaction to it, are handled with sympathetic understatement: "Her eyes looked blacker than they usually looked, and the corners of her mouth were turned down. Adam wished there were some way to make her stop looking like that every time she thought about reading." Adam never tells Susan about his secret code but the two develop their own language of communication, adeptly escaping parental notice. While the frequent references to television programs may date the book, the use of TV as a point of communication between the two main characters is a fresh image in this promising first effort.

913   **Schami**, Rafik. *A Hand Full of Stars*; tr. from the German by Rika Lesser. Dutton, 1990. ISBN 0-525-44535-8. 224p. $14.95.

7-   In a four-year diary detailing daily life in Damascus, Syria, during the political upheavals following World War II, the narrator describes his school, friends, sweetheart, family (especially beloved Uncle Salim), and the steps that lead him to become an underground journalist. The pressures of poverty, constant danger of arrest, and reality of torture in prison emerge from observations of the fate that befalls several of the narrator's intellectual mentors, his father, and a harmless old bum who wanders through the neighborhood. This is a journal of maturation, sometimes slow-moving but vivid in its cumulative effect; within a setting halfway around the world, U.S. readers will find themselves face to face with familiar characters and reactions as the narrator finds the courage to pursue love and career in spite of an oppressive situation.

914   **Schlein**, Miriam. *The Year of the Panda*; illus. by Kam Mak. Crowell, 1990. Library ed. ISBN 0-690-04866-1; Trade ed. ISBN 0-690-04864-5. 83p. Library ed. $12.89; Trade ed. $12.95.

3-5   Soft pencil drawings, composed with restraint, illustrate the story of a child's love for a pet and subsequent interest in animal conservation. Lu Yi, son of a farm family, is aware that the daxion mao (giant panda) is a rare species, and he reluctantly tells a government messenger that he has a very young panda he's rescued. To Lu Yi's joy, he's invited to come along when his pet is flown to the Daxion Mao Rescue Center. Fascinated by the Center's program, Lu Yi decides that he would like to accept the offer to come back, when he is older, and be a student aide. A good cause, an unusual setting, a happy and logical outcome, and an engaging pet are appeals adding to the attraction of a gentle story that is nicely written and nicely paced.

915   **Schmidt**, Diane. *I Am a Jesse White Tumbler*; written and illus. with photographs by Diane Schmidt. Whitman, 1990. ISBN 0-8075-3444-7. 40p. $13.95.

3-5   In an honest and unaffected narrative, Kenyon Conner tells how he practices and performs for the famous Jesse White Tumblers, most of whom come from the Cabrini-Green housing projects and who substitute hard work for the trouble they might otherwise get into.

"You can't drink, smoke, swear, take drugs, or have anything to do with gangs. . . . On some weekends we do 7 shows in a day. I'm really tired after 7 shows; I feel like I don't have legs anymore, and I can barely walk. I just want to go to sleep. . . . Last year we did 570 shows and went to twenty different states." Unlike many glamorous photodocumentaries, this does not gloss over the discipline of performing on the hot streets during a street fair or a freezing field during the intermission of a football game. Kenyon's life is not pampered, but his grandmother and relatives are supportive despite some family trouble ("I guess my mother didn't want me to stay with her") and he's been been honored as a representative of his team as far away as Japan. Schmidt has edited the text for a smooth but natural tone; the organization is unobtrusively self-structured; the color photographs are spontaneous and action-packed. Kenyon will win readers from the pages of this book as surely as he wins fans when he "flies" over his teammates on the mat.

916   **Schnieper**, Claudia. *Lizards*; illus. with photographs by Max Meier. Carolrhoda, 1990. ISBN 0-87614-405-9. 48p. (Nature Watch). $12.95.

4-6   Outstanding color photographs, clearly captioned, illustrate a continuous text that will fit as naturally into classrooms as those ubiquitous terrariums containing the kinds of lizards described here. Focusing on the eye-catching emerald lizard but including many other species as well, Schnieper covers feeding and breeding patterns, physiological characteristics, and widely varied environmental adaptations. Well designed, this combines clear information with stopped-motion subjects that won't disappear in a crack or fade into ground cover before kids can get a good look. A glossary and index are included.

917   **Schotter**, Roni. *Efan the Great*; illus by Rodney Pate. Lothrop, 1986. Library ed. ISBN 0-688-04987-7; Trade ed. ISBN 0-688-04986-9. 28p. Library ed. $11.88; Trade ed. $11.75.

K-3   A touching and unusually substantial Christmas story is set in a poor black neighborhood on 128th street in New York. Ten-year-old Efan is determined, while his sister sleeps and his mother works, to buy the family a Christmas tree with his meager savings. He starts out eagerly (" . . . the whole day lay ahead of him like a huge uneaten cake") but soon finds he doesn't even have funds for the smallest tree. He does however have the determination to work all day at a Christmas tree lot, make a friend of the owner, and drag home the only tree left—an outsize evergreen that's way too big for his apartment but just right for brightening up the whole block. Efan's emotions are varied, genuine, and set into a context of vividly projected secondary characters. Listeners will sympathize with his quest; though the text is long for a picture book, the tight, short-story construction will hold attention. So will the friendly, full-page paintings, which offer some dramatic color contrasts of green and gold in lively scenes from the story.

918   **Schubert**, Dieter, illus. *Where's My Monkey?* Dial, 1987. ISBN 0-8037-0069-5. 23p. $10.95.

4-6 yrs.   This wordless picture book follows the picaresque adventures of a toy monkey, lost by a little boy and picked up by a pack of rats, a family of hedgehogs, and a large bird. Finally, the bedraggled toy is retrieved from a pond by an old man who is fishing and who takes it home to his toy shop for repair. Boy and toy are reunited on the last page. The story has built-in appeal, but the art is all. Vivid, richly colored paintings in cartoon-strip format feature fine drafting and design. The scene progressions are clear, the animals and people expressively detailed. While the endpapers are composed of inviting, vernal landscapes incorporating the tiny cast at a peaceful distance, the closeups as the book progresses reflect the scaled-up drama that enriches the ordinary lives of small creatures from a child's perspective.

919   **Schwartz**, Alvin, comp. *I Saw You in the Bathtub and Other Folk Rhymes;* illus. by Syd Hoff. Harper, 1989. Library ed. ISBN 0-06-025299-5; Trade ed. ISBN 0-06-025298-7. 64p. (I Can Read Books). Library ed. $10.89; Trade ed. $10.95.

K-3   "Nobody knows who made them up. But some of the poets were children. Their rhymes were passed from person to person. And now they have reached you." Beginning with this I-can-read definition of folklore, Schwartz and Hoff go on to offer forty schoolyard chants and taunts, jump-rope rhymes, and other jingles that children have kept alive. From the gross ("Ooey-Gooey was a worm") to the rebellious ("Teacher, teacher made a mistake") to the Freudian ("My father is a butcher, my mother cooks the meat") these chants are likely to be known, in some variant, by most first-graders. Kids may be surprised to see their recess yells on the printed page but will relish the confirmation of significance. Hoff's full-color cartoons interpret the rhymes literally, an approach that leads to some pretty surreal results: "His eyes got so tired they fell from his head," for example. At your own risk, you might want to introduce this at sharing-time.

920   **Schwartz**, Alvin. *Gold and Silver, Silver and Gold: Tales of Hidden Treasure;* illus. by David Christiana. Farrar, 1988. ISBN 0-374-32690-8. 128p. $12.95.

4-6   A conglomeration of true and legendary stories that Schwartz distinguishes from each other in concluding source notes, this will give young readers a taste of the adventure many children long for when they make up treasure maps and dirt-crumple them for authenticity. Here they will meet pirates as famous as Captain Kidd, literary characters, code breakers, underwater explorers, miners, and others who have sometimes destroyed or been destroyed in their search for gold. It's a book to browse through, handsomely designed with pencil sketches and *maps*, and carefully documented, but oddly organized, as treasure hunts probably must be. Thus in the section entitled "No Good Came of It" are juxtaposed a far-fetched Maine account ("probably a legend," according to notes) of a curse on a pirate's treasure, "a true story" of the bad luck entailed in Mexican gold changing hands in the Old West, and a widespread folktale in which one thief kills the other only to drink poisoned wine soon afterwards. Kids will probably blend the genres and skip the notes, much to the heightened enjoyment of their fantasy lives—and reading.

921   **Schwartz**, Amy. *Annabelle Swift, Kindergartner;* written and illus. by Amy Schwartz. Orchard/Watts, 1988. Library ed. ISBN 0-531-08337-3; Trade ed. ISBN 0-531-05737. 28p. Library ed. $12.99; Trade ed. $12.95.

4-7 yrs.   Annabelle figures she's got kindergarten licked. Big sister Lucy has let her in on the trade secrets, "the fancy stuff," like globes ("This is the world, Annabelle. *This* is geography "), colors, and questions: "Remember to ask lots of questions, Annabelle. Teachers like that." But the teacher, Mr. Blum, is a little confused at some of Annabelle's answers the next day: when, for example, Annabelle calls out "Blue Desire!" as the color of a lollipop. Colors from Mom's makeup table are not the same as those in the kindergarten concept corner, it appears. Faithful Lucy, though, is there for a recess pep talk, and Annabelle triumphs when she counts the class milk money, $1.08, without a mistake—addition lessons courtesy of Lucy. This has a lot more verve than most adjustment-to-kindergarten stories, and the funny, deadpan tone is tempered by the strong loyalty between Lucy and Annabelle. As with Beezus and Ramona (whom this cannot but recall) Schwartz's book will be enjoyed by big and little sisters equally, and parents, especially, will appreciate Schwartz's illustrations; with both nostalgia and wit they evoke a 1950s California suburbia-land where being chosen milk monitor could really make a person's day.

922   **Schwartz**, Amy. *Oma and Bobo;* written and illus. by Amy Schwartz. Bradbury, 1987. ISBN 0-02-781500-5. 28p. $13.95.

4-7 yrs.   Alice's grandmother Oma is rather disdainful of Bobo, Alice's new dog. *"Dreckhund,"* she calls him, and, when Bobo refuses to fetch, Oma remarks sardonically "A regular Rin Tin Tin." But Oma does want Alice to win a blue ribbon in obedience class, and slowly, grudgingly, she is won over. "I'm just using up leftovers. And that's all." says Oma when Alice catches her dishing fresh scrambled eggs into Bobo's bowl. This is a fresh portrait of an unlikely friendship that allows room for both humor and dignity. Schwartz's eccentric illustrations have a 50's mood colored by an 80's sensibility, and are filled with witty details and patterns (check out Alice's paisley pedal-pushers) exactly suiting the dry tone of the text.

923   **Schwartz**, David M. *How Much is a Million?*; illus. by Steven Kellogg. Lothrop, 1985. Library ed. ISBN 0-688-04050-0; Trade ed. ISBN 0-688-04049-7. 37p. Library ed. $14.88; Trade ed. $15.00.

K-3   Children are often intrigued by or confused about (sometimes both)
 *   very large numbers. Here Schwartz uses concepts that are simple to help readers conceptualize astronomical numbers like a million, billion, and trillion. Examples: If a million children climbed on each other's shoulders, they would reach higher into the sky than airplanes can fly; if a billion of them made a human tower, it would reach past the moon. Some of the concepts can best be understood if there is previous knowledge (like the distance to the moon) but this is on the whole a successful effort. Extensive notes in small print seem addressed to adults. Kellogg's bouncy, vibrant pictures, however, are colorful and funny and indubitably addressed to children.

924   **Schwartz**, David M. *If You Made a Million*; illus. by Steven Kellogg. Lothrop, 1989. Library ed. ISBN 0-688-07018-3; Trade ed. ISBN 0-688-07017-5. 40p. Library ed. $14.88; Trade ed. $14.95.

2-4   A companion volume to *How Much Is a Million* ?, this has the same oversize format and the same kind of ebulliently comic drawings. The text builds from the known (pictures of coins and bills of familiar denominations, including the various combinations of coins that make one dollar or bills that total one hundred dollars) and proceeds blithely to a million. Each time, the author suggests what you can purchase if you earn a specific amount; you are also invited to consider the interest your money would earn if it were banked. The picture book format indicates a young audience, but the concepts and the appended notes on such subjects as compound interest, checking accounts, and income tax should extend the range of readership.

925   **Schwartz**, Henry. *How I Captured a Dinosaur*; illus. by Amy Schwartz. Orchard, 1989. Library ed. ISBN 0-531-08370-5; Trade ed. ISBN 0-531-05770-4. 32p. Library ed. $12.99; Trade ed. $12.95.

K-2   "I asked Mrs. Fegelman if all the dinos were dead." When her teacher replies in the affirmative, but adds that there have been some "strange sightings," Liz begins to compile a scrapbook of Bigfoot-like newspaper stories, and goes with her family on a serendipitous vacation to Baja (scene of strange sightings), where she finds "Albert" (Albertosaurus) and takes him home. "This seemed like a good time to remind my parents that they had promised me any pet I wanted on my birthday." The text of Schwartz-*papa* provides just the right nonchalant tone for his daughter's funny paintings, which place big blue Albert in her trademark, 1950's-meet-the-80's, California setting. All the kids back home love Albert, of course, and he's a big hit at school assemblies. A touch overextended but nicely told, and it's equally gratifying to see a story that features a *girl* with dino fever.

926   **Scieszka,** Jon. *The True Story of the 3 Little Pigs: by A. Wolf*; illus. by Lane Smith. Viking, 1989. ISBN 0-670-82759-2. 32p. $13.95.

K-3
*

It turns out that Alexander T. Wolf ("You can call me Al") only wanted to borrow a cup of sugar for a birthday cake for his granny (who looks a bit all-the-better-to-*eat*-you-with herself, and is that a pair of bunny ears poking out of the cake batter?). After knocking politely on the first pig's door, Al's nose started to itch. "I felt a sneeze coming on. Well I huffed. And I snuffed. And I sneezed a great sneeze. And do you know what? That whole darn straw house fell down." And lying in the middle of the straw was the First Little Pig, "dead as a doornail." "Think of it as a big cheeseburger just lying there." And so on. The gruesome humor of the text is kept in the line by the breezy style of Al's narration, a natural (if you dare) read-aloud studded with offbeat rhyme: "I called, 'Mr. Pig, Mr. Pig, are you in?' He yelled back, 'Go away wolf. You can't come in. I'm shaving the hairs on my chinny chin chin.'" With a sensibility akin to Henrik Drescher's but informed with more sophisticated draftsmanship, Smith's creepy and witty illustrations get right to the meat of the matter. The Second Little Pig's snuffing leaves his porky bottom posed neatly between a set of fine stick-style tableware; and from our brief glance of the Third (very pink and very mean: "What a pig") we can easily see how A.T. Wolf, "big and bad," soon found himself in Pig Penn. While hardly everyone's cup of tea (or sugar), both read-aloud and read-alone audiences will find a tasty treat.

927   **Scott,** Jack Denton. *Swans;* illus. with photographs by Ozzie Sweet. Putnam, 1988. ISBN 0-399-21406-2. 59p. $13.95.

5-8

As usual, Scott and Sweet have produced a book in which the text and photographs have equal strength, even to the unusual care with which the pictures are placed to make captions unnecessary in almost every instance. The subject lends itself to action pictures of grace and beauty, and to still shots, also beautiful, that extend the text. The continuous text is smooth, seldom formal, never cute or repetitive. Scott gives facts about anatomical structure and flight, about characteristics of species, about habitats and migrations, and about all the patterns of courting, mating, nesting, and rearing cygnets in a book that is pleasant to read and dependably accurate in the information it provides. The index includes italicized entries for illustrations.

928   **Seabrooke**, Brenda. *Judy Scuppernong*; illus. by Ted Lewin. Cobblehill, 1990. ISBN 0-525-65038-5. 64p. $12.95.

5-8   A series of 31 free-verse poems relates, with vivid specifics of detail
  *   and image, the story of a girl who moves into a southern town, captivates three friends her own age (including the narrator) with her imaginative flair, and then disappears as mysteriously as she came. Each poem develops an episode that reveals, with subtlety and depth, a hidden facet of the outsider and of the narrator's discoveries about her. Judy Scupholm, or "Scuppernong" as the girls call her, seems to have the freedom to eat, roam, and dress however she wants. She comes to a birthday party bearing the best gift, nested amidst quantities of tissue, "a tiny bottle of nail polish/ glowing like a ruby in the sun/ . . . Jungle Red." Judy says her absent father is Norwegian. She says nothing about her reclusive mother, but others do: their "voices drifted out/ droning, monotoning, /lifting and dropping,/ like boats on a tantalizing sea. . . . she drinks, you know." And finally the most moving poem, "The Bottles," solves the mystery of a pile of splintered glass "crystals" growing in the greenhouse behind Judy Scuppernong's house. The summer setting is projected with potently selective descriptions: ". . . big-faced fans/ like electric flowers turned/ from side to side on long stems . . . ." The effect is one of a lean but atmospheric narrative, too immediate to slip into the pitfall of nostalgia. Young readers will be drawn to these characters and will see themselves. Lewin's black-and-white watercolors make the most of their half-page space by focusing on parts of people's bodies—feet, backs, torsos, or heads—with unusual perspectives. His images suggest more than they define—an important quality in illustration for poetry.

929   **Segal**, Lore. *The Story of Mrs. Lovewright and Purrless Her Cat*; illus. by Paul O. Zelinsky. Knopf, 1985. Library ed. ISBN 0-394-96817-4; Trade ed. ISBN 0-394-86817-X. 30p. Library ed. $12.99; Trade ed. $12.95.

K-3   Very thin and always cold, Mrs. Lovewright decided that in order to achieve Total Cosiness she needed a cuddly, purring kitten when she sat toasting her toes in front of the fire. The hulking young man who delivers the groceries and who appears periodically to toss in a laconic comment brings a tiny kitten that Mrs. Lovewright immediately names Purrly. Alas, as this saga of a battle of wills progresses, it is clear that Purrly won't purr, won't sit in a lap, and will bite and scratch. As he grows, Purrly becomes harder to evict from the exact center of the footstool or the bed when he establishes squatter's rights. This very funny story has no turnabout ending; it's Purrly Victorious and Mrs.

Lovewright who's tamed, although she does rename her obdurate pet. The artist has that happy combination of just-this-side of exaggeration to achieve humorous effect and a firm control of line and space; he endows each of his characters with a distinct personality that is in judicious accord with the text.

930   **Selden**, George. *Harry Kitten and Tucker Mouse*; illus. by Garth Williams. Farrar, 1986. ISBN 0-374-32860-9. 74p. $11.95.

3-5   A warm but meandering story spiced with occasionally sentimental aphorisms ("And friendship, like a frail tree, grew between them") recounts the meeting of young mouse Tucker and kittenish Harry, close companions in *The Cricket in Times Square*. Here, Tucker chooses a name for himself, inspired by a bakery sign, and stumbles into Harry, who, much to Tucker's surprise, offers him something to eat instead of offering to eat him. The two then explore the basement of the Empire State Building and spend a miserable night on a decaying pier before finding the shelter of a subway hole in Times Square. Even this, they must protect from invading rats before establishing it as their permanent home. Although the story itself lacks the cohesive momentum of Selden's other work, there's humor in the characters and flavor in the New York setting. Fans will be glad to catch up on the backgrounds of these two fabled friends. Garth Williams' pen-and-ink drawings have the dual appeals of familiar style and vigorous line work.

931   **Selden**, George. *The Old Meadow*; illus. by Garth Williams. Farrar, 1987. ISBN 0-374-35616-5. 193p. $12.95.

3-5   Another story about the people and animals in the Old Meadow community has the same appeals—affectionately humorous black-and-white drawings, a text that stresses cooperation and friendship without intruding on the story line, animal characters, and amusing dialogue—as its predecessors. Here a visitor (a mockingbird whose Southern charm and lovely song affect everyone deeply) is instrumental in helping the Old Meadow residents save the home and the independence of the old man who is their closest neighbor.

932   **Selsam**, Millicent E. *A First Look at Caterpillars*; by Millicent E. Selsam and Joyce Hunt; illus. by Harriett Springer. Walker, 1987. Library ed. ISBN 0-8027-6702-8; Trade ed. ISBN 0-8027-6700-1. 32p. Library ed. $11.85; Trade ed. $10.95.

1-3   Beginning with an emphasis on the different shapes of eggs, Selsam leads beginning readers through observations of caterpillar parts, variations in physical appearance, and the process of metamorphosis. With her customary adherence to scientific investigation, the author directs questions at the reader, who can figure out answers from the distinctively drawn, green and gray pictures on every page. Practical application comes with the suggestion to raise a caterpillar ("If it is a moth caterpillar it will spin a cocoon. If it is a butterfly caterpillar it will start to harden and change into a chrysalis"). A concluding identification chart summarizes common identification points to look for: hair, spines, pattern, body movement, horns, forked tails, silky tents. The index comprises a list of caterpillars featured in the book.

933   Selsam Millicent E. *A First Look at Seals, Sea Lions, and Walruses;* by Millicent E. Selsam and Joyce Hunt; illus. by Harriett Springer. Walker, 1988. Library ed. ISBN 0-8027-6788-5; Trade ed. ISBN 0-8027-6787-7. 30p. Library ed. $11.85; Trade ed. $10.95

1-3   Faithful to the tradition of scientific observation, the writers and illustrator collaborate here to help young readers (or preschool listeners) recognize different types of seals and sea lions and to distinguish them from walruses. This is a job complicated by problematic scientific terminology (a "True Seal" is not a "real seal" but a type of seal), and there is a confusing caption in the summary implying that walruses are a type of seal ("To Tell Walruses from Seals"). Overall, however, the book is as useful as it is attractive, especially since seals are often a prime attraction at the zoo. Lots of white space frames accurate pencil drawings that illustrate the answers to textual questions ("How do you tell seals apart?" . . . Which one has ears?" etc.). Two maps show the creatures' global distribution, and a summary list, also illustrated, reviews conclusions on how to classify eared seals, true seals, and walruses. An index doubles as a listing of the species cited in the book.

934   Selsam, Milicent E. *Mushrooms;* illus. with photographs by Jerome Wexler. Morrow, 1986. Library ed. ISBN 0-688-06249-0; Trade ed. ISBN 0-688-06248-2. 38p. Library ed. $11.88; Trade ed. $11.75.

2-5   "There is something mysterious and ghost-like about a plant that is not green, has no leaves or roots, and springs up suddenly after rainstorms." Thus Selsam once again conveys the wonder of science without losing a jot of accuracy in explaining it. In this case the superstitions, myths, and history surrounding the plant are so intriguing that she opens the book with a full chapter devoted to them. There follows an equally interesting description of the mushroom's special features and growth cycle, with suggestions for young researchers to make a spore print at the stage where the cap has opened and the gills are visible. The unusual and fairly complicated methods of mushroom farming and a discussion of the amazing variety of wild mushrooms (including warnings about the poisonous kinds) complete the presentation. As usual, Wexler's clear black-and-white photos, along with a few prints and diagrams, extend the information visually. Well conceived, designed, and executed.

935   **Selsam**, Millicent E. *Strange Creatures That Really Lived;* illus. by Jennifer Dewey. Scholastic, 1987. ISBN 0-590-40707-4. 32p. $13.95.

K-2   Softly drawn and nicely detailed illustrations in colored pencil show creatures that have lived on earth and become extinct. While some of the pictures show size by comparing creature to object (giant land turtle and 13-foot automobile) the artist has not tried to keep species in scale with each other. This is an excellent book for browsing, with varied subjects, not too much information for listeners with a limited attention span, and with a gentle plea for conservation of present, threatened species. A list of creatures, in the order in which they are presented in the text, serves as a finding device although it is not alphabetical in arrangement, and it gives habitats and approximate dates of existence. Selsam's writing, as always, is clear, direct, and accurate.

936   **Service**, Pamela F. *Stinker from Space.* Scribner, 1988. ISBN 0-684-18910-0. 83p. $11.95.

4-6   A first-class, funny science fantasy that will hook middle-grade readers right from the first scene, when Tsynq Yr evades a Zarnk enemy cruiser, crashes to earth, and has to inject his mind into the body of a skunk for lack of a better host. He's found by a lonely girl, Karen, who renames him Stinker and, with the help of her neighbor Jonathan, returns him safely to the Sylon Confederacy in outer space. What gives this traditional plot its punch is the author's consistent detailing of Stinker's transformation: in trying to convince a dog not to attack, he appeals, "We can play together, chase the ball, find loathsome things to eat." Although enamored of peanut butter, Stinker absentmindedly pops the occasional grub into his mouth. The children, too, are realistic in their initial antipathy: "I can't go up there and talk with him .... He's a boy!" ... "She's a girl! Tell her I'm sick or something." Space shuttle officials get their fair share of ridicule when Stinker pirates a craft ("Uh, good morning, Madam, may I use your telephone?" asks an astronaut of Karen's mother after landing in front of her house). The situation is gratifyingly absurd, the development satisfyingly natural.

937   **Seuss**, Dr. *I Am Not Going to Get Up Today;* illus. by James Stevenson. Random House, 1987. ISBN 0-394-89217-8. 36p. (Beginner Books). $5.95.

1-3   The master rhymester catches that moment of morning rebellion when it's just too hard to get up. "My bed is warm./ My pillow's deep./ Today's the day I'm going to sleep,"declares the boy portrayed in

Stevenson's bouncy watercolor cartoons. The lad elaborates his ultimatum with an exaggerated energy that belies his intent. Not food, nor noise, nor prodding, nor police can move him, and his mother finally gives his breakfast egg to the arresting officer. The unrhymed ending is a bit of a textual letdown, but it serves well enough as a joke. Readers won't protest practicing their skills on this one.

938   **Sevela**, Ephraim. *We Were Not Like Other People*; tr. by Antonina Bouis. Harper, 1989. Library ed. ISBN 0-06-025508-0; Trade ed. ISBN 0-06-025507-2. 216p. Library ed. $13.89; Trade ed. $13.95.

6-9   In a tough novel about a Soviet Jewish teenager separated from his parents at the beginning of World War II, the boy wanders from Siberia to Germany, eating when he can, finding temporary caretakers he can trust, and finally joining the last fighting outside Berlin. Whatever the suffering and death in his path, however kind are his occasional helpers, he is aware of a persistent hostility toward Jews: a colonel who grows genuinely fond of him replaces his Jewish name with a nickname; bullies beat another Jewish child with taunts of "Kike, Kike" in a work factory; a friendly soldier betrays the boy with anti-Semitic comments after the fighting is all over. The narrative is not consecutive; an opening battle scene actually happens toward the end of the story, and we don't find out till late in the book how the boy first became separated from his mother (his father was rounded up in one of Stalin's purges of the military). However, the segments are completely developed and totally absorbing, the segmentation serving to give a sense of the way victims of war are dislocated, dumped here or there, and jerked along in trains or other transport. The writing is stark and the translation intense, with a total effect of readers having experienced the situation. Perhaps the concluding reunion seems a bit unrealistic after the rest of the story; the author's dedication suggests that he has tempered the parents' fate for children's reading.

939   **Shalant**, Phyllis. *The Transformation of Faith Futterman*. Dutton, 1990. ISBN 0-525-44570-6. 138p. $13.95.

5-8   Led by Randi Martin ("thin, short, and gray-eyed, with blond hair that she wore in an impossibly smooth ponytail"), Suzanne, Rachel, and Charlie are self-styled "Insiders." The impossibly eager Faith Futterman ("Once she even reminded Mrs. Hayes that she had forgotten to assign homework") is, to recall Randi's phrase, a "Nearly Nerd." Assigned a flute duet for the spring concert, Suzanne and Faith become friends, sort of, until a transformed Faith breezily threatens Suzanne's place in Randi's clique. Suzanne's narration of sixth-grade social vicissitudes has a sharp slant that sets this book above the chatty conventions of the usual school story. The characters are

smoothly engaging and naturally revealed, as when Charlie tells
Suzanne her reasons for so desperately wanting to be an Insider: "At
home we spoke Vietnamese. At school everyone spoke English. Half
the time, I didn't understand the names the kids called me." This is
the best kind of popular realism, informing good storytelling with a
friendly understanding of the everyday events and emotions that kids
find important.

940   **Shalev**, Meir. *My Father Always Embarrasses Me*; tr. from the
Hebrew by Dagmar Herrmann; illus. by Yossi Abolafia. Wellington,
1990. ISBN 0-922984-02-6. 32p. $13.95.

5-8 yrs.   While Mortimer Dunne's mother is a neat, conventional tele
*   vision reporter, his father is an individualist who wears shorts to
weddings, snores at PTA meetings, sings loudly while biking his son to
school (kissing him publicly when they arrive, always late), hides
his head during scary movies, writes stories at night, and—worst of
all—promises to make a cake for the baking contest. When the other
kids' mothers line up with their delicacies—apple strudel, pink-frosted
cupcakes, flaky puffs, chocolate roll, and gingerbread tower—
Mortimer's father presents a confection "the size and color of an
automobile tire." However, the cake has surprising properties that
ultimately redeem Mortimer's father, who confesses to having been
embarrassed by his own father, the baker who invented the
miraculous cake. A picture book that could have bogged down in
bibliotherapy is instead buoyed by witty narrative and watercolor
illustrations featuring Abolafia's funniest details. Mortimer's
estimation of his father is born out by the goodhearted klutz pictorially
developed in each scene. Translated from the Hebrew of the original
Israeli edition into American idiom, this crosses international
boundaries with ease. It's carefree in tone but right on target for
Everychild who knows the agonies of embarrassing parents.

941   **Shamir**, Ilana, ed. *The Young Reader's Encyclopedia of Jewish
History*; ed. and illus. by Ilana Shamir and Shlomo Shavit. Viking
Kestrel, 1987. ISBN 0-670-81738-4. 122p. illus. and with photographs.
$15.95.

5-9   An oversize volume that's liberally illustrated without becoming
cluttered, this is organized into 28 chapters. Each is about four pages
long, from a discussion of early nomadic tribes to an assessment of
contemporary international Jewry. Examples of other topics include
the Babylonian exile, Jewish life in early Christian Europe and in the
Ottoman Empire, Messianism during the Middle Ages, the rise of
Zionism, the Holocaust, the Sinai Campaign and Yom Kippur War,
and problems of Jews in the Eastern Bloc. Necessarily generalized,
these quick-surveys will nevertheless serve to introduce students to

important people, incidents, movements, and issues of religious and political change, with clarifying maps, diagrams, time line charts, and good reproductions of historic art works and photographs. The advantage of this volume over a standard Jewish encyclopedia in a school or public library is its chronological sequence and readability as a browsing item; the book can function either for reference or for home/classroom study.

942   **Sharmat**, Marjorie Weinman. *Hooray for Mother's Day*; illus. by John Wallner. Holiday House, 1986. ISBN 0-8234-0588-5. 29p. $12.95.

5-8 yrs.   This is just ridiculous enough to be truly inventive . . . and very funny. Alaric Chicken is so cautious that he checks to see if the floor is still there before he gets out of bed in the morning. To be prepared for all kinds of weather, he wears rubber boots, shorts, and a fur jacket. To buy his mother a Mother's Day present involves a litany of catastrophes that might accompany any choice of bedroom slippers, candy, perfume, etc. Finally, Alaric buys and presents to his mother, who is barricaded behind padlocks and chains, a huge alligator to join the one already guarding the moat behind her house ("A chicken can't be too careful"). Wallner's solid shapes and primary colors anchor each wild scene in a yellow frame or again, render Alaric's dire fantasies in big, vivid cartoon bubbles. A winning group readaloud for the holiday.

943   **Sharmat**, Marjorie Weinman. *Nate the Great and the Musical Note*; by Marjorie Weinman Sharmat and Craig Sharmat; illus. by Marc Simont. Coward, 1990. ISBN 0-698-20645-2. 48p. (Break-of-Day Books). $11.95.

1-3   Easy-to read mysteries can seem tediously worked out to the adult critic; here Nate the Great laboriously decodes "A note. Step left until you reach the middle. Step up and you will solve this riddle." The note's from Rosamond, who has taken to giving piano lessons (and rewarding her cats with gold stars), and it's addressed to Pip, who badly needs a haircut, so he can . . . "see sharp." While this doesn't have the smooth inevitability of a puzzle naturally solved, the story's clues are clear and logical, encouraging beginning readers to pay word-for-word attention. The easy-reading rhythms are played for humor: "I read the note once. I read the note twice. I read the note three times. Some things get better with time. Rosamond's note just got stranger." Simont's illustrations are cartooned with finesse.

944   **Shepherd**, Elizabeth. *No Bones: A Key to Bugs and Slugs, Worms and Ticks, Spiders and Centipedes, and Other Creepy Crawlies*; illus. by Ippy Paterson. Macmillan, 1988. ISBN 0-02-782880-8. 90p. $13.95.

3-6   This choose-your-own adventure guide to invertebrates combines facts with conceptual game playing. The actual text is organized into informational sections on snails and slugs, earthworms, isopods, centipedes, millipedes, scorpions, daddy longlegs, mites, spiders, insects, maggots and grubs, and caterpillars. A "key" introducing the text, however, offers an alternative to straight reading: "The animal has legs. Go to 2. . . . Animal has ten or more legs. Go to 3. . . . Animal has exactly 14 legs. Turn to page 21 for its story." The idea of groups characterized by certain features is thus reinforced by reader action as well as authorial description. Precisely stippled or hatched black ink drawings add considerably to an easy-to-read text. There's a brief bibliography and an index indicating page numbers where an animal appears in print or picture, along with its range of measurements in millimeters and inches. A science unit bonanza.

945   **Sheppard**, Jeff. *The Right Number of Elephants*; illus. by Felicia Bond. Harper, 1990. Library ed. ISBN 0-06-025616-8; Trade ed. ISBN 0-06-025615-X. 32p. Library ed. $12.89; Trade ed. $12.95.

3-6 yrs.   Counting backwards is a playful challenge for children who have just learned to count up to ten; countdowns also have the inherent suspense of leading to some kind of take-off. Add to that a wildly inventive series of illustrations depicting the number of elephants needed to pull a train out of a tunnel (ten) to paint a ceiling (nine) to supply shade at the beach (eight) etc., and you come up with some thoroughly imaginative picture book entertainment for young counters. Perhaps most satisfying is the scene of the six-elephant phalanx shielding the small protagonist with "a bit of company on a very deserted street at a very deserted time of day." But the flying circus (five), the elephants tripping an opponent in a race (four), and the very special friend (one) are not bad, either. Bond has used neat tricks of linear perspective and color contrast to speed the pictures along, allowing plenty of space for the action to unfold and exaggerating facial expressions and body poses without overdoing them. Ten for tempo.

946   **Shreve**, Susan. *Lucy Forever and Miss Rosetree, Shrinks*. Henry Holt, 1987. ISBN 0-8040-0350-1. 121p. $13.95.

4-5
*
In the consistency and credibility of its sustained imaginative play, this is reminiscent of Zilpha Snyder's *The Egypt Game*, and it, too, develops into a suspenseful thriller. Lucy and Rosie, eleven-year-old best friends, have set up as "psychiatric consultants" in the basement of Lucy's home. Lucy's father is a child psychiatrist, and when one of his younger patients appears at the basement door, the two members of Shrinks, Inc., find her (Cinder, age five, mute and scarred) much more interesting than their pretend patients. The momentum of the story builds as Lucy investigates the children's home in which Cinder lives, and she gets to know both Cinder and the nurse who brings the

child in for therapy sessions with Lucy's father. It soon becomes clear that Lucy's well-meant efforts are endangering her as well as Cinder, and there is a denoument, both dramatic and logical, that ends the novel with fine flair. Good characters and dialogue here, a strong and unusual plot, and excellent narrative flow.

947   **Shub**, Elizabeth. *Cutlass in the Snow;* illus. by Rachel Isadora. Greenwillow, 1986. Library ed. ISBN 0-688-05928-7; Trade ed. ISBN 0-688-05927-9. 35p. Library ed. $11.88; Trade ed. $11.75.

3-5   On a cold Saturday in 1797, Sam and his Grandpa Campbell sail their small boat from Long Island to Fire Island to explore and gather holly for Christmas. A snow forces them to stay overnight, and they are disturbed by some lights along the shore, which they suspect belong to pirates. Sure enough, they find footprints the next morning, a cutlass thrust into the snow, and a buried treasure. A concluding chapter tells how Sam's descendants discovered the story to be true, through some old ledger entries and a gold coin. This is history will told in an easy format, with handsome black-and-white drawings and sure appeal.

948   **Shura**, Mary Francis. *The Josie Gambit.* Dodd, 1986. ISBN 0-396-08810-4. 160p. $10.95.

5-7   "A gambit," Greg explains at the start of his story, "is a very high-risk play you shouldn't try unless you're willing to live with the way the game turns out." Greg is twelve and has just come to stay with his grandmother for six months; Josie, the friend and neighbor whose grandfather had taught both of them to play chess, is delighted that he will be in her school and in its chess club. Her new friend Tory is inexplicably rude to Greg and soon begins being nasty to Josie as well. Shura does a fine job of deftly developing the mystery of Tory's odd behavior and its dramatic, sad ending, for Tory has indeed taken a chance that her gambit would bring her what she most wants—and she loses. This has good pace, strong characters, good dialogue, and an original plot so well controlled by the author that drama never becomes melodrama.

949   **Shura**, Mary Francis. *The Sunday Doll.* Dodd, 1988. ISBN 0-396-09309-4. 138p. $12.95

5-8   Emmy can't think of anything good about turning thirteen. "I can count on the fingers of one hand the number of teenagers I really like." And, as usual, her beloved Aunt Harriet has sent a birthday gift of a doll, a strange one this time, an Amish doll without a face. At first, this novel seems to be (and the cover seems to indicate) a spooky-secrets story, which it is, but the secrets have nothing to do with the supernatural; instead, Emmy's parents and older sister are keeping something from her, not an unusual circumstance. "All my life I've been taken out to buy M & M's and I'm tired of it!" says Emmy, referring to her removal from the movie theater during the gruesome bits. Packed off to Aunt Harriet's, Emmy eventually learns the secret (the breakdown and suicide of her sister's boyfriend) and, perhaps more important, learns to accept her parents' well-meaning imperfections. "Grow up," says a friend of Aunt Harriet's. "Let them off the hook." This thirteen-isn't-so-bad-after-all story has more backbone than most and is written with more than the usual measure of intensity. Readers will share Emmy's desire to know the secret, an effect that adds narrative suspense as well as thematic depth.

950   **Shute**, Linda. *Clever Tom and the Leprechaun*; written and illus. by Linda Shute. Lothrop, 1988. Library ed. ISBN 0-688-07489-8; Trade ed. ISBN 0-688-07488-X. 32p. Library ed. $12.88; Trade ed. $12.95.

5-7 yrs.   Tom Fitzpatrick is a typical dupe of an archetypal leprechaun. Having caught the little man at his work, Tom resists having his attention diverted but falls for a later trick when the leprechaun shows him the plant under which his treasure is buried. Tom marks it with a red garter and makes the leprechaun promise not to remove it, runs for his spade, and returns to find a field of plants all tied with red garters. Traditional wash drawings with bright shades and soft textures play out this folk tale, adapted from Croker's 1825 collection. The excellent source notes that are appended will intrigue storytellers as much as the tale will children.

951   **Siegel**, Beatrice. *Sam Ellis's Island*; illus. by DyAnne diSalvo-Ryan. Four Winds Press, 1985. ISBN 0-02-782720-8. 88p. $11.95.

4-6   Sam Ellis, merchant of Manhattan Island, acquired the small island to which he gave his name in the year before the rebels signed a Declaration of Independence. To Ellis, a Tory, they were rebels, not patriotic heroes. When the war was over, he remained in New York and acquired more property, tried in vain to sell the island that seemed of little value, and eventually moved to New Jersey and lived as a farmer. When he died the ownership of the island was in dispute, and in 1798 the city authorities converted it into a recruiting station. After the War of 1812, Ellis Island was re-named Fort Gibson, and not until 1890 did it become a federal immigration depot. Siegel does an excellent job of making a narrative out of a mass of carefully researched historical information; her style is direct and neither too dry nor too casual, and her text gives many interesting facts about the Revolutionary War and New York City history as well as about Ellis and the small piece of land that was to become internationally known. Author's notes and a list of books suggested for further reading are appended.

952   Sieruta, Peter D. *Heartbeats and Other Stories.* Harper, 1989. Library ed. ISBN 0-06-025849-7; Trade ed. ISBN 0-06-025848-9. 216p. Library ed. $12.89; Trade ed. $12.95.

7-10   These nine short stories—all but one featuring a male protagonist—are characterized by an unpretentious style and generous tone. Their subjects are familiar: getting your own bedroom, finally; missing a girlfriend who has moved away; "25 Good Reasons for Hating My Brother Todd." That last is one of the best stories, combining humor and sharp empathy to tell about a smart and sensitive "nerd" whose older brother is a handsome, popular jock. Emery's reasons are funny (#17: "He has teeth like Chiclets") and touching (#22: "He has lots of dates") and finally wry (#25: "My mother always did like him best"). In "The Attack of the Jolly Green Giant," David knows his teasing of Molly has gotten out of control, "but I'm afraid to stop. Because if I stop, she won't notice me *at all.*" A few of the stories are melodramatic and seem more liked outlined scenarios for longer fiction, but, on the whole, this is an easy, friendly collection, which, because of its humor and directness. should appeal to reluctant as well as more seasoned readers.

953   Sills, Leslie. *Inspirations: Stories About Women Artists.* Whitman, 1989. ISBN 0-8075-3649-0. 56p. illus. with photographs. $16.95.

5-8   This introduction to four women artists is as commendable for its selection as well as its smooth writing and handsome book design. The only subject likely to be familiar to children is Georgia O'Keeffe; her work begins the book, priming the reader for three other individualists, Frida Kahlo, Alice Neel, and Faith Ringgold, who had a much harder time asserting their identities in the artistic establishment. (After graduating from high school in 1948, Ringgold enrolled as an education student because City College of New York did not allow women into the liberal arts program.) In their sometimes bitter struggle and quest for creative vision, these women span the entire twentieth century, with only Ringgold still alive and working. The brief, informal biographies and the full-color reproductions—generous in both quality and size—will be eye-openers for art students and browsers.

954   Silverstein, Alvin. *The Mystery of Sleep;* by Alvin and Virginia Silverstein; illus. by Nelle Davis. Little, 1987. ISBN 0-316-79117-2. 43p. $12.95.

4-6   With their customary clarity, the Silversteins have simplified scientific information on sleeping patterns, needs, and problems. Although they explain the methods researchers have used to investigate dream cycles and other phenomena, they don't forget to include matter-of-fact references to a child's special concerns, such as bed wetting and night terrors, nor the details that would catch his or her interest ("The recordings from one night's sleep use up about half a mile of EEG paper!"). Always aware of a young reader's limited background (although sleep patterns are measured by electric currents, subjects don't get a shock in the process), the authors word the text simply but precisely, as in describing the way the mind arranges experiences of the day into dream stories. The treatment of insomnia is reassuring and the warning against the use of drugs well handled. Although it's a shame there's no index or bibliography, the organization is clear from the table of contents. A first-rate introduction.

955   **Silverstein**, Alvin. *Wonders of Speech;* by Alvin and Virginia Silverstein. Morrow, 1988. ISBN 0-688-06534-1. 154p. $11.95.

7-   Clear writing, good organization of material, broad coverage, and the inclusion of recent research all contribute to an exemplary informational book. The authors discuss the ways in which sound is produced in the human being, the functioning of the brain in storing and sorting bits of the intricate communications network, the learning of language, speech disabilities, artificial languages, and other aspects of speech. Books that are entitled "The Wonders of. . ." don't always seem wonderful; here it is moot which is the more wonderful, the ability of people to speak or the extent to which scientists have discovered the complexities of how the brain operates to produce speech and the memory on which it depends.

956   **Silverstein,** Alvin. *World of the Brain;* written by Alvin and Virginia Silverstein. Morrow, 1986. ISBN 0-688-05777-2. 197p. $11.75.

7-   This is one of the best in the many good books on medical or
  *   biological subjects by the authors. It is serious, comprehensive, well-organized, and clearly written. It discusses the new tools that facilitate and expand the medical profession's ability to diagnose and treat illnesses that emanate from brain malfunction or that affect the brain; it describes in fine detail the brain's structure and its myriad functions; and it informs readers of the results of recent research. An index is provided, as are many photographs, drawings, and diagrams.

957   **Simmie**, Lois. *Auntie's Knitting a Baby;* illus. by Anne Simmie. Ochard/Watts, 1988. Library ed. ISBN 0-531-08362-4; Trade ed. ISBN 0-531-05762-3. 70p. Library ed. $11.99 ; Trade ed. $11.95.

3-6   From the land of Dennis Lee comes another fresh, funny poetic voice. This collection includes lots of nonsense themes that seem to weave in and out of the narrative and lyrical verses for a total effect that's not so nonsensical after all. The Auntie poems (#1-11) pop up periodically with variations on the following: "Auntie's knitting a baby bonnet/ That looks like an airport wind sock;/ If Auntie's baby fits that hat/

She's in for a terrible shock." The baby about which the narrator is so
concerned turns out to be humanly proportioned after all, but many of
the poems spotlight the kind of worried vulnerability that adults learn
to mask with humor. In "Haunted," for instance, a young insomniac
regrets his accidental slaying of a snake, whose "thin little ghost
comes each night to my bed./ He comes every night and he gives me
no rest,/ He curls on my pillow, he lies on my chest;/ He wails in his
little snake voice, so pathetic,/ His little snake sobbings so soft and
poetic . . ." In another poem, a child denies, with poignant protests,
that his dog is getting old. Many of the selections, however, are simply
rhyming high jinks along the lines of "Vampire Poem": "If you think/
Mosquito bites pain ya,/ Be glad you don't live/ In Transylvania." The
spare, pen-and-ink sketches are not as confident as the poems; some
are cleverly cartooned and others amateurishly drafted, especially in
facial expression. The book as a whole, though, is a jolly good
investment.

958   **Simon**, Norma. *The Saddest Time;* illus. by Jacqueline Rogers.
Whitman, 1986. ISBN 0-8075-7203-9. 37p. $10.25.

K-3   Soft pencil drawings illustrate the discussion, through three
anecdotes, in a text that deals with death in differing circumstances
and that is framed by comments (in italics) that explain death as a sad
but natural fact of life. A concluding note to adults makes it clear that
the book was written in part to combat erroneous concepts young
children may have received from television, where they see actors who
"die" but may reappear the following week. The three anecdotes deal
sensitively with the deaths of a young uncle with a terminal illness, of a
classmate killed in an accident, and of a grandparent.

959   **Simon**, Seymour. *101 Questions and Answers about Dangerous
Animals;* illus. by Ellen Friedman. Macmillan, 1985. ISBN 0-02-782710-
0. 88p. $10.95.

3-6   With material divided by types of animals (there are five chapters on
mammalian species, for example) and an index that gives access to
the contents, this question and answer book has minor reference use.
Simon provides facts and refutes commonly-held misconceptions as
he answers such questions as : Are gorillas dangerous? Is there a
dangerous humanlike ape in the world? Is the orang-utan dangerous?
Are chimpanzees dangerous? Are there any dangerous monkeys? The
author doesn't use scare tactics, but he does suggest sensible safety
precautions when they are needed; his writing style is authoritative
and straightforward.

960   **Simon**, Seymour. *Galaxies*. Morrow, 1988. Library ed. ISBN 0-688-
06185-0; Trade ed. ISBN 0-688-06184-2. 30p. illus. with photographs.
Library ed. $12.88; Trade ed. $12.95.

2-4   Part of an astronomy series that already includes books on the sun,
stars, and four planets, this meets the challenge of conveying
immensity by analogy. In describing the more than three hundred
billion stars that make up the Andromeda galaxy, for instance, Simon
says,"If you were to count one star per second nonstop, it would take
you more than nine thousand years to count the stars in that galaxy."
The measurement of light-years gets similar treatment, with reference
to time as well as distance: "The light from the Andromeda spiral that
we see today first started on its journey more than two million years
ago, when our ancestors lived in caves." Dramatic photographs,
computer-colored against black backgrounds, show the shapes of
spiral, elliptical, barred spiral, and irregular galaxies. Although a
concluding statement asserts that the universe is without any
boundary, the map that "plots the locations of one million galaxies"
unfortunately undercuts this idea with a round frame. Outside of such
nitpicking, this is a solid addition to children's understanding of
scientific phenomena.

961   **Simon**, Seymour. *How to Be an Ocean Scientist in Your Own Home*;
illus. by David A. Carter. Lippincott, 1988. Library ed. ISBN 0-397-
32292-5; Trade ed. ISBN 0-397-32291-7. 136p. Library ed. $12.89; Trade
ed. $12.95.

4-7   Salt (sea and table) and water are the primary ingredients for most of
the twenty-four projects and experiments in this collection; other
materials and equipment should be readily available. While a few of
the projects involve plants and animals, including brine shrimp (aka
sea monkeys) most have to do with measuring salinity, waves, and
currents, with bowls, aquariums and bathtubs providing stand-in
service for the ocean. Instructions and diagrams are clear, as are
Simon's explanations of the various phenomena. Good for science
fairs, as well as for those kids who just need a respectable excuse for
playing with water.

962   **Simon**, Seymour. *Stars*. Library ed. ISBN 0-688-05856-6; Trade ed.
ISBN 0-688-05855-8. 28p. The Sun. Library ed. ISBN 0-688-05858-2. 26p.
Both books are Morrow, 1986. illus.; Library ed. $12.88; Trade ed. $13.00.

2-4   These two subjects call upon Simon's greatest gift, which is to inject
*   accurate scientific information with a sense of wonder. The scope of
galaxies requires readers to think in trillions—of years, of miles, of
stars. Simon manages to impart the facts without numbing the brain
with an endless string of figures. He exhorts readers to use the
spaceships of their minds to explore the sun and then proceeds with

an explanation of exemplary clarity describing the size, substance, origin, and movements of the sun, all bolstered with the series' characteristically brilliant graphics. The latter range from diagrams to photographs to paintings and are spaciously incorporated into the careful book design. The introduction to the stars is outstanding for its comparisions and compression of material.

963   **Simon**, Seymour. *Storms*. Morrow, 1989. Library ed. ISBN 0-688-07414-6; Trade ed. ISBN 0-688-07413-8. 30p. illus. with photographs. Library ed. $12.88; Trade ed. $12.95.

4-6
*

Following the format of his stellar series on the sun, stars, and planets, Simon here taps a topic of private terror to many children who have not outgrown early fears of thunder and lightning. There's inherent drama in the information itself, and the book heightens this with bold color photos of cumulonimbus clouds (including a diagram to show air movements), storm cells, squall lines, hailstorms, gust fronts, lightning play, tornados, and hurricanes. The display is awesome, and the text respects it. Explanations are clear but never condescending; the science of radar, satellite, and computer tracking is as astounding as the ancient theory of Thor's chariot striking clouds. Children seeking material for reports will find the real power of facts.

964   **Simon**, Seymour. *Volcanoes*. Morrow, 1988. Library ed. ISBN 0-688-07412-X; Trade ed. ISBN 0-688-07411-1. 32p. illus. with photographs. Library ed. $12.88; Trade ed. $12.95.

1-3

In the same format as the author's *The Sun, Glaciers*, etc., this handsome volume is for younger readers than is Patricia Lauber's *Volcano*. Simon clearly describes how volcanoes are formed and how they erupt, using well-known examples like Mt. Saint Helens and Mauna Loa. The photographs are large, informative, and spectacular, reproduced in brilliant color. Aside from one confusing map of the earth's tectonic plates, this is a solid introduction.

965   **Singer**, Marilyn. *Turtle in July*; illus. by Jerry Pinkney. Macmillan, 1989. ISBN 0-02-782881-6. 32p. $13.95.

3-5
*

The great joy of these fifteen nature poems is the pattern of verbal rhythms that reflect the character of each subject creature. The befuddled bear emerging from hibernation in March asks "Who I?/ Where I?/ When I now?/ No matter/ Need water/ Few berries/ Fresh ants/ Not so hungry/ Or am I?" The timber rattlesnake sibilantly describes summer and winter with long coiling sounds. The beavers in November hurry here and there with the refrain, "This stick here/ That stick there/ Mud, more mud, add mud, good mud . . . ." The joy of the art is Pinkney's venture into new effects without sacrificing his characteristic style. While his human figures are sometimes studied, these animal drawings are anatomically spontaneous. The settings are lusciously simple, with spacious color and sharply focused compositions. Both writer and artist have captured the essence of the fish, fowl, and mammals featured here. Perfect to share in classrooms or story hours emphasizing themes of nature study and seasonal change.

966   Slepian, Jan. *The Broccoli Tapes*. Philomel, 1989. ISBN 0-399-21712-6. 160p. $13.95.

5-7   Using the device of tape transcriptions, Slepian gives a convincing immediacy to Sara Davidson's story of her stay in Hawaii. At the suggestion of her sixth grade teacher at home (Boston) Sara is using the tapes as her way of participating in the class Oral History project. Broccoli is a feral cat that Sara and her brother find, love, and tame, and she becomes very important to the two children, who have left the comfort of familiarity and friends. They do make one friend, Eddie, whose unhappy home situation reaches a crisis and moves on to a happy solution. All of their feelings of displacement are aggravated for Sara and her brother by the rather sudden illness and death of the grandmother who has come to Hawaii with them. This has, then, several plot threads—but they are each about love and especially about the fact that loving exposes one to the possibility of loss and pain. Slepian is a fine writer, and the elements of her story are smoothly meshed, the action and characterization mutually affective. The message that love is worth the chance of pain is given by the people in her story, not didactically imposed by the author.

967   Slepian, Jan. *Getting On With It*. Macmillan, 1985. ISBN 0-02-782930-8. 171p. $11.95.

5-8   Much as she loves her grandmother, thirteen-year-old Berry is unhappy, knowing that she's been sent away from home because her parents are separating. An imaginative and sensitive child, Berry becomes concerned about her neighbors, adults whose lives are interwoven in a pattern Berry comprehends only slowly. Among the things she sees that help her accept the change in her own life are the love between a young man and an older woman and the tenacity of that young man's love for the unhappy father whose guilt (he had been at the wheel when a car crash killed his wife) made him unable to accept a chance to live with his son. As always, Slepian, has created a strong and convincing cast of characters; her protagonist changes in a logical way in response to perceptions and perspectives gained from new experiences and relationships.

968   Slepian, Jan. *Risk n' Roses*. Philomel, 1990. ISBN 0-399-22219-7. 175p. $14.95.

5-7   In a thoughtful period novel set after World War II, Skip, eleven, is as enthralled as the other neighborhood children with Jean, who is tough, daring, and domineering. Sharp-tongued Jean is a manipulator, and one of the people she manipulates is Angela, the beautiful and retarded older sister of Skip. Slepian is an astute and perceptive observer of group dynamics, and her skillfully written story explores the intricacies of the relationships among the children, the cruelty of Jean to Angela, and the way it moves Skip to a new perspective on her feeling for her sister. The characterizations of Angela's overprotective mother and of the elderly neighbor (a victim of Nazi persecution) who is persecuted by Jean are powerful, both adding to the suspense of a story about the effect on others of an unhappy vindictive child.

969   **Slepian**, Jan. *Something Beyond Paradise*. Philomel, 1987. ISBN 0-399-21425-9. 180p. $13.95.

7-10   Franny, sixteen, lives with her mother and grandmother in Honolulu. Save for a close friendship with Akiko, she has focused her time on school, on sharing with her mother the care of her often-irrational grandmother, and on dancing. She has received a letter offering her a dance scholarship in New York, but can't bring herself to tell her mother that she wants to leave. Several new experiences help her decide what to do, and there is a logical catalyst for Franny's final decision. Slepian, a dependably astute and polished writer, here deals capably with the conflict between the adolescent's need for inde-pendence and feelings of duty and family loyalty. Broadening the basic plot, and nicely knit with it, are a first love affair and an exposure to a cult joined by Akiko, resisted by Franny.

970   **Sloan**, Carolyn. *The Sea Child*. Holiday House, 1988. ISBN 0-8234-0723-3. 128p. $12.95.

4-7   "Jessie had never seen another person in all her life. Only Danny." Danny is nine-year-old Jessie's father; her mother left when Jessie was born. The two of them live on The Sands, the only piece left of a village that has been drowned by the sea. Isolated from the mainland by supernaturally dangerous waters, Jenny is happy with their Robinson Crusoe-like existence; as she grows, Danny becomes sad because he knows her mother will come to claim Jenny when she is ten. Part selkie myth, part ghost story, this is an elusive mystery, never too tidied up. The appealing motifs are many, and Jennie's visit to the mainland (through a secret passage), where she meets a girl who has heard of Jenny from a "crazy" old man, gives the story a realistic cast that heightens the unsettling fantasy.

971   Sloat, Teri, ad. *The Eye of the Needle*; based on a Yupik tale as told by Betty Huffman; ad. and illus. by Teri Sloat. Dutton, 1990. ISBN 0-525-44623-0. 32p. $13.95.

4-7 yrs.   From what is evidently a reshaped amalgam of Yupik folktales, Sloat has created a picture book that will make smooth reading aloud to children who appreciate cumulative stories. When Grandmother sends Amik out to hunt after a long Alaska winter, he finds consecutively larger sea creatures, all of which he swallows, from needlefish to a whale. Then, of course, he's too big to fit back into the hut, and Grandmother has to pull him in through the smoke hole with her magic needle. Never mind; he spits everything out, enough to feed the whole community. The rounded shapes of the softly textured, color-pencil drawings fill each page with energetic action. However true this may or may not be to the Yupik tradition, it's a jolly celebration of the oral stage. And who wouldn't love to go out into the world, become a giant, return home, and regain manageable proportions in time to be taken care of? You can have your seal and eat it too.

972   Slote, Alfred. *A Friend Like That*. Lippincott, 1988. Library ed. ISBN 0-397-32311-5; Trade ed. ISBN 0-397-32310-7. 152p. Library ed. $11.89; Trade ed. $11.95.

4-6   In the first book about the eleven-year-old narrator Robby (*Moving In,*), he and his sister are relieved when their widowed father doesn't marry his business partner Mrs. Lowenfeld. Now Robby is apprehensive when another woman seems to have taken Dad's fancy, and he finds a way to avoid going home when Dad invites Mrs. Nathanson to dinner. Having been adjured to get home on time, Robby picks a fight so that he'll have to go to the principal's office, which would mean Dad would have to come to school after work. All does not go according to plan: Robby, who has confessed the truth to the principal, Miss Bradsbury, cannot tell Dad; he runs away, but his friend Beth helps him turn back. Two results: Robby and Dad finally begin to communicate, and Dad becomes smitten with Miss Bradsbury. Like the first book, this has perceptive handling of characters (all well-defined) and relationships, good pace and structure, and a competent style that is especially strong in natural dialogue and quiet humor.

973   Slote, Alfred. *Moving In*. Lippincott, 1988. Library ed. ISBN 0-397-32262-3; Trade ed. ISBN 0-397-32261-5. 167p. Library ed. $11.89; Trade ed. $11.95.

4-6   Robby is the eleven-year-old narrator who, with his sister Peggy (13) and their widowed father, has just moved to a new town where Dad is going into partnership with an old acquaintance, Ruth Lowenfeld, recently divorced. Robby and Peggy dislike Ruth and are appre-

hensive because Dad seems smitten; Peggy's solution is to be openly
hostile, Robby's is to pirate a computer program of Dad's, hoping that
by giving it to Ruth's ex-husband he can be a catalyst to a reunion. Mr.
Lowenfeld, a nice man, quickly returns the stolen material and Dad
never knows, to Robby's relief. This doesn't have the depth of some
earlier Slote books, but it has many strengths: good pace, natural
dialogue, strong characterization, and a pervasive humor.

974   **Small**, David. *Imogene's Antlers;* written and illus. by David Small.
Crown, 1985. ISBN 0-517-55564-6. 26p. $9.95.

K-2   The members of a large household react in different ways when young
Imogene appears one day with a pair of enormous antlers on her
head, an overnight phenomenon. As the day passes, one of the
servants finds the antlers useful for drying towels, and another uses
them as a multiple feeding station for birds. Imogene's mother faints
periodically; Imogene's doctor is baffled. Everyone is delighted, next
day, when Imogene pokes her head around the dining room door,
antler-free. They're delighted, that is, until they see the rest of
Imogene. This ebullient fantasy in the tall tale tradition is told with
pace and flair, and it's illustrated with pictures that are as deft as they
are funny.

975   **Smith**, Alison. *Billy Boone.* Scribner, 1989. ISBN 0-684-18974-7. 128p.
$12.95.

4-6   Trumpet, Billy's mother felt, was not an appropriate instrument for a
young Southern lady. The bandleader told Billy, "the trumpet is a very
masculine instrument." Billy, the narrator, is determined, even
agreeing to take piano lessons (a fiasco) and act as office charlady for
her father if she's allowed to keep up her trumpet lessons. Billy's
musical achievements are kept at a credible level, and her interest is
balanced by familial relationships (particularly in getting along with a
mother and grandmother who do not get along with each other) and in
tenaciously proving that she had not been so negligent as to leave
Dad's office unlocked, facilitating a break-in. This is a good example
of a story about a goal-oriented protagonist whose victory comes
through quiet persistence.

976   **Smith**, Beth. *Castles;* illus. by Anne Canevari Green and with
photographs. Watts, 1988. ISBN 0-531-10511-3. 86p. (First Books). $9.90.

5-8   A solidly instructive text introduces various kinds of castles as they
developed historically, with chapters on castle life and warfare. Terms
are defined in the text as well as the glossary, while black-and-white
photographs and labelled drawings clarify descriptions. Although this
is not as inspiring as David Macaulay's *Castle* , its text is broader in
coverage and also more detailed. The word "wardrobe," for instance,

is traced to the "garderobe" or castle toilet, where clothes were hung because the smell kept the moths away. The geographical emphasis is on England and Wales, but other examples are incorporated as well. A concluding section on legends and ghost stories will whet the reader's appetite for more. Indexed.

977 **Smith**, Doris Buchanan. *Karate Dancer*. Putnam, 1987. ISBN 0-399-21464-X. 169p. $13.95.

6-9 An only child, Troy is a stable, intelligent fourteen-year-old whose parents approve of his talent as a cartoonist (he does work for the local paper) but—without interfering—are unhappy about his other passion, karate. Smith, in a story that has both depth and popular appeal, smoothly knits the several aspects of Troy's life: his relationship with his parents, his disappointment that his own lack of discipline has delayed acquisition of a black belt, and (as per title) his amazed discovery that he enjoys and is good at ballet when a girl on whom he has a crush begs him to partner her for a performance of *Coppelia*. Conflict and drama are added by several sub-plots, and everything that happens is germane to everything else.

978 **Smith**, Doris Buchanan. *Return to Bitter Creek*. Viking, 1986. ISBN 0-670-80783-4. 174p. $11.95.

5-7 Twelve-year-old Lacey returns with her mother, Campbell, and her mother's boyfriend, David, to the small Appalachian town Campbell had fled years before when Lacey was a baby. Now the old family tensions surface again, between defiant Campbell and her tyrannical mother. David acts as peacemaker until his sudden, accidental death, when Lacey finds herself shoring up her mother and fending off her grandmother. Although David seems to good to be true, the other characters show a believable blend of quirky foibles. The mountain setting and wildflowers that Lacey loves form a natural relief to the human dynamics. Lacey's dedication to helping build their house (there's a horse thrown in), David's to his blacksmithing, and Campbell's to her leatherwork cast the drama into a counterculture framework, but the conflicts are as old as the hills.

979 **Smith**, Elizabeth Simpson. *A Dolphin Goes to School: The Story of Squirt, a Trained Dolphin*; illus. by Ted Lewin. Morrow, 1986. Library ed. ISBN 0-688-04816-1; Trade ed. ISBN 0-688-04815-3. 85p. Library ed. $11.88; Trade ed. $11.75.

3-5 Lewin's wonderfully realistic black-and-white paintings are simply composed, accurately detailed, and effective in conveying the physical attributes and actions of dolphins. The text, a good example of nonfiction written with a narrative flow, gives detailed information about how dolphins are captured, protected, transported, and trained by the reward system. Smith's account of the training of one dolphin, Squirt, and of his debut as a performer is informative, impressive, and exciting. An index is provided.

980   **Smith**, Roland. *Sea Otter Rescue: The Aftermath of an Oil Spill*; written and illus. with photographs by Roland Smith. Cobblehill, 1990. ISBN 0-525-65041-5. 64p. $13.95.

4-6   Unlike many perfunctory treatments of current events, this photodocumentary is by an expert with in-depth knowledge of the Valdez oil spill and its effect on wildlife. Smith is an experienced zoologist whose writing and color photographs are both clear and immediate, involving readers in the fate of the sea otters by describing individual animals as well as general rescue operations. The evidence presented here speaks more dramatically than any ecological preaching could, and kids will benefit from discussions of the book in environmental and natural history classes. Although there is no patronizing these animals as "cute," they are undeniably appealing, with a few of the nursery shots downright irresistible. A glossary defines technical terminology, which is kept to a minimum, and an index gives access to the continuous text.

981   **Snelling**, John. *Buddhism*. Bookwright/Watts, 1986. ISBN 0-531-18065-4. 48p. illus. (Religions of the World). $10.90.

4-6   Although unattractive in format (double columns, italicized captions placed too close to the print of the text) this is a sensibly organized and capably written book about one of the world's major religions. Maps and color photographs are amply provided; the glossary, index, and bibliography are brief but adequate. Snelling gives balanced coverage to the topic, describing the life and the philosophy of Siddhartha Gautama, who renounced princely wealth for the poverty of a solitary mendicant. Discussing the principles of Buddhism, the author goes on to explain how, over the centuries, disciples differed and how Buddhism spread from India to other parts of Eastern Asia.

982   **Snyder**, Dianne, ad. *The Boy of the Three-Year Nap*; illus. by Allen Say. Houghton, 1988. ISBN 0-395-44090-4. 32p. $14.95.

5-7 yrs.   A trickster gets tricked in this clever folktale from Japan, with
   *   delicately modulated illustrations that reflect stylistic and narrative techniques of Japanese painting. Taro is a lazy boy who schemes to become the son-in-law of a rich merchant by disguising himself as an ujigami and ordering the merchant to marry off his daughter to "that fine lad who lives on your street" (Taro). Taro's mother in turn tricks Taro into accepting a job as the merchant's storehouse manager. "And as it turned out, the marriage is a happy one. . . . If he is not the busiest man in town, neither is he the laziest." The pictures as well as

the words use an understated irony to suggest the duplicity and gullibility on display here. In fact, several illustrations are witty parodies of well-known *ukiyo-e* woodcuts. Contrasts of color and image are vivid but never exaggerated. The humor of characterization does not detract from the aesthetic appeal of landscape and domestic scenes. Lines are spare and meticulous, with each illustration framed in a black brush-stroked rectangle. A satisfying picture book in every respect.

983   **Snyder**, Zilpha Keatley. *And Condors Danced*. Delacorte, 1987. ISBN 0-385-29575-8. 203p. $14.95.

4-7   This begins with an entry in Carly's journal in 1907, and it is a record of her eleventh year. Living on a ranch in southern California, Carly is bitterly aware of the feud with wealthy Mr. Quigley, a feud that has kept her family poor. She's worried about her languid invalid mother and devoted to the two who had taken her in during the worst of Mama's illness, Great-aunt Mehitabel and her servant Woo Ying. Then there's the local bully, the young Quigley who's her classmate, and the turn of fate that helps her save his life but brings the death of a beloved pet dog. Last, Carly adjusts to her mother's death. This has believable characters and good style, and it gives a convincing picture of place and period, but it is an overcrowded picture, so that while it is an enjoyable read, it lacks impact. The title refers to Carly's interest in observing the reputed ceremonial dancing of the California condor.

984   **Snyder**, Zilpha Keatley. *Janie's Private Eyes*. Delacorte, 1989. ISBN 0-440-50123-7. 212p. $14.95.

4-6   In a fourth book about the Stanley family, the protagonist is thirteen-year-old David, whose investigation into the mystery of who is stealing dogs is spurred by his sister (Jane, age eight) who has set up a "detective agency." Precocious Janie manages, entertainingly, to get in and out of trouble along with the six-year-old twins and two Vietnamese refugee children. The solution of the mystery is nicely woven into the problems of the Vietnamese family. The story is softened by the durable affection within the Stanley family, and is lightened by the deft treatment of the love-struck swain of stepsister Amanda. The mystery is credibly solved in a nicely crafted story that has suspense, humor, and natural dialogue.

985   **Snyder**, Zilpha Keatley. *Libby on Wednesday*. Delacorte, 1990. ISBN 0-385-29979-6. 196p. $14.95.

6-8   Although she lived with her father, grandmother, and great-aunt, it was Libby's absentee mother who had insisted that Libby needed to be "socialized." That was the end of being tutored at home (wonderful) and the beginning of eighth-grade classes (boring) that covered material Libby had learned years before. This isn't a mother-knows-best book, but it does develop into a story of peer relationships, group dynamics, and the evolution of strong friendships emerging from a writing club that Libby had originally resented as part of the abhorred socialization. The background, with its extended and supportive family, gives warmth and solidity to a novel that is percipient in characterization and believably positive in outcome.

986   **Spirin**, Gennady, illus. *The Enchanter's Spell: Five Famous Tales;* comp. and illus. by Gennady Spirin. Dial, 1988. ISBN 0-8037-0320-1. 80p. $14.95.

4-6   A collection of fairy tales by Andersen, Cervantes, Hoffman, Macdonald, and Pushkin is illustrated with wonderfully detailed and textured paintings by a noted Soviet artist. Spirin's work is in the medieval tradition, remarkable for its play of light and shadow and the fidelity of costume detail; within the boundaries of his style, however, there is a varied response to the classic tales he is illustrating, so that the pictures for "The Emperor's New Clothes" are comic, while those for George MacDonald's "Little Daylight" are appropriately eerie. The palette is rich but subdued, the page layout and book design impressive.

987   **Spruyt**, E. Lee. *Behind the Golden Curtain: Hansel and Gretel at the Great Opera House;* written and illus. by E. Lee Spruyt. Four Winds, 1987. ISBN 0-02-786400-6. 30p. $12.95.

3-5   In picture book format, the story of preparation and performance on the occasion of a new production of *Hansel and Gretel* at the Metropolitan Opera House (so announced on the jacket flap if not the title page) is described. The author, long involved with scenic design, gives a full picture of the many services and effects created by the staff as well as of the work of creative performers. What weakens the book are the facts that the descriptions of behind-scenes activities often refer to work done long before production day (lessening the opening-night effect), and that the illustrations, attractive if misty spreads that often have obscure details, may be understood more by those who are experienced opera buffs than by children who are not familiar with the sets, props, and decoration of a large-scale production.

988   **St. Germain**, Sharon. *The Terrible Fight;* illus. by Deborah Zemke. Houghton, 1990. ISBN 0-395-50069-9. 32p. $13.95.

4-7 yrs.   Molly and Becky were best friends, perfectly balancing on the park seesaw, waving good night from their respective bedroom windows. But . . . "that was before the terrible fight." Like most childhood feuds, this one begins with a seemingly inconsequential disagreement (Molly wants to trade dolls) that gathers its own velocity, resulting in a sequence of meannesses far out of proportion to the original offense. "Guess what, Becky? I'm having a birthday party and you're not invited." Although the theme is not new, the appeal of this story lies in its elemental familiarity, and young children appreciate seeing their daily dramas enacted by somebody else. Pen-and-watercolor paintings are big and inviting, with expressively cartooned faces and a sunny tone that implies the happy ending. Like most fights, this one ends when its antagonists decide friendship offers the finer rewards. Becky waves goodnight, "and then, my best friend Molly waved back at me."

989   **Stanek**, Muriel. *All Alone After School;* illus. by Ruth Rosner. Whitman, 1985. ISBN 0-8075-0278-2. 30p. $9.25.

2-4   A small boy describes the way his mother prepared him for being home alone when she took a needed job: there were safety instructions, emergency telephone numbers, and a spare key for the friendly neighbor next door. It's a bit lonely, and there are times when Mom is sorely missed, but the days fall into a familiar pattern; there are chores to do and programs to watch, and homework and telephone calls to fill the time. As the book ends, Josh meets a new girl in class (this is a year later) who admits she has trepidations because she's going to have to be home alone after school. Josh gives her the worry-stone his mother had given him. "Keep it as long as you want," he says, "I don't need it any more." The tone is positive, the information useful, the message and the fictional vehicle nicely combined.

990   **Stanley**, Diane. *A Country Tale;* written and illus. by Diane Stanley. Macmillan, 1985. ISBN 0-02-787680-3. 29p. $12.95.

K-3   An elegant book that spoofs elegance, this gets away with an old-fashioned air because the subject is durably relevant. Two close country friends, Cleo and Lucy, are affected by the arrival of wealthy, snobbish Mrs. Snickers from the city. The grand dame succeeds in making Cleo feel discontented with her lot and in completely rejecting Lucy, who has enough good sense to ride out Cleo's temporary attack of fashion and eventually help her back to her old self. The characters are meticulously drawn cats, each whisker and patch of fur fine-lined. The expressions are both feline and typically human, as in Cleo's careful imitation of Mrs. Snickers' pout. Colors are sometimes sharply patterned and then again, subtly blended. Children will recognize a playground situation in this pastoral, Victorian setting.

991   **Stanley**, Diane. *Peter the Great;* written and illus. by Diane Stanley. Four Winds, 1986. ISBN 0-02-786790-0. 29p. $12.95.

2-4   Peter the Great, although a riveting figure, is an unusual choice of subject for a picture book biography. However, Stanley has compressed a good deal of complex information into a compact text while managing to convey some sense of Peter's wildly unique personality and contributions to Russian history. Her illustrations, rhythmical in coloration and patterning, offer a visual depth that increases the impact of the book considerably. Except for the inevitable odd generalization or two (". . . the Russians never could tell one European from another"), this offers an intriguing perspective on a rare meeting of an implacable force for progress with an immoveable object of traditional society.

992   **Stanley**, Diane. *Shaka: King of the Zulus;* by Diane Stanley and Peter Vennema; illus. by Diane Stanley. Morrow, 1988. Library ed. ISBN 0-688-07343-3; Trade ed. ISBN 0-688-07342-5. 40p. Library ed. $13.88; Trade ed. $13.95.

2-4   Like her middle-grade picture book biography *Peter the Great* , this recounts the life of a major historical figure whose complexities have been subject to much historical investigation. Outcast as a boy, Shaka is driven to prove himself as a warrior, eventually becoming chief of a clan that he builds from obscurity to dominance in a vast empire. Each double spread, with formally coordinated text and full-page pictures, focuses on an important scene in his rise to power. At least twice, his violence and cruelty are explained in context of the times, and his mental instability is suggested, along with his military genius. The format is decorative, with traditional design motifs and illustrations dominated by browns and tans. Although the human figures seem stiff and sometimes glamorized, the rounded shapes and smooth lines render panoramic the movement of the subject, his warriors, and their landscape.

993   **Staples**, Suzanne Fisher. *Shabanu: Daughter of the Wind.* Knopf, 1989. Library ed. ISBN 0-394-94815-7; Trade ed. ISBN 0-394-84815-2. 240p. Library ed. $13.99; Trade ed. $13.95.

7-12   This first novel is, on several counts, one of the most exciting YA books
  *   to appear recently. Staples is so steeped in her story and its Pakistani setting that the problematic use of a first-person voice for a desert child rings authentic—the voice is clear, consistent, and convincing, the narrative all the more immediate. An enormous amount of information on nomadic life surfaces in earthy details that move the story along, build a world, and develop a protagonist who is spirited but bound by the ways of her people. Shabanu and her sister Phulan are to marry brothers as soon as they all come of age. It is an ideal match for family and economic reasons, but accumulating the dowries involves selling Shabanu's beloved camel to cruel Afghans. This is Shabanu's first loss of many: she will eventually lose her betrothed and be promised to a wealthy landowner to settle a blood feud. In the

end, it is only her innermost strength that she can protect, and we feel this sense of self as if it had crossed a world of distance and traditions to become our own. The richness and tragedy of a whole culture are reflected in the fate of this girl's family, each member of whom is rendered with natural clarity. Scenes of dust storms, camels mating and birthing, the onset of menstruation that initiates wedding plans, the burial of an honored grandfather, wedding rituals, the carnival atmosphere of an Asian fair, the binding rites of the Muslim faith are all vividly related. Through an involving plot Staples has given young readers insight into lives totally different from their own, but into emotions resoundingly familiar.

994   **Steig,** William. *Brave Irene*; written and illus by William Steig. Farrar, 1986. ISBN 0-374-30947-7. 28p. $12.95.

K-3   No talking animals or magic pebbles here; Steig instead tells, with vigor and fluency, the adventures of Irene, who braves a blizzard to get the duchess's new ball gown to the palace. Her mother has made the beautiful dress but becomes too ill to deliver it. She doesn't want Irene to go either. "'But I *love* snow,' Irene insisted." It proves to be the wind that torments Irene, driving her "along so rudely she had to hop, skip and go helter-skeltering over the knobbly ground" and telling her to "GO-HO-WO-WOME." Even when the wind rips the dress from its box, Irene presses on, feeling she owes the duchess an explanation. She twists her ankle, gets lost, and falls into a snowdrift and into despair. "Why not freeze to death, she thought, and let all these troubles end. Why not? She was already buried." But Irene's fortitude and resourcefulness get her to the palace, where—mysteriously—the dress awaits. The illustrations of Irene's solid little self, both brave and battered, are as immediate as the text, and the cold and wind are wonderfully evoked. This is one of Steig's simplest stories; it is also one of his best, a sturdily realistic tale that has the force of a legend.

995   **Steig,** William. *Shrek!*; written and illus. by William Steig. Di Capua/Farrar, 1990. ISBN 0-374-36877-5. 32p. $10.95.

2-4   Kids who believe themselves too old for the straightforward rewards of the traditional fairy tale are in for a treat here. Kicked goodbye by his ugly parents, even uglier Shrek goes out into the world on a quest, er, "to do his share of damage." A witch sends him on his way to a princess. After an amusing encounter with a dragon, and a dreadful dream of meeting some friendly children, Shrek finally fights his way into the princess' castle, where, Quixote-like, Shrek confronts himself in a Hall of Mirrors: "They're all me!" he yodeled. 'All ME!' He faced himself, full of rabid self-esteem, happier than ever to be exactly what he was." The princess, of course, is "stunningly ugly," and they live "horribly ever after." An easy joke, perhaps, but Steig's skillful

wordplay adds high gloss to the low humor, as when Shrek and the
princess profess their love: "Your horny warts, your rosy wens,/ Like
slimy bogs and fusty fens,/ Thrill me." The illustrations are cheerfully
mean-spirited, with colors that never hurt anyone crabbed in by little
black lines. Perfect for those bad-mood storyhours.

996   **Steig**, William. *Spinky Sulks*; written and illus. by William Steig.
Farrar, 1988. ISBN 0-374-38321-9. 32p. $13.95.

5-8 yrs.   With an offhand, humorous flair characteristic of his best stories,
*   Steig presents us with an all-too-human protagonist. Spinky has been
offended by his family's outrageous behavior. Though his sister begs
forgiveness for calling him Stinky, though his brother concedes that
Philadelphia *is* the capital of Belgium, though his mother brings him a
lunch tray, though his friends whisper goofy things in his ear and swing
the hammock to which he's retreated, though his father assures him
that he is one of the most popular of the three children, though his
grandmother brings him his favorite candy, though a clown is hired to
pull a triple-dip ice-cream cone out of his pocket, though the whole
family covers him with a tarpaulin and beach umbrella when it starts
raining . . . still Spinky sulks. Actually he begins to reconsider, but he
has to figure out how to give in and still keep his self-respect. That's
exactly what this book will do for sulky children—give them a chance
to laugh at themselves and reconsider their behavior at the same
time. Steig cartoons a green suburban setting with straight walks,
straight fences, straight trees in straight lawns . . . all with a straight
face. Spinky's family itself is a bit square, though they do learn to be
"much more careful about his feelings. Too bad they couldn't keep it
up forever." Fortunately for us, Steig seems to be able to.

997   **Stein**, R. Conrad. *The Story of Mississippi Steamboats*; illus. by Tom
Dunnington. Childrens Press, 1987. ISBN 0-516-04726-4. 32p.
(Cornerstones of Freedom). Library ed. $7.45; Trade ed. $9.95.

4-6   An efficiently brief history of Mississippi steamboats during their
heyday in the mid 1800s describes the development of the vessels and
capitalizes on some of the intriguing detail surrounding them. Stein's
account emphasizes both the romantic allure so eloquently described
by Mark Twain and the constant danger of fire and explosion ("The
dead and missing in the *Sultana* wreck totaled 1,547—more than were
lost in the *Titanic* disaster of 1912"). The format and gray-and-brown
wash drawings are somewhat younger than the tone of the text here,
but the book will be useful in American history studies.

998   **Steptoe**, John. *Mufaro's Beautiful Daughters: An African Tale*; ad.
from a folktale and illus. by John Steptoe. Lothrop, 1987. Library ed.

ISBN 0-688-04046-2; Trade ed. ISBN 0-688-04045-4. 30p. Library ed. $12.88; Trade ed. $13.00.

5-8 yrs.   Dramatic, oversize paintings accompany a story based on an animal-groom tale collected at the end of the nineteenth century from the Zimbabwe region of southern Africa. Two sisters, alike in their beauty but opposite in disposition, are to go with their father to compete for the king's choice of a wife. The mean sister sneaks ahead so she will arrive first, but she is arrogant to three strangers she encounters on the way. The gentle sister, Nyasha, who is kind to the strangers, finds her sister sobbing a story of finding a monster in the palace. Nyasha opens the door and sees the snake she has long befriended in her garden at home. He turns into the king (who had also taken the form of the strangers) and marries Nyasha. The sister who had ridiculed her then becomes a servant in the new queen's household. The art is deep-colored and lush, with sensitive, realistic portraits except in the case of the cruel sister, whose expressions could have been less exaggerated. Sweeping landscapes, textured with fine crosshatch, are thoughtfully composed, though one forest scene loses, in the gutter, the central figure of a bird. The story and art will make an intriguing accompaniment to well-known European versions of "Beauty and the Beast."

999   Stevens, Janet, ad. *How the Manx Cat Lost Its Tail*; ad. and illus. by Janet Stevens. Harcourt, 1990. ISBN 0-15-236765-9. 32p. $14.95.

4-6 yrs.   A pourquoi tale about how the Manx Cat loses its tail by arriving just as Noah slams the door of the Ark gives artist Janet Stevens plenty of latitude to play with her favorite subject, the humorous depiction of animals. Double spreads seem spaciously composed but are, on closer inspection, filled with rollicking details: scenes of Shem, "in charge of all the birds of the air"; Ham, "in charge of all the fish and animals of the sea"; Japhet, "in charge of all the animals of the forest and jungle"; Noah's wife, "in charge of all the pets—dogs, cats, ponies, birds, goldfish, and every other pet you can think of"; and, of course, Noah, frantically calling louder and louder for his favorite cat ("HERE, KITTY, KITTY, KITTY!") until his wife comes along with a soft "Spss, pss, sps sps sps pss" that brings the Manx in, barely. Kids will quickly pick up the escalating refrain and relish the mounting tumult as the waters rise along with the general panic. Stevens' drafting manages to be both accurate and vigorous, with loose, swinging lines surging like the storm and rounded like the waves. Colors are deep but carefully blended to avoid clashes that would overload the action-packed scenes. This one will be a read-aloud favorite for both lap-sitters and large groups.

1000   Stevenson, James. *Are We Almost There?:* written and illus. by James
Stevenson. Greenwillow, 1985. Library ed. ISBN 0-688-04239-2; Trade
ed. ISBN 0-688-04238-4. 30p. Library ed. $11.88; Trade ed. $11.75.

K-3   They may look like animals, Harry and Larry, but no child will be
fooled; the two who squabble and squirm in the back seat are children
testing their parents' patience and stamina on the long ride to the
beach. Stevenson's flyaway drawings, in cartoon strip frames, have
ebullience and humor, and the dialogue (in balloons) should evoke
amused recognition reflexes from most members of the read-aloud
audience. Stevenson also captures the feeling of joyous freedom
children have at the seashore.

1001   Stevenson, James. *Higher on the Door;* written and illus. by James
Stevenson. Greenwillow, 1987. Library ed. ISBN 0-688-06637-2; Trade
ed. ISBN 0-688-06636-4. 30p. Library ed. $11.88; Trade ed. $11.75.

K-3   Stevenson fans who enjoyed *When I Was Nine* should find equal
appeal in this companion volume, with deft watercolor sketches
adding vitality (and often humor) to the author's reminiscences of his
childhood. The read-aloud audience that asks "What was it like
when...?" should enjoy this foray into that primitive era when milkmen
brought milk in bottles, icemen carried in blocks of ice, and small boys
were measured yearly and their height recorded by marks on a door.

1002   Stevenson, James. *The Supreme Souvenir Factory;* written and illus.
by James Stevenson. Greenwillow, 1988. ISBN 0-688-07782-X. 56p.
$11.95.

K-3   Stevenson's pictures, lively despite the sober brown of the line and
wash, echo the text's bland acceptance of the ridiculous as they
picture the adventures of Chester. Chester is a small dog, but he's the
quintessence of the little guy, modest and affable, who achieves heroic
proportions. He is aided in restoring workers' jobs by a friend (Wendy,
a bat) and overcomes the evil machinations of the factory manager (a
weasel) who tries to use crabots (robots with many pincer-like arms) to
take over all jobs. Lightweight fun, but like so many of Stevenson's
picture books, this has some veiled comments on human behavior.

1003   Stevenson, James. *That Dreadful Day;* written and illus. by James
Stevenson. Greenwillow, 1985. Library ed. ISBN 0-688-04035-7; Trade
ed. ISBN 0-688-04036-5. 30p. Library ed. $11.88; Trade ed. $11.75.

K-2   Old fans of the series of tales told by Grandpa will welcome this latest;
new fans will probably be won by the story of Grandpa's first day of
school. As always, his horror stories are designed to make his two
grandchildren feel that theirs is the happier lot; as always, the pictures
showing Grandpa as a boy endow him with his bristly little mustache

(not yet whitened by age) and echo the zestful exaggeration of Grandpa's storytelling. Here Mary Ann and Louis, discouraged by their first day of school, are so struck by the awfulness of Grandpa's memories that they are encouraged by the contrast and decide the second day of school will be better. Message deftly accomplished.

1004   **Stevenson, James.** *The Worst Person in the World at Crab Beach;* written and illus. by James Stevenson. Greenwillow, 1988. Library ed. ISBN 0-688-07299-2; Trade ed. ISBN 0-688-07298-4. Library ed. $11.88; Trade ed. $11.95.

K-3   In a sequel to *The Worst Person in the World,* the elderly grouch-of-all-time goes to a seaside resort that has everything he likes: awful food, lots of mosquitoes and jellyfish, and cold fog. Perfect! Well, almost perfect; there are a mother and son who play wheezing accordion duets, and *the worst,* who is always referred to thus, grudgingly misses the hostility when the pair depart. There *is* a happy if quirky ending. Like the first book, this should amuse Stevenson's fans, since the entertaining cartoon drawings are augmented by some very nice forms-in-fog paintings, the irascible protagonist is a comic non-hero, and the relatively happy ending, after the return from Crab Beach, preserves the cantankerous attitude of *the worst.*

1005   **Stock, Catherine.** *Armien's Fishing Trip;* written and illus. by Catherine Stock. Morrow, 1990. Library ed. ISBN 0-688-08396-X; Trade ed. ISBN 0-688-08395-1. 34p. Library ed. $13.88; Trade ed. $13.95.

5-8 yrs.   Removed with his family to the Cape Flats by the South African government's Group Areas Act, Armien returns for a special weekend at his former seaside home of Kalk Bay. Bragging to his friends that his Uncle Faried is going to take him out for some "real fishing," Armien then stows away on the boat, which is caught in a terrible storm. This is universal adventure specifically set. The town and Armien's friends are an ethnic and cultural mix, a fishing community united by their bond with the sea. Double-page spreads of all the neighbors at the dock are likewise multi-colorful, a strong and sunny contrast to the stormy, blue-washed pages of Armien's heroic rescue of fisherman Sam. Like Stock and Karen Williams' *Galimoto* , set in Malawi, *Armien's Fishing Trip* celebrates the singularity of its cultural context by touching chords common to kids everywhere.

1006   **Stock, Catherine.** *Christmas Time;* ISBN 0-02-788403-1; *Halloween Monster;* ISBN 0-02-788404-X. *Thanksgiving Treat;* ISBN 0-02-788402-3. Each book: written and illus. by Catherine Stock. Bradbury, 1990. 26p. $11.95.

3-5 yrs.   This disarming trio is a toddler-sized introduction to three festive—and often difficult—holiday events. Each book introduces basic traditions (trick-or-treating, Thanksgiving dinner, presents) from a preschool view, not forgetting the anxieties holidays can provoke. In *Halloween*, a young black child is afraid of monsters; the nameless narrator of *Thanksgiving* feels left out of dinner preparations; the little girl in *Christmas* is afraid to talk to Santa. All is resolved, and the holidays are happy. The pencil-and-watercolor illustrations are simple, seasonal, and reassuringly tinted. It's good to see story and concept so smoothly blended; equally good to see a new series so refreshingly gimmick-free.

1007 **Stock**, Catherine. *Sophie's Knapsack*; written and illus. by Catherine Stock. Lothrop, 1988. Library ed. ISBN 0-688-06458-2; Trade ed. ISBN 0-688-06457-4. 32p. Library ed. $11.88; Trade ed. $11.95.

4-6 yrs.
*
An enticing picture book begins with Sophie perched on her]father's shoulders gazing at the skyscrapers looming around them. "It's time to show you some real sky, Sophie . . . . Let's hike up to Purple Cloud Rock next week." Who could resist? Fluent, full-page watercolor paintings show the preparations, drive to the country, hiking, and camping in an idyllically beautiful, isolated mountain setting. The details of every snack or meal are delicious; the expressions and postures of the figures project a warm family feeling that culminates in Sophie's snuggling down between her parents in the tent during a rainstorm. Fresh writing and art, this will inspire either action or envy on the part of young listeners and adult readers.

1008 **Stolz**, Mary. *Bartholomew Fair*; illus. by Pamela Johnson. Greenwillow, 1990. ISBN 0-688-09522-4. 152p. $12.95.

5-8
Queen Elizabeth I of England, a wealthy cloth merchant, a scullery maid, a poor student, his aristocratic schoolmate, and a cruelly treated apprentice all make their way to Bartholomew Fair with high hopes, some of which are fulfilled (even exceeded) and some not. Each character affects another, so that by the time sleep overtakes them, all retain some striking impression of the day. The sense of time antici- pated, passing, and gone is strong, even overtly stated in a lady-in- waiting's reflections on aging. The fair itself fades before the dynamics among those who attend it; yet readers are left with a sense of local hurly-burly and, even stronger, the contrast of rich and poor in Elizabethan England. Stolz's characterizations ring clear as the bells of London, her style is strongly knit with humor, and the plot wends enticingly to a close not entirely foreseen. Picaresque and picturesque, this will enrich many a historical unit with human dimensions.

1009 **Stolz**, Mary. *The Cuckoo Clock*; illus. by Pamela Johnson. Godine, 1987. ISBN 0-87923-653-1. 86p. $12.95.

4-6   Fiction with a fairy tale quality, this is the story of Erich the foundling's friendship with an old clockmaker, Ula, in the Black Forest "once upon a time." Taken in as a baby by a hypocritical do-gooder who resented his presence but used him endlessly for chores, Erich had never experienced companionship until Ula introduced him to the joys of drinking hot chocolate, caring for the aging dog Brangi, and crafting clocks together. It was on the strength of Ula's gifts of tools, a violin, and love that Erich was able to run away, after the old man's death, to seek his fortune as an artist. Stolz' writing is characteristically careful and clean, with the fantasy elements—a wooden cuckoo's coming to life and Ula's ascension to heaven—skillfully built into the reality of the story. The book design and fine-textured pencil drawings are equally strong, creating the total effect of an old-fashioned scene in cameo.

1010   Stolz, Mary. *The Emperor of Barkham Street*; illus. by Emily Arnold McCully. Harper, 1985. Library ed. ISBN 0-06-025977-9; Trade ed. ISBN 0-06-025976-0. 192p. Library ed. $9.89; Trade ed. $9.95.

5-7   It doesn't seem possible that it's a quarter-century since Mary Stolz produced those excellent companion books, *A Dog on Barkham Street* and *The Bully of Barkham Street*, which ingeniously showed the same events from differing viewpoints. This third story about Martin (ex-bully) is just as fresh, just as percipient,and possibly even better written. In a family where there is little demonstration of affection, in a community where he is labelled hostile, too plump, physically awkward, Martin has no close friends, still mourns the dog that had been taken away from him, spends much of his time day-dreaming about being an Arctic explorer. As he gains confidence, makes friends, and adjusts to changes, Martin reappraises some of his close relationships with people. And he discovers that one of the great frontiers of exploration is getting to know and understand oneself.

1011   Stolz, Mary. *Night of Ghosts and Hermits: Nocturnal Life on the Seashore*; illus. by Susan Gallagher. Harcourt, 1985. ISBN 0-15-257333-X. 40p. $12.95.

2-4   This is the kind of story that doesn't interfere with science but enhances it. The book opens with three children building a sand castle. After they go to bed, the narrative picks up on what happens all around their handiwork, starting with a ghost crab that invades it and ending with a hermit crab that walks away in the tiny bottle that served as guard to the castle. Meanwhile, readers learn of the symbiosis, the ongoing search of all creatures for food and shelter, a sea-turtle's egglaying, a specific understanding of the seashore system. The writing is lyrical but never overdramatic, the items of information intriguingly related. Finely shaded drawings are both accurate and aesthetically involving. Glossary, bibliography, and labelled diagrams identifying all the creatures discussed are appended.

1012   **Stolz**, Mary. *Quentin Corn;* illus. by Pamela Johnson. Godine, 1985. ISBN 0-87923-553-5. 122p. $11.95.

4-6   Soft, almost hazy pencil drawings illustrate a fantasy that is smoothly meshed with its realistic matrix, that has an appealing hero, a quietly pervasive humor, and a wonderfully controlled style and development. Finding his life tedious, the pig who names himself Quentin Corn decides to try passing as a man; with adults, Quentin quickly establishes his new identity and becomes a working member of a small-town community—but there are exceptions. Emily knows, and is Quentin's protective friend; Pete knows, and regards Quentin as his enemy. There is a consistent logic within the illogical parameters of the story, which is funny, touching, and entertaining.

1013   **Stolz**, Mary. *Storm in the Night;* illus. by Pat Cummings. Harper, 1988. Library ed. ISBN 0-06-025913-2; Trade ed. ISBN 0-06-025912-4. 30p. Library ed. $12.89; Trade ed. $12.95.

K-3   Effective paintings in dark, vivid colors show a small black boy and his grandfather who go out on the porch during a storm-caused blackout. Thomas discovers that smells and sounds seem more clear in the dark, he comforts his frightened cat, and he has a discussion with Grandfather that leads to an anecdote about another night, another storm, another frightened pet. Gently, in a story told (deftly, smoothly, subtly) primarily in dialogue, Grandfather makes it possible for Thomas to admit his own fear, previously denied, because Grandfather had once been a child frightened by a storm. This doesn't have a lot of action, but it abounds in nuance and should have a lot of impact.

1014   **Stolz**, Mary. *Zekmet the Stone Carver: A Tale of Ancient Egypt;* illus. by Deborah Nourse Lattimore. Harcourt, 1988. ISBN 0-15-299961-2. 28p. $13.95.

2-4   Double-page spreads dominated by stone-gray tints, styled after Egyptian art, and framed with hieroglyphs elaborate this story about the origins of the Sphinx. The Pharaoh, Kafre, commands his vizier to design an "eternal" monument in addition to his pyramid. The vizier happens upon a stone carver, who, during a moonlight walk with his family, sees a lion and conceives of the design for the Sphinx. Both the Pharaoh and the stonecarver die before the work is completed, but the stone carver's son finishes it. This is long for a picture book, but children who have been studying Egypt will be familiar enough with the setting to keep up with Stolz' sophisticated nuances of style. The stonecarver gets in some democratic digs at the vizier, who in turn harbors a twentieth-century irreverence for the Pharaoh. As historical fiction, the book would have benefitted from a note of background distinguishing the factual from the imagined. However, as a graphic and fictional production, this will fit handsomely into ancient history units and feed children's fascination for mummies and all things tomb-like.

1015   **Strauss**, Gwen. *Trail of Stones*; illus. by Anthony Browne. Knopf, 1990. Library ed. ISBN 0-679-90582-0; Paper ed. ISBN 0-679-80582-6. 35p. Library ed. $9.99; Paper ed. $6.95.

10-
*
A dozen sophisticated poems illustrated by Anthony Browne's pen-and-ink drawings are based on fairy tales, mostly from an anti-hero's point of view. The father of Hansel and Gretel confesses his weakness, the witch and a dwarf cast different lights on Snow White, an aging prince celebrates Rapunzel's patience, an ambivalent wolf awaits Red Riding Hood, Cinderella laments her childhood, Bluebeard pursues his solitary madness, the fox-woman reveals her dangerous double life, the frog princess triumphs with temper, the queen who outwitted Rumplestiltskin longs for his company, the Beast despairs of Beauty, and Sleeping Beauty contemplates her sensuous awakening. Strauss' style is lean but resonant with phrases that play on the characters and situation, while Browne's art probes the stories' darker tones of mystery. The wolf's slanted eyes peer enigmatically from a furred space between Grandma's frilly cap and a neatly turned sheet—a picture that deepens the suspense of his anticipation: "She will have the youngest skin/ I have ever touched, her fingers unfurling/ like fiddle heads in spring./ My matted fur will smell to her of forest/ moss at night. She'll wonder about my ears,/ large, pointed, soft as felt,/ my eyes red as her cloak,/ my leather nose on her belly." For high-school students, a meet companion to Anne Sexton's poetic fairy tale variants.

1016   **Strieber**, Whitley. *Wolf of Shadows*. Knopf, 1985. Library ed. ISBN 0-394-97224-4; Trade ed. ISBN 0-394-87224-X. 105p. Library ed. $9.99; Trade ed. $9.95.

6-9
Grim but intriguing, this describes the aftermath of a nuclear holocaust from the point of view of a wolf determined to lead his pack south of the unnatural winter. Joining the wolves in their struggle to survive is an animal ethologist who has escaped from a Minnesota town and managed to keep one of her children alive. While the realities of such a situation are pure conjecture, Strieber (the co-author of *Warday*) has made his scenes convincing with a mixture of scientific detail and fictional development. He never breaks voice with the wolf, yet portrays the humans vividly. Brief, tough, and thought-

provoking fare, especially for junior high discussion groups who can talk out the depressing ramifications.

1017   **Sullivan**, George. *All About Football.* Dodd, 1987. ISBN 0-396-09095-8. 128p. illus. and with photographs. $10.95.

4-7   A dependably good sports writer, Sullivan has pulled together facts about football history, about game play, and about rules and penalties into a text with good organization and sequential flow. His explanations of plays and positions are clear and concise, and since he does not "write down" to his readers, the book can be profitably enjoyed by those older than the target audience. Photographs add interest; diagrams are useful and are carefully placed in relation to the text to which they pertain, and end matter includes a glossary, an index, and a section headed "All-Time Records."

1018   **Sullivan**, George. *Pitcher*; illus. with photographs by the author and line drawings by Don Madden. Crowell, 1986. Library ed. ISBN 0-690-04539-5; Trade ed. ISBN 0-690-04538-7. 55p. Library ed. $10.89; Trade ed. $10.95.

3-5   Photographs that expand the text and comic line drawings that may amuse (but give no information) illustrate a text that is logically arranged, simply written, and crisply informative. Sullivan, a practiced writer of sports information books, describes techniques for pitches, from grip to delivery, discusses strategy of play in different situations, and explains the need for communication with the catcher. All of the pictures and most of the references are to Little League play; the author's advice covers both general topics, such as attitude, and specific ones, such as the windup.

1019   **Sussman**, Susan. *Lies (People Believe) about Animals*; by Susan Sussman and Robert James; photographs by Fred Leavitt. Whitman, 1987. ISBN 0-8075-4530-9. 40p. $9.95.

3-5   Framed black-and-white photographs illustrate a compilation of information about animals, alphabetically arranged, with each section headed "Lie" ("The porcupine can shoot its quills") and "Truth" ("The porcupine cannot shoot its quills any more than you can shoot your hair"). The text is written in a style that is direct and casual; the kind of information in each entry differs and the authors do not attempt to give full information, but they do offer accurate and interesting facts. A bibliography and an index are provided.

1020   **Sutcliff**, Rosemary. *Flame-Colored Taffeta.* Farrar, 1986. ISBN 374-32344-50. 128p. $10.95.

6-8   Set in the mid-eighteenth century in England, this is a novel that subtly incorporates historical details, well-developed characters, and as much action and suspense as any reader of adventure stories could want. Like most of Sutcliff's writing, this is not for facile reading, but it is well worth any extra effort. The story of how two children (Damaris is twelve, Peter thirteen) rescue and hide a wounded stranger at a time of high political tension, is romantic without ever becoming sentimental.

1021   **Sutcliff**, Rosemary. *The Shining Company*. Farrar, 1990. ISBN 0-374-36807-4. 296p. $13.95.

7-10   Set in A.D. 600 and based on "the earliest surviving North British
 *   poem" (actually Welsh), *The Gododdin*, this powerful story is told by Prosper, who is twelve when he first meets Prince Gorthyn and dreams of becoming his shield-bearer. Two years later, Prosper and his bondservant Conn join Gorthyn to attend him in the training of the "shining company," the three hundred young warriors who are responding to the call of the "Golden King," Mynyddog, in preparation for battle against the Saxons. As always, Sutcliff is so immersed in the period that no details of speech or behavior or costume or custom seem obtrusive. Prosper's comments lend immediacy and verisimilitude, as Sutcliff provides pace, drama, color, and historical background.

1022   **Swann**, Brian, ad. *A Basket Full of White Eggs: Riddle-Poems*; illus. by Ponder Goembel. Orchard/Watts, 1988. Library ed. ISBN 0-531-08334-9; Trade ed. ISBN 0-531-05734-8. 30p. Library ed. $14.99; Trade ed. $14.95.

1-3   Richly textured double-page spreads, which look like colored pencil
 *   and pastel drawings on watercolor paper, satisfy the eye of the beholder who considers these fifteen folkloric riddles in poetic form. They are not all easy to guess in spite of broad pictorial hints, and there's a challenging mix of easy and hard ones. The author has drawn lyrically on a range of cultures from Mayan to Lithuanian, Italian, and African, each reflected in the artist's dramatic landscapes. A riddle from the Ten'a of Alaska, for instance, reads "Far off in the distance,/ something white is/ chasing a flash/ of red fire," and the viewer is treated to a sweeping snow scene across which a red fox tracks with bushy tail streaming behind. The Visayan (Philippine) riddle "I run, I run./ When I arrive/ I bend down and/ let fall/ all my white hairs" incorporates the suggestion of a figure in a curling wave of surf against a curving shoreline. For an Aztec riddle, the graceful hands of women slapping tortillas seem to echo the movements of butterflies overhead in dry heat. An eyeful, an earful, a cause to pause . . . .

1023   **Switzer**, Ellen. *Greek Myths: Gods, Heroes and Monsters: Their Sources, Their Stories and Their Meanings;* illus. with photographs by Costas. Atheneum, 1988. ISBN 0-689-31253-9. 208p. $16.95.

7-12   Divided into creation myths, a description of the gods, humans' beginnings, heroes and heroines, popular legends, and the Trojan War and its aftermath, this is more a folkloristic resource than a lyrical retelling. Preceding each story is a brief note discussing its origins, both literary and oral, with historical context or archeological descriptions wherever pertinent. This is an ambitious project, not only for its scope but also for its attempt to relate the tales as they are known in Greece today, with variants favored by different sections of the country and with photographs of the locations. The canon is so large and complex that occasionally the text takes on the tone of a catalogue, and there are a few shortcuts: "the beautiful Helen (who caused all the trouble)" is a description that considerably diminishes the concept of fate described elsewhere; there is also no mention of Achilles heel ("As had been prophesied, Achilles was killed shortly after he defeated Hector, but the war went on relentlessly, with casualties on both sides increasing"). On the whole, however, this draws together and links an extraordinary amount of material with vivid immediacy, an important contribution to the cultural literacy of today's young people, who will be amazed and intrigued at the outrageous behavior of gods and humans alike.

1024   **Tadjo**, Véronique, ad. *Lord of the Dance: An African Retelling;* ad. and illus. by Véronique Tadjo. Lippincott, 1989. Library ed. ISBN 0-397-32352-2; Trade ed. ISBN 0-397-32351-4. 26p. Library ed. $12.89; Trade ed. $12.95.

5-8 yrs.   This picture book almost begs to be chanted and danced, a physical aspect often neglected in the modern representation of folklore in print. The narrative is poetically rhythmic without becoming singsong or forced, the art leaps with color and strikingly balanced shapes. The concept itself is lyrical: the Mask leaves the spirit world and comes among men and women to lead their songs of joy and sadness. Even when traditions are buried in concrete and steel, the voice survives. Folk art motifs border many of the pictures, and a note on the cultural life of the Senufu people, as well as on Tadjo's collection and adaptation of the song, provide valuable context. A map with the Côte d'Ivoire together with photos of a Senufu artist and of Tadjo herself, are also included. An original re-creation in the best storytelling tradition.

1025   **Tafuri**, Nancy. *Who's Counting?* written and illus. by Nancy Tafuri. Greenwillow, 1986. Library ed. ISBN 0-688-06131-1; Trade ed. ISBN 0-688-06130-3. 23p. Library ed. $11.88; Trade ed. $11.75.

3-5 yrs.   One brown puppy is counting: one squirrel, two birds, three moles, etc.
Each number gets a two-page spread, and Tafuri uses the long horizontal space to beautiful advantage. Four geese, for example, are
stark white with orange beaks and feet, stretching across a bright
green background. In the most dramatic spread, two birds, one red,
one yellow, perch in an intense close-up on a flowered tree limb that
reaches back and high over a meadow, puppy looking up from below.
The puppy appears in each picture, sometimes readily seen, sometimes not so apparent, giving this excellent counting book continuity,
as well as the additional pleasure of hide and seek.

1026   **Talbert**, Marc. *Double or Nothing*; illus. by Toby Gowing. Dial, 1990.
Library ed. ISBN 0-8037-0928-5; Trade ed. ISBN 0-8037-0832-7. 129p.
Library ed. $13.89; Trade ed. $13.95.

4-6   Nine-year-old Sam has inherited all of the clothing and the equipment of his Uncle Frank. Sam loved Uncle Frank and had always
wanted to be a professional magician too. With some flashbacks, this
is the story of one day in which Sam goes off by himself, by bus, to a
park where he puts on his first public performance. This is an
intriguing story; it is cohesive, yet it has movement; it is compressed
within the parameters of one day, yet it is not crowded; it has tender
memories of a loving uncle-nephew relationship but is not sentimentalized. Sam is nervous but achieves a degree of success with a first
performance that is modestly believable and very satisfying. There is a
closing section that takes place a few days later, in which Sam's
mother makes it clear that she understands why Sam went off on his
own (it was Uncle Frank's birthday and the performance was Sam's
tribute). There is one scene that can be interpreted as dream or
fantasy, in which Frank steps out of a mirror, tells Sam never to lose
the magic, and then disappears; it doesn't strengthen the story, but it
also is so susceptible to varied interpretations that it doesn't weaken it.

1027   **Talbert**, Marc. *The Paper Knife*. Dial, 1988. ISBN 0-8037-0571-9. 184p.
$14.95.

4-6   George had said he loved Jeremy's mother, but he abused her
physically; ten-year-old Jeremy didn't dare tell her, even after they ran
away, that George had abused him sexually. Taking refuge with
George's sympathetic parents, starting school in a new town, making a
friend like Harriet and having a good teacher like Mr. Williams all
helped. But, as Talbert shows (rather than just telling the reader), the
corrosion and fear of being an abused child don't end easily. Through
a sad mistake the teacher, Mr. Williams, is accused of molesting
Jeremy and is asked to leave. He is proven innocent, but the whole
episode is an example of the ripple effect of child abuse: alienation
from others, suspicion, shame, guilt, distrust. The story deals with

problem behavior but it is solidly enough crafted to be more than a problem novel, since Talbert deals perceptively with other relationships and with other facets of Jeremy's life. He sees children as people, avoiding either condescension or evasion in depicting them.

1028   **Tate**, Eleanora E. *The Secret of Gumbo Grove*. Watts, 1987. ISBN 0-531-10298-X. 256p. $11.95.

5-7   An intriguing novel about eleven-year-old Raisin Stackhouse tracing her black community's history through stories about those buried in a local South Carolina graveyard. The writing occasionally rambles, but that very quality accounts for some delightfully fresh passages of dialogue. The characters are vividly individualized and the setting immediately realized. The ending, when Raisin receives a surprise community service award after some stiff resistance from church and political leaders who haven't wanted to stir up trouble with old memories of racial problems, seems a bit tidy. But it will be satisfying for young readers, who can enjoy this as a leisurely, expansive reading experience on the levels of informal first-person narrative, family story, and black history.

1029   **Taylor**, Mildred D. *The Friendship*; illus. by Max Ginsburg. Dial, 1987. Library ed. ISBN 0-8037-0418-6; Trade ed. ISBN 0-8037-0417-8. Library ed. $11.89; Trade ed. $11.95.

4-7   A bitter short story about race relations in rural Mississippi during the Depression focuses on an incident between an old black man, Mr. Tom Bee, and a white storekeeper, Mr. John Wallace. Indebted to Tom for saving his life as a young man, John had promised they would always be friends. But now, years later, John insists that Tom call him "Mister" and shoots the old man for defiantly—and publicly—calling him by his first name. Narrator Cassie Logan and her brothers, characters from Taylor's previous books, are verbally abused by Wallace's villainous sons before witnessing the encounter, along with a token non-hostile white child, Jeremy. The social drama elicits a naturally powerful response in depicting cruel injustice, and the writing is concentrated to heighten that effect.

1030   **Taylor**, Mildred D. *Mississippi Bridge*; illus. by Max Ginsburg. Dial, 1990. Library ed. ISBN 0-8037-0427-5; Trade ed. ISBN 0-8037-0426-7. 62p. Library ed. $12.89; Trade ed. $12.95.

4-7   Told by the white boy whose attempts at friendship with his black neighbors were recounted in *Roll of Thunder, Hear My Cry* and other books in the series about the Logan family, this is Jeremy's description of a tragedy on the Rosa Lee River. He watches as a store owner insults two black customers and as a bus driver unseats all the black travelers to accommodate a last-minute crowd of whites. His affection for two of the white passengers, a little girl and her grandmother who don't participate in the racism except by being part of a society favoring them, is equalled by his pain over the treatment of the blacks. It is the little girl and her grandmother who die when the bus hurtles over a bridge with rotten planks, and it is this irony that lends more subtle dimension to the story than has characterized some of Taylor's other indictments of racism. The conflict between an unjust father and his ethical son also add power to the scenes, which are smoothly developed in rural Southern dialect. Illustrated with 10 pictures in black and white.

1031   **Taylor**, Theodore. *Walking Up a Rainbow*. Delacorte, 1986. ISBN 0-385-29435-2. 275p. $14.95.

6-9   Susan Carlisle begins her story in 1851, when she's thirteen, newly orphaned, and trying to save her property from the skinflint saloon owner who claims her father had owed him $15,000. That's when Susan craftily arranges to go west with a drover (to whom she lies) without telling her guardian (to whom she lies) so that she can make a profit from selling sheep and get money from a West Coast uncle she doesn't know. This is humorous period fiction, set in the 1850s, in the Patricia Beatty mold, with a feisty, determined heroine who loses her property but gets her man (Bashful Cowboy type) in a long, rollicking novel in which everything that can happen does happen as the wagon "Walking Up a Rainbow," takes Susan's party on an arduous journey to the seamiest parts of San Francisco. Susan writes the first and third parts, the middle section being by the handsome cowboy. All the familiar natural dangers of the trail are here, as well as some incidents (rescue of Susan from a drunken quartet attempting rape, Susan's friendship with a heart-of-gold prostitute) that make this more sophisticated than the Beatty books. The story has lively characters, some of whom seem deliberately typecast to acieve a comic note, and it has variety, pace, and first-person styles that are both convincing and in effective contrast.

1032   **Tehranchian**, Hassan, tr. and ad. *Kalilah and Dimnah: Fables from the Ancient East;* ad. and tr. from the Persian by Hassan Tehranchian; illus. by Anatole Ur. Harmony Books, 1985. ISBN 0-517-55566-2. 75p. $12.95.

3-5   This version of the fables from India makes the stories more accessible than the scholarly *Kalila wa Dimna: Fables from a Fourteenth Century Arabic Manuscript* by Esin Atil, since the writing style is simpler. Most of the fabular material is in the form of beast tales, with pointed commentary by the two jackal characters for whom the book is named. Like most fable collections, this has animal characters who illustrate the foibles of men; it also has human characters.

Occasionally a tag-line moral appears, boxed, in the vividly colored tempera paintings that embellish more than they illustrate the tales.

1033   **Tejima**, Keizaburo. *Fox's Dream;* written and illus. by Keizaburo Tejima. Philomel, 1987. ISBN 0-399-21455-0. 42p. $13.95.

4-6 yrs.   First published in Japan, this story combines a spare but poetic text and, on oversize pages, stunningly dramatic color woodcuts. A fox walks alone in the cold silence of a winter's night; lonely, he imagines he sees companions in the icy forms of the moonlit branches; then he finds a mate. Tejima uses color to accentuate changes: from the blue/white chill of the first pictures through the move to color as the fox fantasizes, and then back to lavender/white (less cold) as the fox finds the vixen. Almost every double-page spread is a picture worth framing.

1034   **Tejima**, Keizaburo. *Owl Lake;* written and illus. by Keizaburo Tejima. Philomel, 1987. ISBN 0-399-21426-7. 38p. $13.95.

4-7 yrs.   The text here is minimal but nevertheless lyrical and dramatic enough
   *   to serve as a story base for a stunning series of oversize woodcuts. Both words and graphics focus on a natural setting, a lake where a father owl is flying out into the evening to hunt for his family. "He keeps his owl eyes open for signs of silver fish. But the lake is silent." The owl waits. Then the centerfold of the book features a heart-stopping spread in which he swooshes down to catch a fish, his wings, the fish, the splash lines, and the frame of the picture forming the point of an arrow. "The Owl Family eats breakfast under the glowing moon. Next, it will be Mother Owl's turn to hunt." The golds, blues, and blacks of the night scenes, the graceful patterns of linework, and the dignity of the subject and its treatment make this an absorbing work of art as well as a durable picture book to share with children.

1035   **Tejima**. *Swan Sky;* written and illus. by Tejima. Philomel, 1988. ISBN 0-399-21547-6. 40p. $13.95.

5-8 yrs.   As much a story about nature's way of accepting death as about the behavioral characteristics of swans, this is a stunning picture book with strong elements of linear design. The text is a simple one: a family of swans waits for one that is sick, flies away, and then recircles back to stay with her till she dies. As he did in *Fox's Dream*, Tejima comes dangerously close to anthropomorphism here; the family is "saddened" but later in the "the morning light . . . thinks of the little swan." Of course, this will only deepen children's empathy with a situation already dramatized by vivid graphics. The play of turquoise, blue, and black with sudden spurts of orange is arresting. So are the shapes, patterned for contrast and repetition, tension and resolution, across the double spreads. The rhythmic cycle of life and death is clearly projected for young listeners to think or talk about.

1036   **Terris,** Susan. *The Latchkey Kids.* Farrar, 1986. ISBN 0-374-34363-2. 167p. $11.95.

4-6   Callie, eleven, wears an apartment key on a chain around her neck, picks up her little brother Rex after school every day, and comes home to an empty apartment—but the real grief in her life is that her father is in a state of severe depression, and that this has affected all the other members of the family. Callie is angry at being confined to the apartment, angry at her parents, angry because her efforts to do chores and watch over Rex seem unappreciated. Two things help. One is that she makes a new friend, Nora, whose Chinese family gives loving support to the latchkey children; the other is that there's some frank, vented anger within the family that clears the air and promises some believable improvement. The story has depth and good pace; characters and dialogue are handled with practiced competence. The one weakness of the book is that there are some scenes that are sharply jarring when they prove to be Callie's imaginings, rather than real events.

1037   **Thiele**, Colin. *Farmer Schultz's Ducks*; illus. by Mary Milton. Harper, 1988. Library ed. ISBN 0-06-026183-8; Trade ed. ISBN 0-06-026182-X. 32p. Library ed. $12.89; Trade ed. $12.95.

5-7 yrs.   A lively story richly told, this relates the dilemma of a farmer in
    *   changing times. His ducks have always crossed the road to the river in the morning and returned at night. With the city expanding, cars rush headlong in a collision course with the birds despite warning signs. Even a bridge over the road crashes, with ducks aboard, before the onslaught of a speeding truck. Finally, the farmer's youngest daughter, who has suggested several sensible solutions, conceives of a duck pipe under the road, through which the ducks waddle safely through the year. "In winter, when the rain poured down and the water swept out of the pipe in a torrent, they came skidding and skiing, swimming and splashing in a wild, rollicking rush—a waterfall of ducks." The descriptions of the birds (like jewels in a fairy tale), the stylistic rhythm and repetition invoking the seasonal landscapes, the humorous commentary on hurried and harried humans (sentences describing the Germanic Mr. Schultz occasionally invert verbs to the end of the sentence) all make this a fitting companion to *Make Way For Ducklings*. Meanwhile, Milton's illustrations are the essence of duck, right down to the medium of watercolor, in which she captures the birds' staid anatomical design, comical varieties of stance, and quizzical stares to feathery perfection (the cow isn't bad either). An unforgettable visit to the Onkaparinga River in South Australia.

1038   Thiele, Colin. *Shadow Shark.* Harper, 1988. Library ed. ISBN 0-06-026179-X; Trade ed. ISBN 0-06-026178-1. 214p. Library ed. $12.89; Trade ed. $12.95.

5-8   This is the story of a hunt for a dangerous sea predator, an immense white pointer shark nicknamed Scarface, who threatens the waters near Cockle Bay in South Australia. To their delight, 12-year-olds Meg and Joe are invited to accompany the great shark hunter George Lane, helping and witnessing the greatest attempt of his career. The hunt itself is exciting, but never romanticized: by turns tedious, dangerous and exhausting, the two attempts fail, the last leaving Meg and Joe stranded with Meg's severely injured father on a lonely island—little food, no signs of rescue. Any combination of shark hunting and survival story has tremendous appeal, of course, and both parts of the novel are filled with you-are-there detail and immediacy. Although lacking the thematic depth of Theodore Taylor's *The Hostage*, this has story, drama, and heroism, and is especially recommended for reluctant readers.

1039   Thomas, Ruth. *The Runaways.* Lippincott, 1989. Library ed. ISBN 0-397-32345-X; Trade ed. ISBN 0-397-32344-1. 297p. Library ed. $13.89; Trade ed. $13.95.

5-7   It is not unusual, in contemporary fiction about friendship between a boy and a girl, to find that the two have been drawn together by the fact that both are loners. In this story from England, two eleven-year-old classmates who happen to be together when they find a thief's cache of money in a deserted house, are so upset by adult inter-rogation that they run off together despite the fact that each dislikes the other. Nathan is small and bright and black and hostile; Julia is tall, lanky, white, an academic laggard who can barely read. This is the story of their days on the road (with one telephone call to tell parents that they are alive and well) and the growth of trust that becomes friendship. Pace and style as well as firm characterization hold the reader's interest to an extent that is remarkable in what is basically a two-character story.

1040   Thompson, Brian, ad. *The Story of Prince Rama;* illus. by Jeroo Roy and with original paintings. Viking, 1985. ISBN 0-670-80117-8. 59p. $12.95.

4-7   An ancient Hindu epic gets action-packed treatment as each story in the cycle unfolds in a brief page of text faced by 300-year-old Indian paintings, with a few contemporary illustrations added. The advantage of Thompson's lively abridgement is its simple organization of a very complex canon, which was more gracefully but less clearly presented in *The Adventures of Rams* by Milo Beach (1983). As an introduction, this should hold the interest of students exploring and comparing the

Eastern folklore of gods and heroes, which is inaccessible to many children simply because of the unfamiliar names and story patterns.

1041   **Thomson, Peggy, ad.** *The King Has Horse's Ears*; illus. by David Small. Simon, 1988. ISBN 0-671-64953-1. 32p. $12.95.

1-3   Where Pevear and Rayevsky's *Our King Has Horns* gave the Midas story a Russian flavor, Small places it in a Louis XIV-like setting, with lots of gold filigree, elegant furnishings (check out the King's shell-shaped bathtub) and identically coiffed poodles and ladies. The king, here named Horace, has everything: gold, a warm dog, all the chocolate he could eat and—horse's ears. Horace is a young king, and it is particularly mortifying to him that his secret, piped by a piper who has plucked the tattletale reed, is revealed at the King's wedding to "Betty." Luckily, she wouldn't have his ears any other way, and horse's ears become the rage, including a new hairstyle: "*Oreilles du Roi surmonté d'un pouf.*" Small stylishly poses limber human figures against operetta-ic palace backgrounds; tongues of both adapter and illustrator are firmly but gracefully in cheek.

1042   **Thomson, Peggy.** *Keepers and Creatures at the National Zoo*; illus. with photographs by Paul S. Conklin. Crowell, 1988. Library ed. ISBN 0-690-04712-6; Trade ed. ISBN 0-690-04710-X. 198p. Library ed. $12.89; Trade ed. $12.95.

5-9   In an informal, enthusiastic style, Thomson describes the work of the National Zoo keepers, with plenty of anecdotes drawn from interviews and observations. Few juvenile books on zoos have given the kind of details included here, from various menus, which may involve frozen mouse, to selective breeding decisions and habitat maintainance. Nursing bats, guarding against affection for animals that may become too dependent, and persuading a tense tiger to transfer into its indoor cage are all part of a day's work for the keepers portrayed here. Plenty of photographs with informative, often witty captions enliven the text and tone. A realistic, yet optimistic book for young people interested in a career working with animals, this gives insight into numerous species as well as the humans responsible for preserving them.

1043   **Titherington, Jeanne.** *A Place for Ben*; written and illus. by Jeanne Titherington. Greenwillow, 1987. Library ed. ISBN 0-688-06494-9; Trade ed. ISBN 0-688-06493-0. 22p. Library ed. $11.88; Trade ed. $11.75.

3-6 yrs.   Ezra's crib has just been moved into Ben's room, and "wherever Ben
  *   turned, there was Ezra." In desperate need of private space, Ben establishes a niche in the garage, furnishes it with his favorite toys and cereal, and then gets lonely. Cat, dog, and parents are all preoccupied, but there's one person who wants to come and play—Ezra! The welcoming look on Ben's face says it all: this is a turning point for two

young brothers. As she demonstrated in *Pumpkin! Pumpkin!*, Titherington has a gift for spare writing and illustration that gets right to the heart of things. Soft but precise, her color pencil drawings capture not only textured scenes but also the expressions of isolation that often haunt children on their own. The picture of Ben talking to the cat, or perched on the porch, and the final spread of his toddler sibling struggling up the stairs toward him, make telling portraits. The text, too, respects the effectiveness of action over description, wherein lies the power of the punch line. Ben sits waiting to see if someone will want to visit him: "And finally someone did." In concept, focus, and execution, this is more than a cut above most books focusing on sibling problems.

1044   **Titherington**, Jeanne. *Pumpkin Pumpkin;* written and illus by Jeanne Titherington. Greenwillow, 1986. Library ed. ISBN 0-688-05696-2; Trade ed. ISBN 0-688-05695-4. 21p. Library ed. $11.88; Trade ed. $11.75.

2-4 yrs.   Tailored for Halloween and gardening activities with nursery school children, this faces a text of one or two lines per page with soft, full-page illustrations; these show a little boy planting his pumpkin seed and watching it grow, flower, and produce a ripe pumpkin, which he turns into a jack-o-lantern with seeds left over to plant in the spring. A reproduction cycle at its simplest gains impact from the finely shaded, subtly colored drawings. Spacious in concept and execution.

1045   **Townsend**, John Rowe. *Downstream.* Lippincott, 1987. Library ed. ISBN 0-397-32189-9; Trade ed. ISBN 0-397-32188-0. 182p. Library ed. $12.89; Trade ed. $12.95.

8-12   A strong problem novel, subtle and sophisticated, is written with Townsend's usual tight structure, smooth narrative flow, and sympathetic perception. It is in the voice of adolescent Alan, so that the abrasion of his parents' bickering, his own crush on a beautiful tutor, and his rage when he discovers that the tutor, Vivien, and his father are lovers, are all seen from his viewpoint. There is no sugared ending, but an honest treatment of the irrevocable damage done to the father-son relationship and to the shaky marriage.

1046   **Townsend**, John Rowe. *Rob's Place.* Lothrop, 1988. ISBN 0-688-07258-5. 202p. $11.95.

5-7   Rob is miserable. He's jealous of his infant stepsister, angry because he is forced to give up his bedroom to her, lonely because his only two friends have gone away, and apprehensive because his father has missed two of their precious Saturdays. The imaginative daydreaming Rob has done about being a heroic castaway on a desert island begins to take over, so that what has been a pleasant escape now becomes an imposed other life in which all of his angers and fears are played out.

Townsend, always a compelling writer, uses a device that is borderline-believable: a girl Rob's age sees that only a visit to the small island in a local park (a place that had given rise to the complex fantasy-life) will help solve the problem, after Rob, on a visit with her and with his stepfather, has narrowly escaped a panic-induced near-drowning. She talks him through a last visit, a purging of anxieties, and an acceptance of the new alignments in family life (stepfather whose friendship has been rejected, father whose marriage plans had engendered rage) to gain new perspective and stability. Save for the heroic role of the girl and the sometimes protracted fantasizing, this is a story that has great strength: vigor, pace, and psychological insight.

1047   **Townsend**, John Rowe. *The Fortunate Isles.* Lippincott, 1989. Library ed. ISBN 0-397-32366-2; Trade ed. 0-397-32365-4. 248p. Library ed. $13.89; Trade ed. $13.95.

7-10   Townsend has created a remarkably doughty and engaging protagonist, Eleni, and has supported her with a cast of characters who are equally strongly drawn. This is set in the unspecified past and in an unspecified land, but it is completely conceived and just as completely convincing. Eleni, with rather timid Andreas and cocky Nikos, runs away (each for a different reason) from their home island hoping to reach the royal city of their island country. (The Fortunate Isles seem to be located in the Aegean.) Their adventures are varied and exciting, and Townsend brings in issues and relationships that give the story depth and color. Fine style, fine story.

1048   **Townsend**, John Rowe. *The Persuading Stick.* Lothrop, 1987. ISBN 0-688-07260-7. 103p. $10.25.

4-6   Beth is a third child, undemanding at home and often disregarded by her classmates. Then one day she finds a strange silvery stick that seems to give her power, a power she asserts half proudly, half fearfully. With the help of the stick, she persuades her mother to have her friends over for tea, her teacher to let the class out early for recess, an old shopkeeper to provide ice cream free for her friends. But Beth is always drained after using the stick, aware of its dangers and unable to get rid of it. The last, climactic use of the "magic wand" comes with her persuading her brother not to commit suicide, after which she realizes "I couldn't do anything with the stick that I wouldn't have been able to do without it." This is a compact story with tight pace and quickly established characterization. The dialogue, brevity, and teasing crossover from science fiction to realism will make it appealing for independent readers or classroom reading aloud.

1049   **Travers**, P. L. *Mary Poppins and the House Next Door;* illus. by Mary Shepard. Delacorte, 1989. ISBN 0-385-29749-1. 93p. $12.95.

3-5 After several years, a new Mary Poppins book revolves, as do the earlier books, around the omniscient nurse in a British household. At times the Banks children wish they could disobey their domestic tyrant, but they do appreciate her magical powers. One is either a Travers fan or not, depending on the amount of whimsy one enjoys. Mary Poppins is a distinctive character, part of her effectiveness lying in the fact that all the other adults of the story are either unpleasant, or credulous, or just plain foolish. Here the ex-governess of Mr. Banks moves into the neighborhood with a small boy who has all the freedom of an indentured servant; when Luti confesses that he longs for home, Mary Poppins cloud-walks him (and the Banks children) to his South Sea island home, stopping to visit the man in the moon.

1050 **Tripp**, Wallace, comp. *Marguerite, Go Wash Your Feet;* comp. and illus. by Wallace Tripp. Houghton, 1985. Library ed. ISBN 0-395-35392-0; Paper ed. ISBN 0-395-40151-8. 46p. Library ed. $14.95; Paper ed. $5.95.

2-5 Tripp's signature cartoon animals are as appealing as ever, but his choice of verse and illustrative farce here leans farther toward adult than the balance in previous collections of nonsense. Shakespeare rubs noses with Spike Milligan, and Jane Taylor's most famous jingle gets updated by a rabbit: "Twinkle, twinkle, little star,/I don't wonder what you are,/You're the cooling down of gases/Forming into solid masses." There is a keen and successful running spoof on culture, which will depend on children's knowing the context. "There's a wonderful family called Stein,/There's Gert and there's Ep and there's Ein;/Gert's poems are bunk/Ep's statues are junk,/And no one can understand Ein." Even where kids don't fully appreciate the references, however, as in the limerick on "God Save the Weasel" and "Pop Goes the Queen," they will enjoy the comic-book aspects of artistic embroidery, in this case a vignette unfolding a corny old joke delivered by characters in Confederate garb. Mr. Tripp cannot help being funny. The number of jokes crammed into a double-spread take-off on the Old Masters may keep parents, teachers, and librarians looking long after their young listeners are ready to turn the page.

1051 **Troughton**, Joanna, ad. *How Stories Came Into the World: A Folktale from West Africa;* ad. and illus. by Joanna Troughton. Bedrick/Blackie, 1990. ISBN 0-87226-411-4. 32p. $13.95.

4-6 yrs. These five abbreviated tales from the Ekoi, Efik Ibibio, and Yoruba peoples are neatly framed in another story about a mouse weaving stories that eventually escape her dwelling to run "up and down all over the earth" forever. "Why the Sun and Moon Live in the Sky" is a well-known Nigerian myth; "Rubber Girl" is a variant of "The Tar

Baby"; "How All Animals Came On Earth," "The Story of Lightning and Thunder," and "Why the Hippo Lives in Water" are less familiar pourquoi tales. The illustrations are bold in both color and design, with thickly textured figures and folk motifs shaped by heavy black outline. Each small white block of text is set against simple but varied compositions for satisfying balance in a book easily shared aloud with very young listeners, either alone or in groups.

1052   **Turner**, Ann. *Grasshopper Summer*. Macmillan, 1989. ISBN 0-02-789511-4. 144p. $12.95.

4-6   The time is 1874, the story begins in Kentucky, and the narrator is Sam White; Sam is irritated by his younger brother Billy (not only a better student but also wasting his time, in Sam's opinion, in teaching ex-slave Harold to read) and worried by the fact that Pa seems to be thinking of going west. Go west they do, and north, to the Dakota Territory. While the writing has occasional stylistic flaws, the story is adequate in pace and structure albeit predictable in following the resistance/adjustment/acceptance pattern of pioneer life fiction, complete with a natural disaster (in this case, a plague of grasshoppers) that tries, but does not daunt, the frontier family. Not stunning, but better-than-average historical fiction, this does have depth in characterization and relationships.

1053   **Turner**, Ann. *Street Talk*; illus. by Catherine Stock. Houghton, 1986. ISBN 0-395-39971-8. 47p. $11.95.

2-4
*   Turner's poetry is full of surprises, a rarity in children's verse. What she sees, the way she sees it, and the way she makes readers see it are full of fresh flashes—and funny sound effects for reading out loud as well. Some effects are light: "Pizza-pepper plucking/ at my throat/ (Hey-hot! hey-hot!)/ fizzy Coke tickling/ my nose (sssz-bam! sssz-bam!)." Some are soft: "I know the long nights, child,/ crickets creaking in the grass/ and the smell of magnolias/ so thick you could cut/ a dress out of it." The 29 poems are all free verse, but none of them lazy (the few less successful ones have an obvious theme, as in "Teacher Talk," with general observations replacing concrete images). There's also enough narrative content to hook readers reluctant to hear poetry.

1054   **Turner**, Ann. *Third Girl from the Left*. Macmillan, 1986. ISBN 0-02-789510-6. 153p. $10.95.

7-10   Sarah Goodhue, a plain, independent 18-year-old, leaves the small Maine town where she has never fit in to become the mail-order bride of a rancher in the Montana Territory. Her journey is a hard one, her husband Alex a 60-year-old man who has deceived her with an old daguerreotype, and the ranch house bitter cold and lonely. Yet Sarah has begun to assert herself and has fallen in love with the mountains by the time her husband is killed in a round-up accident. With the Chinese cook and three ranch hands, Sarah decides to run the ranch. Although the opening scenes seem artificial, Sarah's experiences of adjustment are specifically and convincingly developed, including her ignorance and apprehension of marital sex, her slow-growing friendship with the Chinese cook, and her unexpected sense of loss when Alex dies. Reminiscent of Lampman's *Bargain Bride*, this is a woman's story solidly set in a man's old-West world.

1055   Turner, Gwenda. *Playbook;* written and illus. by Gwenda Turner. Viking, 1986. ISBN 0-670-80660-9. 29p. $9.95.

1-3 yrs.   A prime selection for preparing the intimidated or sharing with the enthusiastic youngster about to set off to day care or nursery school for the first time. The opening page shows a friendly, frumpled, and— most important—motherly woman reading to a couchful of five children. "Miss Williams is our teacher." The atmosphere gets more crowded but no less homey as the first-person-plural narrative enumerates all the activities of painting, sand box, baking, cut-out, building, dress-up, music, eating, and indoor/outdoor games that keep the children busy all day long. The primary element here is, of course, the art, which elaborates with delicately realistic detail and inventively varied page design each child's absorption. A tears-and-comfort scene would have been helpful somewhere in there, but this has plenty of potential for a parent's storytelling what is to come or a child's storytelling what has happened during his or her own day.

1056   Uchida, Yoshiko. *The Happiest Ending*. Atheneum, 1985. ISBN 0-689-50326-1. 111p. $10.95.

4-6   A third book about a Japanese-American community in California during the Depression Era is also narrated by Rinko, now twelve, and romantic enough to overcome her usual diffidence and determine to take a hand in an arranged marriage. What Rinko plans is stopping the union, since she feels the groom is too old for his bride. What she learns is that one shouldn't make hasty judgments and that admitting one's mistakes can be a sign of maturity. Like the other books, this is convincing as a document by a child, it's faithful in its details to the period and the setting, and it's a warm, smoothly written story about family and family friends.

1057   Uchida, Yoshiko, ad. *The Two Foolish Cats;* illus. by Margot Zemach. McElderry, 1987. ISBN 0-689-50397-0. 28p. $12.95.

5-7 yrs.   Big Daizo and Little Suki terrify the mice and birds that inhabit their pine forest in Japan, but one day they turn their wrath on each other in a fight over who gets the larger of the two rice cakes they find beside a stream. Finally they seek judgment from a wise old monkey, who brings out a scale and, in order to equalize the cakes, takes bites from first one and then the other—till they're all gone. Based on a Japanese folktale, this develops the foolish friends and trickster archetypes with simple narrative and some dialogue. Zemach's illustrations are a departure from her characteristic style; the heavy black outlines borrow from the tradition of Japanese painting, as do the shapes and even compositions. The watercolors are delicate, with plenty of white space. The smaller cat looks vaguely like a dog, but the exaggerated expressiveness of all the animals suits their stylized stances. Children will enjoy the story but may not be able to resist asking, as the hungry cats are depicted carrying their rice cakes in their mouths over mountain and marsh, why they don't just chomp down and eat them!

1058   Ure, Jean. *After Thursday*. Delacorte, 1987. ISBN 0-385-29548-0. 181p. $14.95.

7-12   In a sequel to *See You Thursday*, Marianne is now 17, still deeply in love with Abe Shonfeld. Abe is a talented pianist, blind and handsome; he loves Marianne but chafes a bit at her possessiveness and protectiveness. This is primarily a love story in which Marianne's trust is tested when Abe goes off for three weeks to be the accompanist for a singer who is young, lovely, and a childhood friend. Love story, yes; standard romance, no. Ure has controlled style and writes with good pace and flow; her characters have depth and nuance, and the fluctuations in their relationships are those with which any reader can identify.

1059   Ure, Jean. *The Most Important Thing*; illus. by Ellen Eagle. Morrow, 1986. ISBN 0-688-05859-0. 180p. $11.75.

5-7   In a sequel to *Supermouse*, Ure continues the story of two sisters who are proficient in the performing arts: smug and cloying little Rose (who loves to watch her own TV commercials) and Nicola, who is daring to hope that her proficiency at ballet will enable to enter a fine (mythical) ballet school. Everybody thinks Nicola should seize her chance when it comes except her boyfriend Denny, who would miss her; her science teacher, who thinks Nicola would be a fine doctor; and her father, who fears she is losing the chance to choose a lifelong profession to pursue a beloved but impermanent avocation. Anxious as she has been to get into the ballet school, Nicola finds that she really would prefer a science program, and she courageously faces the dismay of her friends and the wrath of her mother. The latter is Ure's best portrayal, an archetypical but highly individual dragon of a stage mother. This isn't strong in plot, but it has excellent characterization, with interesting relationships (Nicola's love/hate feelings about her simpering sister, or her feelings about Denny, who is black), and a smooth writing style that has dialogue and that falls naturally on the ear.

1060   Ure, Jean. *You Win Some, You Lose Some.* Delacorte, 1986. ISBN 0-385-29434-4. 182p. $14.95.

7-10   In *What If They Saw Me Now?* a British adolescent, to help an acquaintance, had filled in as a ballet partner and discovered that—to his surprise—he enjoyed dancing even more than the sports at which he was proficient. In this sequel, Jamie transfers to ballet school; much of the story is about his practice and his prowess, but that theme is nicely and realistically balanced by his first awkward efforts at being a suave Lothario, his surprise when he learns that his flat-mate is gay, his happy discovery that the first girl he's ever loved also loves him, and his gradual achievement of self-confidence and independence. All this happens in a book with a brisk pace, empathetic insight, and a light, witty style that is a good foil for the seriousness of many of the issues and problems of the mid-teen years.

1061   Van Allsburg, Chris. *The Polar Express;* written and illus. by Chris Van Allsburg. Houghton, 1985. ISBN 0-395-38949-6. 29p. $15.95.

K-2   It's the ending that carries the message of this Christmas story: "Though I've grown old, the bell still rings for me as it does for all who truly believe." It's a retrospective story of a child's fantasy experience, a trip by train to a bustling city (a new concept of the North Pole) where hundreds of elves labor in toy factories. Chosen by Santa Claus to receive the first gift of Christmas, the narrator chooses a bell from the harness of the reindeer. Lost, the bell turns up again on Christmas morning and the child discovers that the adults can't hear its sweet tone. Whether the read-aloud audience gets the message or not, they will probably enjoy the several appeals of a story that has Santa Claus and a journey in it; along with older readers-aloud, they will surely appreciate the stunning paintings in which Van Allsburg uses dark, rich colors and misty shapes in contrast with touches of bright white-gold light to create scenes, interior and exterior, that have a quality of mystery that imbues the strong composition to achieve a soft, evocative mood.

1062   Van Allsburg, Chris. *The Z Was Zapped;* written and illus. by Chris Van Allsburg. Houghton, 1987. ISBN 0-395-44612-0. 54p. $15.95.

5-8 yrs.   . . . not to mention B (badly Bitten), F (firmly Flattened), N (Nailed and Nailed again), or any of the others in Van Allsburg's letter-by-letter destruction of the alphabet. Each of the 26 acts of the "play" (performed by the Caslon Players) is devoted to a single center-stage letter and the particular mayhem being visited upon it. Captions are on the versos of the pictures, providing a guessing-game element that may be fun for the first go-through but that ultimately irritates, working against the simple-yet-sinister tone of the book. The Conté-pencilled menace here is quiet, still and sophisticated, etched with impeccably gray shadows. "D," for example, drowning in a *trompe l'oeil* fishbowl, has the elegant repose of a corpse in a British mystery. Even the more innocuous scenes, like the "I," "nicely iced," become perverse in context, as we infer the intent of the icing to be not decoration but suffocation. Handsome, impish, maybe even brilliant in its own peculiar way, but who is this book for?

1063   **Van Leeuwen**, Jean. *More Tales of Amanda Pig;* illus. by Ann Schweninger. Dial, 1985. Library ed. ISBN 0-8037-0224-8; Trade ed. ISBN 0-8037-0223-X. 53p. Library ed. $8.89; Trade ed. $8.95.

K-3   Like the other Oliver and Amanda books, this is both childlike and perceptive, both easy to read and entertaining. The five episodes are built around Amanda and Oliver playing house (all twelve of their babies, of various animal persuasions, get 102° fevers); entertaining relatives, among whom Amanda finally finds a soul mate; washing their toys with a good deal too much bubble bath and shampoo; giving birthday presents to Father, who has the good grace to return Sallie Rabbit to Amanda for safekeeping; and a "Growing up" dialogue that concludes with an Amanda/Mother hugging session. Delicate watercolor illustrations on every page catch the vulnerable, warm quality of these pig children with humor and well-balanced line work. A read-aloud for preschoolers as well as a read-alone for primary graders.

1064   **Van Raven**, Pieter. *A Time of Troubles.* Scribner's, 1990. ISBN 0-684-19212-8. 180p. $13.95.

7-10   In this thoughtful story set in the 1930s, adolescent Roy Purdy goes with his father (newly released from prison) from the East Coast to California. This is a vivid picture of the Depression: the hardships suffered by many, the courage displayed by some, and the desperation that fostered labor resistance. It is also a sensitive story of the relationship between a responsible young man and his irresponsible father who choose opposite sides in a struggle between land owners and field pickers who are trying to unionize. Few juvenile novels have so successfully focused on the plight of migrant farm workers during the Depression, and on their efforts to organize for decent living conditions and wages.

1065   **Vander Els**, Betty. *Leaving Point.* Farrar, 1987. ISBN 0-374-34376-4. 210p. $12.95.

5-7   A sequel to *Bomber's Moon,* which described the trials of two children of a missionary family in China in 1942, is again set in China, where the author spent much of her childhood, and is again told by Ruth, the older child. The setting is Kwangchen, the time is 1950, when the new communist regime was being established. Ruth's family, like the other foreign families, is waiting for permission to leave the country and is unhappily adjusting to being treated with harshness, contempt, and hostility by their Chinese neighbours. The author gives a vivid picture of the groping of the newly-promoted, the crudeness of propaganda methods, and the myriad injustices of a chaotic period, but she never lets the background overpower the story, and she shows in depicting both groups (particularly the mission's teacher and the young Chinese woman who becomes Ruth's friend) that individuals can resist the pressures of hatred or fear to be patient and tolerant.

1066   **Vander Els**, Betty. *The Bombers' Moon*. Farrar, 1985. ISBN 374-30864-0. 167p. $11.95.

4-6   Because of the Japanese invasion of China in 1942, Ruth and her younger brother are sent away by their missionary parents to a safer place than their home city, Nansein. Ruth tells the story, an account of stern (stereotypically stern) teachers, new friendships, the repeated efforts she makes to make timid Simeon feel more courageous or more secure, the harrowing trip to a refuge in India when the war draws closer. Since the author spent much of her childhood in China, this has vividly authentic details. Despite the tendency to typecast and the occasional awkward description of physical act (putting one's head in one's lap, seeing a teacher with "one frowning eye") this is a substantial first novel, adequate in style, interesting because of its setting and the inherent danger, and satisfying in its conclusion, a reunion with parents and a new baby brother in Shanghai.

1067   **Ventura**, Piero. *Michelangelo's World*; written and illus. by Piero Ventura. Putnam, 1989. ISBN 0-399-21593-X. 43p. $13.95.

7-10   Oversize pages are illustrated with meticulously detailed small-scale pictures, line and wash, and formatted with truncated double columns of unfortunately small print. While the text does give information about Michelangelo's world, it is written as though it were auto-biographical. Since many of the illustrations are accompanied by italicized third-person comments about the artist, there's an uncomfortable disparity between sober captions and often-jocular first-person text. The illustrations are, as in other Ventura books, both skillful and diverting, and several pages provide photographs of some of Michelangelo's major works. The text is informative, but its details are not accounted for by any cited sources.

1068   **Ventura**, Piero. *Venice: Birth of a City*; written and illus. by Piero Ventura. Putnam, 1988. ISBN 0-399-21531-X. 36p. $13.95

5-7   Ventura's wonderfully diverse and detailed paintings, miniature in scale but sweeping in composition, are used in effective combination with small blocks of text to tell a cohesive and chronological story of the city called "the bride of the Adriatic." A fine example of presenting history through pictures, this is remarkable for its beauty and its use of perspective; the book closes with a four-page fold-out that shows much of that part of Venice that is most famous.

1069   **Vernon**, Adele, ad. *The Riddle;* illus. by Robert Rayevsky and Vladimir Radunsky. Dodd, 1987. ISBN 0-396-08920-8. 32p. $12.95.

5-8 yrs.   Rayevsky, the witty illustrator of *Mister Cat-and-a-half*, teams up with another Russian-born illustrator to dramatize a clever Catalan tale that will appeal to an older picture-book audience. A king is delighted when a charcoal maker explains a riddle: ten cents a day is plenty to live on, *and* to pay back a debt (take care of his mother), save for his old age (take care of his son), "and still have something left over to throw out the window" (give his daughter a dowry). The charcoal burner promises not to tell anyone else until he's looked upon the king's face one hundred times—which he does when a schemer pays him a hundred coins for the answer. The art work here is strongly stylized, with portraiture that is slyly expressive and scenic panels that suggest stage backdrops. The flat perspectives benefit from back-grounds that are texturally varied; compositions are carefully considered and clean. A good read-aloud to small groups of second and third graders hooked on their own contemporary riddles.

1070   **Vesey**, A. *The Princess and the Frog;* written and illus. by A. Vesey. Atlantic, 1985. ISBN 0-87113-038-6. 28p. $13.95.

K-3   As in most major con jobs, the victim here wants desperately to be duped. When the princess comes home with a squishy frog that has retrieved her golden ball, the queen sees the opportunity for a rich and handsome prince for her seventh daughter ("There are not many rich and handsome princes left") and insists that the frog be extended every courtesy of cuisine and entertainment. Time passes and tempers fray, for the frog is extremely demanding. Finally the queen remembers there was a kiss involved, and the princess forces herself with a peck on his head, only to find that the frog remains a frog, and a married one to boot, with numerous offspring waiting to move into the palace. children familiar with the Grimm version will enjoy this spoof. It has funny lines ("Pond life has its limitations") and spacious, full-color paintings with a Victorian cast, also farcical; the stone lions that guard the palace stick out their tongues at each other in permanent poses of irreverence.

1071   **Vigna**, Judith. *Nobody Wants a Nuclear War;* written and illus. by Judith Vigna. Whitman, 1986. ISBN 0-8075-5739-0. 35p. $10.75.

5-7 yrs.   The youngest book so far to address the issue of nuclear war does so simply and as hopefully as possible. The narrator and her brother confess their fears to each other and build a hideaway in a secret cave in the woods behind their house. After they've stocked it with food and water, they rest, feeling snug and safe until their mother startles them with a flashlight. Over lunch, she discusses briefly the bombing of Hiroshima and her own trauma as a child hiding during air raid drills. She talks about grownups and groups working all over the world to prevent nuclear war and finally helps the children make a banner to photograph and send to the president. The honest warmth of the mother serves as the best reassurance here, as she promises the children family strength and love no matter what. If they are not free of fear, at least they are free of facing fear alone, with the outlet of working toward a world where children can feel safer. Unpretentious in style, under-played in spacious pen-and-wash drawings, this is more than timely; in its quiet way, it is a brave and effective book.

1072   **Vincent**, Gabrielle, illus. *Breakfast Time, Ernest and Celestine.* Greenwillow, 1985. ISBN 0-688-04555-3. 16p. $5.25.

3-5 yrs.   Smaller than earlier Vincent books, this is a brief, wordless story that is very clearly told by the illustrations. Ernest (an amicable bear) wakes his small ward (a mouse) and takes her downstairs for breakfast; Celestine knocks over and breaks a dish, insists on cleaning it up herself, and enjoys the replacement. Deft use of line, soft colors, and a clear sequence of ideas make the book as appealing as it is comprehensible.

1073   **Voigt**, Cynthia. *Jackaroo.* Atheneum, 1985. ISBN 0-689-31123-0. 320p. $14.95.

6-9   Cynthia Voigt moves into the romantic/medieval milieu in a tale that uses the theme of the defender of the poor, and she does it with great success. In a feudal society, the Lords rule, or misrule, with impunity, and for many years there has been legend of Jackaroo, the masked rider who appears to help the poor and oppressed. Clever, confident, courageous, Gwyn the Innkeeper's Daughter assumes the role of Jackaroo when she finds the legendary clothes and mask hidden in a cupboard. Then she knows that there has been a long line of Jackaroos, that he's not a legend—and that anyone who assumes the role may have to pay a price. The end of this carefully structured story may bring a surprise or two to readers, but few are likely to be astonished by the late blooming love affair that the independent and indomitable heroine has not expected. This is a good adventure story, and a believable one; the writing style and characterization are capably controlled, but what gives the book a deep matrix for them is Voigt's full conception of the society and its socioeconomic system.

1074   **Voigt**, Cynthia. *The Runner*. Atheneum, 1985. ISBN 0-689-31069-2. 192p. $11.95.

7-10   Bullet Tillerman is on the school track team, but he doesn't care about the team; he runs for himself; when he's cut from the team—despite being their best performer—he doesn't care, he runs in solitude. He's cut from the team because he refuses the coach's request to help train a black runner, Tamer. Why? He doesn't mix with "colored," he says. However, he does eventually work with, and come to respect, Tamer; he also learns that Patrice, the man he works for and one of the few people he likes, has one black ancestor, and he accepts this. What Voigt is showing is some change, some maturation on the part of a biased adolescent of an earlier generation. Bullet, it develops, is the uncle of Dicey and her siblings (*Homecoming* and its sequels) although this affects the story hardly at all. His mother (Dicey's grandmother) is a potentially strong but almost silent character, totally dominated by Bullet's father, with whom he is in bitter, taciturn conflict. Bullet has no friends, no girl, no ambition. He works for Patrice, he runs, and as soon as he turns eighteen, he drops out of school and joins the Army. In an epilogue, his mother learns he has been killed in action. This has some strong characters and some taut, dramatic situation, but it lacks the cohesion and direction that would make this a powerful novel rather than an interesting but rather puzzling one.

1075   **Voigt**, Cynthia. *Seventeen against the Dealer*. Atheneum, 1989. ISBN 0-689-31497-3. 181p. $13.95.

7-12   Dicey is now twenty-one and proprietor of her own fledgling boat shop in this last (according to the jacket copy) installment in Voigt's series about the Tillerman family. After her workshop is robbed of all of her hard-won boat-building tools, Dicey unwillingly contracts to sand and paint thirty shoddy rowboats built by her landlord. The work is odious and long, allowing Dicey no time to design and build a dinghy, her first order. Unexpected but welcome help comes from a drifter named Cisco, who asks for nothing more than to be allowed to sleep in the shop and share Dicey's hot chocolate. Cisco is a big talker, "like constant rain, the words falling and falling," and an interesting one, describing all the places he's seen and knowledge he's gathered to an increasingly fascinated Dicey. He is also most probably Dicey's father, who abandoned the family before the first book in the series, *Homecoming*, began. While sprinkling hints throughout, Voigt doesn't name Cisco as Frank Verricker, and the relationship will probably be lost on readers unfamiliar with the previous books,

particularly *Sons from Afar*. Dicey herself never realizes who Cisco
really is, which makes his eventual theft of eight hundred dollars from
Dicey all the more shocking, giving a dark irony to Gram's wrap-up
moral that "It's not your failure. It's his. Yours would have been not to
trust him." As was true in the previous books, Gram steals any scene
she appears in, but here she (as well as Maybeth) has acquired a
rather sentimental patina of sainthood, her dignity becoming almost
picturesque. Dicey can be tryingly noble ("Days passed. Dicey
worried and worked") but Voigt shows that Dicey's fortitude and
stubbornness have come at the cost of other essential qualities, such as
curiosity and imagination, lacks that cost her true knowledge of what
she really lost when Cisco betrayed her and disappeared. A brave
finale.

1076   **Voigt**, Cynthia. *Stories about Rosie*; illus by Dennis Kendrick.
Atheneum, 1986. ISBN 0-689-31296-2 . 44p. $12.95.

2-4   These stories are not only about Rosie, they are entirely from Rosie's
point of view, ie., a dog's-eye vision of the world. "The family's job was
to take care of Rosie. . . . Her bed was exactly like Jessie's, only it
smelled better." Rosie's mind works in contradictions, which are
reflected in her conversational barks. When the children leave for
school, for instance, she barks "Hello. Don't go. Good-bye. Take me
with you." The four stories here are not terribly thick on plot: one
establishes Rosie's routine at home, one describes her brief run
outdoors, one romps through an escapade with a bat loose in the
house, and the last is about Rosie's encounter with a deer during the
family's vacation. The style is very simple, however, and funny as well,
with the humor of Rosie's knowledge versus the humans' easily
keeping the text afloat. The cartoon drawings, alternating color with
black-and-white, are energetic in the canine department if stereotypical in the human. Good practice fare for young readers.

1077   **von Tscharner**, Renata. *New Providence: A Changing Cityscape*;
conceived by Renata von Tscharner and Ronald Lee Fleming; illus. by
Denis Orloff. Gulliver/Harcourt, 1987. ISBN 0-15-200540-4. 25p. $10.95.

4-6   An ingeniously conceived and executed visual history of a small,
fictitious but typical American city as it goes through several decades
of change. Full-color double-page spreads depict New Providence in
the years 1910, 1935, 1955, 1970, 1980, and 1987. After each lavishly
detailed illustration is a double-page spread of text pointing out
changes in the socio-economic and cultural climate and how these are
reflected in the buildings and appearance of the town center. Small
black-and-white insets from the paintings are singled out for specific
attention. Without becoming repetitive or boring, this compares
different styles of architecture on the same site; it's effective both

informationally and aesthetically, with the rather idealistic conclusion of a restored inner city serving to inspire readers. Succinct end notes document the actual buildings upon which the scene was constructed. This is, in its own way, as impressively simple as Jorg Müller's *The Changing City* or some of David Macaulay's works on architectural history, though it lacks their perspective of personalizing humor.

1078   **Waber**, Bernard. *Ira Says Goodbye;* written and illus. by Bernard Waber. Houghton, 1988. ISBN 0-395-48315-8. [40p]. $13.95.

K-2   A few years older than when he worried about taking his teddy to Reggie's house in *Ira Sleeps Over* (*BCCB*: 2/73), Ira has just found out that Reggie is moving away. The news is delivered by Ira's sister, who is just as entertainingly obnoxious as she was in the first book: "Far, far away. Oh, I would hate it to pieces if my best friend were moving away. What will you do when your best friend in the whole wide world moves away? Hmmmmmm?" Reggie himself is more excited about the move than is seemly ("Reggie just went on talking about Greendale, as if he had never heard about best friends"), and doesn't even blink when Ira pointedly tells him to take both their pet turtles, rather than split up Felix and Oscar, friends "who are used to being together." Friendship does win in the end, but in the meantime Waber again demonstrates a keen ability to score psychological points through funny and natural dialogue. The illustrations have an offhand air that is similar to the first book, but more spare of line and in full color. The cover art neatly mirrors the first book as well, with a bigger Ira going *up* the stairs (to pack for a visit to Reggie's).

1079   **Waddell**, Martin. *The Park in the Dark;* illus. by Barbara Firth. Lothrop, 1989. Library ed. ISBN 0-688-08517-2; Trade ed. ISBN 0-688-08516-4. [32p]. Library ed. $11.88; Trade ed. $11.95.

3-5 yrs.   A stuffed monkey, a knitted elephant and a toy dog sneak away from their sleeping child for an adventure on the playground. "When the sun goes down/ and the moon comes up/ and the old swing creaks/ in the dark,/ that's when we go/ to the park,/ me and Loopy/ and Little Gee,/ we three." The streets and trees are full of terrors, all graphically reflected in gray-blue watercolor illustrations with faces in surprising places. Yet there's a safe balance between the scary and the secure. Youngsters will love the glorious swoosh of the friends as they swing up into the night sky and the wild run home as they flee from the THING (a passing train). Rhythmic in verse and art, this has a dream quality with plenty of clearcut action that addresses the fears and fantasies of the very young.

1080   **Waddell**, Martin. *The Tough Princess;* illus. by Patrick Benson. Philomel, 1987. ISBN 0-399-21380-5. 28p. $11.95 .

2-4   A handsomely designed book, this nonsexist spoof of the traditional fairy tale has pages that spaciously and artistically accomodate the blocks of clean type and the sprightly, colorful pictures that have wit and vitality—and just occasionally, for contrast, a bit of the macabre. When Princess Rosamund is born to her impoverished parents, they agree to annoy a bad fairy so that their child will go through the usual rescue-by-handsome-prince routine. Alas, our heroine grows up to be very tall, very thin, and very courageous, but not very beautiful or very pitiable. She also slays dragons, knocks the glasses off the Bad Fairy, rescues princes, and bicycles around the kingdom being valiant. When at long last she finds a beautiful prince, fast asleep, she kisses him, he awakens and they fall in love and live happily ever after.

1081   **Wallace**, Barbara Brooks. *Argyle;* illus. by John Sandford. Abingdon, 1987. ISBN 0-687-01724-6. 32p. $10.95.

K-3   Delightful nonsense, this combines a plot with an improbable/impossible twist that is firmly meshed with a realistic base. The style is honed to simplicity and is given humor by the union of fantastic development and bland style. A sheep named Argyle is happiest when he blends with the flock, looking just like the others, doing just what they do. And then. . . Argyle finds a patch of flowers of many colors, and as he eats them, a rainbow band of wool begins to grow. That, of course, is the first step in a process that leads to Argyle socks. The margin-framed paintings are impressive for their composition and their restrained use of color, and they echo the quiet humor of the story to very good effect.

1082   **Walsh**, Jill Paton. *Lost and Found;* illus. by Mary Raynor. Andre Deutsch/Elsevier/Dutton, 1985. ISBN 0-233-97672-8. 30p. $10.95.

2-4   Although the patterned nature of the story strikes an artificial note (each child sent on an errand loses what he or she is carrying, but finds the article lost by the previous child) most children should delight in the concept of articles that become artifacts as the centuries progress. The first child is a prehistoric cavedweller who loses an arrowhead, the next is a child of medieval times who finds the arrowhead and presents it to her grandmother instead of the jug of cream she's mislaid, and so on to a contemporary child and her grandmother. Simply and effectively told, this has no breaks between incidents, but the clothes show a passage of time, as do the architectural details of an increasingly large and complex bridges crossed by the children. The authors have been careful to keep the language more or less consistent with the period.

1083   Walsh, Jill Paton. *Torch.* Farrar, 1988. ISBN 0-374-37684-0. 171p. $12.95.

6-9   Set, as are so many novels of the future, in a world that has lost its technological knowledge and reverted to a simpler society, this tells of a group of children from Greece who go on a quest. If the setting is familiar, the development is fresh in a story with nuance and suspense. Cal and Dio have agreed, in a deathbed promise to the old Guardian, to take on the quest of finding the "Games" for which he had been guarding the torch. Readers will recognize, as Dio and Cal and the other children move through a series of dangerous adventures, references to the Olympics or variants on names and terms from the past. There is one fantastic element, the torch that dims or lights again in response to their behavior as they search for the place and race that feels right. An intriguing adventure story is written with the author's usual flair, nicely knitting history, legend, and quest.

1084   Warren, James A. *Portrait of a Tragedy: America and the Vietnam War.* Lothrop, 1990. ISBN 0-688-07454-5. 208p. illus. with photographs. $17.95.

7-12   Summarizing thirty years of history in fewer than two hundred pages is no easy feat. Warren's introductory survey of America's longest war gives his readers the big picture, providing concise descriptions and thought-provoking analysis. Beginning with the French colonialization of Vietnam, Warren explains the rise of Vietnamese nationalism, the role of Ho Chi Minh, and the reasons for American involvement. Emphasizing the politics behind the war and the attitudes of American presidents from Truman to Nixon, *Portrait* shows multiple points of view: the attitudes of the North Vietnamese, Vietcong, South Vietnamese, American military, and public are all considered. Particularly helpful is Warren's ability to capture key concepts (counterinsurgency, containment) in a few sentences. Making judicious use of secondary sources, the author highlights key conflicts, military engagements and operations, providing the reader with enough background information to understand their significance. Unfortunately, some of the army-issue black-and-white photographs have a generic quality. One, captioned "A B-52 Stratofortress in flight over Vietnam" could have been shot anywhere. Maps, which would have been useful throughout the book, are limited to a handful in the first chapter. The map with the most information is also the hardest to read. But the oversize format, double-spaced text, bibliography, and chronology make this an accessible and helpful resource. Warren successfully proves his thesis that the tragedy of Vietnam was not only the massive loss of life but also the fact that the conflict ultimately was unwinnable, given the lack of popular support for the South Vietnamese government.

1085   **Watanabe**, Shigeo. *It's My Birthday!*; illus. by Yasuo Ohtomo. Philomel, 1988. ISBN 0-399-21492-5. 32p. (I Love Special Days Books). $10.95.

3-5 yrs.   For all their emphasis on action and achievement (*I Can Take a Walk*, etc.) Watanabe's gentle stories about Bear and his family make soothing bedtime reading. Ohtomo's pictures are soft and brushed and quiet, the texts approving and reassuring. On his birthday, Bear's grandparents give him a photo album filled with pictures of Bear as a baby and toddler, allowing the birthday boy to contemplate his tiny triumphs: learning to take a bath, to dress, to walk. The last space in the album is blank—the perfect place, it turns out, for a shot of Bear's surprise party-picnic down by the river. "What a wonderful birthday!"

1086   **Waters**, Marjorie. *The Victory Garden Kid's Book: A Beginner's Guide to Growing Vegetables, Fruits, and Flowers*; illus. with photographs by Gary Mottau and drawings by George Ulrich. Houghton, 1988. Trade ed. ISBN 0-395-42730-4; paper ed. ISBN 0-395-46560-5. 148p. Trade ed. $19.95; paper ed. $12.95

3-7   The co-author of several books for adult gardeners, Waters has produced a how-to book that is clearly written, that provides authoritative information, that is illustrated with well-placed diagrams and photographs, and that is logically organized. The first section describes, chronologically, the garden project of seven children (assorted ages), from choosing the site in the spring to closing the garden in the fall; choosing tools, preparing to compost, and coping with garden pests are included. The second part of the book is an alphabetical arrangement of "Kids' Crops," a list of fruits, vegetables, and flowers that are easy to grow; here special instructions for each plant supplement the information given in the first section. An index gives access to the contents of a book that is, if a bit long for younger children, both simple enough for easy reference for them and not too simplified for the older child's cover-to-cover use.

1087   **Watkins**, Yoko Kawashima. *So Far from the Bamboo Grove*. Lothrop, 1986. ISBN 0-688-06110-9. 183p. $10.25.

7-   In an autobiographical story of World War II and its aftermath, the author begins in 1945 when she was eleven, living with her parents and an older brother and sister in Korea. Most Koreans bitterly resented Japanese rule so the Kawashimas, like other Japanese residing in North Korea, were in grave danger. This is the often-harrowing account of their flight from their home, a journey that began with a long march for the three women, separated from father and brother, and that often included incidents of brutality and harrowing cruelty. Eventually the two girls, after getting to Japan, adjust to their mother's death, ostracism at school, and dire poverty. They learn to fend for themselves and are reunited with their brother and with a kindly man they had met in Korea. Effective, affective, candid, and compelling as personal history, this is a testament to the resilience of the young and a reminder that in war we are all losers.

1088   **Weiss**, Harvey. *Submarines and Other Underwater Craft*; written and illus. by Harvey Weiss and with photographs. Crowell, 1990. Library ed. ISBN 0-690-04761-4; Trade ed. ISBN 0-690-04759-2. 64p. Library ed. $12.89; Trade ed. $12.95.

4-7   Weiss explains clearly the physical principles and history of submarines, using a well-organized text and a combination of photographs and humorous black-and-white cartoons. The writing style is lucid as well as light-hearted. Weiss does not lose his reader's attention by taking his subject too seriously ("The idea was to come up under an enemy warship and drill holes in the bottom. Then, with luck, the submarines would be able to duck away from under the sinking boat!"). Reminiscent of Macaulay's work, the cartoon illustrations are in keeping with the levity of the text. One drawing of "art and artifacts . . . found on the sea bottom" depicts what is meant to be a bust but looks more like a decapitated head—probably for the amusement of the detail-searching reader. Some material about scuba diving, submersibles, underwater treasure, and undersea commercial operations, although interesting, seems tacked on to extend the book. However, the concise information about submarines, accessible by an index, will be invaluable to young researchers and sub devotees.

1089   **Weiss**, Nicki. *Where Does the Brown Bear Go?*; written and illus. by Nicki Weiss. Greenwillow, 1989. Library ed. ISBN 0-688-07863-X; Trade ed. ISBN 0-688-07862-1. 24p. Library ed. $11.88; Trade ed. $11.95.

1-3 yrs.   Offering reassurance through rhythm, story, and soothingly textured colored-pencil drawings, this bedtime chant has some of the same hypnotic comfort as *Goodnight, Moon*. "When the lights go down/ On the city street,/ Where does the white cat go, honey?/ Where does the white cat go?/ When evening settles on the jungle heat,/ Where does the monkey go, honey?/ Where does the monkey go?" Cat, monkey, brown bear, and all the rest are headed to the same place: "They are on their way. They are on their way home." Toddlers will have this one memorized in two nights flat and will love the last picture, which shows all the animals as stuffed toys surrounding a sleeping child. "And everyone is home." Clear white type on black pages with colored borders face pictures of the off-to-bed animals, which are simple, shadowless shapes in felt-like landscapes lit by a crescent moon. Warm as a blanket.

1090   **Wells**, Rosemary. *Hazel's Amazing Mother;* written and illus. by
Rosemary Wells. Dial, 1985. Library ed. ISBN 0-8037-0210-8; Trade ed.
ISBN 0-8037-0209-4. 28p. Library ed. $10.89; Trade ed. $10.95.

4-6 yrs.   The power of maternal love may be exaggerated here, but the lap
audience will understand that mothers are their defenders and will do
extraordinary things for their young. As is true of other books by
Wells, the characters are small animals in appearance; in behavior
they are people. Here a youngster is sent on a pre-picnic errand, loses
her way, arrives at a park where she is beset by bullies who rip her doll
and dump the doll's carriage in the pond, and cries for her mother.
Mother, picnic basket in hand, is caught by a strong wind, the picnic
basket she's holding serving as parachute. She comes down just in
time to force the bullies to tidy up their damage, and the picnic
proceeds, with—a typical Wellsian touch—more food than could ever
have fit in the basket. Breezy and funny, but also touching, this should
appeal to children's sense of justice as well as their faith in parental
omnipotence.

1091   **Wells**, Rosemary , ad. *The Little Lame Prince;* based on a story by
Dinah Maria Mulock Craik; ad. and illus. by Rosemary Wells. Dial,
1990. Library ed. ISBN 0-8037-0789-4; Trade ed. ISBN 0-8037-0788-6.
32p. Library ed. $12.89; Trade ed. $12.95.

5-8 yrs.   Rosemary Wells has benefited children's literature with a versatility
   *   ranging from toddler board books to YA novels. Whether funny or
serious, her style is original, and this adaptation of Dinah Craik's
British classic (1874) celebrates a dramatic plot wrung free of
sentimentality by twists of wildly imaginative illustration. For starters,
the cast has been recast as animals, a choice that displays Wells'
drafting to best advantage and that also allows her to play with visual
satire—the royal family are pigs. When the plump but ailing queen
dies and the king wastes away, an evilly militaristic brother of the king
banishes Prince Francisco to a faraway tower. There, Francisco's fairy
godmother, who always appears with the sound of popcorn, bestows on
him a patched magic cape that helps him recover the suffering
kingdom. Quite apart from Wells' artful abridgement of a Victorian
soap opera, the narrative graphics expand from self-contained
domestic scenes characteristic of her past work to a larger canvas
including landscapes and complex changes of detail, expression, and
composition. The villains "Osvaldo, his porky wife, Isabella, and their
seven wild and whiney sons" are a richly portrayed set of bad actors.
The hero himself, while occasionally reminiscent of Wells' endearing
Max and company, expands considerably on their repertoire of
reactions. Ambitiously colorful, slyly funny—a real porker!

1092   **Wells**, Rosemary. *Max's Bath;* written and illus. by Rosemary Wells. Dial, 1985. ISBN 0-8037-0162-4. 10p. $3.50.

1-2 yrs.   Wells does it again; like the first four books about Max (a very young rabbit) this is realistic, funny, beguiling, and as deft in its minimal text as in its simple and expressive pictures. Older sister Ruby, a long-suffering character, tries repeatedly to get Max clean. Since he is apt to take purple grape juice or orange sherbet into the bath, Max usually comes out as stained as when he went in. Finally Ruby puts Max in the shower; he emerges in white and fluffy state but pointing gleefully at Ruby (who's collected some of his stains) and says balefully "Dirty." His bedtime, his birthday, and his breakfast are the subject of three other new books about Max. They're equally delectable, and they should be as useful for very young children as they are appealing.

1093   **Wells**, Rosemary. *Max's Chocolate Chicken;* written and illus. by Rosemary Wells. Dial, 1989. Library ed. ISBN 0-8037-0586-7; Trade ed. ISBN 0-8037-0585-9. 24p. Library ed. $8.89; Trade ed. $8.95.

3-5 yrs.   It's superego vs. id all the way this Easter, with Ruby telling Max what to do and Max eating the chocolate chicken anyway. What cares he about finding the stupid eggs? A mudpuddle he finds, acorns, a spoon, ants, even. ("Pull yourself together," says Ruby. "Otherwise you'll never get the chocolate chicken.") While Ruby counts her gold egg with purple stripes and her turquoise egg with silver swirls and her lavender egg with orange polka dots, Max makes ant-and-acorn pancakes in the mud. While Ruby declares herself the winner of the egg hunt, Max claims the prize and hides with it in a convenient hole under the tree. While Ruby offers to share it if he will come out, he consumes it all, tail first, head next, wings last. Thoughtfully, a benign Easter Rabbit (not unlike Max in appearance) provides a chocolate duck as well, but Max is closing in on that by the concluding picture. Bright in color and concept, this is as fresh as the spring-green grass that dominates every spread.

1094   **Wells**, Rosemary. *Shy Charles;* written and illus. by Rosemary Wells. Dial, 1988. Library ed. ISBN 0-8037-0564-6; Trade ed. ISBN 0-8037-0563-8. 32p. Library ed. $11.89; Trade ed. $11.95.

5-7 yrs.   Charles is a happy child whose mode of communication is minimal. He is content to accept Mrs. Belinski's chocolate surprise . . . silently. When it's time to say good-bye, Charles simply disappears into a flower bin. In ballet class, he pretends to be asleep. But when the babysitter falls down the stairs, Charles gets right on the phone, summoning the emergency service and saying everything necessary until the crisis is over. "He's a prince, a gem, a hero! / And everyone shouted, 'Thank you, Charles!' / But Charles said . . . / Zero." Like many of Wells' picture-book characters, this mouseling is quirkily endearing, with more of the humor conveyed in the illustrations than in the rhyming text. One full-page spread, for example, shows the ballet students cavorting colorfully across the floor upon which Charles lies, back to the audience, dressed in black, his tail and ears stretched stiff. Shy listeners will empathize, others will sympathize— with a smile.

1095   **Wersba**, Barbara. *Fat: A Love Story*. Harper, 1987. Library ed. ISBN 0-06-026415-2; Trade ed. ISBN 0-06-026400-4. 156p. Library ed. $11.89; Trade ed. $11.50.

7-10   The narrator is Rita Formica, who is sixteen, weighs two hundred pounds, and is five foot three. She has been deeply, hopelessly smitten by Robert Swann, the golden youth who is a member of Sag Harbor's wealthy summer colony. Rita joins a health club just to be near Robert, who simply doesn't see her. He does, however, see her French friend Nicole, who has volunteered to act as bait; her proposal that she trap Robert and then give him to Rita doesn't work, for Nicole and Robert have a torrid affair that ends in marriage. Readers will have noticed, before Rita does, that someone else is in love with her. Arnold is her employer, twice her age, a gentle nonconformist who manages for a time to resist Rita's sexual invitations once she recovers from her crush and realizes that she loves Arnold. This is a frank, cheerful, sophisticated but romantic comedy. Rita is an engaging character, shrewd (save when smitten) and sensitive, whose story is just poignant enough to be touching without being maudlin.

1096   **Wersba**, Barbara. *Just Be Gorgeous*. Harper, 1988. Library ed. ISBN 0-06-026360-1; Trade ed. ISBN 0-06-026359-8. 156p. Library ed. $11.89; Trade ed. $11.95.

7-10   Heidi Rosenbloom, the sixteen-year-old narrator, has little self-esteem and little hope of changing this. Her divorced mother wants Heidi to wear pretty clothes. Heidi prefers shopping in second-hand clothing stores. She's a miserable loner—until she meets a homeless street performer, Jeffrey; he's dancing, hoping to be "discovered" and to break into show business. Heidi falls deeply, generously in love; unfortunately, although Jeffrey returns her affection, he is gay. She accepts this, still loving him. By the time Jeffrey moves on, however, he has given Heidi some appreciation of her own worth as a human being. This is a nicely structured story, and there is depth in the characterization and compassion that never becomes sticky and is, indeed, occasionally lightened by touches of humor in the badinage between the protagonists. There are some minor weaknesses in plot details (would Heidi's mother really fail to realize that when she went off for weekends Jeffrey moved in, for an unspecified period?) but they detract little from the bittersweet quality of the story.

1097   **Wersba**, Barbara. *Love is the Crooked Thing.* Harper, 1987. Library ed. ISBN 0-06-026367-9; Trade ed. ISBN 0-06-026366-0. 167p. Library ed. $11.89; Trade ed. $11.95.

7-10   In the first book about (and narrated by) plump Rita Formica, sixteen, she is desolate as the story ends, for her lover Arnold—twice her age, quiet and gentle—has agreed with her parents that he is too old for her, and has left town. In this sequel to *Fat: A Love Story*, Rita decides that she will somehow get the money to go to Zurich and find Arnold; she has no address but knows he's in that city. Wersba manages, just, to keep Rita's visit (undisclosed to parents) credible, and to make the means (working for a paperback romance mill) refreshingly amusing. This is just as adroit as the first book and just as witty, but a bit more bittersweet.

1098   **Westall**, Robert. *Ghost Abbey.* Scholastic, 1989. ISBN 0-590-41692-8. 176p. $12.95.

5-9   Here's a haunted house story that, from the spooky cover to the happy but unsettling ending, delivers the goods. Twelve-year-old Maggi Adams, her younger brothers, and their father go to Foxwist Abbey when Dad gets a job there supervising its restoration. Maggi, overburdened and bereaved since the death of her mother, hopes it will be a new start for the family. The Abbey has it all: gargoyles, locked rooms, a garden maze . . . as well as a real ghost and mysterious singing voices. It also, suprisingly enough, provides a warm and funny romance for Dad in the person of Ms. McFarlane, owner of the Abbey and a fervent believer in "faith." The Abbey and its inhabitants are filled with secrets, and Maggi is content to explore them until she realizes the nature of its stern protection: the Abbey gives new life to the caretakers it calls, but strikes with a vengeance against anyone who seems to be harming it in any way. While providing all requisite thrills, this is gentler than most of Westall's fiction, even to the characterization of the Abbey, which is really the main character here.

1099   **Wetterer**, Margaret K. *Kate Shelley and the Midnight Express*; illus. by Karen Ritz. Carolrhoda, 1990. ISBN 0-87614-425-3. 48p. (On My Own Books). $8.95.

2-5   "Someone may still be alive in Honey Creek and I have to stop the midnight express." There is a terrible storm and fifteen-year-old Kate Shelley hears the bridge collapse under the weight of a locomotive. Can she save the crew? Can she stop the express in time? Easy-readers are rarely this dramatic, and the author's note indicating that the story actually happened in late nineteenth-century Iowa adds a frisson of authenticity. Rather than burdening the story with exclamation points or hyperbole, the author wisely relies on the events themselves to convey excitement, and the styling is simple, not choppy: "She held up the lantern to light her way over the bridge. But as she did, a fierce wind blew out the lantern's small flame. Kate stared into the darkness." Watercolor and charcoal illustrations are strong and stormy, with enough dignity to make the book appealing to older reluctant readers. The teenaged protagonist, as well, should widen the potential audience.

1100   **Wexler**, Jerome. *Pet Mice*; written and illus. with photographs by Jerome Wexler. Whitman, 1989. ISBN 0-8075-6524-5. 48p. $12.95.

3-6
*

Even for those whose idea of a good time is *not* something that will "run up your arm and poke in your pocket for a treat," Wexler makes pet mice seem like a lot of fun. With a friendly, personal tone, the author explains the details of buying healthy mice, housing and feeding them, training and playing with them, and mating them. "Let's do a little math." Using examples from his own mousekeeping experience, Wexler is frank about problems ("After taking care of my wound, I put my hand back—this time moving more slowly") and contagiously enthusiastic about the pleasures, especially in a remarkable sequence of photographs showing the birth and development of mouse babies. (Unfortunately, a diagram showing how to tell a male from a female mouse is confusing.) The many color photographs throughout are informative, well-keyed to the text, and adorable.

1101   **Wheatley**, Nadia. *My Place*; illus. by Donna Rawlins. Australia in Print, 1990. ISBN 0-7328-0010-2. 48p. $14.95.

3-6

Beginning in 1988 and reaching back at ten-year intervals to 1788, this is a capsule history of Australia as reflected by a succession of children living in the same Sydney house. Laura's house (in 1988) was previously lived in (in 1978) by Mike, named for his father Michaelis (1958), who came with his family from Greece "because there wasn't enough work on our island." Before the house was built in 1888, the Müllers had their store there; the same German family changed their name to Miller sometime between 1908 and 1918. The first inhabitant, Barangaroo, loved to play in the same big tree enjoyed by all those who came later. The tree stands behind a McDonalds now, but Laura's family hangs an Aboriginal flag in their window to remind them of their roots. Each double-page spread represents a decade and is eye-fillingly detailed with a portrait of the child-narrator, a picture of the house and its happenings, and a personalized map illustrating a child's-eye view of the changing neighborhood: 1938—"Boot Factory (Almost no one works here)"; 1918—"Boot factory where Ev makes soldiers' boots") as well as those things that remain the same. The pattern is more than a clever scheme, with family stories as well as history unfolding when each child recalls stories he or she has heard about the past. Some stories, such as one that discreetly touches upon illegitimacy, will be more apparent to adult readers than to children. A natural accompaniment to oral history projects, this book also has the admirable virtue of being just as much fun to read backwards as forwards.

1102   **Whelan**, Gloria. *Next Spring an Oriole;* illus. by Pamela Johnson. Random House, 1987. Library ed. ISBN 0-394-99125-7; Paper ed. ISBN 0-394-89125-2. (Stepping Stone). 64p. Library ed. $5.99; Paper ed. $1.95.

2-4   Historical fiction at an easy level is hard to find, and this pioneer story, narrated by 10-year-old Libby Mitchell on her journey from Virginia to Michigan in 1837, is smoothly written and appealing. The wagon trail is not easy, and Whelan is careful to include a taste of the physical and emotional hardships, from the discomfort of head lice to tension between Mama and Papa. She's also careful in her presentation of the Potawatomi Indians, who figure in the story when the Mitchells nurse one of their children back to health after a bout of measles. Papa mentions the whites' unfair treatment of the Indians, and later the little girl's family shows up with food to help the Mitchells survive their first winter. There's even an ecological theme in Papa's love of the trees he refuses to girdle for farming, but the story, though brief, is well enough developed to outweigh the messages.

1103   **Whelan**, Gloria. *Silver;* illus. by Stephen Marchesi. Random House, 1988. Library ed. ISBN 0-394-99611-9; Paper ed. ISBN 0-394-89611-4. 60p. (Stepping Stone Books). Library ed. $5.99; Paper ed. $1.95

3-5   Nine-year-old Rachel is keenly involved in her father's dog-sled racing. The story is framed between his placing second in an Anchorage competition and third in the Iditarod. Meanwhile, he gives her the runt of a litter from his lead dog, which occasions her own adventure; she follows the puppy through a storm after it has been taken by a wolf to replace a dead cub. The plot is unpretentious if predictable, the setting is crisply delineated, and the writing smooth at a low reading level. Black-and-white illustrations, which have a screened effect, are competently drafted and well composed to balance the text. Although there's nothing unusual here, this has, like other titles in the Stepping Stone series, effectively planned appeal for transitional readers.

1104   **Whipple**, Laura, comp. *Eric Carle's Animals Animals;* illus. by Eric Carle. Philomel, 1989. ISBN 0-399-21744-4. 93p. $18.95.

2-4   This poetry anthology is a splendid showcase for Carle's dramatic
  *   double image. Two haiku by Demaru and Issa, for instance, make
        perfect companions in describing "butterflies dancing through falling
        snow" on one page, and facing it, the observation of "how sadly the
        bird in his cage/ Watches the butterflies." The front part of a whale
        stretches across two pages that illustrate two lines from Genesis: the
        tail, surrounded by fish, extends onto the next two pages, which
        contain an African Pygmy chant and a haiku by Koson, both about
        fish. Prelutsky's poem, "Long Gone," is perched beside a painted
        Tyrannosaurus Rex that looms over John Gardner's "The Lizard,"
        under which hides a childlike miniature of a dinosaur in the same
        brilliant green. Carle's textures are unfailingly intriguing, his colors
        eye-catching, his designs bold, his patterns innovative. Whipple's
        selection should be credited for its variety, quality, and appeal. It's a
        winning combination.

1105   **White**, Ellen Emerson. *White House Autumn.* Avon, 1985. ISBN 0-
        380-89780-6. 209p. Paper. $2.95.

6-9   A sequel to *The President's Daughter* is written with equal restraint,
        humor, and control of the pace and flow of the narrative. The first
        book, in which Meg was also the adolescent protagonist, dealt
        convincingly with the campaign, election, and installation of Meg's
        mother as the first woman president of the United States, and with the
        adjustment that Meg and her younger brothers had to make to public
        prominence. Here the focus is on an assassination attempt and on the
        repercussions it has in inter-familial and other relationships,
        especially for Meg. The setting is unusual, the insight into peer
        relationships is perceptive, and the treatment of family affection and
        tension sensitive.

1106   **Whitney**, Sharon. *Women in Politics*; by Sharon Whitney and Tom
        Raynor. Watts, 1986. ISBN 0-531-10243-2. 135p. illus. with photographs.
        $11.40.

7-10   Although they discuss the careers of many individual women,
        Whitney and Traynor are primarily concerned with the political
        process: how women have gained political recognition and
        appointment, where the support comes from, what those who have
        been elected or appointed have achieved, what inequity in
        representation remains. The book, capably written and candid in
        approach, gives historical background about women's suffrage, early
        political involvement (the first congresswoman, the first women to
        serve as mayor or governor), and then devotes separate chapters to
        such areas of service as municipal offices, state offices, or congres-
        sional office. There's also a good deal of information about the

political process in the United States. An index and a bibliography are included.

1107 **Wiesner**, David. *Hurricane*; written and illus. by David Wiesner. Clarion, 1990. ISBN 0-395-54382-7. 32p. $14.95.

5-8 yrs. Like the author's *Free Fall*, this picture book explores imaginative extensions of reality, but is all the more involving for its basis in ordinary child life, rather than in the murky depths of a dream. A hurricane is coming, and brothers David and George enjoy the drama of the "green blizzard" of leaves, the creaking of the house, the lights going out, and a cozy supper by the fireplace. The hurricane leaves in its wake a legacy of a large fallen-down tree, "a sleeping giant" that provides the boys (and their cat) with a vehicle for fantastic journeying as they imagine themselves on safari, riding the seven seas, in space, and sometimes just sitting enjoying the view. "It just feels good being here." With the hurricane providing its own meteorological excitement, the imaginary games allow Wiesner plenty of scope for phantasmagoric landscaping; *Jumanji*-like, all the games are foreshadowed in the wallpaper pattern in the boys' bedroom. The tree makes a likely-looking space capsule landed on a distant planet, or pirate ship awash in stormy seas; its allure in plain dappled sunlight is also apparent, and readers will share the boys' dismay when the chainsaw turns it into firewood. But as the book closes, the wind is kicking up, and another tree just might fall. Robust and real, this one is guaranteed to get them outdoors.

1108 **Wilcox**, Charlotte. *Trash*; illus. with photographs by Jerry Bushey. Carolrhoda, 1988. ISBN 0-87614-311-7. 40p. $12.95

2-5 Excellent color photographs accompany a continuous text that explains routine trash disposal, the problems that have accrued with the almost one billion pounds of solid waste accumulated in the U.S. daily, the pollution of ground water from unsanitary landfills, and the importance of responsible recycling. The matter-of-fact tone of the text is much more effective than hysterical preaching, though a dramatic story such as New York City's garbage barge crisis would not have been amiss. The pictured trucks, dumpsters, forklifts, bulldozers, and compactors add natural appeal to the book. Most childen are assigned the chore, at some point, of helping to carry out the garbage, and recycling is an area where they can really contribute. "The recycling process begins at home, where different types of waste can be sorted. The three types of trash that can be recycled are paper, glass, and metals. If they are sorted out before being thrown away, they can be taken to recycling centers." This will give readers the incentive to do so and will boost class conservation projects as well.

1109   **Wilhelm**, Hans. *I'll Always Love You;* written and illus. by Hans
Wilhelm. Crown, 1985. ISBN 0-517-55648-0. 29p. $8.95.

2-5 yrs.   "This is a story about Elfie—the best dog in the whole world." Since
pets are often a child's introduction to the wonders of birth and the
sadness of death, the young narrator's account is most appropriate for
sharing with listeners bound to experience the aging of their animals.
Gentle, appealing watercolors and a brief text unfold the friendship of
a puppy, Elfie, and his boy as they both learn to pee in the right place,
romp, rest, and dream together. When Elfie gets older and rounder,
his boy must carry her up the stairs to bed, yet never forgets to say "I'll
always love you" every night. That's what makes it easier in the end,
when Elfie dies in her sleep, and that's what will leave children with a
renewed commitment to all creatures small. Wilhelm displays a
graphic sense of dogginess in scenes of Elfie's mischief and amusing
reluctance to move out of comfortable positions as time wears on. Like
Viorst's *Tenth Good Thing About Barney* and its successors, this will
have an assured spot in family reading.

1110   **Willard**, Nancy. *East of the Sun & West of the Moon:* A Play; illus. by
Barry Moser. Harcourt, 1989. ISBN 0-15-224750-5. 64p. $14.95.

4-7
 *   The best thing about this adaptation is that children who must
memorize parts for a play will have something worthwhile to remember. Willard's poetry here is as good or better than in *William
Blake's Inn* and in fact recalls some of the most lilting rhythms and
imagery of that book. Here's what the woodcutter's daughter sings on
the way to the Bear's palace: "When you go through the forest at
midnight,/ and your friends and relations are few,/ just remember the
crow and the cricket/ are twice as nervous as you./ Just remember the
Bear who brings you/ knows all the best people by name;/ the sun and
the moon are friendly,/ and so is the wind and the rain." And
returning: "When you're going back home through the forest/ and
the road feels lonely and long,/ the violets will lay you a carpet,/ and
the sparrows will pipe you a song,/ and a Bear is just one of the family/
if you know your relations by name./ Blow from the east, and blow
from the west,/ and blow till we're home again!" Not all the script is
poetry; colloquial modern idiom offers a balance for the stylized verse,
so that the total effect is witty and never precious. Most important,
Willard does not violate the basic elements of the story in elaborating
her own inventions. Barry Moser's watercolor portraits are characteristically astute in expression and pose, with the occasional scene lit
like a stage backdrop. This is lovely to look at, but performing it will
transform classroom dramatics.

1111   **Willey,** Margaret. *Finding David Dolores.* Harper, 1986. Library ed.
ISBN 0-06-026484-5; Trade ed. ISBN 0-06-026483-7. 150p. Library ed.
$10.89; Trade ed. $11.50.

6-9
*
As she did in her first novel, *The Bigger Book of Lydia,* Willey here
uses a pair of girls to explore a special preoccupation of adolescence,
in this case, romantic fantasizing. Thirteen, Arly has become irritable
and solitary, pushing her mother away: "My goal in life was to avoid
her." On one of her long aimless walks, she spies a handsome, older
boy named David Dolores, and without speaking to him, falls in love.
Not with him, exactly, but with the romance of him. *"Oh, God,* I
whispered, drifting back to the edges of my own neighborhood. *At last
I've found someone."* The darker side of fantasies is shown by Arly's
friend Regina. Obsessively hating her mother ("It's like having a
secret every single day of your life."), Regina comforts herself with a
cloak of glamorous, self-conscious alienation, and believes she finds a
soulmate in David's bohemian mother. "She makes it seem like life is
so interesting and there's so much to look forward to. Isn't she
absolutely inspiring, Arly?" The two girls—one growing up, the other
becoming more and more disturbed—mirror and collide with each
other, constantly refining and adjusting the reader's perspective.
Likewise, the characterizations of the three mothers resonate off each
other, showing them to be both more and less ideal than the girls
perceive. While all is resolved in a too tidy scene of Arly-as-therapist,
the multiple tensions between characters are remarkably well played
in a deceptively simple and compelling story.

1112   **Willey,** Margaret. *If Not for You.* Harper, 1988. Library ed. ISBN 0-06-
026499-3; Trade ed. ISBN 0-06-026494-2. 154p. Library ed. $11.89; Trade
ed. $11.95.

5-9
In her third novel, Willey is once again concerned with examining the
geometry of friendship; one can almost see the points and lines and
angles, connections made and missed. Bonnie idolizes Linda, a
beautiful, popular, older girl who has dropped out of school, pregnant,
and married her handsome beach bum boyfriend. Bonnie admiringly
says,"They were such a *couple."* Bonnie's best friend Jennie, Linda's
younger sister, is mortified by Linda's behavior. The younger girls'
friendship ends, and Bonnie becomes Linda's babysitter and
confidante. The ever-downward spiral of Ray and Linda's marriage is
didactically predictable, but Willey is less interested in the trials of
teen marriage than she is with the breakdown of illusions: Linda's
about Ray, and Bonnie's about Linda. The author writes quietly but
pointedly about her characters, with a respectful and innocent tone
not often heard in books for younger adolescents. Readers may be far
ahead of Bonnie in understanding the disastrous marriage, but at the
same time they will know how difficult it can be to give up a dream.

1113   Willey, Margaret. *Saving Lenny*. Bantam, 1990. ISBN 0-553-05850-9. [160p]. $13.95.

7-10
*

Kay had convinced her best friend Jesse to ask Lenny for a date—she couldn't have known then how fast the new couple would shut her out. In alternating, distinctively voiced chapters, the two girls recall what happened to their friendship while Jesse and Lenny have "the undisputed romance of the century." Willey deftly combines empathy for her adolescent characters and readers with a seasoned perspective on their dramas. While readers may, like Kay, soon become impatient with Jesse's infatuation, they will understand it, and perhaps be a little jealous, "the kind of jealousy that makes you wonder what it would be like to be so crazy about someone. When it hasn't happened to you." As was true in Willey's last book, *If Not for You*, the sad spiral of the romance is inevitable and believable: it isn't until they run away together to an isolated beach cottage that Jesse understands that Lenny isn't a dark romantic figure; he's clinically depressed, a condition that the author renders with considerable acuity and a welcome lack of problem-novel melodrama. With a prose style that is at once quiet and forthright, Willey demonstrates an unassuming respect for her readers and their passions.

1114   **Williams,** Barbara. *Beheaded, Survived*. Watts, 1987. ISBN 0-531-10403-6. 150p. illus. with maps. $12.90.

6-9

The title alludes to a mnemonic phrase referring to the wives of Henry VIII, and it's offered by Lowell to the other teenagers who are touring historic sites in England and Wales. Lowell is moody and seldom talks to the others; Jane is nevertheless attracted to him. The story is told effectively through the separate comments of the two. It is clear that Lowell has a serious emotional problem, so that the title has a second meaning; only gradually do readers (like other characters in the story) learn what Lowell's problem is. He does, indeed, survive, and a genuine affection develops between the silent boy and Jane, who has been afraid that the others would discover she is diabetic. Natural dialogue, excellent characterization of major and minor characters, and a smooth development of plot make this an eminently readable story that is embellished but not overcome by details of cathedrals, palaces, and cultural events.

1115   **Williams,** Karen. *Galimoto*; illus. by Catherine Stock. Lothrop, 1990. Library ed. ISBN 0-688-08790-6; Trade ed. ISBN 0-688-08789-2. 32p. Library ed. $12.88; Trade ed. $12.95.

4-6 yrs.

You won't get more than three pages into this without listeners insisting "What's a galimoto?"—a suspense (*we're* not telling) well served and fairly resolved in this simple story set in Malawi. Kondi wants to make a galimoto, but he doesn't have enough wire in his "box of things." Undeterred, he trades his knife, combs junkyards and backyards, and teaches a little girl how to use a stick to probe an anthill—all industrious strategies for getting more wire to build a galimoto. Refreshingly contemporary details about life in Kondi's village are casually inflected in the text and pictures, with children playing at an anthill twice as big as themselves, another child wearing a "Disco" t-shirt, mothers shopping at a store that sells aspirin as well as colorful cloth. Stock's watercolors, summer-green and flexibly lined, inform Kondi's quest with good-natured dignity. To the satisfaction of all, the book closes with a double-page close-up of a galimoto in action. Better have on hand an ample supply of old hangers and paper clips—even the most sophisticated American kid will want to attempt the construction of this elegant little toy.

1116   **Williams**, Sue. *I Went Walking*; illus. by Julie Vivas. Gulliver/Harcourt, 1990. ISBN 0-15-200471-8. 32p. $13.95.

2-4 yrs.   As effective with a large group as it will be with a lap-seated audience of one, this has a simple text that invites chanting along or call-and-response; either way, toddlers will have it memorized after just one hearing. "I went walking. What did you see? I saw a black cat (brown horse, red cow, green duck, pink pig, yellow dog) looking at me." Reminiscent of Bill Martin's *Brown Bear, Brown Bear, What Do You See*, this is as easy as could be, with a diversity of appeals that belies the simplicity. Too often, such toddler-sized texts are inundated by brassy graphics, but Vivas' watercolors, cleanly set and balanced among lots of white space, are elemental. The "I" is an inquisitive toddler (a boy, according to the jacket; an Everychild, according to the pictures) whose play with the animals is gentle and affectionate. The animals, while true to their colors, are elegantly shaped and shaded, with the green duck, for example, sporting orange feet and purple feathers along with its dominant hue. The final double spread ("I saw a lot of animals following me!") is a down-to-earth rumpus.

1117   **Willis**, Jeanne. *Earthlets, as Explained by Professor Xargle*; illus. by Tony Ross. Dutton, 1989. ISBN 0-525-44465-3. 26p. $12.95.

K-2   Any dethroned child who feels that the new arrival looks like something from outer space will find a sympathetic note in Professor Xargle's lecture: "Earthlets are born without fangs. At first, they drink only milk, through a hole in their faces called a mouth. When they finish the milk, they are patted and squeezed so they won't explode." It's a toss-up as to who looks funnier here: green, fuzzy, many-eyed Professor Xargle or the jowly, messy, little monster who is the subject of his instructive discourse—"to quiet the Earthlet, the father Earthling flings it into the atmosphere". Good fun for brothers and sisters big enough to get the joke, and perhaps a useful prod to get them to help with Earth's quaint baby rituals. Remember: "After soaking they must be dried carefully so they won't shrink. Then they are sprinkled with dust so they won't stick to things."

1118   **Willis**, Val. *The Secret in the Matchbox;* illus. by John Shelley. Farrar, 1988. ISBN 0-374-36603-9. 30p. $12.95.

K-3   Innovative, sensitive without being sentimental, and nicely balanced
  *   in the storytelling functions of text and illustration, this is a very impressive first team effort. No one is particularly interested in seeing what "secret" Bobby has in his matchbox until Helen Wells, a "good and polite little girl," says "Yes, please," and screams when she sees a little dragon inside. The idea of a dragon tiny enough to fit in a matchbox should appeal to the read-aloud audience, and the development of a multiethnic classroom-set fantasy in which the dragon grows (and grows and grows, pupils holding their nervous breaths, teacher oblivious) is beautifully paced. The simple text and the subtle humor of understated dialogue are as effective as the line and composition of the paintings, which are framed by borders with designs and figures that echo the zest of the action and the appropriately frenetic appearance of the classroom. Nifty.

1119   **Winthrop**, Elizabeth. *Lizzie and Harold;* illus. by Martha Weston. Lothrop, 1986. Library ed. ISBN 0-688-02712-1; Trade ed. ISBN 0-688-02711-3. 28p. Library ed. $11.88; Trade ed. $11.75.

4-6 yrs.   This focuses on two children who are best friends—but one of them doesn't know it. Lizzie continuously yearns for a best friend, often out loud to her neighbor Harold, who volunteers for the job. The mythical creature Lizzie fantasizes is a girl exactly her own age, and Lizzie goes after her with a vengeance. None of Harold's persistent gestures work until, when he finally tries and fails to desert the obtuse Lizzie, she begins to value him. Lizzie's picky obstinacy is very real, Harold's honesty very appealing, and the full-color illustrations roomy enough for some expressive scenes.

1120   **Winthrop**, Elizabeth. *Tough Eddie;* illus. by Lilian Hoban. Dutton, 1985. ISBN 0-525-44164-6. 28p. $10.95.

K-2   Hoban's slightly raffish looking children are an appealing extension of the text, in which young children can enjoy familiar situations and relationships, a convincing demonstration of bravery, and a shift from the stereotypical sex role. Eddie, who likes to play tough roles, is embarrassed when his sister tells two friends that he has a dollhouse, with furniture made by his father; because of his chagrin, he's huffy and doesn't respond to Philip's and Andrew's genuine interest. In fact, he doesn't thaw until after an incident that he feels proves his bravery: standing very still until a bee on his face flies away. There's a message

here, but it doesn't swamp the light but realistic story of peer
relationships.

1121   **Wolf**, Bernard. *Amazing Grace: Smith Island and the Chesapeake
Watermen;* written and photographed by Bernard Wolf. Macmillan,
1986. ISBN 0-02-793330-X. 76p. $14.95.

5-7   In a lively, sometimes witty text, Wolf describes the work and way of
life traditonal to the crabbing community on a small island of
Chesapeake Bay. Shoreline "scraping" from small boats called
barcats, crabbing from the bigger boats rigged with hydraulic scrapes,
checking crab pots, culling crabs—all mean work from pre-dawn to
dark for these watermen. (Women are given short shrift; the focus
here, as defined by the title, in on men.) Wolf also describes their links
with the mainland, including the mail boat captain who does all their
banking and hauls their catches to waiting buyers. In spite of some
odd organizational shifts in the text (from duck-banding in the wildlife
refuge to a celebration of one couple's fiftieth wedding anniversary to
another islander's unprofitable morning on the water), Wolf has
projected the character of the community, even to the deeply felt and
daily lived religious ties that bind individuals in strong, ongoing
dynamics of faith. The black-and-white photographs capture,
naturally and specifically, the common sights and stances of Wolf's
subjects.

1122   **Wolf**, Bernard. *Cowboy;* written and illus. with photographs by
Bernard Wolf. Morrow, 1985. Library ed. ISBN 0-688-03878-6; Trade
ed. ISBN 0-688-03877-8. 77p. Library ed. $10.88; Trade ed. $10.25..

5-9   As he has in earlier photodocumentary books, Wolf combines good
photography and a conversational but controlled writing style. His text
does not romanticize the cowboy and his work, but it does explain what
aspects of the cowboy's life make him prefer it. It's hard work, and the
book describes that work very crisply, as it focuses on Wally McRae
and his family as they operate their cattle ranch, cooperate with
neighbors, fight against the strip mining that depletes their water
supply and the power plants that pollute the atmosphere in that part
of Montana, and enjoy participating in rodeos and other social events.
Good photojournalism.

1123   **Wolff**, Virginia Euwer. *Probably Still Nick Swansen.* Holt, 1988. ISBN
0-8050-0701-6. 144p. $13.95.

6-10   When kids leave the special ed. program in Room 19 to become
  *   mainstreamed in the regular classrooms, the commencement is
called "Going Up." "Where is Up?" asks 16-year-old Nick, left behind
when pretty Shana leaves the class. He asks her to the prom anyway,
saves his money, learns to dance, gets Shana a corsage to match the

dress she plans to wear—and then she stands him up. Because the narration is so closely tied to Nick's perceptions, we never quite understand what's wrong with him, except that he has trouble reading and writing, and works out his thoughts literally, slowly, and sometimes over-logically, as when he assumes (as do readers) that Shana stood him up because she didn't want to be associated with the "droolers" anymore. Not at all, instead, Shana has distracting new problems of her own: "I've figured out where Up is. It's where you flunk tests all the time, and everybody wants you to be so smart all the time, it's so much faster . . ." This is less a narrative than a character study, but few characters have been more intensively realized in recent YA fiction than Nick. The unsentimental narration follows his thoughts rather than his speech or actions, vividly conveying Nick's pride in his talents, his stubborn love and need for a long-dead older sister, and his frustrations in communicating with others. "What do you mean, Nick? Inside his brain was a terrible asking voice, almost yelling at him: what do you *mean*?"

1124   Wood, Audrey. *The Horrible Holidays*; illus. by Rosekrans Hoffman. Dial, 1988. Library ed. ISBN 0-8037-0546-8; Trade ed. ISBN 0-8037-0544-1. 48p. Library ed. $9.89; Trade ed. $9.95.

1-3   A listing of the three stories set in easy-to-read format here gives an idea of the book's unconventional tone: "The No-Thanksgiving, The Crummy Christmas, and The Unhappy New Year." Alf is the anti-hero of three celebratory occasions when his relatives, especially cousin Mert, beleaguer him. Mert prays until the food is cold (Alf is sent to his room for over-reacting); she ruins his Christmas surprises by telling him what's in each present (Alf is sent to his room for getting even); she pursues him when he tries to retreat from the New Year's party (Alf is *already* in his room, and this time he gets revenge in peace). Wood's somehat cynical text is more than matched by Hoffman's quirky animal characters, whose slightly distorted expressions suit the Scrooge effect. Children tipped over the edge of excitement into grouchiness may well appreciate a look at the holidays' downside.

1125   Wood, Audrey. *King Bidgood's in the Bathtub*; illus. by Don Wood. Harcourt, 1985. ISBN 0-15-242730-9. 31p. $12.95.

4-6 yrs.
*   A worthy successor to this author/illustrator team's super-romp, *The Napping House*, poles fun at adults (and royalty yet) for something children often do—refuse to get out of the tub. King Bidgood, however, carries it to extremes, demanding that the knight join him for a morning mock battle, the queen for a noon luncheon, the duke for afternoon fishing, and the court for a nighttime masquerade ball. All of these important persons look disconcertingly soggy when they

remove from the suds, but King Bidgood is not persuaded to leave until the little page, who has slaved and perspired through cleanup and activities, pulls the plug ("Glub, Glub, Glub!"). This is rhythmically told with a few lines to each page and an imaginative assortment of detail in double-spread oil paintings dominated by purple and blue. Perhaps the fishing scene is most memorable, with trout arching over waterlilies and a perplexed duke struggling with hook and worm. Some tub.

1126   **Wright**, Betty Ren. *The Pike River Phantom*. Holiday House, 1988. ISBN 0-8234-0721-7. 153p. $13.95.

4-8   Betty Ren Wright can always be depended upon for an appealing ghost story, and here, as usual, she fills out the frights with believable human relations and complications. Twelve-year-old Charlie has moved to a small Wisconsin town to live with his grandparents, cousin, and father, who has just recently been freed after five years in prison. Charlie is embarrassed by his father, hot-tempered, impulsive, childlike; but he becomes disappointed in his grandparents as well when they refuse to believe Charlie's story about the strange woman who lives in an old, decaying house. The woman is a ghost, set upon revenge for a long-past event that involves both Charlie's grand-mother and his cousin Rachel. Suspenseful and fast-moving, this offers an ending that is both hair-raising and heartwarming, as Charlie discovers something new and valuable about his dad.

1127   **Wrightson**, Patricia. *Balyet*. McElderry, 1989. ISBN 0-689-50468-3. [144p]. $12.95.

5-8   Like other Aborigine spirits Wrightson has written about, Balyet is both playful and dangerous, her thousand years of solitude making her yearn for the company of young humans whom she lures to their deaths for the sake of a moment's warmth. Mrs. Willet, "an aboriginal Australian and a Clever Woman" on a trip to tend the sacred sites of her people, finds teenage Jo stowed away in her old car. Rebellious Jo repeatedly breaks promises to stay safe in camp: she wanders into rocky gullies, trysts with two brothers motorcycling nearby, and neglects a babysitting charge who wanders into the wild and almost dies at the hands of Balyet. Yet it is Jo who precipitates the crisis that lays the spirit to rest, through Mrs. Willet's ancient magic. The author's note acknowledges a nineteenth-century source for the legend of Balyet and advises readers that she, rather than the human characters, is the center of the story. Indeed, none except Mrs. Willet is more than functionally developed, but the intensity of the triangle between spirit, old one, and youngster is magnetic enough to hold the book together, and Wrightson's verbal landscapes are, as always, vividly rendered.

1128   **Wrightson**, Patricia. *Moon-Dark.*. McElderry, 1988. ISBN 0-689-
50451-9. $11.95.

5-8   With her customary and sometimes uncanny sense of the Australian
wildlife and countryside, Wrightson builds a situation, sometimes too
slowly, from a seemingly minor ecological imbalance. The "flying
foxes" (bats), turned out of their traditional habitat by humans, raid
the fruit trees upriver, which causes a shortage among bush rats and
bandicoots, who start a war. Gradually the entire environment is drawn
into the conflict, until one of them—a young wallaby—calls on a
mythical moon man to help resolve the problem. The key figure in all
this is Blue, a dog that witnesses the action and plays a crucial part in
it. The plot is of minor importance compared to the characterization of
the cast, which involves a good deal of humor as well as sensitive
articulation of animal behavior. Often the animals try to avoid
problems by laying low (*"I am not here. I was never here. I am
somewhere else"*). There are certain codes of behavior that Blue
maintains in his relationship to his master, but he is not above lying
and trickery when the occasion requires it. Afterwards, he is penitent;
his apologies and contradictory excuses after becoming injured in a
fight with Red Dog form an unforgettably funny passage. This will
frustrate readers who need a quick start and fast pace, but animal
lovers will revel in the patient development of creature
communication.

1129   **Yee**, Paul. *Tales from the Gold Mountain: Stories of the Chinese in the
New World*; illus. by Simon Ng. Macmillan, 1990. ISBN 0-02-793621-X.
64p. $14.95.

5-
*   Eight original stories—brilliantly illustrated with eerily textured, mask-
like portraits—make a haunting companion to use with the tales in
Laurence Yep's *The Rainbow People*, which were drawn from a WPA
oral narrative project. Yee never indulges in stylistic pretensions as he
releases these dramatic blends of realism and legend from what
seems long silence. The manager of a fish cannery turns trickster to
foil a greedy boss, a young man arranges burial for a group of Chinese
railroad workers after meeting his father's ghost in a deserted tunnel
("Take chopsticks; they shall be our bones"), a young woman's gift of
ginger root saves her betrothed's life and, eventually, their love. A few
of the tales focus on the personal price of clashes between old
traditions and new influences. From romance to sly humor to conflicts
of the living and dead, these carry mythical overtones that lend the
characters unforgettable dimension—humans achieving supernatural power in defying their fate of physical and cultural oppression.
The combination of Yee's piercing portrayals and Ng's monumental
images against background effects of cracked canvas must—as the
author hopes in his afterword—"carve a place in the North American

imagination for the many generations of Chinese who have settled here as Canadians and Americans, and help them stake their claim to be known as pioneers, too."

1130   **Yep**, Laurence. *Mountain Light*. Harper, 1985. Library ed. ISBN 0-06-026759-3; Trade ed. ISBN 0-06-026758-5. 256p. Library ed. $11.89; Trade ed. $11.95.

6-9   In a sequel to *The Serpent's Children* Yep continues the story of that fierce child of a militant family, Cassia, who was the narrator. Here the story is told by Squeaky Lau, who meets Cassia and her father after they have all been fighting against the oppressive Manchus. Since they come from neighboring villages in Kwangtung Province, Cassia and Squeaky keep in touch, a development that is strange because their families have had a vendetta for generations, and because they are so unlike: she is serious and belligerent, he is a clown and self-confessed coward. Their friendship grows into love, but they separate when Squeaky decides he must follow Foxfire (Cassia's brother, now a gold miner in America) and make the fortune that will bring him respectability and will make it possible for them to marry. The story, told with pace and vigor, is set in 1855, and it gives a vivid picture of the conflicts within the Chinese community both at home and in the United States. Like all good historical fiction it has strong characters whose adventures reveal rather than compete with the historical background.

1131   **Yep**, Laurence. *The Rainbow People*; illus. by David Wiesner. Harper, 1989. Library ed. ISBN 0-06-026761-5; Trade ed. ISBN 0-06-026760-7. 194p. Library ed. $13.89; Trade ed. $13.95.

5-9   Divided into sections entitled Tricksters, Fools, Virtues and Vices, In Chinese America, and Love, these 20 stories are adapted from a 1930s WPA oral narrative project in Oakland's Chinatown. Yep's introduction notes the difference between this kind of collection and the more common ones drawn primarily from the northern provinces of China. "Trying to understand Chinese-Americans from these [latter] tales is like trying to comprehend Mississippian ancestors by reading a collection of Vermont folktales." How much understanding of immigrants' experience the stories will convey is arguable, but most of them have what makes folktales last—a vivid or haunting core. The first tale, "Bedtime Snacks," is one of the best and the most shivery of several ghoul stories. In it, the monster Dagger Claws has a satisfying meal ("crunch, crunch, crunch") of the hero's greedy, obnoxious little brother, while Shakey the fearful one stays safe and sound. Several, such as "The Professor of Smells," project a sly or deadpan humor. The majority, however, are suspenseful ("Snake-spoke") or ghostly ("The Butterfly Man") or mystical ("The Homecoming") enough to satisfy readers keen on terror tales. What they get beyond that is all cultural bonus.

1132   **Yolen**, Jane. *Best Witches: Poems for Halloween*; illus. by Elise Primavera. Putnam, 1989. ISBN 0-399-21639-5. 48p. $14.95.

3-5   There's nice control of form, meter, rhyme, and scansion in this collection; there are moments of spine-chill that middle-grades readers will enjoy; there is, as prime appeal, a humor that has verve and sophistication but is never inaccessible. The ebullience of Yolen's poetry is matched by that of Primavera's paintings, which are colorful but pleasantly gruesome, with a great deal of vitality and antic humor.

1133   **Yolen**, Jane. *Bird Watch: A Book of Poetry*; illus. by Ted Lewin. Philomel, 1990. ISBN 0-399-21612-X. 40p. $15.95.

3-5   Like Marilyn Singer's fine *Turtle in July*, this nature poetry is paired
*   with evocative watercolor art that gives young readers plenty of space to consider the graphic verbal images. Some of the lines are solemn: "From the lake/ laughs the last joke/ of a solitary loon./ Winter silences us all." Others are satirical, as in the poem about choosing a supermarket tom over a wild turkey ("In matters of eating,/ our minds do what they can"). "Swan" offers rhymed humor with a contrast of the bird's stately appearance above the water, versus its functional feet underneath. Lewin's pictures strike just the right tonal balance, neither glamorizing the birds nor distracting from the poetry. The swan picture, for example, is a deep blue wash with the white bird framing the poem in white print. A last page gives the names and a bit of information about each bird.

1134   **Yolen**, Jane. *Owl Moon;* illus. by John Schoenherr. Philomel, 1987. ISBN 0-399-21457-7. 30p. $13.95.

K-2   Oversize pages are used in a remarkably effective way by Schoenherr, whose watercolor paintings, in double-page spreads, are economically composed scenes of a winter night that are strikingly dramatic and truly evocative of the cold and silence described in the text. The latter is also spare and poetic, a child's account of going, silently, with her father in hopes that an owl will answer Pa's imitation of an owl's cry. This is a fragment, but a memorable one, in which story and pictures are nicely matched, each reinforcing the other.

1135   **Yolen**, Jane. *Piggins;* illus. by Jane Dyer. Harcourt, 1987. ISBN 0-15-261685-3. 28p. $13.95.

5-8 yrs.   A witty, sophisticated collaboration between author and artist results
*   in a mystery-spoof of Sherlock Holmes vintage. Piggins, the portly butler at Mr. and Mrs. Reynard's wealthy home, welcomes the guests

one night at a dinner party arranged to show off—and sell—Mrs. Reynard's diamond lavaliere, reputed to have a curse that brings bad luck. In the midst of the soup course, the lights go out and the necklace disappears. Even Inspector Bayswater finds only a few disparate clues. Piggins however, is not stumped. He collars the thieves, Lord and Lady Ratsby, plucks the lavaliere from the chandelier, and finishes the evening as he had begun it, trit-trotting up and down stairs to finish his chores. Both the narrative and art contain nuances that lend depth to rereadings. In addition to consistently elegant drafting and watercolor detail, the pictures characterize each of the guests in perfect coordination with the verbal descriptions. Professor T. Ortoise, who "is famous for his conversation," introduces the evening with a comment on the weather. The "world-famous explorer Pierre Lapin" has three unmarried sisters and mutters, after the dining room commotion, "In my youth, I stole into a farmer's garden and made much too much noise." The rats, particularly, are expressive in showing their greed as they pocket the cheese hors d'oeuvres and scamper toward the table before the rest of the company. Yolen's pacing and use of the present tense add an immediacy that counteracts any off-putting effects of the elitist tone, which listeners will actually enjoy once they catch on to the setting. Dyer, too, has taken special care to reflect the upper-crust atmosphere in costumes, furnishings, and design touches such as the shadow profiles facing several full-page illustrations. This has all the appeal *Upstairs Downstairs* had for adults, plus notes of humor and suspense that flavor it for child's palate.

1136 **Yolen**, Jane. *Ring of Earth: A Child's Book of Seasons*; illus. by John Wallner. Harcourt, 1986. ISBN 0-15-267140-4. 32p. $14.95.

3-6   The picture book format is a bit deceptive here, for both the poetry and the art have a more sophisticated appeal. The first of the four poems, "Winter Song of the Weasel," is best, its verbal music almost perfectly cadenced with end-rhymes that never seem forced and imagery that takes a reader by surprise and ends with a rich chant. "I reproduce upon my hide/ the wintering I feel inside./For I was dark and now am light./ For I was brown and now am white./ For I was summer, now am snow./ Upon my back the seasons grow./ And—now again—I know." The last poem, "Autumn Song of the Goose," has the same ringing urgency, but is interrupted by a refrain of bird calls ("Kerhonk, kerhonk, kerhonk") that is not as melodic in print as it is in nature. "Song of the Spring Peeper" and "Dragonfly's Summer Song" are occasionally forced ("And who else waits? Bears new awoke"), but with lyrical flashes: "I am the wind's own stepchild,/ wings colorless as air,/ veins like stained glass ribbings/ trapping all the sun's light there." Wallner's mottled paintings are gracefully composed across double-page spreads to pick up Yolen's circle motifs with interlocking rings and overlapping round frames connecting the cyclical flora and fauna reflected in the verses. A rewarding selection for classroom poetry groups or family sharing in a quieter context.

1137   **Yorinks**, Arthur. *Bravo Minski;* illus. by Richard Egielski. Farrar, 1988. ISBN 0-374-30951-5. 32p. $13.95.

K-2   You name it, and Minski either discovered it, invented it, or did it better than anyone else. There's a touch, in this entertaining picture book, of the child Mozart being shown off by his crafty papa, as little Minski ("the greatest scientist known to man") takes continental audiences by storm. His greatest talent? Singing. A few of his inventions? Oh, the automobile, the airplane, the toaster, eyeglasses. Aspirin. All this is made funnier by the crisp writing style, and by the glowing extravagances of full-color illustrations that show elaborate costumes (mixed vintage) on the gaping, adoring spectators of all ranks.

1138   **Yorinks**, Arthur. *Oh, Brother;* illus. by Richard Egielski. Di Capua/Farrar, 1989. ISBN 0-374-35599-1. 40p. $15.95.

5-8 yrs.   "It was a sorry accident at sea many years ago that caused Milton and Morris, twins from England, to be left all alone in the world, fending as best they could." This rags-to-riches story of two brothers whose ship goes down, leaving them washed up on the streets of New York, will claim instant attention from young listeners, partly because of the ingenuity of text and art, partly because of the slapstick effects of the boys' constant bickering. Whether it's performing for a circus or selling apples, they never stop arguing. Then an old tailor (whom they've tried to pickpocket) takes them in. After his death, they disguise themselves and practise his trade so successfully that Mrs. Guggenheim takes them to meet the queen in England, where the royal gardener and nanny recognize their longlost scoundrels . . . er, children. The early-twentieth-century setting is a perfect showcase for Egielski's satirical combination of softly rounded shapes and absurdly deadpan characters. Even the literal colors project an earnestness that never betrays the tongue-in-cheek tone of the text. Fun for all ages.

1139   **Yorinks**, Arthur. *Ugh;* illus. by Richard Egielski. di Capua/Farrar, 1990. ISBN 0-374-38028-7. 32p. $13.95.

5-8 yrs.   "Many, many, many, many, many, many years ago, there lived a boy.
*   His name was Ugh." Everything about this picture book spells spoof, and it's spoof that's inventive enough to offer laughs at every level, from kids to adults. It's so inventive that it spoofs invention. Ugh, oppressed by the sisters and brothers who make him do all the work around the cave while they go off and watch dinosaurs eat trees, makes prehistory by inventing the bicycle. When Oy the scientist, Eh

the Hunter, Um the spear maker, Ah the doctor, and Ick the dirt seller convene their weekly world meeting, Ugh happens to ride by on his bike, loses control (no brakes), and runs away to hide, thinking that the crowd chasing him is mad. They are not mad. "Hey, what a thing!' said Ick, admiring the abandoned bicycle. 'Whoever make this, he be king!'" True to the Cinderella tradition, the hero is found and identified, while his siblings are eaten by a whale. "Ugh be big-shot boy the rest of his happy life." Well, who wouldn't want to be Ugh, riding his two-wheeler with both hands raised in triumph and a saber-tooth crown on? Short of that, who wouldn't want to *hear* about Ugh, every night, and look at the hysterical pictures Egielski has cooked up to go with this uniquely American tall tale of material success? With a dinosaur on the cover. And endpapers that depict the whole myth in cave paintings. The shapes and colors of the artwork are sturdy enough to support stone bicycle wheels, while the compositions balance dinosaurian perspectives with mammoth spaces. The characters sport some pretty monumental hairdos, too. Yorinks and Egielski's past award books are all very well, but this one is the real winner.

1140   **Yoshida**, Toshi. *Young Lions*; written and illus. by Toshi Yoshida. Philomel, 1989. ISBN 0-399-21546-8. 32p. $14.95.

5-8 yrs.   Unlike Ryder's *White Bear, Ice Bear*, this handsome volume
*   confronts head-on the most pressing reason animals run: eat or be eaten. Three lion cubs, bored with napping, set out for their first solo hunt. Passing by the intimidating rhinoceroses and water buffaloes, the cubs make their first attempt at a group of zebras, "but the alert zebras see the hiding lions, and the entire herd runs off through the trees." The gnus escape as well, and there's a final misbegotten attempt at a porcupine. "Even for strong, grown-up lions more animals escape than are caught." A brave if futile quest, then, but the cubs have sharpened their stalking and hiding skills and, almost inci-dentally, provided readers with a realistic view of animal life on the African plains. The text is minimal, never anthropomorphic, and is choice in the details it provides: "Rhinoceroses cannot see well, but their noses and ears are keen." "Cheetahs are good hunters and good runners, but they cannot run for very long." The subtly and naturally colored pencil drawings use wide double-page spreads to tremendous advantage, showing predators chasing herds across the plain and giving a striking evocation of movement through texturally graded horizontal lines that increase in intensity to illustrate relative speeds. After the sun sets (gorgeous shot of Kilimanjaro here) there's a surprise vertical spread, where the cubs are confronted by a leopard high in a tree, eyes glowing as he stands above a dead antelope draped across a limb. Honest but never brutal, this informs natural selection with natural suspense.

1141 **Young,** Ed. *Lon Po Po: A Red-Riding Hood Story from China;* tr. and illus. by Ed Young. Philomel, 1989. ISBN 0-399-21619-7. 32p. $14.95.

5–8 yrs. As he did in A-Ling Louie's*Yeh Shen: A Cinderella Story from China,*
  *   Young illustrates an intriguing Asian variant of a favorite folktale, in this case one in which a young girl saves herself and her sisters instead of waiting around in the wolf's stomach for rescue by a hunter. Said to be more than a thousand years old, "Lon Po Po" is definitely the most liberated version of Little Red Riding Hood, including an early French version in which LRRH manages to save herself but not to dispense with the wolf. Here, three girls have been tricked into opening the door for a wolf disguised as their grandmother. When the oldest realizes the truth ("Po Po, Po Po, your hand has thorns on it"), she convinces him to try the nuts of the ginko tree, after she and her sisters have climbed safely, by letting them haul him up in a basket. Once, twice, three times they drop the basket ("I am so small and weak, Po Po, I could not hold the rope alone"), bumping the wolf's head and breaking "his heart to pieces." The wolf makes an eerie appearance in Young's art, with white staring eyes, a long sinister muzzle, and shadowy textured fur. Rendered in watercolor and pastel, impressionistic images in each panel offer the kind of illustrative suggestion best suited to symbols from oral narrative. A must for folklore and storytelling collections.

1142 **Zemach,** Margot. *The Three Wishes: An Old Story;* written and illus by Margot Zemach. Farrar, 1986. ISBN 0-374-37529-1. 30p. $13.95.

4–6 yrs. Although the story of the three wishes has appeared in anthologies, it is a natural for the picture-book format, and Zemach has taken full advantage of the humor with her watercolor illustrations. As a woodcutter and his wife discuss what they will do with the three wishes bestowed on them by an imp they've freed from a fallen log, the man accidentally sighs for a pan of sausages, angering the woman so much that she wishes the sausages were hanging from his nose. Of course the third wish must go for removing the sausages, but in the end the hungry couple gets what they want anyway — not gold or jewels but humble, filling food. The colors are a departure from the artist's usual concentration on earthtones with purple, mauve, and pink accents. Here, there are rich blues and turquoise to highlight the basic browns and grays of forest and hearth (note that the imp is the same shade as the man's jacket and the sky—mischief is in and all around us). The characters are homely and affectionate, their dog an amusing echo of their own lively expressions. This has always been a successful storytelling choice; now it will serve as a popular book to share aloud.

1143 **Ziebel,** Peter. *Look Closer!;* written and illus. with photographs by Peter Ziebel. Clarion, 1989. ISBN 0-89919-815-5. 32p. $13.95.

1-3 yrs.   A great graphic guessing game starts with a color closeup of bristles and the line "What keeps your teeth clean?" Turn the page and find a child using a toothbrush. The following pages feature a comb ("What untangles your hair?"), yarn ("What do you use to knit?"), a sweater ("What do you wear to feel warm?"), a cat ("What is a warm and furry friend?"), a succulent sequence on food, etc. The photography here is brilliant in color, texture, and composition. The concept is clear, relevant, and naturally organized with attention to association of words and/or graphic images. Similar to but simpler than Tana Hoban's *Look! Look! Look!*, this reaches younger listeners more effectively. It's too bad the answer to "What can you eat for breakfast?" wasn't "cereal" instead of "shredded wheat," just to keep things generically familiar to the audience, but that's a quibble. Ziebel's photography, set off by striking book design, makes this a stand-out in the concept-book genre.

1144   **Ziefert**, Harriet. *A New Coat for Anna*; illus. by Anita Lobel. Knopf, 1986. Library ed. ISBN 0-394-97426-3; Trade ed. ISBN 0-394-87426-9. 30p. Library ed. $10.99; Trade ed. $10.95.

4-7 yrs.   Anna's old coat is too small and thin, but there is no money for a new one. In fact, there are no coats for sale, anyway, because the war has just ended, and manufactured goods, as well as food, are scarce. So Anna and her mother begin trading heirlooms: a gold watch for wool; a lamp, to have the wool spun into yarn; a necklace, to have the yarn woven into cloth...until the bright red coat is made. This has the sequencing and rhythm of a folktale, and the post Second World War setting is unusual. Lobel's detailed paintings, soft-edged and lovely, are particularly evocative in their depictions of the changing seasons: the fading light of an autumn day, Anna and her mother gathering lingonberries in a summer forest, a bucolic springtime setting for the shearing of the sheep.

1145   **Zolotow**, Charlotte, comp. *Early Sorrow: Ten Stories of Youth*. Harper, 1986. Library ed. ISBN 0-06-026937-5; Trade ed. ISBN 0-06-026936-7. 212p. Library ed. $12.89; Trade ed. $12.95.

7-12   A companion volumer to *An Overpraised Season*, this represents a range of styles, from Carson McCullers' "Like That" to Stephen Vincent Benet's "Too Early Spring" that blend smoothly despite their differences because of a sympathetic tone that runs throughout the selections. The sorrows each young protagonist feels may be loss for a parent, loss of innocence, loss of a friend or first love. In each case, the story is tightly crafted and accessible, conveying that sense of a full world briefly visited that distinguishes the best of the genre. E.L. Doctorow's "The Writer in the Family" and James Purdy's "Short Papa" are especially memorable.

1146   **Zolotow**, Charlotte. *Everything Glistens and Everything Sings: New and Selected Poems;* illus. by Margot Tomes. Harcourt, 1987. ISBN 0-15-226488-4. 96p. $11.95.

2-4   Of the 72 poems included here, only 17 are previously published, and the 55 new ones show Zolotow's gift for evocative description. Diction and device are always kept simple and clear, but perceptions are often more complex, witness "In the Museum": "The horse from 200 B.C./ is made of stone,/ but the way he holds his head/ shows/ someone long ago/ loved a horse like him,/ though now/ both horse and sculptor/ are dead." Many verses focus vividly on the child's feelings: "I remember that night,/ with the snow/ white, white, white,/ and my mother's arms around me/warm and tight." As a collection, the poetry is marked by verbal contrast, internal and end rhyme in free verse forms, and observation of ordinary detail to focus a young reader's attention on nature and human nature. Empathetic.

Title Index

Developmental Values Index

Curricular Use Index

Reading Level Index

Subject Index

Type of Literature Index